내공
중학영어듣기 ③
모의고사 20회

DARAKWON

저자 약력

이소영 EBS 변형문제(모자이크), 천기누설 EBS 고난도 변형문제(비투비) 외 집필
De La Salle University 교육 심리학과 졸

이연홍 맨처음 수능영어 독해모의고사(다락원), EBS 우수문항 고난도 변형문제(모자이크) 외 집필
현 창원 명장학원 원장, 모자이크 EBS 변형문제 출제위원
경북대 졸

김소원 체크체크(천재교육), EBS 변형문제(모자이크) 외 집필

서재교 EBS 수능변형문제 시리즈(모자이크), 맨처음 수능영어 독해모의고사(다락원) 외 집필
현 대전 스카이피아 원장, 모자이크 EBS 변형문제 출제위원

이건희 맨처음 수능영어[기본·완성·실력·독해모의고사], 내공[영문법·구문·단어·듣기](다락원)
체크체크, 싱크로드, 열공(천재교육), Grammar In(비상), EBS 변형문제(모자이크) 외 집필
인스타그램 http://instagram.com/gunee27

내공 중학영어듣기 ❸
모의고사 20회

지은이 이소영, 이연홍, 김소원, 서재교, 이건희
펴낸이 정규도
펴낸곳 (주)다락원

초판 1쇄 발행 2019년 9월 30일
초판 6쇄 발행 2024년 6월 24일

편집 정지인, 서민정, 이동호
디자인 윤지영, 엘림
삽화 양현숙
영문 감수 Michael A. Putlack

다락원 경기도 파주시 문발로 211
내용문의 (02)736-2031 내선 506, 505
구입문의 (02)736-2031 내선 250~252
Fax (02)732-2037
출판등록 1977년 9월 16일 제 406-2008-000007호

Copyright © 2019, 이소영, 이연홍, 김소원, 서재교, 이건희

저자 및 출판사의 허락 없이 이 책의 일부 또는 전부를 무단 복제·
전재·발췌할 수 없습니다. 구입 후 철회는 회사 내규에 부합하는
경우에 가능하므로 구입문의처에 문의하시기 바랍니다. 분실·파
손 등에 따른 소비자 피해에 대해서는 공정거래위원회에서 고시한
소비자 분쟁 해결 기준에 따라 보상 가능합니다. 잘못된 책은 바꿔
드립니다.

ISBN 978-89-277-0853-7 54740
978-89-277-0850-6 54740 (set)

http://www.darakwon.co.kr
다락원 홈페이지를 방문하시면 상세한 출판 정보와 함께 동영상
강좌, MP3 자료 등 다양한 어학 정보를 얻으실 수 있습니다.

내공
중학영어듣기 ③
모의고사 20회

DARAKWON

Structures & Features
이 책의 구성과 특징

실전 모의고사 20회

최근 시·도 교육청 영어듣기능력평가를 분석·반영하여 실전에 대비할 수 있도록
구성하였습니다. 실제 시험과 유사한 모의고사를 20회 풀어보게 하였으며, 매회
영국식 발음을 5문항씩 제공하여 다양한 발음에 노출되도록 합니다.

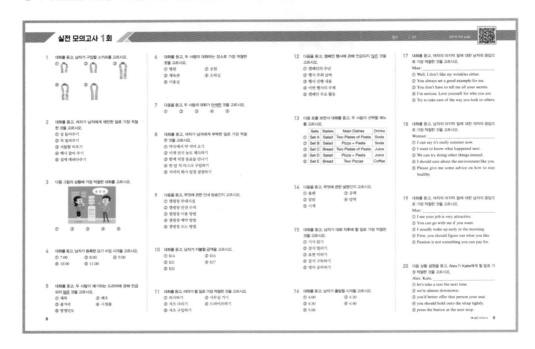

Listen and Check

모의고사를 다시 한 번 들은 후 들은
내용을 한 번 더 확인해 봅니다.

Dictation Test

모의고사 전 지문의 받아쓰기를 통해 다시 한번 내용을 확인하고 중요 표현들과 연음을 학습할 수 있습니다. 발음과 표현 팁을 통해 심층 학습을 할 수 있습니다.

Vocabulary Test

모의고사에 나온 단어를 듣고 영어 단어와 한글 뜻을 같이 써 보면서 어휘를 학습합니다. 또한, 모의고사에 나온 문장들을 다시 듣고 빈칸을 채우며 중요 표현을 복습합니다.

온라인 부가 자료 제공

www.darakwon.co.kr

미국식 발음 100%로 녹음된 파일과 영국식 발음 100%로 녹음된 파일 2종 MP3 파일을 제공합니다. 또한, 0.8배속/1.0배속/1.2배속 MP3 파일을 제공하여 실력에 따라 듣기 속도를 다르게 하여 학습할 수 있습니다.

모의고사에 나온 단어와 표현을 정리한 휴대용 미니 암기장으로 언제 어디서든 학습이 가능합니다.

Contents

목차

실전 모의고사

1 대화를 듣고, 남자가 구입할 스카프를 고르시오.

①   ②   ③

④   ⑤

2 대화를 듣고, 여자가 남자에게 제안한 일로 가장 적절한 것을 고르시오.
① 짐 들어주기
② 차 빌려주기
③ 사물함 비우기
④ 택시 잡아 주기
⑤ 집에 데려다주기

3 다음 그림의 상황에 가장 적절한 대화를 고르시오.

①   ②   ③   ④   ⑤

4 대화를 듣고, 남자가 등록한 요가 수업 시각을 고르시오.
① 7:00   ② 8:00   ③ 9:00
④ 10:00   ⑤ 11:00

5 대화를 듣고, 두 사람이 얘기하는 드라마에 관해 언급되지 않은 것을 고르시오.
① 제목   ② 배우
③ 줄거리   ④ 시청률
⑤ 방영년도

6 대화를 듣고, 두 사람이 대화하는 장소로 가장 적절한 곳을 고르시오.
① 병원   ② 공원
③ 체육관   ④ 오락실
⑤ 미용실

7 다음을 듣고, 두 사람의 대화가 어색한 것을 고르시오.
①   ②   ③   ④   ⑤

8 대화를 듣고, 여자가 남자에게 부탁한 일로 가장 적절한 것을 고르시오.
① 약국에서 약 지어 오기
② 미세 먼지 농도 체크하기
③ 함께 직장 동료들 만나기
④ 한 달 치 마스크 구입하기
⑤ 저녁의 회사 일정 설명하기

9 다음을 듣고, 무엇에 관한 안내 방송인지 고르시오.
① 캠핑장 부대시설
② 캠핑장 안전 수칙
③ 캠핑장 이용 방법
④ 캠핑장 예약 방법
⑤ 캠핑장 오는 방법

10 대화를 듣고, 남자가 지불할 금액을 고르시오.
① $14   ② $16
③ $21   ④ $27
⑤ $32

11 대화를 듣고, 여자가 할 일로 가장 적절한 것을 고르시오.
① 외식하기   ② 사무실 가기
③ 셔츠 다리기   ④ 드라이브하기
⑤ 셔츠 구입하기

12 다음을 듣고, 캠페인 행사에 관해 언급되지 <u>않은</u> 것을 고르시오.
① 캠페인의 주년
② 행사 주최 날짜
③ 행사 진행 내용
④ 이번 행사의 주제
⑤ 캠페인 주요 활동

13 다음 표를 보면서 대화를 듣고, 두 사람이 선택할 메뉴를 고르시오.

	Sets	Starters	Main Dishes	Drinks
①	Set A	Salad	Two Plates of Pasta	Soda
②	Set B	Salad	Pizza + Pasta	Soda
③	Set C	Bread	Two Plates of Pasta	Juice
④	Set D	Salad	Pizza + Pasta	Juice
⑤	Set E	Bread	Two Pizzas	Coffee

14 다음을 듣고, 무엇에 관한 설명인지 고르시오.
① 볼펜   ② 공책
③ 알람   ④ 달력
⑤ 시계

15 대화를 듣고, 남자가 대화 직후에 할 일로 가장 적절한 것을 고르시오.
① 기사 읽기
② 잡지 빌리기
③ 표현 익히기
④ 잡지 구독하기
⑤ 영어 공부하기

16 대화를 듣고, 남자가 출발할 시각을 고르시오.
① 4:00   ② 4:20
③ 4:30   ④ 4:40
⑤ 5:00

17 대화를 듣고, 여자의 마지막 말에 대한 남자의 응답으로 가장 적절한 것을 고르시오.
Man: _____
① Well, I don't like my wrinkles either.
② You always set a good example for me.
③ You don't have to tell me all your secrets.
④ I'm serious. Love yourself for who you are.
⑤ Try to take care of the way you look to others.

18 대화를 듣고, 남자의 마지막 말에 대한 여자의 응답으로 가장 적절한 것을 고르시오.
Woman: _____
① I can say it's really summer now.
② I want to know what happened next.
③ We can try doing other things instead.
④ I should care about the environment like you.
⑤ Please give me some advice on how to stay healthy.

19 대화를 듣고, 여자의 마지막 말에 대한 남자의 응답으로 가장 적절한 것을 고르시오.
Man: _____
① I see your job is very attractive.
② You can go with me if you want.
③ I usually wake up early in the morning.
④ First, you should figure out what you like.
⑤ Passion is not something you can pay for.

20 다음 상황 설명을 듣고, Alex가 Kate에게 할 말로 가장 적절한 것을 고르시오.
Alex: Kate, _____
① let's take a taxi the next time.
② we're almost downtown.
③ you'd better offer that person your seat.
④ you should hold onto the strap tightly.
⑤ press the button at the next stop.

Listen and Check

● 대화를 다시 듣고, 알맞은 것을 고르시오.

1 The one with the flower pattern is the best-selling scarf with elderly women.
  ☐ True   ☐ False

2 The man borrowed the car from his sister.
  ☐ True   ☐ False

3 Does the man drink more than two glasses of water a day?
  ☐ Yes   ☐ No

4 When does the man want to take a yoga class?
  ☐ in the morning   ☐ in the afternoon

5 The woman has watched the drama the man is talking about.
  ☐ True   ☐ False

6 Will the woman get treatment before the game?
  ☐ Yes   ☐ No

7 The man is expecting to see a woman.
  ☐ True   ☐ False

8 Why is the woman going out in the evening?
  ☐ to buy masks
  ☐ to meet her co-workers

9 How many rules does the man mention to visitors?
  ☐ two   ☐ three

10 Does the man only buy two wooden photo frames?
  ☐ Yes   ☐ No

11 The man and the woman will go for a drive tomorrow.
  ☐ True   ☐ False

12 How often does the event take place?
  ☐ once a year   ☐ every three years

13 Do the man and the woman both like to have pizza?
  ☐ Yes   ☐ No

14 The main use of the thing is to remember important events.
  ☐ True   ☐ False

15 Why does the woman read the magazine?
  ☐ to read the news   ☐ to learn English

16 Did the man know that there was a firework festival that day?
  ☐ Yes   ☐ No

17 The man is upset about having wrinkles.
  ☐ True   ☐ False

18 What does the man do to save electricity?
  ☐ save water   ☐ turn off the lights

19 Did the woman find what she liked to do?
  ☐ Yes   ☐ No

20 What did Alex do for his sister and the old woman?
  ☐ offer her seat   ☐ carry her baggage

그림 정보 파악

1 대화를 듣고, 남자가 구입할 스카프를 고르시오.

①   ②   ③

④   ⑤

1

W   Good afternoon. What can I do for you?

M   Hi. I'm looking for scarfs _____ _____ _____.

W   Which do you prefer, plain or patterned ones?

M   I guess she would like _____ _____ _____ _____.

W   How about this one with a flower pattern on it? This is _____ _____ _____ with elderly women.

M   That looks beautiful. She may love it, too. Do you have one that's _____ _____ _____?

W   Yes, we do. Here you are.

제안한 일 파악

2 대화를 듣고, 여자가 남자에게 제안한 일로 가장 적절한 것을 고르시오.

① 짐 들어주기
② 차 빌려주기
③ 사물함 비우기
④ 택시 잡아 주기
⑤ 집에 데려다주기

> ♥ **Don't mention it.**
> : 상대방의 감사 표현에 대한 정중한 인사를 할 때 사용하는 표현으로, '천만에', '별말씀을'이라는 뜻이다.
> = You're welcome.
> = Forget it.
> = My pleasure.

2   🇬🇧

W   What are all those things?

M   Today is my last day at school, so I had to _____ _____ _____ and bring everything back home.

W   Did you bring your car?

M   No, my sister _____ _____ _____ my car today, so I let her have it. I can take a taxi.

W   Your house is far from here. It'll *cost a lot. I can _____ _____ _____.

M   Can you really do that for me? Thanks.

W   ♥Don't mention it. What _____ _____ _____?

★ cost a lot [코스트] [어랏] → [코스터랏]

그림 상황 파악

3 다음 그림의 상황에 가장 적절한 대화를 고르시오.

① ② ③ ④ ⑤

3

① **W**   _____ _____ _____ _____ to drink?
   M   I just want some water.

② **W**   _____ _____ _____ do you drink a day?
   M   I normally drink three glasses of water.

③ **W**   Don't you _____ _____?
   M   I'm fine. Do you?

④ **W**   _____ _____ _____ _____ yesterday?
   M   I hung out with my friends.

⑤ **W**   I played in the water for _____ _____.
   M   That's why you caught a cold.

4 대화를 듣고, 남자가 등록한 요가 수업 시각을 고르시오.

① 7:00
② 8:00
③ 9:00
④ 10:00
⑤ 11:00

4

W　Hello. Are you here to _____ _____ _____ a class?

M　Yes. How do I register for a yoga class?

W　We have classes in the morning and afternoon. When is _____ _____ _____?

M　Morning is better.

W　There are classes starting at 7:00, 9:00, and 11:00. What time would you like to come?

M　I'll choose _____ _____ _____.

W　Okay. You can join the class _____ _____ _____.

M　Thank you.

5 대화를 듣고, 두 사람이 얘기하는 드라마에 관해 언급되지 <u>않은</u> 것을 고르시오.

① 제목
② 배우
③ 줄거리
④ 시청률
⑤ 출시년도

5

W　_____ _____ _____ _____ you're watching now?

M　It's *The Study Master*. It was released in 2010.

W　It's quite an old drama. What is it about?

M　It's about some troublemakers at a high school _____ _____ _____ _____ to the best university in the country.

W　That _____ _____.

M　This drama got high viewer ratings at the time.

W　How high were they?

M　Its ratings were 25.1%.

W　That's such _____ _____ _____.

6 대화를 듣고, 두 사람이 대화하는 장소로 가장 적절한 곳을 고르시오.

① 병원
② 공원
③ 체육관
④ 오락실
⑤ 미용실

♥ **So do I.**
: 상대방의 말에 동감할 때 쓰는 표현으로, '나도 그래.', '마찬가지야.'라는 뜻이다. 부정적인 것에 대한 동감을 나타낼 경우, 'Neither do I.'라고 표현한다.

6

M　How's your leg?

W　It feels better. Can I _____ _____ _____ _____?

M　Let me see. Your ankle is swollen. You'd better go to see a doctor now.

W　I'm really fine. I want to practice. We only have _____ _____ _____ until the game.

M　I know how you feel, but I do not approve you doing that.

W　Okay. I'll go to a hospital and _____ _____ _____.

M　I hope your _____ _____ _____ _____.

W　♥ So do I.

어색한 대화 찾기

7 다음을 듣고, 두 사람의 대화가 <u>어색한</u> 것을 고르시오.

① ② ③ ④ ⑤

7

① M Could you _____ _____ _____ _____?

W What can I do for you?

② M Please _____ _____ _____ our homework.

W Okay. When do you want me to *text you?

③ M You're not supposed to come here.

W Sorry. I went _____ _____ _____.

④ M I'm looking forward to meeting her.

W Of course you should not _____ _____.

⑤ M What would you do if you were in my shoes?

W I might tell _____ _____ _____.

★ text you [텍스트] [유] → [텍스츄]

부탁한 일 파악

8 대화를 듣고, 여자가 남자에게 부탁한 일로 가장 적절한 것을 고르시오.

① 약국에서 약 지어 오기
② 미세 먼지 농도 체크하기
③ 함께 직장 동료들 만나기
④ 한 달 치 마스크 구입하기
⑤ 저녁의 회사 일정 설명하기

8

M Today, _____ _____ _____ _____ is high. You should wear a mask.

W Today again? Oh, no. We don't have any _____ _____ to wear.

M You can buy some on your way back home later.

W I can't do that. I have plans with my coworkers in the evening.

M You're quite busy these days.

W I really am. Anyway, I have no time to _____ _____ _____ _____. Could you buy some for me?

M Okay, I will. How many do you need?

W Please _____ _____ _____. That will be enough for one month.

M No problem.

화제·주제 파악

9 다음을 듣고, 무엇에 관한 안내 방송인지 고르시오.

① 캠핑장 부대시설
② 캠핑장 안전 수칙
③ 캠핑장 이용 방법
④ 캠핑장 예약 방법
⑤ 캠핑장 오는 방법

9

M Welcome to the Moonlight Campground. To make sure of _____ _____, here are some rules to follow. When you are inside your tent, you must not use anything that can _____ _____ _____. Although the materials used in the campground are fireproof, it's still important to _____ _____ _____ _____ _____. Moreover, children under five should be accompanied by their parents. Since the campground is by the river, leaving kids alone can _____ _____ _____. Thank you for your cooperation.

숫자 정보 파악

10 대화를 듣고, 남자가 지불할 금액을 고르시오.

① $14
② $16
③ $21
④ $27
⑤ $32

💙 **May I + V?**
: 상대방에게 허락을 구할 때 나타내는 표현으로, '~해도 될까요?'라는 뜻이다.
= Can I + V?

10

W Hello. How can I help you?

M I'd like to buy _____ _____ _____.

W We have wooden and metal ones. Which do you want?

M _____ _____ _____ _____?

W A wooden one is seven dollars, *and an _____ _____ is eight dollars.

M I'll buy _____ _____ _____. 💙May I use this 10% off coupon?

W Sure. Here you are.

M Thank you.

★ and an [앤드] [언] → [앤던]

할 일 파악

11 대화를 듣고, 여자가 할 일로 가장 적절한 것을 고르시오.
① 외식하기
② 사무실 가기
③ 셔츠 다리기
④ 드라이브하기
⑤ 셔츠 구입하기

11

W Honey, shall we _____ _____ _____ _____ tomorrow?

M Sorry, but I need to go to the office.

W But tomorrow's Saturday.

M It's our company's _____ _____.

W I see. Do you need to wear a white shirt?

M Of course, I do.

W Then I should _____ _____ _____ first.

M Thanks. Let's _____ _____ when I come back home.

언급 유무 파악

12 다음을 듣고, 캠페인 행사에 관해 언급되지 <u>않은</u> 것을 고르시오.
① 캠페인의 주년
② 행사 주최 날짜
③ 행사 진행 내용
④ 이번 행사의 주제
⑤ 캠페인 주요 활동

12 🇬🇧

W Good evening, everyone. Today is the day we've been waiting for. It's _____ _____ _____ of our Save the Earth campaign. This yearly event _____ _____ on the fifteenth of April. For first-time visitors, let me tell you about the event. You can see _____ _____ _____ _____ over the past year and even changes that occurred. We have a theme every year, and for this year, it is "_____ _____." Please enjoy the event. Thank you!

13

13 다음 표를 보면서 대화를 듣고, 두 사람이 선택할 메뉴를 고르시오.

	Sets	Starters	Main Dishes	Drinks
①	Set A	Salad	Two Plates of Pasta	Soda
②	Set B	Salad	Pizza + Pasta	Soda
③	Set C	Bread	Two Plates of Pasta	Juice
④	Set D	Salad	Pizza + Pasta	Juice
⑤	Set E	Bread	Two Pizzas	Coffee

M The atmosphere in this restaurant is _____ _____.

W Yes, it is. It's one of the must-go restaurants for _____

_____.

M I see. What do you want to eat? There are many sets for two.

W First of all, I heard the salad here _____ _____.

M Okay. Let's try it. What about pizza for the main dish?

W That sounds great. I also want some pasta. Here are sets that have salad, pizza, and pasta together.

M All right. All sets _____ _____ _____, too. What do you want to drink?

W Soda _____ _____ _____ cheesy food.

14

14 다음을 듣고, 무엇에 관한 설명인지 고르시오.

① 볼펜
② 공책
③ 알람
④ 달력
⑤ 시계

W You use this when you _____ _____ _____ something important like birthdays. It helps you _____ _____

_____ significant events. It also *reminds you of _____

_____. It comes in _____ _____. You can hang it on

the wall or _____ _____ _____ your desk. The one on

a smartphone lets you know your _____ _____ by ringing

an alarm.

＊ reminds you [리마인즈] [유] → [리마인쥬]

15

15 대화를 듣고, 남자가 대화 직후에 할 일로 가장 적절한 것을 고르시오.

① 기사 읽기
② 잡지 빌리기
③ 표현 익히기
④ 잡지 구독하기
⑤ 영어 공부하기

W This expression _____ _____.

M What are you reading?

W It's a magazine, which is really good for _____ _____.

M _____ _____ _____ _____ with it?

W I read an article and _____ _____ I'm not familiar with.

M That must be _____ _____. Where can I buy it?

W You can _____ _____ _____ online. It's cheaper if you buy a one-year subscription.

M Thanks.

숫자 정보 파악

16 대화를 듣고, 남자가 출발할 시각을 고르시오.

① 4:00   ② 4:20   ③ 4:30
④ 4:40   ⑤ 5:00

16

W   It's already 4 o'clock. Why are you still here?

M   I _____ _____ _____ at 5, so it's fine.

W   You should consider _____ _____ _____ _____ _____ to get there.

M   It only takes twenty minutes by car.

W   There's a _____ _____ in the evening. There will be _____ _____ on the way.

M   Oh, I totally forgot about that. I think I should leave now.

W   Yeah. Drive safely.

적절한 응답 찾기

17 대화를 듣고, 여자의 마지막 말에 대한 남자의 응답으로 가장 적절한 것을 고르시오.

Man: _____

① Well, I don't like my wrinkles either.
② You always set a good example for me.
③ You don't have to tell me all your secrets.
④ I'm serious. Love yourself for who you are.
⑤ Try to take care of the way you look to others.

17

W   Look at _____ _____ _____.

M   I can't really see them.

W   I feel like I am really getting old. I _____ _____.

M   Everybody _____ _____. Don't be too upset.

W   I would look much younger if I didn't have any wrinkles.

M   You are beautiful _____ _____ _____ _____ _____.

W   Do you really mean that?

M   I'm serious. Love yourself for who you are.

적절한 응답 찾기

18 대화를 듣고, 남자의 마지막 말에 대한 여자의 응답으로 가장 적절한 것을 고르시오.

Woman: _____

① I can say it's really summer now.
② I want to know what happened next.
③ We can try doing other things instead.
④ I should care about the environment like you.
⑤ Please give me some advice on how to stay healthy.

♥ **You can say that again.**
: 상대방의 말에 강한 동의를 나타낼 때 사용하는 표현으로, '네 말에 전적으로 동의해.'라는 뜻이다.
= I'm with you.
= I hear you.
= I can't agree with you more.

18 🇬🇧

W   Thanks for _____ _____ to lunch.

M   It's my pleasure. You helped me a lot yesterday.

W   That wasn't _____ _____ _____. By the way, why are the _____ _____?

M   Since it's bright and enough sunlight is coming in, I don't _____ _____ _____ _____ in the afternoon.

W   I see. That's a good habit.

M   And because the weather's getting hot, I feel hotter when the lights are on.

W   ♥You can say that again.

M   Above all, I believe we should _____ _____ to make the Earth healthier.

W   I should care about the environment like you.

19 대화를 듣고, 여자의 마지막 말에 대한 남자의 응답으로 가장 적절한 것을 고르시오.

Man: _____

① I see your job is very attractive.
② You can go with me if you want.
③ I usually wake up early in the morning.
④ First, you should figure out what you like.
⑤ Passion is not something you can pay for.

19

W Are you _____ _____ today?

M I'm planning to visit a new café and _____ _____ _____.

W You are _____ _____. Blogging regularly is never easy.

M It's just what I love to do.

W Isn't that camera too heavy to _____ _____?

M If I can take good pictures, the weight doesn't matter.

W How can I be _____ _____ _____ like you?

M First, you should figure out what you like.

20 다음 상황 설명을 듣고, Alex가 Kate에게 할 말로 가장 적절한 것을 고르시오.

Alex: Kate, _____

① let's take a taxi the next time.
② we're almost downtown.
③ you'd better offer that person your seat.
④ you should hold onto the strap tightly.
⑤ press the button at the next stop.

20

M Alex and his sister Kate _____ _____ _____ to go downtown. On the bus, there is _____ _____ _____, and Kate *sits in it. When they _____ _____ _____ _____ of their destination, the bus is already full. At the next stop, an old woman gets on the bus. She _____ _____ _____ _____ where Kate is sitting. In this situation, what would Alex most likely say to Kate?

Alex Kate, you'd better offer that person your seat.

* sits in [시츠] [인] → [싣친]

1 대화를 듣고, 여자가 만든 모자를 고르시오.

① ② ③

④ ⑤

2 대화를 듣고, 남자가 여자에게 부탁한 일로 가장 적절한 것을 고르시오.
① 옷 골라주기　　② 집 청소하기
③ 영화 예매하기　　④ 여동생 돌보기
⑤ 저녁 준비하기

3 다음 그림의 상황에 가장 적절한 대화를 고르시오.

①　　②　　③　　④　　⑤

4 대화를 듣고, 여자가 치과에 방문할 요일을 고르시오.
① 월요일　　② 화요일
③ 수요일　　④ 목요일
⑤ 금요일

5 대화를 듣고, 연기 동아리에 관해 언급되지 않은 것을 고르시오.
① 모집 인원　　② 연기 주제
③ 심사위원　　④ 오디션 장소
⑤ 오디션 요일

6 대화를 듣고, 두 사람이 대화하는 장소로 가장 적절한 곳을 고르시오.
① 배　　　　② 산　　　　③ 카페
④ 자동차　　⑤ 수영장

7 다음을 듣고, 두 사람의 대화가 어색한 것을 고르시오.
①　　②　　③　　④　　⑤

8 대화를 듣고, 여자가 남자에게 부탁한 일로 가장 적절한 것을 고르시오.
① 방 정돈하기
② 자동차 점검하기
③ 안 입는 옷 고르기
④ 옷장 새로 구입하기
⑤ 자선 단체로 옷 나르기

9 다음을 듣고, 무엇에 관한 안내 방송인지 고르시오.
① 미술관 견학
② 오늘의 일기 예보
③ 개교기념일 안내
④ 준비 운동의 중요성
⑤ 폭풍으로 인한 단축 수업

10 대화를 듣고, 남자가 지불할 금액을 고르시오.
① $70　　② $80　　③ $90
④ $100　　⑤ $110

11 대화를 듣고, 여자가 할 일로 가장 적절한 것을 고르시오.
① 일 마무리하기　　② 컴퓨터 구입하기
③ 수영복 사러 가기　　④ 수영 강습 등록하기
⑤ 의사에게 진찰 받기

12 다음을 듣고, Happy Farm에 관해 언급되지 <u>않은</u> 것을 고르시오.
① 개장 시간　　　② 농장 위치
③ 이용 요금　　　④ 체험 활동
⑤ 문의 연락처

13 대화를 듣고, 두 사람이 앉을 테이블을 고르시오.

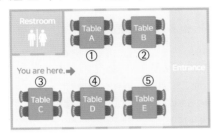

14 다음을 듣고, 무엇에 관한 설명인지 고르시오.
① 책　　　② 거울　　　③ 시계
④ 액자　　　⑤ 달력

15 대화를 듣고, 남자가 대화 직후에 할 일로 가장 적절한 것을 고르시오.
① 오른쪽 귀 뚫기
② 손 깨끗이 씻기
③ 친구와 쇼핑하기
④ 귀걸이 선물하기
⑤ 의사에게 진찰 받기

16 대화를 듣고, 여자가 책을 되돌려 받기로 한 날짜를 고르시오.
① 10월 9일　　　② 10월 10일
③ 10월 11일　　　④ 10월 12일
⑤ 10월 13일

17 대화를 듣고, 남자의 마지막 말에 대한 여자의 응답으로 가장 적절한 것을 고르시오.
Woman: _____
① Excuse me? I don't understand.
② You look great in the gray suit.
③ I appreciate it. You are so kind.
④ Sorry. I want to buy black jeans.
⑤ I'd like to pay in cash if possible.

18 대화를 듣고, 여자의 마지막 말에 대한 남자의 응답으로 가장 적절한 것을 고르시오.
Man: _____
① If so, I will support your dream.
② You should sell the piano tomorrow.
③ We traveled to Thailand this summer.
④ Let me buy tickets for the piano concert.
⑤ I recommend that you take tennis lessons.

19 대화를 듣고, 남자의 마지막 말에 대한 여자의 응답으로 가장 적절한 것을 고르시오.
Woman: _____
① Let's go to see a movie together.
② You need to read books in the library.
③ I already handed in my report yesterday.
④ I will help you to write your essay after school.
⑤ All right. I'll go to the library to write the report.

20 다음 상황 설명을 듣고, Ashley가 Michael에게 할 말로 가장 적절한 것을 고르시오.
Ashley: Michael, _____
① can you help me pack?
② how was your date last night?
③ will you take me to the airport?
④ can I treat you to dinner tonight?
⑤ would you mind if I stayed here tonight?

Listen and Check

● 대화를 다시 듣고, 알맞은 것을 고르시오.

1 Vivian knitted a hat for her little sister.
☐ True   ☐ False

2 Is today the woman's wedding anniversary?
☐ Yes   ☐ No

3 What is the woman interested in?
☐ a vacuum cleaner   ☐ a refrigerator

4 When is Dr. Min going to attend the seminar?
☐ Tuesday   ☐ Wednesday

5 The man needs to act like he is crying.
☐ True   ☐ False

6 Where are the man and the woman heading?
☐ a coral island   ☐ a volcano

7 The man wants to know how many people will go to the baseball game.
☐ True   ☐ False

8 What does Juha want to donate to charity?
☐ money   ☐ clothes

9 Who is speaking to the students?
☐ a principal   ☐ a weather reporter

10 Does the man want to register for the beginner course?
☐ Yes   ☐ No

11 Kaitlyn has some pain in her shoulder.
☐ True   ☐ False

12 Is the Happy Farm open on weekdays?
☐ Yes   ☐ No

13 What is the café famous for?
☐ cakes   ☐ coffee

14 People usually use this to check their appearance.
☐ True   ☐ False

15 When did the man get his ear pierced?
☐ two days ago   ☐ three days ago

16 Did Benjamin finish reading the book?
☐ Yes   ☐ No

17 What does the woman want to do?
☐ get a refund   ☐ exchange a shirt

18 What does Summer want to be?
☐ a teacher   ☐ a pianist

19 What's the deadline for the report?
☐ tomorrow   ☐ two days from now

20 Is Ashley visiting Switzerland to meet her friend?
☐ Yes   ☐ No

그림 정보 파악

1 대화를 듣고, 여자가 만든 모자를 고르시오.

① ② ③

④ ⑤

1

M Vivian, did you ★make that hat by yourself?

W Yes, I did. I _____ _____ for my little sister.

M You made it well. The striped hat is so cute.

W Thank you. _____ _____ to the hat was really hard.

M _____ _____ _____ _____ a pompom to the hat?

W I wanted to. But I didn't know _____ _____ _____

_____.

M Still, it's so cute. I'm sure your sister will like it.

★ make that hat [메이크] [댓] [햇] → [메이크댓햇]

부탁한 일 파악

2 대화를 듣고, 남자가 여자에게 부탁한 일로 가장 적절한 것을 고르시오.

① 옷 골라주기
② 집 청소하기
③ 영화 예매하기
④ 여동생 돌보기
⑤ 저녁 준비하기

2

W Dad, why are you _____ _____ _____ today?

M I _____ _____ _____ with your mom. As you know, today is our wedding anniversary.

W I totally forgot. Sorry, Dad.

M That's okay. If you're not busy, I need you to _____ _____ _____ while we are gone.

W Sure. I can do that. When will you come back?

M We'll be back _____ _____ _____ _____.

W I see. Have a great time, Dad!

그림 상황 파악

3 다음 그림의 상황에 가장 적절한 대화를 고르시오.

① ② ③ ④ ⑤

3

① W Are there any good Italian restaurants around here?

M Of course. There's one _____ _____ _____ _____.

② W How much is this refrigerator?

M It's _____ _____. It costs two thousand dollars.

③ W _____ _____ _____ _____ _____ for breakfast?

M Potato soup and an omelet, please.

④ W I like this jacket. _____ _____ _____ it?

M Sure, but I need it back before Friday.

⑤ W Wow! Your sofa is very comfortable.

M Thank you. I _____ _____ _____ _____.

특정 정보 파악

4 대화를 듣고, 여자가 치과에 방문할 요일을 고르시오.

① 월요일　　　② 화요일
③ 수요일　　　④ 목요일
⑤ 금요일

♥ **Hold on a second.**
: 통화 도중에 잠시 다른 일을 해야 하거나, 대화 도중에 급한 일로 상대방에게 기다려 달라고 부탁할 때 쓰는 표현으로, '잠시만 기다리세요.'라는 뜻이다.
= Wait a minute.
= One moment, please.

4 🇬🇧

[*Telephone rings.*]

M　Hello. This is the Min Dental Clinic. How can I help you?

W　Hello. I'd like to _____ _____ _____ for this week.

M　Okay. Which day do you want?

W　Is Wednesday at 2 p.m. possible?

M　Sorry. Dr. Min has to _____ _____ _____ on Wednesday afternoon.

W　Then _____ _____ _____ at 2 p.m.?

M　♥ Hold on a second. [*Pause*] _____ _____.

W　Great. See you then.

언급 유무 파악

5 대화를 듣고, 연기 동아리에 관해 언급되지 **않은** 것을 고르시오.

① 모집 인원
② 연기 주제
③ 심사위원
④ 오디션 장소
⑤ 오디션 요일

5

W　Kyusung, what are you looking at?

M　The _____ _____ _____ on the bulletin board. I want to join it.

W　That would be perfect for you. When and where is the audition taking place?

M　In the school auditorium next Friday afternoon. They will _____ _____ _____ _____.

W　You must be nervous. What do you have to do at the audition?

M　We _____ _____ to do anything specific. But I need to *act like I am crying.

W　If you want, I'll _____ _____ _____ _____ when you practice.

M　Really? Thank you so much!

★ act like [액트] [라이크] → [액라잌]

장소 추론

6 대화를 듣고, 두 사람이 대화하는 장소로 가장 적절한 곳을 고르시오.

① 배　　　　② 산
③ 카페　　　④ 자동차
⑤ 수영장

♥ **That's a relief.**
: 안 좋은 상황을 무사히 넘기거나 걱정했던 일이 잘 풀렸을 때 쓰는 표현으로, '그거 다행이다.'라는 뜻이다.
= What a relief.
= It's a good thing S + V.

6

W　Are you all right? You _____ _____.

M　This ship is rolling from side to side. I feel like I'm going to throw up.

W　Are you _____ _____? Let's go on the deck.

M　Good idea. I need to _____ _____ _____ _____.

W　[*Door closes.*] How do you feel now?

M　Much better. [*Pause*] Look! I see a coral island.

W　♥ That's a relief. I think we're _____ _____ _____ our destination.

어색한 대화 찾기

7 다음을 듣고, 두 사람의 대화가 <u>어색한</u> 것을 고르시오.

①   ②   ③   ④   ⑤

7

① **M** What do you do in your free time?

   W I usually _____ _____ _____ or listen to music.

② **M** The weather is so hot! My ice cream is melting.

   W _____ _____ _____ your ice cream.

③ **M** Is there _____ _____ _____?

   W I don't think so. We should order some food.

④ **M** How many people are going to the baseball game?

   W The game is supposed _____ _____ _____

   _____ _____.

⑤ **M** Are you done _____ _____ _____ _____?

   W Yes, I just finished.

부탁한 일 파악

8 대화를 듣고, 여자가 남자에게 부탁한 일로 가장 적절한 것을 고르시오.

① 방 정돈하기
② 자동차 점검하기
③ 안 입는 옷 고르기
④ 옷장 새로 구입하기
⑤ 자선 단체로 옷 나르기

> 💗 **What for?**
> : 어떤 일의 목적이나 이유를 묻기 위해 쓰는 표현으로, '무엇 때문에?' 또는 '왜?'라는 뜻이다.
> = For what reason?
> = How come?

8

M Juha, are you organizing your closet?

W Actually, I'm _____ _____ _____ that I never wear or that don't _____ _____.

M 💗 What for?

W I want to _____ _____ _____ _____.

M That's a good deed. Do you need any help?

W Hmm... Can you help me to _____ _____ _____ to a charity?

M Sure. I'll be right back with my car.

화제·주제 파악

9 다음을 듣고, 무엇에 관한 안내 방송인지 고르시오.

① 미술관 견학
② 오늘의 일기 예보
③ 개교기념일 안내
④ 준비 운동의 중요성
⑤ 폭풍으로 인한 단축 수업

9

W Pay attention, students! This is _____ _____ _____. Because a _____ _____ _____ _____ _____, we have decided to _____ _____ _____. It is raining worse, and the wind is blowing heavily. The weather forecast says that the storm is expected to be severe. Students should go home right now and _____ _____ _____. We will keep you informed if anything happens.

숫자 정보 파악

10 대화를 듣고, 남자가 지불할 금액을 고르시오.

① $70
② $80
③ $90
④ $100
⑤ $110

10

W Welcome to the Beijing Chinese Language School. How may I help you?

M I'd like to _____ _____ _____ _____ _____ .

W Okay. The beginner course is 100 dollars a month.

M That's kind of expensive. Is there a discount for beginners?

W Let me see. We're _____ _____ _____ _____ to new students.

M Sounds perfect! Is the _____ _____ ?

W Sorry. You have to buy it at a bookstore.

할 일 파악

11 대화를 듣고, 여자가 할 일로 가장 적절한 것을 고르시오.

① 일 마무리하기
② 컴퓨터 구입하기
③ 수영복 사러 가기
④ 수영 강습 등록하기
⑤ 의사에게 진찰 받기

> ♥ **I have no choice.**
> : 다른 선택의 여지가 없어서 어떤 일을 할 수 밖에 없을 때 쓰는 표현으로, '그럴 수밖에 없어.'라는 뜻이다.
> = I don't have any other choice.

11

M Kaitlyn, you're always sitting in front of your computer.

W ♥I have no choice. I'm _____ _____ on it.

M That's why you have _____ _____ _____ _____ . You need to exercise regularly.

W You're right. I should _____ _____ _____ _____ .

M Why don't you _____ _____ with me?

W That sounds good. But I don't have a swimsuit.

M You can buy one. Let's go to a store.

언급 유무 파악

12 다음을 듣고, Happy Farm에 관해 언급되지 **않은** 것을 고르시오.

① 개장 시간
② 농장 위치
③ 이용 요금
④ 체험 활동
⑤ 문의 연락처

12

M Welcome to Happy Farm. We are _____ _____ _____ from 10 a.m. to 5 p.m. We offer _____ _____ _____ _____ . You can experience life on a farm. Admission is 10 dollars for adults and 5 dollars for children. You can feed and water the horses. You can also _____ _____ _____ _____ _____ . When you get close to the animals, please be careful. If you need help or more information, call us at 010-1234-5678.

13 대화를 듣고, 두 사람이 앉을 테이블을 고르시오.

♥ **I can't wait to ~.**
: 어떤 일을 몹시 하고 싶어서 더 이상 기다릴 수 없다는 의미를 가진 표현으로, '너무 ~ 하고 싶어.'라는 뜻이다.

13

M Look! This café is crowded with people.

W The reason is that it is _____ _____ its cakes.

M Is it? ♥I can't wait to taste one.

W Okay. _____ _____ _____ at Table A.

M I don't want to. It's _____ _____ _____ _____.

W Then how about Table E?

M _____ _____ _____? It must be noisy there. Let's sit
*next to Table E.

W Do you mean between Table C and Table E? Okay.

★ next to [넥스트] [투] → [넥스투]

화제·주제 파악

14 다음을 듣고, 무엇에 관한 설명인지 고르시오.

① 책
② 거울
③ 시계
④ 액자
⑤ 달력

14

W Most people have this in their homes. This may be on your wall or desk. It has many different shapes. The surface is smooth, and it can _____ _____. When you look at this, you can _____ _____ _____ or _____ _____ _____. It is also fragile. Some people believe that if you break this, it will _____ _____ _____.

할 일 파악

15 대화를 듣고, 남자가 대화 직후에 할 일로 가장 적절한 것을 고르시오.

① 오른쪽 귀 뚫기
② 손 깨끗이 씻기
③ 친구와 쇼핑하기
④ 귀걸이 선물하기
⑤ 의사에게 진찰 받기

15 🇬🇧

W What's the matter with your left ear?

M I got _____ _____ _____ three days ago. Nice, huh?

W No. I mean that your ear is bleeding.

M Are you sure? In fact, I _____ _____ because it was itching.

W That's the problem. You should never touch your ear after _____ _____ _____.

M Oh, no! What should I do?

W You seem to _____ _____ _____. Go to see a doctor.

16 대화를 듣고, 여자가 책을 되돌려 받기로 한 날짜를 고르시오.

① 10월 9일
② 10월 10일
③ 10월 11일
④ 10월 12일
⑤ 10월 13일

16

W   Benjamin, here is the _____ _____ _____.

M   Wow! Thank you. Did you finish reading it?

W   Of course I did. It was so interesting!

M   I can't wait to read it. By the way, _____ _____ _____ _____ this book?

W   How about next Friday? On October 10.

M   Sorry, but I have to _____ _____ _____ that day. Is October 12 possible?

W   Do you mean next Sunday? I think that's fine.

M   That's good. Let's meet on October 12 after lunch.

W   Okay. _____ _____ the book.

17 대화를 듣고, 남자의 마지막 말에 대한 여자의 응답으로 가장 적절한 것을 고르시오.

Woman: _____

① Excuse me? I don't understand.
② You look great in the gray suit.
③ I appreciate it. You are so kind.
④ Sorry. I want to buy black jeans.
⑤ I'd like to pay in cash if possible.

17

M   Welcome. What can I do for you?

W   I'd like to _____ _____ _____ on this shirt. I *bought it three days ago.

M   Is there _____ _____ with it?

W   Let me show you. There is a hole here.

M   Oh, I'm sorry. Do you _____ _____ _____?

W   No. I'm afraid I lost it.

M   Sorry. We can give you a refund _____ _____ _____ _____ the receipt.

W   Excuse me? I don't understand.

* bought it [보우트] [잇] → [보릿]

18 대화를 듣고, 여자의 마지막 말에 대한 남자의 응답으로 가장 적절한 것을 고르시오.

Man: _____

① If so, I will support your dream.
② You should sell the piano tomorrow.
③ We traveled to Thailand this summer.
④ Let me buy tickets for the piano concert.
⑤ I recommend that you take tennis lessons.

18

M   Summer, I think you should _____ _____ _____ _____.

W   Why? I really enjoy them a lot.

M   But you need to _____ _____ _____ _____.

W   I understand what you're saying. But I want to be a pianist.

M   Do you? I thought you play the piano _____ _____.

W   No, Dad. I want to _____ _____ _____ someday.

M   If so, I will support your dream.

적절한 응답 찾기

19 대화를 듣고, 남자의 마지막 말에 대한 여자의 응답으로 가장 적절한 것을 고르시오.

Woman: _____

① Let's go to see a movie together.
② You need to read books in the library.
③ I already handed in my report yesterday.
④ I will help you to write your essay after school.
⑤ All right. I'll go to the library to write the report.

♥ **Are you serious?**
: 어떤 일에 대해서 진심인지 여부를 확인하려고 물어볼 때 쓰는 표현으로, '정말이니?'라는 뜻이다.
= Seriously?

19

M Seoyoung, where are you going?

W I'm going to the theater to watch a movie.

M ♥Are you serious? You didn't _____ _____ _____ _____, right?

W No, but I can do it tomorrow.

M The report is _____ _____. You should _____ _____ _____ _____.

W Oh, no. I don't want to _____ _____ _____ in the library.

M If you don't *submit it tomorrow, you will _____ _____ _____.

W All right. I'll go to the library to write the report.

* submit it [썹미트] [잇] → [썹미릿]

상황에 맞는 말 찾기

20 다음 상황 설명을 듣고, Ashley가 Michael에게 할 말로 가장 적절한 것을 고르시오.

Ashley: Michael, _____

① can you help me pack?
② how was your date last night?
③ will you take me to the airport?
④ can I treat you to dinner tonight?
⑤ would you mind if I stayed here tonight?

20

M Ashley is visiting Switzerland _____ _____ _____ _____ Michael. Michael is so happy to see her that he invites her to his place. He introduces some beautiful tourist sites to her. He also drives her to the sites and _____ _____ _____ _____. Ashley has to leave tomorrow. She _____ _____ _____ _____ _____ during her visit. She wants to _____ _____ _____ _____ _____ _____ at a nice restaurant. In this situation, what would Ashley most likely say to Michael?

Ashley Michael, can I treat you to dinner tonight?

1 대화를 듣고, 남자가 구입할 시계를 고르시오.

① ② ③

④ ⑤

2 대화를 듣고, 남자가 여자에게 전화한 목적으로 가장 적절한 것을 고르시오.
① 추천 수업을 확인하려고
② 수업 취소를 알리려고
③ 수업 내용을 문의하려고
④ 수업 신청을 함께하려고
⑤ 다른 강의를 신청하려고

3 다음 그림의 상황에 가장 적절한 대화를 고르시오.

① ② ③ ④ ⑤

4 대화를 듣고, 여자가 이동할 교통수단을 고르시오.
① 지하철 ② 열차 ③ 택시
④ 버스 ⑤ 자전거

5 다음을 듣고, Eiffel Tower에 대해 언급되지 않은 것을 고르시오.
① 높이 ② 건설년도
③ 건설 기간 ④ 건설 인원
⑤ 연간 방문객 수

6 대화를 듣고, 두 사람의 관계로 가장 적절한 것을 고르시오.
① 청소부 — 고객 ② 세탁소 직원 — 고객
③ 미용사 — 손님 ④ 진행자 — 작가
⑤ 호텔리어 — 투숙객

7 대화를 듣고, 두 사람의 대화가 어색한 것을 고르시오.
① ② ③ ④ ⑤

8 대화를 듣고, 남자가 여자에게 부탁한 일로 가장 적절한 것을 고르시오.
① 콘서트 표 예매하기
② 수학여행 일정 확인하기
③ 콘서트 출연진 확인하기
④ 서점에서 표 구매하기
⑤ 현장 학습 도와주기

9 대화를 듣고, 여자의 마지막 말에 담긴 의도로 가장 적절한 것을 고르시오.
① 사과 ② 감사 ③ 제안
④ 동의 ⑤ 유감

10 대화를 듣고, 남자가 지불할 금액을 고르시오.
① $180 ② $200 ③ $220
④ $225 ⑤ $360

11 대화를 듣고, 여자가 할 일로 가장 적절한 것을 고르시오.
① 피트니스 클럽에 등록한다.
② 집에서 유산소 운동을 시작한다.
③ 친구와 함께 운동을 한다.
④ 매일 학교까지 걸어 다닌다.
⑤ 새로운 옷을 구매한다.

12 다음을 듣고, power generation에 관해 언급되지 않은 것을 고르시오.
① 댐이 만들어지는 장소 ② 수력 발전의 장점
③ 화력 발전의 단점   ④ 화력 발전의 원리
⑤ 원자력 발전의 원리

13 다음 표를 보면서 대화를 듣고, 남자가 탑승할 기차를 고르시오.

	Train Number	Departure	Time	Arrival	Time
①	5315	Busan	5:00	Seoul	8:30
②	2665	Busan	6:00	Seoul	9:30
③	0509	Seoul	1:30	Busan	5:00
④	6358	Seoul	2:30	Busan	6:00
⑤	4244	Seoul	3:00	Gunpo	6:30

14 다음을 듣고, 무엇에 관한 설명인지 고르시오.
① 한국 전쟁의 원인
② UN군의 역사
③ UN군의 구성 국가
④ 전쟁에 대한 찬반양론
⑤ 한국군 파병에 대한 논쟁

15 대화를 듣고, 남자가 할 일로 가장 적절한 것을 고르시오.
① 매일 철자 쓰기 연습을 한다.
② 도서관에서 관련된 책을 빌린다.
③ 발음 연습을 시작한다.
④ 영어 단어 학습 강의를 듣는다.
⑤ 여자와 함께 영어를 공부한다.

16 대화를 듣고, 여자가 구입할 물건을 고르시오.
① 청바지   ② 강아지 인형
③ 고양이 인형   ④ 강아지 그림 티셔츠
⑤ 애완견용 옷

17 대화를 듣고, 여자의 마지막 말에 대한 남자의 응답으로 가장 적절한 것을 고르시오.
Man: _____
① The line is busy right now.
② I'm sorry, but do I know you?
③ Your reservation is complete.
④ No problem. Does he have your number?
⑤ Thanks for calling.

18 대화를 듣고, 남자의 마지막 말에 대한 여자의 응답으로 가장 적절한 것을 고르시오.
Woman: _____
① Don't be too hard on yourself.
② The total is 8 dollars.
③ By next Friday.
④ Of course. It doesn't matter.
⑤ From 10 a.m. to 5 p.m.

19 대화를 듣고, 여자의 마지막 말에 대한 남자의 응답으로 가장 적절한 것을 고르시오.
Man: _____
① I'm allergic to meat.
② Korean food is out of style.
③ People should eat more vegetables.
④ I'd love to go there then.
⑤ *Bulgogi* is my favorite.

20 다음 상황 설명을 듣고, Jiwoo가 Ryan에게 할 말로 가장 적절한 것을 고르시오.
Jiwoo: Ryan, _____
① I had a great time at the party.
② why didn't you come to the party?
③ cheer up. You can do better the next time.
④ the bus is more comfortable.
⑤ how terrible. That must have been embarrassing.

Listen and Check

정답 및 해설 p.016

● 대화를 다시 듣고, 알맞은 것을 고르시오.

1 The woman wants a round clock for her living room.
☐ True   ☐ False

2 Students who sign up for the English class together will get a ten-percent discount.
☐ True   ☐ False

3 The displayed coat is not for sale.
☐ Yes   ☐ No

4 A person can get to the Seoul Foreign School by train.
☐ Yes   ☐ No

5 How tall is the Eiffel Tower?
☐ 324 meters   ☐ 889 meters

6 What time does the laundry service end?
☐ 6 p.m.   ☐ 9 p.m.

7 If you want to open a bank account, you should fill out a registration form.
☐ True   ☐ False

8 What day does the man go on a field trip?
☐ Saturday   ☐ Monday

9 Why did the man have to wait so long?
☐ because he didn't put his name on the waiting list
☐ because he was standing in the wrong line

10 A room with a mountain view costs a hundred dollars for the night.
☐ True   ☐ False

11 The woman is going to join the gym to lose weight.
☐ True   ☐ False

12 Burning fossil fuels to make electricity may cause global warming.
☐ True   ☐ False

13 The man will take the train that gets to Busan today.
☐ True   ☐ False

14 How many countries fought for South Korea during the Korean War?
☐ 21   ☐ 12

15 The man will study English with the woman.
☐ True   ☐ False

16 Why doesn't the woman buy the white T-shirt with the black dog on the left?
☐ because her father doesn't like it
☐ because her father says it will not look good on her

17 Dr. Carter is attending a seminar being held in Chicago.
☐ True   ☐ False

18 Can the man borrow all the book he wants?
☐ Yes   ☐ No

19 The man's favorite Korean food is *bibimbap*.
☐ True   ☐ False

20 Ryan didn't go to the party, but he met Jiwoo when he was on the subway.
☐ True   ☐ False

1 대화를 듣고, 남자가 구입할 시계를 고르시오.

① ② ③

④ ⑤

1 🇬🇧

M Hello. I want to get a clock to hang in the nursing home I work at.

W Sure. We have various shapes and designs _____ _____ _____. Do you have _____ _____ _____?

M Yes. I want a _____ _____ with big numbers on it.

W Um, what about this one with the green background? It's a plain design that's very simple.

M The numbers are _____ _____ _____ to see.

W Then this would be perfect. It's white, and the numbers on it are _____ _____ _____ _____ _____.

M I like it.

목적 파악

2 대화를 듣고, 남자가 여자에게 전화한 목적으로 가장 적절한 것을 고르시오.

① 추천 수업을 확인하려고
② 수업 취소를 알리려고
③ 수업 내용을 문의하려고
④ 수업 신청을 함께하려고
⑤ 다른 강의를 신청하려고

♥ **Are you done with ~?**
: 어떤 일이 다 끝났는지를 물을 때 사용하는 표현으로, '너 ~ 끝났니?'라고 물을 때 'Did you finish ~?'라는 표현보다 자주 쓰인다.

2

[*Cellphone rings.*]

M Hi, Melissa. It's me, Jason.

W Hi, Jason. ♥Are you done with English class?

M Yes. And guess what. Now I'm at the _____ _____ to pay for next month's class.

W So why are you calling? Is there a problem?

M No. I am calling you because I want to know if you want to _____ _____ _____ _____ _____ next month.

W Do you mean Mr. Taylor's grammar class?

M Yes. The sign says that we can get a _____ _____ if we register for an English class together. Isn't that great?

W That's a good deal, but I _____ _____ _____ _____ _____. Sorry, Jason.

그림 상황 파악

3 다음 그림의 상황에 가장 적절한 대화를 고르시오.

① ② ③ ④ ⑤

3

① **W** This dress is so nice. How much does it cost?

　M The original price is 50 dollars, but _____ _____ a 20-percent discount on it.

② **W** Let's change the clothes on the mannequin in our display window.

　M Okay. _____ _____ _____ in the outfit that arrived yesterday.

③ **W** I don't think these shoes go with these pants.

　M I'll find some other shoes that _____ _____ _____.

④ **W** _____ _____ _____ _____ this coat?

　M I'm sorry, but it is not for sale. It's only for display.

⑤ **W** Where is the _____ _____ _____?

　M There's one on the third floor next to the pharmacy.

교통수단 파악

4 대화를 듣고, 여자가 이동할 교통수단
을 고르시오.

① 지하철
② 열차
③ 택시
④ 버스
⑤ 자전거

♥ **What can I do for you?**

: 상대방에게 도움을 주려고 먼저 물어볼 때
쓰는 표현으로, '도와 드릴까요?'라는 뜻이
다.
= How may I help you?

4

M Welcome to the Seoul Tourist Information Center. ♥What can I do for
you?

W I want to go to the Seoul Foreign School. What is _____
_____ _____ _____ _____ _____? Can I
take the subway?

M Well, there isn't a subway station near the Seoul Foreign School. You
_____ _____ _____ _____ or taxi.

W Which do you think would be better?

M I think a taxi would be _____ _____ _____.

W Good. Then I'll take a taxi. Thank you.

언급 유무 파악

5 다음을 듣고, Eiffel Tower에 대해 언급
되지 <u>않은</u> 것을 고르시오.

① 높이
② 건설년도
③ 건설 기간
④ 건설 인원
⑤ 연간 방문객 수

5

M Thank you for visiting the Eiffel Tower. The Eiffel Tower is _____
_____ _____ that stands 324 meters tall. It was built
in Paris in 1889. It is currently the most famous symbol of Paris.
Famous _____ _____ _____ to design the monument,
which took over two years to finish. Currently, the Eiffel Tower is the
_____ _____ in the world with over 7 million visitors a year.
If it's your first time in Paris, going up the Eiffel Tower is _____
_____. Have a nice trip.

관계 추론

6 대화를 듣고, 두 사람의 관계로 가장 적
절한 것을 고르시오.

① 청소부 ― 고객
② 세탁소 직원 ― 고객
③ 미용사 ― 손님
④ 진행자 ― 작가
⑤ 호텔리어 ― 투숙객

♥ **Exactly!**

: 상대방의 말에 대한 강한 수긍을 나타낼 때
사용하는 표현으로, '바로 그거에요.'라는 뜻
이다.
= That's it!
= You got it!
= There you go!

6 🇬🇧

M Hello. How can I help you?

W Can you give me a morning call at 6 tomorrow?

M Do you mean a wakeup call? Sure. Your room _____ _____
_____, right?

W ♥Exactly.

M Okay. Is there anything else I can do for you?

W Well, I wonder if _____ _____ _____ _____ now.

M I'm sorry. You can only _____ _____ _____
_____ until 9 p.m.

W All right. Thanks.

어색한 대화 찾기

7 대화를 듣고, 두 사람의 대화가 <u>어색한</u> 것을 고르시오.

① ② ③ ④ ⑤

7

① M Do you want more bread?

  W No, thanks. _____ _____ _____.

② M How often do you go to the movies?

  W I usually go _____ _____ _____.

③ M How *have you been?

  W _____ _____ _____ to Japan.

④ M I'd like to open an account.

  W Okay. Can you _____ _____ _____ _____?

⑤ M How long will it take to get there?

  W It will take _____ _____ _____ _____.

★ Have you been [해브] [유] [빈] → [해뷰빈]

부탁한 일 파악

8 대화를 듣고, 남자가 여자에게 부탁한 일로 가장 적절한 것을 고르시오.

① 콘서트 표 예매하기
② 수학여행 일정 확인하기
③ 콘서트 출연진 확인하기
④ 서점에서 표 구매하기
⑤ 현장 학습 도와주기

8

W Thomas, this is Emily. Did you hear that TWICE _____ _____ _____ _____ in our town?

M Are you serious? When is it?

W In a month.

M I'm a _____ _____ _____ _____. Let's book tickets before they _____ _____.

W I'd like to, but tickets go on sale next week.

M Oh, I'm going on a field trip next Monday. Emily, could you _____ _____ _____ _____?

W Do you mean I should get you a ticket? Don't worry about that. I'll do that for you.

M Thanks, Emily. I owe you one.

의도 파악

9 대화를 듣고, 여자의 마지막 말에 담긴 의도로 가장 적절한 것을 고르시오.

① 사과
② 감사
③ 제안
④ 동의
⑤ 유감

9

M Excuse me, but how long do I have to wait? I _____ _____ _____ _____ _____ 30 minutes.

W Oh, I'm sorry. Let me check. What's your name?

M Samson Lee. But _____ do you need my name _____?

W Well, you didn't put your name on the waiting list.

M The waiting list? I didn't know about that. I just lined up and _____ _____ _____ _____!

W I'm sorry to hear that, but there is nothing I can do for you. You _____ _____ _____ our policy in advance.

숫자 정보 파악

10 대화를 듣고, 남자가 지불할 금액을 고르시오.

① $180
② $200
③ $220
④ $225
⑤ $360

10

W Park Hotel. How can I help you?

M I want to reserve a single room for two nights _____ _____ June 6.

W Hold on, please. We have several rooms with an ocean view and one with a mountain view _____.

M How much is an ocean view?

W It's 150 dollars _____ _____ _____, but we can give you a 10% discount if you stay for two nights.

M I see. Then how about the room with the mountain view?

W It costs 50 dollars less, and we _____ _____ _____ _____ _____.

M Okay. I'll take that one.

할 일 파악

11 대화를 듣고, 여자가 할 일로 가장 적절한 것을 고르시오.

① 피트니스 클럽에 등록한다.
② 집에서 유산소 운동을 시작한다.
③ 친구와 함께 운동을 한다.
④ 매일 학교까지 걸어 다닌다.
⑤ 새로운 옷을 구매한다.

♥ **Are you sure?**
: 상대방에게 확인을 요청할 때 사용하는 표현으로, '확실한가요?'라는 뜻이다.
= Are you certain?

11

W I've gained _____ _____ _____ _____.

M ♥Are you sure? I don't think you're _____ _____ _____.

W I can't *fit into any of the clothes I bought a year ago.

M How about going to a fitness club?

W There is not one near my house.

M Then _____ _____ _____ _____ at home.

W I don't want to do that at home. For me, home is a place of rest.

M Then why don't you _____ _____ _____ going to school on foot?

W That sounds good. I'll try to do that.

★ fit into [핏] [인투] → [피린투]

언급 유무 파악

12 다음을 듣고, power generation에 관해 언급되지 <u>않은</u> 것을 고르시오.

① 댐이 만들어지는 장소
② 수력 발전의 장점
③ 화력 발전의 단점
④ 화력 발전의 원리
⑤ 원자력 발전의 원리

12 🇬🇧

W There are several ways to generate electricity. A long time ago, people built waterwheels and _____ _____ _____ of flowing water into useful forms of power, but nowadays, we build dams on rivers to produce electricity. Another way we use to make electricity is to _____ _____ _____. But many people are worried that this method of power generation may have harmful effects on the environment and cause global warming. Yet another way is by using nuclear energy. Nuclear power _____ _____ _____ _____ to produce electricity.

표 파악

13 다음 표를 보면서 대화를 듣고, 남자가 탑승할 기차를 고르시오.

	Train Number	Departure	Time	Arrival	Time
①	5315	Busan	5:00	Seoul	8:30
②	2665	Busan	6:00	Seoul	9:30
③	0509	Seoul	1:30	Busan	5:00
④	6358	Seoul	2:30	Busan	6:00
⑤	4244	Seoul	3:00	Gunpo	6:30

13

W Good morning. What can I do for you?

M I'd like to _____ _____ _____ for Busan tomorrow.

W Okay. For what time?

M Are there any trains that _____ _____ _____ _____ to Busan at 5:30?

W Sorry. We have _____ _____ _____ _____ 5 p.m. and another train arriving at 6:00 p.m.

M I'll take a seat on _____ _____ _____. Here is my credit card.

W Okay. Your ticket is reserved. Please check the date, the time, and the number of your train. Thank you.

화제·주제 파악

14 다음을 듣고, 무엇에 관한 설명인지 고르시오.

① 한국 전쟁의 원인
② UN군의 역사
③ UN군의 구성 국가
④ 전쟁에 대한 찬반양론
⑤ 한국군 파병에 대한 논쟁

14

M The Korean War was a war between North Korea and South Korea. Twenty-one countries in the United Nations helped South Korea keep the peace. Nowadays, South Korea is one of those countries which is asked to send _____ _____ _____ _____ _____ of the world. Some Koreans are _____ doing this, but others agree with _____ _____ _____. They say that Koreans need to pay back _____ _____ _____ during the Korean War.

할 일 파악

15 대화를 듣고, 남자가 할 일로 가장 적절한 것을 고르시오.

① 매일 철자 쓰기 연습을 한다.
② 도서관에서 관련된 책을 빌린다.
③ 발음 연습을 시작한다.
④ 영어 단어 학습 강의를 듣는다.
⑤ 여자와 함께 영어를 공부한다.

💜 **Would you like to +V?**

: 상대방에게 무언가를 제안하거나 권유할 때 사용하는 표현으로, '~하고 싶으세요?'라는 뜻이다.

15

M You won first prize in the spelling bee. Congratulations!

W Thanks. _____ _____ _____ the results.

M Can you give me _____ _____ _____ on memorizing how to spell words?

W Well, I have practiced spelling 10 words every day since the seventh grade. And I *make a list of difficult words and _____ _____ _____.

M I think the old saying is "Practice makes perfect."

W Oh, I'm looking for someone to study English together with. 💜 Would you like to do that?

M Sure. That will help _____ _____ _____ _____.

★ make a list [메이크] [어] [리스트] → [메이커리스트]

16

특정 정보 파악

16 대화를 듣고, 여자가 구입할 물건을 고르시오.

① 청바지
② 강아지 인형
③ 고양이 인형
④ 강아지 그림 티셔츠
⑤ 애완견용 옷

W Dad, what are you going to buy me for my birthday?

M Anything you want, honey. Go ahead and _____ _____ _____ _____ _____.

W Okay. I like this white T-shirt with the black dog on the left.

M Well, I don't think that will _____ _____ _____ _____.

W How about this white round one with _____ _____ and the cat in the middle?

M I don't like that one either.

W Then I'll just take the black V-neck T-shirt _____ _____ _____ _____ in the middle.

M That one looks nice.

17

적절한 응답 찾기

17 대화를 듣고, 여자의 마지막 말에 대한 남자의 응답으로 가장 적절한 것을 고르시오.

Man: _____
① The line is busy right now.
② I'm sorry, but do I know you?
③ Your reservation is complete.
④ No problem. Does he have your number?
⑤ Thanks for calling.

[*Telephone rings.*]

M Hello. Doctor Smith's office.

W Hello. Can I speak to Dr. Smith?

M I'm afraid he _____ _____ _____ _____ _____.

W What time do you _____ _____ _____ _____ _____?

M He's not going to be here today. He is attending _____ _____ _____ _____ in Chicago. Can I take a message?

W Yes, please. This is Jessica Carter from UCLA. Would you ask him to call me back?

M No problem. Does he have your number?

18

적절한 응답 찾기

18 대화를 듣고, 남자의 마지막 말에 대한 여자의 응답으로 가장 적절한 것을 고르시오.

Woman: _____
① Don't be too hard on yourself.
② The total is 8 dollars.
③ By next Friday.
④ Of course. It doesn't matter.
⑤ From 10 a.m. to 5 p.m.

W What can I do for you?

M I'd like to _____ _____ _____ _____.

W Sure. Can I see your student ID?

M Here you are.

[*Keyboard sounds*]

W You have _____ _____ _____. So you can only borrow four books at this time.

M Oh, sorry. I'll put _____ _____ _____ _____.

W Okay, four books to check out. And please don't forget you must return the overdue one by tomorrow.

M All right. When do I _____ _____ _____ these books?

W By next Friday.

19 대화를 듣고, 여자의 마지막 말에 대한 남자의 응답으로 가장 적절한 것을 고르시오.

Man: _____

① I'm allergic to meat.
② Korean food is out of style.
③ People should eat more vegetables.
④ I'd love to go there then.
⑤ *Bulgogi* is my favorite.

♥ I'd love to ~
: 상대방의 제안을 수락할 때 사용하는 표현으로, '~ 하고 싶다'라는 뜻이다. 때때로 제안을 받아들이고 싶지만, 거절을 해야 할 때는 'I'd love to, but ~'을 사용하기도 하며 '고맙지만 사양할게.'라는 뜻을 가진다.

19

M Whew! It's time to eat lunch. What shall we have today?

W _____ _____ _____ Korean Food World?

M No, not yet. Is it nice?

W Yeah. It's clean, and the food _____ _____. And we can have the lunch special there for only 9 dollars. _____ _____ _____?

M I think _____ _____ _____ _____. What *kind of food does it have?

W *Bibimbap*, *bulgogi*, *japchae*, and lots of other Korean foods as well as a nice _____ _____!

M ♥ I'd love to go there then.

* kind of [카인드] [오브] → [카인덥]

20 다음 상황 설명을 듣고, Jiwoo가 Ryan에게 할 말로 가장 적절한 것을 고르시오.

Jiwoo: Ryan, _____

① I had a great time at the party.
② why didn't you come to the party?
③ cheer up. You can do better the next time.
④ the bus is more comfortable.
⑤ how terrible. That must have been embarrassing.

♥ How + 형용사!
: 감탄을 나타낼 때 사용하는 표현으로, '~하구나!'라는 뜻이다.

20

W Ryan meets Jiwoo _____ _____ _____ _____ school. Ryan tells her that he was embarrassed by _____ _____ _____ last night. He _____ _____ _____ _____ to a party at his best friend's house, but he couldn't go there. After leaving his home, he took the subway, but he _____ _____ when he was on the subway. He wanted to go to the party, but due to his mistake, he ended up going to a station _____ _____ _____ his friend's house. In this situation, what would Jiwoo most likely say to him?

Jiwoo Ryan, ♥ how terrible. That must have been embarrassing.

1 대화를 듣고, 두 사람이 선택한 책표지로 알맞은 것을 고르시오.

① ② ③

④ ⑤

2 대화를 듣고, 여자가 남자에게 전화한 목적으로 가장 적절한 것을 고르시오.
① 책의 대출 비용을 알기 위해
② 책의 환불을 요구하기 위해
③ 책을 추가 주문하기 위해
④ 파손된 책을 교환하기 위해
⑤ 책의 배송 날짜를 알기 위해

3 다음 그림의 상황에 가장 적절한 대화를 고르시오.

① ② ③ ④ ⑤

4 대화를 듣고, 두 사람이 만나기로 한 요일을 고르시오.
① 월요일 ② 화요일 ③ 수요일
④ 목요일 ⑤ 금요일

5 다음을 듣고, 공원의 규칙에 대해 언급되지 <u>않은</u> 것을 고르시오.
① 쓰레기를 버리지 말 것
② 꽃을 꺾지 말 것
③ 계곡에서 수영을 하지 말 것
④ 동물에게 먹이를 주지 말 것
⑤ 담배를 피우지 말 것

6 대화를 듣고, 두 사람의 관계로 가장 적절한 것을 고르시오.
① 상담원 — 고객
② 검침원 — 주택 관리사
③ 마트 배달원 — 고객
④ 이삿짐센터 직원 — 고객
⑤ 농부 — 농산물 검사관

7 대화를 듣고, 두 사람의 대화가 <u>어색한</u> 것을 고르시오.
① ② ③ ④ ⑤

8 대화를 듣고, 여자가 남자에게 충고한 일로 가장 적절한 것을 고르시오.
① 좀 더 일찍 시작하라.
② 계획을 세워서 하라.
③ 반성하는 삶을 살아라.
④ 스스로 힘으로 해라.
⑤ 약속을 어기지 마라.

9 대화를 듣고, 남자의 마지막 말에 담긴 의도로 가장 적절한 것을 고르시오.
① 격려 ② 동의 ③ 기대
④ 걱정 ⑤ 감사

10 대화를 듣고, 여자가 지불할 금액을 고르시오.
① $20 ② $18 ③ $16
④ $10 ⑤ $9

11 대화를 듣고, 남자가 할 일로 가장 적절한 것을 고르시오.
① 샤워하러 간다.
② 알람 시계를 구매한다.
③ 친구들에게 전화를 건다.
④ 어려운 문제를 다시 풀어 본다.
⑤ 엄마에게 일어날 시간을 알려 준다.

12 다음을 듣고, Hines Ward에 관해 언급되지 <u>않은</u> 것을 고르시오.
① 직업
② 출생지
③ 소속팀 이름
④ 재단 설립 이유
⑤ MVP 수상 횟수

13 다음 표를 보면서 대화를 듣고, 여자가 구입할 선풍기를 고르시오.

	Model	Blades	Remote	Timer
①	A	Metal	○	X
②	B	Plastic	○	○
③	C	Metal	X	X
④	D	Plastic	X	○
⑤	E	Metal	X	X

14 다음을 듣고, 무엇에 관한 설명인지 고르시오.
① 씨름　　　　　② 유도
③ 활쏘기　　　　④ 합기도
⑤ 태권도

15 대화를 듣고, 남자가 할 일로 가장 적절한 것을 고르시오.
① 연 사러 가기
② 간식 사러 가기
③ 배드민턴 치기
④ 보드게임 하기
⑤ 집에서 TV보기

16 대화를 듣고, 택배 기사가 방문할 시각을 고르시오.
① 3시 20분　　　② 3시 40분
③ 3시 50분　　　④ 4시 정각
⑤ 4시 20분

17 대화를 듣고, 남자의 마지막 말에 대한 여자의 응답으로 가장 적절한 것을 고르시오.
Woman: _____
① She teaches us English every Sunday.
② I'm writing this as my homework.
③ I write in it at least 3 times a week.
④ It takes 20 minutes to write a diary entry.
⑤ I'm very interested in English.

18 대화를 듣고, 여자의 마지막 말에 대한 남자의 응답으로 가장 적절한 것을 고르시오.
Man: _____
① Can I use your cellphone?
② I should obey the traffic rules.
③ My tire was completely flat.
④ I'm afraid I cannot ride a bicycle.
⑤ Okay. Thank you for understanding.

19 대화를 듣고, 남자의 마지막 말에 대한 여자의 응답으로 가장 적절한 것을 고르시오.
Woman: _____
① That is my favorite bag.
② Thank you. I'd love that.
③ You're right. I'm sorry.
④ Have you seen my bag?
⑤ The order number is missing.

20 다음 상황 설명을 듣고, Ted가 Jason에게 할 말로 가장 적절한 것을 고르시오.
Ted: _____
① why don't you go to another shop?
② how much is a bottle of water?
③ don't worry. Just follow me.
④ let's take the bus.
⑤ the grocery store is already closed.

Listen and Check

정답 및 해설 p.020

● 대화를 다시 듣고, 알맞은 것을 고르시오.

1 Their school's symbol is a bear.
☐ True   ☐ False

2 Shipping has been delayed because of a traffic jam.
☐ True   ☐ False

3 Does the woman go to the hospital due to a high fever?
☐ Yes   ☐ No

4 When will the woman go to the children's center to volunteer?
☐ Thursday   ☐ Friday

5 There is a smoking area in Seoraksan National Park.
☐ True   ☐ False

6 Does the man want to check the state of the delivered products?
☐ Yes   ☐ No

7 The man gives the woman confidence that she can do it.
☐ True   ☐ False

8 Why can't the man go to the movie?
☐ because he forgot to reserve a ticket
☐ because he hasn't done his homework

9 Where is Alice staying now?
☐ at Jason's house   ☐ at John's house

10 They are going to ride their bikes for 2 hours.
☐ True   ☐ False

11 What time is Eddie going to meet his friends?
☐ 10:30   ☐ 11:00

12 Hines Ward lived in Seoul for more than a year.
☐ True   ☐ False

13 The fan with metal blades is powerful.
☐ True   ☐ False

14 Can athletes of this Korean traditional martial art participate in the Olympic Games?
☐ Yes   ☐ No

15 What does the woman want to do?
☐ fly a kite   ☐ play a board game

16 There are no staffers available at the time the woman wants them to come.
☐ True   ☐ False

17 Does the woman write in her diary in English at least 3 times a week?
☐ Yes   ☐ No

18 The man thinks he can't repair the brakes of his bike.
☐ True   ☐ False

19 The woman will finally get what she wants.
☐ True   ☐ False

20 Jason knows where a convenience store is.
☐ True   ☐ False

그림 정보 파악

1 대화를 듣고, 두 사람이 선택한 책표지로 알맞은 것을 고르시오.

① 　② 　③

④ 　⑤

1

M　We _____ _____ _____ the school magazine.

W　Yeah. It *was a really tough time.

M　By the way, we _____ _____ _____ the design of the front cover yet. Do you have any ideas?

W　Um... Let's put the name of the school at the center of the bottom.

M　Then how about _____ _____ _____ _____, our school's symbol, in the center?

W　That's good. And let's put the year 2019 in the center at the top.

M　Okay. That seems simple and neat.

★ **was a really** [워즈] [어] [리얼리] → [워저리얼리]

목적 파악

2 대화를 듣고, 여자가 남자에게 전화한 목적으로 가장 적절한 것을 고르시오.

① 책의 대출 비용을 알기 위해
② 책의 환불을 요구하기 위해
③ 책을 추가 주문하기 위해
④ 파손된 책을 교환하기 위해
⑤ 책의 배송 날짜를 알기 위해

♥ **How may I help you?**

: 상대방에게 도움을 주려고 먼저 물어볼 때 쓰는 표현으로, '어떻게 도와 드릴까요?'라는 뜻이다.

2

[*Telephone rings.*]

M　Hello. Future Online Bookstore. ♥How may I help you?

W　I ordered three books the other day but have received only one of them. I want to know when I can get the rest of the books.

M　I'm very sorry for _____ _____. What is your order number?

W　It's 24605315.

M　Let me check... [*Keyboard sound*] I'm afraid those items are _____ _____ _____ _____, and it will take two days for us to receive new books.

W　So when can I get them?

M　It may _____ _____ _____ three business days.

W　Okay. I'll wait.

그림 상황 파악

3 다음 그림의 상황에 가장 적절한 대화를 고르시오.

① 　② 　③ 　④　⑤

3

① W　_____ _____ _____ do I have to take a day?

　M　Take one three times a day.

② W　I think I have an ear infection.

　M　Let me _____ _____ _____.

③ W　My eyesight is _____ _____.

　M　That's too bad. I think _____ _____ _____.

④ W　How are you feeling today?

　M　Much better. Thanks, Dr. Brown.

⑤ W　You should listen to _____ _____ _____.

　M　Okay. I will.

특정 정보 파악

4 대화를 듣고, 두 사람이 만나기로 한 요일을 고르시오.

① 월요일
② 화요일
③ 수요일
④ 목요일
⑤ 금요일

> ♥ **shall we ~?**
> : '우리 ~할까요?'라는 표현으로 격식을 갖추어 권유할 때 쓰인다.
> = why don't we ~?
> = let's ~

4 🇬🇧

M Are you finished preparing for the presentation, or are you _____ _____ the information for your part?

W _____ _____ _____.

M You know we have to review each other's information by this weekend. We're going to _____ _____ _____ _____ next week.

W All right, Jeremy. It'll be ready by Wednesday.

M Then ♥ shall we meet on Thursday?

W _____ _____ _____. I'm volunteering at the children's center on Thursday.

M Then how about the day after that?

W Okay. _____ _____ _____ _____ on that day.

언급 유무 파악

5 다음을 듣고, 공원의 규칙에 대해 언급되지 <u>않은</u> 것을 고르시오.

① 쓰레기를 버리지 말 것
② 꽃을 꺾지 말 것
③ 계곡에서 수영을 하지 말 것
④ 동물에게 먹이를 주지 말 것
⑤ 담배를 피우지 말 것

5

W Welcome to Seoraksan National Park. _____ _____ _____, please observe the following rules. First of all, don't litter. The mountain is suffering from trash _____ _____ everywhere by visitors. Second, smoking in the park _____ _____ _____ at all times. Even a small fire could turn into a forest fire. Third, don't feed the animals and don't pick any flowers or other plants. Thank you very much _____ _____ _____.

관계 추론

6 대화를 듣고, 두 사람의 관계로 가장 적절한 것을 고르시오.

① 상담원 — 고객
② 이삿짐센터 직원 — 고객
③ 마트 배달원 — 고객
④ 택배 접수원 — 고객
⑤ 농부 — 농산물 검사관

> ♥ **Excuse me?**
> : 상대방의 말을 못 들었을 경우, 혹은 제대로 들은 게 맞는지 확인하고 싶을 때 쓰는 표현으로, '뭐라고?(다시 말해 줄래?)'라는 뜻이다.
> = Pardon me?
> = What did you say?

6

W ♥ Excuse me, but are you John Hwang?

M Yes, I _____ _____ _____ you all morning.

W Here's what you ordered. Please _____ _____ _____ and sign here.

M Before that, I want to check if the products are in good condition.

W Of course. _____ _____ _____ _____. I'll wait.

M Thank you... [*Pause*]... Well, everything *is in good condition. Can I sign here?

W Yes. Thank you for using Mart Plus.

★ is in good condition [이즈] [인] [굿] [컨디션] → [이진굿컨디션]

어색한 대화 찾기

7 대화를 듣고, 두 사람의 대화가 <u>어색한</u> 것을 고르시오.

① ② ③ ④ ⑤

7

① W I'm not sure I can pass the exam.

   M _____ _____ _____ _____ _____ _____ _____.

② W This is for you. I hope _____ _____ _____.

   M Thank you so much.

③ W Are you following what I'm saying?

   M No, I'll _____ _____ _____.

④ W _____ _____ _____ movies do you like?

   M I like science-fiction movies the most.

⑤ W I'll _____ _____ _____ _____.

   M Thanks. I'll try my best.

충고한 일 파악

8 대화를 듣고, 여자가 남자에게 충고한 일로 가장 적절한 것을 고르시오.

① 좀 더 일찍 시작하라.
② 계획을 세워서 하라.
③ 반성하는 삶을 살아라.
④ 스스로 힘으로 해라.
⑤ 약속을 어기지 마라.

> ♥ **Maybe ~**
> : 확실하지는 않지만 약간의 가능성을 나타낼 때 쓰는 표현으로, '아마도'라는 뜻이다.
> =Perhaps ~
> =Possibly ~

8

M Erin, have you done the school project?

W Yes. _____ _____ _____ it yet?

M No, I completely *forgot about it, so I just started _____ _____ _____ yesterday.

W ♥Maybe you can't go to the movies tonight. I think it will take more than 10 hours to do it.

M That's why I need your help. Will you please help me?

W Do you remember the same thing happened before?

M I know, but can you help me _____ _____ _____?

W No. You should be _____ _____ _____. Everyone in our class has been doing this alone.

★ forgot about it [폴갓] [어바웃] [잇] → [폴가러바우릿]

의도 파악

9 대화를 듣고, 남자의 마지막 말에 담긴 의도로 가장 적절한 것을 고르시오.

① 격려
② 동의
③ 기대
④ 걱정
⑤ 감사

---

9 🇬🇧

W Have you heard about Alice?

M No, I haven't. _____ _____ _____ _____ her?

W She came here last night and now is staying at Jason's house.

M Really? Oh, _____ _____ _____ _____ _____.

W Yes, it's already December.

M How is she? Is she fine?

W She _____ _____ _____ _____ than I expected.

M I'm _____ _____ _____ her soon.

숫자 정보 파악

10 대화를 듣고, 여자가 지불할 금액을 고르시오.

① $20
② $18
③ $16
④ $10
⑤ $9

10

W　Hi. I'd like to know your _____ _____ _____.

M　It is 3 dollars an hour.

W　_____ _____ _____ _____ _____ to rent a tandem bike?

M　It is 7 dollars an hour.

W　Okay. We want one bike and one tandem bike.

M　How long do you want the bikes for?

W　Two hours. If I rent _____ _____ _____, can I get a discount?

M　All right. I'll give you a 20% _____ _____ _____.

W　Thank you so much.

할 일 파악

11 대화를 듣고, 남자가 할 일로 가장 적절한 것을 고르시오.

① 샤워하러 간다.
② 알람 시계를 구매한다.
③ 친구들에게 전화를 건다.
④ 어려운 문제를 다시 풀어 본다.
⑤ 엄마에게 일어날 시간을 알려 준다.

11 🇬🇧

M　Oh, no! I overslept!

W　Why are you in a hurry, Eddie? It's Sunday morning. You _____ _____ _____ _____ to school. Calm down, honey.

M　Mom, I have an important meeting with my friends at 11:00. But it's already 10:30.

W　Oh, you should have told me _____ _____ _____ _____ _____. Anyway, you can't make it by 11:00.

M　What should I do first, Mom? _____ _____ _____.

W　Relax first. And _____ _____ _____ _____ your friend and say that you'll be late.

언급 유무 파악

12 다음을 듣고, Hines Ward에 관해 언급되지 <u>않은</u> 것을 고르시오.

① 직업
② 출생지
③ 소속팀 이름
④ 재단 설립 이유
⑤ MVP 수상 횟수

12

W　Hines Ward is a _____ _____ _____ _____. He was born in Seoul, Korea, and moved to the United States when he was one year old. He played for the same team for 14 years. During his career, _____ _____ 3 team MVP awards. He won the Super Bowl MVP award in 2006. That _____ _____ _____ in Korea. He was the first Korean-American to succeed at American football. When he came back to Korea, he made a _____ _____ _____ _____ _____ _____ to help protect mixed-race children like himself from discrimination.

표 파악

13 다음 표를 보면서 대화를 듣고, 여자가 구입할 선풍기를 고르시오.

	Model	Blades	Remote	Timer
①	A	Metal	○	X
②	B	Plastic	○	○
③	C	Metal	X	X
④	D	Plastic	X	○
⑤	E	Metal	X	X

13

W Hello. Can I help you find something?

M Hi. I'm _____ _____ _____ _____ _____ for my living room.

W How about this one? It has _____ _____ and is very powerful.

M It looks too heavy. I don't think _____ _____ _____ _____ _____.

W I see. Well, these fans with plastic blades, a remote, and an auto timer are really light.

M Um... I don't need a remote. But I'd like one with a timer.

W All right. Then this model _____ _____ _____.

M It looks perfect. I'll take it.

화제·주제 파악

14 다음을 듣고, 무엇에 관한 설명인지 고르시오.

① 씨름
② 유도
③ 활쏘기
④ 합기도
⑤ 태권도

14

W This is a Korean traditional martial art. This is a _____ _____ which mainly requires the use of the hands and feet. This is _____ _____ _____ _____ _____ harmony between the body and the mind. Its trainees wear a white uniform with a belt that can be various colors. This _____ _____ Korea, but it has become the world's most popular martial art and has been an Olympic event since 2000.

할 일 파악

15 대화를 듣고, 남자가 할 일로 가장 적절한 것을 고르시오.

① 연 사러 가기
② 간식 사러 가기
③ 배드민턴 치기
④ 보드게임 하기
⑤ 집에서 TV보기

♥ **Why don't we + V ~?**

: 어떤 것을 함께 하자고 제안할 때 쓰는 표현으로, '~는 어때?'라는 뜻이다.
= How about + -ing?
= Let's + V.

15

M I'm so bored. Time is _____ _____ today.

W How about playing a board game?

M ♥ Why don't we do something outdoors? It's the best season to _____ _____ _____ like playing badminton.

W But it's windy outside.

M Windy? _____ _____ _____ _____ _____ then?

W A kite? _____ _____ _____ a kite.

M We can buy one at a store. Let's go out.

16 대화를 듣고, 택배 기사가 방문할 시각을 고르시오.

① 3시 20분
② 3시 40분
③ 3시 50분
④ 4시 정각
⑤ 4시 20분

16

M ABC Shipping Company. May I help you?

W Hi. I'd like to send a _____ _____ _____ _____ this afternoon.

M Okay. Can I _____ _____ _____, please?

W Sure. 135 Main Street, Arlington District.

M What time do you want a member of the staff to visit?

W Around 4 p.m., please.

M I'm sorry, but nobody on the staff can go there by 4:00. _____ _____ _____ with you if someone goes there at 4:20?

W _____ _____ _____ _____.

17 대화를 듣고, 남자의 마지막 말에 대한 여자의 응답으로 가장 적절한 것을 고르시오.

Woman: _____

① She teaches us English every Sunday.
② I'm writing this as my homework.
③ I write in it at least 3 times a week.
④ It takes 20 minutes to write a diary entry.
⑤ I'm very interested in English.

17

M What are you doing, Yujin?

W I'm _____ _____ _____ _____ _____ now.

M Really? _____ _____ _____? I thought that you don't like English.

W I didn't. But my English teacher _____ _____ _____ _____ my English. So now I keep a diary in English.

M So you're keeping an English diary, right? How often do you *write in it?

W I write in it at least 3 times a week.

★ write in it [롸이트] [인] [잇] → [롸잇이닛]

18 대화를 듣고, 여자의 마지막 말에 대한 남자의 응답으로 가장 적절한 것을 고르시오.

Man: _____

① Can I use your cellphone?
② I should obey the traffic rules.
③ My tire was completely flat.
④ I'm afraid I cannot ride a bicycle.
⑤ Okay. Thank you for understanding.

18 🇬🇧

M Mom, I think I have to buy a new bicycle.

W _____ _____ _____ _____ _____?

M The brakes are not working. Yesterday, when I used the brakes, my bike didn't stop. I _____ _____ _____ _____.

W Oh, no. Were you okay?

M Fortunately, _____ _____.

W Well, let's find out if we can repair the brakes first. Then, we can decide _____ _____ _____ _____ a new one.

M Okay. Thank you for understanding.

적절한 응답 찾기

19 대화를 듣고, 남자의 마지막 말에 대한 여자의 응답으로 가장 적절한 것을 고르시오.

Woman: _____

① That is my favorite bag.
② Thank you. I'd love that.
③ You're right. I'm sorry.
④ Have you seen my bag?
⑤ The order number is missing.

19

M What can I do for you?

W I'd like to buy a bag that I saw _____ _____ _____.

M Can I have the model number?

W 52...3... [*Pause*] Oh, I'm sorry, but I can't remember it.

M That's okay. Can you tell me _____ _____ _____ _____ ?

W It's like this red one _____ _____ _____ _____ _____ and has a red strap. The price is 85 dollars.

M Oh, I know what you're talking about. But it _____ _____ _____ _____. I can order one for you if you want.

W <u>Thank you. I'd love that.</u>

상황에 맞는 말 찾기

20 다음 상황 설명을 듣고, Ted가 Jason에게 할 말로 가장 적절한 것을 고르시오.

Ted: Jason, _____

① why don't you go to another shop?
② how much is a bottle of water?
③ don't worry. Just follow me.
④ let's take the bus.
⑤ the grocery store is already closed.

20

W Ted and Jason _____ _____ _____ _____ _____ one weekend. After riding a long distance, they feel thirsty and decide to find a convenience store. Since he _____ _____ _____ _____ this area before, Jason _____ _____ _____ where a convenience store is. But Ted _____ _____ _____ _____ on his smartphone and sees where a convenience store is. In this situation, what would Ted say to Jason?

Ted Jason, <u>don't worry. Just follow me.</u>

1 대화를 듣고, 남자가 사용할 포장 상자를 고르시오.

①   ②   ③

④   ⑤

2 대화를 듣고, 남자가 여자에게 부탁한 일로 가장 적절한 것을 고르시오.
① 물건 골라주기
② 같이 쇼핑하기
③ 현금 빌려주기
④ 계좌 이체하기
⑤ 지갑 맡아주기

3 다음 그림의 상황에 가장 적절한 대화를 고르시오.

①   ②   ③   ④   ⑤

4 대화를 듣고, 남자가 녹음을 시작한 시각을 고르시오.
① 1:00   ② 1:30   ③ 2:00
④ 2:30   ⑤ 3:00

5 대화를 듣고, 두 사람이 얘기하는 장소에 관해 언급되지 <u>않은</u> 것을 고르시오.
① 나라   ② 투숙객   ③ 주요 활동
④ 편의 시설   ⑤ 가는 방법

6 대화를 듣고, 두 사람이 대화하는 장소로 가장 적절한 곳을 고르시오.
① 학교   ② 호텔   ③ 도서관
④ 박물관   ⑤ 경기장

7 다음을 듣고, 두 사람의 대화가 <u>어색한</u> 것을 고르시오.
①   ②   ③   ④   ⑤

8 대화를 듣고, 여자가 남자에게 부탁한 일로 가장 적절한 것을 고르시오.
① 설문지 돌리기   ② 준비물 챙기기
③ 영상 촬영하기   ④ 참가자 모으기
⑤ 설문지 작성하기

9 다음을 듣고, 무엇에 관한 기사 내용인지 고르시오.
① 스마트폰의 기능
② 다양한 직업 소개
③ 미래의 직업 형태
④ 적성을 찾는 방법
⑤ 기술 발전의 역사

10 대화를 듣고, 남자가 지불할 금액을 고르시오.
① $210   ② $240   ③ $330
④ $378   ⑤ $420

11 대화를 듣고, 여자가 할 일로 가장 적절한 것을 고르시오.
① 전구 구입하기
② 전등 설치하기
③ 전구 사진 찍기
④ 남편과 시장 가기
⑤ 여분의 전구 찾기

12 다음을 듣고, Blue Car에 관해 언급되지 <u>않은</u> 것을 고르시오.
① 서비스 신청 방법
② 서비스 이용 시간
③ 서비스 이용 제한
④ 서비스 이용 시 유의점
⑤ 회사가 제공하는 서비스

13 다음 표를 보면서 대화를 듣고, 두 사람이 선택할 여행 상품을 고르시오.

	Types	Periods	Places	Options
①	Type A	July – September	Saipan	Bus Tour
②	Type B	July – September	Saipan	River Tour
③	Type C	July – September	London	River Tour
④	Type D	December – February	London	Bus Tour
⑤	Type E	December – February	Saipan	River Tour

14 다음을 듣고, 무엇에 관한 설명인지 고르시오.
① 소　　② 개　　③ 닭　　④ 돼지　　⑤ 오리

15 대화를 듣고, 남자가 대화 직후에 할 일로 가장 적절한 것을 고르시오.
① 출석 기록하기
② 무료 쿠폰 받기
③ 이벤트 광고하기
④ 신규 계정 만들기
⑤ 웹사이트 출석하기

16 대화를 듣고, 기차가 출발할 시각을 고르시오.
① 7:30　　　② 8:00　　　③ 8:30
④ 9:00　　　⑤ 9:30

17 대화를 듣고, 여자의 마지막 말에 대한 남자의 응답으로 가장 적절한 것을 고르시오.
Man: _____
① I'd rather start my own business.
② Whatever you do, take responsibility for it.
③ Nobody can force you to make a decision.
④ You have no idea how much I want to do it.
⑤ It helps you get a job in the career you want.

18 대화를 듣고, 남자의 마지막 말에 대한 여자의 응답으로 가장 적절한 것을 고르시오.
Woman: _____
① That's such a systematic approach.
② I can help you solve your problem.
③ I still wonder whether I am good at it.
④ The more you do, the better you can be.
⑤ Things would be better if you worried less.

19 대화를 듣고, 여자의 마지막 말에 대한 남자의 응답으로 가장 적절한 것을 고르시오.
Man: _____
① I understand raising a child is never easy.
② You don't seem to care about the matter.
③ I suggest you find a trustworthy babysitter.
④ You'd better get a job as soon as you can.
⑤ It would be better if you did both at the same time.

20 다음 상황 설명을 듣고, Rachel이 Nick에게 할 말로 가장 적절한 것을 고르시오.
Rachel: Nick, _____
① try to think of something positive.
② I know you like science the most.
③ I believe every person has potential.
④ you just showed me your report card.
⑤ rewards are given only to those who work hard.

Listen and Check

대화를 다시 듣고, 알맞은 것을 고르시오.

1 Which pattern does the man prefer?

☐ the banana pattern ☐ the peach pattern

2 The man lends money to the woman.

☐ True ☐ False

3 Is the man's right eye in pain?

☐ Yes ☐ No

4 What time does the man usually finish the radio recording?

☐ 1:00 ☐ 2:00

5 The woman knows a lot about Diver's Resort.

☐ True ☐ False

6 Is it the first time for the man and the woman to visit the building?

☐ Yes ☐ No

7 The man asks the woman to help him tomorrow.

☐ True ☐ False

8 What's the problem the man and the woman have with the survey?

☐ no survey papers ☐ no participants

9 How many jobs does the paper say a person can have at the same time?

☐ two ☐ unlimited

10 Does the man buy more chairs with a height-adjustment function?

☐ Yes ☐ No

11 The man will go to the market to buy a bulb.

☐ True ☐ False

12 What is the woman's purpose in talking about Blue Car?

☐ to promote it ☐ to complain about it

13 The man and the woman will visit Saipan this summer.

☐ Yes ☐ No

14 This animal is raised only for food production.

☐ True ☐ False

15 What is the gift from accessing the website every day for thirty days?

☐ free books ☐ free coupons

16 It takes thirty minutes for the man to get to his destination.

☐ True ☐ False

17 The woman is confident about her plans for the future.

☐ True ☐ False

18 What does the woman want to learn from the man?

☐ to run a book club ☐ to manage time

19 Does the man have the same problem as the woman?

☐ Yes ☐ No

20 Where do the man and the woman study for the exam?

☐ at the library ☐ at Nick's house

정답 및 해설 *p.021*

그림 정보 파악

1 대화를 듣고, 남자가 사용할 포장 상자를 고르시오.

1 🇬🇧

W Welcome to Happy Wrappings. _____ _____ _____ _____ _____?

M I'd like to buy a gift box.

W We have _____ _____ _____, rounded and square. Which do you want?

M _____ _____ _____, please.

W We have different patterns for square ones, too.

M Hmm... _____ _____ _____ looks fine.

W Okay. Here you are.

부탁한 일 파악

2 대화를 듣고, 남자가 여자에게 부탁한 일로 가장 적절한 것을 고르시오.

① 물건 골라주기
② 같이 쇼핑하기
③ 현금 빌려주기
④ 계좌 이체하기
⑤ 지갑 맡아주기

♥ **Go ahead.**
: 상대방에게 무언가를 먼저 하도록 양보할 때 사용하는 표현으로, '먼저 해.', '먼저 가.'라는 뜻이다.
= You can go first.

2

W Are you done _____ _____ _____ _____?

M Yes, let me pay for everything first.

W ♥Go ahead.

M Oh, no. Do you _____ _____ _____? It says "Cash Only." I don't have any cash now.

W _____ _____ _____ _____ _____?

M Five dollars. I'll transfer the money to your account later.

W Okay.

그림 상황 파악

3 다음 그림의 상황에 가장 적절한 대화를 고르시오.

① ② ③ ④ ⑤

3

① W How often do you exercise?

　 M I exercise _____ _____ _____.

② W How many hours do you sleep?

　 M I usually _____ _____ _____ _____.

③ W How do you _____ _____?

　 M I keep talking about it.

④ W Are you a representative of your class?

　 M Yes, I'm _____ _____.

⑤ W Is your _____ _____ _____ _____?

　 M Yes, very much.

숫자 정보 파악

4 대화를 듣고, 남자가 녹음을 시작한 시각을 고르시오.

① 1:00   ② 1:30
③ 2:00   ④ 2:30
⑤ 3:00

4

W   You're late _____ _____ _____.

M   I'm so sorry. The radio recording _____ _____ _____ _____ than I had expected.

W   It was supposed to finish at 2:00, right?

M   You're right. It normally _____ _____ _____ _____, but it took longer today.

W   So how was the recording?

M   It was _____ _____ _____.

언급 유무 파악

5 대화를 듣고, 두 사람이 얘기하는 장소에 관해 언급되지 <u>않은</u> 것을 고르시오.

① 나라   ② 투숙객
③ 주요 활동   ④ 편의 시설
⑤ 가는 방법

5

W   I heard you're going to Diver's Resort. Where is it?

M   How _____ _____ _____? It's in the Philippines.

W   Why does the resort's name have the word divers?

M   The reason is that most of the guests there are divers. They do free diving and sometimes scuba diving.

W   Can _____ _____ _____, too?

M   Of course. There's a training course for beginners.

W   I see. _____ _____ do you do _____ _____?

M   There are spa facilities, restaurants, and a bar.

W   Sounds cool. Have a safe trip.

장소 추론

6 대화를 듣고, 두 사람이 대화하는 장소로 가장 적절한 곳을 고르시오.

① 학교   ② 호텔
③ 도서관   ④ 박물관
⑤ 경기장

6

M   This is huge. It's a three-story building.

W   Look. Here's _____ _____ _____.

M   The whole first floor is for history from prehistoric times to the modern day.

W   There are a library and a café _____ _____ _____ _____.

M   _____ _____ the first floor first.

W   Okay. After that, let's _____ _____ _____ _____.

M   All right.

W   I'll get a brochure.

어색한 대화 찾기

7 다음을 듣고, 두 사람의 대화가 <u>어색한</u> 것을 고르시오.

① ② ③ ④ ⑤

💙 **What do you do for a living?**

: 상대방의 직업을 물어볼 때 사용하는 표현으로, '직업이 어떻게 되세요?'라는 뜻이다. 축약해서 'What do you do?'라고 표현하기도 한다.

7

① **M** I _____ _____ what I said to you.

W Promise me you won't do it again.

② **M** How do you help slow students?

W I _____ _____ _____ _____.

③ **M** _____ _____ _____ _____ tomorrow?

W Sorry. I can do it by myself.

④ **M** What *motivates you to _____ _____ ?

W My family.

⑤ **M** 💙What do you do for a living?

W I teach people _____ _____ _____ _____

_____.

＊ motivates you [모리베이츠] [유] → [모리베이츄]

부탁한 일 파악

8 대화를 듣고, 여자가 남자에게 부탁한 일로 가장 적절한 것을 고르시오.

① 설문지 돌리기
② 준비물 챙기기
③ 영상 촬영하기
④ 참가자 모으기
⑤ 설문지 작성하기

💙 **as soon as possible**

: 무언가를 최대한 빨리 하는 것을 나타낼 때 사용하는 표현으로, '가능한 한 빨리'라는 뜻이다. 줄임말로 ASAP이라고 쓰기도 하며, 말할 때에는 '에이에스에이피'라고 한다.

= as quickly as possible

8 🇬🇧

M We should start the survey 💙as soon as possible.

W Are the survey papers and video ready?

M Yes. But there are no participants.

W _____ _____ _____ do we need?

M We need fifteen.

W Could you try calling your *friends and _____ _____

_____ _____ here?

M My friends? Sure.

W I'll tell _____ _____ _____ _____, too.

＊ friends and [프렌즈] [엔드] → [프랜즈드]

화제·주제 파악

9 다음을 듣고, 무엇에 관한 기사 내용인지 고르시오.

① 스마트폰의 기능
② 다양한 직업 소개
③ 미래의 직업 형태
④ 적성을 찾는 방법
⑤ 기술 발전의 역사

9

M Today's paper talks about what workplaces _____ _____

_____ in the future. First, _____ _____ _____

do you think one person can have at the same time? One? Two?

Actually, the number is unlimited. One can be a businessman, author,

and photographer _____ _____ _____ _____.

It's possible because of smartphones. This handheld device connects

everything so fast that users can access anything easily and become

professionals with it. Just think about _____ _____

_____ and follow your heart.

숫자 정보 파악

10 대화를 듣고, 남자가 지불할 금액을 고르시오.

① $210 ② $240
③ $330 ④ $378
⑤ $420

10

W Hello. What are you _____ _____?

M I'm looking for chairs for an office.

W Here, we have _____ _____ _____ _____, ones with a height-adjustment function and ones without that function.

M How much are they?

W A chair _____ _____ _____ is 120 dollars, and one without it is 90 dollars.

M I'll buy two of each.

W We are selling them at a ten-percent discount now. You _____ _____ _____ _____.

M Thank you. Here's my credit card.

할 일 파악

11 대화를 듣고, 여자가 할 일로 가장 적절한 것을 고르시오.

① 전구 구입하기
② 전등 설치하기
③ 전구 사진 찍기
④ 남편과 시장 가기
⑤ 여분의 전구 찾기

♥ **Wait a moment.**
: 상대방에게 기다려 줄 것을 요구할 때 사용하는 표현으로, '잠시만.', '잠깐 기다려 봐.'라는 뜻이다.
= Wait a minute.
= Wait a second.

11 🇬🇧

W Honey, this light keeps going *off and on.

M We should change the bulb.

W Do we have _____ _____ _____?

M There might be some. ♥Wait a moment.

W Okay.

M Oh, it looks like _____ _____ _____ _____.

W It's okay. I can buy one at the market later.

M _____ _____ _____ _____ _____ before you go out to make sure you buy the same *type of bulb.

★ off and [어프] [엔드] → [어펜드]
★ type of [타입] [어브] → [타이버브]

언급 유무 파악

12 다음을 듣고, Blue Car에 관해 언급되지 않은 것을 고르시오.

① 서비스 신청 방법
② 서비스 이용 시간
③ 서비스 이용 제한
④ 서비스 이용 시 유의점
⑤ 회사가 제공하는 서비스

12

W Hi. This is Samantha Park, the CEO of Blue Car. Blue Car _____ _____ _____ _____ and provides car owners with the opportunity to make money. Users can use the service anytime and anywhere. The rental fee varies depending on the condition of the car and the car model. Please make sure you _____ _____ _____ _____ _____ and return them on time. Smoking inside the cars is strictly banned. If you receive a warning from a car owner more than three times, you can't use the rental service for a month. Our company will try to provide a cleaner, more comfortable, and _____ _____ _____ for everyone.

표 파악

13 다음 표를 보면서 대화를 듣고, 두 사람이 선택할 여행 상품을 고르시오.

	Types	Periods	Places	Options
①	Type A	July – September	Saipan	Bus Tour
②	Type B	July – September	Saipan	River Tour
③	Type C	July – September	London	River Tour
④	Type D	December – February	London	Bus Tour
⑤	Type E	December – February	Saipan	River Tour

13

M　Amy, where do you want to go this summer?

W　How about _____ _____ _____?

M　Won't it be too hot to go there in summer?

W　Then _____ _____ _____ _____ this time.

M　Okay. We can choose options such as a river tour and a bus tour. Which do you like better?

W　_____ _____ _____ seems better. The night view of London is _____ _____.

M　I'm so excited!

W　I hope time passes quickly.

화제·주제 파악

14 다음을 듣고, 무엇에 관한 설명인지 고르시오.

① 소　　　　② 개
③ 닭　　　　④ 돼지
⑤ 오리

14

W　This is an animal _____ _____ _____. It has a red comb on the head and cannot fly well, but it has strong legs. That's why people _____ _____ _____ _____ when they have one-legged fights. Farmers *raise it for eggs and meat. These days, people eat this a lot as a _____ _____. In addition, when people _____ _____, they cook this in a soup.

★ raise it [레이즈] [잇] → [레이짓]

할 일 파악

15 대화를 듣고, 남자가 대화 직후에 할 일로 가장 적절한 것을 고르시오.

① 출석 기록하기
② 무료 쿠폰 받기
③ 이벤트 광고하기
④ 신규 계정 만들기
⑤ 웹사이트 출석하기

♥ **I got it.**
: 상대방의 말을 이해했다는 것을 나타낼 때 사용하는 표현으로, '이해했어.', '알겠어.'라는 뜻이다.
= I understood it.

15

W　Matthew, do you know what?

M　What?

W　There's an event going on that is _____ _____ _____ on the Books.com website.

M　Really? How can you get a coupon?

W　You just need to _____ _____ _____ every day for thirty days.

M　That's easy. How will they know that I go there every day?

W　You will _____ _____ _____ _____ on the right side of the website. Just *click on it, and it will automatically record your visit.

M　♥I got it. I should _____ _____ _____ first.

★ click on it [클릭] [언] [잇] → [클리커닛]

숫자 정보 파악

16 대화를 듣고, 기차가 출발할 시각을 고르시오.

① 7:30　　② 8:00
③ 8:30　　④ 9:00
⑤ 9:30

16

[*Telephone rings.*]

W　William, are you _____ _____ _____ _____?

M　Yes, I am. But the train was _____ _____ _____ _____.

W　So what time will you arrive here?

M　I will arrive there at 9:30.

W　How many hours does it take to come here?

M　It takes two hours.

W　Okay. I'll _____ _____ _____ _____ near the station.

적절한 응답 찾기

17 대화를 듣고, 여자의 마지막 말에 대한 남자의 응답으로 가장 적절한 것을 고르시오.

Man: _____

① I'd rather start my own business.
② Whatever you do, take responsibility for it.
③ Nobody can force you to make a decision.
④ You have no idea how much I want to do it.
⑤ It helps you get a job in the career you want.

17 🇬🇧

W　There's something _____ _____ _____.

M　What is it?

W　I'm not sure if I should go to a university or get a job.

M　What is it that you want to do in the future? If you want to work at a company, I recommend that you _____ _____ _____ _____.

W　Why do you say that?

M　There is _____ _____ _____ _____ _____ between college graduates and high school graduates.

W　What else is good about getting a degree?

M　It helps you get a job in the career you want.

적절한 응답 찾기

18 대화를 듣고, 남자의 마지막 말에 대한 여자의 응답으로 가장 적절한 것을 고르시오.

Woman: _____

① That's such a systematic approach.
② I can help you solve your problem.
③ I still wonder whether I am good at it.
④ The more you do, the better you can be.
⑤ Things would be better if you worried less.

18

W　Joseph, do you have any plans for this Thursday?

M　I'm meeting some people in my book club.

W　You do so many things. How do you _____ _____ _____?

M　It's _____ _____. You just have to know what type of person you are.

W　How do I know that?

M　_____ _____ _____ _____ when you can concentrate on things best and worst.

W　Well, I can focus on things best in the early morning.

M　Then you're _____ _____ _____. Try to manage your time according to your biorhythm.

W　That's such a systematic approach.

적절한 응답 찾기

19 대화를 듣고, 여자의 마지막 말에 대한 남자의 응답으로 가장 적절한 것을 고르시오.

Man: _____

① I understand raising a child is never easy.

② You don't seem to care about the matter.

③ I suggest you find a trustworthy babysitter.

④ You'd better get a job as soon as you can.

⑤ It would be better if you did both at the same time.

19

W I'm so tired of _____ _____ _____ _____ _____.

M I know what you mean. You work at home and at a workplace.

W That's true. I don't know _____ _____ _____.

M You're really struggling. You don't want to _____ _____ _____, right?

W No. If I quit my job, I may get very depressed.

M I think every mother _____ _____ _____ _____.

W I know. Is there a good way to *solve it?

M <u>I suggest you find a trustworthy babysitter.</u>

★ solve it [쏠브] [잇] → [쏠빗]

적절한 응답 찾기

20 다음 상황 설명을 듣고, Rachel이 Nick에게 할 말로 가장 적절한 것을 고르시오.

Rachel: Nick, _____

① try to think of something positive.

② I know you like science the most.

③ I believe every person has potential.

④ you just showed me your report card.

⑤ rewards are given only to those who work hard.

20

M Nick wants to _____ _____ _____ on his final exams. He regrets not _____ _____ _____ _____ on his midterm exams. Nick promises Rachel, his best friend, to _____ _____ _____ _____ to study every day. Although Nick goes to the library every day, he _____ _____ and often gets up and *walks around. He _____ _____ Rachel that he still wants to get good grades. In this situation, what would Rachel most likely say to Nick?

Rachel Nick, <u>rewards are given only to those who work hard.</u>

★ walks around [웍쓰] [어라운드]→ [웍써라운드]

1 대화를 듣고, 여자가 그린 그림을 고르시오.

①   ②   ③

④   ⑤

2 대화를 듣고, 남자가 여자에게 부탁한 일로 가장 적절한 것을 고르시오.
① 물 건네주기　　　② 땀 닦아 주기
③ 고추 사 오기　　　④ 텔레비전 켜기
⑤ 요리 강좌 수강하기

3 다음 그림의 상황에 가장 적절한 대화를 고르시오.

①　　　②　　　③　　　④　　　⑤

4 대화를 듣고, 여자가 유모차를 구입하게 될 요일을 고르시오.
① 월요일　　　② 화요일　　　③ 수요일
④ 목요일　　　⑤ 금요일

5 대화를 듣고, 양로원 자원봉사에 관해 언급되지 <u>않은</u> 것을 고르시오.
① 지원 자격　　　② 해야 할 일
③ 봉사 활동 시간　　④ 식사 제공 여부
⑤ 확인서 발급 유무

6 대화를 듣고, 두 사람이 대화하는 장소로 가장 적절한 곳을 고르시오.
① 학교　　　② 박물관　　　③ 매표소
④ 비행기　　　⑤ 콘서트장

7 다음을 듣고, 두 사람의 대화가 <u>어색한</u> 것을 고르시오.
①　　　②　　　③　　　④　　　⑤

8 대화를 듣고, 여자가 남자에게 부탁한 일로 가장 적절한 것을 고르시오.
① 새로운 집 구하기
② 구직 활동 같이 하기
③ 방송국에서 취재하기
④ 이사하는 거 도와주기
⑤ 직장으로 함께 통근하기

9 다음을 듣고, 무엇에 관한 안내 방송인지 고르시오.
① 교복 물려주기
② 공장 견학하기
③ 학교 대청소하기
④ 졸업식 일정 안내
⑤ 봉사 활동 신청하기

10 대화를 듣고, 남자가 지불할 금액을 고르시오.
① $170　　　② $180　　　③ $190
④ $200　　　⑤ $210

11 대화를 듣고, 여자가 할 일로 가장 적절한 것을 고르시오.
① 야채 구입하기
② 운동복 세탁하기
③ 아이스크림 사주기
④ 친구와 함께 조깅하기
⑤ 새로 나온 옷 구입하기

12 다음을 듣고, golden pass에 관해 언급되지 않은 것을 고르시오.
① 유효 기간   ② 적용 혜택
③ 구입 방법   ④ 회원권 가격
⑤ 환불 관련 정보

13 대화를 듣고, 두 사람이 사용할 회의실을 고르시오.

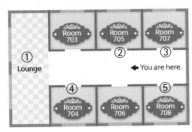

14 다음을 듣고, 무엇에 관한 설명인지 고르시오.
① 옷 오래 입는 방법
② 좋은 향수를 고르기
③ 모기를 피하는 방법
④ 효과적으로 운동하기
⑤ 화상 입었을 때 주의점

15 대화를 듣고, 남자가 대화 직후에 할 일로 가장 적절한 것을 고르시오.
① 독서하기
② 집에서 쉬기
③ 외출 준비하기
④ 친구에게 전화하기
⑤ 밖에 나가서 농구하기

16 대화를 듣고, 여자가 우편물을 받기로 한 날짜를 고르시오.
① 1월 20일   ② 1월 21일
③ 1월 22일   ④ 1월 23일
⑤ 1월 24일

17 대화를 듣고, 남자의 마지막 말에 대한 여자의 응답으로 가장 적절한 것을 고르시오.
Woman: _____
① I'm afraid I can't give you an answer.
② I like to study English more than math.
③ It was nothing. You really did study hard.
④ You need to pay attention to your studies.
⑤ Don't be sad. You can do better the next time.

18 대화를 듣고, 여자의 마지막 말에 대한 남자의 응답으로 가장 적절한 것을 고르시오.
Man: _____
① Don't worry. I'll walk you home.
② My place is far from your place.
③ I think you should buy a new car.
④ Why not? I love to travel by train.
⑤ All right. You have to keep your word.

19 대화를 듣고, 남자의 마지막 말에 대한 여자의 응답으로 가장 적절한 것을 고르시오.
Woman: _____
① We should attend his funeral.
② Maybe we should go upstairs.
③ Same here. I'm afraid of ghosts.
④ I love taking pictures of the mountains.
⑤ You took the words right out of my mouth.

20 다음 상황 설명을 듣고, Eunsung이 버스 기사님께 할 말로 가장 적절한 것을 고르시오.
Eunsung: _____
① Can I take a photo of the bus?
② How can I get to the bus stop?
③ How much should I pay for the exhibition?
④ Which bus goes to the National Museum of Korea?
⑤ How many more stops to the National Museum of Korea?

Listen and Check

정답 및 해설 *p.030*

● 대화를 다시 듣고, 알맞은 것을 고르시오.

1 The man is looking at the picture that the woman drew.

☐ True   ☐ False

2 Has the man ever studied how to cook?

☐ Yes   ☐ No

3 The man wants to take a seat in the café.

☐ True   ☐ False

4 How long did the baby use the stroller?

☐ for one year   ☐ for two years

5 What day will the woman do volunteer work?

☐ Saturday   ☐ Sunday

6 Bryce took a picture of himself with a poster.

☐ True   ☐ False

7 Why does the man tell the woman to call back later?

☐ The man is busy working.

☐ The man is watching TV.

8 Samantha got hired by a TV station.

☐ True   ☐ False

9 Will the school event be held from Tuesday to Friday?

☐ Yes   ☐ No

10 Who broke the man's earphones?

☐ his dog   ☐ his brother

11 Why couldn't the woman go jogging with the man?

☐ because she was hurt

☐ because she was busy

12 The golden pass is the name of the annual pass to the amusement park.

☐ True   ☐ False

13 Was today's meeting canceled?

☐ Yes   ☐ No

14 What likes the scent of sweat or perfume?

☐ mosquitos   ☐ butterflies

15 Who suggested playing basketball outside?

☐ the woman   ☐ the man

16 Is the woman at home now?

☐ Yes   ☐ No

17 How long did the man and the woman study math in the library?

☐ four hours   ☐ five hours

18 The man has been waiting for Brianna for 30 minutes.

☐ True   ☐ False

19 What did the man and the woman see in the middle of climbing Mt. Everest?

☐ a dead tree   ☐ a corpse

20 Is the National Museum of Korea located near Eunsung's place?

☐ Yes   ☐ No

그림 정보 파악

1 대화를 듣고, 여자가 그린 그림을 고르시오.

① ② ③ ④ ⑤

1

M   Congratulations! I heard you won the drawing contest.

W   Thank you. I'm so pleased to _____ _____ _____ _____. I didn't expect to do that.

M   Let me guess _____ _____ _____ _____ your drawing is. You drew the big house _____ _____, right?

W   That's correct. And I drew trees to the right of the house.

M   Did you draw a bench under the trees?

W   No. Instead, I _____ _____ _____ to the left of the house.

M   Oh, I got it. That's your painting.

부탁한 일 파악

2 대화를 듣고, 남자가 여자에게 부탁한 일로 가장 적절한 것을 고르시오.

① 물 건네주기
② 땀 닦아 주기
③ 고추 사 오기
④ 텔레비전 켜기
⑤ 요리 강좌 수강하기

2

W   Wow! These egg fried rice noodles taste fantastic!

M   Thanks. I _____ _____ _____ with chili peppers.

W   *Have you ever studied how to cook?

M   Not really. I just watch TV cooking shows and follow _____ _____ _____ _____.

W   Wow, you're such a good chef. By the way, what's wrong with you? You are sweating.

M   It's much too spicy for me. Can you _____ _____ _____ _____, please?

W   Sure. Here it is.

★ have you [해브] [유] → [해뷰]

그림 정보 파악

3 다음 그림의 상황에 가장 적절한 대화를 고르시오.

① ② ③ ④ ⑤

💗 **Can I have a bite?**
: 상대방의 음식을 맛보고 싶을 때 쓰는 표현으로, '내가 먹어봐도 될까?'라는 뜻이다.
= Can I try it?

3

① W   Where did you buy this table?
   M   I got it _____ _____ _____ _____ yesterday.

② W   Can you _____ _____ _____? It's not working.
   M   Sure. What seems to be the problem?

③ W   Hello. I want to have a part-time job here.
   M   _____ _____ _____ to me first.

④ W   Excuse me. Is _____ _____ _____?
   M   Not at all. You can have a seat here.

⑤ W   Your pancake looks so good. 💗Can I have a bite?
   M   Sorry. I _____ _____ _____ with you. I have a cold.

4 대화를 듣고, 여자가 유모차를 구입하게 될 요일을 고르시오.

① 월요일
② 화요일
③ 수요일
④ 목요일
⑤ 금요일

4

[*Telephone rings.*]

W   Hello. I'm calling about your used stroller ad on the website. Is it _____ _____ ?

M   Yes, I _____ _____ _____ _____ yet. It's almost new. My baby used it for just one year.

W   Can I buy it after looking *at it in person?

M   Sure. _____ _____ _____ _____ _____ to see it?

W   I'm thinking of this Tuesday.

M   Sorry. I _____ _____ then. How about the next day?

W   That's fine with me. See you on Wednesday.

     ★ at it [앳] [잇] → [애릿]

---

5 대화를 듣고, 양로원 자원봉사에 관해 언급되지 <u>않은</u> 것을 고르시오.

① 지원 자격
② 해야 할 일
③ 봉사 활동 시간
④ 식사 제공 여부
⑤ 확인서 발급 유무

5 🇬🇧

W   Excuse me. I hear that you are _____ _____ _____ to volunteer here.

M   That's right. But we need someone _____ _____.

W   _____ _____ at a nursing home for fifteen hours.

M   That's not bad. Can you do volunteer work on Sundays from 12 p.m. to 7 p.m.?

W   No problem. What kind of work is needed here?

M   You will help _____ _____ _____ _____ and clean their rooms.

W   Can I get a volunteer confirmation letter?

M   Of course. Please inform us a week before you need it.

---

6 대화를 듣고, 두 사람이 대화하는 장소로 가장 적절한 곳을 고르시오.

① 학교
② 박물관
③ 매표소
④ 비행기
⑤ 콘서트장

♥ **It's no big deal.**

: 문제가 되거나 어려울 만한 것이 없는 상황이라고 말할 때 쓰는 표현으로, '별거 아니야.'라는 뜻이다.

= It's nothing.
= It's no bother.
= it's not that hard.

6

W   I can't believe that we are here.

M   Neither can I. I'm _____ _____ _____ _____ BTS perform their songs live.

W   It's all thanks to you. You _____ _____ _____ the concert tickets.

M   ♥It was no big deal. Anyway, did you bring the official cheer stick?

W   Of course I did. Bryce, can you _____ _____ _____ _____ _____ with this poster in the background?

M   Okay. _____ _____ the camera. [*Camera shutter sounds*]

W   Now, let's go inside. The concert is about to start.

어색한 대화 찾기

7 다음을 듣고, 두 사람의 대화가 어색한 것을 고르시오.

① ② ③ ④ ⑤

💙 **I feel the same way.**
: 상대방의 생각이나 의견에 대해 동의할 때 쓰는 표현으로, '나도 그래.'라는 뜻이다.
= Same here.

7

① **M** How long have you been _____ _____ _____?
  W About 30 minutes.

② **M** I was _____ _____ the musical.
  W I know! 💙 I felt the same way.

③ **M** I'm _____ _____ right now. Can I call you later?
  W My cellphone broke down again. Let's buy a new one together.

④ **M** Excuse me. Where can I find the soap?
  W You can see it in section 5. It's _____ _____ _____ _____.

⑤ **M** Naomi, why did you open my package _____ _____ _____?
  W Sorry. I thought it was addressed to me.

부탁한 일 파악

8 대화를 듣고, 여자가 남자에게 부탁한 일로 가장 적절한 것을 고르시오.

① 새로운 집 구하기
② 구직 활동 같이 하기
③ 방송국에서 취재하기
④ 이사하는 거 도와주기
⑤ 직장으로 함께 통근하기

8

M Sarah, I'm so glad you _____ _____ by a TV station.

W Thanks. You know, I tried really hard to get that job.

M Anyway, can you _____ _____ _____? The TV station is far from your place.

W That's why I decided to _____ _____ _____ _____.

M Oh, when do you *move in to your new place?

W This Saturday. If you don't mind, can you _____ _____ _____ _____?

M Sure. I'll be at your house on Saturday.

★ move in to [무브] [인] [투] → [무빈투]

화제·주제 파악

9 다음을 듣고, 무엇에 관한 안내 방송인지 고르시오.

① 교복 물려주기
② 공장 견학하기
③ 학교 대청소하기
④ 졸업식 일정 안내
⑤ 봉사 활동 신청하기

9

W Good morning, middle school seniors. Congratulations on your graduation. As you know, our school has a tradition to _____ _____ _____ _____ _____ _____ to new students. School uniforms are kind of costly to buy. If you donate yours, students from lower-income families can _____ _____ your kindness. Please wash your uniform and _____ _____ _____ _____ _____ next to the school gate from Wednesday to Friday. Thank you for your cooperation in advance.

10 대화를 듣고, 남자가 지불할 금액을 고르시오.

① $170
② $180
③ $190
④ $200
⑤ $210

10

W Welcome to Smart Electronics. How may I help you?

M I'd like to buy some earphones. My dog _____ _____ _____ _____ on mine.

W That's too bad. Then _____ _____ _____ _____ these wireless earphones?

M Hmm... They look good. How much are they?

W They are 200 dollars. They were developed by a major international company.

M Wow. They're _____ _____ _____ _____ _____.

W If you want, you can use this 10% off coupon.

M Okay. I'll take them.

11 대화를 듣고, 여자가 할 일로 가장 적절한 것을 고르시오.

① 야채 구입하기
② 운동복 세탁하기
③ 아이스크림 사주기
④ 친구와 함께 조깅하기
⑤ 새로 나온 옷 구입하기

11

M Minseo, you are eating ice cream now. You told me that you were on a diet!

W I am, but this ice cream is my favorite, and it's on sale.

M No way! _____ _____ _____ and go jogging with me.

W I wish I could, but I can't. Yesterday, I fell down and _____ _____ _____.

M Then you have to _____ _____ _____ to lose weight.

W [Sigh] Okay. I'll go to a market to _____ _____ _____ for dinner.

M Let's go together.

12 다음을 듣고, golden pass에 관해 언급되지 않은 것을 고르시오.

① 유효 기간
② 적용 혜택
③ 구입 방법
④ 회원권 가격
⑤ 환불 관련 정보

12

M Hello, everyone. We hope you're having a great time. We would like to tell you about the annual pass to the amusement park. If you _____ _____ _____ a golden pass, you can _____ _____ _____ _____ _____ _____ in the park for free. In addition, you don't need to *wait in line for the rides. A golden pass is 300 dollars for adults and 150 dollars for children for a year. If you want to become a member here, please visit the information desk and _____ _____ _____ _____ _____.

★ wait in line [웨이트] [인] [라인] → [웨이린라인]

그림 정보 파악

13 대화를 듣고, 두 사람이 사용할 회의실을 고르시오.

① Lounge

← You are here.

♥ **How come?**
: 어떠한 상황이나 상대방의 말, 행동에 대해서 이유를 물어볼 때 쓰는 표현으로, '어째서?', '왜?'라는 뜻이다.
= How's that?
= Why?

13

M   Jiwoo, we should _____ _____ _____ for today's meeting.

W   ♥ How come? It's scheduled to be held in Room 707.

M   It was. But the projector in Room 707 is _____ _____ _____.

W   Well, which meeting room is available?

M   We can use Room 705.

W   Okay. We should _____ _____ _____ of this.

M   Don't worry. I'll send a message to them.

W   Thank you. I'll _____ _____ the meeting in the room.

화제·주제 파악

14 다음을 듣고, 무엇에 관한 설명인지 고르시오.

① 옷 오래 입는 방법
② 좋은 향수를 고르기
③ 모기를 피하는 방법
④ 효과적으로 운동하기
⑤ 화상 입었을 때 주의점

14 🇬🇧

W   We spend a lot of time outdoors on summer nights to escape the heat. Soon, mosquitoes start to attack people. If you _____ _____ _____ _____ than others, listen carefully. First, avoid excessive physical activity. Mosquitos are usually _____ _____ _____ _____ of sweat. Not using perfume is a good idea, too. Second, when you go out, _____ _____ _____ _____. Mosquitos love dark clothes to protect themselves.

할 일 파악

15 대화를 듣고, 남자가 대화 직후에 할 일로 가장 적절한 것을 고르시오.

① 독서하기
② 집에서 쉬기
③ 외출 준비하기
④ 친구에게 전화하기
⑤ 밖에 나가서 농구하기

15

W   Yechan, are you still reading that book?

M   Why not? It's so interesting.

W   But you need some exercise. It's not a good idea _____ _____ _____ _____ _____.

M   Is that so? I think somebody _____ _____.

W   You're right. I feel bored. Let's play basketball.

M   Just the two of us? Wait. I'll call my friends and _____ _____ _____ _____.

W   Wonderful! I'll get ready to go out.

숫자 정보 파악

16 대화를 듣고, 여자가 우편물을 받기로 한 날짜를 고르시오.

① 1월 20일
② 1월 21일
③ 1월 22일
④ 1월 23일
⑤ 1월 24일

16 🇬🇧

[*Cellphone rings.*]

W Hello. Who's this?

M This is the postman. I've got some mail for you.

W Can you _____ _____ _____ _____ _____ in front of the door?

M Sorry. This is registered mail. So I _____ _____ _____.

W But I'm away from home. I'm on a business trip.

M _____ _____ _____ _____ _____ to your place?

W On January 21. Can I get it on January 22?

M Let me check the schedule. [*Pause*] Yes, that's possible.

W That's great. Thank you.

적절한 응답 찾기

17 대화를 듣고, 남자의 마지막 말에 대한 여자의 응답으로 가장 적절한 것을 고르시오.

Woman: _____

① I'm afraid I can't give you an answer.
② I like to study English more than math.
③ It was nothing. You really did study hard.
④ You need to pay attention to your studies.
⑤ Don't be sad. You can do better the next time.

17

M Jaekyoung, do you remember you _____ _____ _____?

W Sure I do. We went to the library and studied math for 5 hours.

M Finally, I had a math test yesterday.

W Do you _____ _____ _____ or something?

M Yes! I _____ _____ _____ on the math test.

W Really? I'm so happy to hear that.

M Thank you. I _____ _____ _____ it without your help.

W <u>It was nothing. You really did study hard.</u>

적절한 응답 찾기

18 대화를 듣고, 여자의 마지막 말에 대한 남자의 응답으로 가장 적절한 것을 고르시오.

Man: _____

① Don't worry. I'll walk you home.
② My place is far from your place.
③ I think you should buy a new car.
④ Why not? I love to travel by train.
⑤ All right. You have to keep your word.

18

[*Telephone rings.*]

M Brianna, are you on the way? I've been waiting for you for 20 minutes.

W I'm almost there, but I'm _____ _____ _____.

M Are you _____ _____ _____ _____?

W Sorry. The roads are _____ _____ _____. I didn't *expect that.

M Come on. Today is a holiday. Traffic is always terrible on holidays.

W I'm so sorry. I _____ _____ _____ again.

M <u>All right. You have to keep your word.</u>

* expect that [익스펙트] [댓] → [익스펙댓]

66

적절한 응답 찾기

19 대화를 듣고, 남자의 마지막 말에 대한 여자의 응답으로 가장 적절한 것을 고르시오.

Woman: _____
① We should attend his funeral.
② Maybe we should go upstairs.
③ Same here. I'm afraid of ghosts.
④ I love taking pictures of the mountains.
⑤ You took the words right out of my mouth.

♥ **Nobody knows.**
: 확실하지 않은 정보, 혹은 정확하지 않은 상황에 대해서 말할 때 쓰는 표현으로, '아무도 몰라.'라는 뜻이다.
= Who knows?

19 🇬🇧

M   Look at the mountains _____ _____ _____. I can't believe that I'm climbing Mt. Everest.
W   I agree. They are amazing. But calm down a bit.
M   Why? We should enjoy this great view.
W   Well, do you see the _____ _____ _____ _____? It is called Green Boots.
M   Oh, no! Who is it?
W   ♥Nobody knows. But the corpse stays there and _____ _____ _____ _____ to climbers.
M   I feel bad. I must be more careful.
W   You took the words right out of my mouth.

상황에 맞는 말 찾기

20 다음 상황 설명을 듣고, Eunsung이 버스 기사님께 할 말로 가장 적절한 것을 고르시오.

Eunsung: _____
① Can I take a photo of the bus?
② How can I get to the bus stop?
③ How much should I pay for the exhibition?
④ Which bus goes to the National Museum of Korea?
⑤ How many more stops to the National Museum of Korea?

20

M   Today, there is a special photo exhibition at the National Museum of Korea. Although the National Museum of Korea is _____ _____ _____ _____, Eunsung decides to go there. He finds directions on _____ _____ _____ to the museum. He gets on the bus. A few minutes later, he feels worried. He can't find _____ _____ _____ on the bus route map. So he decides to ask the bus driver _____ _____ _____ _____ there are to go. In this situation, what would Eunsung most likely say to the bus driver?

Eunsung   How many more stops to the National Museum of Korea?

1 대화를 듣고, 여자가 구입할 시계를 고르시오.

 ① ② ③

 ④ ⑤

2 대화를 듣고, 남자가 여자에게 전화한 목적으로 가장 적절한 것을 고르시오.
① 수술 결과를 알리기 위해
② 수술 일정을 알리기 위해
③ 면담 일정을 조정하기 위해
④ 수업에 결석함을 알리기 위해
⑤ 학생부 내용을 확인하기 위해

3 다음 그림의 상황에 가장 적절한 대화를 고르시오.

① ② ③ ④ ⑤

4 대화를 듣고, 여자가 친구를 만날 요일을 고르시오.
① 월요일 ② 화요일 ③ 수요일
④ 목요일 ⑤ 금요일

5 다음을 듣고, 한글에 대해 언급되지 <u>않은</u> 것을 고르시오.
① 만든 사람 ② 한글의 장점
③ 만들어진 년도 ④ 문자 개수의 변화
⑤ 외국의 활용 사례

6 대화를 듣고, 두 사람의 관계로 가장 적절한 것을 고르시오.
① 계산원 — 손님 ② 공무원 — 민원인
③ 경찰관 — 행인 ④ 상담원 — 고객
⑤ 식당 점원 — 손님

7 대화를 듣고, 두 사람의 대화가 <u>어색한</u> 것을 고르시오.
① ② ③ ④ ⑤

8 대화를 듣고, 여자가 남자에게 부탁한 일로 가장 적절한 것을 고르시오.
① 음식을 먹지 마라.
② 휴대 전화를 꺼라.
③ 대화를 하지 마라.
④ 농담을 하지 마라.
⑤ 앞좌석을 밀지 마라.

9 대화를 듣고, 남자의 마지막 말에 담긴 의도로 가장 적절한 것을 고르시오.
① 사과 ② 감사 ③ 격려
④ 동의 ⑤ 권유

10 대화를 듣고, 남자가 지불할 금액을 고르시오.
① $20 ② $23 ③ $19
④ $18 ⑤ $17

11 대화를 듣고, 여자가 할 일로 가장 적절한 것을 고르시오.
① 창문을 열어 둔다.
② 수화물을 맡긴다.
③ 다른 방으로 옮긴다.
④ 호텔에서 체크아웃한다.
⑤ 에어컨 수리 기사를 기다린다.

12 다음을 듣고, 지구 온난화를 예방할 방법에 관해 언급 되지 <u>않은</u> 것을 고르시오.

① 나무 많이 심기
② 자동차 덜 타고 다니기
③ 적정한 실내 온도 유지하기
④ 에너지 효율적인 제품 구입하기
⑤ 재활용이 가능한 제품 선택하기

13 다음 표를 보면서 대화를 듣고, 남자가 선택할 강좌를 고르시오.

	Subject	Time
①	English	4:30 – 5:30
②	Chinese	3:00 – 4:00
③	History	4:30 – 5:30
④	Spanish	4:00 – 5:00
⑤	Japanese	3:30 – 4:30

14 다음을 듣고, 무엇에 관한 설명인지 고르시오.

① 가로등   ② 등대
③ 신호등   ④ 손전등
⑤ 교통 표지판

15 대화를 듣고, 남자가 할 일로 가장 적절한 것을 고르시오.

① 수학 오답 노트를 만든다.
② 서점에 가서 수학책을 산다.
③ 방과 후 수학 수업을 듣는다.
④ 도서관에서 수학 공부를 한다.
⑤ 인터넷 수학 강의를 신청한다.

16 대화를 듣고, 남자가 구입할 물건을 고르시오.

① 운동복 바지   ② 운동화
③ 헤드폰   ④ 악력기
⑤ 카우보이 부츠

17 대화를 듣고, 여자의 마지막 말에 대한 남자의 응답으로 가장 적절한 것을 고르시오.

Man: _____

① I'm sure you'll like it.
② Cheer up. You can do it.
③ Oh, I'm sorry to hear that.
④ Never. I am afraid of heights.
⑤ No. It's number one on my bucket list.

18 대화를 듣고, 남자의 마지막 말에 대한 여자의 응답으로 가장 적절한 것을 고르시오.

Woman: _____

① I'm sure they will pick you up.
② We'll have the party at your house.
③ Don't worry. He'll participate, too.
④ Everyone in our class.
⑤ I guess it can be a big party.

19 대화를 듣고, 여자의 마지막 말에 대한 남자의 응답으로 가장 적절한 것을 고르시오.

Man: _____

① Yes. They live with me.
② Jeju-do is really far away.
③ They have moved three times so far.
④ They want to go there.
⑤ No. They live in Busan.

20 다음 상황 설명을 듣고, James가 노트북 주인에게 할 말로 가장 적절한 것을 고르시오.

James: _____

① Can I have this delivered?
② Do you have any other designs?
③ Could you cut the price by $30?
④ Can you reset it to the factory settings?
⑤ Is there anything that I need to know?

Listen and Check

정답 및 해설 p.035

대화를 다시 듣고, 알맞은 것을 고르시오.

1 The woman is looking for a watch for her son.
☐ True ☐ False

2 Eric's absence will be listed on his student record.
☐ True ☐ False

3 Will the man help the woman?
☐ Yes ☐ No

4 What will the woman do on Friday?
☐ study with her math tutor
☐ attend her grandfather's birthday party

5 How many letters does modern Hangul consists of?
☐ 24 letters ☐ 28 letters

6 How did the woman know she lost her credit card?
☐ Her card was used.
☐ Someone stole her bag.

7 Does the woman know when the man's parents got married?
☐ Yes ☐ No

8 The man refuses to turn off his cellphone.
☐ True ☐ False

9 Did the woman have an argument with her parents last night?
☐ Yes ☐ No

10 The man gets a discount on two combo meals.
☐ True ☐ False

11 Did the woman unpack her baggage?
☐ Yes ☐ No

12 People can create fewer harmful emissions by driving less.
☐ True ☐ False

13 What class did the woman take last semester?
☐ the Spanish class ☐ the Chinese class

14 A blinking light from this signal means caution.
☐ True ☐ False

15 Does the woman review the errors she made to avoid the same mistakes?
☐ Yes ☐ No

16 Will the man buy the sneakers the woman recommends?
☐ Yes ☐ No

17 What is number one on the man's bucket list?
☐ going to an amusement park
☐ going bungee jumping

18 The man can attend the woman's party next Friday.
☐ True ☐ False

19 The man's parents live in Busan.
☐ True ☐ False

20 James can afford to buy a new laptop.
☐ True ☐ False

그림 정보 파악

1 대화를 듣고, 여자가 구입할 시계를 고르시오.

① ② ③ ④ ⑤

1

M Are you looking for _____ _____ _____?

W I'm looking for a watch for my fourteen-year-old daughter. What would you recommend?

M This _____ watch with a simple band and this digital watch with a _____ _____ are popular with teens.

W Good, but I need a simple one.

M How about this one? It's round, *has a simple band, and _____ _____ _____ on its face.

W It's so cute, and _____ _____ _____ _____ and easy to read. I'll take it.

★ has a [해즈] [어] → [해저]

목적 파악

2 대화를 듣고, 남자가 여자에게 전화한 목적으로 가장 적절한 것을 고르시오.

① 수술 결과를 알리기 위해
② 수술 일정을 알리기 위해
③ 면담 일정을 조정하기 위해
④ 수업에 결석함을 알리기 위해
⑤ 학생부 내용을 확인하기 위해

2

[*Telephone rings.*]

W Hello, This is Kelly Stone at Hana Middle School.

M Hello, Ms. Stone. This is Chris Hacker, Eric Hacker's father.

W Hi, Mr. Hacker. What are you _____ _____ _____?

M Eric's mom is _____ _____ now, and he wants to wait for his mom's surgery to be done. He wants to check on his mother's health. So he can't go to school today.

W I'm sorry to hear that. Don't worry _____ _____ _____ because in this case, _____ _____ _____ _____ on his student record. I hope your wife recovers quickly.

M Thank you, Ms. Stone.

그림 상황 파악

3 다음 그림의 상황에 가장 적절한 대화를 고르시오.

① ② ③ ④ ⑤

3

① **M** _____ _____ _____ _____?
  W I'm afraid I can't.

② **M** Where are you moving?
  W _____ _____.

③ **M** May I help you?
  W Thank you. Would you _____ _____ _____ _____?

④ **M** What can I do for you?
  W I want to buy _____ _____ _____ _____.

⑤ **M** Watch out! _____ _____ _____ _____.
  W Thanks. I nearly fell down.

특정 정보 파악

4 대화를 듣고, 여자가 친구를 만날 요일을 고르시오.

① 월요일   ② 화요일
③ 수요일   ④ 목요일
⑤ 금요일

> 💙 **That's fine with me.**
> : 상대방의 말을 받아들일 때 사용하는 표현으로, '좋아요.', '괜찮아요.', '알겠어요.'라는 뜻이다.
> = Okay.
> = All right.

4 🇬🇧

M Jenny, have you got any free time next week?

W _____ _____ my schedule, I'll be busy all week.

M Let me see it. [*Pause*] Wow, you _____ _____ _____ for the entire week.

W Yeah, on Monday and Thursday, I'll _____ _____ _____ Sam all day long, and on Tuesday and Wednesday, I'll study with my math tutor.

M And on Friday, you'll attend your grandfather's birthday party, right?

W That's right. We are going to have dinner at my grandparents' home.

M Really? Then _____ _____ _____ in the morning on that day?

W Okay. 💙 That's fine with me.

언급 유무 파악

5 다음을 듣고, 한글에 대해 언급되지 <u>않</u>은 것을 고르시오.

① 만든 사람
② 한글의 장점
③ 만들어진 년도
④ 문자 개수의 변화
⑤ 외국의 활용 사례

5

W The Korean alphabet, known as Hangeul, _____ _____ _____ to write the Korean language since its creation by King Sejong the Great in the 15th century. Today, it is _____ _____ _____ _____ of both North and South Korea. The Hangeul alphabet originally consisted of 28 letters when it was created. But modern Hangeul _____ _____ a total of 24 letters. It is said that Hangeul can create any words and express any sound. So in 2009, the Korean alphabet _____ _____ _____ by the town of Baubau, Indonesia, to write the Cia-Cia language.

관계 추론

6 대화를 듣고, 두 사람의 관계로 가장 적절한 것을 고르시오.

① 계산원 — 손님
② 공무원 — 민원인
③ 경찰관 — 행인
④ 상담원 — 고객
⑤ 식당 점원 — 손님

> 💙 **Don't worry.**
> : 낙담하고 있는 상대방을 격려하기 위해서 쓰는 표현으로, '걱정하지 마.'라는 뜻이다.
> = Cheer up!
> = Don't be disappointed.

6

W Hello. _____ _____ _____ _____ a lost credit card.

M What are your card number and name, please?

W My number is 0552-6253-1500-2202, and my name is Ellen Jeong.

M How do you know that you lost it?

W Somebody _____ _____ _____.

M When was the last time you used your card?

W Two days ago.

M I'll check if the card _____ _____ _____ since then. [*Keyboard sound*] Nobody has used it. 💙 Don't worry. I've also _____ _____ _____.

W Thanks.

어색한 대화 찾기

7 대화를 듣고, 두 사람의 대화가 <u>어색한</u> 것을 고르시오.

① ② ③ ④ ⑤

7 🇬🇧

① W Isn't this a nice party?
   M I really _____ _____.
② W I _____ _____ _____ before.
   M I just moved to this town.
③ W Have you finished your project?
   M _____ _____ _____.
④ W What are you doing this Saturday?
   M I don't have _____ _____.
⑤ W When did your parents _____ _____?
   M They've been here for 20 years.

부탁한 일 파악

8 대화를 듣고, 여자가 남자에게 부탁한 일로 가장 적절한 것을 고르시오.

① 음식을 먹지 마라.
② 휴대 전화를 꺼라.
③ 대화를 하지 마라.
④ 농담을 하지 마라.
⑤ 앞좌석을 밀지 마라.

8

W What time does the movie start?
M 10 minutes from now. _____ _____ _____ _____ on YouTube was really exciting.
W Yeah, it really was. But don't expect too much. Maybe _____ _____ _____ the actual movie.
M Are you serious?
W I'm just joking. Hey, the movie is starting now. _____ _____ _____ _____ your cellphone? I already did that.
M Why not? I'm a _____ _____ _____.

의도 파악

9 대화를 듣고, 남자의 마지막 말에 담긴 의도로 가장 적절한 것을 고르시오.

① 사과   ② 감사
③ 격려   ④ 동의
⑤ 권유

💜 **I'm so sorry to hear that.**
: 상대방의 말에 유감이나 동정을 나타낼 때 사용하는 표현으로, '유감이야.', '안됐다.'라는 뜻이다.
= That's too bad.

9

M Karen, can I talk with you for a moment?
W Sure. _____ _____ _____.
M I think you and Minho seem to be having some problems, right?
W *How did you know that?
M I can _____ _____ _____ _____ on your face.
W Actually, I had an argument with him over a _____ _____ last night.
M 💜I'm sorry to hear that. Why don't you _____ _____ _____ _____? That's what friends do.

    * How did you [하우] [디드] [유] → [하우디쥬]

10 대화를 듣고, 남자가 지불할 금액을 고르시오.

① $20
② $23
③ $19
④ $18
⑤ $17

10

W   May I take your order?

M   I'd like two hamburgers and _____ _____ French fries.

W   _____ _____ _____?

M   Two large Cokes, please.

W   Your total is 20 dollars, but you can _____ _____ if you order combo meals.

M   Okay. I will _____ _____ _____.

W   Okay, that's two combo meals. Thank you.

11 대화를 듣고, 여자가 할 일로 가장 적절한 것을 고르시오.

① 창문을 열어 둔다.
② 수화물을 맡긴다.
③ 다른 방으로 옮긴다.
④ 호텔에서 체크아웃한다.
⑤ 에어컨 수리 기사를 기다린다.

> ♥ **I think ~**
> : 자신의 의견을 전달할 때 쓰는 표현으로, '내 생각에는 ~'이라는 뜻이다.
> = In my opinion, ~
> = In my view, ~

11

M   What _____ _____ _____ _____ _____?

W   The air conditioner doesn't seem to be working.

M   I'm sorry for the inconvenience you are experiencing.

W   That's all right. ♥I think _____ _____ _____ _____ _____ if I could open a window.

M   Well, all the windows in our hotel rooms are fixed. We'll *put you in a different room right now.

W   Thanks. It's a good thing I _____ _____ _____ _____.

★ put you in a [풋] [유] [인] [어] → [풋츄이너]

12 다음을 듣고, 지구 온난화를 예방할 방법에 관해 언급되지 **않은** 것을 고르시오.

① 나무 많이 심기
② 자동차 덜 타고 다니기
③ 적정한 실내 온도 유지하기
④ 에너지 효율적인 제품 구입하기
⑤ 재활용이 가능한 제품 선택하기

12 🇬🇧

W   There are many ways to prevent global warming from _____ _____. You can reduce waste by using _____ _____. Recycle paper, cans, and plastic products whenever you can. Drive less and walk more. Less driving means creating _____ _____ _____. When you plan to buy a car or electronics, buy energy-efficient ones. Planting many trees is _____ _____ _____ _____ _____ to reduce global warming.

표 파악

13 다음 표를 보면서 대화를 듣고, 남자가 선택할 강좌를 고르시오.

	Subject	Time
①	English	4:30 – 5:30
②	Chinese	3:00 – 4:00
③	History	4:30 – 5:30
④	Spanish	4:00 – 5:00
⑤	Japanese	3:30 – 4:30

13

W Alex, what are _____ _____ _____?

M I'm looking at this semester's after-school program.

W Why don't you sign up for a foreign language class? I took the Spanish class last semester. It was helpful when I _____ _____.

M Was it? Then I'll take the Spanish class. Oh, no! _____ _____ at 5:00. I have to go _____ _____ _____ by 4:30.

W Then how about taking the Japanese class or the Chinese class?

M Hmm... I'm _____ _____ _____ Chinese characters.

W Come on. I bet it will be useful someday.

화제·주제 파악

14 다음을 듣고, 무엇에 관한 설명인지 고르시오.

① 가로등
② 등대
③ 신호등
④ 손전등
⑤ 교통 표지판

14

M You can find this in most cities and countries _____ _____ _____. This was first installed in London, England, in the late 1800s. This usually has a _____ _____ _____ in three colors. The lights signal when pedestrians and vehicles can proceed or have to stop. In some countries, this has a blinking mode, which _____ _____. These days, sound signals for the blind _____ _____ _____.

할 일 파악

15 대화를 듣고, 남자가 할 일로 가장 적절한 것을 고르시오.

① 수학 오답 노트를 만든다.
② 서점에 가서 수학책을 산다.
③ 방과 후 수학 수업을 듣는다.
④ 도서관에서 수학 공부를 한다.
⑤ 인터넷 수학 강의를 신청한다.

♥ **You should + V**
: 상대방에게 어떤 물건이나 행동을 제안하거나 설득할 때 쓰는 표현으로, '너는 ~해야 해', '너는 ~ 하는 것이 좋을 거야'라는 뜻이다.
= You ought to + V
= You had better + V

15 🇬🇧

M I wish I were good at math, just like you.

W ♥You should always be _____ _____ _____ _____.

M Like what?

W I practice and practice. The more you practice, the better you will get.

M Okay.

W And I always review the errors I make. It can help me _____ _____ _____ _____ in the future.

M Practice and review. That's simple but hard.

W Last, do not try to _____ _____ _____ but master the key concepts. It really works.

M Thank you so much for your advice. I'll go to the library to practice right away.

16 대화를 듣고, 남자가 구입할 물건을 고르시오.

① 운동복 바지
② 운동화
③ 헤드폰
④ 악력기
⑤ 카우보이 부츠

16

W   Can I help you find something?

M   Do you have these in size 6? They're for my son.

W   I'm sorry, but that size is _____ _____ _____. How about these sneakers? _____ _____ _____ with teens who like sports. Why didn't you bring your son with you?

M   I just want to _____ _____ _____ _____ _____.

W   Oh, I see. I bet he'll love them.

M   Okay. I'll take them.

17 대화를 듣고, 여자의 마지막 말에 대한 남자의 응답으로 가장 적절한 것을 고르시오.

Man: _____
① I'm sure you'll like it.
② Cheer up. You can do it.
③ Oh, I'm sorry to hear that.
④ Never. I am afraid of heights.
⑤ No. It's number one on my bucket list.

♥ **It sounds great.**
: 상대방의 말에 대한 동의를 나타낼 때 사용하는 표현으로, '좋은 생각이야.'라는 뜻이다.
= That sounds good.
= That's a great idea.

17   🇬🇧

M   Why don't we go to the Riverside Amusement Park this weekend?

W   ♥It sounds great. I _____ _____ _____ several times, and there are lots of exciting things to do.

M   I agree. I can't wait.

W   By the way, _____ _____ do you want to try the most?

M   Well, I want to _____ _____ _____.

W   Bungee jumping? _____ _____ _____?

M   No. It's number one on my bucket list.

18 대화를 듣고, 남자의 마지막 말에 대한 여자의 응답으로 가장 적절한 것을 고르시오.

Woman: _____
① I'm sure they will pick you up.
② We'll have the party at your house.
③ Don't worry. He'll participate, too.
④ Everyone in our class.
⑤ I guess it can be a big party.

18

[Cellphone rings.]

M   Hi, Betty. What's up?

W   Hi, Jake. I'm calling you _____ _____ _____ _____ _____.

M   If possible, I will help you.

W   Well, I am _____ _____ _____ a new semester party next Friday or Saturday. I need your help.

M   I'm afraid I *can't make it on Friday. I am going to visit my grandma in L.A. next Friday.

W   Oh, no. You _____ _____ _____ _____ _____. To make a fun party, I need your help. How about Saturday? Can you come then?

M   Yeah, okay. Who are you going to invite?

W   Everyone in our class.

★ **can't make it** [캔트] [메이크] [잇] → [캔메이킷]

19 대화를 듣고, 여자의 마지막 말에 대한 남자의 응답으로 가장 적절한 것을 고르시오.

Man: _____

① Yes. They live with me.
② Jeju-do is really far away.
③ They have moved three times so far.
④ They want to go there.
⑤ No. They live in Busan.

19

W _____ _____ _____ _____ do you have?
M Five. I have two younger sisters.
W Where do they live?
M One lives in Jeju-do, and the other lives in Changwon.
W _____ _____ _____ live _____ _____ from here. Do you see them often?
M Usually _____ _____ _____.
W Do your parents live in Jeju-do?
M <u>No. They live in Busan.</u>

20 다음 상황 설명을 듣고, James가 노트북 주인에게 할 말로 가장 적절한 것을 고르시오.

James: _____

① Can I have this delivered?
② Do you have any other designs?
③ Could you cut the price by $30?
④ Can you reset it to the factory settings?
⑤ Is there anything that I need to know?

20

M James is a 16-year-old student who wants to _____ _____ _____ _____. He has _____ _____ _____ for a year. Today, he reads an advertisement for a _____ _____ on a website. The owner wants $530 for it. But he has only saved $500. He _____ _____ _____ _____ _____ _____ that he really wants it. In this situation, what would James write to the owner?

James <u>Could you cut the price by $30?</u>

1 대화를 듣고, 남자가 사기로 한 T-shirt를 고르시오.

① ② ③ ④ ⑤

2 대화를 듣고, 여자가 남자에게 전화한 목적으로 가장 적절한 것을 고르시오.
① 인터넷을 연결하기 위해
② 이미지들을 만들기 위해
③ 친구의 안부를 묻기 위해
④ 마우스의 구매처를 알기 위해
⑤ 컴퓨터 조작법을 배우기 위해

3 다음 그림의 상황에 가장 적절한 대화를 고르시오.

① ② ③ ④ ⑤

4 대화를 듣고, 두 사람이 만나기로 한 요일을 고르시오.
① 금요일 ② 토요일 ③ 일요일
④ 월요일 ⑤ 화요일

5 다음을 듣고, a fire drill에 관해 언급되지 <u>않은</u> 것을 고르시오.
① 내일 학교 여러 곳에서 실시된다.
② 학교 근처 경찰서의 도움을 받는다.
③ 교장 선생님이 안내 방송을 하고 있다.
④ 등교를 하면 우선 학교 강당에 모인다.
⑤ 선생님들을 학생들을 잘 이끌어야 한다.

6 대화를 듣고, 두 사람의 관계로 가장 적절한 것을 고르시오.
① 상담원 — 고객 ② 마트 직원 — 손님
③ 택배원 — 관리인 ④ 방문 교사 — 학생
⑤ 경찰관 — 목격자

7 다음을 듣고, 두 사람의 대화가 <u>어색한</u> 것을 고르시오.
① ② ③ ④ ⑤

8 대화를 듣고, 남자가 여자에게 부탁한 일로 가장 적절한 것을 고르시오.
① 영화표를 예매하기
② 교통수단을 바꾸기
③ 볼 영화를 변경하기
④ 저녁 식사를 주문하기
⑤ 영화관에 대한 정보 찾기

9 대화를 듣고, 여자의 마지막 말에 담긴 의도로 가장 적절한 것을 고르시오.
① 기원 ② 위로 ③ 질책
④ 사과 ⑤ 후회

10 대화를 듣고, 여자가 지불할 금액을 고르시오.
① $100 ② $108 ③ $110
④ $120 ⑤ $132

11 대화를 듣고, 남자가 할 일로 가장 적절한 것을 고르시오.
① 택시 타기
② 집들이 가기
③ 음식 주문하기
④ 친구 데려다주기
⑤ 친구에게 전화하기

12 다음을 듣고, 환경을 보호하는 방법에 관해 언급되지 않은 것을 고르시오.

① 개인 머그컵을 사용하기
② 전기 제품 사용을 자제하기
③ 식료품점에 백을 가져가기
④ 비닐봉지를 사용하지 말기
⑤ 짧은 거리는 자전거를 타기

13 다음 표를 보면서 대화를 듣고, 여자가 선택할 강좌를 고르시오.

	Class	Instructor	Day	Fee
①	A	Jasmine	Tue	$35
②	B	Daisy	Mon	$30
③	C	Helen	Wed	$20
④	D	Jasmine	Thurs	$25
⑤	E	Daisy	Tue	$25

14 다음을 듣고, 무엇에 관한 설명인지 고르시오.

① 쥐   ② 토끼
③ 도마뱀   ④ 너구리
⑤ 개구리

15 대화를 듣고, 남자가 할 일로 가장 적절한 것을 고르시오.

① 컴퓨터 끄기
② 친구 만나기
③ 친구에게 전화하기
④ 여동생 학교에 가기
⑤ 학교 행사에 참여하기

16 대화를 듣고, 비행기의 도착 예정 시각을 고르시오.

① 3시   ② 3시 30분
③ 4시   ④ 4시 30분
⑤ 5시

17 대화를 듣고, 남자의 마지막 말에 대한 여자의 응답으로 가장 적절한 것을 고르시오.

Woman: _____

① Let me help you with this job.
② Nine in the morning is fine with us.
③ I can look after people who are sick.
④ Don't hesitate to ask us if you have a question.
⑤ You can't come to the office without permission.

18 대화를 듣고, 여자의 마지막 말에 대한 남자의 응답으로 가장 적절한 것을 고르시오.

Man: _____

① I can't live like that.
② What are friends for?
③ Don't lie to me, please.
④ I am happy to win a prize.
⑤ You are the best friend ever.

19 대화를 듣고, 남자의 마지막 말에 대한 여자의 응답으로 가장 적절한 것을 고르시오.

Woman: _____

① I am looking forward to it.
② I see. Let's find one together.
③ I wish I had skated well like you.
④ I don't like chilly weather.
⑤ Can I skate without gloves?

20 다음 상황 설명을 듣고, Laura가 Aiden에게 할 말로 가장 적절한 것을 고르시오.

Laura: Aiden, _____

① is it possible to try those shoes on?
② I don't know where the shoe store is.
③ tell me why you want to buy white shoes.
④ the shoes you want to buy are not available.
⑤ you want to buy black shoes, don't you?

Listen and Check

● 대화를 다시 듣고, 알맞은 것을 고르시오.

1 The man already has lots of crew-neck T-shirts.
☐ True   ☐ False

2 Does the woman know how to save images?
☐ Yes   ☐ No

3 It would be too dangerous to swim outside the line.
☐ True   ☐ False

4 When will the man and the woman volunteer?
☐ today   ☐ tomorrow

5 Where should the students gather?
☐ in the auditorium   ☐ at the fire department

6 Is the man doing his last job of the day?
☐ Yes   ☐ No

7 The woman left her brother at the airport.
☐ True   ☐ False

8 Are the man and the woman going to watch the movie the woman chooses?
☐ Yes   ☐ No

9 Was this the man's first job interview?
☐ Yes   ☐ No

10 Did the woman rent the car with large trunk?
☐ Yes   ☐ No

11 Where does the man go by taxi?
☐ to his home   ☐ to a bus station

12 We should use plastic bags to protect the Earth.
☐ True   ☐ False

13 Does the woman have yoga class every Tuesday?
☐ Yes   ☐ No

14 Does the animal use body language to attract a mate?
☐ True   ☐ False

15 Will the man eat lunch with Jessica today?
☐ Yes   ☐ No

16 How long was the flight delayed?
☐ 1 hour
☐ 1 hour and 30 minutes

17 The man has experience volunteering for senior citizens.
☐ True   ☐ False

18 Did the man fail to win the competition?
☐ Yes   ☐ No

19 Why should the woman wear gloves?
☐ because it is dangerous
☐ because it is snowing

20 Aiden wanted to buy black shoes.
☐ True   ☐ False

그림 정보 파악

1 대화를 듣고, 남자가 사기로 한 T-shirt를 고르시오.

① ② ③

④  ⑤

1

M　Would you help me choose a T-shirt?

W　Sure. This shopping site has tons of nice T-shirts.

M　Right. ＿＿＿＿＿ ＿＿＿＿＿ ＿＿＿＿＿ ＿＿＿＿＿ all of them.

W　I think this crew-neck T-shirt looks nice.

M　Oh, it's cool. But I have lots of crew-neck shirts.

W　Well, how about the one with the V-neck?

M　I love it. ＿＿＿＿＿ ＿＿＿＿＿ ＿＿＿＿＿ ＿＿＿＿＿? Do you like the black one or the blue one?

W　The white one would go well with the pants you have.

M　I'll follow your advice. Thanks for helping me.

목적 파악

2 대화를 듣고, 여자가 남자에게 전화한 목적으로 가장 적절한 것을 고르시오.

① 인터넷을 연결하기 위해
② 이미지들을 만들기 위해
③ 친구의 안부를 묻기 위해
④ 마우스의 구매처를 알기 위해
⑤ 컴퓨터 조작법을 배우기 위해

2

[*Cellphone rings.*]

M　Hello, Rose. What's up?

W　Hi, Billy. Can you tell me how to paste ＿＿＿＿＿ ＿＿＿＿＿ ＿＿＿＿＿ ＿＿＿＿＿ onto my report?

M　It's very simple. Are you in front of your computer now?

W　Yes, I'm ready.

M　To begin with, choose an image ＿＿＿＿＿ ＿＿＿＿＿ ＿＿＿＿＿ ＿＿＿＿＿ in your report.

W　I did. And?

M　Right-click on the image on the mouse button, and you will see a menu. Click "Save as" to save it onto the hard drive.

W　Wow. I saved it on my computer.

M　Good job. You can copy and paste the image from your hard ＿＿＿＿＿ ＿＿＿＿＿ ＿＿＿＿＿ ＿＿＿＿＿ now.

W　Thanks, Billy. You are a computer genius.

그림 상황 파악

3 다음 그림의 상황에 가장 적절한 대화를 고르시오.

① ② ③ ④ ⑤

3

① M　Did you put on your swimsuit?

　 W　Of course. Let's ＿＿＿＿＿ ＿＿＿＿＿ now.

② M　You ＿＿＿＿＿ ＿＿＿＿＿ the street when the light is red.

　 W　Oh, I am very sorry.

③ M　How can I help you?

　 W　I'd like ＿＿＿＿＿ ＿＿＿＿＿ ＿＿＿＿＿ swimming lessons.

④ M　Do you see that line? It is very dangerous to swim past it.

　 W　I see. I will ＿＿＿＿＿ ＿＿＿＿＿ ＿＿＿＿＿ ＿＿＿＿＿.

⑤ M　How could you say that to me?

　 W　Calm down. ＿＿＿＿＿ ＿＿＿＿＿ ＿＿＿＿＿ ＿＿＿＿＿.

특정 정보 파악

4 대화를 듣고, 두 사람이 만나기로 한 요일을 고르시오.

① 금요일   ② 토요일
③ 일요일   ④ 월요일
⑤ 화요일

💗 **That happens from time to time.**
: 빈번하게 일어나는 일에 대해 상대방이 걱정이나 미안해할 때 사용할 수 있는 표현이다.

4 🇬🇧

[*Cellphone rings.*]

W   Hi, James. It's me, Ria.

M   Oh, Ria. What's up?

W   Do you remember _____ _____ _____ _____ at the hospital today?

M   Oh, my. I forgot. Thanks for reminding me.

W   Anyway, _____ _____ _____ _____ not to be late.

M   Wait, Ria. What day is it? We're volunteering on Sunday. But today is...

W   Oops. Today is Saturday, not Sunday. I am very sorry. _____ _____ _____ _____ _____.

M   💗 That happens from time to time. Don't worry.

W   Sorry again. See you tomorrow.

---

5 다음을 듣고, a fire drill에 관해 언급되지 <u>않은</u> 것을 고르시오.

① 내일 학교 여러 곳에서 실시된다.
② 학교 근처 경찰서의 도움을 받는다.
③ 교장선생님이 안내 방송을 하고 있다.
④ 등교를 하면 우선 학교 강당에 모인다.
⑤ 선생님들을 학생들을 잘 이끌어야 한다.

5

W   Hello, students. I am your principal, Harriett Brown. We will have a fire drill at school tomorrow. The event is _____ _____ because we have to prepare for disasters such as fires and earthquakes. When you _____ _____ _____ _____ _____, you need to *gather in the auditorium to get instructions on _____ _____ _____ _____ the drill. All your teachers will guide you so that you can learn from this experience. The fire department near our school will assist us during the drill.

     * gather in [개덜] [인] → [개더린]

관계 추론

6 대화를 듣고, 두 사람의 관계로 가장 적절한 것을 고르시오.

① 상담원 — 고객
② 마트 직원 — 손님
③ 택배원 — 관리인
④ 방문 교사 — 학생
⑤ 경찰관 — 목격자

6

M   Hello. I'm here to drop these items off.

W   Okay. How many boxes do you have today?

M   Five. I tried to contact _____ _____ _____, but they didn't answer the phone.

W   I will try to contact them, too. Write the receivers' names and phone numbers here, please.

M   Sure. This is _____ _____ _____ _____.

W   It is hard to do this kind of job, isn't it?

M   Well, sometimes it's very hard, but _____ _____ _____ _____ _____. Thanks for asking.

W   Don't mention it. Have a great day.

M   Okay. See you again.

어색한 대화 찾기

7 다음을 듣고, 두 사람의 대화가 어색한 것을 고르시오.

① ② ③ ④ ⑤

7

① **M** Would you mind _____ _____ _____ that I can't meet her?

 W No. Don't worry.

② **M** I think you had better not cut in line.

 W Oh, I am sorry. I will _____ _____ _____.

③ **M** Next, please.

 W Hi. I would like to order _____ _____ _____ ice americano.

④ **M** Don't push the button! This elevator operates automatically.

 W Sorry. _____ _____ _____ _____.

⑤ **M** _____ _____ _____ _____?

 W I have to pick up my brothers at the airport.

부탁한 일 파악

8 대화를 듣고, 남자가 여자에게 부탁한 일로 가장 적절한 것을 고르시오.

① 영화표를 예매하기
② 교통수단을 바꾸기
③ 볼 영화를 변경하기
④ 저녁 식사를 주문하기
⑤ 영화관에 대한 정보 찾기

8

[*Telephone rings.*]

M Hello, Gloria. Did you buy the movie tickets?

W Not yet. Let's meet at Dream Theater at four o'clock. The movie _____ _____ _____ _____.

M We are going to see *My Last Memory of My Friend*, right?

W Yes. It's very popular these days.

M Actually, I need to *ask you for a favor.

W What is it?

M My favorite animated movie _____ _____ _____ at the theater today. Can we _____ _____ _____?

W Why not? But you have to let me choose dinner. Okay?

M Sure.

* ask you for a favor [애스크] [유] [포] [어] [페이버] → [애스큐포러페이버]

의도 파악

9 대화를 듣고, 여자의 마지막 말에 담긴 의도로 가장 적절한 것을 고르시오.

① 기원
② 위로
③ 질책
④ 사과
⑤ 후회

9 🇬🇧

W Steve, how was your job interview yesterday?

M I think it went quite well.

W Were you nervous?

M I was a little nervous at first. But the interviewers helped me _____ _____. So I could answer most of the questions they asked me.

W That was your first job interview, _____ _____?

M No, actually, it was my second interview. I was _____ _____ _____ _____ at my first job interview. The experience helped me prepare for this one a lot.

W Good for you. I really hope _____ _____ _____ _____.

10 대화를 듣고, 여자가 지불할 금액을 고르시오.

① $100
② $108
③ $110
④ $120
⑤ $132

10

W Excuse me. I'd like to rent a car.

M Yes. What size car _____ _____ _____ _____ _____ ?

W Well, any car is okay if it's not expensive.

M Great. This car is only fifty dollars a day. But as you see, the trunk is not very large.

W I see. How about that one? _____ _____ _____ _____ a larger trunk.

M It's sixty dollars. Do you want it?

W Yes. Sixty dollars is _____ _____ _____ _____ _____, right?

M No. You also have to pay a ten-percent sales tax.

W All right. I want it for two days.

11 대화를 듣고, 남자가 할 일로 가장 적절한 것을 고르시오.

① 택시 타기
② 집들이 가기
③ 음식 주문하기
④ 친구 데려다 주기
⑤ 친구에게 전화하기

💙 **Let's keep in touch.**
: 상대방과 헤어지면서 종종 연락하자고 인사하는 표현이다.

11

M Susan, I didn't know that _____ _____ _____ _____ _____. I should be going now.

W I understand, Robert. Thanks for coming to my housewarming party.

M I was really happy to see you and your friends. The food was awesome, and everything was perfect.

W Thanks. I wish I could drive you _____ _____ _____ _____.

M Don't worry. I can take a taxi.

W Good. _____ _____ _____ _____ home. 💙 Let's keep in touch.

M Yeah. Okay, I'm off.

W So long.

12 다음을 듣고, 환경을 보호하는 방법에 관해 언급되지 <u>않은</u> 것을 고르시오.

① 개인 머그컵을 사용하기
② 전기 제품 사용을 자제하기
③ 식료품점에 백을 가져가기
④ 비닐봉지를 사용하지 말기
⑤ 짧은 거리는 자전거를 타기

12

M Hello. Let me *talk about _____ _____ _____ the environment to save the Earth. One simple way is to walk or ride a bike short distances. And we should bring our own bags to grocery stores and not use plastic bags. It's also a good idea _____ _____ _____ _____ _____ instead of using disposable cups. Lastly, we have to turn off electric devices when we're not using them. Please _____ _____ _____ _____ that small actions can be big steps to protecting the environment.

* talk about [토크] [어바웃] → [토커바웃]

표 파악

13 다음 표를 보면서 대화를 듣고, 여자가 선택할 강좌를 고르시오.

	Class	Instructor	Day	Fee
①	A	Jasmine	Tue	$35
②	B	Daisy	Mon	$30
③	C	Helen	Wed	$20
④	D	Jasmine	Thurs	$25
⑤	E	Daisy	Tue	$25

13

M Hi, Helen. What are you doing here?

W I'm checking the yoga classes on the website.

M _____ _____ _____ _____ _____?

W Sure.

M Oh, I heard that Daisy and Jasmine are popular instructors.

W Are they? Hmm... I can take any classes except the one on Tuesday. _____ _____ _____ _____ every Tuesday.

M I see. Then you can choose one of these two classes.

W The price is different.

M Then why don't you _____ _____ _____ _____?

W Good idea. Thanks for your opinion.

화제·주제 파악

14 다음을 듣고, 무엇에 관한 설명인지 고르시오.

① 쥐
② 토끼
③ 도마뱀
④ 너구리
⑤ 개구리

14

W This can *found around the world except in cold areas. This is _____ _____ _____ _____ _____ as a snake, but it's different in some ways. This has feet and ears, but a snake doesn't have them. This can _____ _____ _____ of its body. This also uses body language to communicate. This uses gestures and other movements _____ _____ _____ _____. What is this?

★ found around [퐈운드] [어라운드] → [퐈운더라운드]

할 일 파악

15 대화를 듣고, 남자가 할 일로 가장 적절한 것을 고르시오.

① 컴퓨터 끄기
② 친구 만나기
③ 친구에게 전화하기
④ 여동생 학교에 가기
⑤ 학교 행사에 참여하기

15 🇬🇧

W Bob, hurry up. We're leaving now.

M Mom, I'm coming. Wait, please.

W Who were you speaking to?

M Jessica. I _____ _____ _____ _____ _____ for lunch and had to explain why I can't join her.

W Oh, okay. Now let's go to your little sister's school now.

M _____ _____ _____ _____ her first school play. Let's go!

W Please make sure to turn your computer off _____ _____ _____.

M I will.

16 대화를 듣고, 비행기의 도착 예정 시각을 고르시오.

① 3시
② 3시 30분
③ 4시
④ 4시 30분
⑤ 5시

16

W Excuse me. Could you let me know if the flight from Seattle _____ _____?

M Did you check the flight information board?

W No. I don't know where it is.

M Okay. What is the flight number?

W It's Aurora Airlines AR582. It was supposed to arrive at three p.m., but _____ _____ _____ _____ _____.

M Let's see… Oh, the flight has been delayed by another 30 minutes _____ _____ _____ _____.

W I see. Thank you.

17 대화를 듣고, 남자의 마지막 말에 대한 여자의 응답으로 가장 적절한 것을 고르시오.

Woman: _____
① Let me help you with this job.
② Nine in the morning is fine with us.
③ I can look after people who are sick.
④ Don't hesitate to ask us if you have a question.
⑤ You can't come to the office without permission.

17

M Hello. I wonder _____ _____ _____ for me to volunteer here for a couple of weeks.

W Have you ever looked after senior citizens before?

M Yes. I volunteered at a local senior citizen center for 20 hours.

W Great. _____ _____ _____ _____ senior citizens clean their rooms, eat meals, and so on. Is that clear?

M Okay. I will try my best.

W Can you start volunteering tomorrow?

M Sure. _____ _____ _____ _____ _____?

W <u>Nine in the morning is fine with us.</u>

18 대화를 듣고, 여자의 마지막 말에 대한 남자의 응답으로 가장 적절한 것을 고르시오.

Man: _____
① I can't live like that.
② What are friends for?
③ Don't lie to me, please.
④ I am happy to win a prize.
⑤ You are the best friend ever.

18 🇬🇧

W Chris, you look down. What's wrong?

M I think I _____ _____ _____ playing the piano.

W Why? What happened?

M I _____ _____ _____ _____ in the piano competition last week.

W I'm sorry to hear that. I heard you practiced very hard.

M I really did my best for the competition. But the results were… I'm so frustrated.

W Cheer up. _____ _____ _____ _____ that I've ever known.

M <u>You are the best friend ever.</u>

19 대화를 듣고, 남자의 마지막 말에 대한 여자의 응답으로 가장 적절한 것을 고르시오.

Woman: _____

① I am looking forward to it.
② I see. Let's find one together.
③ I wish I had skated well like you.
④ I don't like chilly weather.
⑤ Can I skate without gloves?

19 🏴

W It is very cold today, but it is a good time for ice skating.

M That's _____ _____ _____ _____ _____.
Oh, your hands feel cold. Where are your gloves?

W I have them in my bag.

M You'd better wear them. _____ _____ _____
_____ _____ your hands in your pockets.

W Okay, I will. Wait. I don't see my gloves in my bag. _____
_____ _____!

M Without them, you can't skate in this cold weather.

W You're right. What should I do?

M Let's see _____ _____ _____ _____ that sells gloves around here.

W I see. Let's find one together.

20 다음 상황 설명을 듣고, Laura가 Aiden에게 할 말로 가장 적절한 것을 고르시오.

Laura: Aiden, _____

① is it possible to try those shoes on?
② I don't know where the shoe store is.
③ tell me why you want to buy white shoes.
④ the shoes you want to buy are not available.
⑤ you want to buy black shoes, don't you?

20

W Laura and Aiden are going to meet at a shoe store. Aiden wants to buy _____ _____ _____ _____ _____, and Laura wants to buy a pair of black ones. Laura arrives at the store _____ _____ _____ Aiden, so she is looking at the shoes herself. The store staff member says that there are _____ _____ _____ _____, but there aren't any white shoes at the moment. Aiden _____ _____ _____ _____ and meets Laura. In this situation, what would Laura most likely say to Aiden?

Laura Aiden, the shoes you want to buy are not available.

1 대화를 듣고, 남자가 구입할 스탠드를 고르시오.

 ① ② ③

 ④ ⑤

2 대화를 듣고, 남자가 여자에게 부탁한 일로 가장 적절한 것을 고르시오.
① 약속 잡아 주기
② 동료들 만나기
③ 세탁기 돌리기
④ 빨래 널어 주기
⑤ 일찍 귀가하기

3 다음 그림의 상황에 가장 적절한 대화를 고르시오.

① ② ③ ④ ⑤

4 대화를 듣고, 남자가 예매한 비행기 표 시각을 고르시오.
① 6:00 a.m. ② 9:00 a.m.
③ 12:00 p.m. ④ 3:00 p.m.
⑤ 5:00 p.m.

5 대화를 듣고, 두 사람이 얘기하는 작품에 관해 언급되지 <u>않은</u> 것을 고르시오.
① 작품의 묘사 ② 화가의 이름
③ 작품의 이름 ④ 작품의 느낌
⑤ 소장 박물관

6 대화를 듣고, 두 사람이 대화하는 장소로 가장 적절한 곳을 고르시오.
① 학원 ② 공원
③ 문구점 ④ 사진관
⑤ 상담소

7 다음을 듣고, 두 사람의 대화가 <u>어색한</u> 것을 고르시오.
① ② ③ ④ ⑤

8 대화를 듣고, 여자가 남자에게 부탁한 일로 가장 적절한 것을 고르시오.
① 액세서리 사진 찍기
② SNS에 영상 올리기
③ 재생할 음악 고르기
④ 함께 홍보 방법 찾기
⑤ 홍보 영상 메시지 쓰기

9 다음을 듣고, 무엇에 관한 설명인지 고르시오.
① 행복의 조건
② 걷기의 효능
③ 스트레스 증상
④ 통증 완화 방법
⑤ 걷기 축제 광고

10 대화를 듣고, 남자가 지불할 금액을 고르시오.
① $24 ② $40 ③ $44
④ $55 ⑤ $58

11 대화를 듣고, 여자가 할 일로 가장 적절한 것을 고르시오.
① 조언 구하기
② 앱 다운받기
③ 휴식 취하기
④ 업무 끝내기
⑤ 일정 조정하기

12 다음을 듣고, 페인트 작업에 관해 언급되지 <u>않은</u> 것을 고르시오.
① 작업 시간
② 작업 대상
③ 주차 시간
④ 공지 대상
⑤ 작업 장소

13 다음 표를 보면서 대화를 듣고, 두 사람이 선택할 수업을 고르시오.

	Classes	Subjects		Schedule
①	Class A	Listening	Reading	Weekdays
②	Class B	Listening	Speaking	Weekdays
③	Class C	Listening	Speaking	Weekends
④	Class D	Speaking	Reading	Weekends
⑤	Class E	Speaking	Reading	Weekdays

14 다음을 듣고, 무엇에 관한 설명인지 고르시오.
① 신문
② 잡지
③ 앨범
④ 소설
⑤ 사전

15 대화를 듣고, 남자가 대화 직후에 할 일로 가장 적절한 것을 고르시오.
① 답장 쓰기
② 이메일 발송
③ 이메일 확인
④ 약속 정하기
⑤ 전화 기다리기

16 대화를 듣고, 남자가 비행기 표를 예매할 시각을 고르시오.
① 10:00 a.m.
② 12:30 p.m.
③ 3:00 p.m.
④ 5:30 p.m.
⑤ 7:00 p.m.

17 대화를 듣고, 여자의 마지막 말에 대한 남자의 응답으로 가장 적절한 것을 고르시오.
Man: _____
① Ask your friend to drive you to work.
② Let me borrow your car this weekend.
③ I have the same problem that you do.
④ You don't seem to care about your body.
⑤ You'd better exercise at least twice a week.

18 대화를 듣고, 남자의 마지막 말에 대한 여자의 응답으로 가장 적절한 것을 고르시오.
Woman: _____
① It's important to listen to your parents.
② You need to consider it more seriously.
③ How lucky you are to have a good job.
④ I'm not satisfied with what I do at work.
⑤ I knew that you would succeed this much.

19 대화를 듣고, 여자의 마지막 말에 대한 남자의 응답으로 가장 적절한 것을 고르시오.
Man: _____
① An animal can also be my best friend.
② I hope to come back here again soon.
③ What's a good thing about having a pet?
④ Is there something wrong with doing this?
⑤ I can't wait to see the animals at the zoo.

20 다음 상황 설명을 듣고, Adam이 Emilia에게 할 말로 가장 적절한 것을 고르시오.
Adam: Emilia, _____
① we need to take a break.
② sorry that I didn't do it well.
③ remember that we're a team.
④ being a leader is never easy.
⑤ that's what you're supposed to do.

Listen and Check

정답 및 해설 *p.045*

● 대화를 다시 듣고, 알맞은 것을 고르시오.

1 What does the man want the lamp to come with?
☐ a shade ☐ only a bulb

2 The woman will go out with the man.
☐ True ☐ False

3 Does the man hurt?
☐ Yes ☐ No

4 When will the man and the woman leave for Vietnam?
☐ in the morning ☐ in the afternoon

5 The woman is familiar with the painting.
☐ True ☐ False

6 Is it the first time for the man to see blurry photographs?
☐ Yes ☐ No

7 Driving at night isn't hard for the man.
☐ True ☐ False

8 What will the man and the woman promote on social networking sites?
☐ a shop ☐ a hobby

9 What is the negative point of walking too much?
☐ more stress ☐ pain in legs

10 Does the man want to have all the bracelets gift-wrapped?
☐ Yes ☐ No

11 The woman knows how to manage her time well.
☐ True ☐ False

12 Which part of the apartment will be repainted?
☐ the parking lots ☐ the exterior walls

13 The man and the woman will take the English class on weekdays.
☐ Yes ☐ No

14 The origins of words are well explained in the book.
☐ True ☐ False

15 For what does the man apologize to the woman?
☐ replying late ☐ not sending an email

16 Do the man and the woman choose to stay one more week in Bangkok?
☐ Yes ☐ No

17 The man doesn't recognize the difference in the woman's body.
☐ True ☐ False

18 What does the man want to become?
☐ a scientist ☐ a popular YouTuber

19 Will the woman help the man feed the sheep?
☐ Yes ☐ No

20 What are the man and the woman supposed to do at the Internet café?
☐ do research ☐ make a presentation

90

그림 정보 파악

1 대화를 듣고, 남자가 구입할 스탠드를 고르시오.

① ② ③

④ ⑤

1

W Good afternoon. How can I help you?

M I'm looking for _____ _____ _____ to put in the corner of my living room.

W Which do you prefer, one with a shade or one with _____ _____ _____?

M I want one _____ _____ _____.

W We have plain white *shades and also ones with striped patterns.

M Simple is the best. I'll _____ _____ _____ _____.

W Okay.

★ shades and [쉐이즈] [엔드] → [쉐이젠드]

부탁한 일 파악

2 대화를 듣고, 남자가 여자에게 부탁한 일로 가장 적절한 것을 고르시오.

① 약속 잡아 주기
② 동료들 만나기
③ 세탁기 돌리기
④ 빨래 널어 주기
⑤ 일찍 귀가하기

💙 **in + 시간 표현**
: 말하는 순간을 기준으로 특정 '시간' 이후를 나타낼 때 사용하는 표현으로, '(시간) 후에' 라는 뜻이다.

2

W Do you _____ _____ _____ now?

M Yes, with my coworkers.

W What time will you _____ _____ _____?

M I'll be back 💙 in two hours. Do you have any plans _____ _____ _____ today?

W No, I don't. Why?

M I just started the washing machine. Please _____ _____ _____ _____ to dry later.

W All right.

그림 상황 파악

3 다음 그림의 상황에 가장 적절한 대화를 고르시오.

① ② ③ ④ ⑤

3

① **W** Shall we _____ _____ _____?
   M Sure.

② **W** When did you _____ _____ _____?
   M I got it when I was four.

③ **W** What happened, Michael?
   M I _____ _____ _____.

④ **W** Where did you go _____ _____ _____ _____?
   M I went to Gyeongju.

⑤ **W** Is walking _____ _____ exercise?
   M Of course, it is.

4 대화를 듣고, 남자가 예매한 비행기 표 시각을 고르시오.

① 6:00 a.m.
② 9:00 a.m.
③ 12:00 p.m.
④ 3:00 p.m.
⑤ 5:00 p.m.

4

W   We need to _____ _____ _____ to Vietnam.

M   I'm _____ _____ _____ _____ from the early morning to the afternoon.

W   It's better for us to depart _____ _____ _____ we can.

M   There are flights leaving at 6:00 a.m., 9:00 a.m., 12:00 p.m., 3:00 p.m., and 5:00 p.m.

W   Let's _____ _____ _____ _____. But I think 6:00 a.m. is too early.

M   Okay. I'll _____ _____ _____ _____ then.

5 대화를 듣고, 두 사람이 얘기하는 작품에 관해 언급되지 <u>않은</u> 것을 고르시오.

① 작품의 묘사
② 화가의 이름
③ 작품의 이름
④ 작품의 느낌
⑤ 소장 박물관

5 🇬🇧

W   This painting by Vincent van Gogh makes me _____ _____ _____.

M   The people sitting at the café terrace and the stars in the night sky make the mood of the piece _____ _____ _____.

W   You're right. I also like the colors he used in the work.

M   They look warm and _____ _____ _____ _____.

W   I heard it's a place that Vincent van Gogh often visited.

M   Where can I _____ _____ _____ _____?

W   It's in a museum in the Netherlands.

6 대화를 듣고, 두 사람이 대화하는 장소로 가장 적절한 곳을 고르시오.

① 학원
② 공원
③ 문구점
④ 사진관
⑤ 상담소

6

M   Hi. I came to _____ _____ _____ _____.

W   Just a minute. Here you are. I noticed some of them were blurry.

M   It _____ _____ _____. What do you think the problem is?

W   Your film got exposed to sunlight when you took some pictures.

M   Oh, did it? I'm just not used to using a film camera.

W   Just _____ _____ _____ _____ _____ before shooting. Then everything will be fine.

M   Thank you for the advice.

7 다음을 듣고, 두 사람의 대화가 <u>어색한</u> 것을 고르시오.

① ② ③ ④ ⑤

7

① **M** Where is your car?

   W My car's _____ _____ _____ for repairs.

② **M** What happened to your car?

   W My car _____ _____ while it was parked.

③ **M** How often do you _____ _____ _____?

   W I wash it at least *once a week.

④ **M** I can't see well in the dark, so I find it difficult to drive at night.

   W Sunglasses can _____ _____ _____.

⑤ **M** It costs a lot to _____ _____ _____.

   W How much do you spend on your car?

★ once a [원쓰] [어] → [원써]

부탁한 일 파악

8 대화를 듣고, 여자가 남자에게 부탁한 일로 가장 적절한 것을 고르시오.

① 액세서리 사진 찍기
② SNS에 영상 올리기
③ 재생할 음악 고르기
④ 함께 홍보 방법 찾기
⑤ 홍보 영상 메시지 쓰기

♥ **That's why + S + V**
: 어떤 원인에 대한 결과를 얘기할 때 사용하는 표현으로, '그래서 (주어)가 (동사)하는 거야'라는 뜻이다.

8

M What have you been thinking about for so long?

W I'm thinking of a way to _____ _____ _____.

M Try to do it on social networking sites.

W That's my plan, but I haven't decided _____ _____ _____ a promotional video yet.

M Put some good *pictures of some of _____ _____ _____ _____ at your shop and play some music in the video.

W Okay. Could you help me _____ _____ _____ to put in the video?

M Why not? You know I have _____ _____ _____ _____ doing that.

W ♥That's why I am asking you.

M All right. Let's _____ _____ _____ by the end of this week.

★ pictures of [픽철쓰] [어브] → [픽철써브]

화제·주제 파악

9 다음을 듣고, 무엇에 관한 설명인지 고르시오.

① 행복의 조건
② 걷기의 효능
③ 스트레스 증상
④ 통증 완화 방법
⑤ 걷기 축제 광고

9

M Hi. I'm here to tell you _____ _____ _____. How much do you walk a day? You can be healthier and lose weight just by walking. First of all, it _____ _____ _____ and boosts your immune system. It also helps reduce stress and _____ _____ _____. However, if you walk too hard, you _____ _____ _____ in your legs. Walk for thirty minutes a day, and you will live a much healthier and happier life.

10 대화를 듣고, 남자가 지불할 금액을 고르시오.

① $24
② $40
③ $44
④ $55
⑤ $58

10

W Good afternoon. _____ _____ _____ _____ are you looking for?

M I heard that if I buy a twenty-dollar leather bracelet, I can get another one for free.

W You're right. You can choose any bracelets that are _____ _____ _____ _____.

M I'll get a black and white one. How much are the metal bracelets beside the leather ones?

W Each costs 35 dollars, but they're _____ _____ _____.

M I'll buy a golden metal one, please.

W Okay. We _____ _____ _____ if you pay an extra three dollars.

M Cool. I'll take the gift wrapping _____ _____ _____ _____ one, please.

11 대화를 듣고, 여자가 할 일로 가장 적절한 것을 고르시오.

① 조언 구하기
② 앱 다운받기
③ 휴식 취하기
④ 업무 끝내기
⑤ 일정 조정하기

11 🇬🇧

W I want to be more productive at work. How can I _____ _____ _____ more efficiently?

M Well, there are some ways to _____ _____ _____.

W What are they?

M Download an application that _____ _____ _____. It *lets you know how much time you spend on the things you do.

W What a great tool that is!

M And _____ _____ _____. Working on tasks without taking breaks decreases your performance.

W Thanks for the advice. I think I should _____ _____ _____ first.

★ lets you [렛츠] [유] → [렛츄]

12 다음을 듣고, 페인트 작업에 관해 언급되지 <u>않은</u> 것을 고르시오.

① 작업 시간
② 작업 대상
③ 주차 시간
④ 공지 대상
⑤ 작업 장소

12

W This is an _____ _____ _____ of Rainbow Apartment. The exterior walls of Building A will be repainted tomorrow. Please _____ _____ _____ in the parking lot near Building B. The paint job will take _____ _____ _____. It starts at 8 a.m. and will be finished by noon. Please _____ _____ _____ the area and the time. Thank you.

표 파악

13 다음 표를 보면서 대화를 듣고, 두 사람이 선택할 수업을 고르시오.

Classes	Subjects		Schedule
① Class A	Listening	Reading	Weekdays
② Class B	Listening	Speaking	Weekdays
③ Class C	Listening	Speaking	Weekends
④ Class D	Speaking	Reading	Weekends
⑤ Class E	Speaking	Reading	Weekdays

13

M Stella, _____ _____ _____ _____ do you want to take?

W Let's take an English class. I want to be good at English.

M Me, too. Would it be better for us to take _____ _____ _____ _____ classes?

W Yes. I heard that practicing listening and speaking together is a great way to improve your foreign language skills.

M When do you have time? I _____ _____ _____ on weekdays.

W I'm _____ _____ _____ _____, too.

M Okay. Let's sign up for the classes right away.

화제·주제 파악

14 다음을 듣고, 무엇에 관한 설명인지 고르시오.

① 신문
② 잡지
③ 앨범
④ 소설
⑤ 사전

14

W This is _____ _____ _____ _____. We use it when we study a language. It *gives us information _____ _____ _____. It includes words and their definitions, pronunciation, and examples. It comes in different sizes, so we _____ _____ _____ a small one. These days, many people use _____ _____ of this book because they are _____ _____ _____. Another thing about this is that every country has this type of book in its language.

★ gives us [기브쓰] [어쓰] → [깁써쓰]

할 일 파악

15 대화를 듣고, 남자가 대화 직후에 할 일로 가장 적절한 것을 고르시오.

① 답장 쓰기
② 이메일 발송
③ 이메일 확인
④ 약속 정하기
⑤ 전화 기다리기

15

[*Telephone rings.*]

W Hello.

M Hi. This is Jimin Kim.

W Hi, Mr. Kim. What _____ _____ _____ _____?

M I sent you an email last Saturday, but I _____ _____ _____ _____ yet.

W An email? Well, let me check. [*A few seconds later*] Sorry, but I _____ _____ _____ _____ from you.

M Really? Please wait for a minute.

W Sure.

M Sorry. It was my mistake. I sent the email to _____ _____ _____. I'll send it to you right now.

숫자 정보 파악

16 대화를 듣고, 남자가 비행기 표를 예매할 시각을 고르시오.

① 10:00 a.m. ② 12:30 p.m.
③ 3:00 p.m. ④ 5:30 p.m.
⑤ 7:00 p.m.

💙 **You'd better + V**
: 상대방에게 제안이나 조언을 할 때 사용하는 표현으로, '~하는 게 좋겠어'라는 뜻이다. 반대로 '~하지 않는 게 좋겠어'라고 말할 때에는 'You'd better not + V'를 사용한다.

16 🇬🇧

W Have you _____ _____ _____ _____ to Bangkok?

M Not yet. I _____ _____ between the 12:30 p.m. and 7 p.m. flights.

W The earlier, the better.

M Tickets _____ _____ _____ cost more. The price of the earlier ticket is double that of the later one.

W Then 💙 you'd better choose the later one.

M Yes. Then I can stay there for _____ _____ _____.

W That's _____ _____ _____.

적절한 응답 찾기

17 대화를 듣고, 여자의 마지막 말에 대한 남자의 응답으로 가장 적절한 것을 고르시오.

Man: _____
① Ask your friend to drive you to work.
② Let me borrow your car this weekend.
③ I have the same problem that you do.
④ You don't seem to care about your body.
⑤ You'd better exercise at least twice a week.

💙 **No way.**
: 상대방의 말을 믿지 못하고 강하게 부정할 때 사용하는 표현으로, '말도 안 돼.', '그럴 리가.'라는 뜻이다.

17

W I have gained _____ _____ _____.

M 💙 No way. You look the same.

W You _____ _____. I have gained four kilograms in one month.

M What do you think the reason is?

W I don't exercise and _____ _____ for a long time _____ _____.

M And you drive your car every day, which means you _____ _____ _____.

W You're right. _____ _____ _____ _____ to lose weight?

M You'd better exercise at least twice a week.

적절한 응답 찾기

18 대화를 듣고, 남자의 마지막 말에 대한 여자의 응답으로 가장 적절한 것을 고르시오.

Woman: _____
① It's important to listen to your parents.
② You need to consider it more seriously.
③ How lucky you are to have a good job.
④ I'm not satisfied with what I do at work.
⑤ I knew that you would succeed this much.

18

W Why are you _____ _____ _____, Jack?

M Look at this guy. He's a YouTuber. He's so funny.

W Is he doing a science experiment? The video seems _____ _____ _____.

M You're right. You know, popular YouTubers make _____ _____ _____ _____.

W There must be a reward for that kind of an effort.

M _____ _____ _____ I became a game YouTuber?

W You mean as a hobby, don't you?

M Of course not. I meant that I _____ _____ _____ _____ and be a full-time YouTuber. Wouldn't that be cool?

W You need to consider it more seriously.

적절한 응답 찾기

19 대화를 듣고, 여자의 마지막 말에 대한 남자의 응답으로 가장 적절한 것을 고르시오.

Man: _____

① An animal can also be my best friend.

② I hope to come back here again soon.

③ What's a good thing about having a pet?

④ Is there something wrong with doing this?

⑤ I can't wait to see the animals at the zoo.

19

W   It's _____ _____ to come to a sheep ranch.

M   Mom, there is a flock of sheep!

W   They look so cute. I think we can _____ _____ _____ _____ here.

M   Can I try feeding them, please?

W   Sure. Let me _____ _____ _____ _____ _____.

M   Look, Mom! This sheep is so mild. It _____ _____ even when I pet it.

W   Oh, Robert. You don't _____ _____ _____ which is raised on a farm or at a zoo.

M   <u>Is there something wrong with doing this?</u>

적절한 응답 찾기

20 다음 상황 설명을 듣고, Adam이 Emilia에게 할 말로 가장 적절한 것을 고르시오.

Adam: Emilia, _____

① we need to take a break.

② sorry that I didn't do it well.

③ remember that we're a team.

④ being a leader is never easy.

⑤ that's what you're supposed to do.

20 🇬🇧

M   Adam and Emilia _____ _____ _____ _____ together. They are assigned to work as a team and to _____ _____ _____ on Western culture. They decide to meet at an Internet café and _____ _____ on the topic. Adam _____ _____ from different sites and takes notes. But Emilia doesn't do what she is supposed to and _____ _____ _____. In this situation, what would Adam most likely say to Emilia?

Adam   Emilia, <u>remember that we're a team.</u>

1 대화를 듣고, 여자가 만든 크리스마스카드를 고르시오.

① ② ③

④ ⑤

2 대화를 듣고, 남자가 여자에게 부탁한 일로 가장 적절한 것을 고르시오.
① 우산 구입하기　　② 뮤지컬 예매하기
③ 함께 지하철 타기　④ 차로 데려다 주기
⑤ 저녁 식사 같이 하기

3 다음 그림의 상황에 가장 적절한 대화를 고르시오.

①　　②　　③　　④　　⑤

4 대화를 듣고, 여자가 배드민턴 코트를 사용할 요일을 고르시오.
① 월요일　　② 화요일　　③ 수요일
④ 목요일　　⑤ 금요일

5 대화를 듣고, 수영장에서 지켜야 할 점으로 언급되지 않은 것을 고르시오.
① 수영복과 수영모 착용
② 달리기와 다이빙 금지
③ 자신의 레인을 지키기
④ 큰소리로 말하지 않기
⑤ 수영 전 준비 운동 하기

6 대화를 듣고, 두 사람이 대화하는 장소로 가장 적절한 곳을 고르시오.
① 식당　　　　　　② 프랑스
③ 꽃가게　　　　　④ 길 한복판
⑤ 인테리어 가게

7 다음을 듣고, 두 사람의 대화가 어색한 것을 고르시오.
①　　　②　　　③　　　④　　　⑤

8 대화를 듣고, 여자가 남자에게 부탁한 일로 가장 적절한 것을 고르시오.
① 아들을 봐 달라고
② 자리를 바꿔 달라고
③ 행선지를 알려달라고
④ 이물질을 제거해 달라고
⑤ 기차표를 대신 구입해 달라고

9 다음을 듣고, 무엇에 관한 안내 방송인지 고르시오.
① 비행기 출발 안내 방송
② 분실물 습득 관련 방송
③ 운항 도중 안전벨트 지시
④ 전자 기기 사용 시 유의점
⑤ 안전벨트의 올바른 착용법

10 대화를 듣고, 남자가 지불할 금액을 고르시오.
① $25　　② $30　　③ $35
④ $40　　⑤ $45

11 대화를 듣고, 여자가 할 일로 가장 적절한 것을 고르시오.
① 만화책 구입하기　② 대학원 진학하기
③ 아들과 대화하기　④ 독서 목록 만들기
⑤ 가족과 시간 보내기

12 다음을 듣고, 서울 국제 불꽃 축제에 관해 언급되지 <u>않</u>은 것을 고르시오.

① 축제 일정　　② 행사 장소
③ 입장 요금　　④ 참여 국가
⑤ 순환 버스

13 대화를 듣고, 두 사람이 앉을 극장 좌석을 고르시오.

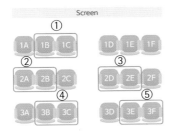

14 다음을 듣고, 무엇에 관한 설명인지 고르시오.
① 피로 누적의 위험성
② 눈을 보호하는 방법
③ 30분 동안 매일 걷기
④ 스마트폰 게임의 단점
⑤ 안경 고를 때 주의할 점

15 대화를 듣고, 남자가 대화 직후에 할 일로 가장 적절한 것을 고르시오.
① 설거지하기
② 식기 구입하기
③ 화장품 교환하기
④ 냉장고 청소하기
⑤ 감자, 당근 구입하기

16 대화를 듣고, 여자가 집을 보러 가기로 한 날짜를 고르시오.
① 6월 14일　　② 6월 15일
③ 6월 16일　　④ 6월 17일
⑤ 6월 18일

17 대화를 듣고, 남자의 마지막 말에 대한 여자의 응답으로 가장 적절한 것을 고르시오.
Woman: _____
① That suit looks good on you.
② I never thought I'd see the singer.
③ I'll be a bit nervous, but I can do it.
④ I won't ever forget hearing the song.
⑤ I can play the piano at your wedding.

18 대화를 듣고, 여자의 마지막 말에 대한 남자의 응답으로 가장 적절한 것을 고르시오.
Man: _____
① It costs 10 dollars and 50 cents.
② Don't rush, or you will fall down.
③ I should return these books today.
④ You have a point. I should start today.
⑤ Come on. It'll take about 2 hours to get there from here.

19 대화를 듣고, 남자의 마지막 말에 대한 여자의 응답으로 가장 적절한 것을 고르시오.
Woman: _____
① You got paint on your shirt.
② Please draw me a nice painting.
③ Be my guest. You can use mine.
④ Let's go to the bank to save money.
⑤ Watermelon is my favorite summer fruit.

20 다음 상황 설명을 듣고, Beatrice가 판매자에게 할 말로 가장 적절한 것을 고르시오.
Beatrice: Hello. _____
① I want to see your bicycle.
② This is just what I'm looking for.
③ I'll ride by your house on my bike.
④ Where are you? I'm waiting for you.
⑤ I'd like to get a refund on this bicycle.

Listen and Check

● 대화를 다시 듣고, 알맞은 것을 고르시오.

1 Santa Claus is hard for Harin to draw.
☐ True   ☐ False

2 What did the man and the woman watch together?
☐ a movie   ☐ a musical

3 Does the woman give her seat to the old man?
☐ Yes   ☐ No

4 When will the final safety inspection be scheduled for?
☐ Monday   ☐ Tuesday

5 What is one of the rules at the pool?
☐ no running   ☐ no jumping

6 The man's business is not doing well.
☐ True   ☐ False

7 What does the man want to know about?
☐ the bank's business hours
☐ how to open an account

8 Are the man and the woman talking in front of the ticket office?
☐ Yes   ☐ No

9 People can't smoke during the entire flight.
☐ True   ☐ False

10 When can the man pick up his clothes?
☐ tomorrow morning   ☐ tomorrow evening

11 Does Harry only love to read comic books?
☐ Yes   ☐ No

12 Four countries will participate in the Seoul International Fireworks Festival.
☐ True   ☐ False

13 What is the name of the movie the man and the woman will watch tonight?
☐ *The Lion King*   ☐ *Aladdin*

14 Blinking your eyes frequently makes your eyes get dry.
☐ True   ☐ False

15 What did the man decide to make for dinner?
☐ pork stew   ☐ pork curry

16 The woman wants to see the two-bedroom apartment.
☐ True   ☐ False

17 Mia is getting married soon.
☐ True   ☐ False

18 Did the man hand in his science report?
☐ Yes   ☐ No

19 When will art class begin?
☐ in 30 minutes   ☐ in 40 minutes

20 What does Beatrice want to buy?
☐ a bicycle   ☐ a helmet

그림 정보 파악

1 대화를 듣고, 여자가 만든 크리스마스 카드를 고르시오.

♥ **I bet (that) S + V**

: 내기할 수 있을 만큼 확신하고 있음을 나타낼 때 쓰는 표현으로, '~은 확실해'라는 뜻이다.

= I'm sure (that) S + V

= I guarantee you (that) S + V

1

M Harin, did you make this Christmas card?

W That's right. This is for my grandmother.

M You ＿＿＿＿＿ ＿＿＿＿＿ ＿＿＿＿＿ ＿＿＿＿＿ in the middle.

W I also drew lots of presents in front of the tree.

M ＿＿＿＿＿ ＿＿＿＿＿ ＿＿＿＿＿ Santa Claus?

W I tried, but it was ＿＿＿＿＿ ＿＿＿＿＿ ＿＿＿＿＿ ＿＿＿＿＿ to draw.

M Still, I like your card. ♥I bet your grandmother will love it, too.

부탁한 일 파악

2 대화를 듣고, 남자가 여자에게 부탁한 일로 가장 적절한 것을 고르시오.

① 우산 구입하기
② 뮤지컬 예매하기
③ 함께 지하철 타기
④ 차로 데려다 주기
⑤ 저녁 식사 같이 하기

2 🇬🇧

W It was a really nice musical.

M I agree. It was so amazing. Now, I need to go home and ＿＿＿＿＿ ＿＿＿＿＿ ＿＿＿＿＿.

W How will you ＿＿＿＿＿ ＿＿＿＿＿ ＿＿＿＿＿ ＿＿＿＿＿?

M I'm thinking of ＿＿＿＿＿ ＿＿＿＿＿ ＿＿＿＿＿. How about you?

W I drove my car here.

M Can you ＿＿＿＿＿ ＿＿＿＿＿ ＿＿＿＿＿ on your way home?

W Why not? That's no problem.

그림 상황 파악

3 다음 그림의 상황에 가장 적절한 대화를 고르시오.

① ② ③ ④ ⑤

3

① **W** There is a ＿＿＿＿＿ ＿＿＿＿＿ ＿＿＿＿＿ ＿＿＿＿＿.

　M I'll try to remove it.

② **W** You can ＿＿＿＿＿ ＿＿＿＿＿ ＿＿＿＿＿ here.

　M Thank you. How kind of you!

③ **W** I'm on my way to the gym.

　M Don't forget to ＿＿＿＿＿ ＿＿＿＿＿ ＿＿＿＿＿ ＿＿＿＿＿.

④ **W** Are you sure you locked the car doors?

　M Don't worry. ＿＿＿＿＿ ＿＿＿＿＿.

⑤ **W** Why don't we take the bus *instead of the subway?

　M We will ＿＿＿＿＿ ＿＿＿＿＿ ＿＿＿＿＿ a serious traffic jam.

＊ instead of [인스테드] [오브] → [인스테러브]

4 대화를 듣고, 여자가 배드민턴 코트를
사용할 요일을 고르시오.

① 월요일
② 화요일
③ 수요일
④ 목요일
⑤ 금요일

4

W Excuse me. Is the badminton court _____ _____ _____?

M Yes. I'm afraid that you can't use it today.

W Hmm... It is _____ _____ _____.

M The repairs are almost done. The _____ _____ _____ is scheduled for Tuesday.

W Then I will _____ _____ _____ _____.

M You can definitely use the court by then.

5 대화를 듣고, 수영장에서 지켜야 할 점
으로 언급되지 <u>않은</u> 것을 고르시오.

① 수영복과 수영모 착용
② 달리기와 다이빙 금지
③ 자신의 레인을 지키기
④ 큰소리로 말하지 않기
⑤ 수영 전 준비 운동 하기

♥ **You can't be too careful.**
: 최대한 신경 쓰고 조심해야 할 상황이라고
말할 때 쓰는 표현으로, '아무리 조심해도 지
나치지 않아.'라는 뜻이다.
= You must be careful.
= It is better to be safe than sorry.

5 🇬🇧

W It's so good to be here. I _____ _____ _____ _____ swimming.

M Let's _____ _____ _____ before we enter the swimming pool.

W Isn't it _____ _____ _____ a swimsuit and a swimming cap?

M ♥You can't be too careful. Did you warm up?

W Of course, I did.

M Good. Be sure you don't run or dive.

W All right. _____ _____?

M You should stay in the lane in the pool.

6 대화를 듣고, 두 사람이 대화하는 장소
로 가장 적절한 곳을 고르시오.

① 식당
② 프랑스
③ 꽃가게
④ 길 한복판
⑤ 인테리어 가게

♥ **It couldn't be better.**
: 정말로 완벽한 상황임을 나타낼 때 쓰는 표
현으로, '이보다 더 좋을 수는 없다.'라는 뜻
이다.
= It's perfect.

6

W Congratulations on _____ _____ _____ _____!

M Thank you. What a beautiful flowerpot!

W I love the interior design of your restaurant. I feel like I'm in France.

M I'm glad to hear that. Do you want me to _____ _____ _____ _____ _____?

W Yes, please. By the way, _____ _____ _____ going?

M Until now, ♥it *couldn't be better.

W That's great.

★ couldn't be [쿠든트] [비] → [쿠든비]

어색한 대화 찾기

7 다음을 듣고, 두 사람의 대화가 <u>어색한</u> 것을 고르시오.

① ② ③ ④ ⑤

7

① M _____ _____ _____ next Friday.

W Sorry. I have to spend some time with my family that day.

② M Look! Why are there _____ _____ _____ here?

W I guess they are watching the street performance.

③ M How can I get to the department store?

W _____ _____ for 3 blocks and then turn right.

④ M Do you know where the coffee mugs are?

W Sure. They are _____ _____ _____ _____.

⑤ M What are the bank's business hours?

W You can _____ _____ _____ _____ today.

부탁한 일 파악

8 대화를 듣고, 여자가 남자에게 부탁한 일로 가장 적절한 것을 고르시오.

① 아들을 봐 달라고
② 자리를 바꿔 달라고
③ 행선지를 알려달라고
④ 이물질을 제거해 달라고
⑤ 기차표를 대신 구입해 달라고

8

W Excuse me. Would you do me a favor?

M What is it?

W I bought two train tickets for my son and me. However, they aren't _____ _____ _____ _____.

M I see. That's why you _____ _____ _____.

W Right. Do you _____ _____ _____ with my son?

M No problem.

W Thank you so much.

화제·주제 파악

9 다음을 듣고, 무엇에 관한 안내 방송인지 고르시오.

① 비행기 출발 안내 방송
② 분실물 습득 관련 방송
③ 운항 도중 안전벨트 지시
④ 전자 기기 사용 시 유의점
⑤ 안전벨트의 올바른 착용법

9

W Good evening, ladies and gentlemen. _____ _____ Happy Air Flight 123 bound for Danang International Airport. It's a pleasure to have you with us. Please make sure that your _____ _____ _____ during takeoff. The use of portable electronic devices is not allowed. In addition, please _____ _____ _____ during the entire flight. If there is anything we can do for you, do not _____ _____ _____. Please enjoy the flight. Thank you.

숫자 정보 파악

10 대화를 듣고, 남자가 지불할 금액을 고르시오.

① $25
② $30
③ $35
④ $40
⑤ $45

10

W   Welcome to White's Cleaners. What can I do for you?

M   I'd like to _____ _____ _____ _____.

W   Okay. Can you show me what you have?

M   I have one leather jacket and two wool coats. How much will that be?

W   Normally, jackets are 10 dollars each. But _____ _____ _____ _____ leather jackets, you have to pay 5 dollars more. And coats are 15 dollars each.

M   Okay. _____ _____ _____ _____ I can pick them up?

W   It's tomorrow evening.

할 일 파악

11 대화를 듣고, 여자가 할 일로 가장 적절한 것을 고르시오.

① 만화책 구입하기
② 대학원 진학하기
③ 아들과 대화하기
④ 독서 목록 만들기
⑤ 가족과 시간 보내기

11 🇬🇧

M   Paige, I'm worried about our son Harry.

W   Why? Did he _____ _____ _____?

M   Harry only reads comic books. I want him to read regular books, too.

W   You're right. He needs to read regular books to _____ _____ _____ _____.

M   So how about making a family reading hour?

W   I can't agree more with you. I'll _____ _____ _____ _____ _____ to read.

M   Okay. That will help.

언급 유무 파악

12 다음을 듣고, 서울 국제 불꽃 축제에 관해 언급되지 <u>않은</u> 것을 고르시오.

① 축제 일정
② 행사 장소
③ 입장 요금
④ 참여 국가
⑤ 순환 버스

12

M   Hello, everyone. The Seoul International Fireworks Festival will be held soon. It is scheduled for Saturday, September 12, and starts at 8 p.m. _____ _____ _____ _____ at Hangang Park in Seoul. Groups from the countries Mexico, Germany, Egypt, and Korea are going to *participate in the festival. Because _____ _____ _____ _____, we decided to provide free shuttle buses from Seoul Station. We recommend that you take the shuttle bus or _____ _____ _____.

★ participate in [팔티시페이트] [인] → [팔티시페이린]

그림 정보 파악

13 대화를 듣고, 두 사람이 앉을 극장 좌석을 고르시오.

Screen

① 1A 1B 1C   1D 1E 1F
②   ③
2A 2B 2C   2D 2E 2F
④   ⑤
3A 3B 3C   3D 3E 3F

♥ **I totally agree with you.**

: 상대방의 의견에 전적으로 동의할 때 쓰는 표현으로, '난 너에게 완전히 동의해.'라는 뜻이다.
= I'm on your side.
= I can't agree with you more.

13

M   Let's go to see a movie tonight.

W   That's a great idea. Do you _____ _____ _____ _____?

M   How about watching *Aladdin*?

W   Sounds fun. Let's make a reservation. Look at this seating chart.

M   I don't like seats in the front row. Sitting there _____ _____ _____ _____.

W   ♥I totally agree with you. How about a middle row?

M   Actually, I like _____ _____ _____ _____.

W   Then let's pick these seats in the back. One is an aisle seat.

화제·주제 파악

14 다음을 듣고, 무엇에 관한 설명인지 고르시오.
① 피로 누적의 위험성
② 눈을 보호하는 방법
③ 30분 동안 매일 걷기
④ 스마트폰 게임의 단점
⑤ 안경 고를 때 주의할 점

14

W   Do your eyes feel dry and a little itchy? The reason is that you are _____ _____ _____ by looking at screens so much. Here are some tips on how to protect your eyes. Take regular breaks. Just looking _____ _____ _____ _____ every 30 minutes helps a lot. In addition, make sure you _____ _____ while you are using your smartphone. Blinking helps _____ _____ _____ and protects your eyes from getting too dry.

할 일 파악

15 대화를 듣고, 남자가 대화 직후에 할 일로 가장 적절한 것을 고르시오.
① 설거지하기
② 식기 구입하기
③ 화장품 교환하기
④ 냉장고 청소하기
⑤ 감자, 당근 구입하기

15

W   Dad, I'm hungry. Is there anything to eat?

M   It's almost dinnertime. Let's check what is _____ _____ _____.

W   I've already checked it, but there's _____ _____ _____ pork.

M   That's _____ _____ _____. I'll make you pork stew.

W   Sounds tasty! But don't we need potatoes and carrots?

M   Right. Can you _____ _____ _____ for me? I'll do the dishes.

W   No problem. I'll be back in a flash.

숫자 정보 파악

16 대화를 듣고, 여자가 집을 보러 가기로
한 날짜를 고르시오.

① 6월 14일
② 6월 15일
③ 6월 16일
④ 6월 17일
⑤ 6월 18일

16

[*Cellphone rings.*]

W   Hello. I'm _____ _____ the two-bedroom apartment you advertised online. Is it _____ _____?

M   Let me check. [*Pause*] Yes, it's available.

W   Can I _____ _____ _____ _____ the house on June 15?

M   Sorry, but I'll _____ _____ _____. How about on June 17?

W   It's okay. Can I go to the real estate agency at 4:00 p.m. on that day?

M   Great. See you then.

적절한 응답 찾기

17 대화를 듣고, 남자의 마지막 말에 대한
여자의 응답으로 가장 적절한 것을 고
르시오.

Woman: _____

① That suit looks good on you.
② I never thought I'd see the singer.
③ I'll be a bit nervous, but I can do it.
④ I won't ever forget hearing the song.
⑤ I can play the piano at your wedding.

💙 **I'm supposed to ~**
: 어떤 일을 해야 할 때 쓰는 표현으로, '나는
~하기로 되어 있다'라는 뜻이다.
= I'm expected to ~
= I ought to ~

17 🇬🇧

M   Mia, can I _____ _____ _____ _____ _____?

W   What is it?

M   My best friend is _____ _____ soon.

W   Wow! Please congratulate your friend for me.

M   Okay. I will. By the way, 💙I'm supposed to sing at the wedding. But I chose a duet.

W   Do you mean you need a _____ _____ _____ _____ _____?

M   That's correct. Can you sing with me?

W   <u>I'll be a bit nervous, but I can do it.</u>

적절한 응답 찾기

18 대화를 듣고, 여자의 마지막 말에 대한
남자의 응답으로 가장 적절한 것을 고
르시오.

Man: _____

① It costs 10 dollars and 50 cents.
② Don't rush, or you will fall down.
③ I should return these books today.
④ You have a point. I should start today.
⑤ Come on. It'll take about 2 hours to get there from here.

18

M   Do you want to go to the museum?

W   Maybe next time. I should _____ _____ _____ _____ now.

M   You're going to the library? What for?

W   Nick, we have to _____ _____ _____ _____ _____ by Friday.

M   But we still have three days until the due date.

W   I know. But I prefer finishing assignments _____ _____ _____ _____. I don't like to be rushed.

M   <u>You have a point. I should start today.</u>

19

적절한 응답 찾기

19 대화를 듣고, 남자의 마지막 말에 대한 여자의 응답으로 가장 적절한 것을 고르시오.

Woman: _____

① You got paint on your shirt.
② Please draw me a nice painting.
③ Be my guest. You can use mine.
④ Let's go to the bank to save money.
⑤ Watermelon is my favorite summer fruit.

♥ **What a pity!**
: 상대방이 처한 상황이 안타까울 때 쓰는 표현으로, '안됐다!', '안타깝다!'라는 뜻이다.
= That's too bad.
= What a bad luck!

19

M Oh, my! I left my paint on my desk at home.
W Why don't you call your mom and _____ _____ _____ _____ _____ _____ _____ ?
M That's impossible. My mom is working now.
W ♥ What a pity! Art class will _____ _____ _____ _____ .
M Dohee, if you don't mind, can you _____ _____ _____ *with me?
W Be my guest. You can use mine.

★ with me [위드] [미] → [윗미]

상황에 맞는 말 찾기

20 다음 상황 설명을 듣고, Beatrice가 판매자에게 할 말로 가장 적절한 것을 고르시오.

Beatrice: Hello. _____

① I want to see your bicycle.
② This is just what I'm looking for.
③ I'll ride by your house on my bike.
④ Where are you? I'm waiting for you.
⑤ I'd like to get a refund on this bicycle.

20

M Beatrice becomes _____ _____ _____ _____ . However, a brand-new bicycle is too expensive for her to buy. So she decides to buy a used one. She searches the Internet to find a good one. At last, she finds one she likes. She calls the person who is selling the bicycle and _____ _____ _____ to meet him. However, the seller _____ _____ _____ at the appointed hour. So she _____ _____ _____ where he is. In this situation, what would Beatrice most likely say to the seller?
Beatrice Hello. Where are you? I'm waiting for you.

1 대화를 듣고, 여자가 구입할 컵을 고르시오.

① ② ③

④ ⑤

2 대화를 듣고, 남자가 여자에게 전화한 목적으로 가장 적절한 것을 고르시오.
① Drake와 통화하려고
② 약속 시간을 정하려고
③ 수학 문제를 물어보려고
④ 함께 책을 빌리러 가려고
⑤ 영화 시작 시간을 물어보려고

3 다음 그림의 상황에 가장 적절한 대화를 고르시오.

① ② ③ ④ ⑤

4 대화를 듣고, 여자가 친구를 만날 요일을 고르시오.
① 월요일 ② 화요일 ③ 수요일
④ 금요일 ⑤ 토요일

5 다음을 듣고, 한국에 대해 언급되지 <u>않은</u> 것을 고르시오.
① 한국의 오랜 역사
② 많은 외세의 침입
③ 한복을 덜 입게 된 이유
④ 전통적인 난방 시스템
⑤ 현대 주거 난방 시스템

6 대화를 듣고, 두 사람의 관계로 가장 적절한 것을 고르시오.
① 학생 — 학생 ② 아빠 — 딸
③ 교사 — 학생 ④ 교사 — 학부모
⑤ 교장 — 교사

7 대화를 듣고, 두 사람의 대화가 <u>어색한</u> 것을 고르시오.
① ② ③ ④ ⑤

8 대화를 듣고, 여자가 남자에게 부탁한 일로 가장 적절한 것을 고르시오.
① 개의 사진을 접수할 것
② 개의 외모를 설명할 것
③ 내일까지 기다릴 것
④ 실종 신고서 작성할 것
⑤ 3시간 이후에 접수할 것

9 대화를 듣고, 남자의 마지막 말에 담긴 의도로 가장 적절한 것을 고르시오.
① 격려 ② 충고 ③ 동의
④ 사과 ⑤ 감사

10 대화를 듣고, 남자가 지불할 금액을 고르시오.
① $27 ② $26 ③ $24
④ $21 ⑤ $18

11 대화를 듣고, 여자가 할 일로 가장 적절한 것을 고르시오.
① 문자를 보낸다. ② 파티에 참석한다.
③ 집안일을 한다. ④ 병문안을 간다.
⑤ 친구를 데리러 간다.

12 다음을 듣고, 행사와 관련하여 언급되지 <u>않은</u> 것을 고르시오.
① 최대 할인 비율 ② 세일 판매 기간
③ 지불 방법 ④ 환불 가능 조건
⑤ 교환 가능 조건

13 다음 표를 보면서 대화를 듣고, 남자가 선택할 강좌를
고르시오.

	Sports Class	Time
①	Golf	7:00 - 8:00 p.m.
②	Swimming	5:00 - 6:00 p.m.
③	Yoga	6:00 - 7:00 p.m.
④	Pilates	6:00 - 7:00 a.m.
⑤	Fitness Training	7:00 - 8:00 a.m.

14 다음을 듣고, 무엇에 관한 설명인지 고르시오.
① 장기   ② 윷놀이
③ 널뛰기   ④ 투호
⑤ 바둑

15 대화를 듣고, 남자가 할 일로 가장 적절한 것을 고르시오.
① 차를 확인한다.
② 경찰서에 신고한다.
③ 분실물 센터를 방문한다.
④ 식당에 전화를 건다.
⑤ 집으로 돌아간다.

16 대화를 듣고, 여자가 구입할 물건을 고르시오.
① 고전 소설책   ② 역사 소설책
③ 역사 만화책   ④ 그림 동화책
⑤ 문학사 만화책

17 대화를 듣고, 여자의 마지막 말에 대한 남자의 응답으
로 가장 적절한 것을 고르시오.
Man: _____
① How often do you study English?
② I bet you'll be a spelling bee master.
③ I don't have time to study words.
④ Is it hard to memorize English words?
⑤ I'll try it your way and see if it works for me.

18 대화를 듣고, 남자의 마지막 말에 대한 여자의 응답으
로 가장 적절한 것을 고르시오.
Woman: _____
① I'm sorry I can't go there.
② Right! It's a piece of cake.
③ Good for you. That was really nice of you.
④ That sounds all right. Can I see your license?
⑤ What did you say? How could you waste
such an opportunity?

19 대화를 듣고, 여자의 마지막 말에 대한 남자의 응답으
로 가장 적절한 것을 고르시오.
Man: _____
① It can't be true.
② I doubt I can do that.
③ Sorry. Maybe next time.
④ I couldn't agree with you more.
⑤ I know how you feel.

20 다음 상황 설명을 듣고, 엄마가 Jason에게 할 말로 가
장 적절한 것을 고르시오.
Mom: Jason, _____
① how long have you played the game?
② you cannot use your computer anymore.
③ you should stop playing games and go back
to a normal life.
④ could you come to school a little earlier to
take some extra classes?
⑤ you never fail to disappoint. I want nothing
to do with your addiction.

대화를 다시 듣고, 알맞은 것을 고르시오.

1 The woman thinks the plain cup is too expensive.
☐ True   ☐ False

2 Is the woman going to the library today?
☐ Yes   ☐ No

3 The man wants to order right now.
☐ True   ☐ False

4 How long will it take to arrive at Jinhae?
☐ 5 hours   ☐ 4 hours

5 Did Korean people usually wear traditional clothes in the 1980s?
☐ Yes   ☐ No

6 Who has a positive attitude?
☐ the man   ☐ the woman

7 The man already watched the movie.
☐ True   ☐ False

8 The woman can report a missing dog today.
☐ True   ☐ False

9 When did the woman buy new sneakers?
☐ a couple of days ago
☐ yesterday

10 Did the man buy a tie for his friend?
☐ Yes   ☐ No

11 The woman will not go to the party because she has to do housework.
☐ True   ☐ False

12 Sale items can be paid for only in cash.
☐ Yes   ☐ No

13 How many classes are held in the evening?
☐ 2 classes   ☐ 3 classes

14 People can't move their tokens six spaces at a time.
☐ True   ☐ False

15 Does the man think he left his wallet at the restaurant?
☐ Yes   ☐ No

16 Does the woman decide to buy a comic book?
☐ Yes   ☐ No

17 The man thinks that it is easy for him to memorize English words.
☐ True   ☐ False

18 Did the man take a picture with BTS?
☐ Yes   ☐ No

19 The woman will join the environmental club.
☐ True   ☐ False

20 Jason concentrates on his schoolwork during class.
☐ True   ☐ False

그림 정보 파악

1 대화를 듣고, 여자가 구입할 컵을 고르
시오.

① ②   ③

④ ⑤

1

M Can I help you?

W Yes. How much is that cup with the dinosaur on it?

M 15 dollars. _____ _____ and _____ _____
_____.

W That's too expensive.

M Then how about _____ _____ _____ with two
handles?

W I don't think it's handy. Do you have anything else?

M What about _____ _____ _____ with the rose on it?

W That looks good. I'll take that.

목적 파악

2 대화를 듣고, 남자가 여자에게 전화한
목적으로 가장 적절한 것을 고르시오.

① Drake와 통화하려고
② 약속 시간을 정하려고
③ 수학 문제를 물어보려고
④ 함께 책을 빌리러 가려고
⑤ 영화 시작 시간을 물어보려고

♥ **What's the matter?**
: 구체적인 원인이 무엇인지 궁금할 때 쓰는
표현으로, '무슨 일이니?'라는 뜻이다.
= What's wrong?

2

[*Cellphone rings.*]

M Hello, Miho.

W Hi, Jun. _____ _____?

M Could you come to the library this evening?

W Why? ♥What's the matter?

M Actually, I'm _____ _____ _____ _____
_____ some math problems. I need your help.

W I'm sorry, but I have plans to meet Drake. How about 11 o'clock
tomorrow morning?

M Okay. _____ _____ _____ tomorrow morning.

그림 상황 파악

3 다음 그림의 상황에 가장 적절한 대화
를 고르시오.

① ② ③ ④ ⑤

3

① W I waited for you _____ _____ _____ _____
_____.

　 M I'm sorry, but I got *caught up in traffic.

② W How much is this?

　 M I'm sorry, but _____ _____ _____, too.

③ W Would you care for anything else?

　 M I've eaten _____ _____ _____. Thanks.

④ W How can I get to Kim's Bakery?

　 M It is _____ _____ _____ _____.

⑤ W May I _____ _____ _____?

　 M Can you give me a bit more time?

* caught up in [컷] [업] [인] → [커럽인]

특정 정보 파악

4 대화를 듣고, 여자가 친구를 만날 요일을 고르시오.

① 월요일
② 화요일
③ 수요일
④ 금요일
⑤ 토요일

4

M Vanessa, are you free next week?

W What for?

M There's a cherry blossom festival in Jinhae next week. Do you want to _____ _____ _____ _____?

W _____ _____ _____. But final exams are next week. When is the last day of the festival?

M Let me check.... Oh, it's next Saturday.

W Next Saturday? Then I can go.

M Great. It takes about 5 hours to get to Jinhae. So _____ _____ _____ _____ _____ _____ _____.

W Okay. See you then.

언급 유무 파악

5 다음을 듣고, 한국에 대해 언급되지 <u>않</u>은 것을 고르시오.

① 한국의 오랜 역사
② 많은 외세의 침입
③ 한복을 덜 입게 된 이유
④ 전통적인 난방 시스템
⑤ 현대 주거 난방 시스템

5

M Korea is said to have about 5,000 years of history. During this long history, the Korean people have *kept their identity _____ _____ _____ _____ _____. So there have been lots of unique traditions passed down up to modern times. The traditional clothes known as *hanbok* have a unique beauty and _____ _____ _____ until the 1970s. But now Koreans _____ _____ _____ _____ special holidays such as New Year's Day. Traditional Korean houses were equipped with an excellent heating system known as *ondol.* Though many Koreans now live in Western-style residences, they still use heating systems _____ _____ *ondol.*

＊ kept their [켑트] [데얼] → [켑데얼]

관계 추론

6 대화를 듣고, 두 사람의 관계로 가장 적절한 것을 고르시오.

① 학생 — 학생
② 아빠 — 딸
③ 교사 — 학생
④ 교사 — 학부모
⑤ 교장 — 교사

♥ **Cheer up!**
: 상대방이 낙담하고 있는 경우 위로를 해줄 때 사용하는 표현으로, '힘내!'라는 뜻이다.

6

W _____ _____ _____, and I am losing weight, too.

M What's wrong?

W I got my test score, and it is the lowest grade _____ _____ _____ _____.

M Oh, Kate. ♥ Cheer up. You know that grades will not _____ _____ _____.

W Thank you for saying that. Anyway, how about you? Did you do well on the test?

M Me? I _____ _____ _____ _____. But the past is the past. Don't worry too much.

어색한 대화 찾기

7 대화를 듣고, 두 사람의 대화가 <u>어색한</u> 것을 고르시오.

① ② ③ ④ ⑤

7

① **W** Excuse me. Is there a _____ _____ _____

_____?

M Yes, there's one within 2 minutes of here.

② **W** Why do you think _____ _____?

M Because he has a lot of talent.

③ **W** Shall we go to see the movie *Shrek*?

M Sorry. _____ _____ _____ _____.

④ **W** Where is your _____ _____ _____?

M She teaches English to middle school students.

⑤ **W** How do you like today's special?

M _____ _____ _____.

부탁한 일 파악

8 대화를 듣고, 여자가 남자에게 부탁한 일로 가장 적절한 것을 고르시오.

① 개의 사진을 접수할 것
② 개의 외모를 설명할 것
③ 내일까지 기다릴 것
④ 실종 신고서 작성할 것
⑤ 3시간 이후에 접수할 것

8

M Hi. I'm Alex Kim, and I'd like to _____ _____ _____

_____. Here's a photo of my dog.

W When was the last time you saw your dog?

M About 3 hours ago.

W Well, 3 hours is _____ _____ _____ to determine

whether your dog is missing or not. You'll have to wait _____

_____ _____ _____.

M What? It's been over 3 hours since I saw my dog.

W We can help you when you _____ _____ _____.

의도 파악

9 대화를 듣고, 남자의 마지막 말에 담긴 의도로 가장 적절한 것을 고르시오.

① 격려
② 충고
③ 동의
④ 사과
⑤ 감사

9

W Dad, can I _____ _____ _____ from you?

M I think you got your allowance from your mom a couple of days ago.

You've already _____ _____ _____ _____?

W Well, I bought a new pair of sneakers yesterday.

M You already have _____ _____ _____ _____.

W But they're out of style, and nobody wears them anymore.

M I think you just _____ _____ _____. Here is 40 dollars,

but there will be no next time.

숫자 정보 파악

10 대화를 듣고, 남자가 지불할 금액을 고르시오.

① $27
② $26
③ $24
④ $21
⑤ $18

10 🇬🇧

W How may I help you?

M Can I see that red tie _____ _____ _____?

W Sure. This tie is _____ _____ _____ with young people. Is it a gift for someone?

M It's for a friend. How much is it?

W It's 30 dollars.

M I love it, but it's _____ _____ _____ for me.

W Well, I'll give you a special discount of 20%. I hope your friendship _____ _____ _____ _____.

M Thank you so much. Please wrap it as a gift.

할 일 파악

11 대화를 듣고, 여자가 할 일로 가장 적절한 것을 고르시오.

① 문자를 보낸다.
② 파티에 참석한다.
③ 집안일을 한다.
④ 병문안을 간다.
⑤ 친구를 데리러 간다.

11

M Hi, Christine. Where are you going?

W Hi, James. I'm _____ _____ _____ _____.

M Home? I heard you are going to Jessy's party today.

W Yeah, but I have to _____ _____ _____ before going to the party.

M What time do you think you _____ _____ _____? I'll *pick you up.

W That's great. I'll _____ _____ _____ _____ _____ when I'm done.

* pick you up [픽] [유] [업] → [피큐업]

언급 유무 파악

12 다음을 듣고, 행사와 관련하여 언급되지 <u>않은</u> 것을 고르시오.

① 최대 할인 비율
② 세일 판매 기간
③ 지불 방법
④ 환불 가능 조건
⑤ 교환 가능 조건

12

W Attention, please! Thank you for shopping at the Paradise Department Store. As a thank you to all our loyal customers, _____ _____ _____ _____ _____ of up to 70% off for the next three hours. On some products, if you buy one, you can get one free. Out-of-season items are 60% _____ _____ _____ _____. You can pay both in cash and with a credit card. But for items more than 50 percent off, you can pay only in cash. The items _____ _____ _____ 5 days of purchase if they are brought back in _____ _____ _____. Thank you.

표 파악

13 다음 표를 보면서 대화를 듣고, 남자가 선택할 강좌를 고르시오.

	Sports Class	Time
①	Golf	7:00 - 8:00 p.m.
②	Swimming	5:00 - 6:00 p.m.
③	Yoga	6:00 - 7:00 p.m.
④	Pilates	6:00 - 7:00 a.m.
⑤	Fitness Training	7:00 - 8:00 a.m.

13 🇬🇧

M   Excuse me. I want to know _____ _____ _____ _____ _____.

W   Okay. In the evening, we offer golf, swimming, and yoga, and in the morning, you can do fitness training and Pilates.

M   How many times a week do you offer them?

W   All _____ _____ _____ two times a week. The evening classes are held on Monday and Thursday, and the morning classes take place on Tuesday and Friday.

M   Okay. I will take the class that starts at 6:00 a.m.

W   Thank you. _____ _____ _____ _____ _____, please.

화제·주제 파악

14 다음을 듣고, 무엇에 관한 설명인지 고르시오.

① 장기
② 윷놀이
③ 널뛰기
④ 투호
⑤ 바둑

14

M   This is a traditional Korean game, and _____ _____ _____ during Lunar New Year in Korea. To play this, you need a board, two different small tokens or marks, and four sticks. This is usually played with 2 partners or 2 teams. The goal of this game is _____ _____ _____ _____ _____ and to get all your team's tokens or marks to the starting position again. To move your token or mark, toss the four sticks together. You can move one of your tokens or marks 1 to 5 spaces _____ _____ _____ _____.

할 일 파악

15 대화를 듣고, 남자가 할 일로 가장 적절한 것을 고르시오.

① 차를 확인한다.
② 경찰서에 신고한다.
③ 분실물 센터를 방문한다.
④ 식당에 전화를 건다.
⑤ 집으로 돌아간다.

💙 **Calm down.**
: 상대방의 화를 가라앉히거나 불안한 감정을 달래줄 때 쓰는 표현으로, '진정해.'라는 뜻이다.
= Relax.

15

W   Hey, Jack. Why do you have _____ _____ _____ _____ _____ your face?

M   I can't find my wallet. I don't remember _____ _____ _____ _____.

W   💙Calm down. Let's start from the beginning. When was the last time you had it?

M   I can't remember.

W   Maybe you *left it at the restaurant after lunch.

M   No, I clearly remember _____ _____ _____ in my pocket.

W   Well, have you checked your car? It may _____ _____ _____ _____ your back pocket.

M   No, I haven't.

W   You should go there and check. There's a good chance that it is there.

★ left it [레프트] [잇] → [렙팃]

16 대화를 듣고, 여자가 구입할 물건을 고르시오.

① 고전 소설책
② 역사 소설책
③ 역사 만화책
④ 그림 동화책
⑤ 문학사 만화책

16

W Dad, I want to buy this novel. It _____ _____.

M *A Christmas Carol*. It is a classic novel. Do you know who wrote this book?

W Charles Dickens. Actually, I saw _____ _____ _____ _____ _____ _____.

M Well, I think you should learn more about famous authors. You'll be in high school soon.

W I will, Dad. So could you buy another book for me?

M Which one?

W It's a comic book about _____ _____ _____ _____.

M Maybe next time. Let's just buy one at a time.

W Then I will _____ _____ _____.

17 대화를 듣고, 여자의 마지막 말에 대한 남자의 응답으로 가장 적절한 것을 고르시오.

Man: _____

① How often do you study English?
② I bet you'll be a spelling bee master.
③ I don't have time to study words.
④ Is it hard to memorize English words?
⑤ I'll try it your way and see if it works for me.

17

M How can you speak English _____ _____?

W I recommend that you practice speaking English _____ _____ _____ _____.

M Then how about words? It's difficult for me to memorize them.

W I write new words in my notebook and review them _____ _____ _____ _____.

M _____ _____. Do you think that way will work for me?

W Just do it that way until you are comfortable. I'm sure it will work.

M I'll try it your way and see if it works for me.

18 대화를 듣고, 남자의 마지막 말에 대한 여자의 응답으로 가장 적절한 것을 고르시오.

Woman: _____

① I'm sorry I can't go there.
② Right! It's a piece of cake.
③ Good for you. That was really nice of you.
④ That sounds all right. Can I see your license?
⑤ What did you say? How could you waste such an opportunity?

18

M Did I ever tell you that I saw BTS?

W No. What happened?

M I was walking down the street, when I saw a black van just _____ _____ _____ _____ of the road. I was passing by the van, and then the van's door _____ _____, and they _____ _____ _____ the van.

W Did you _____ _____ _____ or take any pictures with them?

M No. I couldn't do anything. I _____ _____ _____.

W What did you say? How could you waste such an opportunity?

19 대화를 듣고, 여자의 마지막 말에 대한 남자의 응답으로 가장 적절한 것을 고르시오.

Man: _____
① It can't be true.
② I doubt I can do that.
③ Sorry. Maybe next time.
④ I couldn't agree with you more.
⑤ I know how you feel.

19

M Which club do you want to join?
W I'm going to join the Green Students Society.
M The Green Students Society? _____ _____ does the club do?
W Its members _____ _____ _____ protecting the environment.
M That sounds great. You _____ _____ _____ _____ _____ _____.
W Yes. I think _____ _____ _____ _____ _____ to protect the environment.
M I couldn't agree with you more.

20 다음 상황 설명을 듣고, 엄마가 Jason에게 할 말로 가장 적절한 것을 고르시오.

Mom: Jason, _____
① how long have you played the game?
② you cannot use your computer anymore.
③ you should stop playing games and go back to a normal life.
④ could you come to school a little earlier to take some extra classes?
⑤ you never fail to disappoint. I want nothing to do with your addiction.

20

W Jason's mom is worried because she thinks something is extremely wrong about him. Recently, he _____ _____ _____, hurries to school, and goes to sleep during class. _____ _____ _____ is that he doesn't do his homework on time. When she *asks him why, he says that he seems to _____ _____ _____ _____ _____. He is often scolded by his homeroom teacher and doesn't _____ _____ _____ _____. So his mother decides to advise him. In this situation, what would Jason's mom most likely say to him?

Mom Jason, you should stop playing games and go back to a normal life.

★ asks him [애스크스] [힘] → [애스킴]

1 대화를 듣고, 두 사람이 구입할 파티 모자를 고르시오.

① 　② 　③

④ 　⑤

2 대화를 듣고, 남자가 여자에게 전화한 목적으로 가장 적절한 것을 고르시오.
① 약속을 취소하려고
② 교통 체증을 알리려고
③ 약속 시간을 늦추려고
④ 약속 장소를 바꾸려고
⑤ 도착 시간을 물어보려고

3 다음 그림의 상황에 가장 적절한 대화를 고르시오.

① 　②　③　④　⑤

4 대화를 듣고, 두 사람이 만나기로 한 요일을 고르시오.
① 월요일　② 수요일　③ 목요일
④ 금요일　⑤ 일요일

5 다음을 듣고, 배달 서비스 앱에 관해 언급되지 <u>않은</u> 것을 고르시오.
① 개발한 목적　② 결제 지불 방법
③ 카드 등록 방법　④ 리뷰 작성 혜택
⑤ 사용자 제한 나이

6 대화를 듣고, 두 사람의 관계로 가장 적절한 것을 고르시오.
① 의사 — 간호사　② 선생님 — 학생
③ 트레이너 — 고객　④ 면접관 — 지원자
⑤ 감독 — 영화배우

7 다음을 듣고, 두 사람의 대화가 어색한 것을 고르시오.
①　②　③　④　⑤

8 대화를 듣고, 여자가 남자에게 부탁한 일로 가장 적절한 것을 고르시오.
① 물건 옮기기
② 식물 그리기
③ 벽지 떼어내기
④ 벽에 그림 달기
⑤ 온라인 주문하기

9 대화를 듣고, 남자의 마지막 말에 담긴 의도로 가장 적절한 것을 고르시오.
① 위로　② 칭찬　③ 감사
④ 유감　⑤ 허락

10 대화를 듣고, 여자가 지불할 금액을 고르시오.
① $20　② $24　③ $40
④ $42　⑤ $44

11 대화를 듣고, 남자가 할 일로 가장 적절한 것을 고르시오.
① 상품 개발하기
② 광고 기획하기
③ 일자리 구하기
④ 감사 편지 쓰기
⑤ 친구와 상담하기

12 다음을 듣고, The Reality Exhibition에 관해 언급되지 <u>않은</u> 것을 고르시오.
① 전시회 주제
② 주최자 이름
③ 전시회 기간
④ 참가 작가 수
⑤ 예술 작품 종류

13 다음 표를 보면서 대화를 듣고, 여자가 구입할 커피 원두를 고르시오.

	Types	Body	Flavors	Geography
①	Type A	Light	Vanilla	Colombia
②	Type B	Light	Caramel	Colombia
③	Type C	Dark	Caramel	Colombia
④	Type D	Dark	Vanilla	Ethiopia
⑤	Type E	Dark	Caramel	Ethiopia

14 다음을 듣고, 무엇에 관한 설명인지 고르시오.
① 보트   ② 튜브
③ 풍선   ④ 뗏목
⑤ 수영복

15 대화를 듣고, 남자가 할 일로 가장 적절한 것을 고르시오.
① 여행 계획 세우기
② 친구 설득하기
③ 학원 알아보기
④ 휴학 신청하기
⑤ 영어 공부하기

16 대화를 듣고, 남자가 조깅하러 갈 시각을 고르시오.
① 7:00   ② 8:00
③ 9:00   ④ 10:00
⑤ 11:00

17 대화를 듣고, 남자의 마지막 말에 대한 여자의 응답으로 가장 적절한 것을 고르시오.
Woman: _____
① No, that's not right. Think about it again.
② I'm already sponsoring another organization.
③ I can't remember what really happened there.
④ Being a help to someone is meaningful to me.
⑤ I can take you to the organization. Come with me.

18 대화를 듣고, 여자의 마지막 말에 대한 남자의 응답으로 가장 적절한 것을 고르시오.
Man: _____
① You can tell me what you really want to do.
② How on earth is it possible to fail that subject?
③ I can help you finish your assignment tonight.
④ What you're doing now is not helpful.
⑤ It's not too late to find your interest during college.

19 대화를 듣고, 남자의 마지막 말에 대한 여자의 응답으로 가장 적절한 것을 고르시오.
Woman: _____
① What is making you so nervous?
② Yes, there are many empty seats.
③ Please come back again tomorrow.
④ Don't tell anyone what happened.
⑤ You should hurry to get on the train now.

20 다음 상황 설명을 듣고, Harry가 커플에게 할 말로 가장 적절한 것을 고르시오.
Harry: Excuse me. _____
① Could you please step aside?
② Could you help me find my way?
③ Is there anything I can help you with?
④ You'd better be careful with your things.
⑤ How can I get to city hall from here?

Listen and Check

정답 및 해설 p.059

● 대화를 다시 듣고, 알맞은 것을 고르시오.

1 What is Jeff interested in?
- ☐ stars
- ☐ robots

2 The man will arrive at the appointed meeting place on time.
- ☐ True
- ☐ False

3 What does the woman recommend the man do to improve his English skills?
- ☐ listen to the radio
- ☐ read books

4 When does the woman have to attend a class?
- ☐ Monday
- ☐ Wednesday

5 One free delivery is offered when a customer writes a review for the delivery service.
- ☐ True
- ☐ False

6 Is the woman disappointed with the results of her checkup?
- ☐ Yes
- ☐ No

7 The man is in a good mood.
- ☐ True
- ☐ False

8 Where is the woman planning to hang the painting?
- ☐ on the wall
- ☐ on the shelf

9 What problem does Sarah have?
- ☐ low concentration in class
- ☐ a fight with a friend

10 Is the woman planning to apply the paint to the wall?
- ☐ Yes
- ☐ No

11 The man and the woman are team members for an advertising project.
- ☐ True
- ☐ False

12 How long will the exhibition last?
- ☐ for a week
- ☐ for a month

13 Does the woman prefer sweet flavors?
- ☐ Yes
- ☐ No

14 Both adults and children can use it to float on the water.
- ☐ True
- ☐ False

15 Why does the man want to take a year off?
- ☐ to study English
- ☐ to earn money

16 Will the man still go jogging tomorrow?
- ☐ Yes
- ☐ No

17 The woman won't make a donation to the charity.
- ☐ True
- ☐ False

18 What are the man and the woman talking about?
- ☐ graduation
- ☐ their future plans

19 Does the man care about having a seat on his trip to Daegu?
- ☐ Yes
- ☐ No

20 What do the tourists seem to need some help with?
- ☐ finding their way
- ☐ carrying their luggage

1 대화를 듣고, 두 사람이 구입할 파티 모 자를 고르시오.

① ② ③

④ ⑤

1

W We have to _____ _____ _____ for Jeff's birthday party.

M Here, we have different designs. Which one would be good for him?

W Since he likes robots, the hats _____ _____ _____ would be good.

M That's a good idea. Is it better to buy the one with letters, too?

W Hmm... How about this one _____ _____ _____ _____?

M That _____ _____ for the party. Let's get this hat for Jeff.

2 대화를 듣고, 남자가 여자에게 전화한 목적으로 가장 적절한 것을 고르시오.

① 약속을 취소하려고
② 교통 체증을 알리려고
③ 약속 시간을 늦추려고
④ 약속 장소를 바꾸려고
⑤ 도착 시간을 물어보려고

♥ **All right.**
: 상대방의 말을 받아들일 때 사용하는 표현 으로, '좋아요.', '괜찮아요.', '알겠어요.'라는 뜻이다.
= Okay.
= I'm fine with that.

2

[*Cellphone rings.*]

M Jane, where are you? Are you on your way?

W I'm on the subway and am five stops away. It will take _____ _____ _____. What about you?

M I'm on the bus and am just three *stops away. The problem is that there is a traffic jam.

W Maybe it's because it's Saturday today. Do you think you will _____ _____ _____?

M I think I will get there a bit late. Can we move our meeting time back by thirty minutes?

W Sure. I'll _____ _____ a coffee shop near our appointed meeting place.

M Okay. I'm so sorry. I'll try to _____ _____ _____.

W ♥All right. See you later!

★ steps away [스텝쓰] [어웨이] → [스텝써웨이]

3 다음 그림의 상황에 가장 적절한 대화 를 고르시오.

① ② ③ ④ ⑤

3

① M Why do we _____ _____ _____?
  W It has a complete definition of each word.

② M _____ _____ _____ should we read every month?
  W At least two.

③ M What's _____ _____ in your life?
  W It is to become a person who keeps my word.

④ M What should I do to speak English _____ _____?
  W I recommend you often read books or watch movies in English.

⑤ M Where is the best place for you _____ _____?
  W I study best inside my room.

특정 정보 파악

4 대화를 듣고, 두 사람이 만나기로 한 요일을 고르시오.

① 월요일
② 수요일
③ 목요일
④ 금요일
⑤ 일요일

4 🇬🇧

[Cellphone rings.]

W Brian, do you know that we need to _____ _____ _____ for our play?

M Of course, I do. When will we have it?

W We should set _____ _____ _____ _____ now. Are you free on Monday?

M No, I'm not. There's a class I have to attend.

W How about on Wednesday?

M I'm _____ _____ _____ _____ but not in the evening.

W I can also meet you in the afternoon. See you then!

언급 유무 파악

5 다음을 듣고, 배달 서비스 앱에 관해 언급되지 <u>않은</u> 것을 고르시오.

① 개발한 목적
② 결제 지불 방법
③ 카드 등록 방법
④ 리뷰 작성 혜택
⑤ 사용자 제한 나이

5

W Hello. I'm Linda, a developer for a _____ _____ _____. We made it to offer more convenient and faster delivery service for customers. Anyone over twelve years of age can sign up. If you _____ _____ _____ _____, you don't need to pay in cash to a deliveryman, but you can instead _____ _____ the application online. We will also provide a discount coupon if you _____ _____ _____ for the service you get. Please contact us through the application when you have any questions. We really appreciate your support.

관계 추론

6 대화를 듣고, 두 사람의 관계로 가장 적절한 것을 고르시오.

① 의사 — 간호사
② 선생님 — 학생
③ 트레이너 — 고객
④ 면접관 — 지원자
⑤ 감독 — 영화배우

6

M Hi, Annie. You _____ _____ _____ today, right?

W That's right. I've *worked out really hard this month, so I'm looking forward to seeing some positive results.

M Please stand on the machine and _____ _____ in each hand. [Pause] Okay, you're done. You can come down.

W How am I doing compared to the last time I was here?

M Wow. There's a decrease in _____ _____ _____ by seven percent, and you gained a lot of muscle mass, too.

W I knew it! Recently, I have felt very _____ _____ _____.

M I hope you exercise as hard as you did this month and achieve your goal soon!

* worked out [웍트] [아웃] → [웍타웃]

7 다음을 듣고, 두 사람의 대화가 어색한 것을 고르시오.

① ② ③ ④ ⑤

7

① M _____ _____ _____ in the movie?

W I play the queen of England.

② M I feel blue today.

W I like _____ _____ _____, too.

③ M I need a spare memory card for my camera.

W Let's go to the mall and buy one.

④ M Let's _____ _____ _____ of the zoo over there.

W We don't need one. I know the way.

⑤ M Are you attending Jenny's wedding?

W Of course. I'm _____ _____ _____.

8 대화를 듣고, 여자가 남자에게 부탁한 일로 가장 적절한 것을 고르시오.

① 물건 옮기기
② 식물 그리기
③ 벽지 떼어내기
④ 벽에 그림 달기
⑤ 온라인 주문하기

💙 **Don't mention it.**
: 상대방이 감사한 마음을 표시할 때, 그에 대한 답변으로 괜찮다는 마음을 나타낼 때 사용하는 표현으로, '괜찮아요.', '별말씀을 요.'라는 뜻이다.
= No problem.
= My pleasure.

8

M Wow. What is _____ _____ _____? It looks cool with all the plants on it.

W I ordered it online and just opened it.

M I see. Where are you going to hang it? Can you do it _____ _____?

W I'm planning to hang it on the wall. But since it's quite big, it's hard for me to do it by myself. Could you _____ _____ _____ _____?

M Sure. Please give me a nail and a hammer.

W You're _____ _____ _____. Thank you.

M 💙 Don't mention it.

9 대화를 듣고, 남자의 마지막 말에 담긴 의도로 가장 적절한 것을 고르시오.

① 위로
② 칭찬
③ 감사
④ 유감
⑤ 허락

💙 **That's too bad.**
: 유감을 나타낼 때 사용하는 표현으로, '그거 참 안됐다.'라는 뜻이다.
= I'm sorry to hear that.
= That's a shame.
= That's a pity.

9 🇬🇧

W Did you _____ _____ _____?

M What news?

W Sarah didn't _____ _____ _____ on the exam.

M Really? But she is a good student. What happened to her?

W She fought with her best friend, and she hasn't been able to _____ _____ _____ recently.

M 💙 That's too bad. I hope she _____ _____ _____ the friend she had a fight with.

10 대화를 듣고, 여자가 지불할 금액을 고르시오.

① $20
② $24
③ $40
④ $42
⑤ $44

10

M Good afternoon. How can I help you?

W I'm looking for some paint _____ _____ _____.

M Then I recommend _____ _____ _____. It dries quickly and smells good.

W How much is it?

M For four hundred milliliters, it _____ _____ _____, and for seven hundred milliliters, it's twenty dollars.

W I'll take two four-hundred-milliliter cans of white paint and one seven-hundred-milliliter can of green paint.

M Okay. Do you _____ _____ _____?

W Here, I have a two-dollar coupon.

11 대화를 듣고, 남자가 할 일로 가장 적절한 것을 고르시오.

① 상품 개발하기
② 광고 기획하기
③ 일자리 구하기
④ 감사편지 쓰기
⑤ 친구와 상담하기

11

M Today will be _____ _____ _____ for me.

W Why is that? Did your team take on a new project?

M Yes. We have to _____ _____ _____ for a new product.

W That sounds tiring. You'll probably have many meetings, right?

M That's right. That _____ _____ whenever a new product is released.

W But how lucky you are to have work to do!

M I know. I'm really grateful for my job although it is _____ _____ _____ sometimes.

12 다음을 듣고, The Reality Exhibition에 해해 언급되지 <u>않은</u> 것을 고르시오.

① 전시회 주제
② 주최자 이름
③ 전시회 기간
④ 참가 작가 수
⑤ 예술 작품 종류

12

M Hello, everyone. I'm Adrian Nelson, the host of the Reality Exhibition. Thank you for taking your time to attend _____ _____ _____. The Reality Exhibition, as the name indicates, *focuses on _____ _____ _____ _____ _____. Eight artists participated in the exhibition, and the type of artwork they produced varies. You can enjoy different kinds of art in _____ _____. The exhibition will last _____ _____ _____, so please feel free to come as many times as you want. Thank you.

★ focuses on [포커시스] [온] → [포커시즌]

표 파악

13 다음 표를 보면서 대화를 듣고, 여자가 구입할 커피 원두를 고르시오.

	Types	Body	Flavors	Geography
①	Type A	Light	Vanilla	Colombia
②	Type B	Light	Caramel	Colombia
③	Type C	Dark	Caramel	Colombia
④	Type D	Dark	Vanilla	Ethiopia
⑤	Type E	Dark	Caramel	Ethiopia

💜 **Which do you prefer?**
: 상대방에게 선호하는 것을 물어볼 때 사용하는 표현으로, '어떤 것을 선호하나요?'라는 뜻이다. 둘 중 하나를 골라야 하는 경우, 'Which do you prefer, A or B?'라고 사용하기도 한다.
= Which do you like more?

13 🇬🇧

M Good afternoon. What kind of coffee beans are you looking for?

W I bought coffee beans with a vanilla flavor here before, but I want to _____ _____ _____ this time.

M 💜Which do you prefer, beans with _____ _____ _____ _____ taste?

W I like beans with a light taste better.

M Then how about these beans from Colombia? They are light and have _____ _____ _____ .

W Isn't that too sweet?

M Not really. You can enjoy _____ _____ _____ that is not too sweet.

W Then I'll take them.

화제·주제 파악

14 다음을 듣고, 무엇에 관한 설명인지 고르시오.

① 보트
② 튜브
③ 풍선
④ 뗏목
⑤ 수영복

14

W This is mostly used _____ _____ . It looks like a donut and has a small hole in it. If we _____ _____ into the hole, it inflates and becomes big. It _____ _____ _____ the water, so if we use it, it can help us float on the water. There are _____ _____ for kids like dolphins and flamingos. This is also _____ _____ _____ who can't swim.

할 일 파악

15 대화를 듣고, 남자가 할 일로 가장 적절한 것을 고르시오.

① 여행 계획 세우기
② 친구 설득하기
③ 학원 알아보기
④ 휴학 신청하기
⑤ 영어 공부하기

15

W Rio, what are you thinking about?

M I am thinking about some things to do when I _____ _____ _____ _____ after this semester.

W Why are you doing that?

M I've been planning to do it for a long time. I want to _____ _____ _____ _____ and take a trip to Europe.

W You must be serious about the matter.

M I am. I'm going to go to the administration office to _____ _____ _____ for a *leave of absence from school now.

★ leave of [리브] [오브] → [리보브]

숫자 정보 파악

16 대화를 듣고, 남자가 조깅하러 갈 시각을 고르시오.

① 7:00
② 8:00
③ 9:00
④ 10:00
⑤ 11:00

16

M How's the weather tomorrow?

W It will rain. Why are you asking about the weather?

M I'm going to go jogging tomorrow morning, but I haven't decided _____ _____ _____ _____ _____.

W _____ _____ _____ _____ by 11:00 a.m. The weather forecast says it will start to rain by that time.

M What time is okay?

W How about jogging first thing in the morning? I heard exercising on _____ _____ _____ is much better.

M Then I'll just go jogging at 7:00 a.m. and _____ _____ after I go back home.

W Great.

적절한 응답 찾기

17 대화를 듣고, 남자의 마지막 말에 대한 여자의 응답으로 가장 적절한 것을 고르시오.

Woman: _____

① No, that's not right. Think about it again.
② I'm already sponsoring another organization.
③ I can't remember what really happened there.
④ Being a help to someone is meaningful to me.
⑤ I can take you to the organization. Come with me.

17

M Excuse me. Can I _____ _____ _____ _____ of your time?

W Sure. What can I do for you?

M I'm a member of a charity named Clean Water in Africa. My organization is currently accepting donations to provide African children with _____ _____ _____ _____.

W I see. I know there is a shortage of clean water in Africa.

M Yes. Many Africans are dying because of it. Are you willing to _____ _____ _____ _____?

W I'd love to, but I can't.

M May I ask you why?

W I'm already sponsoring another organization.

적절한 응답 찾기

18 대화를 듣고, 여자의 마지막 말에 대한 남자의 응답으로 가장 적절한 것을 고르시오.

Man: _____

① You can tell me what you really want to do.
② How on earth is it possible to fail that subject?
③ I can help you finish your assignment tonight.
④ What you're doing now is not helpful.
⑤ It's not too late to find your interest during college.

18

M We only have a few months _____ _____ _____.

W Time really flies.

M Exactly. We should think of _____ _____ _____ _____ _____ _____ and what university to enter.

W What are you going to major in?

M I'm going to major in biotechnology. I'm really interested in this field.

W That means you've already made some plans for the future, right?

M Not really. I will figure out what I can do with my major while I am at college. What about you?

W Well, I don't know what I really want to do. I'm _____ _____ _____ _____.

M It's not too late to find your interest during college.

적절한 응답 찾기

19 대화를 듣고, 남자의 마지막 말에 대한 여자의 응답으로 가장 적절한 것을 고르시오.

Woman: _____

① What is making you so nervous?

② Yes, there are many empty seats.

③ Please come back again tomorrow.

④ Don't tell anyone what happened.

⑤ You should hurry to get on the train now.

19

M Hi. Let me have _____ _____ _____ to Daegu, please.

W What time do you want to leave? There is a train that _____ _____ _____ _____, and the next one leaves two hours from now.

M I'd like to take the former one.

W But since all the seats _____ _____ _____, only standing-room-only tickets are available. Is that okay with you?

M There are no seats at all on the train?

W There's some space in the area connecting each train, but it'll be _____ _____ _____ to sit there.

M Are there any _____ _____ on the next train?

W <u>Yes, there are many empty seats.</u>

상황에 맞는 말 찾기

20 다음 상황 설명을 듣고, Harry가 커플에게 할 말로 가장 적절한 것을 고르시오.

Harry: Excuse me. _____

① Could you please step aside?

② Could you help me find my way?

③ Is there anything I can help you with?

④ You'd better be careful with your things.

⑤ How can I get to city hall from here?

20

M Harry goes down the escalator to take the subway and _____ _____ _____ _____ on the platform. They are carrying luggage and are _____ _____ _____. They seem to be tourists. They are looking at _____ _____ _____ on the wall, but they _____ _____. Harry thinks they might need some help _____ _____ _____. In this situation, what would Harry most likely say to the couple?

Harry Excuse me. <u>Is there anything I can help you with?</u>

1 대화를 듣고, 남자가 구입할 태블릿 커버를 고르시오.

2 대화를 듣고, 남자가 여자에게 부탁한 일로 가장 적절한 것을 고르시오.
① 함께 사진 찍기　　② 사인회 참석하기
③ 티셔츠 구입하기　　④ 옷에 사인해 주기
⑤ 팬클럽 가입하기

3 다음 그림의 상황에 가장 적절한 대화를 고르시오.

①　　②　　③　　④　　⑤

4 대화를 듣고, 남자가 전화를 부탁한 시각을 고르시오.
① 1:00　　② 2:00　　③ 3:00
④ 4:00　　⑤ 5:00

5 대화를 듣고, 두 사람이 이야기하는 작가에 관해 언급되지 <u>않은</u> 것을 고르시오.
① 작가의 이름　　② 작가의 소설
③ 소설의 장르　　④ 작가의 가족
⑤ 소설의 일화

6 대화를 듣고, 두 사람이 대화하는 장소로 가장 적절한 곳을 고르시오.
① 학교　　　② 상점　　　③ 회사
④ 약국　　　⑤ 꽃집

7 다음을 듣고, 두 사람의 대화가 <u>어색한</u> 것을 고르시오.
①　　②　　③　　④　　⑤

8 대화를 듣고, 여자가 남자에게 부탁한 일로 가장 적절한 것을 고르시오.
① 경품 받으러 가기
② 냉장고 구입하기
③ 행운 빌어주기
④ 경품 신청하기
⑤ 신규 계좌 만들기

9 다음을 듣고, 무엇에 관한 설명인지 고르시오.
① 살 빼는 방법
② 공부 방해 요소
③ 아침 식사의 이점
④ 현대인의 바쁜 삶
⑤ 건강 관리의 중요성

10 대화를 듣고, 남자가 지불할 금액을 고르시오.
① $50　　　② $150　　　③ $190
④ $200　　⑤ $250

11 대화를 듣고, 여자가 할 일로 가장 적절한 것을 고르시오.
① 운동하기　　　② 직업 체험하기
③ 취업 준비하기　④ 투자 전략 세우기
⑤ 학생들 가르치기

12 다음을 듣고, 동물 보호 단체에 관해 언급되지 <u>않은</u> 것을 고르시오.

① 보호 단체가 하는 일
② 소식 업데이트 요일
③ 자원봉사 문의 수단
④ 보호 단체 자원봉사자 수
⑤ 보호하고 있는 동물의 수

13 다음 표를 보면서 대화를 듣고, 두 사람이 선택할 세트를 고르시오.

	Sets	Pancakes	Soups	Drinks
①	Set A	Bacon & Pancakes	Tomato Soup	Juice
②	Set B	Bacon & Pancakes	Broccoli Soup	Juice
③	Set C	Sausage & Pancakes	Broccoli Soup	Soda
④	Set D	Sausage & Pancakes	Tomato Soup	Soda
⑤	Set E	Sausage & Pancakes	Broccoli Soup	Juice

14 다음을 듣고, 무엇에 관한 설명인지 고르시오.

① 옷   ② 가방   ③ 신발
④ 지갑   ⑤ 장갑

15 대화를 듣고, 남자가 대화 직후에 할 일로 가장 적절한 것을 고르시오.

① 카페 방문하기
② 만날 장소 정하기
③ 프로젝트 회의하기
④ 멤버에게 연락하기
⑤ 문자 메시지 보내기

16 대화를 듣고, 남자가 출발할 시각을 고르시오.

① 12:30   ② 1:00   ③ 1:30
④ 2:00   ⑤ 3:00

17 대화를 듣고, 여자의 마지막 말에 대한 남자의 응답으로 가장 적절한 것을 고르시오.

Man: _____

① You can't buy happiness with money.
② Don't blame others for what you did.
③ We have to figure out what's going on.
④ Being different doesn't mean being wrong.
⑤ How nice it is that your stress level is low!

18 대화를 듣고, 여자의 마지막 말에 대한 남자의 응답으로 가장 적절한 것을 고르시오.

Man: _____

① Nothing matters except success.
② There's nothing we can do about it.
③ We should try hard to spot fake news.
④ Teenagers should be protected by adults.
⑤ I think it's due to the media and games.

19 대화를 듣고, 여자의 마지막 말에 대한 남자의 응답으로 가장 적절한 것을 고르시오.

Man: _____

① Everyone gets old and loses weight.
② I heard the one-food diet is really helpful.
③ Please give me advice on how to exercise.
④ You'd better eat balanced meals to do that.
⑤ I've also exercised at the gym since last week.

20 다음 상황 설명을 듣고, Owen이 Grace에게 할 말로 가장 적절한 것을 고르시오.

Owen: Grace, _____

① we have a company picnic every year.
② you can use my sunscreen if you want.
③ I used to have some skin problems.
④ it's the best time to get close to the others.
⑤ be careful not to drop your phone in the water.

● 대화를 다시 듣고, 알맞은 것을 고르시오.

1 The man wants to get a cover with small images on it for his table PC.
☐ True   ☐ False

2 The woman will autograph the man's T-shirt.
☐ True   ☐ False

3 Did the man notice the sign in the parking lot?
☐ Yes   ☐ No

4 What does the man ask the woman to do?
☐ listen to his speech
☐ call him before the speech

5 The man and the woman both have a positive impression of the author.
☐ True   ☐ False

6 Does the woman suggest that the man turn on the air conditioner?
☐ Yes   ☐ No

7 The man wants to tell the woman about the dangers of energy drinks.
☐ True   ☐ False

8 What does the man have to do to take part in the event?
☐ make an account
☐ meet the woman

9 What is the first benefit of having breakfast?
☐ improving memory
☐ avoiding extra calories

10 Does the man need the watch with the waterproof function?
☐ Yes   ☐ No

11 The woman wants to build a building for students.
☐ True   ☐ False

12 How does the group help the owners find their lost pets?
☐ by sending email to people
☐ by posting photos of the pets

13 Does the woman express a specific preference for drinks?
☐ Yes   ☐ No

14 This is mainly used for storing things.
☐ True   ☐ False

15 Where will they meet tomorrow?
☐ at a café   ☐ at a school

16 Will the man stay outside for more than three hours?
☐ Yes   ☐ No

17 The man respects differences between people.
☐ True   ☐ False

18 Which issue in the news do they talk about?
☐ the heavy traffic   ☐ teenage crime

19 Does the woman exercise to lose weight?
☐ Yes   ☐ No

20 What is Grace worried about?
☐ going on a company picnic
☐ getting a sunburn

그림 정보 파악

1 대화를 듣고, 남자가 구입할 태블릿 커버를 고르시오.

1

W Hello. What _____ _____ _____ _____ are you looking for?

M I want to buy a cover for my tablet PC.

W We have two types, one that fully covers the tablet and another that _____ _____ _____ attached to it.

M I prefer one without a keyboard. Do you have one with any small images on?

W Sorry, but we don't. But we have _____ _____ _____.

M Then I'll just take a _____ _____ _____.

W Okay.

부탁한 일 파악

2 대화를 듣고, 남자가 여자에게 부탁한 일로 가장 적절한 것을 고르시오.

① 함께 사진 찍기
② 사인회 참석하기
③ 티셔츠 구입하기
④ 옷에 사인해 주기
⑤ 팬클럽 가입하기

🖤 **May I ask a favor of you?**
: 상대방에게 무언가를 부탁할 때 사용하는 표현으로, '부탁을 해도 될까요?'라는 뜻이다.
= Can you do me a favor?

2 🇬🇧

W Hi. Thank you so much for coming to the _____ _____.

M I'm a _____ _____ of your group.

W We're _____ _____ _____ our fans' love.

M 🖤May I ask a favor of you?

W What is it?

M Could I _____ _____ _____ on my T-shirt?

W I'd be glad to do that for you.

그림 상황 파악

3 다음 그림의 상황에 가장 적절한 대화를 고르시오.

① ② ③ ④ ⑤

3

① W Don't _____ _____ _____ in front of the gate.
　 M What's wrong with that?

② W I can tell it's a really _____ _____.
　 M Yes. The parking lot is already full.

③ W How much should I _____ _____ _____?
　 M It's five dollars for an hour.

④ W Excuse me, sir. This parking space is only for _____ _____.
　 M Sorry. I read the sign wrong.

⑤ W You must stop your car when people are _____ _____ _____ _____.
　 M I know. I was just rushed.

숫자 정보 파악

4 대화를 듣고, 남자가 전화를 부탁한 시각을 고르시오.

① 1:00
② 2:00
③ 3:00
④ 4:00
⑤ 5:00

4

W How are _____ _____ for the speech for the seminar tomorrow going?

M They're going fine. I think I can _____ _____ since I've been practicing a lot.

W That's great. The audience will _____ _____ _____. By the way, what time *does it start?

M It starts at 3:00 p.m.

W I will get there _____ _____ _____.

M Okay. Could you call me an hour before the seminar?

W Sure. But why?

M I want to _____ _____ _____ while talking to you on the phone.

* does it [더즈] [잇] → [더짓]

언급 유무 파악

5 대화를 듣고, 두 사람이 이야기하는 작가에 관해 언급되지 <u>않은</u> 것을 고르시오.

① 작가의 이름
② 작가의 소설
③ 소설의 장르
④ 작가의 가족
⑤ 소설의 일화

♥ **I can't agree more.**

: 상대방의 말에 강한 동의를 나타낼 때 사용하는 표현으로, '네 말에 전적으로 동의해.'라는 뜻이다.

= I'm with you.
= I hear you.
= You can say that again.

5

W It's been a long time since we came to _____ _____.

M You're right. We were too busy to come here. Look at this! The book is about J.K. Rowling.

W She's my _____ _____. I really love her books, especially the *Harry Potter* series.

M ♥I can't agree more. Do you know how she came to write them?

W No, I don't. How could she make all those stories?

M She said the story suddenly _____ _____ _____ _____ while she was waiting for a train at the station.

W That's awesome! I think she is one of the _____ _____ _____ in the world.

장소 추론

6 대화를 듣고, 두 사람이 대화하는 장소로 가장 적절한 곳을 고르시오.

① 학교
② 상점
③ 회사
④ 약국
⑤ 꽃집

6 🇬🇧

M Hi. How can I help you?

W I've _____ _____ _____ since last night. I also have a fever.

M Well, I think you might have a cold.

W I guess it's due to _____ _____ _____ at my workplace. It runs all day.

M Take these pills. You will _____ _____ _____.

W Thank you so much.

7 다음을 듣고, 두 사람의 대화가 <u>어색한</u> 것을 고르시오.

① ② ③ ④ ⑤

7

① M You're _____ _____ computer games.

  W I am, and so are you.

② M I _____ _____ _____ about saying something bad to my brother.

  W You'd better apologize to him.

③ M Are you aware of the dangers of energy drinks?

  W You can _____ _____ _____ with them.

④ M What are some fun things to do on a rainy day?

  W You can _____ _____ _____ and read a book.

⑤ M It's obvious that he likes you.

  W No way. Don't _____ _____ _____.

8 대화를 듣고, 여자가 남자에게 부탁한 일로 가장 적절한 것을 고르시오.

① 경품 받으러 가기
② 냉장고 구입하기
③ 행운 빌어주기
④ 경품 신청하기
⑤ 신규 계좌 만들기

8

M Suji, _____ _____ _____?

W The free gift event is _____ _____ _____.

M What is the free gift?

W It's a refrigerator.

M I wish _____ _____ _____.

W By the way, do you _____ _____ _____ on this website?

M No. I'm not a member of it.

W Could you make one for me so that I can _____ _____ _____ _____ _____?

M No problem.

9 다음을 듣고, 무엇에 관한 설명인지 고르시오.

① 살 빼는 방법
② 공부 방해 요소
③ 아침 식사의 이점
④ 현대인의 바쁜 삶
⑤ 건강 관리의 중요성

9

M Do you _____ _____ before you go to school or work? Many people these days are so busy that they often _____ _____. However, do you know that breakfast is the _____ _____ _____ of the day? The first benefit of having breakfast is that you can _____ _____ _____ because it decreases your appetite throughout the day. Next, it _____ _____ _____. Finally, it improves your mood and increases your happiness. Have breakfast and have a healthier, happier life.

숫자 정보 파악

10 대화를 듣고, 남자가 지불할 금액을 고르시오.

① $50
② $150
③ $190
④ $200
⑤ $250

10

W   Good afternoon. What can I help you with?

M   I'd like to buy _____ _____ _____.

W   For sports, one with a rubber band would be better.

M   Is that one _____ _____?

W   No, it isn't. The water-resistant watch is 200 dollars, which is fifty dollars _____ _____ _____ the one without the waterproof function.

M   I'll take the one that has _____ _____ _____. I have a 5% off coupon here.

할 일 파악

11 대화를 듣고, 여자가 할 일로 가장 적절한 것을 고르시오.

① 운동하기
② 직업 체험하기
③ 취업 준비하기
④ 투자 전략 세우기
⑤ 학생들 가르치기

11

W   I have a really cool idea for a business.

M   What is it?

W   It's building _____ _____ _____ where students can study, exercise, and have a job-experience program in one place.

M   That will require _____ _____ _____.

W   I know. There may be some big companies that are willing to _____ _____ _____ here.

M   I guess you should _____ _____ _____ _____ to present your ideas to them.

언급 유무 파악

12 다음을 듣고, 동물 보호 단체에 관해 언급되지 <u>않은</u> 것을 고르시오.

① 보호 단체가 하는 일
② 소식 업데이트 요일
③ 자원봉사 문의 수단
④ 보호 단체 자원봉사자 수
⑤ 보호하고 있는 동물의 수

12

W   Let me introduce our _____ _____ _____. We help owners find their lost pets by posting their photos and descriptions and _____ _____ _____ for abandoned pets. Right now, we are protecting twelve animals at our shelter. We _____ _____ _____ about the animals every Friday. Our group recommends that people adopt animals rather than _____ _____. If you're interested in volunteering at the shelter, please _____ by email.

표 파악

13 다음 표를 보면서 대화를 듣고, 두 사람이 선택할 세트를 고르시오.

Set		Pancakes	Soups	Drinks
①	Set A	Bacon & Pancakes	Tomato Soup	Juice
②	Set B	Bacon & Pancakes	Broccoli Soup	Juice
③	Set C	Sausage & Pancakes	Broccoli Soup	Soda
④	Set D	Sausage & Pancakes	Tomato Soup	Soda
⑤	Set E	Sausage & Pancakes	Broccoli Soup	Juice

13

M Which set should we _____ _____ _____?

W How about the one with bacon and pancakes?

M Can we have sausage _____ _____ _____?

W Sure. What about soup? Do you like broccoli soup?

M I love it. Which do you _____ _____ _____ soda or juice?

W I'm fine with either of them. You can choose.

M Then _____ _____ _____.

W Great.

화제·주제 파악

14 다음을 듣고, 무엇에 관한 설명인지 고르시오.

① 옷
② 가방
③ 신발
④ 지갑
⑤ 장갑

14 🇬🇧

W This is what we use to _____ _____ _____ _____. It has different sizes and is made of different materials depending on how it will be used. Most sports brands sell it with their logos and _____ _____. We usually carry it over our shoulders. This is sometimes so small that we can *hold it with one hand, but we can still _____ _____ _____ inside. This is _____ _____ _____, especially for students and travelers.

★ hold it [홀드] [잇] → [홀딧]

할 일 파악

15 대화를 듣고, 남자가 대화 직후에 할 일로 가장 적절한 것을 고르시오.

① 카페 방문하기
② 만날 장소 정하기
③ 프로젝트 회의하기
④ 멤버에게 연락하기
⑤ 문자 메시지 보내기

15 🇬🇧

W Eunho, _____ _____ _____ _____ tomorrow?

M The café across from school will be a good place to _____ _____ _____ _____.

W We need to set the time, too.

M Let me do it. I'll send you a text message after I _____ _____ _____ _____.

W Okay. I'll wait for _____ _____ _____.

M All right.

16 대화를 듣고, 남자가 출발할 시각을 고르시오.

① 12:30
② 1:00
③ 1:30
④ 2:00
⑤ 3:00

16

W Didn't you say that you _____ _____ _____ today?

M I did. I need to go out thirty minutes before the appointed time.

W What time are you _____ _____ _____?

M At 1:00 p.m.

W I see. What time do you think you _____ _____ _____ _____?

M We'll just _____ _____, so I guess I'll get back by 3:00 p.m.

W I got it.

17 대화를 듣고, 여자의 마지막 말에 대한 남자의 응답으로 가장 적절한 것을 고르시오.

Man: _____

① You can't buy happiness with money.
② Don't blame others for what you did.
③ We have to figure out what's going on.
④ Being different doesn't mean being wrong.
⑤ How nice it is that your stress level is low!

17

W When do you _____ _____ _____?

M It's when I spend time with my loved ones. What about you?

W I'm happy when I _____ _____ _____ while doing what I want. It's weird, isn't it?

M No, it isn't. As _____ _____ _____ from each other, people's ideas about happiness vary, too.

W I just feel very different than _____ _____ _____.

M Being different doesn't mean being wrong.

18 대화를 듣고, 여자의 마지막 말에 대한 남자의 응답으로 가장 적절한 것을 고르시오.

Man: _____

① Nothing matters except success.
② There's nothing we can do about it.
③ We should try hard to spot fake news.
④ Teenagers should be protected by adults.
⑤ I think it's due to the media and games.

18

W Michael, did you _____ _____ _____ yesterday?

M No, I didn't. What happened?

W Two teenagers _____ _____ _____ _____ and ran into _____ _____.

M I see teen issues are getting more serious.

W _____ _____ _____ _____ that is happening?

M I think it's due to the media and games.

적절한 응답 찾기

19 대화를 듣고, 여자의 마지막 말에 대한 남자의 응답으로 가장 적절한 것을 고르시오.

Man: _____

① Everyone gets old and loses weight.
② I heard the one-food diet is really helpful.
③ Please give me advice on how to exercise.
④ You'd better eat balanced meals to do that.
⑤ I've also exercised at the gym since last week.

19

W Do you _____ _____ _____ in my body?

M You seem to have lost weight. Did you start exercising?

W No, I am only _____ _____ _____ a day. It's fairly effective.

M Can you really make it through the day if you _____ _____ _____ ?

W Sometimes I feel hungry, but I _____ _____ _____ if I can have a nice body.

M You'd better eat balanced meals to do that.

상황에 맞는 말 찾기

20 다음 상황 설명을 듣고, Owen이 Grace에게 할 말로 가장 적절한 것을 고르시오.

Owen: Grace, _____

① we have a company picnic every year.
② you can use my sunscreen if you want.
③ I used to have some skin problems.
④ it's the best time to get close to the others.
⑤ be careful not to drop your phone in the water.

20

M Owen and Grace are _____ _____. They go to the beach _____ _____ _____ _____ in the afternoon. Because Owen knows that it will be _____ _____ _____, he brings sunscreen. However, Grace doesn't seem to expect it will be so hot. She says she's worried that she could _____ _____ _____. In this situation, what would Owen most likely say to Grace?

Owen Grace, you can use my sunscreen if you want.

1 대화를 듣고, 여자가 만든 졸업 앨범 표지를 고르시오.

2 대화를 듣고, 남자가 여자에게 부탁한 일로 가장 적절한 것을 고르시오.
① 휴대폰 수리하기
② 자주 문자 보내기
③ 같은 취미를 가지기
④ 마주 보고 대화하기
⑤ 어머니에게 사과하기

3 다음 그림의 상황에 가장 적절한 대화를 고르시오.

① ② ③ ④ ⑤

4 대화를 듣고, 여자가 고양이 카페를 방문할 요일을 고르시오.
① 월요일　　② 화요일　　③ 수요일
④ 목요일　　⑤ 금요일

5 대화를 듣고, 정장에 관해 언급되지 않은 것을 고르시오.
① 가격　　② 색상　　③ 원단
④ 제조 국가　　⑤ 구입 용도

6 대화를 듣고, 두 사람이 대화하는 장소로 가장 적절한 곳을 고르시오.
① 은행　　② 농장　　③ 문구점
④ 정비소　　⑤ 골동품 가게

7 다음을 듣고, 두 사람의 대화가 <u>어색한</u> 것을 고르시오.
① ② ③ ④ ⑤

8 대화를 듣고, 여자가 남자에게 부탁한 일로 가장 적절한 것을 고르시오.
① 콜택시 부르기
② 여행 계획 짜기
③ 비행기 표 예매하기
④ 여행 사진 보내주기
⑤ 우편으로 편지 보내기

9 다음을 듣고, 무엇에 관한 안내 방송인지 고르시오.
① 백화점 정기 세일 일정
② 어린이 놀이방 무료 운영
③ 놀이공원 입장 제한 연령
④ 어린이와 쇼핑할 때 주의점
⑤ 전문가와 함께 하는 육아 강연

10 대화를 듣고, 남자가 지불할 금액을 고르시오.
① $20　　② $25　　③ $30
④ $35　　⑤ $40

11 대화를 듣고, 여자가 할 일로 가장 적절한 것을 고르시오.
① 친구에게 책을 팔기
② 파손된 책을 교환하기
③ 친구와 함께 독서하기
④ 서점에서 책 환불하기
⑤ 아버지를 위한 선물 사기

12 다음을 듣고, 반딧불이 구경에 관해 언급되지 <u>않은</u> 것을 고르시오.
① 적합한 복장　② 소요 시간　③ 기념품 판매
④ 참가 비용　⑤ 제한 연령

13 대화를 듣고, 두 사람이 비행기에서 앉을 좌석을 고르시오.

Aisle

14 다음을 듣고, 무엇에 관한 설명인지 고르시오.
① 플라스틱의 유용성
② 지구 온난화의 원인
③ 바다의 무한한 가능성
④ 해양 동물의 먹이사슬
⑤ 플라스틱 오염의 위험

15 대화를 듣고, 남자가 대화 직후에 할 일로 가장 적절한 것을 고르시오.
① 수박 구입하기
② 잡지 사러 가기
③ 자동차 정비하기
④ 친구에게 전화하기
⑤ 병원 진료 예약하기

16 대화를 듣고, 여자가 침대를 받기로 한 날짜를 고르시오.
① 9월 7일　② 9월 8일　③ 9월 9일
④ 9월 10일　⑤ 9월 11일

17 대화를 듣고, 남자의 마지막 말에 대한 여자의 응답으로 가장 적절한 것을 고르시오.
Woman: _____
① Let's start saving money now.
② Someday I want to travel to Africa.
③ Of course. It's the thought that counts.
④ Don't worry. Your health is more important.
⑤ Thank you for coming to my birthday party.

18 대화를 듣고, 여자의 마지막 말에 대한 남자의 응답으로 가장 적절한 것을 고르시오.
Man: _____
① Then let's go fishing together.
② Forget about it. It's not your fault.
③ Be careful when swimming in the sea.
④ I'm so happy that you had a good day.
⑤ You'd better go home and get some rest.

19 대화를 듣고, 남자의 마지막 말에 대한 여자의 응답으로 가장 적절한 것을 고르시오.
Woman: _____
① Personally, I do not recommend it.
② Well-cooked vegetables taste better.
③ It really was. You should give it a try.
④ You can get vitamin A by eating carrots.
⑤ They have a special meal for vegetarians.

20 다음 상황 설명을 듣고, Eunchan이 David에게 할 말로 가장 적절한 것을 고르시오.
Eunchan: David, _____
① I heard you live alone. How is it?
② don't forget to pay the rent monthly.
③ clean your room with the vacuum cleaner.
④ do you want to share your room with me?
⑤ do you get along well with your roommate?

Listen and Check

정답 및 해설 p.069

● 대화를 다시 듣고, 알맞은 것을 고르시오.

1 Did the man design the cover of the middle school yearbook?

☐ Yes　　　　☐ No

2 The man and the woman are having a date.

☐ True　　　　☐ False

3 Is the man worried about the woman?

☐ Yes　　　　☐ No

4 Wesley plans to read some comic books on Friday.

☐ True　　　　☐ False

5 For what does the man want a suit?

☐ for an interview　　☐ for a wedding

6 The woman wants to change the coins into bills.

☐ True　　　　☐ False

7 Is the woman ready for school?

☐ Yes　　　　☐ No

8 Where will the man and the woman go after the conversation?

☐ to an airport　　☐ to a hotel

9 How many childcare specialists are there in a daycare center?

☐ two　　　　☐ three

10 Where did the man get a coupon from?

☐ a newspaper　　☐ a pet magazine

11 The woman's father lost the book that she had bought.

☐ True　　　　☐ False

12 Who is not allowed to participate in the program due to safety reasons?

☐ the elderly　　☐ children under six

13 Do the man and the woman have to pay extra for the seats which they selected?

☐ Yes　　　　☐ No

14 Some marine animals take plastic for food and eat it.

☐ True　　　　☐ False

15 Is Kihoon in the hospital after a car accident?

☐ Yes　　　　☐ No

16 How did the woman pay for the king-sized bed?

☐ by credit card　　☐ in cash

17 Jaekyung has helped a boy in Africa by donating money.

☐ True　　　　☐ False

18 Did Natalie have a wonderful weekend?

☐ Yes　　　　☐ No

19 The woman's son used to hate vegetables.

☐ True　　　　☐ False

20 Why does David need a roommate?

☐ to share the rent

☐ to move to a new place

정답 및 해설 *p.064*

그림 정보 파악

1 대화를 듣고, 여자가 만든 졸업 앨범 표지를 고르시오.

1

M Nicole, I heard that you designed the cover of our middle school yearbook.

W I did. Look at this cover. How is it?

M In the middle of the cover, you drew a circle, a triangle, and a square _____ _____ _____, right?

W You're correct. And I _____ _____ _____ _____ _____ _____ at the bottom.

M Where did you put the year?

W In the _____ _____ _____. Can you see the year, 2020?

M I see. You really did well. It's simple and neat.

부탁한 일 파악

2 대화를 듣고, 남자가 여자에게 부탁한 일로 가장 적절한 것을 고르시오.

① 휴대폰 수리하기
② 자주 문자 보내기
③ 같은 취미를 가지기
④ 마주 보고 대화하기
⑤ 어머니에게 사과하기

2 🇬🇧

W Daniel, you look upset. Is something bothering you?

M Actually, I think you're _____ _____ _____ _____ at all.

W What do you mean? We are having a date now.

M But when I talk to you, you _____ _____ _____ _____ _____ and texting somebody.

W Sorry. It was my mom.

M Can you _____ _____ _____ _____ _____ during a conversation?

W Okay. I apologize to you for that.

그림 상황 파악

3 다음 그림의 상황에 가장 적절한 대화를 고르시오.

① ② ③ ④ ⑤

3

① W Which dish is quick and _____ _____ _____?
   M I recommend the chicken breast salad.

② W What a mess! I should clean the kitchen floor.
   M Then I'll clear the dinner table.

③ W I'm sorry, Dad. I _____ _____ _____.
   M Are you all right? Be careful about the _____ _____.

④ W Look at these beautiful dishes.
   M I _____ _____ _____ for my mom.

⑤ W I'm getting wet from _____ _____ _____.
   M Let me *help you put this apron on.

★ help you [헬프] [유] → [헬퓨]

4 대화를 듣고, 여자가 고양이 카페를 방문할 요일을 고르시오.

① 월요일
② 화요일
③ 수요일
④ 목요일
⑤ 금요일

4

W Wesley, do you _____ _____ _____ _____ this Friday?

M Maybe I'll just stay home and read some comic books.

W _____ _____ _____ to a cat café? We can buy some snacks for the cats and _____ _____.

M You know, I love cats. Can we go today?

W Today? Sorry, but I _____ _____ _____ my history report.

M Then what about tomorrow? I mean on Tuesday.

W That's perfect. Call me tomorrow.

언급 유무 파악

5 대화를 듣고, 정장에 관해 언급되지 않은 것을 고르시오.

① 가격　　　② 색상
③ 원단　　　④ 제조 국가
⑤ 구입 용도

💙 **That's too much.**
: 예상보다 과하거나 무리한 일이라고 느껴질 때 쓰는 표현으로, '너무하다.', '지나치다.'라는 뜻이다.
= Way too much.

5 🇬🇧

W Welcome to Twinkle Clothes Store. What are you looking for?

M I'm _____ _____ _____ _____ for an interview.

W How about this suit? It was _____ _____ Italy.

M I like it, especially the indigo blue color. But it looks _____ _____ _____.

W That's the only drawback. But you can _____ _____ _____ _____ in Korea.

M Okay. How much is the suit?

W It's three thousand dollars.

M Wow! 💙That's too much.

장소 추론

6 대화를 듣고, 두 사람이 대화하는 장소로 가장 적절한 곳을 고르시오.

① 은행
② 농장
③ 문구점
④ 정비소
⑤ 골동품 가게

6

W Good afternoon. I'd like to put these coins into my *bank account.

M Wow! Did you _____ _____ _____ _____ _____ by yourself?

W Of course. I _____ _____ _____ _____ in my piggy bank for a year.

M Can you put your coins in this coin counting machine?

W Okay. [Coin-falling sounds] How much do I have?

M Just a moment. [Beep] You have 37 dollars in coins.

W That's _____ _____ _____ _____. Please put it into my account.

★ bank account [뱅크] [어카운트] → [뱅커카운트]

7 다음을 듣고, 두 사람의 대화가 <u>어색한</u> 것을 고르시오.

① ② ③ ④ ⑤

7

① M _____ _____ _____ in the late afternoon today.

W Perfect! Let's make a snowman.

② M How much is the dress in the display window?

W _____ _____ _____ for 70 dollars.

③ M Tell me your email account password.

W No way! _____ _____ _____.

④ M Thank you for giving me your seat.

W My pleasure. I'm _____ _____ _____ _____ soon.

⑤ M What are you doing in bed? Get ready for school.

W I can't change the bed sheet. _____ _____ _____.

8 대화를 듣고, 여자가 남자에게 부탁한 일로 가장 적절한 것을 고르시오.

① 콜택시 부르기
② 여행 계획 짜기
③ 비행기 표 예매하기
④ 여행 사진 보내주기
⑤ 우편으로 편지 보내기

💜 **Me neither.**
: 상대방의 부정적인 의견에 동의할 때 쓰는 표현으로, '나도 그렇지 않아.'라는 뜻이다.
= I don't either.
= Neither do I.

8

M I can't believe that today is the last day of our trip to Boracay.

W 💜Me neither. Our vacation _____ _____ _____ _____.

M We have to go back home and _____ _____ _____ _____ soon.

W I know! Now, it's time to pack our stuff. But I don't want to.

M Don't be sad. I took hundreds of nice pictures of us.

W Well done! Can you _____ _____ _____ _____?

M Sure. I'll *send them after we get a taxi to the airport.

★ send them [센드] [뎀] → [센뎀]

9 다음을 듣고, 무엇에 관한 안내 방송인지 고르시오.

① 백화점 정기 세일 일정
② 어린이 놀이방 무료 운영
③ 놀이공원 입장 제한 연령
④ 어린이와 쇼핑할 때 주의점
⑤ 전문가와 함께 하는 육아 강연

9 🇬🇧

W Welcome to the Fancy Department Store. We have a daycare center to _____ _____ _____ _____ in comfort. The daycare center is _____ _____ the 1st floor near the information desk. The operating hours are from 12:00 p.m. to 6:00 p.m. All children ages 3 to 7 are allowed. You don't need to pay for it. There, three childcare specialists will look after your children safely. We _____ _____ _____ _____ _____ to improve your customer experience.

숫자 정보 파악

10 대화를 듣고, 남자가 지불할 금액을 고르시오.

① $20   ② $25

③ $30   ④ $35

⑤ $40

♥ **What about ~?**

: 상대방의 의견을 물어볼 때 쓰는 표현으로, '~은 어때?'라는 뜻이다.

= How about ~?

= What do you think about ~?

10

W   Welcome to Cutie Pet Shop. What do you need?

M   I'm looking for _____ _____ for a small dog.

W   ♥What about this one? It's light to carry and _____ _____ _____ _____.

M   I like it. It's _____ _____ _____ _____. How much do I have to pay for it?

W   It's 35 dollars.

M   Can I use this coupon? I _____ _____ _____ a pet magazine.

W   Absolutely! You'll get 5 dollars off the total price.

할 일 파악

11 대화를 듣고, 여자가 할 일로 가장 적절한 것을 고르시오.

① 친구에게 책을 팔기

② 파손된 책을 교환하기

③ 친구와 함께 독서하기

④ 서점에서 책 환불하기

⑤ 아버지를 위한 선물 사기

11

W   Let's go to the bookstore. I'll _____ _____ _____ _____ on this book.

M   Why? Is it damaged?

W   No, it's fine. I bought it yesterday, and my dad _____ _____ _____ _____ _____ this morning.

M   That's so funny! Then can I _____ _____ _____ from you? I want to read it.

W   That's a brilliant idea. I'll sell this to you.

M   Okay. Here is money for it.

언급 유무 파악

12 다음을 듣고, 반딧불이 구경에 관해 언급되지 <u>않은</u> 것을 고르시오.

① 적합한 복장

② 소요 시간

③ 기념품 판매

④ 참가 비용

⑤ 제한 연령

12

M   Good morning, guests. We're glad to introduce the firefly-watching program to you. Participants will experience a river cruise at night to see the fireflies. We recommend that you wear long sleeves to _____ _____ _____ _____ _____ _____ _____ _____. This program is _____ _____ at 7:00 p.m. and lasts for about an hour and a half. It costs $25 for adults and $15 for children under 12. Children under six are not allowed _____ _____ _____ _____. If you want to take part in this program, please contact us at 012-3456-7890.

그림 정보 파악

13 대화를 듣고, 두 사람이 비행기에서 앉을 좌석을 고르시오.

13

M Look! We can _____ _____ _____ _____ in advance.

W That's very convenient. Let's look at the seat map.

M Which one do you prefer, a window seat or an aisle seat?

W I prefer a window seat. I also need the extra legroom.

M If you want that, then we _____ _____ _____ _____ _____ _____ in the exit row.

W We have to _____ _____ _____ _____ in the exit row, right?

M Right. You take the window seat, and I'll sit next to you.

W Okay.

화제·주제 파악

14 다음을 듣고, 무엇에 관한 설명인지 고르시오.

① 플라스틱의 유용성
② 지구 온난화의 원인
③ 바다의 무한한 가능성
④ 해양 동물의 먹이사슬
⑤ 플라스틱 오염의 위험

14

W Plastic is everywhere in our daily lives. It is a useful material for people. However, when it is _____ _____ _____ _____ carelessly, it can cause huge problems. Plastic is harmful to marine animals. Plastic _____ _____ _____ _____ to break down. Some marine animals take plastic for food and eat it, which injures or even kills them. People should be aware of _____ _____ _____ _____ _____. If this continues, things will get even worse.

할 일 파악

15 대화를 듣고, 남자가 대화 직후에 할 일로 가장 적절한 것을 고르시오.

① 수박 구입하기
② 잡지 사러 가기
③ 자동차 정비하기
④ 친구에게 전화하기
⑤ 병원 진료 예약하기

♥ **It's not that serious.**
: 어떤 일에 대해서 대수롭지 않게 여길 때 쓰는 표현으로, '별 거 아니야.'라는 뜻이다.
= (It's) not that bad.
= It's no big deal.

15

W Kihoon, did you hear the news that Seowoo is in the hospital?

M Yes. I _____ _____ _____ _____ her. She had a car accident. But luckily, ♥it's not that serious.

W Why don't we go to see her?

M Sounds good. Before we do that, let's _____ _____ _____ _____.

W I'll buy a watermelon. That's her favorite fruit.

M I'll buy a magazine. She _____ _____ _____ in the hospital.

W Okay. Let's meet in front of the hospital at 3:00 p.m.

숫자 정보 파악

16 대화를 듣고, 여자가 침대를 받기로 한 날짜를 고르시오.

① 9월 7일
② 9월 8일
③ 9월 9일
④ 9월 10일
⑤ 9월 11일

16

[*Cellphone rings.*]

W Hello? Who's calling, please?

M Ms. Murphy, this is the Cozy Furniture Store. Did you order a king-sized bed 3 days ago?

W Right. I visited the shop and _____ _____ _____ _____ _____ _____.

M We'd like to _____ _____ _____ on September 7. Is that all right?

W Sorry, but I work on weekdays. Could you *deliver it on September 10 or 11?

M Let me _____ _____ _____. [*Pause*] September 10 is possible.

W Good. What time can I expect you?

M At around 11 a.m.

W Okay. See you then.

★ deliver it [딜리벌] [잇] → [딜리버릿]

적절한 응답 찾기

17 대화를 듣고, 남자의 마지막 말에 대한 여자의 응답으로 가장 적절한 것을 고르시오.

Woman: _____

① Let's start saving money now.
② Someday I want to travel to Africa.
③ Of course. It's the thought that counts.
④ Don't worry. Your health is more important.
⑤ Thank you for coming to my birthday party.

17

M Jaekyung, what are you doing?

W I'm _____ _____ _____ to a boy in Africa to celebrate his birthday.

M I didn't know that you have a friend in Africa.

W Actually, I've helped this boy _____ _____ _____ for three years.

M You sound like an angel. I've _____ _____ _____ doing that before.

W It's _____ _____ _____ at all. You can do it with your pocket money.

M Really? Just 10 dollars a month is okay?

W Of course. It's the thought that counts.

적절한 응답 찾기

18 대화를 듣고, 여자의 마지막 말에 대한 남자의 응답으로 가장 적절한 것을 고르시오.

Man: _____

① Then let's go fishing together.
② Forget about it. It's not your fault.
③ Be careful when swimming in the sea.
④ I'm so happy that you had a good day.
⑤ You'd better go home and get some rest.

18 🇬🇧

M Natalie, how was your last weekend?

W It was terrible. I _____ _____ _____ _____ all day.

M What happened to you?

W I _____ _____ _____ _____ after eating some raw fish.

M I'm sorry to hear that. Are you okay now?

W _____ _____ _____ _____. But still I don't feel very well.

M You'd better go home and get some rest.

적절한 응답 찾기

19 대화를 듣고, 남자의 마지막 말에 대한 여자의 응답으로 가장 적절한 것을 고르시오.

Woman: _____

① Personally, I do not recommend it.
② Well-cooked vegetables taste better.
③ It really was. You should give it a try.
④ You can get vitamin A by eating carrots.
⑤ They have a special meal for vegetarians.

19

M Doyeon, do you have time to talk?

W What's up? Do you have a problem?

M My daughter hates vegetables. She never even _____ _____ _____ _____.

W Hmm... Do you remember my son Taeoh? He _____ _____ _____ _____. But he likes eating vegetables now.

M Are you serious? What happened?

W Taeoh and I _____ _____ _____ _____. We planted carrots and cucumbers and watered them together.

M Wow! It must have _____ _____ _____ _____ for him.

W <u>It really was. You should give it a try.</u>

상황에 맞는 말 찾기

20 다음 상황 설명을 듣고, Eunchan이 David에게 할 말로 가장 적절한 것을 고르시오.

Eunchan: David, _____

① I heard you live alone. How is it?
② don't forget to pay the rent monthly.
③ clean your room with the vacuum cleaner.
④ do you want to share your room with me?
⑤ do you get along well with your roommate?

20

M Eunchan _____ _____ _____ _____ _____ his parents' house. He searches for a new place, but he _____ _____ _____. A few days later, Eunchan happens to meet David on the street. David says that he's looking for a roommate _____ _____ _____ _____. David's place is nice to live, and the _____ _____ _____ to Eunchan. So he wants to be David's roommate. In this situation, what would Eunchan most likely say to David?

Eunchan David, <u>do you want to share your room with me?</u>

1 대화를 듣고, 여자가 구입할 시계를 고르시오.

① ② ③

④ ⑤

2 대화를 듣고, 남자가 여자에게 전화한 목적으로 가장 적절한 것을 고르시오.
① 약속 시간을 정하기 위해서
② 소미의 노트북을 빌리기 위해서
③ Jason의 병문안을 함께 가기 위해서
④ 과제에 대한 아이디어를 얻기 위해서
⑤ 함께 과제를 할 것을 제안하기 위해서

3 다음 그림의 상황에 가장 적절한 대화를 고르시오.

① ② ③ ④ ⑤

4 대화를 듣고, 여자가 친구를 만날 시간을 고르시오.
① 5:50 ② 6:00 ③ 6:10
④ 6:20 ⑤ 6:30

5 다음을 듣고, Charles Chaplin에 대해 언급되지 않은 것을 고르시오.
① 태어난 날짜와 고향 ② 부모님의 직업
③ 데뷔 연도 ④ 첫 영화 계약 연도
⑤ 데뷔 영화 제목

6 대화를 듣고, 두 사람의 관계로 가장 적절한 것을 고르시오.
① 승무원 — 기장 ② 환자 — 의사
③ 승객 — 승무원 ④ 손님 — 호텔 직원
⑤ 환자 — 간호사

7 대화를 듣고, 두 사람의 대화가 어색한 것을 고르시오.
① ② ③ ④ ⑤

8 대화를 듣고, 여자가 남자에게 부탁한 일로 가장 적절한 것을 고르시오.
① 일부를 포장해 줄 것
② 음료수를 두 잔으로 변경할 것
③ 불고기 샌드위치를 추가해 줄 것
④ 가능한 한 빨리 준비해 줄 것
⑤ 콜라 두 잔을 취소해 줄 것

9 대화를 듣고, 여자의 마지막 말에 담긴 의도로 가장 적절한 것을 고르시오.
① 격려 ② 동의
③ 충고 ④ 안심
⑤ 질책

10 대화를 듣고, 남자가 지불할 금액을 고르시오.
① $30 ② $25
③ $20 ④ $18
⑤ $15

11 대화를 듣고, 여자가 할 일로 가장 적절한 것을 고르시오.
① 난방기를 끈다. ② 집안 청소를 한다.
③ 환풍기를 켠다. ④ 창문을 연다.
⑤ 가습기를 켠다.

12 다음을 듣고, Seoul Dance Festival과 관련하여 언급되지 <u>않은</u> 것을 고르시오.

① 처음 시작한 해 ② 댄스의 종류

③ 참여 단체 ④ 올해 개최 기간

⑤ 공연 관람 비용

13 다음 표를 보면서 대화를 듣고, 남자가 선택할 강좌를 고르시오.

	Subject	Type
①	Chinese	Community Center
②	Japanese	Community Center
③	Chinese	Online
④	Chinese Characters	Online
⑤	Japanese	Online

14 다음을 듣고, 무엇에 관한 설명인지 고르시오.

① 축구 ② 풋살

③ 컬링 ④ 아이스하키

⑤ 스피드 스케이팅

15 대화를 듣고, 남자가 할 일로 가장 적절한 것을 고르시오.

① 바닥을 청소한다.

② 유리창을 닦는다.

③ 로그아웃한다.

④ 쓰레기를 버린다.

⑤ 와이파이를 끈다.

16 대화를 듣고, 여자가 구입할 물건을 고르시오.

① 디지털 카메라

② 스마트폰

③ USB 메모리

④ 일반 카메라

⑤ 노트북

17 대화를 듣고, 여자의 마지막 말에 대한 남자의 응답으로 가장 적절한 것을 고르시오.

Man: _____

① How can I help you?

② You should have secured the door.

③ Just give me your name and address.

④ Turn it to another channel.

⑤ Don't worry. It's more common than you think.

18 대화를 듣고, 남자의 마지막 말에 대한 여자의 응답으로 가장 적절한 것을 고르시오.

Woman: _____

① You should have called 911.

② Don't take it so seriously.

③ Let's go and see a new model.

④ Be more careful from now on.

⑤ I'm glad you came back home.

19 대화를 듣고, 여자의 마지막 말에 대한 남자의 응답으로 가장 적절한 것을 고르시오.

Man: _____

① My family often eats out at a Vietnamese restaurant.

② Great! Vietnam is famous for its rice noodles.

③ Have you ever been to Vietnam?

④ I'm glad you're having a good time.

⑤ That's a good idea. Let's go there someday.

20 다음 상황 설명을 듣고, 하나가 주호에게 할 말로 가장 적절한 것을 고르시오.

Hana: _____

① It's been a long time.

② Excuse me, but do I know you?

③ Nice meeting you again, Juho.

④ Say hello to your Mom and Dad.

⑤ I'm sorry, but I should call the police.

Listen and Check

정답 및 해설 *p.074*

대화를 다시 듣고, 알맞은 것을 고르시오.

1 The woman wanted to buy a round-shaped alarm clock.
☐ True ☐ False

2 Did the teacher ask the woman to do a group project with Ted?
☐ Yes ☐ No

3 The woman and the man think that they are lost.
☐ True ☐ False

4 How many times has the woman been to the ballpark?
☐ never ☐ two times

5 What made Charlie Chaplin earn a living for himself?
☐ his talent ☐ his disease

6 Does the man feel cold now?
☐ Yes ☐ No

7 Does the man have an electric fan?
☐ Yes ☐ No

8 Does the woman have Coke in her fridge?
☐ Yes ☐ No

9 The woman's temperature is about 40 degrees.
☐ True ☐ False

10 Does the woman ask the man to pick up a table?
☐ Yes ☐ No

11 The man is keeping all of the windows closed.
☐ True ☐ False

12 The festival only promotes the beauty of Korean traditional dance.
☐ True ☐ False

13 What is the man's resolution?
☐ to speak Chinese fluently
☐ to take a Chinese course

14 This game is played by a total of 12 players.
☐ True ☐ False

15 The man's mother will help him take out the garbage.
☐ True ☐ False

16 Does the woman want to back up her photos?
☐ Yes ☐ No

17 Nothing is missing in the woman's house.
☐ True ☐ False

18 Did the man get in a fight with his friend?
☐ Yes ☐ No

19 The man is staying in Vietnam now.
☐ True ☐ False

20 Hana doesn't know who Juho is.
☐ True ☐ False

그림 정보 파악

1 대화를 듣고, 여자가 구입할 시계를 고르시오.

① ② ③ ④ ⑤

1

W Dad, it's so hard to wake up early in the morning. I need something to _____ _____ _____ _____.

M That's the reason why we are here. Look around and choose _____ _____ _____ _____.

W I want something loud to wake me up. How about this one?

M The round-faced one with two bells on top? _____ _____ _____ _____ _____?

W No. I mean the square one with the red and blue light on top. I think it makes the same sound as a police car.

M Maybe it will make you wake up by thinking _____ _____ _____ _____. Let's go with that one.

목적 파악

2 대화를 듣고, 남자가 여자에게 전화한 목적으로 가장 적절한 것을 고르시오.

① 약속 시간을 정하기 위해서
② 소미의 노트북을 빌리기 위해서
③ Jason의 병문안을 함께 가기 위해서
④ 과제에 대한 아이디어를 얻기 위해서
⑤ 함께 과제를 할 것을 제안하기 위해서

♥ **What's up?**
: 상대방의 의도를 묻거나 안부를 물을 때 사용하는 표현으로, '무슨 일이야?', '어떻게 지내?'라는 뜻이다. 안부를 묻는 경우의 표현은 다음과 같다.
= How are you?
= How is it going?
= How have you been?

2

[*Cellphone rings.*]

M Hello, Somi.

W Hi, Chris. ♥What's up?

M Have you found a partner for the group project? Have you _____ _____ _____?

W Jason and I were _____ _____ _____ it together, but the teacher asked him to do it with Ted. So I am looking for a new partner now.

M Really? What about me? I have some _____ _____ for the project. Would you like to work together with me?

W Okay, I can do that. When shall we meet?

M You have to strike when the _____ _____ _____. How about this evening? Oh, don't forget to bring your laptop.

W Okay, I won't. See you later.

그림 상황 파악

3 다음 그림의 상황에 가장 적절한 대화를 고르시오.

① ② ③ ④ ⑤

3

① M It's _____ _____ _____ for a walk.
   W You can say that again.
② M Can I help you?
   W Sure. I need the _____ _____ _____ for this city.
③ M Watch out! You were almost hit by that car.
   W Whew! The driver _____ _____ _____ _____.
④ M Let's go hiking tomorrow.
   W Cool. _____ _____ _____.
⑤ M I guess we are lost.
   W Don't worry. We can ask somebody _____ _____.

4 대화를 듣고, 여자가 친구를 만날 시간
을 고르시오.

① 5:50
② 6:00
③ 6:10
④ 6:20
⑤ 6:30

4

W You are a big fan of baseball, _____ _____?

M Of course, I am. Oh, I have two tickets to the game tomorrow. Do you want to go with me?

W Really? That sounds great. In fact, I _____ _____ _____ _____ the ballpark. Will it be fun?

M Oh, I'm sure you will like it.

W What time shall we meet there?

M The game starts at 6:30. How about meeting at 6:00 at _____ _____ _____?

W I'm sorry, but I _____ _____ _____ at 6:00. My piano lesson finishes at 6:00. It will probably take me 20 minutes to get to the ballpark.

M Then let's meet 10 minutes before the game starts.

W Okay. See you then.

5 다음을 듣고, Charles Chaplin에 대
해 언급되지 <u>않은</u> 것을 고르시오.

① 태어난 날짜와 고향
② 부모님의 직업
③ 데뷔 연도
④ 첫 영화 계약 연도
⑤ 데뷔 영화 제목

5

W The famous comedian and actor Charles Spencer Chaplin was born in London, England, on April 16, 1889. His father was a vocalist and actor, and his mother was _____ _____ _____ and singer in the light opera field. The early death of his father and the illness of his mother _____ _____ _____ for Charlie to earn a living for himself. When he was about twelve, he got his first chance to act in a stage show. Charlie _____ _____ _____ as a comedian when he went to the United States in 1910. In the fall of 1912, Chaplin was offered a _____ _____ _____.

6 대화를 듣고, 두 사람의 관계로 가장 적
절한 것을 고르시오.

① 승무원 ― 기장
② 환자 ― 의사
③ 승객 ― 승무원
④ 손님 ― 호텔 직원
⑤ 환자 ― 간호사

6

M Excuse me, but someone _____ _____ _____. I found it _____ _____ _____ next to my seat.

W Thank you. I'll find out _____ _____ _____ _____.

M Okay. Oh, can I have an extra blanket?

W Yes, of course. Do you feel uncomfortable?

M Not now, but when I got airsick in the past, I _____ _____ _____ a little cold.

W Okay, I'll bring one for you right away.

M Thank you for your kindness.

어색한 대화 찾기

7 대화를 듣고, 두 사람의 대화가 <u>어색한</u> 것을 고르시오.

① ② ③ ④ ⑤

7

① **W** How often does the hotel bus come?
  M You _____ _____ _____ every 30 minutes.

② **W** I bought this electric fan, but it doesn't work.
  M You can work _____ _____ _____.

③ **W** What do you want to know about Korea?
  M I'm very _____ _____ _____.

④ **W** What's the best way to _____ _____ _____ in this city?
  M Most tourists like taking the city bus tour.

⑤ **W** How far do you live from here?
  M About _____ _____ _____ by car.

부탁한 일 파악

8 대화를 듣고, 여자가 남자에게 부탁한 일로 가장 적절한 것을 고르시오.

① 일부를 포장해 줄 것
② 음료수를 두 잔으로 변경할 것
③ 불고기 샌드위치를 추가해 줄 것
④ 가능한 한 빨리 준비해 줄 것
⑤ 콜라 두 잔을 취소해 줄 것

8

M Good afternoon, miss. What do you want to have?
W Hello. I'd like to have a *bulgogi* sandwich and an apple pie.
M Anything to drink? We have soda, juice, and lemonade.
W Two Cokes, please. Oh, I _____ _____ _____ _____ _____ _____ _____.
M Okay. You ordered a *bulgogi* sandwich, an apple pie, and two Cokes to go. _____ _____ _____ _____ 5 minutes.
W Thank you. Oh, wait. Please cancel the two Cokes. _____ _____ that I have some juice in my fridge.
M All right.

의도 파악

9 대화를 듣고, 여자의 마지막 말에 담긴 의도로 가장 적절한 것을 고르시오.

① 격려
② 동의
③ 충고
④ 안심
⑤ 질책

9 🇬🇧

W Dad, I think I have a fever.
M Let me see. Oh, your _____ _____ _____.
W I feel dizzy.
M Let me take your temperature. Hmm... It is almost 40 degrees. You should go to see a doctor now.
W My body is burning from the fever.
M Wait a minute. [*Pause*] Put this ice pack on your forehead _____ _____ _____ _____ _____.
W Thank you, Dad. I'm aching all over.
M Don't worry. I parked the car *in front of the house. Let's go to the hospital right away.
W I'm _____ _____ _____ _____, Dad.

* in front of [인] [프런트] [오브] → [인프런터브]

숫자 정보 파악

10 대화를 듣고, 남자가 지불할 금액을 고르시오.

① $30
② $25
③ $20
④ $18
⑤ $15

10

W Good afternoon. What can I do for you?

M I need five 20-liter standard garbage bags. How much are they?

W They are 3 dollars each. Is that all you need?

M Do you pick up large items that _____ _____ _____ _____?

W Yes, we do.

M How much will it cost to get a table _____ _____ for four people?

W It depends on the size, but it usually costs 10 dollars. Would you like to _____ _____ _____ _____ _____ on the pickup schedule?

M No, thanks. I'm _____ _____ _____ the cost.

W Okay. That's fine. Here are your bags.

M Thank you.

할 일 파악

11 대화를 듣고, 여자가 할 일로 가장 적절한 것을 고르시오.

① 난방기를 끈다.
② 집안 청소를 한다.
③ 환풍기를 켠다.
④ 창문을 연다.
⑤ 가습기를 켠다.

11 🇬🇧

M Jennifer, why are you _____ _____ _____ _____ _____ closed?

W As you know, _____ _____ outside.

M Well, keeping the windows closed makes the indoor air bad.

W To me, that's _____ _____ _____ being cold.

M But think about this... If the indoor air is not fresh, you may get sick or _____ _____! You need to have fresh air.

W All right.

언급 유무 파악

12 다음을 듣고, Seoul Dance Festival과 관련하여 언급되지 않은 것을 고르시오.

① 처음 시작한 해
② 댄스의 종류
③ 참여 단체
④ 올해 개최 기간
⑤ 공연 관람 비용

12

W The Seoul Dance Festival started in 1979 and is a _____ _____ _____ in Korea. It promotes Korean dance, modern dance, ballet, and other creative dance performance genres. The festival _____ _____ _____ _____ _____ weeks, with performances by dance groups from all over Korea and invited arts groups _____ _____ as well as university students majoring in dance and performing arts. This year, the festival _____ _____ _____ in the Sejong Center from October 12 to 31. It will be a good chance for children to enjoy and understand dance performances. Don't miss this opportunity.

13 다음 표를 보면서 대화를 듣고, 남자가 선택할 강좌를 고르시오.

	Subject	Type
①	Chinese	Community Center
②	Japanese	Community Center
③	Chinese	Online
④	Chinese Characters	Online
⑤	Japanese	Online

♥ **I'm thinking of ~**
: 자신의 의도나 현재 고려하고 있는 것을 말하기 위해 쓰는 표현으로, '~에 대해 생각 중이야'라는 뜻이다.

13

W Happy New Year, Eric.

M Happy New Year, Subin. Time really flies.

W It sure does. Do you have _____ _____ this year?

M I want to speak Chinese fluently.

W Don't you _____ _____ _____ _____? You're very interested _____ _____ _____. So do you have any plans to learn Chinese?

M Every journey begins with a single step. I will memorize one Chinese character a day.

W Wow, we have _____ _____ _____. Actually, ♥I'm thinking of taking an online Chinese course. Will you *take it with me?

M Absolutely.

★ take it with me [테이크] [잇] [위드] [미] → [테이킷윗미]

14 다음을 듣고, 무엇에 관한 설명인지 고르시오.

① 축구
② 풋살
③ 컬링
④ 아이스하키
⑤ 스피드 스케이팅

14

M This is a team sport which _____ _____ _____ _____. Six players from each team play at the same time. Players have to _____ _____ _____ _____ a helmet, a mouthpiece, and gloves. This game is played in three 20-minute periods and sometimes goes to overtime if _____ _____ _____ _____. This game is played on an ice rink, and the goalies for both teams must wear facemasks to protect themselves from the rubber puck.

15 대화를 듣고, 남자가 할 일로 가장 적절한 것을 고르시오.

① 바닥을 청소한다.
② 유리창을 닦는다.
③ 로그아웃한다.
④ 쓰레기를 버린다.
⑤ 와이파이를 끈다.

15 🇬🇧

W Honey, you've been playing that mobile game for about 2 hours.

M I started _____ _____ _____ just 10 minutes ago. Let me _____ _____, please.

W No, You said that an hour ago. I'm going to turn off the Wi-Fi.

M Okay! I'm _____ _____. Now what should I do, Mom?

W I'm _____ _____ _____, and your sister is cleaning the windows. You have to take out the garbage.

M All these things? They are too heavy.

W _____ _____ and do what I say.

특정 정보 파악

16 대화를 듣고, 여자가 구입할 물건을 고르시오.

① 디지털 카메라
② 스마트폰
③ USB 메모리
④ 일반 카메라
⑤ 노트북

💙 **by the way**
: '그런데 말이야', '그런데'의 의미로 서로 간의 대화 중에 다른 주제의 이야기를 할 경우 사용하는 표현이다.

16

M   May I help you?
W   Can you show me that digital camera?
M   Here you are. This is the most popular model with YouTubers. It has 128GB of memory and _____ _____ _____ _____ Wi-Fi.
W   Well, it _____ _____ _____ _____.
M   Would you like to see another model?
W   No, thanks. It just _____ _____ _____. Actually, I don't need it. 💙 By the way, I need a memory stick _____ _____ _____ my photos. How much is this one?
M   This memory stick? It's 6 dollars.
W   Okay, I'll take it.

적절한 응답 파악

17 대화를 듣고, 여자의 마지막 말에 대한 남자의 응답으로 가장 적절한 것을 고르시오.

Man: _____
① How can I help you?
② You should have secured the door.
③ Just give me your name and address.
④ Turn it to another channel.
⑤ Don't worry. It's more common than you think.

17

[*Telephone rings.*]
M   Hello. 112 National Police Crime Center.
W   I want to _____ _____ _____.
M   What happened, miss?
W   I think somebody _____ _____ _____ _____ a few hours ago.
M   Was anyone hurt? Or _____ _____ _____?
W   Luckily, nobody was hurt, but my TV, laptop and some _____ _____ _____.
M   I'll send a car there right now.
W   Please hurry. I'm so scared.
M   <u>Just give me your name and address.</u>

적절한 응답 파악

18 대화를 듣고, 남자의 마지막 말에 대한 여자의 응답으로 가장 적절한 것을 고르시오.

Woman: _____
① You should have called 911.
② Don't take it so seriously.
③ Let's go and see a new model.
④ Be more careful from now on.
⑤ I'm glad you came back home.

18 🇬🇧

W   Honey, _____ _____ _____ _____. What happened? Did you get in a fight with your friend?
M   No, I'm not that kind of a boy, Mom. I _____ _____ _____ on the street.
W   How did that happen?
M   I tripped over something when I was walking and watching a movie on my smartphone.
W   Oh, I've told you not to use your smartphone _____ _____.
M   Now I understand why you always tell me that. I'm sorry _____ _____ _____ _____, Mom.
W   <u>Be more careful from now on.</u>

19 대화를 듣고, 여자의 마지막 말에 대한 남자의 응답으로 가장 적절한 것을 고르시오.

Man: _____

① My family often eats out at a Vietnamese restaurant.

② Great! Vietnam is famous for its rice noodles.

③ Have you ever been to Vietnam?

④ I'm glad you're having a good time.

⑤ That's a good idea. Let's go there someday.

19

[*Cellphone rings*.]

M　Hello.

W　Hello, Steve. It's me, Jessy.

M　Jessy? Wow, I was surprised that an _____ _____ _____ _____ _____ my cellphone. Where are you?

W　I'm _____ _____ _____. I'm calling you from Ho Chi Minh City now.

M　Is everything okay?

W　Sure. Right now is _____ _____ _____ _____ _____ to Vietnam.

M　I'm glad you're having a good time.

---

20 다음 상황 설명을 듣고, 하나가 주호에게 할 말로 가장 적절한 것을 고르시오.

Hana: _____

① It's been a long time.

② Excuse me, but do I know you?

③ Nice meeting you again, Juho.

④ Say hello to your Mom and Da.

⑤ I'm sorry, but I should call the police.

20

W　When a boy stops her, Hana is _____ _____ _____ _____. He says hello and that he is really glad to see her again. But Hana _____ _____ who he is. So she _____ _____ _____ _____ _____. He says his name is Juho. Hana _____ _____ _____ _____ _____ _____, but she cannot remember him. Hana doesn't think she has heard his name before. In this situation, what would Hana say to the boy?

Hana　Excuse me, but do I know you?

1 대화를 듣고, 두 사람이 타임캡슐 안에 넣지 <u>않을</u> 물건을 고르시오.

①   ②   ③

④  ⑤ LICENSE

2 대화를 듣고, 여자가 남자에게 전화한 목적으로 가장 적절한 것을 고르시오.
① 카펫을 구매하기 위해서
② 약속 시간을 정하기 위해서
③ 거실의 디자인을 문의하려고
④ 배달 요일을 변경하기 위해서
⑤ 구매한 물건을 확인하기 위해서

3 다음 그림의 상황에 가장 적절한 대화를 고르시오.

①   ②   ③   ④   ⑤

4 대화를 듣고, 두 사람이 만나기로 한 시간을 고르시오.
① 2시   ② 3시   ③ 4시
④ 5시   ⑤ 6시

5 다음을 듣고, French cuisine class에 관해 언급되지 <u>않은</u> 것을 고르시오.
① 요리 재료의 종류   ② 요리 강사 이름
③ 주차 가능 유무   ④ 가져올 준비물
⑤ 강좌의 진행 시간

6 대화를 듣고, 두 사람의 관계로 가장 적절한 것을 고르시오.
① 손님 — 판매원   ② 고객 — 안내원
③ 쇼핑객 — 쇼핑객   ④ 상담사 — 의뢰인
⑤ 디자이너 — 모델

7 다음을 듣고, 두 사람의 대화가 어색한 것을 고르시오.
①   ②   ③   ④   ⑤

8 대화를 듣고, 여자가 남자에게 부탁한 일로 가장 적절한 것을 고르시오.
① 아이스쇼 보러 가기
② 아이스쇼 표 예매하기
③ 사이트를 검색하기
④ 스케이트 구매하기
⑤ 표 가격을 알아보기

9 대화를 듣고, 남자의 마지막 말에 담긴 의도로 가장 적절한 것을 고르시오.
① 감사   ② 거절
③ 격려   ④ 충고
⑤ 실망

10 대화를 듣고, 남자가 지불할 금액을 고르시오.
① $20   ② $30   ③ $34
④ $44   ⑤ $54

11 대화를 듣고, 남자가 할 일로 가장 적절한 것을 고르시오.
① 분실물 검색하기
② 휴대 전화 충전하기
③ 승차권 구매하기
④ 버스 기사에게 전화하기
⑤ 환승 차량을 알아보기

12 다음을 듣고, English class에서 주의할 점에 관해 언급되지 <u>않은</u> 것을 고르시오.
① 시간 엄수　　　　② 수업 준비물
③ 공책의 용도　　　④ 숙제 검사 방법
⑤ 한국어 사용 금지

13 다음 표를 보면서 대화를 듣고, 남자가 구입할 자전거를 고르시오.

	Model	Wheel Size	Type	Price
①	A	22 inches	Foldable	$200
②	B	24 inches	Foldable	$250
③	C	22 inches	Regular	$180
④	D	24 inches	Foldable	$200
⑤	E	22 inches	Regular	$220

14 다음을 듣고, 무엇에 관한 설명인지 고르시오.
① manuals　　　　② video clips
③ illustrations　　④ news articles
⑤ advertisements

15 대화를 듣고, 남자가 할 일로 가장 적절한 것을 고르시오.
① 버린 물건 줍기
② 재활용하기
③ 휴지통 닦기
④ 길거리 청소하기
⑤ 청소 표어 만들기

16 대화를 듣고, 남자가 사무실로 출발할 시각을 고르시오.
① 2시　　　　　② 2시 30분
③ 2시 40분　　　④ 2시 50분
⑤ 3시

17 대화를 듣고, 남자의 마지막 말에 대한 여자의 응답으로 가장 적절한 것을 고르시오.
Woman: _____
① It's very kind of you to say that.
② I'm not satisfied with your opinion.
③ Great idea. Saturday is fine with me.
④ Actually, I don't like department stores.
⑤ Then I'll meet you there at the same time on Sunday.

18 대화를 듣고, 여자의 마지막 말에 대한 남자의 응답으로 가장 적절한 것을 고르시오.
Man: _____
① Sorry. It closes at seven o'clock.
② We don't know the driver's name.
③ Hurry up. We are running out of time.
④ How long will it take to get the station?
⑤ Here it is. I hope you get your phone back.

19 대화를 듣고, 남자의 마지막 말에 대한 여자의 응답으로 가장 적절한 것을 고르시오.
Woman: _____
① We don't talk face to face with others much anymore.
② I appreciate you helping me use the phone.
③ It will give us a lot of useful information.
④ I wish the fonts of the messages were bigger.
⑤ I agree with the bad points the cellphone has.

20 다음 상황 설명을 듣고, Gloria가 Alice에게 할 말로 가장 적절한 것을 고르시오.
Gloria: Alice, _____
① good morning. Wish me luck.
② let's prepare for tomorrow's math test.
③ what should I do to do well on the test?
④ wake up! The exam is going to start soon.
⑤ turn off the TV and go to bed.

Listen and Check

● 대화를 다시 듣고, 알맞은 것을 고르시오.

1 The man will put his album in the time capsule.

☐ True   ☐ False

2 When will the woman get the carpet?

☐ Friday   ☐ Saturday

3 Did the man stay with the woman's family during summer?

☐ Yes   ☐ No

4 Will the man and the woman have lunch together?

☐ Yes   ☐ No

5 Students can take a break in the middle of the class.

☐ True   ☐ False

6 Does the man know where the fitting room is?

☐ Yes   ☐ No

7 Does the woman know how the weather will be tomorrow?

☐ Yes   ☐ No

8 The woman will book a ticket.

☐ True   ☐ False

9 Does the woman think she will fail the science exam?

☐ Yes   ☐ No

10 Does the price include the wrapping fee?

☐ Yes   ☐ No

11 The bus driver found the woman's purse on the bus.

☐ True   ☐ False

12 Should students carry their notebooks for homework?

☐ Yes   ☐ No

13 The man will buy the regular type of the bike.

☐ True   ☐ False

14 The goal of advertisements is to sell certain products.

☐ True   ☐ False

15 Does the woman throw her milk carton on the street?

☐ Yes   ☐ No

16 Why does the woman suggest the man go to the office early?

☐ because of the traffic jam

☐ because of the preparations

17 Will the man and the woman meet on Sunday?

☐ Yes   ☐ No

18 What will the woman do after this conversation?

☐ call the taxi company

☐ call the man on the phone

19 The man thinks the cellphone is a convenient device.

☐ True   ☐ False

20 Gloria and Alice studied all night without sleeping.

☐ True   ☐ False

그림 정보 파악

1 대화를 듣고, 두 사람이 타임캡슐 안에 넣지 <u>않을</u> 물건을 고르시오.

① ② ③

④ ⑤

1 🇬🇧

W: I'm so thrilled about the time capsule event!

M: _____ _____ _____. I think it's such a great idea.

W: What items do you want to put into the capsule?

M: Well, I want to put some of _____ _____ _____ in it.

W: Toys? That's interesting. What else?

M: My photos and some money. What about you?

W: I will _____ _____ _____ to the people of the future. I'll _____ _____ _____ _____, too.

M: Why are you going to put it in your album?

W: The people of the future will see my pictures and messages in it.

목적 파악

2 대화를 듣고, 여자가 남자에게 전화한 목적으로 가장 적절한 것을 고르시오.

① 카펫을 구매하기 위해서
② 약속 시간을 정하기 위해서
③ 거실의 디자인을 문의하려고
④ 배달 요일을 변경하기 위해서
⑤ 구매한 물건을 확인하기 위해서

2

[*Telephone rings.*]

M: Hello. Aladin Carpets. How may I help you?

W: Hi. I'm calling _____ _____ _____ _____.

M: May I have your name, please?

W: This is Jennifer Lee. I ordered a green carpet for my living room yesterday.

M: Just a second, please. I'll _____ _____ _____ _____... Oh, here it is. What do you want to change?

W: Can I get the carpet on Friday instead of on Saturday?

M: Okay. You want _____ _____ _____ _____ _____ from Saturday to Friday, right?

W: Exactly.

그림 상황 파악

3 다음 그림의 상황에 가장 적절한 대화를 고르시오.

① ② ③ ④ ⑤

3

① M: I enjoyed _____ _____ _____ and your family this summer.

　 W: I hope you will visit us again sometime soon.

② M: Congratulations on winning the math contest.

　 W: Thank you. I cannot express _____ _____ _____ _____.

③ M: The train for Gwangju has been delayed, ma'am.

　 W: How long _____ _____ _____ _____?

④ M: I'd like to make a reservation. Do you have any rooms available?

　 W: Yes, _____ _____ _____ _____ a double room.

⑤ M: How much is this big pink bag?

　 W: It's one hundred dollars. You are planning _____ _____ _____, right?

숫자 정보 파악

4 대화를 듣고, 두 사람이 만나기로 한 시간을 고르시오.

① 2시
② 3시
③ 4시
④ 5시
⑤ 6시

4

W Peter, what are you going to do this weekend?

M I'm going to _____ _____ _____ at the national museum this Sunday. Do you want to join me?

W Sounds good. What time shall we meet?

M Let's meet at 1:00 p.m. and have lunch together.

W Oh, I'm sorry, but I am having lunch _____ _____ _____.

M That's okay. Then let's meet after lunch. The museum closes at 6:00 p.m., so how about meeting there _____ _____ _____ _____ _____?

W All right. See you then. And we can have dinner together.

언급 유무 파악

5 다음을 듣고, French cuisine class에 관해 언급되지 않은 것을 고르시오.

① 요리 재료의 종류
② 요리 강사 이름
③ 주차 가능 유무
④ 가져올 준비물
⑤ 강좌의 진행 시간

5

W Hi, everyone. Welcome to French cuisine class. Thank you for joining us for a 6-week course with chef Billy. You _____ _____ _____ _____ of the cooking world. The class will be two hours long _____ _____ _____. If anyone can't attend this morning class, you can attend an afternoon or evening class. We cover the same material in all three classes. _____ _____ _____ _____ _____ in front of the center. Don't forget to bring some containers to take all the lovely French food you cook home with you.

관계 추론

6 대화를 듣고, 두 사람의 관계로 가장 적절한 것을 고르시오.

① 손님 — 판매원
② 고객 — 안내원
③ 쇼핑객 — 쇼핑객
④ 상담사 — 의뢰인
⑤ 디자이너 — 모델

6

M Excuse me. Can I try these *shorts on?

W Well, I don't know. In fact, I'm not a sales clerk. I'm a customer, too.

M Oh, I'm sorry. I just _____ _____ _____ _____ _____.

W Yeah, it looks really busy today. They're probably all helping other customers. I think it's okay for you _____ _____ _____ _____.

M I think so, too. Do you happen to know where the fitting room is?

W Yes, it's over there near that wall.

M Thanks. _____ _____ _____ _____.

W You, too.

* shorts on [숄츠] [언] → [숄천]

7 다음을 듣고, 두 사람의 대화가 어색한 것을 고르시오.

① ② ③ ④ ⑤

7

① M What will the weather be like tomorrow?

W I'm feeling _____ _____ _____ lately.

② M Do you think we should leave a tip?

W Oh, _____ _____ _____ _____.

③ M I'm sorry, ma'am, but can you please _____ _____ _____ of the song?

W It's *The Secret between Us.*

④ M Did you have a good weekend?

W Yes, _____ _____ _____.

⑤ M I'm very sorry. All the tickets for the Saturday show _____ _____ _____.

W No! I really wanted to see it.

8 대화를 듣고, 여자가 남자에게 부탁한 일로 가장 적절한 것을 고르시오.

① 아이스쇼 보러 가기
② 아이스쇼 표 예매하기
③ 사이트를 검색하기
④ 스케이트 구매하기
⑤ 표 가격을 알아보기

💗 **Leave it to me.**
: '나에게 맡겨 줘.'라는 의미로 무슨 일을 해야 하는 경우, 자신이 책임지고 하겠다고 하는 표현이다.
= You can count on me.

8

W The news said there will be an ice show this Saturday.

M I heard that, too. Are you planning to go there?

W I would love to, but tickets are very expensive. They're almost seventy dollars each. I'm not sure _____ _____ _____ _____ _____ _____.

M But it will be _____ _____ _____ _____ _____ Olympic figure skating stars like Yuna Kim.

W Then would you like to see the show together?

M Okay. Let's go there and have a good time.

W Can you _____ _____ _____ for me? I don't know how to do it.

M Sure. 💗Leave it to me.

9 대화를 듣고, 남자의 마지막 말에 담긴 의도로 가장 적절한 것을 고르시오.

① 감사
② 거절
③ 격려
④ 충고
⑤ 실망

9

W I can't believe this. The science exam was really awful.

M What are you talking about? You are _____ _____ _____ _____. Was it really that bad?

W Yes, it was. I think I answered only _____ _____ _____ correctly.

M Really? That's too bad.

W Maybe I will fail the test. _____ _____ _____ _____?

M You don't know that yet. Besides, there's one more exam next month. If you study hard, the results _____ _____ _____ _____.

10 대화를 듣고, 남자가 지불할 금액을 고르시오.

① $20
② $30
③ $34
④ $44
⑤ $54

10 🇬🇧

M Excuse me. I'm shopping for a birthday present for my mother.

W Is there anything you *have in mind?

M These earrings are great. Do you think they are good for my mother's age? She's in her late forties.

W Of course. And _____ _____ _____ _____, so you can get a twenty-percent discount.

M Are you sure? _____ _____ _____ _____.

W The original price is fifty dollars, and since you get twenty percent off, you only have to pay forty dollars.

M Good. Do you _____ _____ _____ _____?

W Yes, that will cost four dollars.

M Okay. Please *wrap it as a gift.

* have in [해브] [인] → [해빈]
* wrap it [뤱] [잇] → [뤠핏]

11 대화를 듣고, 남자가 할 일로 가장 적절한 것을 고르시오.

① 분실물 검색하기
② 휴대 전화 충전하기
③ 승차권 구매하기
④ 버스 기사에게 전화하기
⑤ 환승 차량을 알아보기

11

W Excuse me. Can you help me?

M Of course. What can I do for you?

W I think _____ _____ _____ _____ on the bus from Busan today.

M I am sorry to hear that. What time did your bus arrive here?

W About thirty minutes ago. And my seat number was 09A.

M Wait, please. Well, _____ _____ _____ _____ _____ yet. Maybe the bus driver is around here. I'll call and _____ _____.

W Thank you so much.

12 다음을 듣고, English class에서 주의할 점에 관해 언급되지 <u>않은</u> 것을 고르시오.

① 시간 엄수
② 수업 준비물
③ 공책의 용도
④ 숙제 검사 방법
⑤ 한국어 사용 금지

12

M Hello, everyone. I'm very happy to meet you for English class. I'm Ryan, your English teacher. Since today is _____ _____ _____ _____ _____, I want to explain a few important things to keep. First, you should always carry your textbook and a notebook. The notebook is _____ _____ _____. Second, be on time at all times. If any of you are late, we can't start the lesson together. Third, don't speak Korean in class. _____ _____ _____ _____ _____ is my primary job. Thanks for listening, and if you follow the rules I just gave you, we'll have the best class ever.

표 파악

13 다음 표를 보면서 대화를 듣고, 남자가 구입할 자전거를 고르시오.

	Model	Wheel Size	Type	Price
①	A	22 inches	Foldable	$200
②	B	24 inches	Foldable	$250
③	C	22 inches	Regular	$180
④	D	24 inches	Foldable	$200
⑤	E	22 inches	Regular	$220

13

M   Hi. I'm looking for a bicycle for my 10-year-old daughter.

W   Okay. For that age group, a twenty-two or twenty-four-inch wheel _____ _____ _____.

M   She's tall for her age, so a twenty-four-inch wheel will be better.

W   Which type do you want, a foldable or regular one?

M   I'd prefer a foldable one since _____ _____ _____ _____ _____ _____. How much is this foldable one?

W   It is 250 dollars, including tax.

M   It looks good, but it is a little costly. Do you have anything cheaper?

W   _____ _____ _____, you'll love this one.

M   Good. I'll take it.

화제·주제 파악

14 다음을 듣고, 무엇에 관한 설명인지 고르시오.

① manuals
② video clips
③ illustrations
④ news articles
⑤ advertisements

14 🇬🇧

W   They are designed to catch your eye when you watch TV or read newspapers and magazines. Sometimes they *pop up _____ _____ _____ _____ _____ _____. They tell you that a certain product is great. Their goal is to _____ _____ _____ _____ _____ the product. If you believe what they are saying, you will want to buy the product. However, they don't always tell the truth about the product they're selling, so you should be careful _____ _____ _____ about it.

★ pop up [팝] [업] → [파펍]

할 일 파악

15 대화를 듣고, 남자가 할 일로 가장 적절한 것을 고르시오.
① 버린 물건 줍기
② 재활용하기
③ 휴지통 닦기
④ 길거리 청소하기
⑤ 청소 표어 만들기

15

W   I'm very disappointed with you, Bob.

M   Why? _____ _____ _____ _____ _____?

W   Yes. I can't believe I saw you throw your milk carton on the street.

M   Oh, don't worry about that. Somebody will clean the street later.

W   _____ _____ _____ _____ _____? That's a really bad attitude. We should always keep our streets clean.

M   I see, Kate. Don't be so angry. I'll *pick it up and put it _____ _____ _____ _____.

★ pick it up [픽] [잇] [업] → [피키럽]

숫자 정보 파악

16 대화를 듣고, 남자가 사무실로 출발할
시각을 고르시오.

① 2시   ② 2시 30분

③ 2시 40분   ④ 2시 50분

⑤ 3시

> ♥ **Best of luck.**
> : 상대방에게 행운을 빌어줄 때 사용하는 표
> 현이다.
> = Wish you best luck.
> = I will keep my fingers crossed.
> = Break a leg.

16 🇬🇧

M   Claire, I'm so nervous. I have an important meeting at three o'clock.

W   I remember _____ _____ _____ _____ yesterday.
Are you done preparing for it? You only have twenty minutes left.

M   Yes, I am. It takes ten minutes to get to the office. I don't think
_____ _____ _____ _____.

W   But you could get stuck in a traffic jam at this time. Why don't you
_____ _____ _____ _____?

M   Yeah, you're right. I'll leave now then.

W   ♥ Best of luck, Sam!

적절한 응답 찾기

17 대화를 듣고, 남자의 마지막 말에 대한
여자의 응답으로 가장 적절한 것을 고
르시오.

Woman: _____

① It's very kind of you to say
that.

② I'm not satisfied with your
opinion.

③ Great idea. Saturday is fine
with me.

④ Actually, I don't like
department stores.

⑤ Then I'll meet you there at the
same time on Sunday.

17

W   Chris, _____ _____ _____ _____ _____
_____ this Sunday? Do you have any plans?

M   Yes, I'm going shopping with my sister.

W   Oh, really? Where?

M   Perhaps we will go to the new department store.

W   _____ _____ _____ _____? I have to buy a
present for my father. Can you help me find something nice for him?

M   Of course! What time _____ _____ _____? My sister
and I will go to the department store together at noon.

W   Then I'll meet you there at the same time on Sunday.

적절한 응답 찾기

18 대화를 듣고, 여자의 마지막 말에 대한
남자의 응답으로 가장 적절한 것을 고
르시오.

Man: _____

① Sorry. It closes at seven
o'clock.

② We don't know the driver's
name.

③ Hurry up. We are running out
of time.

④ How long will it take to get the
station?

⑤ Here it is. I hope you get your
phone back.

18

M   What are you looking for?

W   Oh, no! I think I left my phone _____ _____ _____.

M   Oh, that's terrible. Shall I call your number with my phone? Somebody
may answer the phone.

W   It would be of no use. It's probably off. I remember _____
_____ _____ _____.

M   Do you remember the taxi company?

W   Luckily, I remember it. Can I use your cellphone? I think I should call
the taxi company and _____ _____ _____ _____
_____ _____.

M   Here it is. I hope you get your phone back.

적절한 응답 찾기

19 대화를 듣고, 남자의 마지막 말에 대한 여자의 응답으로 가장 적절한 것을 고르시오.

Woman: _____

① We don't talk face to face with others much anymore.

② I appreciate you helping me use the phone.

③ It will give us a lot of useful information.

④ I wish the fonts of the messages were bigger.

⑤ I agree with the bad points the cellphone has.

19 🇬🇧

W   Can you _____ _____ _____ _____?

M   No way. It's very useful in my life. I can't live without one _____ _____ _____ _____.

W   Would you explain why it is so useful?

M   As you know, it _____ _____ _____ _____ such as sending messages, surfing the Internet, and taking photos and videos.

W   I know that it's a convenient device. But _____ _____ _____ _____ _____ some bad points.

M   Like what?

W   We don't talk face to face with others much anymore.

상황에 맞는 말 찾기

20 다음 상황 설명을 듣고, Gloria가 Alice에게 할 말로 가장 적절한 것을 고르시오.

Gloria: Alice, _____

① good morning. Wish me luck.

② let's prepare for tomorrow's math test.

③ what should I do to do well on the test?

④ wake up! The exam is going to start soon.

⑤ turn off the TV and go to bed.

20

W   Gloria and Alice are classmates. They _____ _____ _____ _____ _____. They decide to study together at Alice's house. They promise that they will study all night _____ _____ _____ _____. As time passes, however, both of them lie down and fall asleep. When Gloria wakes up, she sees that it's 7:00 a.m. and that _____ _____ _____ _____ _____ _____ _____. In this situation, what would Gloria most likely say to Alice?

Gloria   Alice, wake up! The exam is going to start soon.

1 대화를 듣고, 남자가 의뢰할 포스터를 고르시오.

2 대화를 듣고, 남자가 여자에게 부탁한 일로 가장 적절한 것을 고르시오.
① 해결법 찾기　　　② 시계 선물하기
③ 구멍 뚫어주기　　④ 시곗줄 교체하기
⑤ 팔목 사이즈 재기

3 다음 그림의 상황에 가장 적절한 대화를 고르시오.

①　　②　　③　　④　　⑤

4 대화를 듣고, 남자가 문자를 부탁한 시각을 고르시오.
① 3:00　　　② 3:30　　　③ 4:00
④ 4:30　　　⑤ 5:00

5 대화를 듣고, 리조트에 관해 언급되지 <u>않은</u> 것을 고르시오.
① 오픈한 달　　　② 객실 가격
③ 리조트 위치　　④ 리조트 시설
⑤ 웹사이트 주소

6 대화를 듣고, 두 사람이 대화하는 장소로 가장 적절한 곳을 고르시오.
① 병원　　　　② 서점　　　　③ 호텔
④ 안경점　　　⑤ 미용실

7 다음을 듣고, 두 사람의 대화가 <u>어색한</u> 것을 고르시오.
①　　②　　③　　④　　⑤

8 대화를 듣고, 여자가 남자에게 부탁한 일로 가장 적절한 것을 고르시오.
① 조언해 주기　　　② 고민 들어주기
③ 문제 해결하기　　④ 맡은 일 끝내기
⑤ 팀 멤버 정하기

9 다음을 듣고, 무엇에 관한 설명인지 고르시오.
① 좋은 결정의 정의　　② 많은 정보의 이점
③ 광고가 미치는 영향　④ 여러 가지 광고 유형
⑤ 집중력을 향상시키는 법

10 대화를 듣고, 남자가 지불할 금액을 고르시오.
① $5　　　　② $10　　　　③ $20
④ $32　　　⑤ $40

11 대화를 듣고, 여자가 할 일로 가장 적절한 것을 고르시오.
① 여행담 나누기　　② 지도 찾아보기
③ 안내원 찾아가기　④ 표지판 따라가기
⑤ 블로그 찾아보기

12 다음을 듣고, 학습 프로그램에 관해 언급되지 <u>않은</u> 것을 고르시오.

① 학습 프로그램 과목
② 학습 프로그램의 수
③ 프로그램 주최 회사명
④ 프로그램 진행자 명단
⑤ 프로그램 참여 신청 방법

13 다음 표를 보면서 대화를 듣고, 두 사람이 선택할 반 티셔츠를 고르시오.

	Types	Sleeves	Colors	Letters
①	Type A	Short Sleeves	Blue	Classroom Number (O)
②	Type B	Short Sleeves	Yellow	Classroom Number (X)
③	Type C	Long Sleeves	Yellow	Classroom Number (X)
④	Type D	Long Sleeves	Blue	Classroom Number (O)
⑤	Type E	Long Sleeves	Yellow	Classroom Number (O)

14 다음을 듣고, 무엇에 관한 설명인지 고르시오.

① 공책   ② 신문   ③ 동화책
④ 장난감   ⑤ 교과서

15 대화를 듣고, 남자가 대화 직후에 할 일로 가장 적절한 것을 고르시오.

① 시장에 가기   ② 정원 가꾸기
③ 딸과 대화하기   ④ 식물에 물 주기
⑤ 식물 구입하기

16 대화를 듣고, 남자가 출발할 시각을 고르시오.

① 1:00   ② 1:20   ③ 1:40
④ 2:00   ⑤ 2:20

17 대화를 듣고, 여자의 마지막 말에 대한 남자의 응답으로 가장 적절한 것을 고르시오.

Man: _____

① It was when I visited here the last time.
② It's good that I can get a full refund.
③ Okay. I'll call you back when I set the date.
④ I heard this hotel provides the best service.
⑤ I would rather take a shuttle bus.

18 대화를 듣고, 남자의 마지막 말에 대한 여자의 응답으로 가장 적절한 것을 고르시오.

Woman: _____

① There's nothing wrong with watching TV.
② I think your idea sounds better than mine.
③ I know it's not easy to keep your promises.
④ You can take a walk or read books together.
⑤ We can easily find a solution to that problem.

19 대화를 듣고, 여자의 마지막 말에 대한 남자의 응답으로 가장 적절한 것을 고르시오.

Man: _____

① What's the use of becoming a leader?
② Never mind. Everything will go smoothly.
③ Sure. Let me know what I can do for you.
④ I couldn't make a decision at that moment.
⑤ You should keep your place clean all the time.

20 다음 상황 설명을 듣고, Joshua가 Vivian에게 할 말로 가장 적절한 것을 고르시오.

Joshua: Vivian, _____

① studying here is so comfortable.
② do you mind closing the window?
③ I don't understand some questions.
④ let's turn on the light. It's too dark.
⑤ why don't we have a snack now?

Listen and Check

정답 및 해설 *p.084*

● 대화를 다시 듣고, 알맞은 것을 고르시오.

1 Where will the picture of the pet be positioned on the poster?

☐ on the left side   ☐ on the right side

2 The man's wrists were thinner when he bought the watch.

☐ True   ☐ False

3 Does the man allow the child to ride the roller coaster?

☐ Yes   ☐ No

4 How will the woman give a signal to the man for the party?

☐ by making a call   ☐ by sending a message

5 The woman recommends the new water park to the man for a family trip.

☐ True   ☐ False

6 Did the woman come to have her hair cut?

☐ Yes   ☐ No

7 The man is good at writing essays.

☐ True   ☐ False

8 Why is the woman angry about her team member?

☐ Her performance is poor.
☐ She has an irresponsible attitude.

9 When does the man think advertisements affect people?

☐ when focusing on work
☐ when making decisions

10 Can the man get fifty percent off with his credit card?

☐ Yes   ☐ No

11 The woman doubts information from blogs.

☐ True   ☐ False

12 What is the main activity of the program?

☐ science experiments
☐ student discussions

13 Will the man and the woman put their names on the T-shirts?

☐ Yes   ☐ No

14 Only children can read this kind of book.

☐ True   ☐ False

15 What does the man often forget to do?

☐ garden   ☐ water plants

16 The man already took his driver's license exam.

☐ True   ☐ False

17 It is possible to get a full refund when making a cancelation one week before the date of a reservation.

☐ True   ☐ False

18 What does the woman suggest that the man do with his children?

☐ watch TV   ☐ read books

19 The man is willing to help the woman if she asks him to help her.

☐ True   ☐ False

20 What is keeping Joshua from focusing on his studies?

☐ the noise from outside
☐ the view from the window

그림 정보 파악

1 대화를 듣고, 남자가 의뢰할 포스터를 고르시오.

1

W Good afternoon. What can I help you with?

M I'd like to _____ _____ _____ to find my lost cat.

W The basic layout of the poster for that is that we place a picture on the left side and _____ _____ _____ on the right side.

M All right. Please write my phone number at _____ _____ _____ the poster. It's 888-1234.

W Okay. Anything else to add?

M I think it would be better to _____ _____.

W I got it. You can _____ _____ _____ _____ by five o'clock.

부탁한 일 파악

2 대화를 듣고, 남자가 여자에게 부탁한 일로 가장 적절한 것을 고르시오.

① 해결법 찾기
② 시계 선물하기
③ 구멍 뚫어주기
④ 시곗줄 교체하기
⑤ 팔목 사이즈 재기

2 🇬🇧

W It's been a while since you _____ _____ _____.

M You're right. But I have a problem.

W What is it?

M I guess my wrists have gotten _____ _____ _____. It's actually very tight for me to wear.

W Then you can _____ _____ _____ in the watchstrap.

M Could you do that for me? I'm terrible at doing things like that.

W Sure. It's not _____ _____ _____ you think.

그림 상황 파악

3 다음 그림의 상황에 가장 적절한 대화를 고르시오.

① ② ③ ④ ⑤

3

① W You _____ _____ than the last time I saw you.

   M That's true. I have gotten five centimeters taller.

② W Is it possible for her to ride the roller coaster?

   M Sorry, but those who are below 130cm in height _____ _____ _____ _____ *ride it.

③ W Oh, no. We have to wait _____ _____ _____ _____ again.

   M We shouldn't have come here on a holiday.

④ W Do you have a membership card for the amusement park?

   M Yes, I do. We only have to _____ _____ _____.

⑤ W I heard it is _____ _____ _____ in the world.

   M That makes me want to ride it more.

★ ride it [라이드] [잇] → [라이딧]

4 대화를 듣고, 남자가 문자를 부탁한 시각을 고르시오.

① 3:00
② 3:30
③ 4:00
④ 4:30
⑤ 5:00

4

W Did you _____ _____ for the surprise party?

M Of course, I did. Stella said she _____ _____ _____ at 4:00.

W Everything _____ _____ _____ by that time.

M You're picking her up soon, right? Please send me a message _____ _____ before you guys arrive here.

W Okay.

M _____ _____ the surprise party to her.

---

5 대화를 듣고, 리조트에 관해 언급되지 **않은** 것을 고르시오.

① 오픈한 달
② 객실 가격
③ 리조트 위치
④ 리조트 시설
⑤ 웹사이트 주소

5

W Do you know that a new ski resort _____ _____ _____?

M Really? Where is the resort?

W It's in Gangwon-do. There are _____ _____ _____ and a water park, too.

M The resort must be huge. How's the water park?

W It's _____ _____ _____. There are many rides for children.

M It sounds nice. Does the resort have _____ _____ _____?

W Yes, it does. It's www.skyresorts.com.

---

6 대화를 듣고, 두 사람이 대화하는 장소로 가장 적절한 곳을 고르시오.

① 병원
② 서점
③ 호텔
④ 안경점
⑤ 미용실

♥ **Long time no see.**
: 상대방을 오랜만에 만났을 때 사용하는 표현으로, '오랜만이야.'라는 뜻이다.
= It's been a while.
= It's been a long time.
= I haven't seen you for ages.

6

M Hi, Ms. Lee. ♥Long time, no see!

W Yeah. I have been _____ _____ these days. Is Jack _____ _____?

M He's talking with one of his clients now. You can stay in the waiting room.

W Okay.

[Pause]

M How would you like to _____ _____ _____ _____?

W I want to dye my hair a bright color.

M I see. I *recommend you _____ _____ _____ light brown. It will look good on you.

W That color could be _____ _____ _____. Thanks.

★ recommend you [레코멘드] [유] → [레코멘쥬]

어색한 대화 찾기

7 다음을 듣고, 두 사람의 대화가 <u>어색한</u> 것을 고르시오.

① ② ③ ④ ⑤

7

① M You're talented at _____ _____.

W That's what my father used to teach me.

② M You did a great job! _____ _____ in your work.

W Thank you for the compliment.

③ M Do you _____ _____ _____ over there?

W I'm not sure. Who is she?

④ M What's _____ _____ as a mother?

W It's raising my child to be independent.

⑤ M I'm having difficulty _____ _____ _____.

W I really appreciate your help.

부탁한 일 파악

8 대화를 듣고, 여자가 남자에게 부탁한 일로 가장 적절한 것을 고르시오.

① 조언해 주기
② 고민 들어주기
③ 문제 해결하기
④ 맡은 일 끝내기
⑤ 팀 멤버 정하기

8 🇬🇧

M Jessica, what's the matter? You look upset.

W I _____ _____ _____ with one of my team members.

M What's the reason?

W She wasn't _____ _____ _____ her responsibilities, so I complained to her.

M Did she _____ _____ _____?

W Not at all.

M So how do you want to _____ _____ _____?

W Could you give me some advice on it?

M You'd better talk with her _____ _____.

화제·주제 파악

9 다음을 듣고, 무엇에 관한 설명인지 고르시오.

① 좋은 결정의 정의
② 많은 정보의 이점
③ 광고가 미치는 영향
④ 여러 가지 광고 유형
⑤ 집중력을 향상시키는 법

9

M _____ _____ _____ do you think we are exposed to every day? I'll explain how it influences our behavior. The type of information I _____ _____ _____ _____ is advertisements. We don't recognize it, but we see *hundreds of ads a day. What matters is they affect us when we _____ _____ on food, books, jobs, and so on. We should develop the ability to distinguish _____ _____ _____ from ones that are formed by ads. When you have to make an important decision, _____ _____ _____ you come up with.

★ hundreds of [헌드레즈] [오브] → [헌드레저브]

숫자 정보 파악

10 대화를 듣고, 남자가 지불할 금액을 고르시오.

① $5
② $10
③ $20
④ $32
⑤ $40

10

M I'd like to _____ _____ _____ for the movie *Toy Story 4* starting at 4:00.

W For an adult, it's ten dollars per ticket.

M Okay. Is there _____ _____ _____ where two people can sit together?

W Yes, there is. You have to buy two tickets, and each ticket is twice as expensive as a regular one.

M I'd like two tickets for adults for a couple seat. I heard I can get fifty percent off when I pay with _____ _____ _____.

W Sorry, but we only offer _____ _____ _____ for that card.

M I see. Here is the card.

할 일 파악

11 대화를 듣고, 여자가 할 일로 가장 적절한 것을 고르시오.

① 여행담 나누기
② 지도 찾아보기
③ 안내원 찾아가기
④ 표지판 따라가기
⑤ 블로그 찾아보기

💜 **That's a good idea.**
: 상대방의 말에 대한 동의를 나타낼 때 사용하는 표현으로, '좋은 생각이야.'라는 뜻이다.
= Sounds great.
= That sounds good.

11

W I think we can _____ _____ _____ _____.

M Wait a second. I wrote down how to get there in my notebook.

W The road sign says we can turn left and walk for about ten minutes until we _____ _____ _____ _____.

M Well, I guess turning right is right. My notebook says so.

W Where did you get that information?

M I got it from a traveler's blog, where he shares _____ _____ _____.

W Let's not depend on what he wrote on his blog. Let's ask someone at an information center to make sure we _____ _____ _____.

M 💜That's a good idea.

언급 유무 파악

12 다음을 듣고, 학습 프로그램에 관해 언급되지 <u>않은</u> 것을 고르시오.

① 학습 프로그램 과목
② 학습 프로그램의 수
③ 프로그램 주최 회사명
④ 프로그램 진행자 명단
⑤ 프로그램 참여 신청 방법

12 🇬🇧

W Hello. I'm _____ _____ _____ at the company Thinking Up. Let me introduce some programs for _____ _____ _____. First of all, four programs, including history, arts, literature, and science, will be held. _____ _____ _____ will be a student discussion. Each of the programs will _____ _____ from Monday to Friday at 10:00 a.m. and 2:00 p.m. for six weeks. You can _____ _____ here at the company or on the website.

표 파악

13 다음 표를 보면서 대화를 듣고, 두 사람이 선택할 반 티셔츠를 고르시오.

	Types	Sleeves	Color	Letter
①	Type A	Short Sleeves	Blue	Classroom Number (O)
②	Type B	Short Sleeves	Yellow	Classroom Number (X)
③	Type C	Long Sleeves	Yellow	Classroom Number (X)
④	Type D	Long Sleeves	Blue	Classroom Number (O)
⑤	Type E	Long Sleeves	Yellow	Classroom Number (O)

13

M What are we going to do about the T-shirts for our class? Here are _____ _____ _____ _____ _____.

W Let me see. Considering the chilly weather, it would be better if we got _____ _____.

M I agree with you. What about the color? How about yellow?

W I heard that another class already has yellow T-shirts. So we should _____ _____ _____.

M That's totally fine. Blue is the color of victory.

W Do you think we should put _____ _____ on the T-shirts?

M No, I don't think so. Just _____ _____ _____ will do.

화제·주제 파악

14 다음을 듣고, 무엇에 관한 설명인지 고르시오.

① 공책
② 신문
③ 동화책
④ 장난감
⑤ 교과서

14

W It is a kind of book which is _____ _____ for children. They can _____ _____ _____ and learn important life lessons through this. It sometimes *tells about the _____ _____ _____ of different countries. In addition, parents read it to their children before they _____ _____ _____. We can _____ _____ _____ only for this in bookstores.

* tells about [텔쓰] [어바웃] → [텔써바웃]

할 일 파악

15 대화를 듣고, 남자가 대화 직후에 할 일로 가장 적절한 것을 고르시오.

① 시장에 가기
② 정원 가꾸기
③ 딸과 대화하기
④ 식물에 물 주기
⑤ 식물 구입하기

♥ **What is the date?**
: 오늘의 날짜를 물어볼 때 사용하는 표현으로, '오늘이 며칠이지?'라는 뜻이다.
= What date is it today?
= What is today's date?

15

W Dad, we have _____ _____ _____ that our house seems like a small garden.

M Is that so?

W And look at those plants in the living room. They are no longer _____ _____ _____.

M Oh, no. ♥What is the date? I guess it's already been more than two weeks since I _____ _____. I need to do that now.

W Dad, let's only have as many plants as we can _____ _____ _____ _____.

M Okay. I'll have to water them more often _____ _____ _____.

숫자 정보 파악

16 대화를 듣고, 남자가 출발할 시각을 고르시오.

① 1:00
② 1:20
③ 1:40
④ 2:00
⑤ 2:20

16

W Is it today that you are taking _____ _____ _____ _____?

M Yes, it is. The test starts at the center at 2:00 p.m.

W It's already 1:00 p.m. Don't you _____ _____ _____ now?

M Four people take the exam one by one, which means I have to _____ _____ _____ _____ for quite a long time.

W Then when are you going to leave?

M I'll _____ _____ _____ before the exam starts.

W Make sure you don't miss it.

적절한 응답 찾기

17 대화를 듣고, 여자의 마지막 말에 대한 남자의 응답으로 가장 적절한 것을 고르시오.

Man: _____

① It was when I visited here the last time.
② It's good that I can get a full refund.
③ Okay. I'll call you back when I set the date.
④ I heard this hotel provides the best service.
⑤ I would rather take a shuttle bus.

17

[*Telephone rings.*]

W Hello. This is Healing Resort. What can I help you with?

M Hi. It's Nathan Park. I'd like to _____ _____ _____.

W Hello, Mr. Park. Did you check the refund policy before you _____ _____ _____?

M What is the policy?

W You can _____ _____ _____ _____ only when you make a cancelation one month before the date of your reservation.

M How about just _____ _____ _____ to another one?

W That's possible if there are rooms available.

M Okay. I'll call you back when I set the date.

적절한 응답 찾기

18 대화를 듣고, 남자의 마지막 말에 대한 여자의 응답으로 가장 적절한 것을 고르시오.

Woman: _____

① There's nothing wrong with watching TV.
② I think your idea sounds better than mine.
③ I know it's not easy to keep your promises.
④ You can take a walk or read books together.
⑤ We can easily find a solution to that problem.

18 🇬🇧

M I'm concerned that my children _____ _____ _____ _____.

W _____ _____ do they usually watch it?

M Around two hours a day.

W That _____ _____ _____. What kinds of TV programs do they watch?

M They watch entertainment shows and dramas.

W How about _____ _____ _____ with them?

M What activities do you think will be _____ _____ _____ at the same time?

W You can take a walk or read books together.

적절한 응답 찾기

19 대화를 듣고, 여자의 마지막 말에 대한 남자의 응답으로 가장 적절한 것을 고르시오.

Man: _____

① What's the use of becoming a leader?
② Never mind. Everything will go smoothly.
③ Sure. Let me know what I can do for you.
④ I couldn't make a decision at that moment.
⑤ You should keep your place clean all the time.

19

W   Minhyeok, _____ _____ _____ your part?

M   I'm finalizing it now. What about you?

W   I just started because there was _____ _____ I had to do first.

M   You don't have enough time. You've only got _____ _____ _____.

W   I know. I should have started much earlier.

M   _____ _____ _____ you need my help.

W   Then could you _____ _____ _____ _____ after you're done with your work?

M   <u>Sure. Let me know what I can do for you.</u>

상황에 맞는 말 찾기

20 다음 상황 설명을 듣고, Joshua가 Vivian에게 할 말로 가장 적절한 것을 고르시오.

Joshua: Vivian, _____

① studying here is so comfortable.
② do you mind closing the window?
③ I don't understand some questions.
④ let's turn on the light. It's too dark.
⑤ why don't we have a snack now?

20

M   Joshua and Vivian go to Vivian's house to _____ _____ _____ together. When they get to the house, they start to do their work. Soon, they hear _____ _____ _____ right outside the window. Joshua notices that there is some _____ _____ _____ beside where they are studying. He _____ _____ _____ his studies and is sitting far from the window. He sees Vivian sitting close to _____ _____ _____. In this situation, what would Joshua most likely say to Vivian?

Joshua   <u>Vivian, do you mind closing the window?</u>

1 대화를 듣고, 여자가 만든 명함을 고르시오.

    ③

    ⑤

2 대화를 듣고, 남자가 여자에게 부탁한 일로 가장 적절한 것을 고르시오.
① 꽃다발 사 주기
② 준비물 가지고 오기
③ 부케 만드는 법 알려 주기
④ 결혼식 날 축가 불러 주기
⑤ 저녁을 위해 식료품 쇼핑하기

3 다음 그림의 상황에 가장 적절한 대화를 고르시오.

① ② ③ ④ ⑤

4 대화를 듣고, 여자가 수영 강습에 참여하게 될 요일을 고르시오.
① 월요일 ② 화요일 ③ 수요일
④ 목요일 ⑤ 금요일

5 대화를 듣고, 인턴십에 관해 언급되지 않은 것을 고르시오.
① 일하는 기간 ② 받게 될 월급
③ 일하게 될 분야 ④ 총 모집 인원
⑤ 지원 가능한 자격

6 대화를 듣고, 두 사람이 대화하는 장소로 가장 적절한 곳을 고르시오.
① 학교 ② 박물관 ③ 동물원
④ 영화관 ⑤ 동물병원

7 다음을 듣고, 두 사람의 대화가 어색한 것을 고르시오.
① ② ③ ④ ⑤

8 대화를 듣고, 여자가 남자에게 부탁한 일로 가장 적절한 것을 고르시오.
① 편지지 사 오기 ② 우편물 찾아오기
③ 부모님께 편지 쓰기 ④ 집에 일찍 들어오기
⑤ 축구 경기에서 이기기

9 다음을 듣고, 무엇에 관한 안내 방송인지 고르시오.
① 계단 보수 공사
② 에스컬레이터 안전 점검
③ 올바른 자세의 중요성
④ 하반기 직원 채용 안내
⑤ 지하철 이용 시 주의 사항

10 대화를 듣고, 남자가 지불할 금액을 고르시오.
① $10 ② $15 ③ $20
④ $25 ⑤ $30

11 대화를 듣고, 여자가 할 일로 가장 적절한 것을 고르시오.
① 학교 가기 ② 책 정돈하기
③ 옷 정리하기 ④ 아침 식사 하기
⑤ 영어 에세이 쓰기

12 다음을 듣고, 청학동 여름 예절 학교에 관해 언급되지 않은 것을 고르시오.

① 참가 비용
② 예절 교육 기간
③ 숙식 제공 여부
④ 담당 강사 연락처
⑤ 참여 가능한 나이

13 대화를 듣고, 두 사람이 묵게 될 호텔을 고르시오.

14 다음을 듣고, 무엇에 관한 설명인지 고르시오.

① 산불을 예방하는 법
② 생태계와 산불의 관계
③ 산불의 긍정적인 효과
④ 산불이 발생하는 이유
⑤ 불을 끄는 다양한 방법

15 대화를 듣고, 남자가 대화 직후에 할 일로 가장 적절한 것을 고르시오.

① 종이컵 버리기
② 머그컵 구입하기
③ 책상 정리정돈 하기
④ 구입한 물건 교환하기
⑤ 재활용품 분리수거 하기

16 대화를 듣고, 여자가 건강 검진을 받기로 한 날짜를 고르시오.

① 4월 5일
② 4월 6일
③ 4월 7일
④ 4월 8일
⑤ 4월 9일

17 대화를 듣고, 남자의 마지막 말에 대한 여자의 응답으로 가장 적절한 것을 고르시오.

Woman: _____

① You need to respect my decision.
② Stop delaying what you should do.
③ Just relax and have a great vacation.
④ It is the biggest aquarium in Europe.
⑤ Okay. I'll prepare some healthy snacks.

18 대화를 듣고, 여자의 마지막 말에 대한 남자의 응답으로 가장 적절한 것을 고르시오.

Man: _____

① Look! I can blow bubbles with gum.
② You should go home and get some rest.
③ I'll ask my mom how to remove it.
④ Let's go to buy some new sneakers.
⑤ Brush your teeth after eating sweets.

19 대화를 듣고, 남자의 마지막 말에 대한 여자의 응답으로 가장 적절한 것을 고르시오.

Woman: _____

① Let me give the leftovers to the dog.
② My sister is a good cook. Help yourself.
③ My grandmother. She's good at organizing.
④ I need more water. This food is very spicy.
⑤ Our teacher will tell us what to do tomorrow.

20 다음 상황 설명을 듣고, Marcus가 자동차 주인에게 할 말로 가장 적절한 것을 고르시오.

Marcus: Hello. _____

① I'm sorry, but your car is damaged.
② What time does the next train arrive?
③ I'd like to know what you bought here.
④ Do you mind moving your car so I can get out?
⑤ Can you tell me where you had your car repaired?

Listen and Check

정답 및 해설 p.089

● 대화를 다시 듣고, 알맞은 것을 고르시오.

1 What is the name of the woman's café?
☐ Corner ☐ Pause

2 The man's sister is getting married.
☐ True ☐ False

3 Did the woman break her leg while surfing on the sea?
☐ Yes ☐ No

4 What does the man study on Fridays?
☐ Chinese ☐ French

5 How much can the man make in a month if he gets the job?
☐ 500 dollars ☐ 700 dollars

6 The lions were hunting small animals.
☐ True ☐ False

7 The man wanted something to eat.
☐ True ☐ False

8 Did the man know that tomorrow is his mother's birthday?
☐ Yes ☐ No

9 How long will it take to complete the inspection?
☐ one week ☐ two weeks

10 How many jars of strawberry jam did the man buy?
☐ two ☐ three

11 Sujin hasn't finished her homework yet.
☐ True ☐ False

12 Can a 12-year-old child attend summer school?
☐ Yes ☐ No

13 The man and the woman's flight includes free meals.
☐ True ☐ False

14 Are forest fires good for ecosystems?
☐ Yes ☐ No

15 Disposable products are bad for the environment.
☐ True ☐ False

16 Did the woman cancel her appointment for her annual physical checkup?
☐ Yes ☐ No

17 Ms. Hanson teaches Brian the cello.
☐ True ☐ False

18 When did Jenny buy the sandals?
☐ 3 days ago ☐ 5 days ago

19 What are the memos attached to the fridge door?
☐ to-do lists ☐ lists of food items

20 Where is Marcus now?
☐ at a repair shop ☐ in a parking lot

정답 및 해설 *p.084*

그림 정보 파악

1 대화를 듣고, 여자가 만든 명함을 고르시오.

① ② ③

④ ⑤

1

M Did you design your business card yourself?

W That's right. At the center, I drew a coffee cup. Three tiny hearts are _____ _____ _____.

M I also see one chocolate muffin to the right of the cup.

W Yes. The coffee cup and the muffin show that this business card is for a café.

M _____ _____ _____ _____ _____ your café?

W I put the name of the café, Pause, in the upper *left corner.

M I really love _____ _____ _____ _____.

★ left corner [레프트] [코너] → [레프코너]

부탁한 일 파악

2 대화를 듣고, 남자가 여자에게 부탁한 일로 가장 적절한 것을 고르시오.

① 꽃다발 사 주기
② 준비물 가지고 오기
③ 부케 만드는 법 알려 주기
④ 결혼식 날 축가 불러 주기
⑤ 저녁을 위해 식료품 쇼핑하기

2

W Why are you _____ _____ _____ _____ _____?

M I'm thinking of making a bouquet for my sister's wedding.

W Wow. You must be a wonderful brother.

M So can you _____ _____ _____ _____ _____ a wedding bouquet?

W My pleasure. Do you have _____ _____ _____?

M Only flowers.

W Please give some scissors, wrapping paper, and ribbons to me.

그림 상황 파악

3 다음 그림의 상황에 가장 적절한 대화를 고르시오.

① ② ③ ④ ⑤

♥ **lucky for me, ~**
: 뜻밖에 일이 잘 되는 경우에 쓰는 표현으로, '운 좋게도', '다행히도'라는 뜻이다.
= fortunately, ~
= by a lucky chance, ~

3 🇬🇧

① W What do you like to do for fun?
   M _____ _____ _____.
② W I heard that you _____ _____ _____ _____.
   M Right. ♥Lucky for me, I was not hurt seriously.
③ W Let's _____ _____ _____ _____.
   M Okay. Please let me know when you want to go.
④ W How long do you need to _____ _____ _____ on your arm?
   M I'm not sure, but maybe for a month.
⑤ W _____ _____ to your leg?
   M I broke it while skateboarding.

4 대화를 듣고, 여자가 수영 강습에 참여하게 될 요일을 고르시오.

① 월요일
② 화요일
③ 수요일
④ 목요일
⑤ 금요일

4

W Look at this brochure. We can _____ _____ this summer.

M That's a great idea. Which class would you like to take?

W What do you *think about _____ _____ _____ together?

M Sounds good.

W There are two swimming classes _____ _____ _____. They are on Tuesday and Friday.

M I have to study Chinese every Friday. How about _____ _____ _____ _____ _____?

W Sure.

* think about [띵크] [어바웃] → [띵커바웃]

5 대화를 듣고, 인턴십에 관해 언급되지 <u>않은</u> 것을 고르시오.

① 일하는 기간
② 받게 될 월급
③ 일하게 될 분야
④ 총 모집 인원
⑤ 지원 가능한 자격

5

W Gold Bank is offering a _____ _____ internship.

M Great! Gold Bank has 50,000 employees.

W If you get the job, you will make 700 dollars a month.

M That's _____ _____ _____ _____ _____.

W You can also _____ _____ _____ in investments.

M What are the qualifications?

W _____ _____ _____ from high school can apply.

M Well, I should apply for it.

6 대화를 듣고, 두 사람이 대화하는 장소로 가장 적절한 곳을 고르시오.

① 학교
② 박물관
③ 동물원
④ 영화관
⑤ 동물병원

♥ **I feel exactly the same way.**
: 상대방과 같은 의견, 감정을 가지고 있다고 말할 때 쓰는 표현으로, '나도 똑같이 느껴.' 라는 뜻이다.
= Same here.

6

W _____ _____ _____ _____ over there. They are so big but look so sad.

M ♥I feel exactly the same way. Maybe they're sad because they have _____ _____ _____.

W Look at the lions. They are _____ _____ _____ and seem to sleep all day.

M Do you think it's okay to keep wild animals here just for our pleasure?

W I don't think so. They're confined to such small spaces.

M We should _____ _____ _____ to their natural habitats.

어색한 대화 찾기

7 다음을 듣고, 두 사람의 대화가 <u>어색한</u> 것을 고르시오.

① ② ③ ④ ⑤

7

① **M** Do you need a hand with that?

W Yes, please. These books are _____ _____ for me _____ _____.

② **M** Make sure you're not late for the meeting.

W Don't worry. I'll _____ _____ _____ _____.

③ **M** Can I borrow your bicycle? I lost mine.

W Sure, but I _____ _____ _____ by this Friday.

④ **M** Do you want to _____ _____ _____ to eat?

W Let's take a walk rather than get a taxi.

⑤ **M** How many people _____ _____ _____ to your housewarming party?

W About 15.

부탁한 일 파악

8 대화를 듣고, 여자가 남자에게 부탁한 일로 가장 적절한 것을 고르시오.

① 편지지 사 오기
② 우편물 찾아오기
③ 부모님께 편지 쓰기
④ 집에 일찍 들어오기
⑤ 축구 경기에서 이기기

8

[*Cellphone rings.*]

M Hey, Bella. What's up?

W Where are you? Are you on your way home?

M Not yet. I'm _____ _____ _____ _____ on the school playground.

W Then can you _____ _____ _____ _____ _____ on your way home?

M No problem. What do you need?

W I need _____ _____ _____ because tomorrow is Mom's birthday.

M Oh, no! I completely forgot about it.

화제·주제 파악

9 다음을 듣고, 무엇에 관한 안내 방송인지 고르시오.

① 계단 보수 공사
② 에스컬레이터 안전 점검
③ 올바른 자세의 중요성
④ 하반기 직원 채용 안내
⑤ 지하철 이용 시 주의 사항

9 🇬🇧

W Good morning, passengers. As we informed you earlier, today we're going to check the escalators located in Anyang Station. It will _____ _____ _____ _____ _____. If needed, the escalators can be _____ _____ _____ _____. During the inspection, please _____ _____ _____. There will also be extra staff members to assist passengers. We apologize for the inconvenience. Thank you for your cooperation!

숫자 정보 파악

10 대화를 듣고, 남자가 지불할 금액을 고르시오.

① $10
② $15
③ $20
④ $25
⑤ $30

10

W   Welcome to Sweet Bakery. What can I _____ _____ _____ ?

M   Hi. Is this strawberry jam homemade? How much is it?

W   Right. My grandmother and I made all of the products at home. The strawberry jam is 5 dollars _____ _____ _____ _____ .

M   Hmm... How much are these butter cookies?

W   They cost 10 dollars per dozen.

M   Then I'll take a dozen of the cookies and two jars of strawberry jam.

W   Okay. I'll _____ _____ _____ _____ _____ _____ .

할 일 파악

11 대화를 듣고, 여자가 할 일로 가장 적절한 것을 고르시오.

① 학교 가기
② 책 정돈하기
③ 옷 정리하기
④ 아침 식사 하기
⑤ 영어 에세이 쓰기

11

M   Sujin, your room is messy. Why are your clothes _____ _____ _____ _____ ?

W   Dad, I got up so late that I had to go to school in a hurry.

M   It's not just today. Look at your desk. Many books are _____ _____ _____ _____ .

W   All right. Can I *clean it up tomorrow? I have to finish my English essay.

M   Sorry, but you have to _____ _____ _____ on the bed first.

W   Okay. After that, I'll do my homework.

★ **clean it up** [클린] [잇] [업] → [클리니럽]

언급 유무 파악

12 다음을 듣고, 청학동 여름 예절 학교에 관해 언급되지 <u>않은</u> 것을 고르시오.

① 참가 비용
② 예절 교육 기간
③ 숙식 제공 여부
④ 담당 강사 연락처
⑤ 참여 가능한 나이

12

M   Cheonghakdong Etiquette Summer School provides various classes for students _____ _____ _____ _____ . Children can _____ _____ _____ _____ _____ and the Internet and focus on themselves. Cheonghakdong Etiquette Summer School will begin on August 1 and end on August 20. It is for children ages 8 to 12. It costs one thousand dollars, _____ _____ _____ _____ . For more information, please visit www.cheonghakschool.com.

그림 정보 파악

13 대화를 듣고, 두 사람이 묵게 될 호텔을 고르시오.

① Hotel A   Restaurant   Airport
② Hotel B   Bakery
③ Hotel C   Flower Shop
Fruit Shop   ④ Hotel D   Bus Station   Train Station   ⑤ Hotel E
You are here.

💜 **I can't agree with you more.**
: 상대방의 생각이나 의견에 완전히 동의한다고 말할 때 쓰는 표현으로, '완전히 동의해.'라는 뜻이다.
= I'm on your side.
= I totally agree with you.

13

M Sweetie, let's select the hotel where we'll stay on our last night in Canada.

W Our flight to Seoul is scheduled early in the morning.

M Then _____ _____ _____ _____ near the
*bus station is much better.

W 💜 I can't agree with you more. And our flight doesn't include any free meals.

M Let's buy fresh bread at a bakery that morning. How about hotel A?

W I don't think so. It's _____ _____ _____ _____
_____. We'll take a bus to the airport.

M What about the hotel _____ _____ _____ _____
_____ _____? It's near the bus station, too.

W That's perfect. I'll make a reservation.

★ bus station [버스] [스테이션] → [버스테이션]

화제·주제 파악

14 다음을 듣고, 무엇에 관한 설명인지 고르시오.

① 산불을 예방하는 법
② 생태계와 산불의 관계
③ 산불의 긍정적인 효과
④ 산불이 발생하는 이유
⑤ 불을 끄는 다양한 방법

14

W Most wildfires are caused by people. Forest fires destroy many big, old trees and the habitats of animals. They also _____
_____ _____ _____. So what can people do to
_____ _____ _____? Above all, people must be more careful with their actions. Make a fire in the forest only if it is absolutely necessary. Make sure you extinguish your fire before leaving.
_____ _____ _____ _____ _____ or cover
it with soil. In addition, don't smoke in the forest. Don't throw burning matches on the ground either.

할 일 파악

15 대화를 듣고, 남자가 대화 직후에 할 일로 가장 적절한 것을 고르시오.

① 종이컵 버리기
② 머그컵 구입하기
③ 책상 정리정돈 하기
④ 구입한 물건 교환하기
⑤ 재활용품 분리수거 하기

15

W Woojin, are you still _____ _____ _____?

M Yes. After using them, I don't need to wash them.

W But you throw them away after a single use. Disposable products are
_____ _____ _____ _____.

M I see what you mean. The environment is _____ _____
_____ _____.

W So why don't you _____ _____ _____ for the office?

M Good idea! I should buy one now. Can you go with me?

W Sure.

숫자 정보 파악

16 대화를 듣고, 여자가 건강 검진을 받기로 한 날짜를 고르시오.

① 4월 5일
② 4월 6일
③ 4월 7일
④ 4월 8일
⑤ 4월 9일

16 🇬🇧

[*Cellphone rings.*]

W Hello. I need to _____ _____ _____ for my annual physical checkup.

M Sure. Who's calling, please?

W This is Natalie White.

M Let me check the schedule. [*Pause*] All right. When would _____ _____ _____ _____ for you?

W Is April 5 possible?

M I'm afraid that day is _____ _____. How about two days after that?

W On April 7? Well, can you check the next day?

M We _____ _____ _____ then. I'll change your reservation to April 8.

W Thank you.

적절한 응답 찾기

17 대화를 듣고, 남자의 마지막 말에 대한 여자의 응답으로 가장 적절한 것을 고르시오.

Woman: _____
① You need to respect my decision.
② Stop delaying what you should do.
③ Just relax and have a great vacation.
④ It is the biggest aquarium in Europe.
⑤ Okay. I'll prepare some healthy snacks.

17 🇬🇧

M Mom, can I _____ _____ _____ _____ _____ with my friends tomorrow?

W Brian, you have a cello lesson tomorrow.

M No, I don't. Ms. Hanson told me that she is _____ _____ _____ this week.

W Really? Anyway, are you done with your vacation homework?

M Absolutely! So can I go to the aquarium?

W All right. Do you _____ _____ _____ tomorrow?

M No, thanks. I can take the bus. Can you _____ _____ _____ for me?

W <u>Okay. I'll prepare some healthy snacks.</u>

적절한 응답 찾기

18 대화를 듣고, 여자의 마지막 말에 대한 남자의 응답으로 가장 적절한 것을 고르시오.

Man: _____
① Look! I can blow bubbles with gum.
② You should go home and get some rest.
③ I'll ask my mom how to remove it.
④ Let's go to buy some new sneakers.
⑤ Brush your teeth after eating sweets.

18

M Why do you _____ _____ _____ _____ _____?

W On my way here, I _____ _____ _____ _____. Chewing gum is stuck to my shoe.

M Oh, no! I know that irritating feeling.

W The worst part is that I bought these sandals 3 days ago. They are so new.

M Calm down. Let's _____ _____ _____ from your shoe.

W But how? The shoe repair shop is closed today.

M <u>I'll ask my mom how to remove it.</u>

적절한 응답 찾기

19 대화를 듣고, 남자의 마지막 말에 대한 여자의 응답으로 가장 적절한 것을 고르시오.

Woman: _____

① Let me give the leftovers to the dog.

② My sister is a good cook. Help yourself.

③ My grandmother. She's good at organizing.

④ I need more water. This food is very spicy.

⑤ Our teacher will tell us what to do tomorrow.

19

M I'm thirsty. Can I _____ _____ _____?

W Of course. There's some in the fridge.

M [*Pause*] What are these memos _____ _____ _____ _____ _____?

W Ah, they are _____ _____ _____ _____ _____ _____ in the fridge. They remind me of what I have.

M That's a great idea!

W It really is. *With these memos, I can _____ _____ _____.

M Brilliant! Who taught you this?

W My grandmother. She's good at organizing.

★ with these [위드] [디즈] → [윗디즈]

상황에 맞는 말 찾기

20 다음 상황 설명을 듣고, Marcus가 자동차 주인에게 할 말로 가장 적절한 것을 고르시오.

Marcus: Hello. _____

① I'm sorry, but your car is damaged.

② What time does the next train arrive?

③ I'd like to know what you bought here.

④ Do you mind moving your car so I can get out?

⑤ Can you tell me where you had your car repaired?

20

M Marcus goes shopping at a department store. He _____ _____ _____ in the parking lot and buys what he needs. After shopping, he returns to his car to go home. He sees that his car is _____ _____ _____ _____. Someone has double-parked, and there's no one in the car. Marcus _____ _____ _____ of the car owner. He wants to call and _____ _____ _____ _____ _____ the car. In this situation, what would Marcus most likely say to the car owner?

Marcus Hello. Do you mind moving your car so I can get out?

1 대화를 듣고, 여자가 입양할 반려동물을 고르시오.

2 대화를 듣고, 남자가 여자에게 전화한 목적으로 가장 적절한 것을 고르시오.
① 구매한 김치에 대해 항의하기 위해
② 우산의 디자인을 설명하기 위해
③ 자신의 우산을 찾기 위해
④ 가게의 위치를 문의하기 위해
⑤ 직원의 이름을 확인하기 위해

3 다음 그림의 상황에 가장 적절한 대화를 고르시오.

① ② ③ ④ ⑤

4 대화를 듣고, 주문한 물건이 배달될 요일을 고르시오.
① 월요일 ② 화요일
③ 수요일 ④ 목요일
⑤ 금요일

5 다음을 듣고, German Village Festival에 대해 언급되지 <u>않은</u> 것을 고르시오.
① 축제 기간 ② 마을의 유래
③ 처음 시작된 년도 ④ 올해 축제의 내용
⑤ 연간 방문객 수

6 대화를 듣고, 두 사람의 관계로 가장 적절한 것을 고르시오.
① 환자 — 의사 ② 손님 — 수의사
③ 손님 — 건축가 ④ 손님 — 카페 주인
⑤ 행인 — 경찰

7 대화를 듣고, 두 사람의 대화가 <u>어색한</u> 것을 고르시오.
① ② ③ ④ ⑤

8 대화를 듣고, 여자가 남자에게 부탁한 일로 가장 적절한 것을 고르시오.
① 반려동물 치료해 주기
② 반려동물 찾아 주기
③ 반려동물 먹이 사주기
④ 반려동물 돌봐 주기
⑤ 반려동물 분양해 주기

9 대화를 듣고, 남자의 마지막 말에 담긴 의도로 가장 적절한 것을 고르시오.
① 격려 ② 원망
③ 기대 ④ 걱정
⑤ 이해

10 대화를 듣고, 남자가 지불할 금액을 고르시오.
① $5 ② $8
③ $9 ④ $10
⑤ $11

11 대화를 듣고, 여자가 할 일로 가장 적절한 것을 고르시오.
① 멀미약을 먹는다.
② 자동차 창문을 연다.
③ 자동차를 운전한다.
④ 잠시 잠을 잔다.
⑤ 차에서 내려 쉰다.

12 다음을 듣고, Seowon과 관련하여 언급되지 <u>않은</u> 것을 고르시오.

① 전통 서원의 기능
② 14번째 세계 유산
③ 지정된 서원의 개수
④ 건물을 배치한 의도
⑤ 남부 지방 서원의 특징

13 다음 표를 보면서 대화를 듣고, 두 사람이 참여할 수 있는 것을 고르시오.

	Attractions	Duration	Thrill Type
①	Hyperspace Mountain	7 mins	Big Drops, Loud
②	Roller Coaster	5 mins	Big Drops, Thrill Rides
③	Water Quest	5 mins	Small Drops, Thrill Rides
④	Bumper Cars	8 mins	Spinning, Loud
⑤	Jungle Cruise	4 mins	Small Drops, Slow Rides

14 다음을 듣고, 무엇에 관한 설명인지 고르시오.

① 일식   ② 운석   ③ 무지개
④ 블랙홀   ⑤ 유성

15 대화를 듣고, 토요일에 남자가 할 일로 가장 적절한 것을 고르시오.

① 영화를 예매한다.   ② 동생을 돌본다.
③ 친척을 방문한다.   ④ 영화를 보러 간다.
⑤ 동생과 부산에 간다.

16 대화를 듣고, 여자가 구입할 물건을 고르시오.

① 스킨로션   ② 천연 향수   ③ 마스크 팩
④ 선크림   ⑤ 립스틱

17 대화를 듣고, 여자의 마지막 말에 대한 남자의 응답으로 가장 적절한 것을 고르시오.

Man: _____

① No kidding.
② That's so unfair.
③ I doubt I can do it.
④ I know how you feel.
⑤ I feel the same way.

18 대화를 듣고, 남자의 마지막 말에 대한 여자의 응답으로 가장 적절한 것을 고르시오.

Woman: _____

① K-pop has made Korea famous.
② She needs to learn Korean, too.
③ You're always trying to study hard.
④ You have an amazing teacher.
⑤ King Sejong the Great made it.

19 대화를 듣고, 여자의 마지막 말에 대한 남자의 응답으로 가장 적절한 것을 고르시오.

Man: _____

① A little knowledge is a dangerous thing.
② A short break can really help you avoid stress.
③ I had a great time there.
④ It's all my fault.
⑤ Your computer screen needs fixing

20 다음 상황 설명을 듣고, 미나가 웨이터에게 할 말로 가장 적절한 것을 고르시오.

Mina: _____

① Are these today's special?
② How much are these?
③ Excuse me, but can I make an additional order?
④ Could I have another plate?
⑤ Sorry, but these are not what we ordered.

Listen and Check

정답 및 해설 *p.094*

● 대화를 다시 듣고, 알맞은 것을 고르시오.

1 Does the woman like reptiles?

☐ Yes ☐ No

2 What does the man's umbrella look like?

☐ It has yellow stripes and blue stars.
☐ It has blue stripes and yellow stars.

3 The woman violated a traffic regulation.

☐ True ☐ False

4 What has delayed the delivery of the man's laptop?

☐ the heavy rain ☐ the heavy snow

5 Has the festival been held every year to honor German people in Korea?

☐ Yes ☐ No

6 The woman can't get a free refill of her coffee.

☐ True ☐ False

7 Is the man not willing to close the window?

☐ Yes ☐ No

8 The man will take care of the woman's cats during her entire trip.

☐ True ☐ False

9 Beth didn't help the man with his school project.

☐ Yes ☐ No

10 How many times has the man gotten the same service so far?

☐ four times ☐ five times

11 The woman has already opened the windows in the back.

☐ True ☐ False

12 Where are *seowons* located?

☐ near palaces and schools in Seoul
☐ near mountains and water sources

13 The woman doesn't like big drops or thrill rides.

☐ True ☐ False

14 Black holes have strong gravity.

☐ True ☐ False

15 What will the man and the woman likely to do on Sunday?

☐ go to Busan ☐ go to the movies

16 What kinds of cosmetics are effective for dry skin?

☐ lotions ☐ facial masks

17 Brian and Dave were in the same class last year.

☐ True ☐ False

18 What is the topic of the man's presentation for Hangeul Day?

☐ the history of Hangeul
☐ the creators of Hangeul

19 Is the woman good at using a computer?

☐ Yes ☐ No

20 Mina and Julie didn't order *bibimbap* and *bulgogi*.

☐ True ☐ False

그림 정보 파악

1 대화를 듣고, 여자가 입양할 반려동물을 고르시오.

① ② ③ ④ ⑤

💙 **such as ~**
: 앞에 특정한 명사를 가리켜 그 명사의 예를 열거할 경우 사용되며, '~와 같은'의 의미이다.

1 🇬🇧

M Hi. May I help you?

W Hi. I'd like to adopt a pet.

M What kind of pet would you like to have? We have _____ _____ _____ _____.

W Could you recommend one for me?

M Well, how long do you stay at home? If you are a busy worker, I'd recommend a reptile.

W A reptile? Do you mean a snake or lizard?

M Yes. Compared to other pets 💙such as dogs and cats, _____ _____ _____ _____ _____. And they don't make any noise.

W I see. But I don't like _____ _____.

M Then how about this cat wearing a ribbon around its neck?

W Oh, _____ _____ _____. I'll take it.

목적 파악

2 대화를 듣고, 남자가 여자에게 전화한 목적으로 가장 적절한 것을 고르시오.

① 구매한 김치에 대해 항의하기 위해
② 우산의 디자인을 설명하기 위해
③ 자신의 우산을 찾기 위해
④ 가게의 위치를 문의하기 위해
⑤ 직원의 이름을 확인하기 위해

💙 **Let me ~**
: 원래는 '내가 ~하도록 허락해 줘'의 의미이지만 '내가 ~하겠어', '내가 ~할게'로 사용된다.
= I will ~

2

[*Telephone rings.*]

W Hello. Kim's Korean Food.

M Hello. I just bought some kimchi at your store. I think I _____ _____ _____. Could you please check to see if it is there?

W Hold on, please. [*Pause*] Mister, someone on my staff found an umbrella _____ _____ _____. Is this yours?

M Can you see six stars when you open the umbrella?

W 💙Let me check. [*Pause*] Yes, it _____ _____ _____ _____. It must be yours then.

M Thank you so much. I'll _____ _____ soon.

그림 상황 파악

3 다음 그림의 상황에 가장 적절한 대화를 고르시오.

① ② ③ ④ ⑤

3

① M What a nice car that is!

　W Thanks. It's _____ _____ _____.

② M Excuse me, but _____ _____ a flat tire.

　W Oh, there must have been something sharp on the road.

③ M Watch out! You _____ _____ _____ _____.

　W Don't worry about that. I'm a good driver.

④ M You ran a red light. Can I _____ _____ _____?

　W Oh, I'm sorry. I didn't see a red light anywhere.

⑤ M _____ _____ _____ back here?

　W I want to learn the traffic rules.

4 대화를 듣고, 주문한 물건이 배달될 요일을 고르시오.

① 월요일
② 화요일
③ 수요일
④ 목요일
⑤ 금요일

♥ **I see.**
: '알겠어.'라는 의미로 상대방의 이야기를 이해했을 때 사용하는 표현이다.
= I understand.

4

[*Telephone rings.*]

M Hello. This is the Neo Computer Mall. What can I do for you?

W Hello. I ordered a laptop last Sunday. It's already Thursday, but I _____ _____ _____ _____.

M Oh, I'm sorry about that. Our delivery service _____ _____ _____ due to the road problems caused by the heavy snow.

W Oh, ♥I see. Then how long will I have to wait?

M Under normal conditions, we offer the speedy delivery within 3 days, but in this case, it will take two more days. It _____ _____ _____ _____ tomorrow.

W Okay. I'll wait.

5 다음을 듣고, German Village Festival에 대해 언급되지 <u>않은</u> 것을 고르시오.

① 축제 기간
② 마을의 유래
③ 처음 시작된 년도
④ 올해 축제의 내용
⑤ 연간 방문객 수

5

W The annual German Village Festival will run this year from October 6 to 8. The German Village was built for Koreans who worked _____ _____ _____ _____ in Germany in the 1960s and returned home to settle down. The festival, launched for the first time in 2010, is now in _____ _____ _____. Every year, visitors can look forward to _____ _____ _____ _____ _____ beer and snacks. This year, visitors can enjoy traditional German performances, concerts, and parties in the evening. The German Village Festival is a unique event where visitors can experience German culture.

6 대화를 듣고, 두 사람의 관계로 가장 적절한 것을 고르시오.

① 환자 — 의사
② 손님 — 수의사
③ 손님 — 건축가
④ 손님 — 카페 주인
⑤ 행인 — 경찰

6 🇬🇧

W Excuse me.

M Yes. What can I do for you?

W I wonder where I can wash my hands.

M There is a restroom _____ _____ _____ _____.

W Thank you. I like the antique atmosphere here, and your coffee was good.

M It's _____ _____ _____ _____ to say that. Is there anything you want?

W Can I get a _____ _____ _____ my coffee?

M Sure. I'd be glad to do that.

어색한 대화 찾기

7 대화를 듣고, 두 사람의 대화가 <u>어색한</u> 것을 고르시오.

① ② ③ ④ ⑤

♥ **Do you mind if I ~?**

: 상대방에게 허락을 구할 때 쓰는 표현으로, '~하면 신경 쓰이니?'라는 뜻이다.

= May/Can I ~?

= Is it all right if I ~?

7

① W Do you know how to make curry and rice?

   M Of course. _____ _____ _____ _____
_____ .

② W Do you expect me to apologize?

   M Yes. It was you who _____ _____ _____ .

③ W ♥Do you mind if I _____ _____ _____ ?

   M Of course, I do. You can do as you like.

④ W _____ _____ _____ I can pass the test.

   M Keep your chin up! I'm sure you can do it.

⑤ W Can I _____ _____ _____ on this jacket?

   M Is there something wrong with it?

부탁한 일 파악

8 대화를 듣고, 여자가 남자에게 부탁한 일로 가장 적절한 것을 고르시오.

① 반려동물 치료해 주기
② 반려동물 찾아 주기
③ 반려동물 먹이 사주기
④ 반려동물 돌봐 주기
⑤ 반려동물 분양해 주기

♥ **No problem.**

: 상대방이 감사한 마음을 표시할 때, 그에 대한 답변으로 괜찮다는 마음을 나타낼 때 사용하는 표현으로, '괜찮아요.', '별 말씀을 요.'라는 뜻이다.

= Don't mention it.

= No worries.

8

M Janet, are you _____ _____ _____ your trip to Paris?

W Yes, but I'm worried about one thing.

M What is it? Tell me.

W You know that I have two cats at home.

M Oh, do you want me to *take care of them?

W Actually, one of my neighbors will _____ _____ _____ , but he said he can only do that for 2 days.

M And you need someone that _____ _____ _____ for the rest of your trip, right?

W Yes. Can you do that for me?

M ♥No problem. _____ _____ _____ _____ ?

        * take care of them [테이크] [케어] [오브] [뎀] → [테익케어럽뎀]

의도 파악

9 대화를 듣고, 남자의 마지막 말에 담긴 의도로 가장 적절한 것을 고르시오.

① 격려
② 원망
③ 기대
④ 걱정
⑤ 이해

♥ **What happened?**

: 실망스럽거나 좋지 않은 상황에 대해서 구체적으로 물어볼 때 쓰는 표현으로, '무슨 일이니?'라는 뜻이다.

= What's wrong?

= What is the matter (with you)?

---

9 🇬🇧

M I don't understand why Beth _____ _____ _____ to me.

W ♥What happened?

M I asked her to help me with my school project, but she said no and commented that I should _____ _____ of myself. How could she say that to me?

W Well, Jake, you know that she didn't _____ _____ _____ _____ . I think she said that for your own sake.

M I know, but she didn't need to talk like that!

W If it were not an individual task, she _____ _____ _____ _____ .

M I didn't mind it at first, but she went too far.

10 대화를 듣고, 남자가 지불할 금액을 고르시오.

① $5
② $8
③ $9
④ $10
⑤ $11

10

W Hello. This is the ABC Car Insurance Service Center. What can I do for you?

M Hello. I _____ _____ _____. I left the key in my car and locked myself out.

W You want us to _____ _____ to open your car, right?

M Yes.

W Let me check your location through the GPS on your smartphone. Hold on, please. [*Pause*] Thank you for waiting. We'll send our staff to you at once.

M That's great. I'll stay here. Thanks. How much is it?

W We usually charge 10 dollars for this service. Isn't this _____ _____ _____ _____?

M Yes, that's right.

W In this case, you have to pay _____ _____ _____ of 10%.

11 대화를 듣고, 여자가 할 일로 가장 적절한 것을 고르시오.

① 멀미약을 먹는다.
② 자동차 창문을 연다.
③ 자동차를 운전한다.
④ 잠시 잠을 잔다.
⑤ 차에서 내려 쉰다.

11

W How long will it take to _____ _____ _____ _____?

M We're almost there. What's up? You look uncomfortable.

W I feel dizzy. Maybe I _____ _____ _____.

M Open the window and _____ _____ _____ _____.

W Can't you see that I already have the window wide open?

M I mean that I'll open the windows in the back, too.

W Oh, I see. I'm _____ _____ _____ because I feel bad.

M It's okay. Do you want to *get out of the car for a while?

W Yes, please. I'll be fine after I get some rest.

* get out of [겟] [아웃] [오브] →[게라롭]

12 다음을 듣고, *Seowon*과 관련하여 언급되지 <u>않은</u> 것을 고르시오.

① 전통 서원의 역할
② 14번째 세계 유산
③ 지정된 서원의 개수
④ 건물을 배치한 의도
⑤ 남부 지방 서원의 특징

12

W Korean traditional academies known as *seowon* _____ _____ _____ _____ South Korea's 14th World Heritage site designated by UNESCO. This site, located in the central and southern parts of Korea, consists of nine *seowons,* representing the Confucian academies of the Joseon Dynasty. Situated near mountains and water sources, they favoured _____ _____ _____ _____ and the cultivation of the mind and the body. So the buildings were _____ _____ _____ _____ _____ with the surrounding landscape. The *seowon* illustrates an historical process in which Confucianism was adapted to Korean conditions.

13

13 다음 표를 보면서 대화를 듣고, 두 사람이 참여할 수 있는 것을 고르시오.

	Attractions	Dura-tion	Thrill Type
①	Hyperspace Mountain	7 mins	Big Drops, Loud
②	Roller Coaster	5 mins	Big Drops, Thrill Rides
③	Water Quest	5 mins	Small Drops, Thrill Rides
④	Bumper Cars	8 mins	Spinning, Loud
⑤	Jungle Cruise	4 mins	Small Drops, Slow Rides

W What do you want to do next?

M I can't do anything now. Let's get some rest _____ _____ _____.

W No way. We don't have _____ _____ _____. Come on. Let's go on the roller coaster.

M The roller coaster? I don't like big drops or _____ _____.

W Then how about the jungle cruise? It is much gentler and shorter than a roller coaster.

M But isn't it just for kids? I don't think _____ _____ _____ _____ _____.

W No, not really. It is popular with everyone on this hot day.

M Okay. Let's go on it.

14

14 다음을 듣고, 무엇에 관한 설명인지 고르시오.

① 일식
② 운석
③ 무지개
④ 블랙홀
⑤ 유성

W These are some of _____ _____ _____ and powerful forces in the universe. These are places where gravity has become so strong that _____ _____ _____ can escape, not even light. These are _____ _____. We can't actually see them because they don't reflect light. But scientists know that they exist _____ _____ _____ _____ _____ around them.

15

15 대화를 듣고, 토요일에 남자가 할 일로 가장 적절한 것을 고르시오.

① 영화를 예매한다.
② 동생을 돌본다.
③ 친척을 방문한다.
④ 영화를 보러 간다.
⑤ 동생과 부산에 간다.

W Do you have _____ _____ _____ for this weekend?

M I have to take care of my brothers because my parents are going to visit our relatives in Busan. How about you? Do you have something in mind?

W Um... I was thinking of going to the movies with you, but _____ _____ _____ you have other things to do.

M Wait! They _____ _____ _____ _____ on Sunday morning. After that, I'll have some time to spend with you.

W Great. Then _____ _____ _____ 2:00 this Sunday afternoon.

M Okay. I can't wait.

특정 정보 파악

16 대화를 듣고, 여자가 구입할 물건을 고르시오.

① 스킨 로션
② 천연 향수
③ 마스크 팩
④ 선크림
⑤ 립스틱

16 🇬🇧

M   May I help you?

W   _____ _____ _____ _____ some information about these cosmetics.

M   Okay. This lotion _____ _____ _____, which are especially good for dry skin. This facial mask helps you keep your skin moisturized and healthy.

W   How about this one?

M   Oh, this sunscreen _____ _____ _____ _____ of your skin caused by UV rays.

W   So how often should I use it?

M   You _____ _____ _____ every 2 to 3 hours on a sunny day.

W   Okay, give me this one.

적절한 응답 찾기

17 대화를 듣고, 여자의 마지막 말에 대한 남자의 응답으로 가장 적절한 것을 고르시오.

Man: _____
① No kidding.
② That's so unfair.
③ I doubt I can do it.
④ I know how you feel.
⑤ I feel the same way.

17

W   Hey, Brian. How was the first day of the new semester?

M   It was okay. _____ _____ _____ a new friend. He said _____ _____ _____ _____ _____ last year.

W   Really? *I was in Class B last year. What is his name?

M   Dave. Dave Jordan.

W   The boy who lives on 17th Street?

M   Maybe. There is _____ _____ _____ in my class.

W   Oh, he's kind and fun. You are lucky to have a nice friend.

M   I feel the same way.

* I was in [아이] [워즈] [인] → [아이워진]

적절한 응답 찾기

18 대화를 듣고, 남자의 마지막 말에 대한 여자의 응답으로 가장 적절한 것을 고르시오.

Woman: _____
① K-pop has made Korea famous.
② She needs to learn Korean, too.
③ You're always trying to study hard.
④ You have an amazing teacher.
⑤ King Sejong the Great made it.

18

W   What are you planning to do for this coming Hangeul Day event?

M   Some of my classmates and I are going to _____ _____ _____ on the history of Hangeul.

W   Sounds great! Who came up with the idea?

M   My English teacher suggested it, and _____ _____ _____ _____.

W   What? Your English teacher? Not a Korean teacher?

M   Yes. She is not Korean, but _____ _____ _____ _____ _____ _____ Hangeul.

W   You have an amazing teacher.

적절한 응답 찾기

19 대화를 듣고, 여자의 마지막 말에 대한 남자의 응답으로 가장 적절한 것을 고르시오.

Man: _____

① A little knowledge is a dangerous thing.
② A short break can really help you avoid stress.
③ I had a great time there.
④ It's all my fault.
⑤ Your computer screen needs fixing.

19

M What are you doing?

W I'm making a UCC video.

M Wow, I didn't know _____ _____ _____ _____ a computer.

W Not really. It is just my homework. I really don't want to do _____ _____ _____ homework.

M When will you be finished *with it?

W I'm not sure. I might work _____ _____ _____ _____.

M Come on. You need to refresh yourself. Let's take a walk.

W _____ _____ _____ _____. I have to finish this by tomorrow morning.

M A short break can really help you avoid stress.

* with it [위드] [잇] → [위딧]

상황에 맞는 말 찾기

20 다음 상황 설명을 듣고, 미나가 웨이터에게 할 말로 가장 적절한 것을 고르시오.

Mina: _____

① Are these today's special?
② How much are these?
③ Excuse me, but can I make an additional order?
④ Could I have another plate?
⑤ Sorry, but these are not what we ordered.

20

W Mina and Julie want to eat out after a _____ _____ _____. Mina and Julie go into a Korean restaurant. They decide _____ _____ _____ _____ _____, and Mina orders. _____ _____ _____ _____, the waiter brings some *bibimbap* and *bulgogi* to them. But they are not what Mina and Julie wanted, so Mina _____ _____ _____. In this situation, what would Mina say to the waiter?

Mina Sorry, but these are not what we ordered.

1 대화를 듣고, 두 사람이 만든 눈사람을 고르시오.

2 대화를 듣고, 여자가 남자에게 전화한 목적으로 가장 적절한 것을 고르시오.
① 방을 청소하라고
② 책상을 수리하라고
③ 건전지를 구입하라고
④ 집에 서둘러서 오라고
⑤ 시간에 맞춰 일어나라고

3 다음 그림의 상황에 가장 적절한 대화를 고르시오.

①   ②   ③   ④   ⑤

4 대화를 듣고, 두 사람이 만나기로 한 요일을 고르시오.
① 수요일   ② 목요일   ③ 금요일
④ 토요일   ⑤ 일요일

5 다음을 듣고, 전기차 Handy에 관해 언급되지 않은 것을 고르시오.
① 구입 가격
② 탑승 가능 인원
③ 정부 보조금 안내
④ 제조 회사 및 국가
⑤ 충전 후 주행 가능 거리

6 대화를 듣고, 두 사람의 관계로 가장 적절한 것을 고르시오.
① 학부모 — 교사   ② 경찰관 — 목격자
③ 문하생 — 화가   ④ 수학자 — 학생
⑤ 운동선수 — 코치

7 다음을 듣고, 두 사람의 대화가 어색한 것을 고르시오.
①   ②   ③   ④   ⑤

8 대화를 듣고, 여자가 남자에게 부탁한 일로 가장 적절한 것을 고르시오.
① 할인 쿠폰을 달라고
② 신발을 수선해 달라고
③ 재고를 확인해 달라고
④ 전화번호를 알려 달라고
⑤ 습득한 휴대 전화를 돌려달라고

9 대화를 듣고, 남자의 마지막 말에 담긴 의도로 가장 적절한 것을 고르시오.
① 위로   ② 안도   ③ 후회
④ 감사   ⑤ 조언

10 대화를 듣고, 여자가 지불할 금액을 고르시오.
① $ 40   ② $ 50   ③ $ 60
④ $ 65   ⑤ $ 75

11 대화를 듣고, 남자가 할 일로 가장 적절한 것을 고르시오.
① 배낭 구입하기
② 은행에서 환전하기
③ 여행 일정 계획하기
④ 여권 재발급 신청하기
⑤ 친구에게 강아지 맡기기

12 다음을 듣고, 자연사 박물관에 관해 언급되지 <u>않은</u> 것을 고르시오.

① 참가비   ② 행사 기간
③ 참가 대상   ④ 접수 장소
⑤ 활동 안내

13 다음 표를 보면서 대화를 듣고, 여자가 구입할 뮤지컬 표를 고르시오.

	Title	Day	Time	Price
①	*The Little Prince*	Fri	5 p.m.	$100
②	*Snow White and the Seven Dwarfs*	Fri	8 p.m.	$120
③	*Little Red Riding Hood*	Sat	3 p.m.	$120
④	*The Lion King*	Sat	7 p.m.	$150
⑤	*The Little Prince*	Sun	3 p.m.	$100

14 다음을 듣고, 무엇에 관한 설명인지 고르시오.

① 군함   ② 비행기
③ 잠수함   ④ 유람선
⑤ 전투기

15 대화를 듣고, 남자가 할 일로 가장 적절한 것을 고르시오.

① 병원으로 가기
② 물 자주 마시기
③ 거실 환기시키기
④ 중고 전자 제품 팔기
⑤ 공기 청정기 구입하기

16 대화를 듣고, 엄마가 아들을 깨울 시각을 고르시오.

① 2:00 p.m.   ② 3:00 p.m.
③ 4:00 p.m.   ④ 5:00 p.m.
⑤ 6:00 p.m.

17 대화를 듣고, 남자의 마지막 말에 대한 여자의 응답으로 가장 적절한 것을 고르시오.

Woman: _____

① I had my wisdom teeth taken out.
② Clean your room before going to bed.
③ Knowledge has little to do with wisdom.
④ My parents want me to become a dentist.
⑤ If you don't go, the pain will get worse and worse.

18 대화를 듣고, 여자의 마지막 말에 대한 남자의 응답으로 가장 적절한 것을 고르시오.

Man: _____

① Good idea. I'm sure it'll help you.
② I can fix your problem in ten seconds.
③ Let's go to see a horror movie tomorrow.
④ In my opinion, *Romeo and Juliet* is better.
⑤ I'm going to the playground to play soccer.

19 대화를 듣고, 남자의 마지막 말에 대한 여자의 응답으로 가장 적절한 것을 고르시오.

Woman: _____

① It's helpful to keep a diary in English.
② I'd like to exchange this one for another.
③ Then I should find a native Korean speaker.
④ English is such a difficult language to learn.
⑤ You should memorize new words every day.

20 다음 상황 설명을 듣고, 소영이 은혁에게 할 말로 가장 적절한 것을 고르시오.

Soyoung: Eunhyuk, _____

① I want you to try to be on time.
② we had better head for the airport.
③ you are in charge of taking photos.
④ I wrote an editorial in the class newspaper.
⑤ give a speech about the economy to the class.

Listen and Check

정답 및 해설 p.099

● 대화를 다시 듣고, 알맞은 것을 고르시오.

1 After making a snowman, the man and the woman took a picture with it.
- ☐ True
- ☐ False

2 Who cleaned Ivan's room?
- ☐ Ivan
- ☐ his mother

3 There are so many people in front of the elevator.
- ☐ True
- ☐ False

4 What does the man plan to do on Wednesday?
- ☐ take a piano lesson
- ☐ attend a family gathering

5 How much is the electric car the Handy?
- ☐ 15,000 dollars
- ☐ 25,000 dollars

6 What does Violet want to be?
- ☐ a scientist
- ☐ a mathematician

7 Was the woman late for the meeting today?
- ☐ Yes
- ☐ No

8 The woman found somebody's cellphone in the department store.
- ☐ True
- ☐ False

9 Sewon is wearing contacts now.
- ☐ True
- ☐ False

10 What did the woman want to buy at the store?
- ☐ a Halloween costume
- ☐ a uniform

11 Where is the man going tomorrow?
- ☐ Vietnam
- ☐ Thailand

12 How much is the registration fee for the Dinosaur Discovery Camp?
- ☐ 13 dollars
- ☐ 30 dollars

13 Did the man and the woman decide to see a musical on Sunday?
- ☐ Yes
- ☐ No

14 This is used for military purposes only.
- ☐ True
- ☐ False

15 After the conversation, where will the man go?
- ☐ to a repair shop
- ☐ to an electronics store

16 Does the man have a math test tomorrow?
- ☐ Yes
- ☐ No

17 The man went to the dentist because of his wisdom tooth.
- ☐ True
- ☐ False

18 What part does Abigail play in *Beauty and the Beast*?
- ☐ Belle
- ☐ the Beast

19 What language does Eleanor learn these days?
- ☐ Korean
- ☐ Spanish

20 Did all of the members arrive at the meeting spot on time?
- ☐ Yes
- ☐ No

그림 정보 파악

1 대화를 듣고, 두 사람이 만든 눈사람을 고르시오.

① ② ③

④ ⑤

♥ **No way!**
: 어떤 상황에 대해 반대하거나 부정할 때 쓰는 표현으로, '말도 안돼'라는 뜻이다.
= That's impossible.

1 🇬🇧

M Charlotte, are you still _____ _____ _____?

W No. Look at this. The snowman is almost done.

M You did great. I'll make him eyes with these buttons.

W Looks nice. I'll _____ _____ _____ around the snowman.

M ♥No way! If you do, you'll catch a cold. How about making his nose and mouth _____ _____ _____?

W Okay. But he looks cold, too. I want to make him warm.

M Then _____ _____ _____ _____ his head.

W We're done! Let's take a picture with the snowman.

목적 파악

2 대화를 듣고, 여자가 남자에게 전화한 목적으로 가장 적절한 것을 고르시오.

① 방을 청소하라고
② 책상을 수리하라고
③ 건전지를 구입하라고
④ 집에 서둘러서 오라고
⑤ 시간에 맞춰 일어나라고

2

[*Cellphone rings.*]

M Hello, Mom. What's up?

W Ivan, where are you? Are you _____ _____ now?

M That's right. Do you _____ _____ from me?

W When I cleaned your room, I found your alarm clock had stopped.

M Oh, is it broken?

W I don't think so. If you _____ _____ _____, it will work.

M I got it. I'll _____ _____ _____ _____ _____ and buy some batteries.

W Okay. See you at home.

그림 상황 파악

3 다음 그림의 상황에 가장 적절한 대화를 고르시오.

① ② ③ ④ ⑤

3

① M Oh, is the elevator broken again?

W I think so. We _____ _____ customer service.

② M This elevator doesn't stop at the second floor.

W Are you sure? _____ _____ _____.

③ M Ouch! You _____ _____ _____!

W I'm so sorry. I didn't notice it.

④ M There are so many people in front of the elevator.

W How about _____ _____ _____ instead of taking the elevator?

⑤ M The elevator suddenly stopped, so I _____ _____ _____ _____.

W That sounds terrible. Were you okay?

특정 정보 파악

4 대화를 듣고, 두 사람이 만나기로 한 요일을 고르시오.

① 수요일
② 목요일
③ 금요일
④ 토요일
⑤ 일요일

4

W   Did you hear that an Indian restaurant _____ _____ _____ _____?

M   I heard that. I really want to go to the restaurant *as soon as possible.

W   How about this Wednesday after school?

M   Sorry. I _____ _____ _____ _____ then. Let's meet on Friday.

W   Let me see. Wait! I _____ _____ _____ a family gathering on that day.

M   Then what about this Thursday?

W   That's perfect! See you then.

　　　　　　　　　　　　　　* as soon as [애즈] [쑨] [애즈] → [애쑤내즈]

언급 유무 파악

5 다음을 듣고, 전기차 Handy에 관해 언급되지 <u>않은</u> 것을 고르시오.

① 구입 가격
② 탑승 가능 인원
③ 정부 보조금 안내
④ 제조 회사 및 국가
⑤ 충전 후 주행 가능 거리

5

W   Ladies and gentlemen, look at this innovative electric car, the Handy. We are so proud to introduce the Handy to you after _____ _____ _____ _____. The Handy was produced by the Star Automobile Company in Korea in 2020. The Handy is designed for four passengers, and it can drive 500 kilometers _____ _____ _____ _____. In addition, the price is 25,000 dollars, _____ _____ _____ compared to other electric cars. The Handy goes on sale next month. Don't miss this chance to protect the environment.

관계 추론

6 대화를 듣고, 두 사람의 관계로 가장 적절한 것을 고르시오.

① 학부모 — 교사
② 경찰관 — 목격자
③ 문하생 — 화가
④ 수학자 — 학생
⑤ 운동선수 — 코치

♥ What's on your mind?
: 할 말이 있는지, 또는 지금 생각하고 있는 것이 무엇인지 물어볼 때 쓰는 표현으로, '무슨 생각을 하고 있니?'라는 뜻이다.
= What are you thinking about?

6

M   Hello, Ms. Duncan. I'm glad to meet you. I'm Violet's father.

W   Ah, nice to meet you. Please _____ _____ _____. ♥What's on your mind?

M   The other day, Violet told me that she _____ _____ _____ a mathematician.

W   A mathematician? I think that's perfect for her.

M   Do you think she _____ _____ _____ to become a mathematician?

W   Absolutely. Violet is a very talented student. If I were you, I would _____ _____ _____.

M   Thank you. I'll talk to Violet more about it.

어색한 대화 찾기

7 다음을 듣고, 두 사람의 대화가 <u>어색한</u> 것을 고르시오.

① ② ③ ④ ⑤

7

① M Can you do me a favor?

W Why not? Tell me _____ _____ _____.

② M Why were you _____ _____ _____ _____ today?

W Unfortunately, I *haven't met them yet.

③ M Do you want to _____ _____ _____?

W Yes! I'll ride on the black horse over there.

④ M I wonder if anybody is home or not.

W I don't think so. Look! The lights _____ _____ _____.

⑤ M This is the _____ _____ _____ I've ever been on.

W It's like this every day during commuting hours.

★ haven't met [해븐트] [멧] → [해븐멧]

부탁한 일 파악

8 대화를 듣고, 여자가 남자에게 부탁한 일로 가장 적절한 것을 고르시오.

① 할인 쿠폰을 달라고
② 신발을 수선해 달라고
③ 재고를 확인해 달라고
④ 전화번호를 알려 달라고
⑤ 습득한 휴대 전화를 돌려달라고

8

[*Telephone rings.*]

M Hello. Sweet Home Department Store Customer Service Center. How can I help you?

W I think I _____ _____ _____ _____ in your store today.

M _____ _____ were you shopping?

W I was in the Comfy shoe store.

M Okay. I'll check if the Comfy shoe store has your cellphone. Hold on a second. [*Ringtone sounds*] Sorry. _____ _____ _____ there.

W Then could you please _____ _____ _____ _____ of the shoe store? I want to call myself.

M Sure. The phone number is 012-3456-7890.

의도 파악

9 대화를 듣고, 남자의 마지막 말에 담긴 의도로 가장 적절한 것을 고르시오.

① 위로
② 안도
③ 후회
④ 감사
⑤ 조언

9

W Sewon, there's _____ _____ about you today.

M I _____ _____ _____ and changed my hair.

W You look great. Where are your glasses? Are you wearing contacts now?

M Nope. I lost my glasses after I got back from my vacation.

W That's too bad. You just _____ _____ _____ _____ not too long ago, right?

M I know. I _____ _____ _____ more careful.

10 대화를 듣고, 여자가 지불할 금액을 고르시오.

① $ 40
② $ 50
③ $ 60
④ $ 65
⑤ $ 75

10

M Welcome to Betty Costume. What are you looking for?

W I'm _____ _____ a Halloween costume for my four-year-old daughter.

M Hmm... How about this princess dress? We got this yesterday.

W Actually, my daughter _____ _____ _____ _____ last year. Oh, I like that witch costume. How much is it?

M It's 50 dollars. And I think you need this broom.

W Perfect! And I like the witch hat. _____ _____ _____ _____?

M The broom is 10 dollars, and the hat is 15 dollars.

W Okay. I'll just take the dress and the hat.

11 대화를 듣고, 남자가 할 일로 가장 적절한 것을 고르시오.

① 배낭 구입하기
② 은행에서 환전하기
③ 여행 일정 계획하기
④ 여권 재발급 신청하기
⑤ 친구에게 강아지 맡기기

♥ **I'd better go.**

: 어떤 일에 대해서 강한 충고나 권유를 할 때 'had better + V'를 쓰며, 본문에서는 '나는 지금 가는 게 좋겠다.'라는 뜻이다.

= I better go.
= I'd best go.

11 🇬🇧

M Finally, by this time tomorrow, I'll be _____ _____ _____.

W Where are you going tomorrow?

M I'm going on a trip to Vietnam. I've _____ _____ _____ _____ there for a long time.

W Did you _____ _____ _____ if you packed everything? Your passport, clothes, money, and other things.

M Let me see. My backpack is ready to go. And I'll go to the bank at the airport tomorrow to _____ _____ _____.

W The exchange rate there is not very good. How about going to a bank around here today?

M Okay. ♥ I'd better go now.

12 다음을 듣고, 자연사 박물관에 관해 언급되지 <u>않은</u> 것을 고르시오.

① 참가비
② 행사 기간
③ 참가 대상
④ 접수 장소
⑤ 활동 안내

12

M Hello, everyone. I'm happy to _____ _____ _____ _____ about the museum of natural history. The museum is going to hold the Dinosaur Discovery Camp this summer. The camp will be held from July 10 to August 9. It is for elementary school students, and the _____ _____ is $30. The camp offers _____ _____ _____. For example, participants will look for dinosaur bones _____ _____ _____ and then put them together.

표 파악

13 다음 표를 보면서 대화를 듣고, 여자가 구입할 뮤지컬 표를 고르시오.

	Title	Day	Time	Price
①	*The Little Prince*	Fri	5 p.m.	$100
②	*Snow White and the Seven Dwarfs*	Fri	8 p.m.	$120
③	*Little Red Riding Hood*	Sat	3 p.m.	$120
④	*The Lion King*	Sat	7 p.m.	$150
⑤	*The Little Prince*	Sun	3 p.m.	$100

화제·주제 파악

14 다음을 듣고, 무엇에 관한 설명인지 고르시오.

① 군함
② 비행기
③ 잠수함
④ 유람선
⑤ 전투기

할 일 파악

15 대화를 듣고, 남자가 할 일로 가장 적절한 것을 고르시오.

① 병원으로 가기
② 물 자주 마시기
③ 거실 환기시키기
④ 중고 전자 제품 팔기
⑤ 공기 청정기 구입하기

13

M Lydia, look at _____ _____ _____ _____. Let's go to see one.

W Sure. But not on Friday. I have to go to my English academy on Friday.

M Oh, I wanted to see *Snow White and the Seven Dwarfs*.

W Sorry. What about *The Lion King*? I hear this one is awesome. We can see an _____ _____.

M Well, I think $150 per person is _____ _____ _____ _____.

W I didn't _____ _____ _____. Anyway, I've already seen *Little Red Riding Hood*.

M Then there's only one thing left.

W That's right. I think *The Little Prince* is a wonderful choice because we can take a picture *with the actors.

M Really? That'll be a great memory.

W Let's reserve tickets now.

* with the actors [위드] [디] [액터즈] → [윗디액터즈]

14

W This is a special vehicle that can _____ _____. This is quite different from ships because it can _____ _____ _____ _____ _____. This is a sealed container which is covered with the strongest steel. People in this can breathe freely and eat food underwater. This is mainly used by the navy and is _____ _____ _____ _____ _____. However, this is also _____ _____ _____, marine research, and undersea exploration.

15

W Honey, we _____ _____ _____ _____ today. It's foggy outside.

M No. That's not just fog. It looks like fine dust.

W Oh, my! That's why I have a _____ _____ _____ _____.

M Do you? You need to drink a lot of water. Honey, I'll go to the electronics store.

W Why?

M To buy an air purifier. We _____ _____, _____ _____.

숫자 정보 파악

16 대화를 듣고, 엄마가 아들을 깨울 시각을 고르시오.

① 2:00 p.m. ② 3:00 p.m.
③ 4:00 p.m. ④ 5:00 p.m.
⑤ 6:00 p.m.

🩶 **That's my boy!**
: 주로 아들에게 잘했다고 칭찬할 때 쓰는 표현으로, '역시 내 아들이야.', '잘했어.'라는 뜻이다. 딸에게는 'That's my girl!'이라고 한다.

16 🇬🇧

M   Mom, I _____ _____ _____ _____ on my English exam.

W   🩶 That's my boy! You finally did it.

M   English is _____ _____ _____, but I kept trying to get a perfect score.

W   Well done! It's already 2 o'clock. Now get some rest.

M   Not today. I have a math test tomorrow. So can you _____ _____ _____ 3 hours from now?

W   Okay. Do you want to get up at 5?

M   That's right. I need to _____ _____ _____ for a while.

W   I got it.

적절한 응답 찾기

17 대화를 듣고, 남자의 마지막 말에 대한 여자의 응답으로 가장 적절한 것을 고르시오.

Woman: _____

① I had my wisdom teeth taken out.
② Clean your room before going to bed.
③ Knowledge has little to do with wisdom.
④ My parents want me to become a dentist.
⑤ If you don't go, the pain will get worse and worse.

17

W   What's the matter with your face? It's _____ _____.

M   I have a terrible toothache. My gums have been bleeding. It's painful.

W   Ugh! You look really sick. _____ _____ _____ _____ start?

M   Since last month, I've had some pain because of a wisdom tooth.

W   Last month? Didn't you see a dentist?

M   No, I didn't. I thought it would _____ _____ _____.

W   No way! Anyway, _____ _____ _____ _____ and go to the dentist today.

M   All right. But I'm really *scared of the dentist.

W   If you don't go, the pain will get worse and worse.

★ scared of [스케얼드] [오브] → [스케얼더브]

적절한 응답 찾기

18 대화를 듣고, 여자의 마지막 말에 대한 남자의 응답으로 가장 적절한 것을 고르시오.

Man: _____

① Good idea. I'm sure it'll help you.
② I can fix your problem in ten seconds.
③ Let's go to see a horror movie tomorrow.
④ In my opinion, *Romeo and Juliet* is better.
⑤ I'm going to the playground to play soccer.

18

M   Abigail, what are you looking at on your laptop?

W   I'm watching the movie *Beauty and the Beast*.

M   I didn't know you're _____ _____ romantic movies.

W   To be honest, I like horror movies.

M   Why are you watching it? It's _____ _____ _____.

W   Actually, I'm _____ _____ _____ Belle from *Beauty and the Beast* in the school play.

M   Wow! That's good news.

W   Yes. That's why I'm watching this. I want to _____ _____ _____ _____.

M   Good idea. I'm sure it'll help you.

19 대화를 듣고, 남자의 마지막 말에 대한 여자의 응답으로 가장 적절한 것을 고르시오.

Woman: _____
① It's helpful to keep a diary in English.
② I'd like to exchange this one for another.
③ Then I should find a native Korean speaker.
④ English is such a difficult language to learn.
⑤ You should memorize new words every day.

19

M   Eleanor, is there something bothering you?

W   You know I'm learning Korean these days. But it's not easy to study Korean.

M   Come on! It's obvious that it _____ _____ _____ _____ a new language.

W   I know that! But after learning a new word, when I try to *use it, I find that I _____ _____ _____ _____.

M   Well, you need more practice. How about _____ _____ _____ _____ partner?

W   Language exchange? What is that?

M   It's a method where two native speakers _____ _____ _____ their native language. You are a native English speaker.

W   Then I should find a native Korean speaker.

* use it [유즈] [잇] → [유짓]

20 다음 상황 설명을 듣고, 소영이 은혁에게 할 말로 가장 적절한 것을 고르시오.

Soyoung: Eunhyuk, _____
① I want you to try to be on time.
② we had better head for the airport.
③ you are in charge of taking photos.
④ I wrote an editorial in the class newspaper.
⑤ give a speech about the economy to the class.

20

M   Soyoung and her classmates are planning to make a class newspaper. Her teacher _____ _____ _____ _____ seven groups. Soyoung's group decides to meet at 6 o'clock after school. At 6:00, Soyoung arrives at the meeting spot. However, she doesn't see Eunhyuk and some other members. About 30 minutes later, _____ _____ _____ _____ _____ _____ except for Eunhyuk. She wants to tell him _____ _____ _____ _____ when Eunhyuk arrives. In this situation, what would Soyoung most likely say to Eunhyuk?

Soyoung   Eunhyuk, I want you to try to be on time.

Vocabulary Test

A 들려주는 단어를 듣고 쓴 뒤, 괄호 안에 우리말 뜻을 쓰시오.

	영어	우리말			영어	우리말
1				6		
2				7		
3				8		
4				9		
5				10		

B 다음 문장을 잘 듣고 빈칸에 들어갈 단어를 채우시오.

1 I can _____ _____ _____.

2 Can I _____ _____ _____ _____?

3 Could you _____ _____ _____ _____?

4 How can I be _____ _____ _____ like you?

5 She _____ _____ _____ _____ where Kate is sitting.

6 It _____ _____ _____ _____ forget significant events.

7 _____ _____ _____ this restaurant is really romantic.

8 You can hang it on the wall or _____ _____ _____ your desk.

9 This yearly event _____ _____ _____ the fifteenth of April.

10 I _____ _____ _____ and highlight expressions I'm not familiar with.

A 들려주는 단어를 듣고 쓴 뒤, 괄호 안에 우리말 뜻을 쓰시오.

	영어	우리말		영어	우리말
1			6		
2			7		
3			8		
4			9		
5			10		

B 다음 문장을 잘 듣고 빈칸에 들어갈 단어를 채우시오.

1 I want to _____ _____ _____ _____.

2 You can also _____ _____ _____ _____ _____.

3 I should _____ _____ _____ _____ _____.

4 This ship is _____ _____ _____ _____ _____.

5 I got _____ _____ _____ three days ago.

6 Sure, but I _____ _____ _____ before Friday.

7 I'd like to _____ _____ _____ _____ _____.

8 She _____ _____ _____ _____ during her visit.

9 When you look at this, you can _____ _____ _____.

10 The weather forecast says that the storm is _____ _____ _____ _____.

A 들려주는 단어를 듣고 쓴 뒤, 괄호 안에 우리말 뜻을 쓰시오.

	영어	우리말		영어	우리말
1			6		
2			7		
3			8		
4			9		
5			10		

B 다음 문장을 잘 듣고 빈칸에 들어갈 단어를 채우시오.

1 _____ _____ _____ _____ English class?

2 _____ _____ _____ Korean Food World?

3 I'll take a seat on _____ _____ _____.

4 I'm afraid he _____ _____ _____ _____ _____.

5 I don't think that _____ _____ _____ _____.

6 I wonder if _____ _____ _____ _____ now.

7 Famous _____ _____ _____ to design the monument.

8 Why don't you _____ _____ _____ _____ going to school on foot?

9 It costs 50 dollars less, and we are _____ _____ _____ _____.

10 Nuclear power _____ _____ _____ _____ to produce electricity.

A 들려주는 단어를 듣고 쓴 뒤, 괄호 안에 우리말 뜻을 쓰시오.

	영어	우리말		영어	우리말
1			6		
2			7		
3			8		
4			9		
5			10		

B 다음 문장을 잘 듣고 빈칸에 들어갈 단어를 채우시오.

1 _____ _____ _____ me.

2 I'm very sorry for _____ _____.

3 _____ _____ _____ _____ them.

4 _____ _____ _____ do something outdoors?

5 Are you _____ _____ _____ _____?

6 I'm _____ _____ _____ _____ her soon.

7 Can you tell me _____ _____ _____ _____?

8 I don't think _____ _____ _____ _____ _____.

9 We _____ _____ the school magazine.

10 I'm afraid those items are _____ _____ _____ _____.

A 들려주는 단어를 듣고 쓴 뒤, 괄호 안에 우리말 뜻을 쓰시오.

	영어	우리말		영어	우리말
1			6		
2			7		
3			8		
4			9		
5			10		

B 다음 문장을 잘 듣고 빈칸에 들어갈 단어를 채우시오.

1 This light keeps going _____ _____ _____.

2 Farmers _____ _____ for _____ _____ meat.

3 What _____ _____ _____ _____ harder?

4 _____ _____ _____ too hot to go _____ _____ summer?

5 You just have to know _____ _____ _____ _____ you are.

6 Click on it, and it will _____ _____ _____ _____.

7 _____ _____ what _____ _____ and follow your heart.

8 Nick hardly _____ _____ often _____ _____ and walks around.

9 Could you try calling your _____ _____ _____ them to come here?

10 Make sure you _____ _____ _____ _____ _____.

A 들려주는 단어를 듣고 쓴 뒤, 괄호 안에 우리말 뜻을 쓰시오.

	영어	우리말			영어	우리말
1				6		
2				7		
3				8		
4				9		
5				10		

B 다음 문장을 잘 듣고 빈칸에 들어갈 단어를 채우시오.

1 The roads are _____ _____ _____.

2 I thought _____ _____ _____ to me.

3 It's _____ _____ _____ in Room 707.

4 They're _____ _____ _____ _____ _____.

5 Yesterday, I fell down and _____ _____ _____.

6 I _____ _____ it without your help.

7 You _____ _____ _____ the concert tickets.

8 Mosquitos are usually _____ _____ _____ _____ of sweat.

9 Let me guess _____ _____ _____ _____ your drawing is.

10 You will help _____ _____ _____ _____ and clean their rooms.

A 들려주는 단어를 듣고 쓴 뒤, 괄호 안에 우리말 뜻을 쓰시오.

	영어	우리말		영어	우리말
1			6		
2			7		
3			8		
4			9		
5			10		

B 다음 문장을 잘 듣고 빈칸에 들어갈 단어를 채우시오.

1 I just want to _____ _____ _____ _____ _____.

2 _____ _____ _____ live _____ _____ from here.

3 I'm _____ _____ _____ Chinese characters.

4 You should always be _____ _____ _____ _____.

5 _____ _____ _____ with teens who like sports.

6 I'm sorry for the _____ _____ _____ _____.

7 _____ _____ _____ _____ on YouTube was really exciting.

8 On Monday and Thursday, I'll _____ _____ _____ Sam all day long.

9 Today, it is _____ _____ _____ _____ of both North and South Korea.

10 I am _____ _____ _____ a new semester party next Friday or Saturday.

A 들려주는 단어를 듣고 쓴 뒤, 괄호 안에 우리말 뜻을 쓰시오.

	영어	우리말		영어	우리말
1			6		
2			7		
3			8		
4			9		
5			10		

B 다음 문장을 잘 듣고 빈칸에 들어갈 단어를 채우시오.

1 The white one ＿＿＿＿＿ ＿＿＿＿＿ ＿＿＿＿＿ ＿＿＿＿＿ the pants you have.

2 But you ＿＿＿＿＿ ＿＿＿＿＿ ＿＿＿＿＿ ＿＿＿＿＿ choose dinner.

3 I wish ＿＿＿＿＿ ＿＿＿＿＿ ＿＿＿＿＿ to the bus station.

4 This uses ＿＿＿＿＿ ＿＿＿＿＿ ＿＿＿＿＿ ＿＿＿＿＿ to attract a mate.

5 Anyway, we have to hurry ＿＿＿＿＿ ＿＿＿＿＿ ＿＿＿＿＿ ＿＿＿＿＿.

6 The experience ＿＿＿＿＿ ＿＿＿＿＿ ＿＿＿＿＿ ＿＿＿＿＿ this one a lot.

7 Have ＿＿＿＿＿ ＿＿＿＿＿ ＿＿＿＿＿ ＿＿＿＿＿ senior citizens before?

8 It's ＿＿＿＿＿ ＿＿＿＿＿ ＿＿＿＿＿ ＿＿＿＿＿ your hands in your pockets.

9 ＿＿＿＿＿ ＿＿＿＿＿ ＿＿＿＿＿ ＿＿＿＿＿ your computer off before you leave.

10 All your teachers will guide you ＿＿＿＿＿ ＿＿＿＿＿ ＿＿＿＿＿ ＿＿＿＿＿ ＿＿＿＿＿ from this experience.

A 들려주는 단어를 듣고 쓴 뒤, 괄호 안에 우리말 뜻을 쓰시오.

	영어	우리말			영어	우리말
1				6		
2				7		
3				8		
4				9		
5				10		

B 다음 문장을 잘 듣고 빈칸에 들어갈 단어를 채우시오.

1 I ＿＿＿＿＿ ＿＿＿＿＿ ＿＿＿＿＿ down.

2 I wash it at least ＿＿＿＿＿ ＿＿＿＿＿ ＿＿＿＿＿.

3 I also like the colors ＿＿＿＿＿ ＿＿＿＿＿ ＿＿＿＿＿ the work.

4 Let's ＿＿＿＿＿ ＿＿＿＿＿ ＿＿＿＿＿ by the end of this week.

5 ＿＿＿＿＿ ＿＿＿＿＿ ＿＿＿＿＿ information in alphabetical order.

6 There must be a reward for that ＿＿＿＿＿ ＿＿＿＿＿ ＿＿＿＿＿ ＿＿＿＿＿.

7 ＿＿＿＿＿ ＿＿＿＿＿ ＿＿＿＿＿ the earlier ticket is double ＿＿＿＿＿ ＿＿＿＿＿ the later one.

8 Adam ＿＿＿＿＿ ＿＿＿＿＿ from different sites and takes notes.

9 However, if you walk too hard, you can ＿＿＿＿＿ ＿＿＿＿＿ ＿＿＿＿＿ your legs.

10 It ＿＿＿＿＿ ＿＿＿＿＿ ＿＿＿＿＿ how much time you ＿＿＿＿＿ ＿＿＿＿＿ the things you do.

A　들려주는 단어를 듣고 쓴 뒤, 괄호 안에 우리말 뜻을 쓰시오.

	영어	우리말		영어	우리말
1			6		
2			7		
3			8		
4			9		
5			10		

B　다음 문장을 잘 듣고 빈칸에 들어갈 단어를 채우시오.

1 I _____ _____ _____ _____ swimming.

2 Do you _____ _____ _____ _____?

3 _____ _____ _____ _____ Santa Claus?

4 It's a pleasure _____ _____ _____ _____ _____.

5 Can you _____ _____ _____ _____ _____ home?

6 We will _____ _____ _____ a serious traffic jam.

7 Is the badminton court _____ _____ _____?

8 I prefer finishing assignments _____ _____ _____.

9 Just looking _____ _____ _____ _____ every 30 minutes helps a lot.

10 Why don't you call your mom and _____ _____ _____ _____ _____ to school?

A 들려주는 단어를 듣고 쓴 뒤, 괄호 안에 우리말 뜻을 쓰시오.

	영어	우리말			영어	우리말
1				6		
2				7		
3				8		
4				9		
5				10		

B 다음 문장을 잘 듣고 빈칸에 들어갈 단어를 채우시오.

1 It's _____ _____ _____ _____ memorize them.

2 It _____ _____ _____ _____ to get to Jinhae.

3 It's _____ _____ _____ _____ since I saw my dog.

4 Could you _____ _____ _____ _____ this evening?

5 He is often _____ _____ _____ _____ _____.

6 I think you _____ _____ _____ _____ famous authors.

7 To move your token or mark, _____ _____ _____ _____ _____.

8 You got your allowance from your mom _____ _____ _____ _____ _____.

9 There have been lots of unique traditions _____ _____ _____ _____ modern times.

10 For items more than 50 percent off, _____ _____ _____ _____ _____.

A 들려주는 단어를 듣고 쓴 뒤, 괄호 안에 우리말 뜻을 쓰시오.

	영어	우리말		영어	우리말
1			6		
2			7		
3			8		
4			9		
5			10		

B 다음 문장을 잘 듣고 빈칸에 들어갈 단어를 채우시오.

1   This is mostly _____ _____ _____.

2   It looks cool with all the _____ _____ _____.

3   Did your team _____ _____ _____ new project?

4   I'm on the bus and am just _____ _____ _____.

5   The weather forecast says it will _____ _____ _____ by that time.

6   I hope she _____ _____ _____ the friend she had a fight with.

7   We should think of what field we will _____ _____.

8   There is a train _____ _____ _____ thirty minutes.

9   Harry _____ _____ _____ _____ on the platform.

10   I am thinking about some things to do when I _____ _____ _____ _____ after this semester.

A 들려주는 단어를 듣고 쓴 뒤, 괄호 안에 우리말 뜻을 쓰시오.

	영어	우리말			영어	우리말
1				6		
2				7		
3				8		
4				9		
5				10		

B 다음 문장을 잘 듣고 빈칸에 들어갈 단어를 채우시오.

1 The audience will _____ _____ _____.

2 You can _____ _____ _____ with them.

3 This is what we use to _____ _____ _____ _____.

4 Could I _____ _____ _____ _____ my T-shirt?

5 Didn't you say that you _____ _____ _____ today?

6 By the way, do you _____ _____ _____ on this website?

7 I'll _____ _____ _____ _____ after I talk with the others.

8 I'm happy when I _____ _____ _____ while doing what I want.

9 Finally, it _____ _____ _____ and increases your happiness.

10 There may be big companies that are willing to _____ _____ _____ here.

A 들려주는 단어를 듣고 쓴 뒤, 괄호 안에 우리말 뜻을 쓰시오.

	영어	우리말		영어	우리말
1			6		
2			7		
3			8		
4			9		
5			10		

B 다음 문장을 잘 듣고 빈칸에 들어갈 단어를 채우시오.

1 You don't _____ _____ _____ _____ _____.

2 Our vacation _____ _____ _____ _____.

3 But you can _____ _____ _____ _____ in Korea.

4 I've _____ _____ _____ doing that before.

5 Actually, I think you're _____ _____ _____ _____ at all.

6 I visited the shop and _____ _____ _____ _____ _____.

7 I _____ _____ _____ _____ after eating some raw fish.

8 People should be aware of _____ _____ _____ _____.

9 David says that he's looking for a roommate _____ _____ _____ _____ _____.

10 If you want that, then we _____ _____ _____ _____ in the exit row.

A 들려주는 단어를 듣고 쓴 뒤, 괄호 안에 우리말 뜻을 쓰시오.

	영어	우리말			영어	우리말
1				6		
2				7		
3				8		
4				9		
5				10		

B 다음 문장을 잘 듣고 빈칸에 들어갈 단어를 채우시오.

1 My body is _____ _____ _____ _____.

2 _____ _____ _____ _____ a new partner now.

3 I need a memory _____ _____ _____ _____ _____ photos.

4 Do you have _____ _____ _____ _____ _____ in the future?

5 Right now is the _____ _____ _____ _____ to Vietnam.

6 Keeping _____ _____ _____ _____ the indoor air bad.

7 It will probably take me 20 minutes _____ _____ _____ _____
_____.

8 When he was about twelve, he got _____ _____ _____ _____
_____ in a stage show.

9 It will be a _____ _____ _____ _____ _____ enjoy and
understand dance performances.

10 I _____ _____ _____ _____ _____ was walking and watching
a movie on my smartphone.

A 들려주는 단어를 듣고 쓴 뒤, 괄호 안에 우리말 뜻을 쓰시오.

	영어	우리말		영어	우리말
1			6		
2			7		
3			8		
4			9		
5			10		

B 다음 문장을 잘 듣고 빈칸에 들어갈 단어를 채우시오.

1 Can _____ _____ _____ _____ something nice for him?

2 Then _____ _____ _____ _____ _____ the show together?

3 What items _____ _____ _____ _____ into the capsule?

4 Do you think _____ _____ _____ _____ my mother's age?

5 But you _____ _____ _____ _____ a traffic jam at this time.

6 If _____ _____ _____ are late, we can't start the lesson together.

7 As time passes, however, _____ _____ _____ lie down and fall asleep.

8 I'm _____ _____ _____ _____ at the national museum this Sunday.

9 If you _____ _____ _____ _____ _____, you will want to buy the product.

10 If anyone _____ _____ _____ _____ _____, you can attend an afternoon or evening class.

A 들려주는 단어를 듣고 쓴 뒤, 괄호 안에 우리말 뜻을 쓰시오.

	영어	우리말		영어	우리말
1			6		
2			7		
3			8		
4			9		
5			10		

B 다음 문장을 잘 듣고 빈칸에 들어갈 단어를 채우시오.

1 That _____ _____ _____.

2 Each ticket is _____ _____ _____ _____ a regular one.

3 I _____ _____ _____ _____ hair light brown.

4 You can _____ _____ _____ _____ by five o'clock.

5 I _____ _____ _____ with one of my team members.

6 Do you think we should put _____ _____ _____ the T-shirts?

7 That's possible if there _____ _____ _____.

8 I guess it's already been more than two weeks _____ _____ _____ _____.

9 It sometimes _____ _____ the history and _____ _____ different countries.

10 When you have to _____ _____ _____ decision, question the ideas you _____ _____ _____.

226

A 들려주는 단어를 듣고 쓴 뒤, 괄호 안에 우리말 뜻을 쓰시오.

	영어	우리말		영어	우리말
1			6		
2			7		
3			8		
4			9		
5			10		

B 다음 문장을 잘 듣고 빈칸에 들어갈 단어를 채우시오.

1   I'll _____ _____ in a(n) _____ _____ .

2   That's _____ _____ _____ _____ _____ .

3   Many books are _____ _____ _____ _____ .

4   On my way here, I _____ _____ _____ _____ .

5   These books are _____ _____ _____ _____ _____ _____ .

6   We should _____ _____ _____ to their natural habitats.

7   The environment is _____ _____ _____ _____ .

8   If needed, the escalators can be _____ _____ _____ _____ .

9   Above all, people must be more _____ _____ _____ .

10 Can you _____ _____ _____ _____ _____ on your way home?

A 들려주는 단어를 듣고 쓴 뒤, 괄호 안에 우리말 뜻을 쓰시오.

	영어	우리말		영어	우리말
1			6		
2			7		
3			8		
4			9		
5			10		

B 다음 문장을 잘 듣고 빈칸에 들어갈 단어를 채우시오.

1 When _____ _____ _____ _____ with it?

2 Could you please _____ _____ _____ _____ it is there?

3 Do you want _____ _____ _____ _____ _____ them?

4 I like _____ _____ _____ _____, and your coffee was good.

5 You _____ _____ _____ _____ _____ to open your car, right?

6 This facial mask _____ _____ _____ _____ moisturized.

7 Under normal conditions, _____ _____ _____ _____ _____ within 3 days.

8 What are _____ _____ _____ _____ _____ this coming Hangeul Day event?

9 Scientists know _____ _____ _____ _____ _____ light and objects around them.

10 The *seowon* illustrates _____ _____ _____ _____ Confucianism was adapted to Korean conditions.

A 들려주는 단어를 듣고 쓴 뒤, 괄호 안에 우리말 뜻을 쓰시오.

	영어	우리말		영어	우리말
1			6		
2			7		
3			8		
4			9		
5			10		

B 다음 문장을 잘 듣고 빈칸에 들어갈 단어를 채우시오.

1 Then there's _____ _____ _____ _____.

2 I _____ _____ _____ more careful.

3 That's why I have a(n) _____ _____ _____ _____.

4 I wonder _____ _____ _____ _____ or not.

5 If I were you, I would _____ _____ _____.

6 Her teacher _____ _____ _____ _____ seven groups.

7 The elevator suddenly stopped, so I _____ _____ _____ _____.

8 Anyway, _____ _____ _____ _____ and go to the dentist today.

9 People in this can _____ _____ and eat food underwater.

10 How about making his nose and mouth _____ _____ _____?

MEMO

MEMO

MEMO

내공
중학영어듣기
모의고사 20회
정답 및 해설

3

이소영
이연홍
김소원
서재교
이건희

DARAKWON

내공
중학영어듣기 ❸
모의고사 20회

정답 및 해설

DARAKWON

실전 모의고사 1회

pp. 08~09

1	④	2	⑤	3	②	4	①	5	②
6	③	7	④	8	④	9	②	10	④
11	③	12	⑤	13	②	14	④	15	④
16	①	17	④	18	④	19	④	20	③

1 　그림 정보 파악　④

W　Good afternoon. What can I do for you?
M　Hi. I'm looking for scarfs <u>for elderly women</u>.
W　Which do you prefer, plain or patterned ones?
M　I guess she would like <u>a patterned one better</u>.
W　How about this one with a flower pattern on it?
　　This is <u>the best-selling scarf</u> with elderly women.
M　That looks beautiful. She may love it, too. Do you have one that's <u>a bit longer</u>?
W　Yes, we do. Here you are.

여　안녕하세요. 무엇을 도와드릴까요?
남　안녕하세요. 나이가 지긋한 여성을 위한 스카프를 찾습니다.
여　무늬가 없는 것과 있는 것 중에서 어떤 걸 선호하시나요?
남　제 생각엔 그녀는 무늬가 있는 것을 더 좋아할 것 같아요.
여　그럼 꽃무늬가 있는 이건 어떠신가요? 나이가 있으신 여성들 사이에서 가장 잘 팔리는 스카프예요.
남　예쁜걸요. 그녀도 좋아할 것 같아요. 그걸로 길이가 더 긴 제품도 있나요?
여　네, 있습니다. 여기 있습니다.

해설　점원이 추천한 꽃무늬에 스카프 중 길이가 더 긴 제품이 있냐고 물었다.
어휘　elderly [éldərli] 연세가 드신　plain [plein] 무늬가 없는, 무지의　patterned [pǽtərnd] 무늬가 있는　best-selling 가장 잘 팔리는

2 　제안한 일 파악　⑤

W　What are all those things?
M　Today is my last day at school, so I had to <u>empty my locker</u> and bring everything back home.
W　Did you bring your car?
M　No, my sister <u>wanted to use</u> my car today, so I let her have it. I can take a taxi.
W　Your house is far from here. It'll cost a lot. I can <u>drive you home</u>.
M　Can you really do that for me? Thanks.
W　Don't mention it. What <u>are friends for</u>?

여　이것들은 다 뭐야?
남　오늘 학교 마지막 날이거든, 그래서 사물함을 비우고 집으로 다시 가지고 와야 했어.
여　차는 가지고 왔어?
남　아니, 여동생이 오늘 내 차를 사용하길 원해서 그녀가 쓰도록 했어. 택시 타면 돼.
여　너희 집은 여기서 멀잖아. 비용이 많이 들 거야. 내가 집에 태워다 줄게.
남　정말 그래 줄 수 있어? 고마워.
여　천만에. 친구 좋다는 게 뭐야?

해설　택시를 타고 가겠다는 남자의 말에 여자는 차로 태워주겠다고 제안하였다.
어휘　empty [émpti] 비우다　locker [lákər] 사물함, 보관함　cost

[kɔ(:)st] (비용이) 들다

3 　그림 상황 파악　②

① W　<u>What do you want</u> to drink?
　　M　I just want some water.
② W　<u>How much water</u> do you drink a day?
　　M　I normally drink three glasses of water.
③ W　Don't you <u>get thirsty</u>?
　　M　I'm fine. Do you?
④ W　<u>What did you do</u> yesterday?
　　M　I hung out with my friends.
⑤ W　I played in the water for <u>too long</u>.
　　M　That's why you caught a cold.

① 여　뭐 마시고 싶어?
　　남　난 그냥 물만 좀 마시고 싶어.
② 여　하루에 물을 얼마나 마셔?
　　남　난 평소에 3잔 마셔.
③ 여　목마르지 않아?
　　남　난 괜찮아. 너 목말라?
④ 여　어제 뭐했어?
　　남　나 친구들이랑 놀았어.
⑤ 여　물속에서 너무 오래 놀았나봐.
　　남　그래서 네가 감기에 걸렸구나.

해설　여자가 하루에 물을 몇 잔 마시는지 물어보자 남자는 3잔을 마신다고 답하는 상황이다.
어휘　get thirsty 목이 마르다　hang out with ~와 어울려 놀다　catch a cold 감기에 걸리다

4 　숫자 정보 파악　①

W　Hello. Are you here to <u>sign up for</u> a class?
M　Yes. How do I register for a yoga class?
W　We have classes in the morning and afternoon. When is <u>convenient for you</u>?
M　Morning is better.
W　There are classes starting at 7:00, 9:00, and 11:00. What time would you like to come?
M　I'll choose <u>the earliest time</u>.
W　Okay. You can join the class <u>starting next Monday</u>.
M　Thank you.

여　안녕하세요. 수업 신청하러 오셨나요?
남　네. 요가 수업은 어떻게 등록하면 되나요?
여　수업이 아침이랑 오후에 있어요. 언제가 편하신가요?
남　아침 시간이 더 좋아요.
여　7시, 9시, 11시에 시작하는 수업이 있어요. 몇 시에 오시는 게 좋으시겠어요?
남　가장 이른 시간으로 할게요.
여　알겠습니다. 다음 주 월요일부터 수업에 참여하실 수 있어요.
남　감사합니다.

해설　오전 수업인 7시, 9시, 11시 중에서 가장 이른 시간으로 등록한다고 하였다.
어휘　sign up for ~을 신청하다　register for ~에 등록하다　convenient [kənví:njənt] 편리한

5 　언급 유무 파악　②

W　<u>What is the drama</u> you're watching now?
M　It's *The Study Master*. It was released in 2010.

W It's quite an old drama. What is it about?

M It's about some troublemakers at a high school struggling to get accepted to the best university in the country.

W That sounds interesting.

M This drama got high viewer ratings at the time.

W How high were they?

M Its ratings were 25.1%.

W That's such a big number.

여 보고 있는 드라마가 뭐야?

남 '공부의 신'이라는 거야. 2010년에 나온 거야.

여 꽤 오래된 드라마구나. 무슨 내용이야?

남 고등학교에 어떤 문제아들이 그 지역에 있는 최고의 대학에 들어가려고 고군분투하는 거야.

여 재밌게 들리는걸.

남 당시에 이 드라마는 시청률이 높았어.

여 얼마나 되었는데?

남 25.1%를 기록했어.

여 대단히 큰 수치네.

해설 배우에 관해서는 언급되지 않았다.

어휘 release [rilíːs] 출시하다   troublemaker [trʌ́blmèikər] 문제아   struggle [strʌ́gl] 고군분투하다   viewer ratings 시청률   record [rékərd] 기록하다

6 장소 추론 ③

M How's your leg?

W It feels better. Can I take part in practice?

M Let me see. Your ankle is swollen. You'd better go to see a doctor now.

W I'm really fine. I want to practice. We only have four days left until the game.

M I know how you feel, but I do not approve you doing that.

W Okay. I'll go to a hospital and get some treatment.

M I hope your injury is not serious.

W So do I.

남 다리는 좀 어때?

여 좀 괜찮아요. 연습에 참여해도 되나요?

남 어디 보자. 발목이 부었구나. 지금 병원에 가는 게 좋겠다.

여 정말 괜찮아요. 연습하고 싶어요. 시합이 4일밖에 안 남았잖아요.

남 네 심정은 이해하지만 네가 그렇게 하도록 허락할 수 없어.

여 알겠어요. 병원에 가서 치료를 받을게요.

남 부상이 심각한 수준이 아니면 좋겠구나.

여 저도요.

해설 여자가 다리를 다쳤지만 연습에 참여하고 싶다고 했고, 남자는 병원에 가라고 하는 상황이다.

어휘 practice [prǽktis] 연습   enough [inʌ́f] 충분한   go see a doctor 병원에 가다

7 어색한 대화 찾기 ④

① M Could you give me a hand?
  W What can I do for you?

② M Please remind me about our homework.
  W Okay. When do you want me to text you?

③ M You're not supposed to come here.
  W Sorry. I went the wrong way.

④ M I'm looking forward to meeting her.

W Of course you should not look backward.

⑤ M What would you do if you were in my shoes?
  W I might tell her the truth.

① 남 날 도와줄 수 있습니까?
  여 무엇을 도와드릴까요?

② 남 내게 숙제 좀 상기시켜줘.
  여 언제 네게 문자를 보내주길 바라니?

③ 남 여기에 오시면 안 됩니다.
  여 죄송합니다. 길을 잘못 들었네요.

④ 남 그녀를 만나는 게 너무 기대돼.
  여 물론 넌 뒤를 보면 안돼.

⑤ 남 네가 내 입장이라면 어떻게 할 거야?
  여 난 그녀에게 사실을 얘기할 거야.

해설 여자를 만나게 되는 것을 기대한다는 말에 뒤를 돌아보지 말라고 답하는 것은 부자연스럽다.

어휘 give a hand 도와주다   remind [rimáind] 상기시키다   be supposed to ~해야 되다   look forward to ~을 기대하다   look backward 뒤돌아 보다   be in one's shoes ~의 입장에 처하다

8 부탁한 일 파악 ④

M Today, the fine dust level is high. You should wear a mask.

W Today again? Oh, no. We don't have any extra masks to wear.

M You can buy some on your way back home later.

W I can't do that. I have plans with my coworkers in the evening.

M You're quite busy these days.

W I really am. Anyway, I have no time to drop by a drugstore. Could you buy some for me?

M Okay, I will. How many do you need?

W Please buy me thirty. That will be enough for one month.

M No problem.

남 오늘 미세 먼지 농도가 높아. 마스크 써야 해.

여 오늘도? 오, 저런. 우리 여유분의 쓸 마스크가 없어.

남 나중에 집으로 돌아오는 길에 좀 사면 되지.

여 그럴 수 없어. 오늘 저녁에 동료들이랑 약속이 있거든.

남 당신 요즘 꽤 바쁘네.

여 나 정말 바빠. 어쨌든 약국에 들를 시간이 없어. 당신이 사다 주면 안 될까?

남 그래, 그럴게. 몇 개나 필요한데?

여 30개 사다 줘. 한 달 치야.

남 알겠어.

해설 여자는 남자에게 한 달 치 마스크를 대신 구입해 줄 것을 부탁하였다.

어휘 fine dust 미세 먼지   level [lévəl] 농도, 정도   extra [ékstrə] 여분의   coworker 동료   drop by 들르다

9 화제·주제 파악 ②

M Welcome to the Moonlight Campground. To make sure of everyone's safety, here are some rules to follow. When you are inside your tent, you must not use anything that can catch on fire. Although the materials used in the campground are fireproof, it's still important to keep places safe and clean. Moreover, children under five should be accompanied by their parents. Since the

정답 및 해설

campground is by the river, leaving kids alone can lead to accidents. Thank you for your cooperation.

남 Moonlight 캠핑장에 오신 것을 환영합니다. 모두의 안전을 확실히 하기 위해 따라야 할 규칙들이 있습니다. 텐트 안에 계실 때에는 불이 날 수 있는 어떤 것도 사용하시면 안 됩니다. 캠핑장에 사용된 재료들이 불연성일지라도 장소를 안전하고 깨끗하게 유지하는 것은 여전히 중요합니다. 게다가, 다섯 살 미만의 어린이는 부모님과 동반되어야 합니다. 캠핑장이 강 옆에 위치하고 있기 때문에 아이들을 혼자 두는 것은 사고로 이어질 수 있습니다. 협조해 주셔서 감사합니다.

해설 캠핑장 이용 시의 안전 수칙에 대해 말하고 있다.
어휘 campground [kǽmpgràund] 캠핑장   make sure of ~을 확실히 하다   material [mətí(:)əriəl] 재료, 자재   accompany [əkʌ́mpəni] 동반하다   cooperation [kouὰpəréiʃən] 협조

10 숫자 정보 파악 ④

W Hello. How can I help you?
M I'd like to buy some photo frames.
W We have wooden and metal ones. Which do you want?
M How much are they?
W A wooden one is seven dollars, and an aluminum one is eight dollars.
M I'll buy two of each. May I use this 10% off coupon?
W Sure. Here you are.
M Thank you.

여 안녕하세요. 무엇을 도와드릴까요?
남 액자를 사고 싶은데요.
여 나무로 된 것과 알루미늄으로 된 것이 있어요. 어떤 걸 원하시나요?
남 얼마인가요?
여 나무로 된 건 7달러이고, 알루미늄으로 된 건 8달러예요.
남 2개씩 살게요. 이 10% 쿠폰을 사용해도 되나요?
여 물론이죠. 여기 있습니다.
남 감사해요.

해설 품목별로 2개씩 구입하고 10% 쿠폰을 사용한다고 하였다.
어휘 photo frame 액자   wooden [wúdən] 나무로 된   aluminum [əljúːmənəm] 알루미늄

11 할 일 파악 ③

W Honey, shall we go for a drive tomorrow?
M Sorry, but I need to go to the office.
W But tomorrow's Saturday.
M It's our company's founding anniversary.
W I see. Do you need to wear a white shirt?
M Of course, I do.
W Then I should iron your shirt first.
M Thanks. Let's eat out when I come back home.

여 여보, 내일 드라이브하러 갈까?
남 미안해, 사무실에 가봐야 해.
여 하지만 내일 토요일이야.
남 우리 회사 창립 기념일이거든.
여 그렇구나. 와이셔츠 입어야 해?
남 물론, 그래야지.
여 그럼 셔츠 먼저 다려야겠네.
남 고마워. 집에 오면 외식하자.

해설 남자가 내일 회사를 가야하고 와이셔츠를 입어야 한다고 하자, 여자가 셔츠를 먼저 다려야겠다고 하였다.

어휘 go for a drive 드라이브하다   founding anniversary 창립 기념일   iron [áiərn] 다림질하다   eat out 외식하다

12 언급 유무 파악 ⑤

W Good evening, everyone. Today is the day we've been waiting for. It's the third anniversary of our Save the Earth campaign. This yearly event takes place on the fifteenth of April. For first-time visitors, let me tell you about the event. You can see all the campaign activities over the past year and even changes that occurred. We have a theme every year, and for this year, it is "No plastic." Please enjoy the event. Thank you!

여 안녕하세요, 여러분. 오늘은 바로 저희가 기다려 온 날이죠. 저희 '지구를 살리자' 캠페인의 3주년이랍니다. 이 연간 행사는 4월 15일에 열립니다. 처음 방문하시는 분들을 위해 행사에 대해 소개해 드리겠습니다. 작년 한 해 동안의 모든 캠페인 활동을 보실 수 있고 심지어 나타난 변화들도 보실 수 있습니다. 매년 저희는 주제를 가지는데, 올해는 '노 플라스틱'이랍니다. 그럼 행사를 즐기시고, 감사합니다!

해설 캠페인에서 하는 주요 활동에 대해서는 언급하지 않았으므로, 정답은 ⑤이다.
어휘 yearly [jíərli] 연간의, 해마다 있는   take place 일어나다, 개최되다   overall [òuvərɔ́ːl] 전체적인   occur [əkə́ːr] 발생하다, 일어나다

13 표 파악 ②

M The atmosphere in this restaurant is really romantic.
W Yes, it is. It's one of the must-go restaurants for young people.
M I see. What do you want to eat? There are many sets for two.
W First of all, I heard the salad here tastes good.
M Okay. Let's try it. What about pizza for the main dish?
W That sounds great. I also want some pasta. Here are sets that have salad, pizza, and pasta together.
M All right. All sets include two drinks, too. What do you want to drink?
W Soda goes perfectly with cheesy food.

남 이 레스토랑 분위기 되게 로맨틱하다.
여 맞아. 젊은 사람들 사이에서 꼭 가봐야 하는 레스토랑 중 한 곳이야.
남 그렇구나. 뭐 먹고 싶어? 2인 메뉴가 많네.
여 우선, 내가 듣기론 여기 샐러드가 맛있대.
남 그래. 먹어보자. 메인 요리로 피자 어때?
여 좋아. 파스타도 먹고 싶어. 여기 샐러드, 피자, 파스타가 같이 있는 세트들이 있어.
남 알겠어. 모든 세트에는 음료 두 잔이 포함이네. 뭘 마실래?
여 느끼한 음식에는 탄산음료가 완벽하지.

해설 샐러드와 피자 그리고 파스타가 함께 있는 세트에 탄산음료를 마시겠다고 하였다.
어휘 atmosphere [ǽtməsfìər] 분위기   must-go 꼭 가봐야 하는   first of all 우선   cheesy [tʃíːzi] 느끼한

14 화제·주제 파악 ④

W You use this when you record or check something important like birthdays. It helps you not to forget significant events. It also reminds you of national holidays. It comes in different sizes. You can hang it on the wall or put it on your desk. The one on a smartphone lets you know your important anniversaries by ringing an alarm.

여 당신은 생일과 같은 중요한 무언가를 기록하거나 확인을 할 때 이것을 사용합니다. 이것은 당신이 중요한 일을 까먹지 않도록 도와줍니다. 이것은 또한 당신에게 공휴일을 상기시키기도 합니다. 이것은 다양한 크기가 있습니다. 당신은 그것을 벽에 걸어둘 수도 있고 책상에 올려둘 수도 있습니다. 스마트폰에 있는 것은 알람을 울리면서 당신에게 중요한 기념일을 알려주기도 합니다.

해설 중요한 날을 잊지 않도록 도와주고 스마트폰 안에 있는 것은 알람을 울리며 중요한 날을 알려준다고 하였다.

어휘 significant [signífikənt] 중요한   national [nǽʃənəl] 국가의

15 **할 일 파악** ④

W This expression seems unfamiliar.
M What are you reading?
W It's a magazine, which is really good for learning English.
M How do you study with it?
W I read an article and highlight expressions I'm not familiar with.
M That must be really helpful. Where can I buy it?
W You can subscribe to it online. It's cheaper if you buy a one-year subscription.
M Thanks.

여 이 표현은 생소한 것 같아.
남 뭘 읽고 있는 거야?
여 잡지인데, 영어를 배우기에 아주 좋아.
남 이걸로 어떻게 공부를 해?
여 기사를 읽고 익숙하지 않은 표현들에 하이라이트 표시를 하는 거야.
남 그거 정말 유용하겠다. 어디서 살 수 있어?
여 온라인으로 구독할 수 있어. 1년 구독을 하면 더 저렴해.
남 고마워.

해설 여자에게 어디서 잡지를 살 수 있는지 물어보고 구독 신청 방법을 알려준 것에 대해 고맙다고 하였다.

어휘 expression [ikspréʃən] 표현   unfamiliar [ʌnfəmíljər] 생소한, 익숙지 않은   article [áːrtikl] 기사   highlight [háilàit] 하이라이트 표시를 하다   subscribe [səbskráib] 구독하다

16 **숫자 정보 파악** ①

W It's already 4 o'clock. Why are you still here?
M I have an appointment at 5, so it's fine.
W You should consider how long it will take to get there.
M It only takes twenty minutes by car.
W There's a firework festival in the evening. There will be heavy traffic on the way.
M Oh, I totally forgot about that. I think I should leave now.
W Yeah. Drive safely.

여 벌써 4시야. 왜 아직 여기에 있어?
남 5시 약속이라서 괜찮아.
여 가는 데 걸리는 시간을 고려해야지.
남 차로 20분밖에 안 걸려.
여 저녁에 불꽃 축제 있잖아. 가는 길에 차가 많이 막힐 텐데.
남 아, 완전히 까먹고 있었네. 지금 나가야겠다.

여 그래. 운전 조심히 해.

해설 지금 시각은 4시이고 차가 막힐 것을 생각하여 지금 나간다고 하였다.

어휘 appointment [əpɔ́intmənt] 약속   consider [kənsídər] 고려하다   traffic [trǽfik] 교통 체증   totally [tóutəli] 완전히

17 **적절한 응답 찾기** ④

W Look at all these wrinkles.
M I can't really see them.
W I feel like I am really getting old. I feel depressed.
M Everybody gets old. Don't be too upset.
W I would look much younger if I didn't have any wrinkles.
M You are beautiful just the way you are.
W Do you really mean that?
M I'm serious. Love yourself for who you are.

여 여기 주름들 좀 봐.
남 잘 안 보이는걸.
여 정말 나이가 든 것 같아. 우울해.
남 모든 사람은 나이가 들어. 너무 속상하지 마.
여 주름만 없으면 훨씬 어려 보일 텐데.
남 있는 모습 그대로의 당신이 아름다워.
여 진심이야?
남 진심이야. 있는 그대로의 자신을 사랑해.

해설 있는 모습 그대로가 아름답다고 하자 진심이냐고 묻는 말에 대한 가장 적절한 응답은 ④ '진심이야. 있는 그대로의 자신을 사랑해.'이다.
① 글쎄, 나도 내 주름이 싫어.   ② 넌 늘 내게 모범을 보여주잖아.
③ 내게 너의 모든 비밀을 얘기할 필요는 없어.
⑤ 다른 사람에게 어떻게 보일지 신경 쓰도록 해.
어휘 wrinkle [ríŋkl] 주름   depressed [diprést] 우울한   mean [miːn] 의도하다, ~을 뜻하다

18 **적절한 응답 찾기** ④

W Thanks for inviting me to lunch.
M It's my pleasure. You helped me a lot yesterday.
W That wasn't a big deal. By the way, why are the lights off?
M Since it's bright and enough sunlight is coming in, I don't turn on the lights in the afternoon.
W I see. That's a good habit.
M And because the weather's getting hot, I feel hotter when the lights are on.
W You can say that again.
M Above all, I believe we should save electricity to make the Earth healthier.
W I should care about the environment like you.

여 점심에 초대해줘서 고마워.
남 내가 좋아서 하는 건데 뭘. 어제 날 많이 도와줬잖아.
여 큰일도 아닌걸. 그건 그렇고, 왜 불이 다 꺼져 있어?
남 햇빛이 충분히 들어와서 밝기 때문에 오후에는 불을 켜지 않아.
여 그렇구나. 좋은 습관이네.
남 그리고 날씨가 더워지고 있어서 불이 켜져 있으면 더 덥더라고.
여 맞아.
남 무엇보다도, 지구를 더 건강하게 하려면 전기를 줄여야 한다고 믿어.
여 나도 너처럼 환경에 대해 신경 써야겠는걸.

해설 지구를 건강하게 하려면 전기를 줄여야 한다는 말에 대한 가장 적절한 응답은 ④ '나도 너처럼 환경에 대해 신경 써야겠는걸.'이다.
① 이제 정말 여름이라고 말할 수 있겠어.

② 그 다음 무슨 일이 있었는지 알고 싶어.
③ 우리는 대신 다른 것들을 해볼 수 있어.
⑤ 건강을 유지하는 법에 대해 조언해 줘.
어휘 pleasure [pléʒər] 기쁨   habit [hǽbit] 습관   above all 무엇보다도   electricity [ilektrísəti] 전기

19   적절한 응답 찾기 ④

W Are you <u>going somewhere</u> today?
M I'm planning to visit a new café and <u>blog it later</u>.
W You are <u>so diligent</u>. Blogging regularly is never easy.
M It's just what I love to do.
W Isn't that camera too heavy to <u>carry around</u>?
M If I can take good pictures, the weight doesn't matter.
W How can I be <u>full of passion</u> like you?
M <u>First, you should figure out what you like.</u>

여 오늘 어디가?
남 새로 오픈한 카페에 가려고 해.
여 너 정말 부지런하다. 규칙적으로 블로그를 기록하는 게 절대 쉽지 않은데 말이야.
남 그저 내가 좋아서 하는 건데 뭘.
여 그 카메라 가지고 다니기에 너무 무겁지 않아?
남 좋은 사진을 찍을 수만 있다면 무게는 중요하지 않아.
여 어떻게 하면 내가 너처럼 열정이 가득할 수 있니?
남 <u>우선, 네가 좋아하는 것이 무엇인지를 찾아야 해.</u>

해설 어떻게 하면 열정적일 수 있느냐는 질문에 대한 가장 적절한 응답은 ④ '우선, 네가 좋아하는 것이 무엇인지를 찾아야 해.'이다.
① 네 직업이 굉장히 매력 있는 것 같아.   ② 원하면 나랑 같이 가도 돼.
③ 난 보통 아침에 일찍 일어나.   ⑤ 열정은 돈으로 살 수 있는 게 아니야.
어휘 blog [blag] (블로그를) 기록하다   diligent [dílidʒənt] 부지런한   matter [mǽtər] 중요하다

20   상황에 맞는 말 찾기 ③

M Alex and his sister Kate <u>take the bus</u> to go downtown. On the bus, there is <u>one empty seat</u>, and Kate sits in it. When they <u>reach the halfway point</u> of their destination, the bus is already full. At the next stop, an old woman gets on the bus. She <u>stands in front of</u> where Kate is sitting. In this situation, what would Alex most likely say to Kate?
Alex Kate, <u>you'd better offer that person your seat.</u>

남 Alex와 그의 여동생인 Kate는 시내로 가기 위해 버스를 탑니다. 버스에는 빈 좌석이 하나 있고, Kate는 거기에 앉습니다. 도착지의 중간 지점에 다다랐을 때, 버스는 이미 만석 상태입니다. 다음 정거장에서 나이가 지긋한 여성이 버스를 탑니다. 그녀는 Kate가 앉은 자리 앞에 서 있습니다. 이 상황에서 Alex는 Kate에게 뭐라고 말을 할까요?
Alex Kate, 자리를 양보해 드리도록 해.

해설 나이가 지긋한 여성이 여동생이 앉은 좌석 앞에 서 있는 상황이므로 가장 적절한 응답은 ③ '자리를 양보해 드리도록 해.'이다.
① 다음에는 택시를 타자.   ④ 우리 시내에 거의 다 왔어.
④ 손잡이를 꽉 잡아야 해.   ⑤ 다음 정거장에서 버튼을 눌러.
어휘 downtown [dàuntáun] 시내로   empty [émpti] 텅 빈   reach [ri:tʃ] 도달하다   halfway point 중간 지점   destination [dèstənéiʃən] 목적지

Listen and Check   *p. 10*

Q1	True	Q11	False
Q2	False	Q12	once a year
Q3	Yes	Q13	Yes
Q4	in the morning	Q14	True
Q5	False	Q15	to learn English
Q6	Yes	Q16	No
Q7	True	Q17	False
Q8	to meet co-workers	Q18	turn off the lights
Q9	two	Q19	No
Q10	No	Q20	offer her seat

해석
Q1 꽃무늬가 있는 것이 나이가 있는 여성들 사이에서 가장 잘 팔리는 스카프이다.
Q2 남자는 그의 여동생에게서 차를 빌렸다.
Q3 남자는 하루에 두 잔 이상의 물을 마시는가?
Q4 남자는 언제 요가 수업을 듣고 싶어 하는가?
Q5 여자는 남자가 말하고 있는 드라마를 본 적이 있다.
Q6 여자는 경기 전에 치료를 받을 것인가?
Q7 남자는 여자를 보기를 기대한다.
Q8 여자는 무엇을 위해서 외출을 하는가?
Q9 남자는 방문객에게 몇 가지의 규칙을 안내하고 있는가?
Q10 남자는 원목 액자 두 개만을 사는가?
Q11 남자와 여자는 내일 드라이브를 하러 갈 것이다.
Q12 그 행사는 얼마나 자주 개최되는가?
Q13 남자와 여자는 둘 다 피자를 먹기를 원하는가?
Q14 그 물건의 주된 사용은 중요한 날을 기억하기 위해서이다.
Q15 그녀는 왜 잡지를 읽는가?
Q16 남자는 그 날 불꽃 축제가 있다는 것을 알았는가?
Q17 남자는 주름살을 가지는 것에 대해 속상해 한다.
Q18 남자는 전기를 절약하기 위해서 무엇을 하는가?
Q19 여자는 자신이 하고 싶은 것을 찾았는가?
Q20 Alex가 나이가 지긋한 여성을 위해 자신의 여동생에게 요청한 것은 무엇인가?

실전 모의고사 2회   *pp. 18~19*

1	⑤	2	④	3	②	4	④	5	③
6	①	7	④	8	⑤	9	⑤	10	③
11	③	12	②	13	④	14	②	15	⑤
16	④	17	①	18	①	19	⑤	20	④

1   그림 정보 파악 ⑤

M Vivian, did you make that hat by yourself?
W Yes, I did. I <u>knitted it</u> for my little sister.
M You made it well. The striped hat is so cute.
W Thank you. <u>Adding stripes</u> to the hat was really hard.
M <u>Why didn't you attach</u> a pompom to the hat?
W I wanted to. But I didn't know <u>how to make one</u>.

M Still, it's so cute. I'm sure your sister will like it.

남 Vivian, 그 모자를 너 혼자서 만든 거야?
여 그럼. 내 여동생을 위해 뜨개질했어.
남 잘 만들었네. 줄무늬 모자가 너무 귀엽다.
여 고마워. 모자에 줄무늬를 추가하는 건 정말 힘들었어.
남 왜 모자에 방울을 달지 않았니?
여 그러고 싶었어. 하지만 어떻게 만드는지 몰랐어.
남 그래도 너무 귀여워. 네 여동생은 분명히 좋아할 거야.

해설 줄무늬 모자이며 방울을 만드는 방법을 몰라서 달지 못했다고 하였다.
어휘 knit [nit] 뜨개질하다   stripe [straip] 줄무늬, 띠   attach [ətǽtʃ] 부착하다, 달다   pompom [pɑ́mpɑ̀m] 모자 위에 달린 방울

2 부탁한 일 파악 ④

W Dad, why are you all dressed up today?
M I have a date with your mom. As you know, today is our wedding anniversary.
W I totally forgot. Sorry, Dad.
M That's okay. If you're not busy, I need you to babysit your sister while we are gone.
W Sure. I can do that. When will you come back?
M We'll be back in about 5 hours.
W I see. Have a great time, Dad!

여 아빠, 오늘 왜 그렇게 차려 입었어요?
남 네 엄마랑 데이트가 있단다. 너도 알다시피 오늘은 우리 결혼기념일이잖아.
여 완전히 잊었어요. 죄송해요, 아빠.
남 괜찮아. 네가 바쁘지 않다면 우리가 없는 동안 네가 여동생을 돌봐주면 좋겠어.
여 그럼요. 할 수 있어요. 언제 돌아오세요?
남 5시간 이내에 돌아올게.
여 알겠어요. 좋은 시간 보내세요, 아빠!

해설 아내와 결혼기념일 데이트를 하게 되어 딸에게 여동생을 돌봐 달라고 부탁하였다.
어휘 dress up 차려 입다   babysit 아기를 돌봐 주다

3 그림 상황 파악 ②

① W Are there any good Italian restaurants around here?
  M Of course. There's one just across the road.
② W How much is this refrigerator?
  M It's brand new. It costs two thousand dollars.
③ W What would you like to eat for breakfast?
  M Potato soup and an omelet, please.
④ W I like this jacket. May I borrow it?
  M Sure, but I need it back before Friday.
⑤ W Wow! Your sofa is very comfortable.
  M Thank you. I bought it last week.

① 여 근처에 좋은 이탈리아 레스토랑이 있니?
  남 물론이지. 길 건너편에 하나 있어.
② 여 이 냉장고는 얼마인가요?
  남 새로 나온 제품이에요. 2천 달러입니다.
③ 여 아침 식사로 무엇을 드시겠어요?
  남 감자 수프랑 오믈렛 주세요.
④ 여 이 재킷이 마음에 든다. 내가 빌려가도 될까?
  남 물론이지. 하지만 금요일 전까지 돌려줘.
⑤ 여 우와! 네 소파는 매우 편하다.
  남 고마워. 저번 주에 구입했어.

해설 냉장고를 가리키며 냉장고에 대한 정보를 묻고 답하는 상황이다.
어휘 refrigerator [rifrídʒərèitər] 냉장고   comfortable [kʌ́mfərtəbl] 편한, 편안한

4 특정 정보 파악 ④

[Telephone rings.]
M Hello. This is the Min Dental Clinic. How can I help you?
W Hello. I'd like to make an appointment for this week.
M Okay. Which day do you want?
W Is Wednesday at 2 p.m. possible?
M Sorry. Dr. Min has to attend a seminar on Wednesday afternoon.
W Then how about Thursday at 2 a.m.?
M Hold on a second. [Pause] It's available.
W Great. See you then.

남 안녕하세요. 민 치과입니다. 무엇을 도와드릴까요?
여 여보세요. 이번 주에 예약하고 싶은데요.
남 네. 어떤 요일을 원하세요?
여 수요일 오후 2시는 가능할까요?
남 죄송해요. 민 박사님이 수요일 오후에는 세미나에 참석하셔야 해요.
여 그러면 목요일 오후 2시는 어때요?
남 잠깐만요. 가능해요.
여 좋아요. 그때 뵈어요.

해설 수요일은 불가능하여 목요일 오후 2시에 방문하기로 하였다.
어휘 attend [əténd] 참석하다   available [əvéiləbl] 이용 가능한

5 언급 유무 파악 ③

W Kyusung, what are you looking at?
M The acting club poster on the bulletin board. I want to join it.
W That would be perfect for you. When and where is the audition taking place?
M In the school auditorium next Friday afternoon. They will pick just one person.
W You must be nervous. What do you have to do at the audition?
M We aren't required to do anything specific. But I need to act like I am crying.
W If you want, I'll be your acting partner when you practice.
M Really? Thank you so much!

여 규성아, 무엇을 보고 있니?
남 게시판에 있는 연기 동아리 포스터를 보는 중이야. 가입하고 싶어.
여 너한테 딱 맞을 것 같아. 오디션이 언제, 어디에서 열려?
남 학교 강당에서 다음 주 금요일 오후야. 1명만 뽑을 거래.
여 긴장되겠다. 오디션에서 무엇을 연기해야 해?
남 구체적으로 정해진 건 없어. 하지만 난 울고 있는 것 같이 연기해야 해.
여 만약 네가 원하면, 내가 연습을 위해 너의 연기 파트너가 되어 줄게.
남 정말? 정말 고마워.

해설 오디션 지원자를 평가하는 심사위원에 대해서는 언급되지 않았다.
어휘 bulletin board 게시판, 공고판   auditorium [ɔ̀ːditɔ́ːriəm] 강당   specific [spisífik] 구체적인, 특정한

6 장소 추론 ①

W Are you all right? You look pale.

M This ship is rolling from side to side. I feel like I'm going to throw up.

W Are you getting seasick? Let's go on the deck.

M Good idea. I need to get some fresh air.

W [Door closes.] How do you feel now?

M Much better. [Pause] Look! I see a coral island.

W That's a relief. I think we're close to reaching our destination.

여 괜찮니? 너 창백해 보여.
남 배가 심하게 흔들려. 나 토할 거 같아.
여 뱃멀미하는 거야? 갑판으로 나가자.
남 좋은 생각이야. 신선한 공기가 필요해.
여 지금은 어때?
남 훨씬 낫다. 저걸 봬! 산호섬이 보여.
여 다행이다. 우리는 목적지에 거의 다 온 것 같아.

해설 뱃멀미를 해서 갑판으로 나가 시원한 바람을 마시고 있는 상황이다.
어휘 pale [peil] 안색이 안 좋은, 창백한   seasick [síːsìk] 뱃멀미가 난   deck [dek] 갑판

7   어색한 대화 찾기 ④

① M What do you do in your free time?
  W I usually take a nap or listen to music.
② M The weather is so hot! My ice cream is melting.
  W Hurry up and finish your ice cream.
③ M Is there anything to eat?
  W I don't think so. We should order some food.
④ M How many people are going to the baseball game?
  W The game is supposed to start at 5 p.m.
⑤ M Are you done vacuuming the living room?
  W Yes, I just finished.

① 남 자유 시간에 무엇을 하니?
  여 나는 보통 낮잠을 자거나 음악을 들어.
② 남 날씨가 너무 더워. 내 아이스크림이 녹고 있어.
  여 서둘러서 아이스크림을 다 먹어.
③ 남 먹을 게 있니?
  여 아닐 거야. 우리는 음식을 주문해야 해.
④ 남 야구 경기에 얼마나 많은 사람들이 올까?
  여 경기는 오후 5시에 시작해.
⑤ 남 거실에 진공청소기 돌렸니?
  여 응. 이제 막 끝냈어.

해설 얼마나 많은 사람들이 오냐고 묻는 질문에 오후 5시에 경기가 시작된다는 대답은 부자연스럽다.
어휘 nap [næp] 낮잠   melt [melt] 녹다

8   부탁한 일 파악 ⑤

M Juha, are you organizing your closet?

W Actually, I'm sorting the clothes that I never wear or that don't fit well.

M What for?

W I want to donate them to charity.

M That's a good deed. Do you need any help?

W Hmm... Can you help me to carry these clothes to a charity?

M Sure. I'll be right back with my car.

남 주하야, 옷장을 정돈하는 중이야?

여 사실은, 전혀 안 입거나 안 맞는 옷을 분류하는 중이야.
남 무엇 때문에?
여 옷을 자선 단체에 기부하고 싶어서.
남 착한 행동이네. 도움이 필요하니?
여 흠, 내가 이 옷을 자선 단체로 나르는 걸 도와줄 수 있니?
남 물론이야. 차를 가지고 다시 올게.

해설 기부하려고 구분해 둔 옷을 자선 단체로 나르는 걸 도와달라고 부탁하였다.
어휘 organize [ɔ́ːrgənàiz] 정리하다, 준비하다   sort [sɔːrt] 분류하다, 선별하다   deed [diːd] 행동, 행위   charity [tʃǽrəti] 자선 단체, 자선

9   화제·주제 파악 ⑤

W Pay attention, students! This is your principal speaking. Because a storm warning has been issued, we have decided to close school today. It is raining worse, and the wind is blowing heavily. The weather forecast says that the storm is expected to be severe. Students should go home right now and avoid outdoor activities. We will keep you informed if anything happens.

여 집중하세요, 학생 여러분! 저는 교장입니다. 폭풍 주의보가 내렸기 때문에 우리는 오늘 학교를 폐쇄하기로 결정했습니다. 바깥은 비가 몹시 내리고 바람이 점점 세게 불고 있습니다. 일기 예보에서 폭풍이 심해질 것으로 예상된다고 합니다. 학생들은 지금 당장 집으로 돌아가서 야외 활동을 피하길 바랍니다. 무슨 일이 생기면 바로 알려주겠습니다.

해설 폭풍 주의보가 내려서 학교 수업을 중단하고 학생들을 집으로 보낸다는 방송을 하고 있다.
어휘 attention [ətènʃ ʌn] 주목, 주의   principal [prínsəpəl] 교장   issue [íʃuː] 내리다, 발행하다   inform [infɔ́ːrm] 알리다

10   숫자 정보 파악 ③

W Welcome to the Beijing Chinese Language School. How may I help you?

M I'd like to register for the beginner course.

W Okay. The beginner course is 100 dollars a month.

M That's kind of expensive. Is there a discount for beginners?

W Let me see. We're giving a 10% discount to new students.

M Sounds perfect! Is the textbook included?

W Sorry. You have to buy it at a bookstore.

여 베이징 중국어 학원에 오신 걸 환영합니다. 어떻게 도와 드릴까요?
남 초보자 과정에 등록하고 싶어요.
여 알겠습니다. 초보자 과정은 한 달에 100달러입니다.
남 조금 비싸네요. 초보자를 위한 할인은 있나요?
여 잠깐만요. 새로운 학생들에게 10%를 할인해 주고 있어요.
남 좋아요! 교재는 포함되어 있나요?
여 아뇨. 교재는 서점에서 구입해야 해요.

해설 학원비는 100달러인데 신규 학생을 위해 10% 할인을 해준다고 하였다.
어휘 register [rédʒistər] 등록하다   include [inklúːd] 포함하다

11   할 일 파악 ③

M Kaitlyn, you're always sitting in front of your computer.

W I have no choice. I'm busy working on it.

M That's why you have some pain in your neck. You

need to exercise regularly.
W You're right. I should take better care of myself.
M Why don't you go swimming with me?
W That sounds good. But I don't have a swimsuit.
M You can buy one. Let's go to a store.

남 Kaitlyn, 넌 항상 컴퓨터 앞에만 앉아 있구나.
여 선택의 여지가 없어. 컴퓨터로 일하느라 바빠.
남 그래서 네가 목이 아픈 거야. 넌 규칙적으로 운동할 필요가 있어.
여 네 말이 맞아. 내 자신을 돌봐야 해.
남 나랑 수영하러 가는 건 어때?
여 좋은 생각이야. 하지만 수영복이 없어.
남 하나 사면 돼. 가게로 가자.

해설 친구와 함께 수영을 하기 위해 수영복을 사러 가기로 하였다.
어휘 regularly [régjələrli] 정기적으로, 규칙적으로 swimsuit
[swímsjùːt] 수영복

12 언급 유무 파악 ②

M Welcome to Happy Farm. We are open only on
weekends from 10 a.m. to 5 p.m. We offer daytime
activities for visitors. You can experience life on
a farm. Admission is 10 dollars for adults and 5
dollars for children. You can feed and water the
horses. You can also milk a cow by hand. When
you get close to the animals, please be careful. If
you need help or more information, call us at 010-
1234-5678.

남 Happy Farm에 오신 걸 환영합니다. 저희는 주말 오전 10시부터 오후
5시까지만 개방합니다. 저희는 방문자를 위한 주간 활동을 제공하고 있
습니다. 여러분은 농장의 삶을 체험할 수 있습니다. 입장료는 성인 10
달러, 어린이 5달러입니다. 여러분은 말에게 먹이를 주거나 물을 먹일
수 있습니다. 또한 여러분은 직접 소의 젖을 짤 수 있습니다. 동물에게
다가갈 때는 부디 주의해 주세요. 만약 도움이나 추가 정보가 필요하다
면, 010-1234-5678로 연락 주세요.

해설 농장이 어디에 있는지에 대해서는 언급되지 않았다.
어휘 admission [ədmíʃən] 입장, 입학 by hand 직접, 손으로

13 그림 정보 파악 ④

M Look! This café is crowded with people.
W The reason is that it is famous for its cakes.
M Is it? I can't wait to taste one.
W Okay. Take a seat at Table A.
M I don't want to. It's next to the restroom.
W Then how about Table E?
M Near the entrance? It must be noisy there. Let's sit
next to Table E.
W Do you mean between Table C and Table E? Okay.

남 저기 봐! 이 카페는 사람으로 가득 차 있네.
여 왜냐하면 여기가 케이크로 유명해서 그래.
남 정말? 케이크를 빨리 맛보고 싶군.
여 그래. A 테이블에 앉자.
남 그러고 싶지 않아. 화장실 옆이잖아.
여 그러면 E 테이블은 어때?
남 입구 근처 말이니? 시끄러울 거야. E 테이블 옆에 앉자.
여 네 말은 C 테이블이랑 E 테이블 사이 말이지? 그래.

해설 화장실 옆이나 입구 근처도 아닌, C 테이블과 E 테이블 사이에 앉기
로 하였다.
어휘 be crowded with ~로 가득 차다 next to ~ 옆에 entrance

[éntrəns] 입구

14 화제·주제 파악 ②

W Most people have this in their homes. This may be
on your wall or desk. It has many different shapes.
The surface is smooth, and it can reflect light.
When you look at this, you can check your teeth
or adjust your appearance. It is also fragile. Some
people believe that if you break this, it will bring
bad luck.

여 대부분의 사람들은 이것을 집에 가지고 있습니다. 이것은 당신의 벽이
나 책상에 있을 겁니다. 이것은 다양한 모양을 가지고 있습니다. 표면은
매끄러우며 빛을 반사할 수 있습니다. 당신이 이것을 볼 때 치아를 확인
하거나 외모를 점검할 수 있습니다. 또한 이것은 깨지기 쉽습니다. 어떤
사람들은 만약 당신이 이것을 깨뜨리면, 그것이 불운을 가져올 거라고
믿습니다.

해설 빛을 반사해서 바라보는 상대의 모습을 보여주는 것은 거울이다.
어휘 surface [sə́ːrfis] 표면 smooth [smuːð] 매끄러운, 부드러운
adjust [ədʒʌ́st] 조정하다, 조절하다 appearance [əpí(ː)ərəns] 외모,
겉모습 fragile [frǽdʒəl] 깨지기 쉬운, 취약한

15 할 일 파악 ⑤

W What's the matter with your left ear?
M I got my ear pierced three days ago. Nice, huh?
W No. I mean that your ear is bleeding.
M Are you sure? In fact, I scratched it because it was
itching.
W That's the problem. You should never touch your
ear after getting it pierced.
M Oh, no! What should I do?
W You seem to have an infection. Go to see a doctor.

여 왼쪽 귀가 왜 그래?
남 3일 전에 귀를 뚫었어. 멋지지, 그렇지?
여 아니. 난 네 귀에서 피가 난다고 말하는 거야.
남 정말? 사실은 가려워서 긁었어.
여 그게 문제네. 귀를 뚫은 후에는 절대 만지면 안 돼.
남 맙소사. 어떻게 해야 하지?
여 염증이 생긴 거 같아. 의사에게 진찰받으러 가.

해설 여자가 남자에게 귀 뚫은 부분에 염증이 생겨 의사에게 진찰을 받으
러 가라고 하였다.
어휘 pierce [piərs] 뚫다 itching [ítʃiŋ] 간지러운, 가려운
infection [infékʃən] 염증

16 숫자 정보 파악 ④

W Benjamin, here is the book you requested.
M Wow! Thank you. Did you finish reading it?
W Of course I did. It was so interesting!
M I can't wait to read it. By the way, when should I
return this book?
W How about next Friday? On October 10.
M Sorry, but I have to visit my aunt that day. Is
October 12 possible?
W Do you mean next Sunday? I think that's fine.
M That's good. Let's meet on October 12 after lunch.
W Okay. Enjoy reading the book.

여 Benjamin, 여기 네가 요청했던 책이야.

남 왜 고마워. 넌 다 읽었어?
여 물론이지. 너무 재미있었어.
남 얼른 읽고 싶다. 그런데 책을 언제 돌려줘야 해?
여 다음 주 금요일은 어때? 10월 10일.
남 미안하지만 그 날은 이모네 방문해야 해. 10월 12일은 가능하니?
여 다음 일요일 말이지? 가능할 거 같아.
남 잘됐네. 10월 12일에 점심 먹은 후에 만나자.
여 그래. 책 재미있게 읽어.
해설 10월 10일에는 다른 계획이 있어서 12일에 책을 돌려주기로 하였다.
어휘 request [rikwést] 요청하다, 요구하다

17 적절한 응답 찾기 ①

M Welcome. What can I do for you?
W I'd like to get a refund on this shirt. I bought it three days ago.
M Is there something wrong with it?
W Let me show you. There is a hole here.
M Oh, I'm sorry. Do you have the receipt?
W No. I'm afraid I lost it.
M Sorry. We can give you a refund only if you have the receipt.
W Excuse me? I don't understand.

남 어서 오세요. 무엇을 도와 드릴까요?
여 이 셔츠를 환불받고 싶어요. 3일 전에 구입했어요.
남 셔츠에 문제가 있나요?
여 보여 드릴게요. 여기 구멍이 있어요.
남 죄송합니다. 영수증은 가져오셨나요?
여 아니요. 잃어버린 것 같아요.
남 죄송합니다. 저희는 영수증이 있는 경우에만 환불을 해 드릴 수 있어요.
여 뭐라고요? 이해가 안 되네요.
해설 영수증이 없어서 환불해 줄 수 없다는 말에 대한 가장 적절한 응답은 ① '뭐라고요? 이해가 안 되네요.'이다.
② 회색 정장이랑 잘 어울리네요.
③ 감사합니다. 당신은 매우 친절하시군요.
④ 죄송하지만 저는 까만 청바지를 사고 싶어요.
⑤ 가능하다면 현금으로 지불할게요.
어휘 refund [rí:fʌnd] 환불   receipt [risí:t] 영수증

18 적절한 응답 찾기 ①

M Summer, I think you should stop taking piano lessons.
W Why? I really enjoy them a lot.
M But you need to spend more time studying.
W I understand what you're saying. But I want to be a pianist.
M Do you? I thought you play the piano for fun.
W No, Dad. I want to perform before audiences someday.
M If so, I will support your dream.

남 Summer, 내 생각에는 넌 피아노 레슨을 그만둬야 할 거 같아.
여 왜요? 전 피아노 레슨이 정말 좋아요.
남 하지만 넌 공부에 시간을 더 써야 해.
여 무슨 말인지 이해해요. 하지만 저는 피아니스트가 되고 싶어요.
남 그러니? 네가 재미로 피아노를 친다고 생각했어.
여 아니요, 아빠. 저는 언젠가 청중 앞에서 공연하고 싶어요.
남 그렇다면, 너의 꿈을 지지해 주마.
해설 피아니스트가 되어 언젠가 청중 앞에서 공연하고 싶다는 말에 대한

가장 적절한 응답은 ① '그렇다면, 내가 너의 꿈을 지지해 주마.'이다.
② 넌 내일 피아노를 팔아야 해.   ③ 우리는 이번 여름에 태국을 여행했어.
④ 내가 피아노 공연 티켓을 사 줄게.   ⑤ 너에게 테니스 강습 받는 것을 추천할게.
어휘 perform [pərfɔ́:rm] 연주하다, 공연하다   audience [ɔ́:diəns] 청중, 관객

19 적절한 응답 찾기 ⑤

M Seoyoung, where are you going?
W I'm going to the theater to watch a movie.
M Are you serious? You didn't hand in your report, right?
W No, but I can do it tomorrow.
M The report is due tomorrow. You should start doing it now.
W Oh, no. I don't want to ruin my weekend in the library.
M If you don't submit it tomorrow, you will get a zero.
W All right. I'll go to the library to write the report.

남 서영아, 어디 가는 중이야?
여 영화 보러 극장으로 가는 중이야.
남 정말이니? 보고서를 아직 안 냈잖아.
여 안 냈지. 근데 내일 할 수 있어.
남 기한이 내일까지야. 지금 당장 시작해야 해.
여 어휴. 내 주말을 도서관에서 망치기 싫어.
남 내일 제출하지 않으면 0점을 받게 될 거야.
여 알겠어. 보고서 쓰러 도서관으로 갈게.
해설 보고서를 내일까지 제출하지 않으면 0점을 받게 될 거라는 말에 대한 가장 적절한 응답은 ⑤ '알겠어. 보고서 쓰러 도서관으로 갈게.'이다.
① 함께 영화 보러 가자.   ② 너는 도서관에서 책을 읽을 필요가 있어.
③ 어제 이미 보고서를 제출했어.   ④ 방과 후에 네가 에세이 쓰는 걸 도와줄게.
어휘 submit [səbmít] 제출하다

20 상황에 맞는 말 찾기 ④

M Ashley is visiting Switzerland to meet her friend Michael. Michael is so happy to see her that he invites her to his place. He introduces some beautiful tourist sites to her. He also drives her to the sites and takes pictures of her. Ashley has to leave tomorrow. She feels grateful for his kindness during her visit. She wants to buy him a big dinner at a nice restaurant. In this situation, what would Ashley most likely say to Michael?
Ashley Michael, can I treat you to dinner tonight?

남 Ashley는 그녀의 친구인 Michael을 만나기 위해 스위스를 방문하는 중입니다. Michael은 그녀를 만나게 되어 너무 기뻐서 그녀를 자신의 집에 초대합니다. 그는 그녀에게 멋진 여행지를 소개합니다. 그는 또한 차를 운전해서 그녀를 여행지로 데려다 주고 사진도 찍어줍니다. Ashley는 내일 떠나야 합니다. 그녀는 방문하는 동안 보여준 그의 친절에 고마워합니다. 그녀는 그에게 근사한 식당에서 멋진 저녁을 사주고 싶습니다. 이런 상황에서, Ashley가 Michael에게 할 말로 가장 적절한 것은 무엇일까요?
Ashley Michael, 내가 오늘 밤 너에게 저녁을 대접해도 될까?
해설 Ashley가 여행 중에 Michael이 자신에게 보여준 친절에 고마워하는 상황이므로 ④ '내가 오늘 밤 너에게 저녁을 대접해도 될까?'라고 하는 것이 가장 적절하다.
① 내가 짐 꾸리는 걸 도와줄래?   ② 어젯밤 데이트 어땠어?

③ 날 공항까지 데려다 줄 수 있니? ⑤ 내가 오늘 밤 여기에 머물러도 될까?

어휘 grateful [gréitfəl] 고마워하는 situation [sìtʃuéiʃən] 상황, 처지

Listen and Check   p. 20

Q1	True	Q11	False
Q2	No	Q12	No
Q3	a refrigerator	Q13	cakes
Q4	Wednesday	Q14	True
Q5	True	Q15	three days ago
Q6	a coral island	Q16	No
Q7	True	Q17	getting a refund
Q8	clothes	Q18	a pianist
Q9	a principal	Q19	tomorrow
Q10	Yes	Q20	Yes

해석

Q1 Vivian은 그녀의 여동생을 위해 모자를 뜨개질했다.
Q2 오늘은 그녀의 결혼기념일인가?
Q3 그녀는 무엇에 관심이 있는가?
Q4 민 박사는 언제 세미나에 참석할 예정인가?
Q5 남자는 울고 있는 것 같이 연기해야 한다.
Q6 남자와 여자는 어디로 가고 있는가?
Q7 남자는 야구 경기에 얼마나 많은 사람들이 올지를 알고 싶어 했다.
Q8 주하는 자선 단체에 무엇을 기부하길 원하는가?
Q9 누가 학생에게 말하고 있을까?
Q10 그는 초보자 과정에 등록하고 싶어 하는가?
Q11 Kaitlyn은 어깨에 통증이 있다.
Q12 Happy Farm은 주중에 문을 열까?
Q13 이 카페는 무엇으로 유명한가?
Q14 사람들은 보통 외모를 확인하기 위해 이것을 사용한다.
Q15 그는 언제 귀를 뚫었을까?
Q16 Benjamin은 그 책을 다 읽었을까?
Q17 여자가 요청하는 것은 무엇인가?
Q18 Summer가 되고 싶어 하는 것은 무엇인가?
Q19 보고서 마감일이 언제인가?
Q20 Ashley는 친구를 만나기 위해 스위스에 방문했을까?

실전 모의고사 3회   pp. 28~29

1	⑤	2	④	3	④	4	③	5	④
6	⑤	7	③	8	①	9	⑤	10	①
11	④	12	②	13	③	14	⑤	15	⑤
16	④	17	④	18	③	19	④	20	⑤

1 그림 정보 파악 ⑤

M Hello. I want to get a clock to hang in the nursing home I work at.
W Sure. We have various shapes and designs for the elderly. Do you have something in mind?
M Yes. I want a round one with big numbers on it.
W Um, what about this one with the green

---

background? It's a plain design that's very simple.
M The numbers are a bit hard to see.
W Then this would be perfect. It's white, and the numbers on it are big and easy to see.
M I like it.

남 안녕하세요. 요양원에 설치할 시계를 찾고 있어요.
여 네, 노인들을 위한 다양한 모양과 디자인이 있답니다. 따로 생각하신 것이 있나요?
남 예, 큰 숫자가 있는 둥근 시계를 원해요.
여 음, 초록색 배경의 이것은 어떠신가요? 매우 단순한 일반 디자인이에요.
남 숫자가 잘 보이지 않네요.
여 그러면, 이것이 완벽할 거예요. 흰색 배경이고, 숫자가 커서 잘 보여요.
남 마음에 드네요.

해설 흰색 배경에 숫자가 큰 것이라고 하였다.
어휘 nursing home 요양원 various [vέ(:)əriəs] 다양한 the elderly 노인들

2 목적 파악 ④

[Cellphone rings.]
M Hi, Melissa. It's me, Jason.
W Hi, Jason. Are you done with English class?
M Yes. And guess what. Now I'm at the registration desk to pay for next month's class.
W So why are you calling? Is there a problem?
M No. I am calling you because I want to know if you want to take English class with me next month.
W Do you mean Mr. Taylor's grammar class?
M Yes. The sign says that we can get a 10-percent discount if we register for an English class together. Isn't that great?
W That's a good deal, but I already enrolled in another class. Sorry, Jason.

남 Melissa. 나야 Jason.
여 Jason, 영어 수업 끝났니?
남 응, 있잖아. 나 지금 다음 달 수업료를 내려고 등록 창구에 있어.
여 왜? 무슨 문제가 있어?
남 아니. 네가 다음 달에 나와 함께 영어 수업을 듣고 싶은지 알려고 전화했어.
여 Taylor 선생님의 문법 수업 말이니?
남 응. 안내문에 함께 등록하면 10퍼센트 할인을 받을 수 있다고 되어 있어. 괜찮지 않아?
여 괜찮네. 하지만, 나는 이미 다른 수업에 등록을 했어. 미안해, Jason.

해설 다음 달 수업을 10% 할인된 금액으로 함께 수강할 것인지를 묻고 있다.
어휘 registration [rèdʒistréiʃən] 등록 enroll [inróul] 등록하다

3 그림 상황 파악 ④

① W This dress is so nice. How much does it cost?
  M The original price is 50 dollars, but we're offering a 20-percent discount on it.
② W Let's change the clothes on the mannequin in our display window.
  M Okay. Get her dressed in the outfit that arrived yesterday.
③ W I don't think these shoes go with these pants.
  M I'll find some other shoes that match your pants.

④ W <u>Can</u> I <u>try on</u> this coat?
  M I'm sorry, but it is not for sale. It's only for display.
⑤ W Where is the <u>nearest</u> <u>shoe</u> <u>store</u>?
  M There's one on the third floor next to the pharmacy.

① 여 이 드레스가 멋지네요. 얼마인가요?
  남 원래 가격은 50달러지만 20퍼센트 할인을 하고 있어요.
② 여 진열창에 있는 마네킹의 옷을 바꿉시다.
  남 좋아요. 어제 도착한 옷을 입히도록 해요.
③ 여 이 신발이 이 바지와 어울리는 것 같지 않아.
  남 네 바지에 어울리는 다른 신발을 찾아볼게.
④ 여 이 코트를 입어 봐도 되나요?
  남 죄송합니다만 판매용이 아닙니다. 전시용이에요.
⑤ 여 가장 가까운 신발 가게가 어디인가요?
  남 3층 약국 옆에 있습니다.

해설 전시되어 있는 코트를 입어볼 수 있는지 묻고 있는 상황이다.
어휘 mannequin [mǽnəkin] 마네킹 outfit [áutfìt] 옷 pharmacy [fɑ́ːrməsi] 약국

4 교통수단 파악 ③

M Welcome to the Seoul Tourist Information Center. What can I do for you?
W I want to go to the Seoul Foreign School. What is <u>the best way to get there</u>? Can I take the subway?
M Well, there isn't a subway station near the Seoul Foreign School. You <u>should</u> <u>take</u> <u>a</u> <u>bus</u> or taxi.
W Which do you think would be better?
M I think a taxi would be <u>comfortable</u> <u>and</u> <u>fast</u>.
W Good. Then I'll take a taxi. Thank you.

남 Seoul Tourist Information Center에 오신 것을 환영합니다. 무엇을 도와드릴까요?
여 저는 서울 외국인 학교에 가고 싶어요. 그곳에 도착할 가장 빠른 방법은 무엇인가요? 지하철을 탈 수 있나요?
남 음, 서울 외국인 학교 근처에는 지하철역이 없습니다. 버스나 택시를 타셔야 해요.
여 어느 것이 더 낫다고 생각하시나요?
남 택시가 편하고 또한 빠르다고 생각합니다.
여 좋습니다. 그럼 택시를 이용할게요. 감사합니다.

해설 목적지까지 택시를 이용할 것을 권유하고 있다.
어휘 get [get] 도착하다

5 언급 유무 파악 ④

M Thank you for visiting the Eiffel Tower. The Eiffel Tower is <u>an iron tower</u> that stands 324 meters tall. It was built in Paris in 1889. It is currently the most famous symbol of Paris. Famous <u>architects</u> <u>were</u> <u>hired</u> to design the monument, which took over two years to finish. Currently, the Eiffel Tower is the <u>most-visited</u> <u>monument</u> in the world with over 7 million visitors a year. If it's your first time in Paris, going up the Eiffel Tower is <u>a must</u>. Have a nice trip.

남 에펠 탑을 방문해 주셔서 감사합니다. 에펠 탑은 높이가 324m인 철탑입니다. 그것은 1889년 파리에 건설되었습니다. 현재 파리에서 가장 유명한 상징이지요. 유명한 건축가들을 고용하여 기념비를 디자인하였고 완료하는 데 2년이 걸렸습니다. 현재 에펠 탑은 1년에 7백만 명이 넘는

방문객이 있는 세계에서 가장 많이 방문한 기념물입니다. 파리가 첫 방문이라면 에펠 탑에 올라가는 것은 필수입니다. 좋은 여행 되십시오.

해설 에펠 탑을 건설하는데 투입된 인원은 언급되지 않았다.
어휘 iron [áiərn] 철 currently [kə́ːrəntli] 현재 monument [mɑ́njəmənt] 기념비 architect [ɑ́ːrkitèkt] 건축가 must [mʌst] 필수

6 관계 추론 ⑤

M Hello. How can I help you?
W Can you give me a morning call at 6 tomorrow?
M Do you mean a wakeup call? Sure. Your room <u>number</u> <u>is</u> <u>604</u>, right?
W Exactly.
M Okay. Is there anything else I can do for you?
W Well, I wonder if <u>laundry</u> <u>service</u> <u>is</u> <u>available</u> now.
M I'm sorry. You can only <u>get</u> <u>your</u> <u>laundry</u> <u>done</u> until 9 p.m.
W All right. Thanks.

남 여보세요. 무엇을 도와드릴까요?
여 내일 오전 6시에 모닝콜을 해줄 수 있나요?
남 모닝콜 말씀이시죠? 물론이죠. 방 번호가 604호이시네요, 그렇죠?
여 정확해요.
남 네, 제가 도와드릴 다른 것이 있나요?
여 음, 지금 세탁 서비스가 가능한지 궁금합니다.
남 죄송하지만, 세탁 서비스는 오후 9시까지 이용할 수 있습니다.
여 네, 감사합니다.

해설 모닝콜을 요청하는 투숙객과 호텔 직원의 대화이다.
어휘 wakeup call 모닝콜 laundry [lɔ́ːndri] 세탁

7 어색한 대화 찾기 ③

① M Do you want more bread?
  W No, thanks. <u>I'm</u> <u>completely</u> <u>stuffed</u>.
② M How often do you go to the movies?
  W I usually go <u>twice</u> <u>a</u> <u>month.</u>
③ M How have you been?
  W <u>I've</u> <u>never</u> <u>been</u> to Japan.
④ M I'd like to open an account.
  W Okay. Can you <u>fill</u> <u>out</u> <u>this</u> <u>form</u>?
⑤ M How long will it take to get there?
  W It will take <u>an</u> <u>hour</u> <u>or</u> <u>so.</u>

① 남 빵 좀 더 먹을래?
  여 고맙지만 괜찮아. 난 완전 배불러.
② 남 얼마나 자주 영화를 보러 가니?
  여 보통 한 달에 두 번 가.
③ 남 어떻게 지냈어?
  여 나는 일본에 가본 적이 없어.
④ 남 계좌를 만들고 싶습니다.
  여 이 양식을 작성해 주시겠어요?
⑤ 남 거기 도착하는 데 얼마나 걸릴까?
  여 한 시간 정도 걸릴 거야.

해설 잘 지냈냐는 말에 대한 대답으로 일본에 가본 적이 없다고 답하는 것은 부자연스럽다.
어휘 stuffed [stʌft] 포식한, 배부른 fill out 기입하다

8 부탁한 일 파악 ①

W Thomas, this is Emily. Did you hear that TWICE <u>is</u>

having a concert in our town?

M Are you serious? When is it?

W In a month.

M I'm a huge fan of theirs. Let's book tickets before they sell out.

W I'd like to, but tickets go on sale next week.

M Oh, I'm going on a field trip next Monday. Emily, could you give me a hand?

W Do you mean I should get you a ticket? Don't worry about that. I'll do that for you.

M Thanks, Emily. I owe you one.

여 Thomas, 나 Emily야. TWICE가 우리 도시에서 콘서트를 개최할 거란 것을 들었니?

남 정말이야? 언젠데?

여 한 달 뒤에.

남 나는 그들의 열혈 팬이야. 매진되기 전에 예매하자.

여 나도 그러고 싶지만, 표는 다음 주부터 판매될 거야.

남 아, 다음 주 월요일에 현장 학습을 가. Emily, 나 좀 도와줄 수 있겠니?

여 표 사는 거 말하는 거지? 걱정하지 마. 내가 구입할게.

남 고마워 Emily. 내가 신세를 졌어.

해설 자신을 대신하여 콘서트 표를 예매해 줄 것을 부탁하고 있다.

어휘 huge fan 열혈 팬   field trip 현장 학습, 수학여행   owe [ou] 신세를 지다

9 의도 파악 ⑤

M Excuse me, but how long do I have to wait? I have been waiting for over 30 minutes.

W Oh, I'm sorry. Let me check. What's your name?

M Samson Lee. But what do you need my name for?

W Well, you didn't put your name on the waiting list.

M The waiting list? I didn't know about that. I just lined up and waited for my turn!

W I'm sorry to hear that, but there is nothing I can do for you. You should have checked our policy in advance.

남 실례합니다만 얼마나 더 기다려야 하나요? 제가 30분 정도 기다렸습니다.

여 죄송합니다. 확인해 볼게요. 성함이 어떻게 되시죠?

남 Samson Lee입니다. 제 이름이 왜 필요하죠?

여 음, 대기자 명단에 이름을 적지 않으셨군요.

남 대기자 명단요? 저는 그것에 대해 몰랐어요. 저는 그냥 제 차례를 기다리면서 줄을 서 있었어요.

여 유감입니다만, 제가 해 드릴 수 있는 것은 없네요. 미리 저희의 정책을 확인하셨어야만 했어요.

해설 대기자 명단에 이름을 올리지 않은 채 기다리고 있었던 고객에게 따로 조치를 취해줄 수 없다는 유감의 뜻을 전하고 있다.

어휘 waiting list 대기자 명단   line up 줄을 서다   policy [pálisi] 정책   in advance 미리

10 숫자 정보 파악 ①

W Park Hotel. How can I help you?

M I want to reserve a single room for two nights starting on June 6.

W Hold on, please. We have several rooms with an ocean view and one with a mountain view available.

M How much is an ocean view?

W It's 150 dollars for each night, but we can give you a 10% discount if you stay for two nights.

M I see. Then how about the room with the mountain view?

W It costs 50 dollars less, and we are offering the same discount.

M Okay. I'll take that one.

여 Park Hotel입니다. 무엇을 도와드릴까요?

남 6월 6일에 2박으로 1인실을 예약하고 싶습니다.

여 잠시만 기다려 주세요. 음, 바다가 보이는 방들과 산이 보이는 방들이 이용 가능하십니다.

남 바다가 보이는 방은 얼마입니까?

여 1박당 150달러이지만, 2박에 대해서 10% 할인을 해드릴 수 있습니다.

남 산이 보이는 방은 어떤가요?

여 50달러가 더 저렴하고, 똑같이 할인해 드립니다.

남 알겠습니다. 그것으로 하겠습니다.

해설 산 전망이 보이는 방에서 2박을 하고 동일한 할인 10%를 적용한다고 하였으므로 180달러가 된다.

어휘 reserve [rizə́:rv] 예약하다

11 할 일 파악 ④

W I've gained a few pounds recently.

M Are you sure? I don't think you're putting on weight.

W I can't fit into any of the clothes I bought a year ago.

M How about going to a fitness club?

W There is not one near my house.

M Then do some light exercise at home.

W I don't want to do that at home. For me, home is a place of rest.

M Then why don't you make a point of going to school on foot?

W That sounds good. I'll try to do that.

여 나 요즘 살찌고 있어.

남 어 정말? 네가 살쪘다는 생각이 들진 않는데.

여 일 년 전에 샀던 옷이 맞질 않아.

남 피트니스 클럽에 가는 건 어때?

여 우리 집 근처에는 없어.

남 그럼 집에서 가벼운 운동을 해.

여 집에서는 운동하고 싶지 않아. 나에게 집은 휴식의 장소거든.

남 그럼 학교에 걸어가는 건 어떻겠니?

여 괜찮은 생각인 것 같아. 한번 해볼게.

해설 살을 빼기 위해 학교까지 걸어가는 것을 권유하고 있다.

어휘 put on weight 살찌다   fit into ~에 들어맞다   fitness club 피트니스 클럽   make a point of ~을 습관으로 삼다

12 언급 유무 파악 ②

W There are several ways to generate electricity. A long time ago, people built waterwheels and converted the energy of flowing water into useful forms of power, but nowadays, we build dams on rivers to produce electricity. Another way we use to make electricity is to burn fossil fuels. But many people are worried that this method of power generation may have harmful effects on the environment and cause global warming. Yet another way is by using nuclear energy. Nuclear power <u>involves</u> <u>using</u> <u>nuclear</u> <u>reactions</u> to produce electricity.

여 전기를 생산하는 몇 가지 방법이 있습니다. 오래전에 사람들은 물레방아를 만들어 흐르는 물의 에너지를 유용한 형태의 힘으로 바꾸었지만, 요즘에는 강에 댐을 만들고 전기를 생산합니다. 전기를 만들기 위해 우리가 사용하는 또 다른 방법은 화석 연료를 태우는 것입니다. 그러나 많은 사람들은 이러한 발전 방식이 환경과 지구 온난화에 해로운 영향을 미칠 수 있다고 우려하고 있습니다. 또 다른 방법은 원자력을 사용하는 것입니다. 원자력은 전기를 생산하기 위해 핵반응을 사용합니다.

[해설] 수력 발전의 장점은 언급되지 않았다.
[어휘] generate [dʒénərèit] 생산하다   waterwheel [wɔ́:tərhwì:l] 물레방아, 수차   convert [kənvə́:rt] 전환하다   fossil [fásl] 화석   nuclear [njú:kliər] 핵의, 원자력의

13 [표 파악] ③

W Good morning. What can I do for you?
M I'd like to <u>book</u> <u>a</u> <u>ticket</u> for Busan tomorrow.
W Okay. For what time?
M Are there any trains that <u>are</u> <u>scheduled</u> <u>to</u> <u>get</u> to Busan at 5:30?
W Sorry. We have <u>a</u> <u>train</u> <u>arriving</u> <u>at</u> 5 p.m. and another train arriving at 6:00 p.m.
M I'll take a seat on <u>the</u> <u>earlier</u> <u>one</u>. Here is my credit card.
W Okay. Your ticket is reserved. Please check the date, the time, and the number of your train. Thank you.

여 안녕하세요. 무엇을 도와 드릴까요?
남 내일 부산행 표를 예매하고 싶습니다.
여 네, 몇 시 열차입니까?
남 부산에 오후 5시 30분에 도착할 예정인 기차가 있나요?
여 죄송합니다. 저희는 5시에 도착하는 열차와 6시에 도착하는 열차가 있습니다.
남 더 이른 시간의 좌석 하나를 예매하겠습니다. 여기 제 신용 카드예요.
여 네. 열차가 예약되었습니다. 날짜와 시간 그리고 열차 번호를 확인해 주세요. 감사합니다.

[해설] 부산에 5시와 6시에 도착하는 열차 중, 더 이른 것은 5시에 도착하는 열차이다.
[어휘] book [buk] 예약하다   be scheduled to ~할 예정이다

14 [화제·주제 파악] ⑤

M The Korean War was a war between North Korea and South Korea. Twenty-one countries in the United Nations helped South Korea keep the peace. Nowadays, South Korea is one of those countries which is asked to send <u>its</u> <u>troops</u> <u>to</u> <u>conflicted</u> <u>parts</u> of the world. Some Koreans are <u>against</u> doing this, but others agree with <u>sending</u> <u>troops</u> <u>abroad</u>. They say that Koreans need to pay back <u>what</u> <u>they</u> <u>received</u> during the Korean War.

남 한국 전쟁은 남한과 북한 사이의 전쟁이었다. 유엔의 21개국이 한국이 평화를 지키도록 도왔다. 이제 한국은 세계의 충돌 지역에 군대를 보내도록 요청을 받고 있는 국가들 중 하나이다. 몇몇 한국인들은 그 요청에 반대하지만, 다른 사람들은 그것에 동의한다. 한국인들은 한국 전쟁 동안에 그들이 받았던 것을 보답할 필요가 있다고 그들은 말한다.

[해설] 분쟁 지역으로 한국군을 보내는 것에 대한 찬성과 반대 의견의 사람

들이 있다고 하였다.
[어휘] troop [tru:p] 군대   conflict [kánflikt] 갈등, 분쟁   abroad [əbrɔ́:d] 해외로

15 [할 일 파악] ⑤

M You won first prize in the spelling bee. Congratulations!
W Thanks. <u>I'm</u> <u>pleased</u> <u>with</u> the results.
M Can you give me <u>some</u> <u>useful</u> <u>tips</u> on memorizing how to spell words?
W Well, I have practiced spelling 10 words every day since the seventh grade. And I make a list of difficult words and <u>practice</u> <u>them</u> <u>separately</u>.
M I think the old saying is "Practice makes perfect."
W Oh, I'm looking for someone to study English together with. Would you like to do that?
M Sure. That will help <u>boost</u> <u>my</u> <u>English</u> <u>level</u>.

남 철자 맞추기 대회에서 우승했다면서. 축하해!
여 고마워. 좋은 결과가 나와서 기뻐.
남 철자를 암기하는 유용한 비결을 말해 줄 수 있니?
여 음, 나는 중학교 1학년 때부터 매일 10단어씩 철자 연습을 해. 그리고 철자가 어려운 단어들 목록을 만들어서 따로 연습해.
남 '연습이 완벽을 만든다.'는 말이 생각나네.
여 나 함께 영어 공부할 사람을 찾고 있어. 같이 할래?
남 물론이야. 내 영어 실력 향상에 도움이 될 거야.

[해설] 함께 공부할 사람을 찾는다는 여자의 말에 그러겠다고 하였다.
[어휘] spelling bee 철자 말하기 대회   boost [bu:st] 증대시키다

16 [특정 정보 파악] ④

W Dad, what are you going to buy me for my birthday?
M Anything you want, honey. Go ahead and <u>pick</u> <u>out</u> <u>what</u> <u>you</u> <u>like</u>.
W Okay. I like this white T-shirt with the black dog on the left.
M Well, I don't think that will <u>look</u> <u>good</u> <u>on</u> <u>you</u>.
W How about this white round one with <u>black</u> <u>stripes</u> and the cat in the middle?
M I don't like that one either.
W Then I'll just take the black V-neck T-shirt <u>with</u> <u>the</u> <u>white</u> <u>dog</u> in the middle.
M That one looks nice.

여 아빠, 제 생일 선물로 뭘 사주실 거예요?
남 네가 원하는 뭐든지, 애야. 가서 마음에 드는 걸 고르렴.
여 네, 저는 왼쪽에 검은 개가 있는 이 티셔츠가 마음에 들어요.
남 음, 내 생각엔 너에게 어울리지 않는 것 같구나.
여 작은 고양이가 가운데 있는 줄무늬 라운드 티셔츠는 어때요?
남 그것 또한 아닌 것 같아
여 그럼, 전 그냥 가운데 흰 개가 있는 검정색 브이넥 티셔츠로 할게요.
남 그게 더 나은 것 같구나.

[해설] 생일 선물로 하얀 강아지가 그려진 티셔츠를 사겠다고 하였다.
[어휘] pick out 고르다   either [í:ðər] (부정문에서) 또한

17 [적절한 응답 찾기] ④

[Telephone rings.]
M Hello. Doctor Smith's office.
W Hello. Can I speak to Dr. Smith?

M I'm afraid he is not here right now.

W What time do you expect him to be back?

M He's not going to be here today. He is attending a seminar being held in Chicago. Can I take a message?

W Yes, please. This is Jessica Carter from UCLA. Would you ask him to call me back?

M No problem. Does he have your number?

남 여보세요. 스미스 박사 사무실입니다.
여 스미스 박사님과 통화할 수 있을까요?
남 미안하지만 박사님은 지금 여기 계시지 않습니다.
여 몇 시에 그가 돌아올 것 같은지요?
남 아마도, 오늘은 오시지 않을 거예요. 박사님은 시카고에서 열리는 세미나에 참석 중이십니다. 메시지를 남겨 드릴까요?
여 네, 부탁드립니다. 저는 UCLA의 Jessica Carter입니다. 박사님께 제게 전화 좀 부탁한다고 말씀 해 주시겠어요?
남 그러죠. 박사님께서 당신의 전화번호를 알고 있나요?

해설 전화를 부탁한다는 말에 대해 가장 적절한 응답은 ④ '그러죠. 그가 당신의 번호를 알고 있나요?'이다.
① 지금 통화 중입니다. ② 미안하지만, 제가 당신을 아나요?
③ 당신의 예약이 완료되었습니다. ⑤ 전화 주셔서 감사합니다.
어휘 seminar [sémənà:r] 세미나

18 적절한 응답 찾기 ③

W What can I do for you?

M I'd like to check out five books.

W Sure. Can I see your student ID?

M Here you are.

[Keyboard sounds]

W You have a book overdue. So you can only borrow four books at this time.

M Oh, sorry. I'll put this one back then.

W Okay, four books to check out. And please don't forget you must return the overdue one by tomorrow.

M All right. When do I need to return these books?

W By next Friday.

여 도와드릴까요?
남 저는 다섯 권의 책을 빌리고 싶습니다.
여 네, 학생증 좀 보여주시겠어요?
남 여기 있습니다.
여 아, 연체된 책이 한 권 있군요. 그래서 이번에는 4권만 빌릴 수 있습니다.
남 아, 죄송합니다. 한 권을 다시 가져다 놓을게요.
여 네, 4권, 대출 완료되었습니다. 연체된 책은 내일까지 반납할 것을 잊지 마세요.
남 알겠습니다. 그러면, 이 책들은 언제 반납해야 하나요?
여 금요일까지요.

해설 언제까지 책을 반납해야 하는지에 대한 가장 적절한 응답은 ③ '다음 금요일까지.'이다.
① 너무 자책하지는 마. ② 모두 8달러입니다.
④ 물론이죠. 상관없습니다. ⑤ 아침 10시부터 오후 5시까지입니다.
어휘 student ID 학생증 overdue [òuvərdjú:] 기한이 지난

19 적절한 응답 찾기 ④

M Whew! It's time to eat lunch. What shall we have today?

W Have you tried Korean Food World?

M No, not yet. Is it nice?

W Yeah. It's clean, and the food tastes good. And we can have the lunch special there for only 9 dollars. Isn't that great?

M I think it's a reasonable price. What kind of food does it have?

W Bibimbap, bulgogi, japchae, and lots of other Korean foods as well as a nice Korean atmosphere!

M I'd love to go there then.

남 휴! 또 점심시간이네. 오늘은 뭘 먹지?
여 Korean Food World에서 먹어 봤니?
남 아니, 아직. 거기 괜찮아?
여 응, 깨끗하고 음식도 맛있어. 그리고, 9달러짜리 점심 특선도 먹을 수 있어. 괜찮지 않아?
남 적당한 가격인 것 같네. 어떤 종류의 음식들이 있지?
여 비빔밥, 불고기, 잡채 그리고 한국 음식에 관한 모든 것이 한국적인 분위기를 물씬 풍기고 있지!
남 그럼 거기 가고 싶어.

해설 무엇을 먹을지에 대한 대화로 식당에서 제공하는 음식에 대한 말에 이어지는 가장 적절한 응답은 ④ '그럼 거기 가고 싶어.'이다.
① 난 고기에 알레르기가 있어. ② 한국음식은 유행이 지났어.
③ 사람들은 더 많은 야채를 먹어야만 해. ⑤ 불고기가 내가 가장 좋아하는 음식이야.
어휘 reasonable [rí:zənəbl] 합리적인, 합당한

20 상황에 맞는 말 찾기 ⑤

W Ryan meets Jiwoo on his way to school. Ryan tells her that he was embarrassed by an unexpected experience last night. He was supposed to go to a party at his best friend's house, but he couldn't go there. After leaving his home, he took the subway, but he fell asleep when he was on the subway. He wanted to go to the party, but due to his mistake, he ended up going to a station far away from his friend's house. In this situation, what would Jiwoo most likely say to him?

Jiwoo Ryan, how terrible. That must have been embarrassing.

여 Ryan은 학교 가는 길에 지우를 만납니다. Ryan은 그녀에게 어젯밤 예기치 못한 경험 때문에 당황했다고 말합니다. 그는 가장 친한 친구의 집에서 하는 파티에 가기로 되어 있었지만 갈 수 없었습니다. 그의 집에서 그는 지하철을 탔는데, 지하철에서 그는 잠이 들어버렸습니다. 그는 파티에 가길 원했지만 그의 실수 때문에 결국 친구의 집에서 멀리 떨어진 지하철역에 가게 되었습니다. 이런 상황에서, 지우는 그에게 무엇이라고 말할까요?
지우 Ryan, 정말 안 됐다. 당황스러웠겠구나.

해설 지하철에서 잠이 들어 파티가 열리는 친구네 집에서 멀리 떨어진 역에 도착하게 된 Ryan의 경험에 대해 Jiwoo가 할 말로 가장 적절한 것은 ⑤ '저런, 당황스러웠겠다.'이다.
① 파티에서 즐거운 시간을 보냈어
② 왜 파티에 오지 않았어?
③ 힘내. 다음에 더 잘할 수 있어.
④ 버스가 더 편안해.
어휘 embarrassed [imbǽrəst] 당황한 asleep [əslí:p] 잠든
due to ~때문에

정답 및 해설

Listen and Check
p. 30

Q1	False	Q11	False
Q2	True	Q12	True
Q3	Yes	Q13	False
Q4	No	Q14	21
Q5	324 meters	Q15	True
Q6	9 p.m.	Q16	because her father says it will not look good on her
Q7	True		
Q8	Monday		
Q9	because he didn't put his name on the waiting list	Q17	False
		Q18	No
		Q19	False
Q10	True	Q20	False

해석
Q1 여자는 그녀의 거실을 위해 둥근 시계를 원한다.
Q2 영어 수업을 등록한 학생들은 10퍼센트 할인을 받을 것이다.
Q3 전시용 코트는 비매품이다.
Q4 당신은 서울 외국인 학교까지 기차를 타고 갈 수 있다.
Q5 에펠탑의 높이는 얼마나 되는가?
Q6 세탁 서비스는 몇 시에 끝나는가?
Q7 은행 계좌를 만들고 싶으면, 신청서를 작성해야 한다.
Q8 남자는 어느 요일에 현장 학습을 가는가?
Q9 남자는 왜 그렇게 오래 기다려야 했는가?
Q10 산 전망인 방은 1박에 100달러이다.
Q11 여자는 살을 빼기 위해 체육관에 갈 것이다.
Q12 전기를 만들기 위해 화석 연료를 태우는 것은 지구 온난화를 초래할지도 모른다.
Q13 남자는 오늘 부산에 가는 열차를 탈 것이다.
Q14 몇 나라가 한국 전쟁 동안 남한을 위해 싸웠는가?
Q15 남자는 여자와 함께 영어 공부를 할 것이다.
Q16 여자는 왜 왼쪽에 검은 개가 있는 티셔츠를 사지 않았나?
Q17 Carter 박사는 시카고에서 열리는 세미나에 참석 중이다.
Q18 남자는 원하는 모든 책을 빌릴 수 있는가?
Q19 남자의 가장 좋아하는 한국 음식은 비빔밥이다.
Q20 Ryan은 파티에 가지 않았지만 지하철에서 지우를 만났다.

실전 모의고사 4회
pp. 38~39

1 ④	2 ⑤	3 ②	4 ⑤	5 ③
6 ③	7 ③	8 ④	9 ③	10 ③
11 ③	12 ③	13 ④	14 ⑤	15 ①
16 ⑤	17 ③	18 ⑤	19 ②	20 ③

1 　그림 정보 파악　④

M We are finally done with the school magazine.
W Yeah. It was a really tough time.
M By the way, we haven't decided on the design of the front cover yet. Do you have any ideas?
W Um... Let's put the name of the school at the center of the bottom.
M Then how about putting a tiger cub, our school's symbol, in the center?
W That's good. And let's put the year 2019 in the center at the top.
M Okay. That seems simple and neat.

남 드디어 학교 잡지를 끝냈어.
여 그래, 정말 힘든 시간이었어.
남 하지만, 아직 앞표지 디자인을 결정하지 않았어. 어떤 생각이 있니?
여 음… 학교 이름은 하단 중앙에 넣자.
남 그럼 우리 학교 상징인 새끼 호랑이를 가운데 넣는 건 어때?
여 좋아. 그리고 2019를 상단 중앙에 넣자.
남 그래. 단순하고 깔끔할 것 같아.

해설 하단 가운데 학교명이 들어가고 학교의 상징인 새끼 호랑이를 가운데 넣고 발행 연도를 상단 가운데 두자고 하였다.
어휘 cub [kʌb] 새끼

2 　목적 파악　⑤

[*Telephone rings.*]
M Hello. Future Online Bookstore. How may I help you?
W I ordered three books the other day but have received only one of them. I want to know when I can get the rest of the books.
M I'm very sorry for the inconvenience. What is your order number?
W It's 24605315.
M Let me check... [*Keyboard sound*] I'm afraid those items are temporarily out of stock, and it will take two days for us to receive new books.
W So when can I get them?
M It may take up to three business days.
W Okay. I'll wait.

남 미래 온라인 서점입니다. 무엇을 도와드릴까요?
여 일전에 세 권의 책을 주문했습니다만, 그중 한 권만 받았어요. 제가 주문한 나머지 책을 언제 받을 수 있는지 알고 싶습니다.
남 불편을 끼쳐 드려서 죄송합니다. 주문 번호가 어떻게 되시나요?
여 24605315입니다.
남 확인해 보겠습니다… 죄송하지만 일시적으로 재고가 없습니다. 저희가 새 책을 받는데 이틀이 걸릴 예정입니다.
여 그러면, 제가 언제 받을 수 있나요?
남 최대 3일 걸릴 것 같습니다.
여 좋아요. 기다릴게요.

해설 배송되지 않은 나머지 책의 배송 날짜를 묻고 있다.
어휘 inconvenience[ìnkənvíːnjəns] 불편　temporarily [tèmpərέ(ː)rəli] 일시적으로　business day 영업일

3 　그림 상황 파악　②

① W How many pills do I have to take a day?
　M Take one three times a day.
② W I think I have an ear infection.
　M Let me examine your ears.
③ W My eyesight is getting worse.
　M That's too bad. I think you need glasses.
④ W How are you feeling today?
　M Much better. Thanks, Dr. Brown.
⑤ W You should listen to what I'm saying.
　M Okay. I will.

① 여 약을 하루에 얼마나 먹어야 하나요?
남 하루에 세 번 한 알씩 드세요
② 여 귀에 염증이 있는 것 같아요.
남 귀를 한번 검사해 봅시다.
③ 여 시력이 점점 나빠지고 있어.
남 안됐구나. 내 생각엔 안경이 필요할 것 같아.
④ 여 오늘 기분이 어떠세요?
남 훨씬 좋아요. 감사합니다, Brown 박사님.
⑤ 여 내가 말하는 것에 귀를 기울여야만 해.
남 응, 그럴게.

해설 귀가 아픈 환자를 진료하고 있는 상황이다.
어휘 pill [pil] 알약   infection [infékʃən] 감염   eyesight [áisàit] 시력

4 특정 정보 파악 ⑤

M Are you finished preparing for the presentation, or are you still organizing the information for your part?
W I'm almost done.
M You know we have to review each other's information by this weekend. We're going to make a joint presentation next week.
W All right, Jeremy. It'll be ready by Wednesday.
M Then shall we meet on Thursday?
W I'm afraid not. I'm volunteering at the children's center on Thursday.
M Then how about the day after that?
W Okay. Anytime will be good on that day.

남 발표 준비는 다 끝났니, 아니면 아직 네가 할 부분의 자료를 정리 중이니?
여 거의 다해 가.
남 알다시피 이번 주말까지 서로의 자료를 검토해야만 하잖아. 다음 주에 우리 합동 발표를 해야 해.
여 알았어, Jeremy. 수요일까지 준비될 거야.
남 그럼 목요일에 만날까?
여 미안하지만 안 돼. 목요일에 아동 센터에서 자원봉사를 하거든.
남 그럼 그 다음 날은 어떠니?
여 좋아. 그날은 어느 시간이든 괜찮아.

해설 자원봉사를 한 다음 날에 만나기로 하였다.
어휘 joint [dʒɔint] 공동의   volunteer [vɑ̀ləntíər] 자원봉사하다

5 언급 유무 파악 ③

W Welcome to Seoraksan National Park. To conserve nature, please observe the following rules. First of all, don't litter. The mountain is suffering from trash being thrown everywhere by visitors. Second, smoking in the park is strictly prohibited at all times. Even a small fire could turn into a forest fire. Third, don't feed the animals and don't pick any flowers or other plants. Thank you very much for your cooperation.

여 설악산 국립 공원에 오신 것을 환영합니다. 우리의 자연을 보호하기 위해, 다음의 규칙을 지켜주세요. 먼저, 쓰레기를 버리지 마십시오. 방문객들이 도처에 버린 쓰레기로 산이 고통을 겪고 있습니다. 두 번째, 공원 내 흡연은 항상 강력히 금지됩니다. 작은 불이 산불로 바뀔 수 있습니다. 세 번째, 동물에게 먹이를 주지 마시고, 어떤 꽃이나 식물도 꺾지 마세요. 협조해 주셔서 감사합니다.

해설 계곡에서 수영을 금지한다는 내용은 언급되지 않았다.
어휘 conserve [kánsəːrv] 보존하다   observe [əbzɔ́ːrv] 준수하다 litter [lítər] 쓰레기를 버리다   strictly [stríktli] 엄격하게   prohibit [prouhíbit] 금지하다

6 관계 추론 ③

W Excuse me, but are you John Hwang?
M Yes, I have been expecting you all morning.
W Here's what you ordered. Please read this order sheet and sign here.
M Before that, I want to check if the products are in good condition.
W Of course. Feel free to inspect them. I'll wait.
M Thank you... [Pause]... Well, everything is in good condition. Can I sign here?
W Yes. Thank you for using Mart Plus.

여 실례합니다, John Hwang씨 되시나요?
남 예, 오전 내내 기다리고 있었어요.
여 여기 주문하신 것이 있습니다. 그리고, 이 주문서를 읽어보시고, 여기 서명해 주세요.
남 그 전에, 제품의 상태가 좋은지 확인하고 싶어요.
여 물론이죠. 편하게 살펴보세요. 기다리겠습니다.
남 감사합니다… 음… 제품의 상태가 다 좋네요. 여기 사인할까요?
여 네, Mart Plus를 이용해 주셔서 감사합니다.

해설 배달된 제품을 확인하고 있는 상황이다.
어휘 order [ɔ́ːrdər] 주문하다; 주문   inspect [inspékt] 검사하다

7 어색한 대화 찾기 ③

① W I'm not sure I can pass the exam.
   M I bet you'll do just fine.
② W This is for you. I hope you like it.
   M Thank you so much.
③ W Are you following what I'm saying?
   M No, I'll follow his advice.
④ W What kinds of movies do you like?
   M I like science-fiction movies the most.
⑤ W I'll keep my fingers crossed.
   M Thanks. I'll try my best.

① 여 내가 시험에 통과할 수 있을지 모르겠어.
   남 넌 잘 할 거라고 확신해.
② 여 네게 주는 거야. 마음에 들길 바래.
   남 정말 고마워.
③ 여 내 말 이해하니?
   남 아니, 난 그의 조언을 따를 거야.
④ 여 어떤 종류의 영화를 가장 좋아하니?
   남 난 공상 과학 영화가 제일 좋아.
⑤ 여 네게 행운을 빌어 줄게.
   남 고마워. 최선을 다할게.

해설 이해하고 있는지 묻는 말에 그의 조언을 따르겠다고 답하는 것은 부자연스럽다.
어휘 science-fiction movie 공상 과학 영화   keep one's fingers crossed 행운을 빌다

8 충고한 일 파악 ④

M Erin, have you done the school project?
W Yes. Haven't you finished it yet?

정답 및 해설

M No, I completely forgot about it, so I just started working on it yesterday.

W Maybe you can't go to the movies tonight. I think it will take more than 10 hours to do it.

M That's why I need your help. Will you please help me?

W Do you remember the same thing happened before?

M I know, but can you help me one more time?

W No. You should be ashamed of yourself. Everyone in our class has been doing this alone.

남 Erin, 학교 숙제 다 끝냈어?
여 응. 넌 아직 못 끝냈어?
남 응, 완전히 잊고 있었어. 그래서 어제 겨우 시작했어.
여 아마 오늘 밤에 영화 보러 못 가겠구나. 숙제를 끝내는데 10시간 더 걸리는 것 같더라.
남 그게 바로 내가 너의 도움을 필요한 이유야. 나 좀 도와줄래?
여 전에도 똑같은 일이 있었던 거 기억하니?
남 알아. 하지만, 이번 한 번만 더 도와주면 안 되겠니?
여 안 돼. 넌 자신에 대해 부끄럽게 생각해야만 해. 우리 반 아이들 모두 혼자서 하고 있단 말이야.

[해설] 숙제를 도와달라는 남자의 요청에 부끄럽게 생각하라고 충고하고 있다.
[어휘] be ashamed of ~을 부끄러워 하다

9 의도 파악 ③

W Have you heard about Alice?

M No, I haven't. What's going on with her?

W She came here last night and now is staying at Jason's house.

M Really? Oh, time flies like an arrow.

W Yes, it's already December.

M How is she? Is she fine?

W She looks a lot healthier than I expected.

M I'm looking forward to seeing her soon.

여 최근에 Alice 소식 들어본 적 있니?
남 아니, 그녀에게 무슨 일이 있었니?
여 그녀가, 어젯밤 여기에 왔고, 지금 Jason의 집에 머무르고 있어.
남 정말? 오, 시간이 화살처럼 빨리 간다.
여 그러게. 벌써 12월이야.
남 그녀는 어때? 건강하니?
여 예상했던 것보다 훨씬 더 건강해 보여.
남 그녀를 빨리 만나보고 싶네.

[해설] Alice를 빨리 만나고 싶다는 기대를 나타내고 있다.
[어휘] arrow [ǽrou] 화살

10 숫자 정보 파악 ③

W Hi. I'd like to know your bike rental rates.

M It is 3 dollars an hour.

W How much does it cost to rent a tandem bike?

M It is 7 dollars an hour.

W Okay. We want one bike and one tandem bike.

M How long do you want the bikes for?

W Two hours. If I rent both of them, can I get a discount?

M All right. I'll give you a 20% discount for each.

W Thank you so much.

여 안녕하세요. 자전거 빌리는 요금을 알고 싶습니다.
남 한 시간에 3달러입니다.
여 2인승 자전거를 빌리는 데는 얼마나 드나요?
남 한 시간에 7달러요.
여 좋아요. 자전거 한 대와 2인승 자전거 한 대 주세요.
남 몇 시간 동안 타기를 원하시나요?
여 두 시간 동안요, 그런데 깎아주실 수는 있나요?
남 좋습니다. 각각 20% 할인해 드릴게요.
여 정말 감사합니다.

[해설] 한 시간당 자전거는 3달러, 2인승 자전거는 7달러이고, 두 시간 동안 빌리는 경우 20% 할인이 된다고 하였다.
[어휘] rental [réntal] 임대   rate [reit] 비율, 요금   tandem bike 2인승 자전거

11 할 일 파악 ③

M Oh, no! I overslept!

W Why are you in a hurry, Eddie? It's Sunday morning. You don't have to go to school. Calm down, honey.

M Mom, I have an important meeting with my friends at 11:00. But it's already 10:30.

W Oh, you should have told me to wake you up early. Anyway, you can't make it by 11:00.

M What should I do first, Mom? I'm totally confused.

W Relax first. And you had better call your friend and say that you'll be late.

남 오 이런! 늦잠 잤어요!
여 왜 그렇게 서두르니, Eddie. 일요일 아침이야. 학교에 갈 필요가 없단다. 진정하렴, 애야.
남 엄마, 11시에 친구들과 중요한 모임이 있어요. 하지만, 벌써 10시 30분 걸요.
여 오, 엄마에게 일찍 깨워달라고 말했어야지. 어쨌거나, 11시까지 약속에 못 갈 것 같구나.
남 무엇을 먼저 해야 하죠, 엄마? 완전히 헷갈려요.
여 침착하렴. 그리고 친구에게 전화해서 늦을 것 같다고 말하는 게 좋겠어.

[해설] 약속 시간에 늦은 남자에게 미리 전화로 사정을 말하라고 조언하였다.
[어휘] oversleep [òuvərslí:p] 늦잠 자다   confused [kənfjú:zd] 혼란스러운   relax [rilǽks] 긴장을 풀다

12 언급 유무 파악 ③

W Hines Ward is a former American football player. He was born in Seoul, Korea, and moved to the United States when he was one year old. He played for the same team for 14 years. During his career, he won 3 team MVP awards. He won the Super Bowl MVP award in 2006. That made him famous in Korea. He was the first Korean-American to succeed at American football. When he came back to Korea, he made a big donation to create a foundation to help protect mixed-race children like himself from discrimination.

여 Hines Ward는 이전 미식축구 선수이다. 그는 서울에서 태어났고, 한 살 때 미국으로 이주했다. 그는 한 팀에서 14년 동안 경기를 했다. 그의 경력 동안, 그는 3번의 팀 MVP에 올랐다. 그는 2006년 the Super Bowl MVP를 수상한다. 그것이 그를 한국 사회에서 유명해지게 했다. 그는 미식축구에서 성공한 최초의 한국계 미국인이었다. 그가 한국으로 돌아왔을 때, 그는 자신과 같은 혼혈 아동들을 차별로부터 보호하기 위한 재단을 만드는데 거액을 기부하였다.

남 정말? 어렵지 않니? 난 네가 영어를 싫어한다고 생각했어.
여 그랬지, 그러나 영어 선생님께서 나에게 영어를 향상시키라고 조언하셨어. 그래서 지금 영어로 일기를 쓰는 거야.
남 그래서, 영어 일기를 쓰고 있는 거구나. 얼마나 자주 영어로 일기를 쓰니?
여 적어도 일주일에 세 번은 쓰고 있어.

해설 영어 일기를 쓰는 빈도를 묻는 말에 대한 가장 적절한 응답은 ③ '적어도 일주일에 세 번은 쓰고 있어.' 이다.
① 일요일마다 그녀가 우리에게 영어를 가르쳐 주셔.
② 난 숙제로 이걸 쓰고 있는 거야.   ④ 일기를 쓰는데 20분이 걸려.
⑤ 난 영어에 흥미가 많아.
어휘 improve [imprúːv] 향상시키다

18 적절한 응답 찾기 ⑤

M Mom, I think I have to buy a new bicycle.
W Why do you think so?
M The brakes are not working. Yesterday, when I used the brakes, my bike didn't stop. I almost hit a car.
W Oh, no. Were you okay?
M Fortunately, nothing happened.
W Well, let's find out if we can repair the brakes first. Then, we can decide whether to buy you a new one.
M Okay. Thanks for understanding.

남 엄마, 저 새 자전거를 사야만 할 것 같아요.
여 왜 그렇게 생각하니?
여 브레이크가 작동하지 않아요. 어제, 제가 브레이크를 잡았을 때, 자전거가 멈추지 않았어요. 차와 거의 부딪힐 뻔했어요.
여 오, 저런. 너 괜찮은 거니?
남 다행스럽게도, 아무 일도 일어나지 않았어요.
여 음, 먼저 브레이크가 수리 가능한지 알아보도록 하자꾸나. 그런 다음 새 자전거를 살지 결정할 수 있을 거야.
남 네. 이해해 주셔서 고마워요.

해설 수리 가능 여부를 확인한 후 새 자전거를 살지 결정하자는 말에 대한 가장 적절한 응답은 ⑤ '네, 이해해 주셔서 감사해요.'이다.
① 당신의 전화를 사용할 수 있을까요?   ② 전 교통 규칙을 따라야만 해요.
③ 타이어가 완전히 펑크가 났어요.   ④ 자전거를 탈 수 없을까 걱정이 되요.
어휘 almost [ɔ́ːlmoust] 거의   repair [ripέər] 수리하다

19 적절한 응답 찾기 ②

M What can I do for you?
W I'd like to buy a bag that I saw in your brochure.
M Can I have the model number?
W 52... 3... [Pause] Oh, I'm sorry, but I can't remember it.
M That's okay. Can you tell me what it looks like?
W It's like this red one but is brown in color and has a red strap. The price is 85 dollars.
M Oh, I know what you're talking about. But it is out of stock. I can order one for you if you want.
W Thank you. I'd love that.

남 도와드릴까요?
여 예, 저는 소책자에서 봤던 가방을 사고 싶어요.
남 모델 번호를 받을 수 있을까요?
여 52… 3… 오, 죄송하지만 정확히 기억나지 않네요.
남 괜찮습니다. 어떻게 생겼는지 말씀해 주실 수 있나요?
여 이 빨간 가방처럼 생겼지만 갈색에 빨간 끈이 있었어요. 가격은 85달러

예요.
남 아, 어떤 것을 말씀하시는지 알겠습니다. 그러나, 재고가 없네요. 원하신다면 주문을 해드릴 수 있습니다.
여 감사합니다. 그렇게 해주세요.

해설 현재 재고는 없지만 원할 경우 주문을 해주겠다는 말에 대한 가장 적절한 응답은 ② '감사합니다. 그렇게 해주세요.'이다.
① 그것이 제가 가장 좋아하는 가방입니다.
③ 당신이 옳아요. 죄송합니다.   ④ 제 가방을 보셨나요?
⑤ 주문 번호를 잊어버렸습니다.
어휘 brochure [bróuʃuər] 팸플릿   strap [stræp] 끈

20 상황에 맞는 말 찾기 ③

W Ted and Jason go on a bike trip one weekend. After riding a long distance, they feel thirsty and decide to find a convenience store. Since he has never been in this area before, Jason is not sure where a convenience store is. But Ted has a map application on his smartphone and sees where a convenience store is. In this situation, what would Ted say to Jason?
Ted Jason, don't worry. Just follow me.

여 어느 주말에 Ted와 Jason은 자전거 여행을 떠납니다. 자전거를 타고 먼 거리를 이동한 이후에, 그들은 목마름을 느끼고 편의점을 찾기로 결정합니다. Jason은 전에 이 지역에 왔던 적이 없기 때문에, 편의점이 어디에 있는지 확신하지 못합니다. 그러나 Ted는 그의 스마트폰에 지도 어플리케이션을 가지고 있고, 길을 앞장섭니다. 이 상황에서 Ted가 Jason에게 무엇이라고 말할까요?
Ted Jason, 걱정하지 마. 그냥 날 따라와.

해설 Jason이 편의점의 위치를 알지 못할 때 Ted가 지도 어플리케이션으로 편의점의 위치를 알아낸 상황이므로 ③ '걱정하지 마, 그냥 날 따라와.'라고 말하는 것이 가장 적절하다.
① 다른 가게로 가는 게 어때?
② 물 한 병은 얼마야?
④ 버스를 타자.
⑤ 식료품 가게가 이미 문을 닫았어.
어휘 go on a trip 여행을 가다   distance [dístəns] 거리
application [æ̀pləkéiʃən] 응용 프로그램

Listen and Check   p. 40

Q1	False	Q11	11:00
Q2	False	Q12	False
Q3	No	Q13	True
Q4	Thursday	Q14	Yes
Q5	False	Q15	play a board game
Q6	Yes	Q16	True
Q7	True	Q17	Yes
Q8	because he hasn't done his homework	Q18	False
Q9	at Jason's house	Q19	True
Q10	True	Q20	False

해석
Q1 그들의 학교 상징은 곰이다.
Q2 배송이 교통 체증 때문에 지체되었다.
Q3 여자는 고열로 인해 병원에 가는가?
Q4 여자는 언제 자원봉사 활동을 위해 아동 센터에 가는가?
Q5 설악산 국립 공원에는 흡연 구역이 있다.

Q6 남자는 배달 제품의 상태를 점검하기를 원하는가?
Q7 남자는 여자에게 그녀가 그것을 할 수 있다는 자신감을 주고 있다.
Q8 남자는 왜 영화를 보러 갈 수 없는가?
Q9 Alice는 지금 어디에 머무는가?
Q10 그들을 2시간 동안 자전거를 탈 것이다.
Q11 Eddie는 몇 시에 친구들을 만날 것인가?
Q12 Hines Ward는 1년 이상 서울에 살았다.
Q13 금속 날개로 된 선풍기는 강력하다.
Q14 이 한국 전통 무술의 선수들은 올림픽 게임에 참여할 수 있다.
Q15 여자는 무엇을 하고 싶은가?
Q16 여자가 오기를 바라는 시간에 올 수 있는 직원이 없다.
Q17 여자는 적어도 일주일에 세 번쯤 영어로 일기를 쓰는가?
Q18 남자는 자기 자전거의 브레이크를 수리할 수 없다고 생각한다.
Q19 여자는 마침내 자신이 원하는 것을 얻었다.
Q20 Jason은 편의점이 어디 있는지를 안다.

실전 모의고사 5회
pp. 48~49

1	⑤	2	③	3	⑤	4	①	5	⑤
6	④	7	③	8	④	9	③	10	④
11	③	12	①	13	③	14	③	15	④
16	①	17	⑤	18	①	19	③	20	⑤

1 그림 정보 파악 ⑤
W Welcome to Happy Wrappings. How can I help you?
M I'd like to buy a gift box.
W We have two different shapes, rounded and square. Which do you want?
M A square one, please.
W We have different patterns for square ones, too.
M Hmm... That banana pattern looks fine.
W Okay. Here you are.

여 Happy Wrappings에 오신 걸 환영합니다. 무엇을 도와드릴까요?
남 선물 상자를 사고 싶어서요.
여 두 가지 다른 모양이 있는데, 동그란 모양과 정사각형 모양이 있어요. 어떤 걸 원하시나요?
남 정사각형으로 할게요.
여 정사각형 상자에도 역시 다양한 무늬가 있습니다.
남 음… 바나나 무늬가 있는 게 좋아 보이네요.
여 네. 여기 있습니다.

해설 정사각형 상자에 바나나 무늬가 있는 것을 원한다고 하였다.
어휘 rounded [ráundid] 둥근 모양의 tie [tai] 묶다

2 부탁한 일 파악 ③
W Are you done choosing things to buy?
M Yes, let me pay for everything first.
W Go ahead.
M Oh, no. Do you have some cash? It says "Cash Only." I don't have any cash now.
W How much do you need?
M Five dollars. I'll transfer the money to your account

later.
W Okay.

여 살 것들 다 고른 거야?
남 응, 내가 먼저 계산할게.
여 먼저 해.
남 오, 이런. 현금 가지고 있는 거 있어? 현금만 받는다고 되어있네. 지금 현금이 없어.
여 얼마가 필요한데?
남 5달러. 나중에 계좌 이체를 해 줄게.
여 알겠어.

해설 남자가 여자에게 현금 5달러를 빌리며 나중에 계좌 이체해 주겠다고 했다.
어휘 pay for 결제하다, 지불하다 bring [briŋ] 가져오다 transfer [trǽnsfər] 옮기다, 넘겨주다 account [əkáunt] 계좌

3 그림 상황 파악 ⑤
① W How often do you exercise?
  M I exercise twice a week.
② W How many hours do you sleep?
  M I usually sleep for five hours.
③ W How do you overcome stress?
  M I keep talking about it.
④ W Are you a representative of your class?
  M Yes, I'm the class president.
⑤ W Is your left eye in pain?
  M Yes, very much.

① 여 얼마나 자주 운동하나요?
  남 일주일에 두 번 운동합니다.
② 여 몇 시간 잠을 주무시나요?
  남 보통 다섯 시간 잡니다.
③ 여 스트레스를 어떻게 극복하나요?
  남 그것에 대해 계속해서 얘기를 해요.
④ 여 네가 반의 대표니?
  남 네, 반장이에요.
⑤ 여 왼쪽 눈이 아픈가요?
  남 네, 아주 많이요.

해설 남자가 왼쪽 눈이 아프다고 하는 상황이다.
어휘 overcome [òuvərkám] 극복하다 representative [rèprizéntətiv] 대표 president [prézidənt] 반장, 회장

4 숫자 정보 파악 ①
W You're late by twenty minutes.
M I'm so sorry. The radio recording took a bit longer than I had expected.
W It was supposed to finish at 2:00, right?
M You're right. It normally lasts for an hour, but it took longer today.
W So how was the recording?
M It was fun as usual.

여 20분 늦었네.
남 정말 미안해. 라디오 녹음이 조금 길어졌어.
여 2시에 끝나야 하는 거잖아, 그렇지?
남 맞아. 보통 한 시간 하는데, 오늘 우리가 더 했어.
여 그래서 녹음은 어땠어?
남 평소처럼 재미있었어.

해설 평소 1시간 동안 녹음을 하며, 여자가 원래 2시에 끝났어야 하는 거라

고 하였다.

어휘 recording [rikɔ́ːrdiŋ] 녹음 normally [nɔ́ːrməli] 보통
as usual 평상시처럼 broadcasting station 방송국

5 [언급 유무 파악] ⑤

W I heard you're going to Diver's Resort. Where is it?
M How <u>did you know</u>? It's in the Philippines.
W Why does the resort's name have the word divers?
M The reason is that most of the guests there are divers. They do free diving and sometimes scuba diving.
W Can <u>beginners go diving</u>, too?
M Of course. There's a training course for beginners.
W I see. <u>What else</u> do you do <u>besides diving</u>?
M There are spa facilities, restaurants, and a bar.
W Sounds cool. Have a safe trip.

여 Diver's 리조트에 간다고 들었어. 그건 어디에 있어?
남 어떻게 알았어? 필리핀에 있는 거야.
여 왜 리조트 이름에 divers라는 단어가 있는 거야?
남 왜냐하면 오는 대부분의 투숙객들이 다이버거든. 사람들은 무료로 다이빙을 하고 가끔 스쿠버 다이빙을 하기도 해.
여 초보자도 다이빙을 할 수 있어?
남 물론이지. 초보자들을 위한 훈련 과정이 있어.
여 그렇구나. 다이빙 이외에 다른 건 뭘 해?
남 온천 시설도 있고, 음식점이랑 바도 있어.
여 멋진걸. 잘 다녀와.

해설 리조트에 가는 방법에 관해서는 언급되지 않았다.
어휘 guest [gest] 투숙객 beginner [bigínər] 초보자 course [kɔːrs] 과정 facility [fəsíləti] 편의 시설

6 [장소 추론] ④

M This is huge. It's a three-story building.
W Look. Here's <u>the information map</u>.
M The whole first floor is for history from prehistoric times to the modern day.
W There are a library and a café <u>on the second floor</u>.
M <u>Let's tour</u> the first floor first.
W Okay. After that, let's <u>go to the café</u>.
M All right.
W I'll get a brochure.

남 정말 크다. 3층 건물이야.
여 이것 봐. 안내도야.
남 1층 전체는 선사 시대부터 현대까지의 역사에 대한 거네.
여 2층에는 도서관하고 카페가 있어.
남 우선 1층부터 구경하자.
여 그래. 그러고 나서 카페에 가자.
남 알았어.
여 안내 책자를 가지고 올게.

해설 한 층이 모두 역사에 관련된 곳이라고 하였다.
어휘 three-story 3층의 information map 안내도 prehistoric times 선사시대 modern [mádərn] 현대의

7 [어색한 대화 찾기] ③

① M I <u>apologize for</u> what I said to you.
　W Promise me you won't do it again.
② M How do you help slow students?
　W I <u>give them extra homework</u>.

③ M <u>Could you assist me</u> tomorrow?
　W Sorry. I can do it by myself.
④ M What motivates you to <u>work harder</u>?
　W My family.
⑤ M What do you do for a living?
　W I teach people <u>how to play the piano</u>.

① 남 네게 말한 것에 대해 사과할게.
　여 다시는 그러지 않겠다고 약속해.
② 남 어떻게 공부 못하는 학생들을 돕나요?
　여 저는 추가 숙제를 준답니다.
③ 남 내일 나를 도와줄 수 있어?
　여 미안하지만 나 혼자서 할 수 있어.
④ 남 무엇이 당신을 더 열심히 일하도록 동기를 부여하나요?
　여 저의 가족입니다.
⑤ 남 하시는 일이 어떻게 되나요?
　여 전 피아노 치는 방법을 가르쳐요.

해설 도와줄 수 있냐는 남자의 요청에 혼자서 할 수 있다고 답하는 것은 대화의 흐름상 부자연스럽다.
어휘 apologize [əpálədʒàiz] 사과하다 punish [pʌ́niʃ] 처벌하다
assist [əsíst] 돕다 by oneself 혼자서 motivate [móutəvèit] 동기를 부여하다

8 [부탁한 일 파악] ④

M We should start the survey as soon as possible.
W Are the survey papers and video ready?
M Yes. But there are no participants.
W <u>How many participants</u> do we need?
M We need fifteen.
W Could you try calling your friends and <u>asking them to come</u> here?
M My friends? Sure.
W I'll tell <u>my friends and family</u>, too.

남 우리 가능한 한 빨리 설문 조사를 시작해야 해.
여 우리 설문지 종이랑 동영상은 준비됐어?
남 응. 그런데 참가자가 없어.
여 몇 명의 참가자가 필요하지?
남 15명이 필요해.
여 친구들에게 전화해서 여기에 와 달라고 부탁할 수 있어?
남 내 친구들? 물론이지.
여 나도 내 가족과 친구들한테 얘기할게.

해설 여자가 남자에게 그의 친구들에게 설문 조사를 위해 와달라고 해달라고 부탁했다.
어휘 survey [sə́ːrvei] 설문 조사 as soon as possible 가능한 한 빨리 participant [pɑːrtísəpənt] 참가자

9 [화제·주제 파악] ③

M Today's paper talks about what workplaces <u>will be like</u> in the future. First, <u>how many jobs</u> do you think one person can have at the same time? One? Two? Actually, the number is unlimited. One can be a businessman, author, and photographer <u>at the same time</u>. It's possible because of smartphones. This handheld device connects everything so fast that users can access anything easily and become professionals with it. Just think about <u>what interests you</u> and follow your heart.

남 오늘의 기사는 미래의 직장은 어떠할 것인지에 대해 얘기합니다. 먼저,

여러분은 한 사람이 동시에 몇 개의 직업을 가질 수 있다고 생각하시나요? 하나? 또는 두 개? 그 수는 무한합니다. 한 사람이 동시에 회사원, 작가, 그리고 사진작가가 될 수도 있습니다. 이것은 스마트폰 때문에 가능합니다. 이 한손에 들어오는 기기는 모든 것을 매우 빠르게 연결하여 사용자들은 어떤 것에든 쉽게 접근할 수 있고, 그것에 대한 전문가가 될 수 있습니다. 단지 무엇이 당신을 흥미롭게 하는지를 생각하고 하고 싶은 일을 하세요.

해설 스마트폰 덕분에 미래에 한 사람이 하나가 아닌 무한개의 직업을 가질 수 있다고 말하고 있다.

어휘 workplace [wəːrkpleis] 직장   unlimited [ʌnlímitid] 무한의   handheld [hǽndheld] 손에 들어오는   device [diváis] 기기, 장치   professional [prəféʃənəl] 전문가   interest [íntərəst] 흥미롭게 하다

10 숫자 정보 파악 ④

W Hello. What are you <u>looking for</u>?
M I'm looking for chairs for an office.
W Here, we have <u>two types of chairs</u>, ones with a height-adjustment function and ones without that function.
M How much are they?
W A chair <u>with the function</u> is 120 dollars, and one without it is 90 dollars.
M I'll buy two of each.
W We are selling them at a ten-percent discount now. You <u>made a good choice</u>.
M Thank you. Here's my credit card.

여 안녕하세요. 무엇을 찾으시나요?
남 사무실용 의자를 찾고 있어요.
여 여기 두 종류의 의자가 있는데, 높이 조정 기능이 있는 것과 없는 것이에요.
남 얼마인가요?
여 그 기능이 있는 의자는 120달러이고, 기능이 없는 것은 90달러입니다.
남 각각 두 개씩 살게요.
여 현재 10프로 할인된 가격에 팔고 있어요. 잘 선택하신 겁니다.
남 감사합니다. 여기 신용 카드 있습니다.

해설 각 2개씩 구입을 하고 10% 할인된 가격에 살 수 있다고 하였다.

어휘 adjustment [ədʒʌ́stmənt] 조절   function [fʌ́ŋkʃən] 기능   make a choice 선택을 하다

11 할 일 파악 ③

W Honey, this light keeps going off and on.
M We should change the bulb.
W Do we have <u>any spare bulbs</u>?
M There might be some. Wait a moment.
W Okay.
M Oh, it looks like <u>we used them all</u>.
W It's okay. I can buy one at the market later.
M <u>Take a picture of it</u> before you go out to make sure you buy the same type of bulb.

여 여보, 이 전등이 계속 깜박거려.
남 전구를 갈아야겠네.
여 여분의 전구가 있어?
남 몇 개 있을 거야. 잠시만 기다려봐.
여 알겠어.
남 흠, 다 쓴 것 같아.
여 괜찮아. 나중에 마트에서 하나 사면 돼.
남 꼭 똑같은 전구를 사야 하니까 나가기 전에 사진을 찍어.

해설 전구를 새로 구입을 해야 하는 상황에서 남자가 여자에게 전구 사진부터 찍으라고 하였다.

어휘 light [lait] 전등, 빛   bulb [bʌlb] 전구   spare [spɛər] 여분의

12 언급 유무 파악 ①

W Hi. This is Samantha Park, the CEO of Blue Car. Blue Car <u>lets people rent cars</u> and provides car owners with the opportunity to make money. Users can use the service anytime and anywhere. The rental fee varies depending on the condition of the car and the car model. Please make sure you <u>keep your rental cars clean</u> and return them on time. Smoking inside the cars is strictly banned. If you receive a warning from a car owner more than three times, you can't use the rental service for a month. Our company will try to provide a cleaner, more comfortable, and <u>more satisfying service</u> for everyone.

여 안녕하세요, 저는 Samantha Park이고 Blue Car의 대표입니다. Blue Car는 사람들에게 차를 대여할 수 있는 서비스를 제공하고 차 주인에게는 돈을 벌 수 있는 기회를 제공합니다. 사용자는 언제 어디서나 서비스를 이용하실 수 있습니다. 대여료는 차의 상태와 차의 모델에 따라 다릅니다. 대여하신 차를 반드시 깨끗이 유지하고 제시간에 반납해 주세요. 차 안에서의 흡연은 엄격히 금지됩니다. 만약 차 주인으로부터 세 번 이상의 경고를 받게 된다면 한 달간 대여 서비스를 이용하실 수 없습니다. 저희 회사는 모든 분들을 위해 더 깨끗하고, 편안하고, 만족스러운 서비스를 만들도록 노력하겠습니다.

해설 서비스 신청 방법에 관해서는 언급되지 않았다.

어휘 provide [prəváid] 제공하다   rental fee 대여료   vary [vɛ́(ː)əri] 다양하다   depending on ~에 따라   ban [bɑːn] 금지하다   satisfying [sǽtisfàiiŋ] 만족스러운

13 표 파악 ③

M Amy, where do you want to go this summer?
W How about <u>going to Saipan</u>?
M Won't it be too hot to go there in summer?
W Then <u>let's go to London</u> this time.
M Okay. We can choose options such as a river tour and a bus tour. Which do you like better?
W <u>The river tour</u> seems better. The night view of London is <u>really spectacular</u>.
M I'm so excited!
W I hope time passes quickly.

남 Amy, 이번 여름에는 어디를 가고 싶어?
여 Saipan을 가는 건 어때?
남 여름에 관광하기엔 거긴 너무 덥지 않을까?
여 그럼 이번에는 London으로 가자.
남 그래. 강 투어랑 버스 투어 중에서 옵션을 고를 수 있어. 어떤 게 더 좋겠어?
여 강 투어가 더 좋은 것 같아. London의 야경은 정말 화려하잖아.
남 너무 설렌다!
여 시간이 빨리 흐르면 좋겠어.

해설 여름에 런던에 가기로 했고 선택 관광으로 강 투어를 골랐다.

어휘 tour around 관광하다   spectacular [spektǽkjələr] 화려한, 눈부신   pass by (시간이) 흐르다

14 [화제·주제 파악] ③

W This is an animal we're familiar with. It has a red comb on the head and cannot fly well, but it has strong legs. That's why people mimic its physical features when they have one-legged fights. Farmers raise it for eggs and meat. These days, people eat this a lot as a late-night snack. In addition, when people lack energy, they cook this in a soup.

여 이것은 우리와 친숙한 동물입니다. 이것은 빨간색이 볏을 머리 위에 가지고 있고 잘 날지는 못하지만 튼튼한 다리를 가지고 있습니다. 그래서 사람들은 닭싸움을 할 때 이것의 신체적 특징을 흉내냅니다. 농부들은 이것을 계란과 고기 생산의 목적으로 키웁니다. 오늘날 사람들은 야식으로 이것을 많이 먹습니다. 또한, 사람들은 기력이 없을 때, 이것을 이용해 요리를 하고 탕을 만듭니다.

해설 볏을 가지고 있으며 사람들이 야식으로 먹거나 기력이 없을 때 즐겨 먹는다고 하였다.

어휘 be familiar with ~와 친숙한 comb [koum] 벼슬 mimic [mímik] 흉내를 내다 feature [fíːtʃər] 특징 fold [fould] 접다

15 [할 일 파악] ④

W Matthew, do you know what?
M What?
W There's an event going on that is providing free coupons on the Books.com website.
M Really? How can you get a coupon?
W You just need to access the website every day for thirty days.
M That's easy. How will they know that I go there every day?
W You will see a stamp icon on the right side of the website. Just click on it, and it will automatically record your visit.
M I got it. I should make an account first.

여 Matthew, 그거 알아?
남 뭔데?
여 Books.com 웹사이트에서 무료 쿠폰을 주는 이벤트를 하고 있거든.
남 정말? 어떻게 쿠폰을 받는 건데?
여 웹사이트에 30일간 매일 접속을 하면 돼.
남 꽤 쉬운걸. 어떻게 그들이 내가 매일 출석을 했다는 걸 알지?
여 웹사이트 우측에 도장 아이콘을 볼 수 있을 거야. 클릭만 하면 자동으로 기록이 돼.
남 알겠어. 계정 먼저 만들어야겠네.

해설 남자는 계정을 먼저 만들어야겠다고 하였다.
어휘 go on 진행되다, 계속되다 access [ǽksès] 접속하다
automatically [ɔːtəmǽtik(ə)li] 자동적으로

16 [숫자 정보 파악] ①

[Telephone rings.]
W William, are you on the train yet?
M Yes, I am. But the train was delayed by thirty minutes.
W So what time will you arrive here?
M I will arrive there at 9:30.
W How many hours does it take to come here?
M It takes two hours.

W Okay. I'll wait inside a café near the station.

여 William, 네가 탄 기차 출발했어?
남 응. 기차가 30분 연착됐어.
여 여기 몇 시에 도착해?
남 9시 30분에 도착할 거야.
여 여기까지 얼마나 걸려?
남 2시간 걸려.
여 알겠어. 도착역 가까이에 있는 카페 안에서 기다릴게.

해설 도착역까지 2시간이 걸리며 30분이 연착되어 9시 30분에 도착한다고 하였다.
어휘 delay [diléi] 연착시키다, 연기하다 arrive [əráiv] 도착하다
take [teik] (시간이) 걸리다

17 [적절한 응답 찾기] ⑤

W There's something I'm concerned about.
M What is it?
W I'm not sure if I should go to a university or get a job.
M What is it that you want to do in the future? If you want to work at a company, I recommend that you go to a university.
W Why do you say that?
M There is a big gap in incomes between college graduates and high school graduates.
W What else is good about getting a degree?
M It helps you get a job in the career you want.

여 나 고민되는 게 있어.
남 뭔데?
여 대학에 가야 할지 취직을 해야 할지 모르겠어.
남 미래에 네가 하고 싶은 게 뭔데? 만약 네가 회사를 다니려고 한다면, 대학을 가는 걸 추천해.
여 왜 그렇게 말하는 거야?
남 대학교 졸업자랑 고등학교 졸업자 사이에 수입 격차가 크거든.
여 학위를 받는 것에 대한 다른 좋은 점은 뭘까?
남 그것은 네가 일하고 싶은 분야에서 직업을 갖도록 도와줘.

해설 학위 취득의 장점을 묻는 말에 대한 가장 적절한 응답은 ⑤ '그것은 네가 일하고 싶은 분야에서 직업을 갖도록 도와줘.'이다.
① 나는 사업을 시작하는 걸 선택하는 게 낫겠어.
② 네가 무엇을 하든, 그것에 대한 책임을 져야 해.
③ 누구도 네가 결정을 내리도록 강요할 수 없어.
④ 넌 내가 이것을 얼마나 하고 싶은지 모를 거야.
어휘 income [ínkʌm] 수입 graduate [grǽdʒəwət] 졸업자
degree [digríː] 학위 responsibility [rispὰnsəbíləti] 책임감

18 [적절한 응답 찾기] ①

W Joseph, do you have any plans for this Thursday?
M I'm meeting some people in my book club.
W You do so many things. How do you manage your time?
M It's nothing special. You just have to know what type of person you are.
W How do I know that?
M Try to write down when you can concentrate on things best and worst.
W Well, I can focus on things best in the early morning.
M Then you're a morning person. Try to manage your

time according to your biorhythm.

W That's such a systematic approach.

여 Joseph, 이번 주 목요일에 계획이 있어?

남 독서 모임에서 사람들을 만나.

여 넌 정말 많은 일을 하는구나. 어떻게 시간 관리를 하는 거야?

남 특별한 건 없어. 그저 네가 어떤 유형의 사람인지 알아야 해.

여 내가 어떻게 알 수 있어?

남 네가 가장 집중을 잘 할 수 있는 시간과 최악인 시간을 적어 봐.

여 음, 난 이른 아침에 가장 집중을 잘해.

남 그렇다면 넌 아침형 인간이네. 너의 신체 리듬에 따라서 시간을 관리해 봐.

여 그거 정말 체계적인 접근인걸.

해설 신체 리듬에 따라서 시간을 관리해 보라는 말에 대한 가장 적절한 응답은 ① '그거 정말 체계적인 접근인걸.'이다.
② 네가 문제를 해결하도록 도울 수 있어.
③ 난 여전히 이걸 내가 잘하는지 모르겠어.
④ 더 하면 할수록 더 나아질 수 있어.
⑤ 걱정을 덜 하면 상황은 더 좋아질 거야.

어휘 manage [mǽnidʒ] 관리하다   concentrate [kánsəntrèit] 집중하다   according to ~에 따라서   biorhythm [báiouərìðəm] 생체리듬   systematic [sìstəmǽtik] 체계적인   approach [əpróutʃ] 접근

19 적절한 응답 찾기 ③

W I'm so tired of combining work and child care.

M I know what you mean. You work at home and at a workplace.

W That's true. I don't know what to do.

M You're really struggling. You don't want to leave your job, right?

W No. If I quit my job, I may get very depressed.

M I think every mother shares the same problem.

W I know. Is there a good way to solve it?

M I suggest you find a trustworthy babysitter.

여 일과 육아를 병행하는 게 너무 지쳐.

남 그럴 것 같아. 집 안에서도 밖에서도 일하잖아.

여 그건 사실이야. 어떻게 해야 할지 모르겠어.

남 정말 힘들겠다. 일을 그만둘 수도 없잖아, 그렇지?

여 맞아. 직장을 그만두면 난 너무 우울할 것 같아.

남 내가 보기에 모든 엄마들이 같은 문제를 공유하는 것 같아.

여 맞아. 해결할 좋은 방법이 있을까?

남 신뢰할 만한 아기 봐주는 사람을 알아보는 걸 제안해.

해설 일과 육아의 병행이 힘들다는 말에 대한 적절한 응답은 ③ '신뢰할 만한 아기 봐주는 사람을 알아보는 걸 제안해.'이다.
① 아이를 키우는 게 절대 쉽지 않다는 것 이해해.
② 넌 그 문제에 대해 신경을 쓰지 않는 것 같아.
④ 할 수 있는 한 빨리 직업을 구하는 게 좋겠어.
⑤ 두 가지를 동시에 하는 게 좋겠어.

어휘 combine [kəmbáin] 병행하다. 결합하다   struggling [strʌ́gliŋ] 힘든, 어려운   quit [kwit] 그만두다   raise [reiz] 키우다   trustworthy [trʌ́stwə̀ːrði] 신뢰   babysitter [béibisítər] 아기 돌봐주는 사람

20 적절한 응답 찾기 ⑤

M Nick wants to get high grades on his final exams. He regrets not having done his best on his midterm exams. Nick promises Rachel, his best friend, to go to the library to study every day. Although Nick goes to the library every day, he hardly studies and often gets up and walks around. He keeps telling

Rachel that he still wants to get good grades. In this situation, what would Rachel most likely say to Nick?

Rachel Nick, rewards are given only to those who work hard.

남 Nick은 기말고사에서 높은 성적을 얻기를 원합니다. 그는 중간고사에서 최선을 다하지 않았던 것을 후회합니다. Nick과 그의 친한 친구인 Rachel은 매일 공부를 하기 위해 도서관을 갈 것을 약속합니다. 비록 Nick이 매일 도서관을 가지만, 그는 공부를 거의 하지 않고 자주 외출을 합니다. 그는 Rachel에게 여전히 좋은 성적을 받고 싶다고 계속해서 말을 합니다. 이 상황에서 Rachel은 Nick에게 뭐라고 말을 할까요?

Rachel Nick, 보상은 열심히 노력하는 사람에게만 주어지는 거야.

해설 노력은 하지 않고 좋은 성적을 받고 싶다는 말에 대한 가장 적절한 응답은 ⑤ '보상은 열심히 노력하는 사람에게만 주어지는 거야.'이다.
① 긍정적인 것을 생각하려고 노력해 봐.
② 나는 네가 과학을 가장 좋아하는 걸 알고 있어.
③ 모든 사람은 그들만의 잠재력을 가지고 있다고 믿어.
④ 나에게 방금 성적표를 보여줬잖아.

어휘 grade [greid] 성적   final exam 기말고사   midterm exam 중간고사   hardly [háːrdli] 거의 ~않는   reward [riwɔ́ːrd] 보상

Listen and Check

p. 50

Q1	the banana pattern	Q11	False
Q2	False	Q12	to promote it
Q3	No	Q13	No
Q4	2:00	Q14	False
Q5	False	Q15	free coupons
Q6	Yes	Q16	False
Q7	False	Q17	False
Q8	no participants	Q18	to manage time
Q9	unlimited	Q19	No
Q10	No	Q20	at the library

해석

Q1 남자는 어떤 무늬를 선호하는가?

Q2 남자가 여자에게 돈을 빌려준다.

Q3 남자의 오른쪽 눈이 아픈가?

Q4 남자는 보통 몇 시에 라디오 녹음을 끝내는가?

Q5 여자는 Diver's 리조트에 관해 잘 알고 있다.

Q6 남자와 여자는 그 건물을 방문하는 것이 처음인가?

Q7 남자는 여자에게 내일 그를 도와달라고 요청한다.

Q8 남자와 여자가 설문 조사에 관해 가지는 문제점이 무엇인가?

Q9 기사는 한 사람이 동시에 몇 개의 직업을 가질 수 있다고 말하는가?

Q10 남자는 높이 조정 기능이 있는 의자를 더 구입하는가?

Q11 남자는 전구를 사기 위해 시장에 갈 것이다.

Q12 Blue Car에 관해 얘기하는 여자의 목적이 무엇인가?

Q13 남자와 여자는 이번 여름에 사이판을 방문할 것이다.

Q14 이 동물은 음식 생산을 위해서만 길러진다.

Q15 30일간 매일 웹사이트에 접속하는 것으로부터 얻는 선물은 무엇인가?

Q16 남자가 그의 목적지까지 도달하는 데에는 30분이 걸린다.

Q17 여자는 미래에 대한 그녀의 계획에 확신을 가진다.

Q18 여자는 남자에게서 무엇을 배우고 싶어 하는가?

Q19 남자는 여자와 같은 문제를 가지는가?

Q20 남자와 여자는 어디에서 시험공부를 하는가?

정답 및 해설

실전 모의고사 6회

pp. 58~59

1	②	2	①	3	④	4	③	5	④
6	⑤	7	③	8	④	9	①	10	②
11	①	12	⑤	13	②	14	③	15	④
16	③	17	③	18	⑤	19	⑤	20	⑤

1 그림 정보 파악 ②

M Congratulations! I heard you won the drawing contest.

W Thank you. I'm so pleased to <u>have won first prize</u>. I didn't expect to do that.

M Let me guess <u>which of those pictures</u> your drawing is. You drew the big house <u>in the middle</u>, right?

W That's correct. And I drew trees to the right of the house.

M Did you draw a bench under the trees?

W No. Instead, I <u>drew a pond</u> to the left of the house.

M Oh, I got it. That's your painting.

남 축하해! 네가 사생 대회에서 상 받았다고 들었어.

여 고마워. 1등상을 받게 되어 너무 기뻐. 기대하지 않았는데.

남 저 그림들 중에 네 그림이 무엇인지 맞춰 볼게. 중앙에 큰 집을 그렸어, 맞지?

여 맞아. 그리고 난 집의 오른쪽에 나무들도 그렸어.

남 나무 아래에 벤치도 그렸니?

여 아니. 대신에 집의 왼쪽에 연못을 그렸어.

남 알겠다. 저게 네 그림이구나.

해설 큰 집이 중앙에 그려져 있고 집의 오른편에는 나무, 왼편에는 연못이 있다고 하였다.

어휘 congratulation [kəngrætʃəléiʃən] 축하하다   contest [kántest] 대회   instead [instéd] 대신에

2 부탁한 일 파악 ①

W Wow! These egg fried rice noodles taste fantastic!

M Thanks. I <u>made them spicier</u> with chili peppers.

W Have you ever studied how to cook?

M Not really. I just watch TV cooking shows and follow <u>what the chefs do</u>.

W Wow, you're such a good chef. By the way, what's wrong with you? You are sweating.

M It's much too spicy for me. Can you <u>pass me the water</u>, please?

W Sure. Here it is.

여 우와! 이 계란 볶음 쌀국수는 맛이 환상적인걸!

남 고마워. 고추를 넣어서 더 맵게 만들었어.

여 요리하는 법을 배운 적이 있니?

남 그렇지는 않아. 단지 TV 요리 프로그램을 보고 셰프가 하는 걸 따라서 해.

여 와, 너 진짜 요리 잘한다. 그런데 너 괜찮니? 땀 흘리고 있어.

남 내게는 너무 매워. 물 좀 줄래?

여 물론이야. 여기 있어.

해설 음식을 먹다가 매워서 물을 달라고 부탁하였다.

어휘 fantastic [fæntǽstik] 환상적인   chili pepper 고추   sweat [swet] 땀을 흘리다

3 그림 상황 파악 ④

① W Where did you buy this table?

　 M I got it <u>at a flea market</u> yesterday.

② W Can you <u>fix my computer</u>? It's not working.

　 M Sure. What seems to be the problem?

③ W Hello. I want to have a part-time job here.

　 M <u>Send your résumé</u> to me first.

④ W Excuse me. Is <u>this seat taken</u>?

　 M Not at all. You can have a seat here.

⑤ W Your pancake looks so good. Can I have a bite?

　 M Sorry. I <u>can't share it</u> with you. I have a cold.

① 여 어디에서 이 테이블을 구입했니?

　 남 어제 벼룩시장에서 구했어.

② 여 내 컴퓨터를 고쳐줄 수 있니? 작동을 하지 않아.

　 남 물론이지. 내게 줘 봐.

③ 여 안녕하세요. 여기에서 아르바이트를 하고 싶어요.

　 남 우선 당신의 이력서를 보내주세요.

④ 여 실례합니다. 여기 자리 있나요?

　 남 아뇨. 여기 앉으세요.

⑤ 여 팬케이크가 너무 맛있어 보여. 한 입 먹어도 돼?

　 남 미안해. 너랑 나눠먹을 수 없어. 나 감기 걸렸어.

해설 테이블이 비어있는지 여자가 물어보는 상황이다.

어휘 flea market 벼룩시장   resume [rizjúːm] 이력서

4 특정 정보 파악 ③

[Telephone rings.]

W Hello. I'm calling about your used stroller ad on the website. Is it <u>still available</u>?

M Yes, I <u>have not sold it</u> yet. It's almost new. My baby used it for just one year.

W Can I buy it after looking at it in person?

M Sure. <u>What day do you want</u> to see it?

W I'm thinking of this Tuesday.

M Sorry. I <u>have plans</u> then. How about the next day?

W That's fine with me. See you on Wednesday.

여 여보세요. 인터넷에 있는 당신의 중고 유모차 광고를 보고 전화했어요. 아직 구입할 수 있나요?

남 네, 아직 팔리지 않았어요. 거의 새 거예요. 제 아기가 단지 1년 사용했어요.

여 직접 본 후에 구입해도 될까요?

남 그럼요. 무슨 요일에 보길 원하세요?

여 이번 화요일을 생각하고 있어요.

남 죄송해요. 제가 다른 약속이 있어요. 그 다음 날은 어떠세요?

여 괜찮아요. 수요일에 뵈어요.

해설 화요일에는 남자가 선약이 있어서 다음날인 수요일에 보기로 하였다.

어휘 stroller [stróulər] 유모차   in person 직접

5 언급 유무 파악 ④

W Excuse me. I hear that you are <u>looking for someone</u> to volunteer here.

M That's right. But we need someone <u>with experience</u>.

W <u>I've volunteered</u> at a nursing home for fifteen hours.

M That's not bad. Can you do volunteer work on Sundays from 12 p.m. to 7 p.m.?

26

W No problem. What kind of work is needed here?
M You will help <u>the</u> <u>elderly</u> <u>eat</u> <u>meals</u> and clean their rooms.
W Can I get a volunteer confirmation letter?
M Of course. Please inform us a week before you need it.

여 실례합니다. 여기서 자원봉사할 사람을 찾는다고 들었어요.
남 맞아요. 하지만 우리는 경력이 있는 분만 필요해요.
여 저는 양로원에서 15시간 동안 봉사 활동을 했어요.
남 나쁘지 않군요. 일요일마다 점심 12시부터 오후 7시까지 봉사 활동을 하실 수 있나요?
여 네. 어떤 일을 해야 하나요?
남 어르신들이 식사하시는 것을 도와드리고 방 청소를 할 거예요.
여 봉사 활동 확인서를 받을 수 있나요?
남 물론이죠. 일주일 전에 알려 주세요.

[해설] 자원봉사자에게 식사가 제공되는지에 관해서는 언급되지 않았다.
[어휘] nursing home 양로원   the elderly 고령자, 어르신
confirmation [kὰnfərméiʃən] 확인, 입증

6 [장소 추론] ⑤

W I can't believe that we are here.
M Neither can I. I'm <u>so</u> <u>excited</u> <u>to</u> <u>see</u> BTS perform their songs live.
W It's all thanks to you. You <u>succeeded</u> <u>in</u> <u>buying</u> the concert tickets.
M It was no big deal. Anyway, did you bring the official cheer stick?
W Of course I did. Bryce, can you <u>take</u> <u>a</u> <u>picture</u> <u>of</u> <u>me</u> with this poster in the background?
M Okay. <u>Pose</u> <u>for</u> the camera. [Camera shutter sounds.]
W Now, let's go inside. The concert is about to start.

여 우리가 여기에 있다는 게 믿기지 않아.
남 나도 그래. BTS가 그들의 노래를 라이브로 공연하는 걸 보게 되다니 너무 신나.
여 모두 너 덕분이야. 네가 콘서트 표를 구입하는 것에 성공했잖아.
남 별거 아니었어. 그런데 공식 응원봉은 가져왔어?
여 물론이지. Bryce, 이 포스터를 배경으로 내 사진을 찍어 줄래?
남 그래. 포즈를 취해 봐.
여 이제 안으로 들어가자. 콘서트가 곧 시작할 거야.

[해설] 콘서트가 시작하기를 기다리며 포스터를 배경으로 사진을 찍는 상황이다.
[어휘] official [əfíʃəl] 공식의, 공인된   cheer stick (빛이 나오는) 응원봉
pose [pouz] 자세, 포즈

7 [어색한 대화 찾기] ③

① M How long have you been <u>waiting</u> <u>in</u> <u>line</u>?
　W About 30 minutes.
② M I was <u>disappointed</u> <u>with</u> the musical.
　W I know! I felt the same way.
③ M I'm <u>busy</u> <u>working</u> right now. Can I call you later?
　W My cellphone broke down again. Let's buy a new one together.
④ M Excuse me. Where can I find the soap?
　W You can see it in section 5. It's <u>just</u> <u>around</u> <u>the</u> <u>corner</u>.
⑤ M Naomi, why did you open my package <u>without</u> <u>asking</u> <u>me</u>?
　W Sorry. I thought it was addressed to me.

① 남 얼마나 오랫동안 줄 서 있는 거니?
　여 대략 30분 정도야.
② 남 뮤지컬에 실망했어.
　여 그러게. 나도 너처럼 생각해.
③ 남 지금 당장은 일하느라 바빠. 내가 나중에 전화해도 될까?
　여 내 휴대폰이 또 고장났어. 함께 새로 하나 사러 가자.
④ 남 실례합니다. 비누를 어디에서 찾을 수 있나요?
　여 5번 구역에서 볼 수 있어요. 모퉁이 근처에 있어요.
⑤ 남 Naomi, 왜 나한테 물어보지 않고 내 소포를 열었니?
　여 미안해. 나한테 온 거라고 생각했어.

[해설] 일하느라 바빠서 다음에 전화해도 되냐는 말에 자신의 휴대폰이 고장났으니 함께 사러 가자고 답하는 것은 부자연스럽다.
[어휘] disappointed [dìsəpɔ́intid] 실망한   section [sékʃən] 구역, 부분

8 [부탁한 일 파악] ④

M Sarah, I'm so glad you <u>got</u> <u>hired</u> by a TV station.
W Thanks. You know, I tried really hard to get that job.
M Anyway, can you <u>commute</u> <u>to</u> <u>work</u>? The TV station is far from your place.
W That's why I decided to <u>move</u> <u>closer</u> <u>to</u> <u>work</u>.
M Oh, when do you move in to your new place?
W This Saturday. If you don't mind, can you <u>help</u> <u>me</u> <u>move</u> <u>out</u>?
M Sure. I'll be at your house on Saturday.

남 Sarah, 네가 방송국에 고용되었다니 너무 기쁘다.
여 고마워. 너도 알다시피 이 일을 얻으려고 너무 열심히 일했어.
남 그런데 직장으로 통근할 수 있니? 그 방송국은 너희 집에서 멀잖아.
여 그래서 직장이랑 가까운 곳으로 이사 가려고 결심했어.
남 아, 언제 새로운 집으로 이사하는데?
여 이번 토요일이야. 괜찮다면 내가 이사하는 걸 도와줄 수 있니?
남 물론이지. 토요일에 너희 집으로 갈게.

[해설] 직장과 가까운 곳으로 집을 옮기게 되어 이사하는 걸 도와달라고 부탁하고 있다.
[어휘] hire [haiər] 고용하다, 채용하다   TV station 텔레비전 방송국
commute [kəmjúːt] 통근하다

9 [화제·주제 파악] ①

W Good morning, middle school seniors. Congratulations on your graduation. As you know, our school has a tradition to <u>hand</u> <u>your</u> <u>used</u> <u>school</u> <u>uniforms</u> <u>down</u> to new students. School uniforms are kind of costly to buy. If you donate yours, students from lower-income families can <u>benefit</u> <u>from</u> your kindness. Please wash your uniform and <u>put</u> <u>it</u> <u>in</u> <u>a</u> <u>box</u> next to the school gate from Wednesday to Friday. Thank you for your cooperation in advance.

여 중학교 3학년 여러분, 좋은 아침입니다. 졸업을 축하합니다. 여러분도 아시다시피, 우리 학교는 입었던 교복을 신입생에게 물려주는 전통이 있습니다. 교복은 다소 비쌉니다. 만약 여러분이 교복을 기증한다면, 저소득 가구의 학생들은 여러분의 친절함을 통해 도움을 얻을 수 있습니다. 교복을 세탁해서 학교 정문 옆에 있는 상자에 수요일부터 금요일까지 놓아 주세요. 협조에 미리 감사합니다.

[해설] 저소득 가구 학생들을 돕기 위해 졸업하는 학생들에게 교복을 기증해

달라고 하였다.

어휘 graduation [græ̀dʒəwéiʃən] 졸업   hand down ~을 물려주다
costly [kɔ́(:)stli] 값비싼   donate [dóuneit] 기부하다, 기증하다

10 숫자 정보 파악 ②

W Welcome to Smart Electronics. How may I help you?
M I'd like to buy some earphones. My dog chewed the cable wire on mine.
W That's too bad. Then why don't you use these wireless earphones?
M Hmm... They look good. How much are they?
W They are 200 dollars. They were developed by a major international company.
M Wow. They're more expensive than I expected.
W If you want, you can use this 10% off coupon.
M Okay. I'll take them.

여 Smart Electronics에 오신 걸 환영합니다. 어떻게 도와 드릴까요?
남 이어폰을 사고 싶어요. 제 강아지가 케이블 선을 씹었어요.
여 안됐네요. 그러면 이 무선 이어폰을 사용하는 건 어때요?
남 흠... 좋아 보이네요. 얼마인가요?
여 200 달러입니다. 세계적인 기업에서 만들어진 거예요.
남 와. 예상했던 것보다 비싸네요.
여 원하신다면, 10% 쿠폰을 쓰셔도 됩니다.
남 알겠어요. 구입할게요.

해설 10% 할인 쿠폰을 적용해서 200달러짜리 무선 이어폰을 구입하겠다고 하였다.
어휘 electronics [ilèktrániks] 전자 제품   chew [tʃuː] 씹다
wireless [wáiərlis] 무선의

11 할 일 파악 ①

M Minseo, you are eating ice cream now. You told me that you were on a diet!
W I am, but this ice cream is my favorite, and it's on sale.
M No way! Stop eating that and go jogging with me.
W I wish I could, but I can't. Yesterday, I fell down and hurt my knee.
M Then you have to change your diet to lose weight.
W [Sigh] Okay. I'll go to a market to buy some vegetables for dinner.
M Let's go together.

남 민서야, 너 지금 아이스크림 먹고 있구나. 나한테 다이어트하는 중이라고 말했잖아.
여 하는 중이야. 하지만 이 아이스크림이 내가 제일 좋아하는 것이고, 할인 판매 중이란 말이야.
남 말도 안 돼! 그거 그만 먹고 나랑 조깅하러 가자.
여 그러고 싶지만 그럴 수 없어. 어제 실수로 넘어져서 무릎을 다쳤어.
남 그러면 체중을 줄이기 위해 식단을 바꿔야겠다.
여 알겠어. 저녁으로 먹을 야채를 사러 마켓에 갈게.
남 나랑 같이 가.

해설 식단을 바꾸기 위해 마켓으로 야채를 사러 간다고 하였다.
어휘 favorite [féivərit] 좋아하는 물건   fall down 넘어지다

12 언급 유무 파악 ⑤

M Hello, everyone. We hope you're having a great time. We would like to tell you about the annual

pass to the amusement park. If you sign up for a golden pass, you can go on all of the rides in the park for free. In addition, you don't need to wait in line for the rides. A golden pass is 300 dollars for adults and 150 dollars for children for a year. If you want to become a member here, please visit the information desk and fill out an application form.

남 안녕하세요, 여러분. 저희는 여러분이 좋은 시간을 보내고 있기를 바랍니다. 저희 놀이공원의 연간 회원권에 대해 소개해 드리고자 합니다. 만약 golden pass에 가입하신다면, 놀이공원에 있는 모든 놀이 기구를 무료로 이용 가능합니다. 게다가 놀이 기구를 타기 위해 줄을 서서 기다릴 필요도 없습니다. golden pass는 성인은 연간 300달러이고 어린이는 연간 150달러입니다. 참여하고 싶으시면, 안내 데스크를 방문하셔서 신청서를 작성해 주시기 바랍니다.

해설 연간 회원권의 환불에 관해서는 언급되지 않았다.
어휘 annual [ǽnjuəl] 연간의, 매년의   amusement park 놀이공원
in addition 게다가   application [æ̀pləkéiʃən] 신청, 지원

13 그림 정보 파악 ②

M Jiwoo, we should change the room for today's meeting.
W How come? It's scheduled to be held in Room 707.
M It was. But the projector in Room 707 is out of order.
W Well, which meeting room is available?
M We can use Room 705.
W Okay. We should inform our clients of this.
M Don't worry. I'll send a message to them.
W Thank you. I'll prepare for the meeting in the room.

남 지우씨, 오늘 회의실 바꿔야 해요.
여 왜요? 707번 회의실에서 회의하기로 예정되어 있잖아요.
남 그랬죠. 하지만 707번 회의실에 있는 빔 프로젝터가 고장이 났어요.
여 음, 어떤 회의실이 이용 가능할까요?
남 705번 회의실을 사용할 수 있어요.
여 알겠어요. 우리 고객들에게 이것을 알려야겠군요.
남 걱정하지 마세요. 제가 문자를 보낼게요.
여 감사합니다. 저는 방에서 회의를 준비할게요.

해설 707번 회의실에 있는 빔 프로젝터가 고장이 나서 705번 회의실을 사용하기로 하였다.
어휘 projector [prədʒéktər] 빔 프로젝터   client [kláiənt] 고객, 거래처

14 화제·주제 파악 ③

W We spend a lot of time outdoors on summer nights to escape the heat. Soon, mosquitoes start to attack people. If you get more mosquito bites than others, listen carefully. First, avoid excessive physical activity. Mosquitos are usually attracted to the scent of sweat. Not using perfume is a good idea, too. Second, when you go out, put on bright clothes. Mosquitos love dark clothes to protect themselves.

여 우리는 여름밤에 더위를 피하기 위해 실외에서 많은 시간을 보냅니다. 곧, 모기가 사람을 공격하기 시작합니다. 만약 당신이 다른 사람보다 모기에 더 많이 물린다면, 잘 들으세요. 첫째, 과도한 신체 활동은 피하세요. 모기는 보통 땀 냄새에 끌립니다. 향수를 사용하지 않는 것도 좋은 생각입니다. 두 번째, 외출할 때 밝은 옷을 입으세요. 모기는 자신을 보호하기 위해 어두운 옷을 좋아합니다.

15 할 일 파악 ④

W Yechan, are you still reading that book?
M Why not? It's so interesting.
W But you need some exercise. It's not a good idea <u>to stay</u> <u>home</u> <u>all</u> <u>day</u>.
M Is that so? I think somebody <u>feels</u> <u>bored</u>.
W You're right. I feel bored. Let's play basketball.
M Just the two of us? Wait. I'll call my friends and <u>ask</u> <u>them</u> <u>to</u> <u>join</u> <u>us</u>.
W Wonderful! I'll get ready to go out.

여 예찬아, 아직도 책 읽는 중이니?
남 왜? 이거 정말 재미있어?
여 하지만 넌 운동이 필요해. 하루 종일 집에 있는 건 좋은 생각이 아니야.
남 그러니? 누군가는 지루할 거 같기는 해.
여 맞아. 나 지루해. 나가서 나랑 농구하자.
남 우리 둘이서? 기다려 봐. 내가 친구들에게 전화해서 같이 하자고 물어 볼게.
여 좋아! 난 나갈 준비를 할게.

해설 친구들에게 함께 농구하자고 물어보기 위해 전화를 하겠다고 하였다.
어휘 still [stil] 여전히, 아직도

16 숫자 정보 파악 ③

[*Cellphone rings.*]
W Hello. Who's this?
M This is the postman. I've got some mail for you.
W Can you <u>put</u> <u>it</u> <u>into</u> <u>the</u> <u>mailbox</u> in front of the door?
M Sorry. This is registered mail. So I <u>need</u> <u>your</u> <u>signature</u>.
W But I'm away from home. I'm on a business trip.
M <u>When</u> <u>will</u> <u>you</u> <u>come</u> <u>back</u> to your place?
W On January 21. Can I get it on January 22?
M Let me check the schedule. [*Pause*] Yes, that's possible.
W That's great. Thank you.

여 여보세요? 누구세요?
남 집배원입니다. 우편이 하나 있어요.
여 문 앞에 있는 우편함에 넣어 주시겠어요?
남 죄송하지만 이게 등기 우편이에요. 그래서 고객님의 서명이 필요해요.
여 하지만 저는 집에 없어요. 출장 중이에요.
남 언제 집으로 돌아오시나요?
여 1월 21일이요. 제가 그걸 1월 22일에 받을 수 있을까요?
남 일정을 확인해 볼게요. 가능합니다.
여 잘됐네요. 감사합니다.

해설 1월 21일에 집으로 돌아오기 때문에 1월 22일에 우편을 받기로 하였다.
어휘 registered [rédʒistərd] 등록된, 등기의   signature [sígnətʃər] 서명   schedule [skédʒuːl] 일정, 예정

17 적절한 응답 찾기 ③

M Jaekyoung, do you remember you <u>helped</u> <u>me</u> <u>study</u>?
W Sure I do. We went to the library and studied math for 5 hours.

M Finally, I had a math test yesterday.
W Do you <u>have</u> <u>good</u> <u>news</u> or something?
M Yes! I <u>got</u> <u>an A</u> on the math test.
W Really? I'm so happy to hear that.
M Thank you. I <u>couldn't</u> <u>have</u> <u>done</u> it without your help.
W <u>It was nothing. You really did study hard.</u>

남 재경아, 내 공부를 네가 도와줬던 걸 기억하니?
여 물론이지. 우리는 도서관에 가서 5시간 동안 수학 공부했잖아.
남 드디어 나 어제 수학 시험을 봤어.
여 그러면 뭔가 좋은 소식이 있는 거야?
남 응! 나 수학 시험에서 A 받았어.
여 그거 정말이니? 그 소식을 듣게 되어 너무 기쁘다.
남 고마워. 네 도움이 없었으면 하지 못했을 거야.
여 별거 아니었어. 네가 정말 열심히 했잖아.

해설 여자의 도움으로 수학 시험에 A를 받게 되어 고마워하는 말에 대한 가장 적절한 응답은 ③ '별거 아니었어. 네가 정말 열심히 했잖아.'이다.
① 너에게 대답을 해 줄 수 없어서 미안해.
② 나는 수학보다 영어를 공부하고 싶어.   ④ 너는 공부에 더 집중해야 해.
⑤ 슬퍼하지 마. 다음에 더 잘할 거야.
어휘 finally [fáinəli] 마침내, 결국

18 적절한 응답 찾기 ⑤

[*Telephone rings.*]
M Brianna, are you on the way? I've been waiting for you for 20 minutes.
W I'm almost there, but I'm <u>stuck</u> <u>in</u> <u>traffic</u>.
M Are you <u>still</u> <u>on</u> <u>the</u> <u>bus</u>?
W Sorry. The roads are <u>jammed</u> <u>with</u> <u>cars</u>. I didn't expect that.
M Come on. Today is a holiday. Traffic is always terrible on holidays.
W I'm so sorry. I <u>won't</u> <u>be</u> <u>late</u> again.
M <u>All right. You have to keep your word.</u>

남 Brianna, 오는 길이니? 난 너를 20분 동안 기다리는 중이야.
여 나 거의 도착했어. 하지만 교통 체증에 갇혔어.
남 여전히 버스 안에 있는 거야?
여 미안해. 도로가 차로 가득 찼어. 이걸 예상하지 못했어.
남 맙소사. 오늘 휴일이야. 휴일에는 늘 교통 체증이 심하다고.
여 정말 미안해. 다시는 늦지 않을게.
남 알겠어. 그 말 꼭 지켜야 해.

해설 다시는 늦지 않겠다는 여자의 말에 대한 남자의 응답으로 가장 적절한 것은 ⑤ '알겠어. 그 말 꼭 지켜야 해.'이다.
① 걱정하지 마. 내가 집까지 걸어서 데려다줄게.
② 우리 집은 너희 집에서 멀어.
③ 내 생각에는 네가 새 차를 사야 할 거 같아.
④ 당연하지. 기차 타고 여행하는 거 좋아해.
어휘 stuck in traffic 교통이 정체된   jammed [dʒæmd] 꼼짝 못하게 된

19 적절한 응답 찾기 ⑤

M Look at the mountains <u>covered</u> <u>with</u> <u>snow</u>. I can't believe that I'm climbing Mt. Everest.
W I agree. They are amazing. But calm down a bit.
M Why? We should enjoy this great view.
W Well, do you see the <u>dead</u> <u>body</u> <u>over</u> <u>there</u>? It is called Green Boots.

정답 및 해설

M Oh, no! Who is it?

W Nobody knows. But the corpse stays there and <u>serves as a warning</u> to climbers.

M I feel bad. I must be more careful.

W <u>You took the words right out of my mouth.</u>

남 눈으로 뒤덮인 산을 봐. 내가 에베레스트산을 등반하고 있다는 게 믿을 수 없어.

여 동의해. 멋지지. 하지만 조금 침착해.

남 왜? 우리는 이 멋진 광경을 즐겨야 해.

여 음, 저기에 시체가 보이지? 그건 Green Boots라고 말해져.

남 맙소사. 누구야?

여 아무도 몰라. 하지만 저 시체는 저기에 계속 머물러서 등반가들에게 경고의 역할을 하지.

남 안됐다. 난 좀 더 조심해야겠어.

여 내 말이 그 말이야.

해설 에베레스트산에 남겨진 시체를 보며 조심해야겠다는 말에 대한 가장 적절한 응답은 ⑤ '내 말이 그 말이야.'이다.
① 우리는 그의 장례식에 참석해야 해.
② 우리는 위층으로 올라가야 할 것 같아.
③ 나도 그래. 유령이 무서워.   ④ 난 산의 사진 찍는 것을 좋아해.

어휘 corpse [kɔːrps] 시체   serve as ~의 역할을 하다   warning [wɔ́ːrniŋ] 경고, 주의

20 상황에 맞는 말 찾기 ⑤

M Today, there is a special photo exhibition at the National Museum of Korea. Although the National Museum of Korea is <u>far from his place</u>, Eunsung decides to go there. He finds directions on <u>how to get</u> to the museum. He gets on the bus. A few minutes later, he feels worried. He can't find <u>where he is</u> on the bus route map. So he decides to ask the bus driver <u>how many more stops</u> there are to go. In this situation, what would Eunsung most likely say to the bus driver?

Eunsung <u>How many more stops to the National Museum of Korea?</u>

남 오늘은 국립 중앙 박물관에서 특별 사진 전시회가 있습니다. 국립 중앙 박물관은 그의 집에서 멀리 떨어져 있지만, 은성이는 전시회에 가기로 결심합니다. 그는 국립 중앙 박물관으로 가는 길에 대한 정보를 얻습니다. 그는 버스에 오릅니다. 몇 분 후에, 그는 걱정됩니다. 그는 버스 노선도에서 자신이 어디에 있는지 찾을 수 없습니다. 그래서 그는 버스 기사님께 몇 정거장을 더 가야 하는지 물어보기로 결심합니다. 이러한 상황에서, 은성이가 버스 기사님께 할 말로 가장 적절한 것은 무엇일까요?

은성 국립 중앙 박물관까지 몇 정거장을 더 가야 하나요?

해설 처음 가보는 곳에 가는 도중에 자신이 얼마나 더 가야 하는지 궁금한 상황이므로 은성이 버스 기사님께 할 말로 가장 적절한 것은 ⑤ '국립 중앙 박물관까지 몇 정거장을 더 가야 하나요?'이다.
① 제가 버스 사진을 찍어도 될까요?
② 버스 정거장까지 어떻게 가야 하나요?
③ 전시회에 가려면 얼마를 지불해야 하나요?
④ 국립 중앙 박물관으로 가는 버스가 몇 번인가요?

어휘 exhibition [èksəbíʃən] 전시회   bus route map 버스 노선도

Listen and Check
p. 60

Q1	True	Q11	because she was hurt
Q2	No		
Q3	False	Q12	True
Q4	for one year	Q13	No
Q5	Sunday	Q14	mosquitos
Q6	False	Q15	the woman
Q7	The man is busy working	Q16	No
Q8	True	Q17	five hours
Q9	No	Q18	False
Q10	his dog	Q19	a corpse
		Q20	No

해석
Q1 남자는 여자가 그린 그림을 보고 있는 중이다.
Q2 남자는 요리를 배운 적이 있을까?
Q3 남자는 카페에서 자리에 앉고 싶다.
Q4 아기는 유모차를 몇 년 동안 사용했을까?
Q5 여자는 무슨 요일에 자원봉사 활동을 해야 할까?
Q6 Bryce는 포스터를 배경으로 자신의 사진을 찍었다.
Q7 왜 남자는 여자에게 나중에 전화하겠다고 말했을까?
Q8 Samantha는 방송국에 취업했다.
Q9 이 학교 행사는 화요일부터 금요일까지 열릴 예정인가?
Q10 누가 남자의 이어폰을 망가뜨렸나?
Q11 왜 여자는 남자와 함께 조깅하러 갈 수 없었을까?
Q12 golden pass는 놀이공원의 연간 회원권의 이름이다.
Q13 오늘 회의는 취소되었나?
Q14 무엇이 땀 냄새나 향수 냄새를 좋아할까?
Q15 누가 밖에서 농구할 것을 제안했는가?
Q16 여자는 지금 집에 있는가?
Q17 남자와 여자는 도서관에서 얼마나 오랫동안 수학 공부를 했을까?
Q18 남자는 Brianna를 30분 동안 기다리는 중이다.
Q19 남자와 여자는 에베레스트산을 오르던 도중에 무엇을 보았을까?
Q20 국립 중앙 박물관은 은성이네 집에서 가까운 곳에 위치해 있을까?

실전 모의고사 7회
pp. 68~69

1	④	2	④	3	③	4	⑤	5	③
6	④	7	⑤	8	②	9	⑤	10	⑤
11	③	12	③	13	②	14	③	15	④
16	②	17	⑤	18	④	19	⑤	20	③

1 그림 정보 파악 ④

M Are you looking for <u>something in particular</u>?

W I'm looking for a watch for my fourteen-year-old daughter. What would you recommend?

M This <u>heart-shaped</u> watch with a simple band and this digital watch with a <u>square shape</u> are popular with teens.

W Good, but I need a simple one.

M How about this one? It's round, has a simple band, and has a bear on its face.

W It's so cute, and the numbers are big and easy to read. I'll take it.

남 특별한 무언가를 찾고 있으세요?

여 14살짜리 딸을 위한 시계를 찾고 있어요. 무엇을 추천해 주시겠어요?

남 하트 모양에 단순한 밴드가 있는 시계와 사각형 모양의 디지털 손목 시계가 십 대들 사이에서 인기가 있습니다.

여 좋네요, 하지만 저는 약간 더 단순한 것을 원합니다.

남 이건 어떠신가요? 둥근 모양에 평범한 손목 밴드, 그리고 배경에 곰이 있어요.

여 귀엽네요. 숫자가 커서 읽기도 쉽고요. 이걸로 할게요.

해설 평범한 손목 밴드에 시계 표면에는 곰이 있다고 하였다.

어휘 particular [pərtíkjələr] 특별한, 특정한   recommend [rèkəménd] 추천하다, 권고하다   square [skwɛər] 정사각형

2   목적 파악 ④

[Telephone rings.]

W Hello, This is Kelly Stone at Hana Middle School.

M Hello, Ms. Stone. This is Chris Hacker, Eric Hacker's father.

W Hi, Mr. Hacker. What are you calling in for?

M Eric's mom is having surgery now, and he wants to wait for his mom's surgery to be done. He wants to check on his mother's health. So he can't go to school today.

W I'm sorry to hear that. Don't worry about his absence because in this case, it won't be listed on his student record. I hope your wife recovers quickly.

M Thank you, Ms. Stone.

여 여보세요, 하나 중학교 Kelly Stone입니다.

남 Stone 선생님, 저는 Eric Hacker의 아빠 Chris Hacker입니다.

여 안녕하세요, Hacker씨. 무슨 일로 전화를 주셨나요?

남 Eric의 엄마가 지금 수술 중이에요. Eric은 엄마의 수술이 끝나길 기다리길 원해요. Eric은 수술 뒤 엄마의 건강 상태를 확인하길 원합니다. 그래서, 오늘 학교에 못 갈 것 같아요.

여 유감입니다. 결석에 대해 걱정하지 마세요. 왜냐하면, 이런 경우에는 학생부에 기록되지 않습니다. 그녀가 빨리 회복하시길 바랍니다.

남 감사합니다, Stone 선생님.

해설 남자는 아들이 엄마의 수술 결과를 보기 위해 학교를 갈 수 없다고 하였다.

어휘 have surgery 수술을 받다   absence [ǽbsəns] 결석

3   그림 상황 파악 ③

① M Could you help me?
  W I'm afraid I can't.
② M Where are you moving?
  W Next door.
③ M May I help you?
  W Thank you. Would you hold these for me?
④ M What can I do for you?
  W I want to buy all of these books.
⑤ M Watch out! The floor is slippery.
  W Thanks. I nearly fell down.

① 남 저 좀 도와주시겠습니까?
  여 미안하지만, 도와드릴 수 없습니다.

② 남 어디로 이사 가니?
  여 옆집으로.
③ 남 도와 드릴까요?
  여 고맙습니다. 이것들을 좀 들어주실래요?
④ 남 무엇을 도와 드릴까요?
  여 이 책을 모두 사겠습니다.
⑤ 남 조심해! 바닥이 미끄러워.
  여 고마워. 거의 넘어질 뻔했어.

해설 남자가 많은 책을 들고 있는 여성을 도와주려는 상황이다.

어휘 slippery [slípəri] 미끄러운

4   특정 정보 파악 ⑤

M Jenny, have you got any free time next week?

W According to my schedule, I'll be busy all week.

M Let me see it. [Pause] Wow, you are tied up for the entire week.

W Yeah, on Monday and Thursday, I'll babysit my cousin Sam all day long, and on Tuesday and Wednesday, I'll study with my math tutor.

M And on Friday, you'll attend your grandfather's birthday party, right?

W That's right. We are going to have dinner at my grandparents' home.

M Really? Then shall we meet in the morning on that day?

W Okay. That's fine with me.

남 Jenny, 다음 주에 편한 시간 있니?

여 내 일정을 보니 다음 주 내내 바쁠 것 같아.

남 어디 한번 보자. 와, 너 일주일 내내 바쁘겠구나.

여 응, 월요일과 목요일엔 하루 종일 나의 사촌 Sam을 돌봐야 하고, 화요일과 수요일엔 수학 과외 선생님과 공부를 해야만 해.

남 그리고, 금요일엔 할아버지 생신 파티에 갈 거고, 그지?

여 맞아. 우리는 할아버지 댁에서 저녁 식사를 할 거야.

남 정말? 그럼 그날 오전에 만날까?

여 그래, 좋아.

해설 할아버지 댁에서 저녁을 먹기로 한 날 오전에 만나기로 하였다.

어휘 be tied up for ~동안 바쁘다

5   언급 유무 파악 ③

W The Korean alphabet, known as Hangeul, has been used to write the Korean language since its creation by King Sejong the Great in the 15th century. Today, it is the official writing system of both North and South Korea. The Hangeul alphabet originally consisted of 28 letters when it was created. But modern Hangeul consists of a total of 24 letters. It is said that Hangeul can create any words and express any sound. So in 2009, the Korean alphabet was unofficially adopted by the town of Baubau, Indonesia, to write the Cia-Cia language.

여 한글이라고 알려진, 한국어 알파벳은 15세기에 세종대왕에 의해 창제된 이래 한국어를 쓰는데 사용되어 왔습니다. 오늘날, 그것은 한국과 북한 모두의 공식적인 문자 체계입니다. 한글 알파벳은 창제되었을 때 28자로 구성되었습니다. 그러나 현대 한글은 총 24자로 구성되어 있습니다. 한글은 어떤 단어도 만들어 낼 수 있고, 어떤 소리도 표현할 수 있다고 합니다. 그래서 2009년에, 인도네시아의 Baubau시에 의해 Cia-

Cia 언어를 쓰기 위해 한글이 비공식적으로 채택되었습니다.

해설 한글의 만들어진 년도에 대해서는 언급되지 않았다.

어휘 creation [kriéiʃən] 창조, 창작   consist [kənsíst] 구성되다
unofficially [ənəfíʃəli] 비공식적으로

6 관계 추론 ④

W Hello. I'd like to report a lost credit card.
M What are your card number and name, please?
W My number is 0552-6253-1500-2202, and my name is Ellen Jeong.
M How do you know that you lost it?
W Somebody stole my bag.
M When was the last time you used your card?
W Two days ago.
M I'll check if the card has been used since then. [Keyboard sound] Nobody has used it. Don't worry. I've also canceled your card.
W Thanks.

여 여보세요. 분실된 신용 카드를 신고하려 합니다.
남 카드 번호와 성함이 어떻게 되나요?
여 0552-6253-1500-2202이고, 제 이름은 Ellen Jeong입니다.
남 카드를 잃어버린 걸 어떻게 아셨나요?
여 누군가 제 가방을 훔쳐 갔어요.
남 마지막으로 카드를 사용하신 게 언제죠?
여 이틀 전이요.
남 그때부터의 카드 사용 여부를 확인하겠습니다. 사용한 내역은 없습니다. 걱정하지 마세요. 또한 카드는 취소시켰습니다.
여 감사합니다.

해설 신용 카드 분실 신고를 하고 있는 상황이다.

어휘 credit card 신용 카드   cancel [kǽnsəl] 취소하다

7 어색한 대화 찾기 ⑤

① W Isn't this a nice party?
   M I really like it.
② W I haven't seen you before.
   M I just moved to this town.
③ W Have you finished your project?
   M I'm almost done.
④ W What are you doing this Saturday?
   M I don't have anything planned.
⑤ W When did your parents get married?
   M They've been here for 20 years.

① 여 멋진 파티이지 않나요?
   남 정말 좋습니다.
② 여 처음 뵙는 것 같습니다.
   남 이곳에 막 이사 왔어요.
③ 여 과제 다 끝냈어?
   남 거의 다 했어.
④ 여 이번 토요일에 무엇을 할 거니?
   남 계획한 것은 없어.
⑤ 여 네 부모님은 언제 결혼하셨니?
   남 그들은 20년째 여기 살고 계셔.

해설 부모님께서 언제 결혼하셨는지를 묻는 말에 결혼한지 20년째가 되었다고 답하는 것은 부자연스럽다.

8 부탁한 일 파악 ②

W What time does the movie start?
M 10 minutes from now. The preview I watched on YouTube was really exciting.
W Yeah, it really was. But don't expect too much. Maybe we won't enjoy the actual movie.
M Are you serious?
W I'm just joking. Hey, the movie is starting now. How about turning off your cellphone? I already did that.
M Why not? I'm a man of manners.

여 몇 시에 영화가 시작하니?
남 10분 뒤야. 유튜브에서 보았던 예고편은 정말로 흥미진진했어.
여 응, 정말 그렇더라. 하지만, 너무 기대하지 마. 아마, 우리가 진짜 영화를 즐길지 못할 수도 있어.
남 뭐라고?
여 농담이야. 야, 영화가 지금 시작하려고 해. 휴대 전화를 꺼두는 게 어때? 난 이미 껐어.
남 물론이지. 난 매너 있는 남자야.

해설 영화가 시작하기 전에 휴대폰을 끌 것을 제안하고 있다.

어휘 preview [príːvjùː] 미리 보기   turn off 끄다

9 의도 파악 ⑤

M Karen, can I talk with you for a moment?
W Sure. I'd love to.
M I think you and Minho seem to be having some problems, right?
W How did you know that?
M I can tell by the expression on your face.
W Actually, I had an argument with him over a trivial matter last night.
M I'm sorry to hear that. Why don't you make up with him? That's what friends do.

남 Karen, 잠깐 이야기할 수 있을까?
여 물론이지. 그러자.
남 음, 내 생각엔 너와 민호 사이에 문제가 있는 것 같아, 그렇지 않니?
여 너 어떻게 알았어?
남 네 표정만 봐도 알 수 있어.
여 사실, 어젯밤에 사소한 문제로 민호와 말다툼을 했어.
남 그랬다니 유감이구나. 민호와 화해하는 게 어떻겠니? 친구는 그런 거야.

해설 남자는 여자에게 민호와 화해할 것을 권유하고 있다.

어휘 expression [ikspréʃən] 표현, 표정   argument [ɑ́ːrgjumənt] 논쟁   trivial [tríviəl] 사소한

10 숫자 정보 파악 ⑤

W May I take your order?
M I'd like two hamburgers and two orders of French fries.
W Anything to drink?
M Two large Cokes, please.
W Your total is 20 dollars, but you can save 15% if you order combo meals.
M Okay. I will order combo meals.
W Okay, that's two combo meals. Thank you.

여 주문하시겠습니까?
남 햄버거 2개와 감자튀김 2개 부탁합니다.

여 마실 것은요?
남 콜라 큰 걸로 2개 부탁합니다.
여 총 20달러입니다. 하지만, 세트 메뉴로 주문하시면 15퍼센트를 절약하실 수 있어요.
남 좋아요. 세트 메뉴로 주문할게요.
여 세트 메뉴 두 개를 주문하셨습니다. 감사합니다.

해설 세트 메뉴에 대해 15%의 할인을 적용하면 총액인 20달러에서 3달러가 할인된다.

어휘 combo meal 세트 메뉴

11 할 일 파악 ③

M What seems to be the problem?
W The air conditioner doesn't seem to be working.
M I'm sorry for the inconvenience you are experiencing.
W That's all right. I think it wouldn't be so bad if I could open a window.
M Well, all the windows in our hotel rooms are fixed. We'll put you in a different room right now.
W Thanks. It's a good thing I didn't unpack my baggage.

남 무엇이 문제인 것 같습니까?
여 에어컨이 작동하지 않는 것 같아요.
남 불편을 끼쳐 드려서 죄송합니다.
여 괜찮아요. 제 생각엔 창문을 열면 나쁘지 않을 것 같아요.
남 호텔 객실의 모든 창문은 고정되어 있습니다. 지금 바로 다른 방으로 바꿔 드리겠습니다.
여 감사합니다. 제 짐을 풀지 않아서 다행이네요.

해설 에어컨이 작동하지 않고, 창문도 열리지 않아 다른 방으로 이동한다고 하였다.

어휘 air conditioner 에어컨   unpack [ʌnpǽk] (짐을) 풀다
baggage [bǽɡidʒ] 수화물, 짐

12 언급 유무 파악 ③

W There are many ways to prevent global warming from becoming worse. You can reduce waste by using reusable products. Recycle paper, cans, and plastic products whenever you can. Drive less and walk more. Less driving means creating fewer harmful emissions. When you plan to buy a car or electronics, buy energy-efficient ones. Planting many trees is one of the best ways to reduce global warming.

여 지구 온난화가 악화되는 것을 예방할 수 있는 여러 가지 방법들이 있습니다. 재사용이 가능한 제품을 선택하여 낭비를 줄일 수 있습니다. 가능하면 종이, 캔 및 플라스틱을 재활용하십시오. 덜 운전하고 더 많이 걸으십시오. 운전을 덜 하는 것은 더 적은 해로운 배기가스를 배출하는 것을 의미합니다. 자동차나 전자 제품을 구입할 때는 에너지 효율적인 제품을 구입하십시오. 많은 나무를 심는 것은 지구 온난화를 줄이는 최선의 방법 중 하나입니다.

해설 지구 온난화를 예방하는 방법으로 온도를 조절하는 방법은 언급되지 않았다.

어휘 prevent [privént] 예방하다   reusable [riúːzəbəl] 재사용할 수 있는   emission [imíʃən] 배출 가스   efficient [ifíʃənt] 효율적인

13 표 파악 ②

W Alex, what are you looking at?

M I'm looking at this semester's after-school program.
W Why don't you sign up for a foreign language class? I took the Spanish class last semester. It was helpful when I traveled abroad.
M Was it? Then I'll take the Spanish class. Oh, no! It ends at 5:00. I have to go to the gym by 4:30.
W Then how about taking the Japanese class or the Chinese class?
M Hmm... I'm really terrible at Chinese characters.
W Come on. I bet it will be useful someday.

여 Alex, 뭘 보고 있니?
남 이번 학기 방과 후 프로그램을 보고 있는 중이야.
여 외국어 강좌를 등록하는 게 어때? 난 지난 학기에 스페인어 수업을 들었어. 외국 여행할 때 그게 도움이 되더라구.
남 그랬어? 그럼, 나도 스페인어 수업을 들어야겠다. 오, 저런! 수업이 5시에 끝나네. 나는 체육관에 4시 30분까지 가야 해.
여 그럼, 일본어 수업이나 중국어 수업을 듣는 건 어때?
남 흠... 나 한자에 아주 약한데.
여 해 봐. 그게 언젠가 도움이 될 거라고 확신해.

해설 체육관에 가야 하는 시간 전에 끝나고, 한자를 사용하는 수업이어야 한다.

어휘 sign up for ~에 등록하다   gym [dʒim] 체육관

14 화제·주제 파악 ③

M You can find this in most cities and countries around the world. This was first installed in London, England, in the late 1800s. This usually has a set of lights in three colors. The lights signal when pedestrians and vehicles can proceed or have to stop. In some countries, this has a blinking mode, which means caution. These days, sound signals for the blind have been added.

남 당신은 전 세계 대부분의 도시와 시골에서 이것을 찾을 수 있습니다. 이것은 1800년대 후반, 영국의 런던에 처음 설치되었습니다. 이것은 대개 세 개의 색깔이 있는 등을 가지고 있습니다. 그 불빛은 보행자와 차량들이 진행해야 할 때와 멈춰야 할 때를 표시합니다. 몇몇 나라에서는 깜빡임 모드가 있는데, 그것은 주의를 의미합니다. 요즘, 시각 약자를 위해서 소리 신호가 추가되고 있습니다.

해설 대개 세 가지 색깔이 있는 등으로 이루어지고 차량과 보행자의 흐름을 통제한다고 하였다.

어휘 install [instɔ́ːl] 설치하다   signal [síɡnəl] 표시하다, 신호로 보내다   pedestrian [pədéstriən] 보행자   vehicle [víːikl] 자동차, 탈 것   blink [bliŋk] 깜빡이다   caution [kɔ́ːʃən] 주의, 경고

15 할 일 파악 ④

M I wish I were good at math, just like you.
W You should always be faithful to the basics.
M Like what?
W I practice and practice. The more you practice, the better you will get.
M Okay.
W And I always review the errors I make. It can help me avoid the same mistakes in the future.
M Practice and review. That's simple but hard.
W Last, do not try to memorize the processes but master the key concepts. It really works.
M Thank you so much for your advice. I'll go to the

library to practice right away.

남 나도 너처럼 수학을 잘하면 좋을 텐데.
여 너는 언제나 기본에 충실해야만 해.
남 예를 들면?
여 난 연습하고 연습해. 더 많이 연습할수록 더 나아질 거야.
남 알겠어.
여 그리고 언제나 틀린 걸 복습해. 다음에 같은 실수를 피하는데 도움이 되거든.
남 연습하고 복습한다. 간단하지만 어렵네.
여 마지막으로, 과정을 외우려고 하지 말고 주요 개념에 숙달해. 그건 정말 효과가 있지.
남 조언 정말 고마워. 당장 도서관에 가서 연습해야겠어.

해설 수학 공부에 대한 조언을 듣고 도서관을 가겠다고 하였다.
어휘 faithful [féiθfəl] 충실한 memorize [méməràiz] 암기하다

16 특정 정보 파악 ②

W Can I help you find something?
M Do you have these in size 6? They're for my son.
W I'm sorry, but that size is out of stock. How about these sneakers? They're really popular with teens who like sports. Why didn't you bring your son with you?
M I just want to give him a surprise gift.
W Oh, I see. I bet he'll love them.
M Okay. I'll take them.

여 무엇을 찾으시나요?
남 이것으로 치수 6이 있나요? 제 아들이 신을 건데요.
여 죄송하지만, 그 사이즈의 재고는 없습니다. 이 운동화는 어떠신가요? 그것들은 운동을 좋아하는 십대들에게 아주 인기가 있어요. 아들을 데려오지 그러셨어요?
남 아들에게 깜짝 선물을 해주고 싶어서요.
여 아 그렇군요. 그는 분명히 이것을 좋아할 거예요.
남 알겠습니다. 그걸로 할게요.

해설 십 대에게 인기 있는 운동화를 아들을 위한 깜짝 선물로 구매하고 있다.
어휘 stock [stɑk] 재고 bet [bet] 단언하다, 확신하다

17 적절한 응답 파악 ⑤

M Why don't we go to the Riverside Amusement Park this weekend?
W It sounds great. I have been there several times, and there are lots of exciting things to do.
M I agree. I can't wait.
W By the way, which ride do you want to try the most?
M Well, I want to go bungee jumping.
W Bungee jumping? Aren't you scared?
M No. It's number one on my bucket list.

남 이번 주말에 Riverside Amusement Park에 가는 게 어때?
여 멋진데. 나는 거기 여러 번 가본 적이 있는데 많은 흥미진진한 것들이 있어.
남 나도 그렇게 생각해. 정말 가고 싶어.
여 그런데, 어느 것을 가장 해보고 싶니?
남 음, 나는 번지 점프를 하러 갈 거야.
여 번지 점프라고? 무섭지 않니?
남 아니, 그게 나의 버킷 리스트 중 첫 번째야.

해설 번지 점핑이 무섭지 않은지 묻는 말에 대한 가장 적절한 응답은 ⑤ '아

니. 그것이 나의 버킷리스트 중 첫 번째야.'이다.
① 분명히 너도 좋아할 거야. ② 힘내. 너도 할 수 있어.
③ 오, 그 말을 들으니 유감이구나. ④ 전혀. 난 높은 곳이 무서워.
해설 scared [skɛərd] 무서워하는, 겁먹은 bucket list (죽기 전에) 해보고 싶은 일 목록

18 적절한 응답 파악 ④

[Cellphone rings.]
M Hi, Betty. What's up?
W Hi, Jake. I'm calling you to ask for a favor.
M If possible, I will help you.
W Well, I am thinking of having a new semester party next Friday or Saturday. I need your help.
M I'm afraid I can't make it on Friday. I am going to visit my grandma in L.A. next Friday.
W Oh, no. You should be at the party. To make a fun party, I need your help. How about Saturday? Can you come then?
M Yeah, okay. Who are you going to invite?
W Everyone in our class.

남 Betty, 무슨 일이야?
여 Jake. 부탁이 있어서 전화했어.
남 가능하다면 들어줄게.
여 음, 다음 주 금요일이나 토요일에 새 학기 파티를 열까 생각 중이야. 네 도움이 필요해.
남 미안하지만, 금요일엔 안 돼. 다음 주 금요일에 LA에 계시는 할머니를 뵈러 갈 예정이거든.
여 저런, 안 돼. 넌 파티에 참석해야만 해. 즐거운 파티가 되기 위해서는 네 도움이 필요해. 그럼, 토요일은 어때? 올 수 있어?
남 응, 좋아. 누굴 초대할 거야?
여 우리 반 모두.

해설 누구를 초대할 예정인지를 묻는 말에 대한 가장 적절한 응답은 ④ '우리 반 모두.'이다.
① 틀림없이 그들이 널 데리러 갈 거야. ② 너희 집에서 파티를 열거야.
③ 걱정 마. 그도 또한 참가할 거야. ⑤ 내 생각엔 큰 파티가 될 거야.
어휘 ask for ~을 요청하다 favor [féivər] 호의 invite [inváit] 초대하다

19 적절한 응답 파악 ⑤

W How many family members do you have?
M Five. I have two younger sisters.
W Where do they live?
M One lives in Jeju-do, and the other lives in Changwon.
W Both of them live pretty far from here. Do you see them often?
M Usually once a year.
W Do your parents live in Jeju-do?
M No. They live in Busan.

여 넌 가족이 몇 명이니?
남 다섯 명. 나는 두 명의 여동생이 있어.
여 그들은 어디에 살아?
남 한 명은 제주도에 살고, 다른 한 명은 창원에 살아.
여 그들 둘 다 꽤 먼 곳에 사는구나. 자주 만나니?
남 거의 일 년에 한 번 만나.
여 너의 부모님도 제주도에 사시니?
남 아니. 그들은 부산에 살고 계셔.

해설 부모님도 제주도에 살고 계시는지를 묻는 말에 대한 가장 적절한 응답은 ⑤ '아니. 그들은 부산에 살고 계셔.'이다.
① 응. 그들은 나와 함께 살아.   ② 제주도는 정말 먼 곳이야.
③ 그들은 지금까지 세 번 이사를 하셨어.   ④ 그들은 그곳에 가길 원하셔.

20 상황에 맞는 말 찾기 ③

M James is a 16-year-old student who wants to <u>get</u> <u>his</u> <u>own</u> laptop. He has <u>saved</u> <u>his</u> <u>allowance</u> for a year. Today, he reads an advertisement for a <u>second-hand</u> <u>laptop</u> on a website. The owner wants $530 for it. But he has only saved $500. He <u>leaves</u> <u>a</u> <u>comment</u> <u>beneath</u> <u>the</u> <u>post</u> that he really wants it. In this situation, what would James write to the owner?

James <u>Could you cut the price by $30?</u>

남 James는 자신의 노트북을 갖길 원하는 16세 학생입니다. 그는 용돈을 일 년 동안 저축해 왔습니다. 오늘 그는 웹사이트에서 중고 노트북의 광고를 보았습니다. 소유자는 530달러에 팔기를 원합니다. 그러나 그가 저축한 금액은 500달러입니다. 그는 게시된 글에 그가 정말로 노트북을 원한다고 글을 남깁니다. 이 상황에서 James가 소유자에게 할 말로 가장 적절한 것은 무엇일까요?

James <u>30달러만 깎아 주실 수 있나요?</u>

해설 노트북은 530달러인데 James가 가진 돈은 500달러이므로, James가 판매자에게 할 말로 가장 적절한 것은 ③ '30달러만 깎아 주실 수 있나요?'이다.
① 배달로 받을 수 있나요?   ② 다른 디자인은 없나요?
④ 공장 설정 상태로 초기화해 주실 수 있나요?
⑤ 제가 알아야 할 것이 있나요?

어휘 allowance [əláuəns] 용돈   second-hand 중고의   beneath [biní:θ] ~아래에

Listen and Check   p. 70

Q1	False	Q10	True
Q2	False	Q11	No
Q3	Yes	Q12	True
Q4	attend her grandfather's birthday party	Q13	the Spanish class
		Q14	True
Q5	24 letters	Q15	Yes
Q6	Someone stole her bag.	Q16	Yes
Q7	No	Q17	going bungee jumping
Q8	False	Q18	False
Q9	No	Q19	True
		Q20	False

해석
Q1 여자는 그녀의 아들을 위한 시계를 찾고 있다.
Q2 Eric의 결석은 학생부에 기록될 것인가?
Q3 남자는 여자를 도울 것인가?
Q4 여자는 금요일에 무엇을 할 것인가?
Q5 현대 한글은 몇 개의 글자로 구성되어 있는가?
Q6 그녀는 어떻게 자신의 신용 카드를 잃어버린 것을 알았는가?
Q7 여자는 남자의 부모가 언제 결혼했는지 아는가?
Q8 남자는 휴대 전화 끄는 것을 거부했다.
Q9 여자는 어젯밤에 부모님과 말다툼을 했는가?
Q10 남자는 세트 메뉴 두 개에 대해 할인을 받았다.
Q11 여자는 자기 짐을 풀었는가?

Q12 사람들은 차를 덜 운전함으로서 더 적은 해로운 배기가스를 배출한다.
Q13 여자는 지난 학기에 어떤 수업을 들었는가?
Q14 이 신호에서 깜박이는 불빛은 주의를 의미한다.
Q15 여자는 같은 실수를 반복하는 것을 피하기 위해 자신이 틀린 것을 복습하는가?
Q16 남자는 여자가 추천한 운동화를 살 것인가?
Q17 남자의 버킷 리스트 중 첫 번째는 무엇인가?
Q18 남자는 다음 주 금요일에 여자의 파티에 참석할 수 있다.
Q19 남자의 부모님은 부산에 살고 계신다.
Q20 James는 새 노트북을 살 여유가 있다.

실전 모의고사 8회   pp. 78~79

1	④	2	⑤	3	④	4	③	5	②
6	③	7	⑤	8	③	9	①	10	⑤
11	①	12	②	13	④	14	③	15	①
16	④	17	②	18	⑤	19	②	20	④

1 그림 정보 파악 ④

M Would you <u>help</u> <u>me</u> <u>choose</u> a T-shirt?
W Sure. This shopping site has tons of nice T-shirts?
M Right. <u>I'd</u> <u>like</u> <u>to</u> <u>buy</u> all of them.
W I think this crew-neck T-shirt looks nice.
M Oh, it's cool. But I have lots of crew-neck shirts.
W Well, how about the one with the V-neck?
M I love it. <u>How</u> <u>about</u> <u>the</u> <u>color</u>? Do you like the black one? Or the blue one?
W The white one would go well with the pants you have.
M I'll follow your advice. Thanks for helping me.

남 내가 티셔츠 고르는 것 좀 도와줄래?
여 물론이야. 이 쇼핑몰은 아주 많은 멋진 티셔츠들이 있구나.
남 맞아. 난 그것들 모두를 사고 싶어.
여 이 둥근 목선의 티셔츠가 멋져 보이는걸.
남 오, 그거 멋지다. 하지만 난 많은 둥근 목선의 티셔츠들이 있어.
여 음, 브이넥 스타일을 가진 것은 어때?
남 매우 마음에 들어. 색깔은 어때? 검은색이 좋아? 아니면 파란색?
여 흰색 셔츠가 네가 갖고 있는 바지들과 잘 어울릴 거야.
남 너의 충고를 따르게. 나를 도와줘서 고마워.

해설 흰색을 고르겠다는 여자의 말을 따르겠다고 하였다.
어휘 crew-neck 둥근 목선의

2 목적 파악 ⑤

[Cellphone rings.]
M Hello, Rose. What's up?
W Hi, Billy. Can you tell me how to paste <u>images</u> <u>on</u> <u>the</u> <u>Internet</u> onto my report?
M It's very simple. Are you in front of your computer now?
W Yes, I'm ready.
M To begin with, choose an image <u>you</u> <u>want</u> <u>to</u> <u>use</u> in

your report.

W I did. And?

M Right-click on the image on the mouse button, and you will see a menu. Click "Save as" to save it onto the hard drive.

W Wow. I saved it on my computer.

M Good job. You can copy and paste the image from your hard <u>drive</u> <u>anytime</u> <u>you</u> <u>want</u> now.

W Thanks, Billy. You are a computer genius.

남 안녕, Rose. 무슨 일이야?

여 안녕, Billy. 너 나에게 인터넷에 있는 이미지들을 내 보고서에 붙이는 방법을 말해줄 수 있니?

남 매우 간단해. 너 지금 컴퓨터 앞에 있어?

여 그래, 준비됐어.

남 우선, 네 보고서에 사용하고 싶은 이미지들을 골라봐.

여 그렇게 했어. 그리고?

남 마우스 버튼으로 그 이미지를 오른쪽 클릭하면, 메뉴들이 보일거야. 이미지를 하드 드라이브에 저장하기 위해서 '다른 이름으로 저장' 메뉴를 클릭해 봐.

여 와. 나 컴퓨터에 저장했어.

남 잘 했어. 네가 원할 때 언제나 하드 드라이브에서 그 이미지를 복사해서 붙일 수 있어.

여 고마워, Billy. 너 컴퓨터 천재구나.

해설 여자는 남자에게 인터넷에 있는 이미지를 보고서에 붙이는 방법을 배우고 있다.

어휘 paste [peist] 붙이다, 첨부하다 to begin with 우선, 먼저 right-click 오른쪽 클릭(을 하다) anytime ~ ~하면 언제라도

3 그림 상황 파악 ④

① M Did you put on your swimsuit?

  W Of course. Let's <u>go</u> <u>swimming</u> now.

② M You <u>can't</u> <u>cross</u> the street when the light is red.

  W Oh, I am very sorry.

③ M How can I help you?

  W I'd like <u>to</u> <u>register</u> <u>for</u> swimming lessons.

④ M Do you see that line? It is very dangerous to swim past it.

  W I see. I will <u>keep</u> <u>that</u> <u>in</u> <u>mind</u>.

⑤ M How could you say that to me?

  W Calm down. I <u>didn't</u> <u>mean</u> <u>it</u>.

① 남 너 수영복 입었니?

  여 물론이야. 이제 수영하러 가자.

② 남 넌 빨간불이 켜질 때 길을 건너면 안 돼.

  여 오, 미안해.

③ 남 어떻게 도와드릴까요?

  여 저는 수영 강좌에 등록하고 싶습니다.

④ 남 넌 저 선이 보이니? 그것을 넘어서 수영을 하는 것은 매우 위험해.

  여 알겠어. 명심할게.

⑤ 남 넌 어떻게 내게 그런 말을 할 수 있어?

  여 진정해. 그런 의도가 아니었어.

해설 바닷가에서 두 남녀가 수영복을 입은 채 바다 먼 곳을 가리키며 대화하는 상황이다.

4 특정 정보 파악 ③

[Cellphone rings.]

W Hi, James. It's me, Ria.

M Oh, Ria. What's up?

W Do you remember <u>we</u> <u>have</u> <u>to</u> <u>volunteer</u> at the hospital today?

M Oh, my. I forgot. Thanks for reminding me.

W Anyway, <u>we</u> <u>have</u> <u>to</u> <u>hurry</u> not to be late.

M Wait, Ria. What day is it? We're volunteering on Sunday. But today is...

W Oops. Today is Saturday, not Sunday. I am very sorry. <u>I</u> <u>mistook</u> <u>today</u> <u>for</u> <u>Sunday</u>.

M That happens from time to time. Don't worry.

W Sorry again. See you tomorrow.

여 안녕, James. 나야, Ria.

남 오, Ria. 아침에 무슨 일 있어?

여 너 오늘 우리가 병원으로 자원봉사를 가야 하는 거 기억하지?

남 오, 이런. 나 거의 잊을 뻔 했네. 상기시켜 줘서 고마워.

여 어쨌든, 우리는 늦지 않도록 서둘러야 해.

남 기다려, Ria. 오늘이 무슨 요일이지? 자원봉사 날은 일요일이야. 근데 오늘은…

여 이런. 오늘은 일요일이 아니라 토요일이구나. 너무 미안해. 내가 오늘을 일요일로 잘못 알았어.

남 그럴 수도 있지. 걱정하지 마.

여 다시 한 번 미안해. 내일 보자.

해설 여자는 토요일을 일요일로 착각하고 남자에게 전화를 하였다.

어휘 mistake [mistéik] 잘못 알다, 실수하다 things [θiŋs] 상황, 것들, 물건들

5 언급 유무 파악 ②

W Hello, students. I am your principal, Harriett Brown. We will have a fire drill at school tomorrow. The event is <u>very</u> <u>important</u> because we have to prepare for disasters such as fires and earthquakes. When you <u>come</u> <u>to</u> <u>the</u> <u>school</u> <u>tomorrow</u>, you need to gather in the auditorium to get instructions on <u>how</u> <u>to</u> <u>participate</u> <u>in</u> the drill. All your teachers will guide you so that you can learn from this experience. The fire department near our school will assist us during the drill.

여 안녕하세요, 여러분. 저는 교장인 Harriett Brown입니다. 우리는 내일 학교 여러 곳에서 소방 훈련을 갖게 됩니다. 그 행사는 우리가 화재, 지진 같은 재해에 대비해야 하기 때문에 매우 중요합니다. 여러분들이 내일 학교에 오면, 여러분들은 훈련 참여 방법에 대한 지시를 받기 위해 학교 강당에 모여 있을 필요가 있습니다. 선생님들 전원은 여러분이 그 경험에서 배울 수 있도록 여러분을 잘 이끌어주실 겁니다. 그 훈련 동안 우리 학교 근처 소방서는 우리를 지원해 주실 겁니다.

해설 경찰서의 도움으로 소방 훈련이 실시된다는 내용은 언급되지 않았다.

어휘 fire drill 화재 훈련 disaster [dizǽstər] 재해, 재앙 gather [gǽðər] 모이다 participate in ~ ~에 참여하다

6 관계 추론 ③

M Hello. I'm here to drop these items off.

W Okay. How many boxes do you have today?

M Five. I tried to contact <u>all</u> <u>the</u> <u>customers</u>, but they didn't answer the phone.

W I will try to contact them, too. Write the receivers' names and phone numbers here, please.

M Sure. This is <u>my</u> <u>last</u> <u>job</u> <u>today</u>.

W It is hard to do this kind of job, isn't it?

M Well, sometimes it's very hard, but <u>I</u> <u>am</u> <u>used</u> <u>to</u> <u>it</u>.

Thanks for asking.

W Don't mention it. Have a great day.

M Okay. See you again.

남 안녕하세요. 저는 이 물건들을 놓고 가려고 여기에 왔습니다.

여 좋아요. 오늘은 몇 개의 상자들을 놓아야 하나요?

남 다섯 개요. 저는 모든 고객들에게 전화해 봤지만 그들은 내 전화를 받지 않았어요.

여 저도 그들과 연락해 볼게요. 이곳에 수신인들의 이름과 전화번호를 적어주세요.

남 네. 이것이 오늘 저의 마지막 일이에요.

여 이런 종류의 직업이 때로는 힘들죠, 그렇죠?

남 음, 가끔은 매우 힘들지만, 저는 익숙해졌어요. 물어봐 주셔서 감사해요.

여 천만에요. 오늘 수고 많이 하셨어요.

남 알겠습니다. 다음에 봴게요.

해설 남자는 고객에게 배달할 수 없었던 택배를 놓고 가기 위해 택배 영업 사무소에 들른 상황이다.

어휘 leave [liːv] 남겨놓다, 떠나다   contact [kɑ́ntækt] 연락하다, 접촉하다   receiver [risíːvər] 수령자, 수신인

7 어색한 대화 찾기 ⑤

① M Would you mind telling your sister that I can't meet her?

W No. Don't worry.

② M I think you had better not cut in line.

W Oh, I am sorry. I will be more careful.

③ M Next, please.

W Hi. I would like to order two glasses of ice americano.

④ M Don't push the button! This elevator operates automatically.

W Sorry. I didn't know that.

⑤ M What brings you here?

W I have to pick up my brothers at the airport.

① 남 네 여동생에게 내가 그녀와의 약속을 지킬 수가 없다고 말해줄 수 있겠니?

여 그럼. 걱정하지 마.

② 남 저는 당신이 공공장소에서 새치기를 하지 말아야 한다고 생각해요.

여 오, 죄송합니다. 제가 좀 더 조심하겠습니다.

③ 남 다음 손님, 와주십시오.

여 안녕하세요. 저는 아이스 아메리카노 두 잔을 주문하고 싶어요.

④ 남 버튼을 누르지 마세요! 이 엘리베이터는 자동으로 작동됩니다.

여 미안해요. 저는 몰랐어요.

⑤ 남 여기에 어떻게 오셨나요?

여 제 남동생을 공항에서 데리고 와야 해요.

해설 무슨 일로 여기까지 왔느냐는 질문에 동생을 공항에서 데리고 와야 한다고 답하는 것은 부자연스럽다.

어휘 had better ~ ~하는 것이 낫다   cut in line 새치기 하다   operate [ɑ́pərèit] 작동하다, 운영하다, 수술하다

8 부탁한 일 파악 ③

[Telephone rings.]

M Hello, Gloria. Did you buy the movie tickets?

W Not yet. Let's meet at Dream Theater at four o'clock. The movie starts at four thirty.

M We are going to see *My Last Memory of My Friend*, right?

W Yes. It's very popular these days.

M Actually, I need to ask you for a favor.

W What is it?

M My favorite animated movie is being shown at the theater today. Can we watch it instead?

W Why not? But you have to let me choose dinner. Okay?

M Sure.

남 안녕, Gloria. 너 영화표 샀니?

여 아직이야. Dream 극장에서 4시에 만나자. 영화는 4시 30분에 시작해.

남 우리 *My Last Memory of My Friend*를 볼 거지, 그렇지?

여 응. 그거 요즘 아주 인기거든.

남 실은 나 부탁이 하나 있어.

여 뭔데?

남 내가 제일 좋아하는 애니메이션이 오늘 개봉하거든. 오늘은 그걸 볼 수 있을까?

여 왜 안 되겠어. 하지만 대신 저녁 식사 메뉴는 내가 정할게. 알겠지?

남 물론이지!

해설 남자는 원래 보기로 했던 영화 대신 자신이 좋아하는 애니메이션을 보자고 부탁하는 상황이다.

어휘 animated [ǽnəmèitid] 만화 영화의

9 의도 파악 ①

W Steve, how was your job interview yesterday?

M I think it went quite well.

W Were you nervous?

M I was a little nervous at first. But the interviewers helped me feel relaxed. So I could answer most of the questions they asked me.

W That was your first job interview, wasn't it?

M No, actually, it was my second interview. I was too nervous to speak at my first job interview. The experience helped me prepare for this one a lot.

W Good for you. I really hope you get the job.

여 Steve. 어제 취업 면접은 어땠어?

남 꽤 잘한 것 같아.

여 긴장했었니?

남 처음에는 약간 긴장됐었지. 하지만 면접관들이 나를 편안하게 해주었어. 그래서 난 그들이 내게 하는 질문의 대부분을 대답할 수 있었지.

여 그게 네 첫 번째 취업 면접이었지, 그렇지 않니?

남 아니, 실은 내 두 번째 면접이었어. 첫 번째 취업 면접에서는 너무 긴장해서 말을 못했거든. 그 경험이 이번 인터뷰를 준비하는 데 많은 도움이 되었지.

여 잘됐구나. 난 네가 면접에 통과하기를 진심으로 바래.

해설 여자는 남자가 취업 면접에 통과하기를 기원하고 있다.

어휘 result [rizʌ́lt] 결과   nervous [nə́ːrvəs] 긴장한, 초초한   relaxed [rilǽkst] 편안한   most of ~ ~의 대부분

10 숫자 정보 파악 ⑤

W Excuse me. I'd like to rent a car.

M Yes. What size car do you have in mind?

W Well, any car is okay if it's not expensive.

M Great. This car is only fifty dollars a day. But as you see, the trunk is not very large.

W I see. How about that one? It seems to have a larger trunk.

M It's sixty dollars. Do you want it?

W Yes. Sixty dollars is all I have to pay, right?

M No. You also have to pay a ten-percent sales tax.

W All right. I want it for two days.

여 실례합니다. 차 한 대를 빌리고 싶어요.

남 네, 어느 크기의 차를 생각하고 계신가요?

여 글쎄요, 비싸지 않다면 어느 차라도 괜찮아요.

남 좋습니다. 이 자동차는 하루에 겨우 50달러예요. 하지만 고객님이 보시는 것처럼, 트렁크가 그다지 크지는 않죠.

여 알겠습니다. 저것은 어때요? 그것은 더 큰 트렁크를 가진 것 같네요.

남 60달러예요. 그걸로 하시겠어요?

여 네. 60달러가 제가 지불하는 전부죠, 그렇죠?

남 아니오. 10퍼센트의 판매세 역시 내셔야 합니다.

여 알겠습니다. 저는 이틀 동안 그것을 사용할게요.

해설 여자는 하루 대여료가 60달러인 자동차를 이틀 동안 빌릴 것이고, 10퍼센트의 세금이 부과된다고 하였다.

어휘 rent [rent] 빌리다

11 할 일 파악 ①

M Susan, I didn't know that so much time had passed. I should be going now.

W I understand, Robert. Thanks for coming to my housewarming party.

M I was really happy to see you and your friends. The food was awesome, and everything was perfect.

W Thanks. I wish I could drive you to the bus station.

M Don't worry. I can take a taxi.

W Good. Have a safe trip home. Let's keep in touch.

M Yeah. Okay, I'm off.

W So long.

남 Susan, 시간이 이렇게 빨리 지날 줄 몰랐네. 나는 이제 가봐야 해.

여 알겠어, Robert. 집들이에 와줘서 고마워.

남 난 너와 너의 친구들과 함께해서 정말로 행복했어. 음식도 매우 좋았고 모든 것이 완벽하더라.

여 고마워. 내가 버스 터미널까지 너를 데려다주면 좋을 텐데.

남 걱정하지 마. 택시를 타면 돼.

여 좋아. 집까지 조심해서 가.

남 그래. 그럼 나는 갈게.

여 또 봐.

해설 남자는 버스 터미널까지 택시를 타고 간다고 하였다.

어휘 housewarming party 집들이 파티 awesome[ɔ́:səm] 매우 멋진, 굉장한 perfect[pə́:rfikt] 완벽한 keep in touch 연락을 주고받다 be off 떠나다

12 언급 유무 파악 ②

M Hello. Let me talk about how to protect the environment to save the Earth. One simple way is to walk or ride a bike short distances. And we should bring our own bags to grocery stores and not use plastic bags. It's also a good idea to carry a personal mug instead of using disposable cups. Lastly, we have to turn off electric devices when we're not using them. Please make sure to remember that small actions can be big steps to protecting the environment.

남 안녕하세요. 저는 지구를 살리기 위해 환경을 보호하는 방법을 말하려고 합니다. 하나의 간단한 방법은 짧은 거리는 걷거나 자전거를 타는 것입니다. 그리고 우리는 식료품점에 각자의 백을 가져와야 하고 비닐봉투를 사용하지 말아야 합니다. 또한, 일회용 컵을 사용하지 않고 개인용

머그컵을 지니는 것도 좋은 생각입니다. 마지막으로, 우리는 사용하지 않을 때 전기 제품을 꺼야 합니다. 작은 행동이 환경을 보호하는 데 큰 발걸음이 된다는 것을 반드시 기억해 주세요.

해설 지구를 살리기 위해 환경을 보호하는 방법으로 전기 기구를 사용하지 않는 것은 언급되지 않았다.

어휘 protect[prətékt] 보호하다 environment[inváiərənmənt] 환경 plastic bag 비닐봉투 personal[pə́rsənal] 개인의 instead of ~ ~ 대신에 electronic device 전기 제품 make sure 확실히 하다

13 표 파악 ④

M Hi, Helen. What are you doing here?

W I'm checking the yoga classes on the website.

M Can I take a look?

W Sure.

M Oh, I heard that Daisy and Jasmine are popular instructors.

W Are they? Hmm... I can take any classes except the one on Tuesday. I have baseball practice every Tuesday.

M I see. Then you can choose one of these two classes.

W The price is different.

M Then why don't you pick the cheaper one?

W Good idea. Thanks for your opinion.

남 안녕, Helen. 여기서 뭐하고 있어?

여 난 웹사이트에서 요가 수업을 알아보는 중이야.

남 내가 봐도 돼?

여 물론이지.

남 오, 난 Daisy와 Jasmine이 유명한 강사라고 들었어.

여 그래? 흠… 화요일만 제외하면 어떤 수업이든 들을 수 있어. 매주 화요일마다 야구 연습이 있거든.

남 그럼 이 두 수업 중 하나를 고를 수 있겠네.

여 가격 차이가 있네.

남 그럼 더 저렴한 것을 고르면 어떨까?

여 좋은 생각이야. 의견 고마워.

해설 화요일을 제외한 Daisy와 Jasmine의 요가 수업 중 비용이 더 저렴한 수업을 듣는다고 하였다.

어휘 expensive [ikspénsiv] 비싼 opinion [əpínjən] 의견

14 화제·주제 파악 ③

W This can be found around the world except in cold areas. This is the same kind of animal as a snake, but it's different in some ways. This has feet and ears, but a snake doesn't have them. This can change the color of its body. This also uses body language to communicate. This uses gestures and other movements to attract a mate. What is this?

여 이것은 추운 지역을 제외하고 전 세계에서 발견될 수 있습니다. 이것은 뱀과 같은 종류이지만, 어떤 면에서는 다릅니다. 이것은 발과 귀가 있지만, 뱀은 그것들이 없습니다. 이것은 그들의 몸 색깔을 바꿀 수 있습니다. 이것은 또한 의사소통을 하기 위해서 몸짓 언어를 사용하기도 합니다. 몸짓과 동작들은 짝에게 구애를 하기 위해 사용됩니다. 이것은 무엇일까요?

해설 뱀과 같은 종류의 파충류이지만 뱀과는 다르게 발과 귀가 있고 몸 색깔을 바꿀 수 있다고 하였다.

어휘 across [əkrɔ́:s] 여기저기에, ~을 가로질러 except [iksépt]

~을 제외하고   communicate [kəmjú:nəkèit] 의사소통을 하다
gesture [dʒéstʃər] 몸짓   movement [mú:vmənt] 동작, 움직임
mate [meit] 짝, 친구

15 할 일 파악 ①

W Bob, hurry up. We're leaving now.
M Mom, I'm coming. Wait, please.
W Who were you speaking to?
M Jessica. I <u>was</u> <u>supposed</u> <u>to</u> <u>meet</u> <u>her</u> for lunch and had to explain why I can't join her.
W Oh, okay. Now let's go to your little sister's school now.
M <u>I'm</u> <u>excited</u> <u>to</u> <u>see</u> her first school play. Let's go!
W Please make sure to turn your computer off <u>before</u> <u>you</u> <u>leave</u>.
M I will.

여 Bob, 서두르렴. 우리 지금 출발해.
남 엄마, 가고 있어요. 기다려 주세요.
여 누구랑 통화하고 있었니?
남 Jessica요. 점심 먹으러 그녀를 만날 예정이었기 때문에 왜 함께할 수 없는지 설명해야 했어요.
여 오, 그렇구나. 이제 네 여동생 학교에 가도록 하자.
남 그녀의 첫 학예회를 보게 되어 너무 신나요. 가요!
여 떠나기 전에 반드시 너의 컴퓨터를 끄렴.
남 그럴게요.

해설 엄마는 남자에게 출발 전에 컴퓨터를 끄라고 하였다.

16 숫자 정보 파악 ④

W Excuse me. Could you let me know if the flight from Seattle <u>has</u> <u>arrived</u>?
M Did you check the flight information board?
W No. I don't know where it is.
M Okay. What is the flight number?
W It's Aurora Airlines AR582. It was supposed to arrive at three p.m., but <u>it</u> <u>was</u> <u>delayed</u> <u>by</u> <u>one</u> <u>hour</u>.
M Let's see… Oh, the flight has been delayed by another 30 minutes <u>because</u> <u>of</u> <u>bad</u> <u>weather</u>.
W I see. Thank you.

여 실례합니다. 시애틀에서 오는 비행기가 도착했는지를 알 수 있을까요?
남 비행 정보 게시판을 확인해 보셨나요?
여 아니오. 저는 그것이 어디에 있는지를 알지 못해요.
남 알겠습니다. 비행기 번호는 무엇인가요?
여 그것은 Aurora 항공사의 AR582편입니다. 그것은 오후 세시에 도착할 예정이었습니다만, 한 시간 지연되었어요.
남 어디 볼까요… 오, 나쁜 기상 상태로 인해 비행기가 30분이 더 지연되었네요.
여 알겠습니다. 감사합니다.

해설 3시 도착 예정이던 시애틀발(發) 비행기가 1시간 뒤인 4시로 지연된데 이어 날씨가 안 좋아 30분이 더 지연되었다고 하였다.
어휘 flight[flait] 비행(편), 비행기   be delayed 지연되다, 연기되다

17 적절한 응답 찾기 ②

M Hello. I wonder <u>if</u> <u>it's</u> <u>possible</u> for me to volunteer here for a couple of weeks.
W Have you ever looked after senior citizens before?
M Yes. I volunteered at a local senior citizen center for 20 hours.

W Great. <u>You</u> <u>have</u> <u>to</u> <u>help</u> senior citizens clean their rooms, eat meals, and so on. Is that clear?
M Okay. I will try my best.
W Can you start volunteering tomorrow?
M Sure. <u>What</u> <u>time</u> <u>should</u> <u>I</u> <u>come</u>?
W <u>Nine in the morning is fine with us.</u>

남 안녕하세요. 저는 제가 여기서 몇 주 동안 자원봉사를 하는 것이 가능한지가 궁금해요.
여 당신은 전에 어르신들을 돌본 적이 있나요?
남 네. 저는 20시간 동안 지역의 양로원에서 자원봉사를 했어요.
여 훌륭하네요. 당신은 노인들이 방을 청소하고, 식사 하시는 것 등을 도우셔야 합니다. 아시겠나요?
남 네. 최선을 다하겠습니다.
여 내일부터 자원봉사를 시작할 수 있나요?
남 물론이죠. 몇 시에 제가 와야 하나요?
여 아침 9시가 우리에게는 좋아요.

해설 내일 몇 시에 와야 하는지를 묻는 말에 대한 가장 적절한 응답은 ② '아침 9시가 우리에게는 좋아요.'이다.
① 제가 이 일을 하는 것을 돕겠습니다.
③ 저는 아픈 사람들을 돌볼 수 있습니다.
④ 질문이 있으시면 언제라도 우리에게 물어보세요.
⑤ 당신은 허락 없이 사무실에 들어올 수 없습니다.
어휘 wonder [wʌ́ndər] 궁금히 여기다   a couple of ~ 두 개의, 몇몇의   local [lóukəl] 지역의; 지역   senior citizen (격식) 노인   and so on 기타 등등   clear [kliər] 분명한, 명확한, 깨끗한

18 적절한 응답 찾기 ⑤

W Chris, you look down. What's wrong?
M I think I <u>should</u> <u>give</u> <u>up</u> playing the piano.
W Why? What happened?
M I <u>failed</u> <u>to</u> <u>win</u> <u>first</u> <u>place</u> in the piano competition last week.
W I'm sorry to hear that. I heard you practiced very hard.
M I really did my best for the competition. But the results were… I'm so frustrated.
W Cheer up. <u>You</u> <u>are</u> <u>the</u> <u>best</u> <u>pianist</u> that I've ever known.
M <u>You are the best friend ever.</u>

여 Chris. 너 우울해 보여. 무슨 일 있어?
남 난 피아노 치는 거 포기해야 할 것 같아.
여 왜? 무슨 일이 있는 건데?
남 난 지난주에 피아노 대회에서 1등을 하지 못했어.
여 저런 안됐구나. 난 네가 열심히 연습했다고 들었는데.
남 난 그 대회를 위해서 정말 최선을 다했어. 하지만 결과가… 난 실망이 매우 커.
여 기운 내. 넌 내가 아는 사람 중에서 최고의 피아노 연주가야.
남 넌 정말 최고의 친구야.

해설 낙담한 친구를 격려하는 말에 대한 가장 적절한 응답은 ⑤ '넌 정말 최고의 친구야.'이다.
① 난 이대로 살 수 없어.   ② 친구 좋다는 게 뭐야.
③ 제발 내게 거짓말하지 마.   ④ 난 그 상을 받아서 매우 기뻐.
어휘 down [daun] 낙담한, 우울한   fail to ~ ~하지 못하다
competition [kàmpití∫ən] 대회, 경쟁   frustrated [frʌ́strèitid] 매우 실망한, 좌절한

19 적절한 응답 찾기 ②

W It is very cold today, but it is a good time for ice

skating.

M That's <u>what</u> I <u>want</u> <u>to</u> <u>say</u>. Oh, your hands feel cold. Where are your gloves?

W I have them in my bag.

M You'd better wear them. <u>It's</u> <u>dangerous</u> <u>to</u> <u>walk</u> <u>with</u> your hands in your pockets.

W Okay, I will. Wait. I don't see my gloves in my bag. <u>They</u> <u>are</u> <u>gone</u>!

M Without them, you can't skate in this cold weather.

W You're right. What should I do?

M Let's see <u>if</u> <u>there's</u> <u>a</u> <u>place</u> that sells gloves around here.

W I see. <u>Let's find one together.</u>

여 오늘은 매우 춥지만, 아이스 스케이팅 타기에 좋은 때야.

남 그것이 내가 말하고 싶은 거야. 오, 너의 손이 차가워 보여. 네 장갑은 어디에 있니?

여 난 가방 속에 두었어.

남 장갑을 끼는 것이 좋아. 너의 손을 주머니에 꽂은 채로 걷는 것은 위험해.

여 좋아, 그렇게. 기다려 봐. 가방 안에 장갑이 보이지 않아. 그것들은 사라졌어!

남 그것들이 없으면, 이런 추운 날씨에 스케이트를 탈 수 없어.

여 네 말이 맞아. 어떻게 해야 하지?

남 여기 주위에 장갑을 파는 장소가 있는지 보자.

여 <u>알겠어. 함께 그곳을 찾아보자.</u>

해설 장갑이 없어져 장갑 파는 곳을 알아보자는 말에 대한 가장 적절한 응답은 ② '알겠어. 함께 그곳을 찾아보자.'이다.
③ 난 그것을 고대하고 있어.
③ 내가 너처럼 스케이트를 잘 타면 좋을 텐데.
④ 난 쌀쌀한 날씨를 좋아하지 않아.
⑤ 내가 장갑 없이 스케이트를 탈 수 있을까?
어휘 gone [ɡɔ(ː)n] 사라진, 죽은   if ~ ~인지 아닌지 (여부)

20 상황에 맞는 말 찾기 ④

W Laura and Aiden are going to meet at a shoe store. Aiden wants to buy <u>a pair of</u> <u>brand-new</u> <u>white</u> <u>shoes</u>, and Laura wants to buy a pair of black ones. Laura arrives at the store <u>ten minutes before</u> Aiden, so she is looking at the shoes herself. The store staff member says that there are <u>black shoes in stock</u>, but there aren't any white shoes at the moment. Aiden <u>gets to the store</u> and meets Laura. In this situation, what would Laura most likely say to Aiden?

Laura Aiden, <u>the shoes you want to buy are not available.</u>

여 Aiden과 Laura는 신발 가게에서 만날 예정입니다. Aiden은 신상품의 흰색 신발을 사고 싶고, Laura는 검은색 신발을 사고 싶습니다. Laura는 가게에 Aiden보다 10분 전에 도착해서, 혼자서 다양한 그 종류의 신발을 보고 있습니다. 가게 점원은 검은색 신발은 재고로 가지고 있지만, 지금 당장은 흰색 신발이 없다고 말합니다. Aiden이 가게에 도착해서 Laura를 만납니다. 이런 상황에서, Laura가 Aiden에게 할 말로 가장 적절한 것은 무엇일까요?

Laura Aiden, 네가 사고 싶어하는 신발을 살 수가 없어.

해설 Aiden이 사고 싶어 하는 흰색 신발이 없는 상황이므로, Laura가 Aiden에게 할 말로 가장 적절한 것은 ④ '네가 사고 싶어 하는 신발을 살 수가 없어.'이다.
① 저 신발을 한번 신어보는 것이 가능할까?

② 난 그 신발 가게가 어디에 있는지 모르겠어.
③ 내게 왜 흰색 신발을 사고 싶은지 말해줘.
⑤ 넌 검정색 신발을 사고 싶지, 그렇지?
어휘 a pair of ~ ~ 한 벌, 한 켤레   brand-new 신상품의   kind [kaind] 종류; 친절한   have ~ in stock ~을 재고로 갖고 있다   at the moment 지금 당장, 현재   most likely 아마도

Listen and Check
p. 80

Q1	True	Q12	False
Q2	No	Q13	No
Q3	True	Q14	True
Q4	tomorrow	Q15	No
Q5	in the auditorium	Q16	1 hour and 30 minutes
Q6	Yes	Q17	True
Q7	False	Q18	Yes
Q8	No	Q19	because it is dangerous
Q9	No	Q20	False
Q10	Yes		
Q11	to a bus station		

해석
Q1 남자는 이미 둥근 목선의 티셔츠를 많이 가지고 있다.
Q2 여자는 이미지를 저장하는 방법을 알고 있는가?
Q3 선 밖에서 수영하는 것은 매우 위험할 것이다.
Q4 남자와 여자는 언제 봉사 활동을 할 것인가?
Q5 학생들은 어디로 모여야 하는가?
Q6 남자는 그날의 마지막 일을 하고 있는가?
Q7 여자는 그녀의 남동생을 공항에 내려놓고 왔다.
Q8 남자와 여자는 여자가 고른 영화를 볼 예정인가?
Q9 이번이 남자의 첫 번째 면접이었나?
Q10 여자는 큰 트렁크가 있는 차를 빌렸나?
Q11 남자는 택시를 타고 어디로 가는가?
Q12 우리는 지구를 지키기 위해 비닐봉투를 사용해야 한다.
Q13 여자는 매주 화요일에 요가 수업을 받는가?
Q14 그 동물은 짝에게 구애를 하기 위해 몸짓 언어를 사용하는가?
Q15 남자는 오늘 Jessica와 같이 점심을 먹을 것인가?
Q16 비행기는 얼마 동안이나 지연되었는가?
Q17 남자는 노인들을 위한 봉사 활동을 한 경험이 있다.
Q18 남자는 대회에서 우승하지 못했는가?
Q19 여자는 왜 장갑을 껴야 하는가?
Q20 Aiden은 검은색 신발을 사고 싶었다.

실전 모의고사 **9회**
pp. 88~89

1 ③	2 ④	3 ③	4 ②	5 ③
6 ④	7 ④	8 ⑤	9 ②	10 ⑤
11 ②	12 ③	13 ③	14 ⑤	15 ②
16 ⑤	17 ⑤	18 ②	19 ④	20 ③

1 그림 정보 파악 ③

W Good afternoon. How can I help you?

M I'm looking for a floor lamp to put in the corner of my living room.
W Which do you prefer, one with a shade or one with only a bulb?
M I want one with a shade.
W We have plain white shades and also ones with striped patterns.
M Simple is the best. I'll buy a plain one.
W Okay.

여 안녕하세요. 무엇을 도와드릴까요?
남 거실 모퉁이에 놓을 플로어 스탠드를 찾고 있어요.
여 갓이 있는 것 또는 전구로만 되어있는 것 중 어떤 것을 더 선호하시나요?
남 갓이 있는 것이요.
여 저희는 화이트 색상의 무지로 된 갓도 있고 줄무늬 패턴이 들어간 갓도 있어요.
남 심플한 게 최고죠. 무늬가 없는 걸로 살게요.
여 알겠습니다.

해설 무늬가 없는 심플한 갓이 쓰인 플로어 스탠드로 구입한다고 하였다.
어휘 floor lamp 플로어 스탠드 (바닥에 세우는 키 큰 스탠드) prefer [prifə́ːr] 선호하다 shade [ʃeid] (전등의) 갓 striped [straipt] 줄무늬의

2 부탁한 일 파악 ④

W Do you have any plans now?
M Yes, with my coworkers.
W What time will you come back home?
M I'll be back in two hours. Do you have any plans to go out today?
W No, I don't. Why?
M I just started the washing machine. Please hang up the laundry to dry later.
W All right.

여 지금 약속 있어?
남 응, 동료들이랑.
여 집에 몇 시에 와?
남 2시간 안에 올 거야. 오늘 나갈 계획 있어?
여 아니, 없어. 왜?
남 방금 막 세탁기를 돌렸거든. 있다가 빨래 좀 넣어줘.
여 알겠어.

해설 남자가 여자에게 빨래를 넣어줄 것을 부탁하였다.
어휘 washing machine 세탁기 hang up 넣어놓다

3 그림 상황 파악 ③

① W Shall we take a walk?
M Sure.
② W When did you get that scar?
M I got it when I was four.
③ W What happened, Michael?
M I tripped and fell down.
④ W Where did you go on a field trip?
M I went to Gyeongju.
⑤ W Is walking good enough exercise?
M Of course, it is.

① 여 우리 산책할까?
남 좋아.

② 여 그 상처는 언제 생긴 거야?
남 내가 4살 때 생겼어.
③ 여 무슨 일이야, Michael?
남 발을 헛디뎌서 땅에 넘어졌어.
④ 여 넌 현장 학습을 어디로 갔니?
남 경주로 갔어.
⑤ 여 걷는 것만으로 운동하기에 충분해?
남 당연히 그렇지.

해설 남자가 넘어져서 다친 상황이다.
어휘 take a walk 산책하다 scar [skɑːr] 상처, 흉터 trip [trip] 발을 헛디디다

4 숫자 정보 파악 ②

W We need to book plane tickets to Vietnam.
M I'm checking out the schedule from the early morning to the afternoon.
W It's better for us to depart as early as we can.
M There are flights leaving at 6:00 a.m., 9:00 a.m., 12:00 p.m., 3:00 p.m., and 5:00 p.m.
W Let's take a morning flight. But I think 6:00 a.m. is too early.
M Okay. I'll book the next flight then.

여 우리 베트남 가는 비행기 표를 예매해야 해.
남 이른 아침부터 오후까지 일정을 확인 중이야.
여 가능한 한 일찍 출발하는 게 나아.
남 오전 6시, 9시, 오후 12시, 3시, 5시에 출발하는 비행기가 있어.
여 아침 비행기를 타자. 하지만 6시는 너무 일러.
남 알겠어. 그럼 다음 항공편으로 예매할게.

해설 오전 6시는 너무 이른 시간이어서 다음 비행기로 예매를 한다고 하였다.
어휘 book [buk] 예매하다 check out 확인하다 depart [dipɑ́ːrt] 출발하다

5 언급 유무 파악 ③

W This painting by Vincent van Gogh makes me feel so comfortable.
M The people sitting at the café terrace and the stars in the night sky make the mood of the piece seem very peaceful.
W You're right. I also like the colors he used in the work.
M They look warm and make me feel relaxed.
W I heard it's a place that Vincent van Gogh often visited.
M Where can I see the original work?
W It's in a museum in the Netherlands.

여 빈센트 반 고흐의 그림은 나를 정말 편안하게 만들어.
남 카페테라스에 앉아 있는 사람들과 밤하늘에 있는 별들이 작품의 분위기를 되게 평온하게 해주네.
여 맞아. 나는 또한 그가 이 작품에서 사용한 색채도 좋아.
남 그건 따뜻해 보이고 나를 느긋한 기분을 느끼게 해 주네.
여 내가 듣기로는 저기는 빈센트 반 고흐가 자주 방문했던 곳이래.
남 원본 작품은 어디에서 볼 수 있을까?
여 이건 네덜란드에 있는 박물관에 있어.

해설 작품의 이름에 관해서는 언급되지 않았다.
어휘 peaceful [píːsfəl] 평온한 original [ərídʒənəl] 원본의

정답 및 해설

6 장소 추론 ④

M Hi. I came to <u>pick</u> <u>up</u> <u>my</u> <u>photos</u>.
W Just a minute. Here you are. I noticed some of them were blurry.
M It <u>happens</u> <u>quite</u> <u>often</u>. What do you think the problem is?
W Your film got exposed to sunlight when you took some pictures.
M Oh, did it? I'm just not used to using a film camera.
W Just <u>close</u> <u>the</u> <u>film</u> <u>cover</u> <u>firmly</u> before shooting. Then everything will be fine.
M Thank you for the advice.

남 안녕하세요. 제 사진을 찾으러 왔어요.
여 잠시만요. 여기 있습니다. 사진 중 몇 개는 흐릿하더라고요.
남 꽤 자주 그런 일이 생겨요. 문제가 뭐라고 생각하세요?
여 사진을 찍을 때 필름이 햇빛에 노출이 되어서 그렇답니다.
남 그랬어요? 제가 필름 카메라를 사용하는 데 익숙하질 않아요.
여 사진을 찍기 전에 필름 뚜껑을 꽉 닫으세요. 그러면 괜찮을 거예요.
남 조언 감사드려요.

해설 사진을 찾으러 온 남자에게 여자가 사진 찍을 때 주의할 점을 이야기해 주고 있다.
어휘 blurry [blə́:ri] 흐릿한, 모호한 quite [kwait] 꽤, 상당히 be exposed to ~에 노출되다 advice [ədváis] 조언, 충고

7 어색한 대화 찾기 ④

① M Where is your car?
 W My car's <u>at</u> <u>the</u> <u>garage</u> for repairs.
② M What happened to your car?
 W My car <u>got</u> <u>scratched</u> while it was parked.
③ M How often do you <u>wash</u> <u>your</u> <u>car</u>?
 W I wash it at least once a week.
④ M I can't see well in the dark, so I find it difficult to drive at night.
 W Sunglasses can <u>protect</u> <u>your</u> <u>eyes</u>.
⑤ M It costs a lot to <u>maintain</u> <u>my</u> <u>car</u>.
 W How much do you spend on your car?

① 남 너 차 어디 있어?
 여 수리를 위해 정비소에 있어.
② 남 차 어떻게 된 거야?
 여 주차를 하다가 차를 긁혔어.
③ 남 얼마나 자주 세차를 해?
 여 일주일에 최소 한번 해.
④ 남 나는 밤눈이 어두워서 밤에 운전하기가 힘들어.
 여 선글라스는 눈을 보호해 줄 수 있어.
⑤ 남 차를 유지하는데 돈이 많이 들어.
 여 차에 얼마나 비용을 쓰는데?

해설 밤눈이 어두워 운전을 못한다는 말에 선글라스가 눈을 보호해 준다고 답하는 것은 부자연스럽다.
어휘 garage [gərá:ʤ] 정비소 repairs [ripɛ́ərs] 수리 작업 scratch [skræʧ] 긁다 at least 최소한 maintain [meintéin] 유지하다

8 부탁한 일 파악 ⑤

M What have you been thinking about for so long?
W I'm thinking of a way to <u>promote</u> <u>my</u> <u>shop</u>.
M Try to do it on social networking sites.

W That's my plan, but I haven't decided <u>how</u> to <u>make</u> a promotional video yet.
M Put some good pictures of some of <u>the</u> <u>accessories</u> <u>you</u> <u>sell</u> at your shop and play some music in the video.
W Okay. Could you help me <u>write</u> <u>some</u> <u>messages</u> to put in the video?
M Why not? You know I have <u>a</u> <u>lot</u> <u>of</u> <u>experience</u> doing that.
W That's why I am asking you.
M All right. Let's <u>get</u> <u>it</u> <u>done</u> by the end of this week.

남 무엇을 그렇게 오래 생각을 해?
여 내 가게를 홍보할 방법을 생각 중이야.
남 SNS에 홍보해 봐.
여 그럴 생각인데 아직 홍보 영상을 어떻게 만들지 정하지 못했어.
남 가게에서 파는 액세서리가 잘 나온 사진들을 넣고 비디오에서 재생할 음악을 골라.
여 알았어. 비디오에 넣을 메시지 쓰는 것을 도와줄 수 있겠니?
남 물론이야. 나 많이 해본 거 알잖아.
여 그래서 너한테 부탁하는 거야.
남 그래. 이번 주 내로 끝내 보자.

해설 홍보 영상에 넣을 메시지를 써 줄 것을 부탁하였다.
어휘 promote [prəmóut] 홍보하다 decide [disáid] 결정하다 promotional [prəmóuʃənl] 홍보의 get something done 무언가를 끝내다

9 화제·주제 파악 ②

M Hi. I'm here to tell you <u>something</u> <u>about</u> <u>walking</u>. How much do you walk a day? You can be healthier and lose weight just by walking. First of all, it <u>strengthens</u> <u>your</u> <u>muscles</u> and boosts your immune system. It also helps reduce stress and <u>improves</u> <u>your</u> <u>memory</u>. However, if you walk too hard, you <u>can</u> <u>get</u> <u>aches</u> in your legs. Walk for thirty minutes a day, and you will live a much healthier and happier life.

남 안녕하세요, 저는 여러분들에게 걷기에 대한 것을 말씀드리러 왔습니다. 여러분은 하루에 얼마나 걸으시나요? 걷는 것만으로 여러분은 더 건강해지고 살을 빼실 수 있습니다. 우선, 이것은 여러분의 근육을 강화시키고 면역 체계를 높여줍니다. 이것은 또한 스트레스를 줄여 주고 기억력을 향상시키는 것을 도와줍니다. 하지만 너무 무리해서 걸으면 다리에 통증을 느끼실 수도 있습니다. 하루에 30분씩 걸으세요, 그러면 여러분은 훨씬 더 건강하고 행복한 삶을 사실 수 있을 겁니다.

해설 걷기의 좋은 점을 말하며 하루에 30분씩 걷는 것을 장려하고 있다.
어휘 strengthen [stréŋkθən] 강화시키다 boost [bu:st] 높이다, 올리다 immune system 면역 체계 reduce [ridʤú:s] 줄이다, 감소시키다 ache [eik] 통증

10 숫자 정보 파악 ⑤

W Good afternoon. <u>What</u> <u>type</u> <u>of</u> <u>bracelet</u> are you looking for?
M I heard that if I buy a twenty-dollar leather bracelet, I can get another one for free.
W You're right. You can choose any bracelets that are <u>displayed</u> <u>on</u> <u>the</u> <u>table</u>.
M I'll get a black and white one. How much are the metal bracelets beside the leather ones?

42

W Each costs 35 dollars, but they're <u>not</u> <u>on</u> <u>sale</u>.

M I'll buy a golden metal one, please.

W Okay. We <u>provide</u> <u>gift</u> <u>wrapping</u> if you pay an extra three dollars.

M Cool. I'll take the gift wrapping <u>only</u> <u>for</u> <u>the</u> <u>metal</u> one, please.

여 안녕하세요. 어떤 유형의 팔찌를 찾으시나요?

남 제가 듣기로는 20달러 하는 팔찌 하나를 사면 또 하나를 무료로 얻을 수 있다고 들었어요.

여 맞습니다. 테이블 위에 전시되어있는 팔찌를 고르시면 되세요.

남 검은색이랑 하얀색으로 할게요. 가죽 팔찌들 옆에 있는 금속 팔찌는 얼마인가요?

여 각각 35달러인데 할인 중이 아니에요.

남 금속 팔찌로 하나 주세요.

여 알겠습니다. 3달러를 추가로 지불하시면 선물 포장도 해드려요.

남 좋네요. 금속 팔찌만 선물 포장해 주세요.

해설 20달러짜리 가죽 팔찌와 35달러짜리 금속 팔찌를 하나씩 사고 금속 팔찌만 포장한다고 하였다.

어휘 bracelet [bréislit] 팔찌   leather [léðər] 가죽   for free 무료로   display [displéi] 전시하다   wrapping [rǽpiŋ] 포장

11 할 일 파악 ②

W I want to be more productive at work. How can I <u>manage</u> <u>my</u> <u>time</u> more efficiently?

M Well, there are some ways to <u>improve</u> <u>your</u> <u>productivity</u>.

W What are they?

M Download an application that <u>helps</u> <u>track</u> <u>your</u> <u>time</u>. It lets you know how much time you spend on the things you do.

W What a great tool that is!

M And <u>take</u> <u>regular</u> <u>breaks</u>. Working on tasks without taking breaks decreases your performance.

W Thanks for the advice. I think I should <u>download</u> <u>the</u> <u>application</u> first.

여 직장에서 더 생산적이고 싶어. 어떻게 하면 내 시간을 좀 더 효율적으로 관리할 수 있을까?

남 음, 생산성을 높이는 몇 가지 방법이 있어.

여 뭔데?

남 네 시간을 추적하는 걸 도와주는 어플리케이션을 다운받아. 네가 하는 일들에 시간을 얼마나 쓰는지 알려 주거든.

여 좋은 도구네!

남 그리고 규칙적인 휴식을 가져. 휴식 없이 일하면 성과를 감소시키거든.

여 조언 고마워. 어플리케이션을 먼저 다운받아야 할 것 같아.

해설 여자는 남자가 추천한 시간 추적 앱을 먼저 다운받겠다고 하였다.

어휘 productive [prədʌ́ktiv] 생산적인   productivity [pròudʌktívəti] 생산성   efficiently [ifíʃəntli] 효율적으로   track [træk] 추적하다   decrease [díːkriːs] 감소시키다

12 언급 유무 파악 ③

W This is an <u>announcement for residents</u> of Rainbow Apartment. The exterior walls of Building A will be repainted tomorrow. Please <u>park your car</u> in the parking lot near Building B. The paint job will take <u>about four hours</u>. It starts at 8 a.m. and will be finished by noon. Please <u>be aware of</u> the area and the time. Thank you.

여 Rainbow 아파트 주민 여러분께 알려드립니다. 내일 빌딩 A의 외벽이 다시 페인트칠이 될 예정입니다. 주차는 빌딩 B 가까이에 있는 주차장에 하시길 부탁드립니다. 페인트 작업은 대략 4시간이 걸릴 것입니다. 아침 8시에 시작해서 낮 12시까지는 끝날 것입니다. 구역과 시간에 유의해 주십시오. 감사합니다.

해설 주차를 할 수 있는 시간에 관해서는 언급되지 않았다.

어휘 announcement [ənáunsmənt] 공지, 발표   resident [rézidənt] 주민   exterior [ikstí(ː)əriər] 외부의   be aware of ~을 알다

13 표 파악 ③

M Stella, <u>which foreign language class</u> do you want to take?

W Let's take an English class. I want to be good at English.

M Me, too. Would it be better for us to take <u>both</u> <u>listening</u> <u>and</u> <u>speaking</u> classes?

W Yes. I heard that practicing listening and speaking together is a great way to improve your foreign language skills.

M When do you have time? I <u>can't</u> <u>make</u> <u>it</u> on weekdays.

W I'm <u>more</u> <u>comfortable</u> <u>with</u> <u>weekends</u>, too.

M Okay. Let's sign up for the classes right away.

남 Stella, 어떤 외국어 강좌를 듣고 싶어?

여 영어 수업을 듣자. 난 영어를 잘하고 싶어.

남 나도 그래. 듣기와 말하기 수업을 같이 듣게 나을까?

여 응. 듣기와 말하기를 함께 연습하는 게 외국어 능력을 향상시키는 데 좋은 방법이래.

남 언제 시간이 되니? 난 평일 동안은 할 수가 없어.

여 나도 주말이 더 편해.

남 좋아. 지금 수업 등록하러 가자.

해설 듣기와 말하기를 함께 연습하는 것이 외국어 능력 향상에 좋다고 말하며 주말에 수업을 듣기로 하였다.

어휘 foreign [fɔ́ːrin] 외국의   practice [prǽktis] 연습하다

14 화제·주제 파악 ⑤

W This is a <u>kind</u> <u>of</u> <u>book</u>. We use it when we study a language. It gives us information <u>in</u> <u>alphabetical</u> <u>order</u>. It includes words and their definitions, pronunciation, and examples. It comes in different sizes, so we <u>can</u> <u>carry</u> <u>around</u> a small one. These days, many people use <u>online</u> <u>versions</u> of this book because they are <u>easy</u> <u>to</u> <u>use</u>. Another thing about this is that every country has this type of book in its language.

여 이것은 책의 한 종류입니다. 우리는 이것을 언어를 공부할 때 사용합니다. 이것은 우리에게 알파벳 순서로 정보를 줍니다. 이것은 단어와 정의, 발음, 그리고 예시들을 포함합니다. 크기가 다양해서 작은 것을 가지고 다닐 수 있습니다. 요즘은 많은 사람들이 사용하기 쉽기 때문에 인터넷 사전을 사용합니다. 이것에 대한 또 다른 것은 모든 나라에 그들의 언어로 된 이런 종류의 책이 있다는 것입니다.

해설 언어를 공부할 때 사용하고, 단어와 발음 등을 포함하는 책이라고 하였다.

어휘 alphabetical [æ̀lfəbétikəl] 알파벳의   order [ɔ́ːrdər] 순서   include [inklúːd] 포함하다   definition [dèfəníʃən] 정의   example [igzǽmpl] 예시

정답 및 해설

15 할 일 파악 ②

[*Telephone rings.*]
W Hello.
M Hi. This is Jimin Kim.
W Hi, Mr. Kim. What <u>are</u> <u>you</u> <u>calling</u> <u>for</u>?
M I sent you an email last Saturday, but I <u>haven't</u> <u>received</u> a <u>reply</u> yet.
W An email? Well, let me check. [*A few seconds later*] Sorry, but I <u>didn't</u> <u>get</u> <u>an</u> <u>email</u> from you.
M Really? Please wait for a minute.
W Sure.
M Sorry. It was my mistake. I sent the email to <u>the</u> <u>wrong</u> <u>address</u>. I'll send it to you right now.

여 여보세요?
남 안녕하세요. 저 김지민입니다.
여 안녕하세요, 김 선생님. 어떤 일로 전화를 하셨어요?
남 저번 주 토요일에 이메일을 보내드렸는데, 아직 답장을 못 받았거든요.
여 이메일요? 음, 확인해 볼게요. 죄송하지만 이메일 받은 게 없어요.
남 정말요? 잠시만 기다려 주세요.
여 물론이죠.
남 죄송해요, 제 실수네요. 이메일을 다른 주소로 잘못 보냈네요. 지금 바로 메일 보낼게요.

해설 남자가 여자에게 바로 이메일을 보낸다고 하였다.
어휘 send [send] 보내다   receive [risíːv] 받다   mistake [mistéik] 실수

16 숫자 정보 파악 ⑤

W Have you <u>booked</u> a <u>plane</u> <u>ticket</u> to Bangkok?
M Not yet. I <u>can't</u> <u>decide</u> between the 12:30 p.m. and 7 p.m. flights.
W The earlier, the better.
M Tickets <u>for</u> <u>early</u> <u>times</u> cost more. The price of the earlier ticket is double that of the later one.
W Then you'd better choose the later one.
M Yes. Then I can stay there for <u>one</u> <u>more</u> <u>day</u>.
W That's <u>a</u> <u>good</u> <u>plan</u>.

여 방콕 가는 비행기 표 예매했어?
남 아직. 12시 30분이랑 7시 시간표 중에서 언제 출발할지 고민 중이야.
여 물론 빠를수록 좋지.
남 너도 알다시피 빠른 시간대 표들이 비용이 더 많이 들어. 일찍 출발하는 표 가격이 나중에 출발하는 표 가격의 두 배야.
여 그렇다면 늦게 출발하는 걸 선택하는 게 좋겠네.
남 응. 그리고 하루 더 머무를 수 있어.
여 좋은 계획이네.

해설 늦게 출발하는 비행기로 예약하되 하루 더 머무르기로 하였다.
어휘 double [dʌ́bl] 두 배의

17 적절한 응답 찾기 ⑤

W I have gained <u>too</u> <u>much</u> <u>weight</u>.
M No way. You look the same.
W You <u>don't</u> <u>understand</u>. I have gained four kilograms in one month.
M What do you think the reason is?
W I don't exercise and <u>stay</u> <u>seated</u> for a long time <u>at</u> <u>work</u>.
M And you drive your car every day, which means

you <u>hardly</u> <u>ever</u> <u>walk</u>.
W You're right. <u>What</u> <u>should</u> I <u>do</u> to lose weight?
M <u>You'd better exercise at least twice a week.</u>

여 나 살이 너무 많이 쪘어.
남 말도 안 돼. 똑같아 보이는걸.
여 넌 이해 못 해. 한 달 안에 4킬로그램이나 쪘어.
남 원인이 뭐라고 생각하는데?
여 운동을 하지 않고 직장에서 장시간 앉아 있어.
남 그리고 매일 넌 차를 운전하잖아, 즉 네가 거의 걷지 않는다는 걸 의미하지.
여 네 말이 맞아. 살을 빼려면 무엇을 해야 할까?
남 일주일에 최소 두 번은 운동을 하는 게 좋겠어.

해설 살을 빼는 법을 묻는 말에 대한 가장 적절한 응답은 ⑤ '일주일에 최소 두 번은 운동을 하는 게 좋겠어.'이다.
① 친구한테 직장까지 태워달라고 부탁해 봐.
② 이번 주말에 네 차를 빌리게 해 줘.
③ 나도 너와 같은 문제를 가지고 있어.
④ 넌 네 몸에 신경 쓰지 않는 것 같아.
어휘 gain weight 살이 찌다   stay seated 계속 앉아있다

18 적절한 응답 찾기 ②

W Why are you <u>laughing</u> <u>so</u> <u>hard</u>, Jack?
M Look at this guy. He's a YouTuber. He's so funny.
W Is he doing a science experiment? The video seems <u>fun</u> <u>and</u> <u>informative</u>.
M You're right. You know, popular YouTubers make <u>large</u> <u>amounts</u> <u>of</u> <u>money</u>.
W There must be a reward for that kind of an effort.
M <u>How</u> <u>about</u> if I became a game YouTuber?
W You mean as a hobby, don't you?
M Of course not. I meant that I <u>would</u> <u>quit</u> <u>my</u> job and be a full-time YouTuber. Wouldn't that be cool?
W <u>You need to consider it more seriously.</u>

여 왜 그렇게 심하게 웃어, Jack?
남 이 남자 좀 봐. 유튜버야. 정말 웃겨.
여 과학 실험을 하는 건가? 영상이 재밌고 유익해 보이네.
남 그렇지? 인기 있는 유튜버들은 돈을 정말 많이 벌어.
여 저 부단한 노력에 보상이 있어야지.
남 내가 게임 유튜버가 되는 건 어떨까?
여 네 말은 취미 삼아 말이지, 그렇지 않니?
남 당연히 아니지. 내 말은 직장을 그만두고 방송을 한다는 거지. 멋있지 않아?
여 넌 좀 더 진지하게 고려해 볼 필요가 있어.

해설 유튜버가 되기 위해 퇴사하겠다는 말에 대한 가장 적절한 응답은 ② '넌 좀 더 진지하게 고려해 볼 필요가 있어.'이다.
① 부모님 말씀을 듣는 것은 중요해.
③ 좋은 직업을 갖고 있다는 게 얼마나 행운이야.
④ 직장에서 내가 하는 일에 만족이 안 돼.
⑤ 난 네가 이만큼 성공할 줄 알았어.
어휘 experiment [ikspérəmənt] 실험   informative [infɔ́ːrmətiv] 유익한   amount [əmáunt] 액수, 양

19 적절한 응답 찾기 ④

W It's <u>so</u> <u>relaxing</u> to come to a sheep ranch.
M Mom, there is a flock of sheep!
W They look so cute. I think we can <u>feed</u> <u>them</u> <u>dry</u> <u>grass</u> here.

M Can I try feeding them, please?
W Sure. Let me take a picture of you.
M Look, Mom! This sheep is so mild. It stays still even when I pet it.
W Oh, Robert. You don't pet an animal which is raised on a farm or at a zoo.
M Is there something wrong with doing this?

여 양 목장에 오니까 마음이 정말 느긋하다.
남 엄마, 저기 양 떼가 있어요!
여 정말 귀엽다. 여기 건초를 먹여도 되는 것 같아.
남 제가 한 번 먹여 줘도 되나요?
여 물론이지. 사진 찍어 줄게.
남 보세요, 엄마! 이 양 정말 순해요. 제가 쓰다듬어도 가만히 있어요.
여 오, Robert. 개방된 장소와 동물원에서 키워지는 동물은 만지는 게 아니란다.
남 만지면 어떤 문제가 있나요?

해설 동물원의 동물을 만지면 안 된다는 말에 대한 가장 적절한 응답은 ④ '만지면 어떤 문제가 있나요?'이다.
① 동물도 저의 친한 친구가 될 수 있어요.
② 조만간 여기 다시 오기를 바라요.
③ 반려동물을 키우면 좋은 점이 뭐예요?
⑤ 동물원에 있는 동물들을 얼른 보고 싶어요.
어휘 relaxing [riléksiŋ] 마음이 느긋한, 편한   flock [flɑk] 떼, 무리
feed [fi:d] 먹이를 주다   dry grass 건초   mild [maild] 온순한
pet [pet] 어루만지다

20 적절한 응답 찾기 ③

M Adam and Emilia take a history class together. They are assigned to work as a team and to make a presentation on Western culture. They decide to meet at an Internet café and do research on the topic. Adam collects information from different sites and takes notes. But Emilia doesn't do what she is supposed to and keeps playing games. In this situation, what would Adam most likely say to Emilia?
Adam Emilia, remember that we're a team.

남 Adam과 Emilia는 같이 역사 수업을 듣습니다. 그들은 한 팀으로 서양 문화에 대해 알아보고 발표를 하라고 배정을 받습니다. 그들은 인터넷 카페에서 만나서 주제에 관해 조사하기로 합니다. Adam은 다양한 사이트에서 정보를 모으고 필기를 합니다. 하지만 Emilia는 그녀가 해야 할 일을 하지 않고 계속해서 게임만 합니다. 이 상황에서 Adam은 Emilia에게 뭐라고 말을 할까요?
Adam Emilia, 우리가 한 팀이라는 걸 기억해.

해설 자료 조사는 하지 않고 계속 게임만 하는 Emilia에게 할 수 있는 가장 적절한 말은 ③ '우리가 한 팀이라는 걸 기억해.'이다.
① 우리 휴식을 취해야겠어.   ② 내가 이것을 잘 하지 못해서 미안해.
④ 리더가 되는 것을 절대 쉽지 않아.   ⑤ 그게 네가 해야 하는 일이야.
어휘 assign [əsáin] 배정하다   Western [wéstərn] 서양의
presentation [prì:zəntéiʃən] 발표   do research 조사하다
collect [kəlékt] 모으다, 수집하다

Listen and Check p. 90

Q1 a shade
Q2 False
Q3 Yes
Q4 in the morning
Q5 True
Q6 No
Q7 False
Q8 a shop
Q9 pain in legs
Q10 No
Q11 False
Q12 the exterior walls
Q13 No
Q14 False
Q15 not sending an email
Q16 No
Q17 True
Q18 a popular YouTuber
Q19 No
Q20 do research

해석
Q1 남자는 스탠드에 무엇이 달려 있기를 원하는가?
Q2 여자는 남자와 함께 외출할 것이다.
Q3 남자는 다쳤는가?
Q4 남자와 여자는 언제 베트남으로 떠날 것인가?
Q5 여자는 그림을 잘 알고 있다.
Q6 남자는 흐릿한 사진을 보는 것이 처음인가?
Q7 밤에 운전하는 것은 남자에게 어렵지 않다.
Q8 남자와 여자는 SNS에 무엇을 홍보할 것인가?
Q9 너무 오래 걷는 것의 부정적인 면이 무엇인가?
Q10 남자는 모든 팔찌를 포장하기를 원하는가?
Q11 여자는 시간을 잘 관리하는 방법을 알고 있다.
Q12 아파트의 어떤 부분이 다시 페인트가 칠해질 것인가?
Q13 남자와 여자는 평일에 영어 수업을 들을 것이다.
Q14 그 책에는 단어의 유래가 잘 설명되어 있다.
Q15 남자는 어떤 것에 대해 여자에게 사과를 하는가?
Q16 남자와 여자는 방콕에 일주일 더 머물기로 선택하였는가?
Q17 남자는 여자의 몸에 나타난 차이를 알아채지 못한다.
Q18 남자는 무엇이 되기를 바라는가?
Q19 여자는 남자가 양에게 먹이를 주는 것을 도와줄 것인가?
Q20 남자와 여자는 인터넷 카페에서 무엇을 해야만 하는가?

실전 모의고사 10회 pp. 98~99

1	①	2	④	3	②	4	③	5	④
6	①	7	⑤	8	②	9	①	10	⑤
11	④	12	③	13	④	14	②	15	①
16	④	17	③	18	④	19	③	20	④

1 그림 정보 파악 ①

M Harin, did you make this Christmas card?
W That's right. This is for my grandmother.
M You drew a big tree in the middle.
W I also drew lots of presents in front of the tree.
M Why didn't you draw Santa Claus?
W I tried, but it was too hard for me to draw.
M Still, I like your card. I bet your grandmother will

love it, too.

남 하린아, 네가 이 크리스마스카드를 만들었니?
여 맞아. 이건 우리 할머니를 위한 거야.
남 중간에 큰 나무를 그렸구나.
여 그리고 나무 앞에는 많은 선물도 그렸지.
남 산타클로스는 왜 안 그렸어?
여 시도해 봤는데, 내가 그리기에는 너무 어려웠어.
남 그래도, 네 카드가 좋아. 너희 할머니도 좋아하실 거라고 확신해.

해설 산타클로스는 그리기 어려워서 그리지 못했다고 하였다.
어휘 present [prézənt] 선물

2 부탁 한 일 파악 ④

W It was a really nice musical.
M I agree. It was so amazing. Now, I need to go home and get some rest.
W How will you get to your place?
M I'm thinking of taking the bus. How about you?
W I drove my car here.
M Can you drop me off on your way home?
W Why not? That's no problem.

여 정말 멋진 뮤지컬이야.
남 동의해. 너무 멋졌어. 이제 난 집으로 가서 좀 쉬어야겠다.
여 집에 어떻게 갈 거야?
남 난 버스 타고 가려고. 너는?
여 난 차를 가지고 왔어.
남 집으로 가는 길에 나를 내려줄래?
여 물론이지.

해설 차를 가져왔다는 여자의 말에 집으로 가는 길에 내려다 달라고 부탁하였다.
어휘 amazing [əméiziŋ] 굉장한   drop off 내려 주다, 바래다주다

3 그림 상황 파악 ②

① W There is a stain on the chair.
  M I'll try to remove it.
② W You can have a seat here.
  M Thank you. How kind of you!
③ W I'm on my way to the gym.
  M Don't forget to bring your water bottle.
④ W Are you sure you locked the car doors?
  M Don't worry. I double-checked.
⑤ W Why don't we take the bus instead of the subway?
  M We will get caught in a serious traffic jam.

① 여 의자에 얼룩이 있어요.
  남 내가 제거해 볼게.
② 여 여기 앉으세요.
  남 고마워. 정말 친절하구나!
③ 여 저는 체육관에 가는 길이예요.
  남 물병을 가져가는 것을 잊지 말아라.
④ 여 자동차 문을 확실히 잠갔나요?
  남 걱정 마. 내가 두 번이나 확인했어.
⑤ 여 지하철 대신에 버스를 타는 게 어때요?
  남 우리는 심각한 교통 체증에 갇힐 거야.

해설 여자아이가 할아버지께 자리를 양보하고 있는 상황이다.
어휘 stain [stein] 얼룩, 오염   remove [rimúːv] ~을 제거하다
traffic jam 교통 체증

4 특정 정보 파악 ③

W Excuse me. Is the badminton court still being repaired?
M Yes. I'm afraid that you can't use it today.
W Hmm... It is taking so long.
M The repairs are almost done. The final safety inspection is scheduled for Tuesday.
W Then I will use it on Wednesday.
M You can definitely use the court by then.

여 실례합니다. 배드민턴 코트가 여전히 수리 중인가요?
남 네. 오늘은 사용하지 못할 것 같네요.
여 흠, 오래 걸리네요.
남 수리는 거의 끝났어요. 최종 안전 검사가 화요일로 예정되어 있어요.
여 그러면 수요일에 사용할게요.
남 그때까지는 코트를 확실히 사용하실 수 있을 겁니다.

해설 수리 중인 배드민턴 코트의 최종 안전 검사가 화요일로 예정되어 있고 그 이후인 수요일에는 사용이 가능할 것이라고 하였다.
어휘 inspection [inspékʃən] 검사, 조사   schedule [skédʒuːl] 예정하다

5 언급 유무 파악 ④

W It's so good to be here. I can't wait to go swimming.
M Let's read the rules before we enter the swimming pool.
W Isn't it enough to wear a swimsuit and a swimming cap?
M You can't be too careful. Did you warm up?
W Of course, I did.
M Good. Be sure you don't run or dive.
W All right. Anything else?
M You should stay in the lane in the pool.

여 여기에 와서 너무 좋아. 얼른 수영하고 싶어.
남 수영장에 들어가기 전에 규칙을 읽어 보자.
여 수영복과 수영모를 착용한 걸로 충분하지 않니?
남 조심해서 나쁠 건 없잖아. 준비 운동 했니?
여 물론 했어.
남 좋아. 안전을 위해 달리거나 다이빙을 해선 안 돼.
여 알겠어. 다른 건 없니?
남 풀장 안에서는 네 레인을 지켜야 해.

해설 수영장에서 큰소리로 말하는 것에 관해서는 언급되지 않았다.
어휘 lane [lein] 레인, 항로

6 장소 추론 ①

W Congratulations on opening your new restaurant!
M Thank you. What a beautiful flowerpot!
W I love the interior design of your restaurant. I feel like I'm in France.
M I'm glad to hear that. Do you want me to get you something to drink?
W Yes, please. By the way, how's your business going?
M Until now, it couldn't be better.
W That's great.

여 새로운 식당을 개업한 거 축하해.
남 고마워. 정말 예쁜 화분이구나.

여 식당의 인테리어가 마음에 든다. 마치 내가 프랑스에 있는 기분이야.
남 그 말을 들으니 기쁘다. 마실 것을 좀 가져다줄까?
여 응. 부탁해. 그런데 장사는 잘 되니?
남 지금까지는 더할 나위 없을 만큼 좋아.
여 잘 됐네.

해설 새로운 식당을 개업한 친구를 축하하기 위해 화분을 들고 찾아간 상황이다.

어휘 flowerpot [fláuərpàt] 화분   by the way 그런데

7 어색한 대화 찾기 ⑤

① M Let's play baseball next Friday.
  W Sorry. I have to spend some time with my family that day.
② M Look! Why are there so many people here?
  W I guess they are watching the street performance.
③ M How can I get to the department store?
  W Walk straight for 3 blocks and then turn right.
④ M Do you know where the coffee mugs are?
  W Sure. They are in the first cabinet.
⑤ M What are the bank's business hours?
  W You can open a bank account today.

① 남 다음 금요일에 야구하자.
  여 미안해. 그 날 가족들과 시간을 보내야 해.
② 남 이걸 봐! 여기에 왜 많은 사람들이 있지?
  여 그들은 길거리 공연을 보는 중인 거 같아.
③ 남 백화점까지 어떻게 갈 수 있나요?
  여 3블록 직진해서 오른쪽으로 도세요.
④ 남 커피 머그잔이 어디에 있는지 아시나요?
  여 물론이죠. 첫 번째 수납장에 있어요.
⑤ 남 은행 영업시간이 어떻게 되나요?
  여 당신은 오늘 은행 계좌를 만들 수 있습니다.

해설 은행 영업시간이 언제인지 묻는 말에 오늘 은행 계좌를 만들 수 있다고 답하는 것은 부자연스럽다.

어휘 cabinet [kǽbənit] 보관함, 수납장   business hours 영업시간

8 부탁 한 일 파악 ②

W Excuse me. Would you do me a favor?
M What is it?
W I bought two train tickets for my son and me. However, they aren't in the same row.
M I see. That's why you keep looking back.
W Right. Do you mind changing seats with my son?
M No problem.
W Thank you so much.

여 실례합니다. 부탁 좀 드려도 될까요?
남 뭔데요?
여 저와 어린 아들을 위한 기차표를 2장을 구입했어요. 하지만 연석이 아니에요.
남 그렇군요. 그래서 당신이 계속 뒤돌아 본 거군요.
여 맞아요. 제 아들과 자리를 바꿔 주실 수 있을까요?
남 물론이죠.
여 정말 감사합니다.

해설 기차표를 연석으로 구입하지 못해 아들과 떨어져 앉게 되어서 옆자리에 앉은 남자에게 자리를 바꿔 달라고 부탁하고 있다.

어휘 row [rou] 줄   look back 뒤돌아 보다

9 화제·주제 파악 ①

W Good evening, ladies and gentlemen. Welcome aboard Happy Air Flight 123 bound for Danang International Airport. It's a pleasure to have you with us. Please make sure that your seatbelt is fastened during takeoff. The use of portable electronic devices is not allowed. In addition, please refrain from smoking during the entire flight. If there is anything we can do for you, do not hesitate to ask. Please enjoy the flight. Thank you.

여 신사 숙녀 여러분, 좋은 저녁입니다. 다낭 국제공항으로 향하는 Happy 항공 123편에 탑승하신 것을 환영합니다. 함께할 수 있게 되어 기쁩니다. 이륙하는 동안 안전벨트를 매주십시오. 휴대용 전자 기기의 사용은 허용되지 않습니다. 또한 전체 비행 동안 담배는 삼가 주십시오. 저희가 도와드릴 일이 있으면 주저 말고 요청해 주세요. 즐거운 비행이 되시기를 바랍니다. 감사합니다.

해설 비행기가 이륙하면서 승객들에게 주의 사항을 알려주고 있다.

어휘 bound for ~ ~행의   fasten [fǽsən] 매다, 고정하다   portable [pɔ́:rtəbl] 휴대용의   refrain [rifréin] 자제하다, 삼가다   hesitate [hézitèit] 주저하다, 망설이다

10 숫자 정보 파악 ⑤

W Welcome to White's Cleaners. What can I do for you?
M I'd like to have these clothes dry-cleaned.
W Okay. Can you show me what you have?
M I have one leather jacket and two wool coats. How much will that be?
W Normally, jackets are 10 dollars each. But in the case of leather jackets, you have to pay 5 dollars more. And coats are 15 dollars each.
M Okay. When is the fastest I can pick them up?
W It's tomorrow evening.

여 White 세탁소에 오신 걸 환영합니다. 무엇을 도와 드릴까요?
남 이 옷을 드라이클리닝 맡기고 싶어요.
여 네. 어떤 옷을 가져왔는지 볼 수 있을까요?
남 가죽 재킷 1개랑 울 코트 2개요. 얼마인가요?
여 보통 재킷은 개당 10달러입니다. 하지만 가죽 재킷의 경우 5달러를 더 내야 합니다. 그리고 코트는 개당 15달러입니다.
남 네. 찾아갈 수 있는 가장 빠른 때가 언제인가요?
여 내일 저녁입니다.

해설 코트 1개당 15달러, 가죽 재킷은 1개당 기본 10달러에 추가 비용 5달러, 총 45달러이다.

어휘 in the case of ~의 경우에는

11 할 일 파악 ④

M Paige, I'm worried about our son Harry.
W Why? Did he do something wrong?
M Harry only reads comic books. I want him to read regular books, too.
W You're right. He needs to read regular books to get good general knowledge.
M So how about making a family reading hour?
W I can't agree more with you. I'll make a list of books to read.
M Okay. That will help.

남 Paige, 난 우리 아들 Harry가 걱정이 돼.
여 왜? 뭐 잘못이라도 했어?
남 Harry는 만화책만 읽어. 난 그가 일반 책도 읽기를 바라.
여 당신 말이 맞아. 그는 좋은 일반 지식을 얻기 위해 일반 책을 읽을 필요가 있어.
남 그래서 말인데, 가족 독서 시간을 만드는 건 어떨까?
여 완전히 동의해. 내가 읽어야 할 책 목록을 만들게.
남 그래. 도움이 될 거야.

해설 만화책만 읽는 아들을 위해 가족 독서 모임을 만들고, 여자가 독서 목록을 작성하기로 하였다.
어휘 regular [régjulər] 보통의, 정규의

12 언급 유무 파악 ③

M Hello, everyone. The Seoul International Fireworks Festival will be held soon. It is scheduled for Saturday, September 12, and starts at 8 p.m. It will be held at Hangang Park in Seoul. Groups from the countries Mexico, Germany, Egypt, and Korea are going to participate in the festival. Because bad traffic is expected, we decided to provide free shuttle buses from Seoul Station. We recommend that you take the shuttle bus or use public transportation.

남 여러분, 안녕하세요? 서울 국제 불꽃 축제가 곧 시작됩니다. 그것은 9월 12일 토요일로 예정되어 있으며 저녁 8시에 시작합니다. 축제는 서울에 있는 한강 공원에서 열릴 것입니다. 멕시코, 독일, 이집트 그리고 한국으로 구성된 4개의 나라가 축제에 참여할 예정입니다. 심각한 교통 체증이 예상되어 우리는 서울역에서 무료 순환 버스를 제공하기로 결정했습니다. 순환버스를 타거나 대중교통을 이용하시기를 추천 드립니다.

해설 서울 국제 불꽃 축제의 입장 요금에 관해서는 언급되지 않았다.
어휘 international [ìntərnǽʃənəl] 국제의   participate [pɑːrtísəpèit] 참여하다, 참가하다   public transportation 대중교통

13 그림 정보 파악 ④

M Let's go to see a movie tonight.
W That's a great idea. Do you have anything in mind?
M How about watching *Aladdin*?
W Sounds fun. Let's make a reservation. Look at this seating chart.
M I don't like seats in the front row. Sitting there makes my neck stiff.
W I totally agree with you. How about a middle row?
M Actually, I like sitting in the back.
W Then let's pick these seats in the back. One is an aisle seat.

남 오늘 영화 보러 가자.
여 좋아. 생각해 둔 게 있니?
남 '알라딘'을 보는 건 어때?
여 재미있겠다. 예매하자. 여기 좌석 배치도를 봐.
남 난 앞자리는 싫어. 내 목을 뻐근하게 하거든.
여 완전히 동의해. 중간 자리는 어때?
남 사실은 나는 뒤에 앉는 걸 좋아해.
여 그러면 뒤에 있는 통로 좌석을 고르자.

해설 맨 뒤에 있는 통로 자리를 예매하기로 하였다.
어휘 reservation [rèzərvéiʃən] 예약   stiff [stif] 뻣뻣한   aisle [ail] 통로, 복도

14 화제·주제 파악 ②

W Do your eyes feel dry and a little itchy? The reason is that you are straining your eyes by looking at screens so much. Here are some tips on how to protect your eyes. Take regular breaks. Just looking at a distant object every 30 minutes helps a lot. In addition, make sure you blink frequently while you are using your smartphone. Blinking helps moisten your eyes and protects your eyes from getting too dry.

여 당신의 눈이 건조하거나 약간 가렵다고 느끼나요? 그건 당신이 화면을 보는데 많은 시간을 쓰면서 눈을 혹사시키고 있기 때문입니다. 눈을 보호하는 조언을 드릴게요. 규칙적으로 쉬세요. 30분마다 멀리 있는 물체를 보는 것도 도움이 됩니다. 또한 스마트폰을 사용하는 동안 눈을 자주 깜박이세요. 깜박이는 것은 당신의 눈을 촉촉하게 하는데 도움이 되어 당신의 눈이 지나치게 건조해지는 걸 막아 줍니다.

해설 건조한 눈을 보호하기 위한 몇 가지의 조언을 하고 있다.
어휘 itchy [ítʃi] 가려운, 근질근질한   strain [strein] 무리하게 사용하다   distant [dístənt] 먼   frequently [frí:kwəntli] 빈번히, 자주   moisten [mɔ́isən] 촉촉하게 하다

15 할 일 파악 ①

W Dad, I'm hungry. Is there anything to eat?
M It's almost dinnertime. Let's check what is in the refrigerator.
W I've already checked it, but there's nothing except for pork.
M That's not so bad. I'll make you pork stew.
W Sounds tasty! But don't we need potatoes and carrots?
M Right. Can you go grocery shopping for me? I'll do the dishes.
W No problem. I'll be back in a flash.

여 아빠, 저 배고파요. 먹을 게 있을까요?
남 거의 저녁 시간이구나. 냉장고에 무엇이 있는지 보자.
여 제가 이미 확인했어요. 하지만 돼지고기 빼고는 아무것도 없어요.
남 나쁘지 않구나. 내가 돼지고기 스튜를 만들어 줄게.
여 맛있을 거 같아요! 음, 감자랑 당근이 필요하죠?
남 맞아. 식료품 쇼핑을 다녀오겠니? 나는 설거지를 할게.
여 문제없어요. 순식간에 다녀올게요.

해설 딸이 감자와 당근을 사러 식료품 가게에 가는 동안 아빠는 설거지를 하겠다고 하였다.
어휘 except for ~을 제외하고   grocery [gróusəri] 식료품   in a flash 순식간에

16 숫자 정보 파악 ④

[Cellphone rings.]
W Hello. I'm calling about the two-bedroom apartment you advertised online. Is it still available?
M Let me check. [Pause] Yes, it's available.
W Can I take a look at the house on June 15?
M Sorry, but I'll be on vacation. How about on June 17?
W It's okay. Can I go to the real estate agency at 4:00 p.m. on that day?

M Great. See you then.

여 여보세요. 인터넷에 당신이 광고한 방 2개짜리 아파트를 보고 전화 드리는데요. 여전히 이용 가능한가요?

남 확인해 볼게요. 네, 가능해요.

여 6월 15일에 집을 볼 수 있을까요?

남 죄송하지만 제가 휴가 기간이에요. 6월 17일은 어떠세요?

여 괜찮아요. 그 날 오후 4시에 부동산으로 가면 될까요?

남 좋아요. 그때 봬어요.

해설 6월 17일에 부동산에서 만나 집을 보러 가기로 하였다.

어휘 advertise [ǽdvərtàiz] 광고하다   real estate agency 부동산

17 적절한 응답 찾기 ③

M Mia, can I ask you for a favor?

W What is it?

M My best friend is getting married soon.

W Wow! Please congratulate your friend for me.

M Okay. I will. By the way, I'm supposed to sing at the wedding. But I chose a duet.

W Do you mean you need a woman to sing with you?

M That's correct. Can you sing with me?

W I'll be a bit nervous, but I can do it.

남 Mia, 부탁 하나만 들어 줄래?

여 뭔데? 말해 봐.

남 사실은 제일 친한 친구가 곧 결혼을 해.

여 와! 친구에게 축하한다고 전해 줘.

남 그럴게. 그런데, 내가 결혼식 때 노래를 부르기로 했거든. 그리고 내가 듀엣곡을 골랐어.

여 네 말은 너랑 같이 노래할 여자가 필요하다는 거구나.

남 맞아. 나랑 같이 노래해 줄래?

여 약간 긴장되지만 할 수 있을 거 같아.

해설 친구의 결혼식 축가를 위해 여성 파트를 노래해 달라는 말에 대한 가장 적절한 응답은 ③ '약간 긴장되지만 할 수 있을 거 같아.'이다.

① 그 정장은 너에게 잘 어울린다.

② 내가 그 가수를 볼 거라고는 전혀 생각하지 못했어.

④ 그 노래를 들은 걸 잊을 수 없을 거야.

⑤ 네 결혼식을 위해 피아노를 연주할게.

어휘 duet [dju(ː)ét] 2중창

18 적절한 응답 찾기 ④

M Do you want to go to the museum?

W Maybe next time. I should go to the library now.

M You're going to the library? What for?

W Nick, we have to hand in our science reports by Friday.

M But we still have three days until the due date.

W I know. But I prefer finishing assignments as early as possible. I don't like to be rushed.

M You have a point. I should start today.

남 박물관에 갈래?

여 다음에. 난 지금 도서관에 가야 해.

남 도서관으로 간다고? 왜?

여 Nick, 우리는 금요일 전까지 과학 보고서를 제출해야 해.

남 하지만 마감일까지 3일 남았잖아.

여 알아. 하지만 난 가능한 일찍 숙제를 끝내는 걸 좋아해. 쫓기는 걸 안 좋아해.

남 일리가 있네. 오늘 시작해야겠다.

해설 시간에 쫓기는 것을 좋아하지 않아 숙제를 빨리 끝낸다는 말에 대한

가장 적절한 응답은 ④ '일리가 있네. 나도 오늘 시작해야겠다.'이다.

① 10달러 50센트입니다.   ② 서두르지 마, 그렇지 않으면 넘어질 거야.

③ 난 오늘 이 책을 돌려줘야 해.   ⑤ 서둘러. 여기서부터 2시간이 걸릴 거야.

어휘 due date 마감일, 예정일   rush [rʌʃ] 서두르다, 돌진하다

19 적절한 응답 찾기 ③

M Oh, my! I left my paint on my desk at home.

W Why don't you call your mom and ask her to bring it to school?

M That's impossible. My mom is working now.

W What a pity! Art class will start in 30 minutes.

M Dohee, if you don't mind, can you share your paint with me?

W Be my guest. You can use mine.

남 맙소사! 물감을 집에 있는 책상에 두고 왔어.

여 음, 엄마한테 전화해서 가져다 달라고 하는 건 어때?

남 불가능해. 우리 엄마는 지금 일하고 계셔.

여 안됐다! 30분 후에 미술 수업 시작할 거야.

남 도희야, 괜찮다면, 네 물감을 나랑 같이 쓸 수 있니?

여 그럼. 내 거 써도 돼.

해설 미술 준비물인 물감을 가져오지 않아 같이 쓸 수 있냐고 물어보는 말에 대한 가장 적절한 응답은 ③ '그럼. 내 거 써도 돼.'이다.

① 너 셔츠에 물감 묻었어.   ② 내게 예쁜 그림을 그려줘.

④ 돈을 저축하러 은행으로 가자.

⑤ 수박은 내가 여름에 제일 좋아하는 과일이야.

어휘 impossible [impásəbl] 불가능한   paint [peint] 물감

pity [píti] 안타까운 일

20 상황에 맞는 말 찾기 ④

M Beatrice becomes interested in riding bikes. However, a brand-new bicycle is too expensive for her to buy. So she decides to buy a used one. She searches the Internet to find a good one. At last, she finds one she likes. She calls the person who is selling the bicycle and makes an appointment to meet him. However, the seller doesn't show up at the appointed hour. So she calls him to know where he is. In this situation, what would Beatrice most likely say to the seller?

Beatrice Hello. Where are you? I'm waiting for you.

남 Beatrice는 자전거 타는 것에 흥미가 있습니다. 하지만 새 자전거는 그녀가 구입하기에 비쌉니다. 그래서 그녀는 중고를 사기로 결심합니다. 그녀는 좋은 것을 찾기 위해 인터넷을 검색합니다. 마침내 그녀가 마음에 드는 것을 발견합니다. 그녀는 자전거를 판매하는 사람에게 전화를 해서 그를 만날 약속을 정합니다. 하지만 판매자는 약속된 시간에 나타나지 않습니다. 그래서 그녀는 그가 어디 있는지 알기 위해 그에게 전화를 합니다. 이런 상황에서, Beatrice가 판매자에게 할 말로 가장 적절한 것은 무엇일까요?

Beatrice 여보세요. 어디세요? 저는 기다리는 중이에요.

해설 약속 시간에 나타나지 않는 자전거 판매자에게 전화를 걸어 어디 있는지 알아보는 상황에서 Beatrice가 판매자에게 할 말로 가장 적절한 것은 ④ '어디세요? 저는 기다리는 중이에요.'이다.

① 당신의 자전거를 보고 싶어요.   ② 이것은 바로 제가 찾던 거예요.

③ 자전거를 타고 당신의 근처로 갈게요.

⑤ 이 자전거를 환불하고 싶어요.

어휘 search [səːrtʃ] 검색하다, 찾다   seller [sélər] 판매자   show up 나타나다

정답 및 해설

p. 100

Listen and Check

Q1 True	Q11 Yes
Q2 a musical	Q12 True
Q3 Yes	Q13 *Aladdin*
Q4 Tuesday	Q14 False
Q5 no running	Q15 pork stew
Q6 False	Q16 True
Q7 the bank's business hours	Q17 False
Q8 No	Q18 No
Q9 True	Q19 in 30 minutes
Q10 tomorrow evening	Q20 a bicycle

해석

Q1 산타클로스는 하린이 그리기에 어렵다.
Q2 남자와 여자는 무엇을 함께 봤을까?
Q3 여자는 할아버지께 자리를 양보하는가?
Q4 최종 안전 검사는 언제 예정되어 있었는가?
Q5 수영장에서 규칙 중 하나는 무엇인가?
Q6 남자의 사업은 잘 되지 않는다.
Q7 남자가 알고 싶은 것은 무엇인가?
Q8 남자와 여자는 매표소 앞에서 대화하고 있는가?
Q9 사람들은 전체 비행 동안에 담배를 피울 수 없다.
Q10 남자는 언제 그의 옷을 찾을 수 있는가?
Q11 Harry는 만화책 읽기만을 좋아하는가?
Q12 4개 나라가 서울 국제 불꽃 축제에 참가할 것이다.
Q13 남자와 여자가 오늘 보게 될 영화의 이름은 무엇인가?
Q14 눈을 자주 깜박이는 것은 당신의 눈을 건조하게 만든다.
Q15 남자는 저녁으로 무엇을 만들기로 결정했을까?
Q16 여자는 방 2개짜리 아파트를 보고 싶어 한다.
Q17 Mia는 곧 결혼할 예정이다.
Q18 그는 과학 보고서를 제출했을까?
Q19 미술 수업이 언제 시작할까?
Q20 Beatrice는 무엇을 사고 싶어 하는가?

실전 모의고사 11회

pp. 108~109

1	④	2	③	3	⑤	4	④	5	③
6	①	7	④	8	③	9	②	10	③
11	③	12	⑤	13	④	14	②	15	①
16	⑤	17	⑤	18	⑤	19	④	20	③

1 그림 정보 파악 ④

M Can I help you?
W Yes. How much is that cup with the dinosaur on it?
M 15 dollars. It's light and doesn't break easily.
W That's too expensive.
M Then how about this plain one with two handles?
W I don't think it's handy. Do you have anything else?
M What about this green one with the rose on it?

W That looks good. I'll take that.

남 도와 드릴까요?
여 예. 공룡 그림이 있는 저 컵은 얼마인가요?
남 15달러입니다. 가볍고 쉽게 깨지지 않아요.
여 비싸군요.
남 그럼 손잡이가 두 개 있는 이 무늬 없는 것은 어떠신가요?
여 편리하지 않을 것 같아요. 다른 것 없나요?
남 장미가 그려진 녹색 컵은 어떠신가요?
여 좋아 보이네요. 그걸로 하겠습니다.

해설 장미가 있는 녹색 컵을 구매하겠다고 하였다.
어휘 dinosaur[dáinəsɔ̀ːr] 공룡

2 목적 파악 ③

[Cellphone rings.]
M Hello, Miho.
W Hi, Jun. What's up?
M Could you come to the library this evening?
W Why? What's the matter?
M Actually, I'm having a hard time solving some math problems. I need your help.
W I'm sorry, but I have plans to meet Drake. How about 11 o'clock tomorrow morning?
M Okay. Let's make it tomorrow morning.

남 안녕, 미호야.
여 안녕, 준. 무슨 일이야?
남 오늘 저녁에 도서관에 올 수 있겠니?
여 왜? 무슨 일인데?
남 사실 내가 수학 문제 푸는 데 어려움이 있거든. 너의 도움이 필요해.
여 미안하지만, 이미 Drake와 만날 계획이야. 내일 아침 11시는 어때?
남 좋아. 그럼 내일 아침에 보자.

해설 수학 문제 풀이에 어려움이 있다고 하였다.
어휘 solve[salv] 풀다 have a hard time -ing ~하는데 어려움이 있다

3 그림 상황 파악 ⑤

① W I waited for you for more than an hour.
  M I'm sorry, but I got caught up in traffic.
② W How much is this?
  M I'm sorry, but I am shopping, too.
③ W Would you care for anything else?
  M I've eaten too much already. Thanks.
④ W How can I get to Kim's Bakery?
  M It is located one floor down.
⑤ W May I take your order?
  M Can you give me a bit more time?

① 여 한 시간 넘게 동안 기다렸어.
  남 미안해. 차가 많이 막혔어.
② 여 얼마인가요?
  남 죄송하지만, 저도 손님이랍니다.
③ 여 다른 거 뭐 더 드시겠어요?
  남 이미 많이 먹었어요. 고마워요.
④ 여 Kim's Bakery가 어디에 있나요?
  남 한 층 아래에 있습니다.
⑤ 여 주문하시겠습니까?
  남 잠시 뒤에 주문할 수 있을까요?

해설 주문을 받고 있는 상황이다.

어휘 get caught up in traffic 차가 막히다

4 특정 정보 파악하기 ④

M Vanessa, are you free next week?
W What for?
M There's a cherry blossom festival in Jinhae next week. Do you want to go there with me?
W That sounds tempting. But final exams are next week. When is the last day of the festival?
M Let me check.... Oh, it's next Saturday.
W Next Saturday? Then I can go.
M Great. It takes about 5 hours to get to Jinhae. So let's meet the day before the last day.
W Okay. See you then.

남 Vanessa, 다음 주에 시간 있니?
여 왜?
남 다음 주에 진해에서 벚꽃 축제가 있어. 나랑 거기 같이 갈래?
여 가고 싶지만 기말고사가 다음 주야. 축제의 마지막 날이 언제니?
남 확인해 볼게... 오, 다음 주 토요일이야.
여 다음 주 토요일? 그럼 나 갈 수 있어.
남 좋아. 진해까지는 대략 5시간 정도 걸리거든. 그러니까 축제의 마지막 전날에 만나자.
여 좋아. 그때 보자.

해설 축제 마지막 일자의 전날에 만나자고 하였다.
어휘 tempting [témptiŋ] 솔깃한, 유혹하는

5 언급 유무 파악 ③

M Korea is said to have about 5,000 years of history. During this long history, the Korean people have kept their identity despite lots of foreign invasions. So there have been lots of unique traditions passed down up to modern times. The traditional clothes known as *hanbok* have a unique beauty and were widely worn until the 1970s. But now Koreans wear these clothes on special holidays such as New Year's Day. Traditional Korean houses were equipped with an excellent heating system known as *ondol*. Though many Koreans now live in Western-style residences, they still use heating systems similar to *ondol*.

남 한국은 약 5,000 년의 역사를 가지고 있다고 합니다. 이러한 오랜 역사 속에서, 한국인들은 많은 외국의 침략에도 불구하고 그들의 정체성을 유지해 왔습니다. 그래서 오늘날까지 이어진 고유한 전통이 많이 있습니다. 한복으로 알려진 전통 의상은 고유한 아름다움을 지니고 있으며 1970년대까지 널리 착용되었습니다. 그러나 이제 한국인들은 새해 첫날 같은 특별한 명절에 한복을 입습니다. 전통적인 한국의 집에는 온돌이라고 알려진 우수한 난방 시스템이 갖추어져 있었습니다. 비록 많은 한국인들이 지금은 서양식 주거지에 살고 있지만, 그들은 여전히 전통적인 온돌 시스템과 비슷한 난방 시스템을 사용합니다.

해설 한복을 덜 입게 된 이유에 관해서는 언급되지 않았다.
어휘 identity [aidéntəti] 정체성   invasion [invéiʒən] 침입
be equipped with ~을 갖추다   residence [rézidəns] 주택, 거주지
similar [símələr] 비슷한

6 관계 추론 ①

W I'm so depressed, and I am losing weight, too.
M What's wrong?

W I got my test score, and it is the lowest grade that I've ever gotten.
M Oh, Kate. Cheer up. You know that grades will not completely decide your life.
W Thank you for saying that. Anyway, how about you? Did you do well on the test?
M Me? I didn't do well either. But the past is the past. Don't worry too much.

여 나 굉장히 우울하고 살도 빠지고 있어.
남 무슨 일인데?
여 시험 결과가 나왔는데, 내가 받는 것 중 가장 낮은 점수야.
남 저런, Kate, 힘내. 점수가 네 인생을 완전히 결정하지 않는다는 걸 너도 알잖아.
여 그렇게 말해줘서 고마워. 여하튼 넌 어때? 시험 잘 봤어?
남 나? 나도 성적이 좋지 않아. 그렇지만 지나간 건 지나간 거잖아. 너무 걱정하지 마.

해설 시험 결과에 대한 친구 사이의 대화이다.
어휘 completely [kəmplíːtli] 완전히   past [pæst] 과거

7 어색한 대화 찾기 ④

① W Excuse me. Is there a convenience store near here?
  M Yes, there's one within 2 minutes of here.
② W Why do you think he's attractive?
  M Because he has a lot of talent.
③ W Shall we go to see the movie *Shrek*?
  M Sorry. I've already seen it.
④ W Where is your English teacher from?
  M She teaches English to middle school students.
⑤ W How do you like today's special?
  M It tastes wonderful.

① 여 실례합니다만 근처에 편의점이 있나요?
  남 네, 걸어서 2분 거리에 있습니다.
② 여 왜 그가 매력적이라고 생각해?
  남 왜냐하면 재능이 많거든.
③ 여 영화 'Shrek' 보러 갈래?
  남 미안하지만, 난 이미 봤어.
④ 여 너희 영어 선생님은 어디 출신이시니?
  남 그녀는 중학생에게 영어를 가르치셔.
⑤ 여 오늘의 특별 메뉴는 어떤가요?
  남 매우 훌륭한 맛이네요.

해설 출신을 묻는 말에 중학생에게 영어를 가르친다고 답하는 것은 부자연스럽다.
어휘 attractive [ətræktiv] 매력적인   already [ɔːlrédi] 이미

8 부탁한 일 파악 ③

M Hi. I'm Alex Kim, and I'd like to report a missing dog. Here's a photo of my dog.
W When was the last time you saw your dog?
M About 3 hours ago.
W Well, 3 hours is not enough time to determine whether your dog is missing or not. You'll have to wait until this time tomorrow.
M What? It's been over 3 hours since I saw my dog.
W We can help you when you follow our policy.

남 안녕하세요, 제 이름은 Alex Kim인데요, 개의 실종 신고를 하고 싶습니

다. 여기 제 개의 사진입니다.
여 당신의 개를 본 마지막이 언제였죠?
남 약 3시간 전이요.
여 음, 3시간은 당신의 개가 실종인지 아닌지를 결정하기에 충분한 시간이 아닙니다. 내일 이 시간까지 기다리셔야 합니다.
남 뭐라구요? 제 개를 본지 세 시간 이상이 되어가고 있어요.
여 당신이 우리의 정책을 따를 때 우리가 당신을 도울 수 있습니다.

해설 정책을 따라야만 개를 찾는 것을 도울 수 있다고 하였다.
어휘 report [ripɔ́ːrt] 보고하다 determine [ditə́ːrmin] 결정하다

9 의도 파악 ②

W Dad, can I <u>borrow</u> <u>40 dollars</u> from you?
M I think you got your allowance from your mom a couple of days ago. You've already <u>run</u> <u>out</u> <u>of</u> <u>money</u>?
W Well, I bought a new pair of sneakers yesterday.
M You already have <u>several</u> <u>pairs</u> <u>of</u> <u>sneakers</u>.
W But they're out of style, and nobody wears them anymore.
M I think you just <u>wasted</u> <u>your</u> <u>money</u>. Here is 40 dollars, but there will be no next time.

여 아빠, 40달러만 빌려주실 수 있어요?
남 며칠 전에 엄마에게 용돈을 좀 받은 것 같은데. 벌써 다 썼어?
여 음, 어제 새 운동화를 샀어요.
남 이미 운동화 여러 켤레를 가지고 있잖아.
여 그건 유행이 지나서 아무도 그런 건 신지 않아요.
남 내 생각엔 그건 돈 낭비인 것 같구나. 여기 40달러야. 하지만 이번이 마지막이다.

해설 새 운동화를 사는데 용돈을 쓴 것에 대해 충고를 하고 있다.
어휘 sneaker [sníːkər] 운동화(주로 복수로 사용) run out of ~을 다 써버리다

10 숫자 정보 파악 ③

W How may I help you?
M Can I see that red tie <u>with</u> <u>white</u> <u>dots</u>?
W Sure. This tie is <u>high</u> <u>in</u> <u>demand</u> with young people. Is it a gift for someone?
M It's for a friend. How much is it?
W It's 30 dollars.
M I love it, but it's <u>a</u> <u>bit</u> <u>expensive</u> for me.
W Well, I'll give you a special discount of 20%. I hope your friendship <u>lasts</u> <u>a</u> <u>long</u> <u>time</u>.
M Thank you so much. Please wrap it as a gift.

여 무엇을 도와 드릴까요?
남 흰색 점이 있는 빨간 넥타이 좀 볼 수 있을까요?
여 물론이죠. 이 넥타이는 젊은이들에게 인기가 많습니다. 누군가를 위한 선물인가요?
남 네, 친구를 위한 거예요. 얼마인가요?
여 30달러입니다.
남 마음에 들지만 약간 비싸군요.
여 음, 제가 20% 특별 할인을 해드릴게요. 당신의 우정이 오래 지속되길 바랍니다.
남 정말 감사합니다. 선물 포장 부탁드리겠습니다.

해설 20% 할인된 금액으로 판매한다고 하였다.
어휘 dot [dɑt] 점 demand [dimǽnd] 수요 last [læst] 지속하다

11 할 일 파악 ③

M Hi, Christine. Where are you going?
W Hi, James. I'm <u>on</u> <u>my</u> <u>way</u> <u>home</u>.
M Home? I heard you are going to Jessy's party today.
W Yeah, but I have to <u>do</u> <u>some</u> <u>housework</u> before going to the party.
M What time do you think you <u>will</u> <u>be</u> <u>done</u>? I'll pick you up.
W That's great. I'll <u>send</u> <u>you</u> <u>a</u> <u>text</u> <u>message</u> when I'm done.

남 안녕, Christine. 어디 가는 길이니?
여 안녕, James. 집에 가고 있는 길이야.
남 집에? 오늘 Jessy의 파티에 네가 온다고 들었어.
여 맞아, 하지만 파티에 가기 전에 집안일을 좀 해야 해.
남 몇 시에 다 끝날 거 같아? 내가 데리러 갈게.
여 잘 됐네. 다 끝나면 문자 보낼게.

해설 파티에 가기 전에 집안일을 해야 한다고 하였다.

12 언급 유무 파악 ⑤

W Attention, please! Thank you for shopping at the Paradise Department Store. As a thank you to all our loyal customers, <u>we're</u> <u>having</u> <u>a</u> <u>surprise</u> <u>sale</u> of up to 70% off for the next three hours. On some products, if you buy one, you can get one free. Out-of-season items are 60% <u>off</u> <u>their</u> <u>original</u> <u>prices</u>. You can pay both in cash and with a credit card. But for items more than 50 percent off, you can pay only in cash. The items <u>are</u> <u>refundable</u> <u>within</u> 5 days of purchase if they are brought back in <u>their</u> <u>original</u> <u>condition</u>. Thank you.

여 안내 말씀 드립니다! Paradise 백화점을 이용해주셔서 감사합니다. 우리의 모든 단골 고객님들께 감사의 의미로 지금부터 3시간 동안 최대 70%를 할인하는 깜짝 할인을 실시합니다. 일부 제품은 한 개를 구입하시면 한 개를 공짜로 드립니다. 이월 상품은 원래 가격에서 60%를 할인합니다. 현금과 신용 카드로 지불하실 수 있습니다. 하지만 50% 이상 할인된 제품은 현금으로만 지불할 수 있습니다. 제품은 구입 후 5일 이내에 사용하지 않은 상태에서 환불 가능합니다. 감사합니다.

해설 교환 가능 조건에 관해서는 언급되지 않았다.
어휘 loyal [lɔ́iəl] 충실한 out-of-season 제철이 아닌 refundable [rifʌ́ndəbl] 환불 가능한

13 표 파악 ④

M Excuse me. I want to know <u>what</u> <u>sports</u> <u>classes</u> <u>you</u> <u>offer</u>.
W Okay. In the evening, we offer golf, swimming, and yoga, and in the morning, you can do fitness training and Pilates.
M How many times a week do you offer them?
W All <u>classes</u> <u>are</u> <u>held</u> two times a week. The evening classes are held on Monday and Thursday, and the morning classes take place on Tuesday and Friday.
M Okay. I will take the class that starts at 6 a.m.
W Thank you. <u>Fill</u> <u>out</u> <u>this</u> <u>registration</u> <u>form</u>, please.

남 실례합니다. 어떤 스포츠 수업을 제공하는지 알고 싶습니다.
여 네, 저녁에는 골프, 수영, 요가가 가능하며 아침에는 피트니스 트레이닝

과 필라테스를 이용하실 수 있습니다.
남 일주일에 몇 번이나 수업이 진행되나요?
여 모든 수업은 일주일에 두 번 열려요. 저녁 수업은 월요일과 목요일, 아침 수업은 화요일과 금요일이죠.
남 알겠습니다. 오전 6시에 시작하는 수업을 선택하겠습니다.
여 감사합니다. 등록 신청서를 작성해 주세요.

해설 오전 6시에 시작하는 강좌를 선택하겠다고 하였다.
어휘 offer [ɔ́(ː)fər] 제공하다

14 화제·주제 파악 ②

M This is a traditional Korean game, and it's usually played during Lunar New Year in Korea. To play this, you need a board, two different small tokens or marks, and four sticks. This is usually played with 2 partners or 2 teams. The goal of this game is to go around the board and to get all your team's tokens or marks to the starting position again. To move your token or mark, toss the four sticks together. You can move one of your tokens or marks 1 to 5 spaces depending on the result.

남 이 게임은 한국의 전통 게임으로, 보통 한국에서 음력설에 하는 놀이입니다. 이 게임을 하기 위해서는 보드, 두 가지 다른 말들, 그리고 4개의 막대가 필요합니다. 이것은 보통 두 명의 파트너 또는 두 팀과 함께 진행됩니다. 이 게임의 목표는 보드를 돌아서 팀의 모든 말들을 다시 시작 위치로 데려오는 것입니다. 말을 옮기려면, 4개의 막대기를 함께 던지십시오. 결과에 따라 당신의 말들 중 하나를 1칸에서 5칸을 움직일 수 있습니다.

해설 두 팀으로 나누어 4개의 막대를 던져서 하는 전통 놀이에 대한 설명이다.
어휘 lunar [lúːnər] 달의   token [tóukən] (보드 게임의) 말
toss [tɔːs] 던지다

15 할 일 파악 ①

W Hey, Jack. Why do you have such a serious look on your face?
M I can't find my wallet. I don't remember where I put it.
W Calm down. Let's start from the beginning. When was the last time you had it?
M I can't remember.
W Maybe you left it at the restaurant after lunch.
M No, I clearly remember putting it back in my pocket.
W Well, have you checked your car? It may have fallen out of your back pocket.
M No, I haven't.
W You should go there and check. There's a good chance that it is there.

여 Jack, 왜 그렇게 심각한 얼굴을 하고 있어?
남 지갑을 찾지 못하겠어. 어디에 뒀는지 기억이 안나.
여 침착해. 처음부터 생각해 보자. 지갑을 마지막으로 본 게 언제야?
남 기억이 안나.
여 아마, 점심 먹고 식당에 두고 온 것 같아.
남 아니야, 내 호주머니에 다시 넣은 것은 분명히 기억나.
여 음, 차는 확인해 봤니? 지갑이 호주머니에서 떨어졌을 수도 있잖아.
남 아니, 확인 안 해 봤어.
여 가서 확인해 봐. 지갑이 차에 있을 확률이 높아.

해설 호주머니에서 지갑이 떨어졌을 수도 있으니 먼저 차에 가보라고 조언을 하였다.
어휘 wallet [wάlit] 지갑

16 특정 정보 파악 ⑤

W Dad, I want to buy this novel. It looks interesting.
M *A Christmas Carol.* It is a classic novel. Do you know who wrote this book?
W Charles Dickens. Actually, I saw the author's name on the cover.
M Well, I think you should learn more about famous authors. You'll be in high school soon.
W I will, Dad. So could you buy another book for me?
M Which one?
W It's a comic book about the history of literature.
M Maybe next time. Let's just buy one at a time.
W Then I will choose the latter.

여 아빠, 저 이 소설책 사고 싶어요. 재미있어 보여요.
남 ≪크리스마스 캐롤≫이요. 고전 소설이구나. 이 책을 누가 썼는지 아니?
여 음… Charles Dickens. 사실 표지에서 작가의 이름을 봤어요.
남 유명한 작가에 대해서 더 많이 배울 필요가 있어. 너 곧 고등학생이잖아.
여 그럴게요, 아빠. 그럼 또 다른 책 한 권 사주실 수 있어요?
남 뭔데?
여 문학사에 관한 만화책이에요.
남 다음번에 사자. 한 번에 하나씩 사자.
여 그럼, 저는 후자를 고를게요.

해설 한 권만 사라는 아빠의 말에 후자를 선택하겠다고 하였다.
어휘 author [ɔ́ːθər] 작가   literature [lítərətʃùər] 문학   latter [lǽtər] 둘 중 후자의

17 적절한 응답 찾기 ⑤

M How can you speak English so fluently?
W I recommend that you practice speaking English as much as possible.
M Then how about words? It's difficult for me to memorize them.
W I write new words in my notebook and review them whenever I have time.
M You're awesome. Do you think that way will work for me?
W Just do it that way until you are comfortable. I'm sure it will work.
M I'll try it in your way and see if it works for me.

남 넌 어떻게 영어를 그렇게 유창하게 말할 수 있니?
여 가능한 영어로 말하는 연습을 많이 하길 추천해.
남 그럼 단어는? 나는 단어 외우는 게 너무 힘들어.
여 난 새로운 단어들을 공책에 쓰고 시간 날 때마다 복습해.
남 대단하네. 내게도 효과가 있을까?
여 그냥 익숙해질 때까지 해 봐. 분명 효과가 있을 거야.
남 너처럼 해 보고 내게 효과가 있는지 볼게.

해설 익숙할 때까지 해보라는 조언에 대한 가장 적절한 응답은 ⑤ '너처럼 해보고 내게 효과가 있는지 볼게.'이다.
① 얼마나 자주 영어를 공부하니?
② 난 네가 철자 맞추기의 달인이 될 거라고 확신해.
③ 난 단어를 공부할 시간이 없어.   ④ 영어 단어를 암기하는 게 어렵니?

어휘 fluently [flúːəntli] 유창하게

18 적절한 응답 찾기 ⑤

M Did I ever tell you that I saw BTS?
W No. What happened?
M I was walking down the street, when I saw a black van just parked on the side of the road. I was passing by the van, and then the van's door suddenly opened, and they jumped out of the van.
W Did you get their autographs or take any pictures with them?
M No. I couldn't do anything. I was scared stiff.
W What did you say? How could you waste such an opportunity?

남 내가 전에 BTS 본 거 이야기했었니?
여 아니. 무슨 일인데?
남 내가 거리를 걸어가는 중에 검정색 밴이 길 옆에 주차된 걸 봤어. 내가 그 밴을 지나칠 때 갑자기 문이 열렸고, 그들이 밴에서 뛰어 내렸어.
여 그들의 사인을 받았니? 아님 사진을 함께 찍었어?
남 아니, 아무 것도 못했어. 긴장해서 얼어버렸거든.
여 뭐라고? 어떻게 그런 기회를 놓칠 수가 있니?

해설 연예인을 만났지만 아무것도 못했다는 말에 대한 가장 적절한 응답은 ⑤ '뭐라고? 어떻게 그런 기회를 놓칠 수가 있니?'이다.
① 유감스럽게도 거기에 갈 수 없었어. ② 맞아! 식은 죽 먹기지.
③ 잘했어. 정말로 네게 잘됐어.
④ 괜찮게 들리는군요. 면허증을 좀 볼 수 있을까?
어휘 van [væn] 승합차   autograph [ɔ́ːtəgræf] 사인, 서명

19 적절한 응답 찾기 ④

M Which club do you want to join?
W I'm going to join the Green Students Society.
M The Green Students Society? What activities does the club do?
W Its members are engaged in protecting the environment.
M That sounds great. You must be interested in environmental problems.
W Yes. I think we need to do more to protect the environment.
M I couldn't agree with you more.

남 어떤 동아리에 가입하고 싶니?
여 난 Green Students Society에 가입할 거야.
남 Green Students Society? 그 동아리에서는 어떤 활동을 하는데?
여 동아리 회원들은 환경을 보호하는 일을 해.
남 멋지네. 너 환경 문제에 관심이 많구나.
여 응. 난 환경 보호를 위해 우리가 더 많이 힘써야 한다고 생각해.
남 나도 전적으로 동의해.

해설 환경 보호를 위해 더 많이 힘써야 한다는 말에 대한 가장 적절한 응답은 ④ '나도 전적으로 동의해.'이다.
① 그건 사실일 리 없어. ② 내가 그걸 할 수 있을지 의문이야.
③ 미안해. 다음번에 하자. ⑤ 네가 어떻게 느끼는지 알아.
어휘 be engaged in ~에 참여하다

20 상황에 맞는 말 찾기 ③

W Jason's mom is worried because she thinks something is extremely wrong about him. Recently, he gets up late, hurries to school, and goes to sleep during class. What is worse is that he doesn't do his homework on time. When she asks him why, he says that he seems to be addicted to mobile games. He is often scolded by his homeroom teacher and doesn't concentrate on his schoolwork. So his mother decides to advise him. In this situation, what would Jason's mom most likely say to him?

Mom Jason, you should stop playing games and go back to a normal life.

여 Jason의 엄마는 그에게 심각하게 문제가 있다고 생각을 하기 때문에, Jason을 걱정하고 있습니다. 최근에 그는 늦게 일어나고, 서둘러 학교에 가며, 수업 중에는 잠을 잡니다. 더 나쁜 것은, 그가 제시간에 숙제를 하지 않는다는 것입니다. 그녀가 그에게 이유를 물었을 때, 그는 그가 모바일 게임에 중독된 것 같다고 말합니다. 그는 종종 담임 선생님께 혼이 나고, 학업에 집중하지 못합니다. 그래서 그녀는 그에게 조언하기로 결정합니다. 이 상황에서 Jason의 엄마가 그에게 무엇이라고 말할까요?
엄마 Jason, 넌 게임을 그만 하고 정상적인 생활로 돌아와야 해.

해설 모바일 게임 때문에 늦잠을 자고, 학업을 소홀히 하는 Jason에게 할 수 있는 엄마의 조언으로 가장 적절한 것은 ③ '게임을 그만하고 정상적인 생활로 돌아와야 해.'이다.
① 얼마나 오랫동안 게임을 해왔니?
② 더 이상 컴퓨터를 사용할 수가 없어.
④ 보충 수업을 듣기 위해 학교에 좀 더 일찍 올 수 있겠니?
⑤ 나를 실망시키지 않은 적이 없구나. 너의 게임 중독에 대해 신경 쓰고 싶지 않아.
어휘 extremely [ikstríːmli] 매우   addicted [ədíktid] 중독된
scold [skould] 비난하다

Listen and Check   *p. 110*

Q1	False	Q11	False
Q2	No	Q12	No
Q3	False	Q13	3 classes
Q4	5 hours	Q14	True
Q5	No	Q15	No
Q6	the man	Q16	Yes
Q7	True	Q17	False
Q8	False	Q18	No
Q9	yesterday	Q19	True
Q10	Yes	Q20	False

해석
Q1 여자는 무늬 없는 컵이 비싸다고 생각한다.
Q2 여자는 오늘 도서관에 갈 것인가?
Q3 남자는 지금 당장 주문하고 싶어 한다.
Q4 진해에 도착하기까지 시간이 얼마나 걸릴까?
Q5 한국인들은 1980년대에 주로 전통 의상을 입었는가?
Q6 누가 긍정적인 태도를 지녔는가?
Q7 남자는 이미 영화를 보았다.
Q8 여자는 개의 실종 신고를 오늘 할 수 있다.
Q9 여자는 언제 새 운동화를 샀는가?
Q10 남자는 친구를 위해 넥타이를 샀는가?
Q11 여자는 집안일을 해야 하기 때문에 파티에 가지 않을 것이다.
Q12 세일 제품들은 현금으로만 구매할 수 있다.
Q13 저녁에는 몇 개의 수업이 열리는가?
Q14 사람들은 말들을 한 번에 여섯 칸씩 옮길 수 없다.

Q15 남자는 자기 지갑을 식당에 두고 왔다고 생각하는가?
Q16 여자는 만화책을 사기로 결정했는가?
Q17 남자는 영어 단어 외우는 것이 쉽다고 생각한다.
Q18 남자는 BTS와 사진을 찍었는가?
Q19 여자는 환경 동아리에 가입할 것이다.
Q20 Jason은 수업 중에 학교 공부에 집중한다.

실전 모의고사 **12회**
pp. 118~119

1 ④	2 ③	3 ④	4 ②	5 ③
6 ③	7 ②	8 ④	9 ④	10 ④
11 ②	12 ⑤	13 ②	14 ②	15 ④
16 ①	17 ②	18 ⑤	19 ②	20 ③

1 그림 정보 파악 ④

W We have to buy party hats for Jeff's birthday party.
M Here, we have different designs. Which one would be good for him?
W Since he likes robots, the hats with robot images would be good.
M That's a good idea. Is it better to buy the one with letters, too?
W Hmm... How about this one with the word "birthday"?
M That seems perfect for the party. Let's get this hat for Jeff.

여 Jeff의 생일 파티를 위해 파티 모자를 사야 해.
남 여기 다양한 디자인이 있어. 그에게 어떤 게 좋을까?
여 로봇을 좋아하니까 로봇 이미지가 있는 모자가 좋을 것 같아.
남 좋은 생각이야. 글자도 있는 것을 사는 게 나을까?
여 흠… 'birthday'라는 단어가 있는 이건 어때?
남 파티에 완벽한 것 같아. Jeff에게 이것을 사주자.

해설 로봇 이미지가 그려져 있고 'birthday'라는 단어가 적힌 것을 구입하자고 하였다.
어휘 letter [létər] 글자, 편지

2 목적 파악 ③

[Cellphone rings.]
M Jane, where are you? Are you on your way?
W I'm on the subway and am five stops away. It will take about twenty minutes. What about you?
M I'm on the bus and am just three stops away. The problem is that there is a traffic jam.
W Maybe it's because it's Saturday today. Do you think you will arrive on time?
M I think I will get there a bit late. Can we move our meeting time back by thirty minutes?
W Sure. I'll stay inside a coffee shop near our appointed meeting place.
M Okay. I'm so sorry. I'll try to get there faster.
W All right. See you later!

남 Jane, 어디야? 오는 중이야?
여 전철 안인데 다섯 정거장 남았어. 20분 정도 걸릴 거야. 너는?
남 나는 버스 안이고 세 정거장 남았어. 문제는 교통 체증이 있다는 거야.
여 아마도 오늘이 토요일이라서 그런 것 같아. 제 시간에 도착할 수 있을 것 같아?
남 조금 늦게 도착할 것 같아. 시간을 30분 늦춰도 될까?
여 물론이야. 우리 약속 장소에서 가까운 커피숍 안에 있을게.
남 그래. 정말 미안해. 더 빨리 도착하도록 할게.
여 알겠어. 나중에 봐!

해설 남자가 교통 체증으로 인해 늦을 것 같아서 약속 시간을 30분 늦추는 것이 괜찮은지 물어보았다.
어휘 away [əwéi] (거리가) 떨어져 on time 정각에, 시간을 어기지 않고

3 상황에 맞는 대화 찾기 ④

① M Why do we need a dictionary?
   W It has a complete definition of each word.
② M How many books should we read every month?
   W At least two.
③ M What's your challenge in your life?
   W It is to become a person who keeps my word.
④ M What should I do to speak English more fluently?
   W I recommend you often read books or watch movies in English.
⑤ M Where is the best place for you to study?
   W I study best inside my room.

① 남 우리는 왜 사전이 필요할까?
   여 각 단어의 완전한 뜻을 알 수 있거든.
② 남 매달 몇 권의 책을 읽어야 할까?
   여 최소한 두 권이야.
③ 남 너는 네 삶에서 도전이 뭐야?
   여 약속을 잘 지키는 사람이 되는 거야.
④ 남 영어를 더 유창하게 하려면 무엇을 해야 할까?
   여 영어로 된 책 또는 영화를 자주 볼 것을 추천해.
⑤ 남 네가 공부하기에 최고의 장소는 어디야?
   여 나는 내 방 안에서 가장 공부가 잘 돼.

해설 남자에게 영어를 공부하는 방법을 알려주고 있는 상황이다.
어휘 challenge [tʃælindʒ] 도전 keep one's word 약속을 지키다

4 특정 정보 파악 ②

[Cellphone rings.]
W Brian, do you know that we need to have a rehearsal for our play?
M Of course, I do. When will we have it?
W We should set the day and time now. Are you free on Monday?
M No, I'm not. There's a class I have to attend.
W How about on Wednesday?
M I'm available in the afternoon but not in the evening.
W I can also meet you in the afternoon. See you then!

여 Brian, 우리 연극을 위해 리허설을 해야 하는 거 알아?
남 물론 알지. 언제 하는 거야?
여 지금 요일이랑 시간을 정해야 해. 월요일에 시간 되니?
남 아니. 들어야 할 수업이 있어.
여 그럼 수요일은 어때?
남 오후에는 가능한데, 저녁에는 안 돼.
여 나도 오후에는 너를 만날 수 있어. 그럼 그 때 봐!

정답 및 해설

해설 수요일 오후에 둘 다 시간이 가능하다고 하였다.
어휘 rehearsal [rihə́:rsəl] 리허설, 예행연습 set [set] 정하다, 결정하다

5 언급 유무 파악 ③

W Hello. I'm Linda, a developer for a <u>delivery</u> <u>service</u> <u>application</u>. We made it to offer more convenient and faster delivery service for customers. Anyone over twelve years of age can sign up. If you <u>register</u> <u>your</u> <u>credit</u> <u>card</u>, you don't need to pay in cash to a deliveryman, but you can instead <u>pay</u> <u>through</u> the application online. We will also provide a discount coupon if you <u>write</u> <u>a</u> <u>review</u> for the service you get. Please contact us through the application when you have any questions. We really appreciate your support.

여 안녕하세요. 저는 배달 서비스 앱 개발자인 Linda입니다. 저희는 더 편하고 빠른 배달 서비스를 고객들에게 제공해 드리기 위해서 이것을 만들었습니다. 12살 이상의 어느 누구든지 가입이 가능합니다. 만약 신용 카드를 등록해 놓으시면 배달원에게 현금으로 지불하실 필요 없이 온라인으로 앱을 통해 지불하시면 됩니다. 제공되는 서비스에 리뷰를 써 주시면 할인 쿠폰을 제공해 드립니다. 더 문의 사항이 있으시면 앱을 통해 연락을 주시기를 바랍니다. 저희는 당신의 지지를 정말 감사해 합니다.

해설 카드를 등록하는 방법에 대해서는 구체적으로 언급되지 않았다.
어휘 developer [divéləpər] 개발자

6 관계 추론 ③

M Hi, Annie. You <u>have</u> <u>a</u> <u>checkup</u> today, right?

W That's right. I've worked out really hard this month, so I'm looking forward to seeing some positive results.

M Please stand on the machine and <u>hold</u> <u>the</u> <u>sticks</u> in each hand. [Pause] Okay, you're done. You can come down.

W How am I doing compared to the last time I was here?

M Wow. There's a decrease in <u>your</u> <u>body</u> <u>fat</u> by seven percent, and you gained a lot of muscle mass, too.

W I knew it! Recently, I have felt very <u>light</u> <u>and</u> <u>stronger</u>.

M I hope you exercise as hard as you did this month and achieve your goal soon!

남 안녕하세요, Annie씨. 오늘 신체 검진하는 날이죠?
여 맞아요. 이번 달에 정말 열심히 운동해서 긍정적인 결과를 기대해요.
남 기계에 올라 서주시고 양 손에 스틱을 잡아주세요. 네, 됐습니다. 내려오셔도 됩니다.
여 여기 마지막으로 왔을 때와 비교해서 제가 어떤가요?
남 와. 체지방이 7퍼센트 가량 감소했고 근육량도 많이 증가했는걸요.
여 그럴 줄 알았어요! 최근에 정말 가볍고 튼튼해진 기분이었거든요.
남 이번 달 열심히 하신 것만큼 운동하셔서 곧 목표를 달성하시길 바라요!

해설 신체 검진을 받고 운동을 열심히 해서 체지방을 감소시키고 근육량을 늘렸다고 하였다.
어휘 checkup [tʃékʌ̀p] 검진 work out 운동하다 compare [kəmpέər] 비교하다 gain [gein] 얻다 muscle [mʌ́sl] 근육 mass [mæs] 덩어리 achieve [ətʃíːv] 달성하다

7 어색한 대화 찾기 ②

① M <u>What's</u> <u>your</u> <u>role</u> in the movie?
  W I play the queen of England.
② M I feel blue today.
  W I like <u>the</u> <u>color</u> <u>blue</u>, too.
③ M I need a spare memory card for my camera.
  W Let's go to the mall and buy one.
④ M Let's <u>get</u> <u>a</u> <u>map</u> of the zoo over there.
  W We don't need one. I know the way.
⑤ M Are you attending Jenny's wedding?
  W Of course. I'm <u>her</u> <u>best</u> <u>friend</u>.

① 남 영화에서 너의 역할이 뭐야?
  여 나는 영국의 여왕을 연기해.
② 남 오늘 나 울적해.
  여 나도 파란색 좋아해.
③ 남 내 카메라에 여분의 메모리 카드가 필요해.
  여 쇼핑몰 가서 하나 사자.
④ 남 저기서 동물원 지도를 가져오자.
  여 필요 없어. 내가 길을 알아.
⑤ 남 너 Jenny의 결혼식에 가니?
  여 당연하지. 난 그녀의 가장 친한 친구인걸.

해설 울적하다는 남자의 말에 파랑색을 좋아한다고 답하는 것은 부자연스럽다.
어휘 play [plei] 연기하다 feel blue 울적함을 느끼다

8 부탁한 일 파악 ④

M Wow. What is <u>that</u> <u>big</u> <u>painting</u>? It looks cool with all the plants on it.

W I ordered it online and just opened it.

M I see. Where are you going to hang it? Can you do it <u>by</u> <u>yourself</u>?

W I'm planning to hang it on the wall. But since it's quite big, it's hard for me to do it by myself. Could you <u>give</u> <u>me</u> <u>a</u> <u>hand</u>?

M Sure. Please give me a nail and a hammer.

W You're <u>a</u> <u>big</u> <u>help</u>. Thank you.

M Don't mention it.

남 우와. 저 큰 그림은 뭐야? 식물 그림들이 멋있네.
여 온라인으로 주문하고 방금 뜯었어.
남 그렇구나. 어디에 걸려고? 혼자 할 수 있겠어?
여 벽에 걸려고 해. 그런데 크기가 꽤 커서 혼자 걸기가 어려워. 날 도와줄 수 있겠니?
남 물론이지. 못이랑 망치는 내게 줘.
여 정말 큰 도움이 된다. 고마워.
남 천만에.

해설 여자가 남자에게 그림을 벽에 거는 것을 도와달라고 요청하였다.
어휘 hang [hæŋ] (벽에) 걸다, 매달다 actually [ǽktʃuəli] 사실은 balance [bǽləns] 균형을 잡다 nail [neil] 못 hammer [hǽmər] 망치

9 의도 파악 ④

W Did you <u>hear</u> <u>the</u> <u>news</u>?
M What news?
W Sarah didn't <u>do</u> <u>very</u> <u>well</u> on the exam.
M Really? But she is a good student. What happened to her?

W She fought with her best friend, and she hasn't been able to <u>concentrate</u> in <u>class</u> recently.
M That's too bad. I hope she <u>makes</u> <u>up</u> <u>with</u> the friend she had a fight with.

여 너 그 소식 들었어?
남 어떤 소식?
여 Sarah가 이번 시험을 망쳤대.
남 정말? 그녀는 공부를 정말 잘하잖아. 분명 이유가 있을 거야. 분명 이유가 있을 거야.
여 그녀는 가장 친한 친구와 싸워서 최근에 수업에 집중할 수 없었대.
남 그것 참 안 됐다. 그녀가 싸운 친구와 화해하기를 바랄게.

해설 남자가 Sarah의 상황에 관해 안쓰러워하였고 화해하기를 바란다고 하였다.
어휘 fight with ~와 싸우다   recently [ríːsəntli] 최근에   make up with ~와 화해하다

10 숫자 정보 파악 ④

M Good afternoon. How can I help you?
W I'm looking for some paint <u>for</u> <u>wooden</u> <u>furniture</u>.
M Then I recommend <u>this</u> <u>ecofriendly</u> <u>paint</u>. It dries quickly and smells good.
W How much is it?
M For four hundred milliliters, it <u>costs</u> <u>twelve</u> <u>dollars</u>, and for seven hundred milliliters, it's twenty dollars.
W I'll take two four-hundred-milliliter cans of white paint and one seven-hundred-milliliter can of green paint.
M Okay. Do you <u>have</u> <u>a</u> <u>coupon</u>?
W Here, I have a two-dollar coupon.

남 안녕하세요. 무엇을 도와드릴까요?
여 원목 가구를 위한 페인트를 찾고 있어요.
남 그렇다면 이 친환경 페인트를 추천합니다. 빨리 마르고 냄새가 좋아요.
여 얼마인가요?
남 400ml는 12달러이고, 700ml는 20달러입니다.
여 400ml 하얀색 페인트 2개하고 700ml 초록색 페인트 하나 주세요.
남 알겠습니다. 쿠폰 가지고 계신 게 있나요?
여 여기 2달러 쿠폰이 있습니다.

해설 400ml 두 개에 24달러이고, 700ml 한 개에 20달러인데 2달러 쿠폰을 제시하였다.
어휘 wooden [wúdən] 원목의, 나무로 된   ecofriendly [ékoufréndli] 친환경적인

11 할 일 파악 ②

M Today will be <u>a</u> <u>long</u> <u>day</u> for me.
W Why is that? Did your team take on a new project?
M Yes. We have to <u>plan</u> <u>an</u> <u>advertisement</u> for a new product.
W That sounds tiring. You'll probably have many meetings, right?
M That's right. That <u>always</u> <u>happens</u> whenever a new product is released.
W But how lucky you are to have work to do!
M I know. I'm really grateful for my job although it is <u>stressful</u> <u>and</u> <u>tiring</u> sometimes.

남 오늘은 힘든 하루가 될 거야.
여 왜? 너희 팀이 새로운 프로젝트 맡았어?
남 응. 신상품 광고 기획을 해야 해.

여 피곤할 것 같다. 회의도 많을 거잖아, 그렇지?
남 맞아. 신상품이 출시되면 늘 이렇지.
여 하지만 할 수 있는 일이 있다는 건 복 받은 거야!
남 나도 알아. 가끔 스트레스도 많고 피곤하긴 해도 내 직업을 감사히 여겨.

해설 신상품에 대한 광고 기획을 해야 한다고 하였다.
어휘 take on 떠맡다   advertisement [ædvərtáizmənt] 광고   tiring [táiəriŋ] 피곤하게 만드는, 피곤한   stressful [strésfəl] 스트레스가 많은

12 언급 유무 파악 ⑤

M Hello, everyone. I'm Adrian Nelson, the host of the Reality Exhibition. Thank you for taking your time to attend <u>the</u> <u>opening</u> event. The Reality Exhibition, as the name indicates, focuses on <u>the</u> <u>reality</u> <u>of</u> <u>our</u> <u>society</u>. Eight artists participated in the exhibition, and the type of artwork they produced varies. You can enjoy different kinds of art in <u>every</u> <u>corner</u>. The exhibition will last <u>for</u> <u>a</u> <u>week</u>, so please feel free to come as many times as you want. Thank you.

남 안녕하세요, 여러분. 저는 Reality Exhibition의 주최자인 Adrian Nelson입니다. 오프닝 행사에 참여해주시는 데에 시간을 할애해주셔서 감사합니다. The Reality Exhibition은 이름이 보여주듯이 우리 사회의 현실에 대해 이야기합니다. 8명의 작가가 전시회에 참여하였고 그들의 작품의 종류들은 모두 다릅니다. 모든 코너에서 다양한 작품을 즐기실 수 있습니다. 전시회는 일주일간 지속이 될 것이니 원하는 횟수만큼 방문해 주세요. 감사합니다.

해설 다양한 예술 작품이 있다고 했지만 어떤 종류가 있는지에 관해서는 언급되지 않았다.
어휘 host [houst] 주최자, 진행자   indicate [índəkèit] 보여주다, 나타내다   society [səsáiəti] 사회   last [læst] 지속되다

13 표 파악 ②

M Good afternoon. What kind of coffee beans are you looking for?
W I bought coffee beans with a vanilla flavor here before, but I want to <u>try</u> <u>something</u> <u>else</u> this time.
M Which do you prefer, beans with <u>a</u> <u>light</u> <u>or</u> <u>dark</u> taste?
W I like beans with a light taste better.
M Then how about these beans from Colombia? They are light and have <u>a</u> <u>caramel</u> <u>flavor</u>.
W Isn't that too sweet?
M Not really. You can enjoy <u>a</u> <u>smooth</u> <u>taste</u> that is not too sweet.
W Then I'll take them.

남 안녕하세요. 어떤 종류의 커피 원두를 찾으시나요?
여 전에 바닐라 맛이 나는 커피 원두를 구입했고 이번엔 다른 것을 맛보고 싶어요.
남 가벼운 맛과 진한 맛 중에서 어떤 걸 선호하시나요?
여 저는 가벼운 걸 더 좋아해요.
남 그렇다면 콜롬비아에서 온 이 원두는 어떠세요? 가볍고 캐러멜 향이 나요.
여 너무 달지 않은가요?
남 그렇지는 않아요. 너무 달지 않은 부드러운 맛을 즐길 수 있으실 겁니다.
여 그걸로 살게요.

해설 가벼운 것을 좋아하고 콜롬비아산에서 오는 캐러멜 향이 나는 콜롬비

아산 원두를 산다고 하였다.

어휘 coffee beans 커피 원두   flavor [fléivər] 맛

14 화제·주제 파악 ②

W This is mostly used in summer. It looks like a donut and has a small hole in it. If we blow air into the hole, it inflates and becomes big. It can float on the water, so if we use it, it can help us float on the water. There are various shapes for kids like dolphins and flamingos. This is also useful for adults who can't swim.

여 이것은 주로 여름에 사용됩니다. 도넛처럼 생겼고 위에 작은 구멍이 하나 있습니다. 만약 우리가 그 구멍에 공기를 불어 넣으면, 부풀어 오르고 커집니다. 이것은 물에 뜰 수 있어서 우리가 우리를 이것에 끼워 넣으면 물에 뜨도록 도와줍니다. 돌고래와 플라밍고와 같이 아이들을 위한 다양한 모양이 있습니다. 수영을 못하는 성인들에게 유용합니다.

해설 공기를 불어 넣으면 부풀어 오르고 물에 뜨도록 해주는 것이라고 하였다.

어휘 mostly [móustli] 주로, 일반적으로   blow [blou] (입으로) 불다   inflate [infléit] 부풀다   float [flout] (물에) 뜨다   useful [júːsfəl] 유용한

15 할 일 파악 ④

W Rio, what are you thinking about?

M I am thinking about some things to do when I take a year off after this semester.

W Why are you doing that?

M I've been planning to do it for a long time. I want to improve my English skills and take a trip to Europe.

W You must be serious about the matter.

M I am. I'm going to go to the administration office to submit an application for a leave of absence from school now.

여 Rio, 무슨 생각해?

남 이번 학기 이후에 1년 쉬면서 할 것들에 대해서 생각 중이었어.

여 왜 쉬려는 거야?

남 오랫동안 계획해 온 거야. 난 영어 실력도 향상시키고 싶고 유럽으로 여행도 가고 싶어.

여 넌 그 문제에 대해 진지하게 생각해야 해.

남 난 지금 진지해. 난 휴학계를 내기 위해 지금 행정실에 갈 거야.

해설 영어 실력을 향상시키고 유럽으로 여행을 가기 위해 휴학계를 내러 행정실에 갈 거라고 하였다.

어휘 take a year off 1년 휴학하다   apply for 신청하다   leave of absence 휴학   administration office 행정실

16 특정 숫자 파악 ①

M How's the weather tomorrow?

W It will rain. Why are you asking about the weather?

M I'm going to go jogging tomorrow morning, but I haven't decided what time to go out.

W You'd better finish jogging by 11:00 a.m. The weather forecast says it will start to rain by that time.

M What time is okay?

W How about jogging first thing in the morning? I heard exercising on an empty stomach is much better.

M Then I'll just go jogging at 7:00 a.m. and have breakfast after I go back home.

W Great.

남 내일 날씨가 어떻지?

여 비가 내릴 거야. 날씨는 왜 물어보는 거야?

남 내일 아침에 조깅을 하러 가려고 하는데 아직 몇 시에 나갈지 안 정했거든.

여 오전 11시에는 조깅을 끝내는 게 좋겠어. 일기 예보에서 그 시간쯤에 비가 내리기 시작한다고 하거든.

남 몇 시가 좋을까?

여 일어나자마자 조깅하는 건 어때? 내가 듣기로 공복에 운동하는 게 더 좋대.

남 그렇다면 그냥 7시에 조깅을 하고 돌아와서 아침을 먹어야겠다.

여 좋아.

해설 7시에 조깅을 간다고 하였다.

어휘 go jogging 조깅을 하다   weather forecast 일기 예보   empty stomach 공복

17 적절한 응답 찾기 ②

M Excuse me. Can I have a few minutes of your time?

W Sure. What can I do for you?

M I'm a member of a charity named Clean Water in Africa. My organization is currently accepting donations to provide African children with food and clean water.

W I see. I know there is a shortage of clean water in Africa.

M Yes. Many Africans are dying because of it. Are you willing to donate to our charity?

W I'd love to, but I can't.

M May I ask you why?

W I'm already sponsoring another organization.

남 실례지만 시간을 좀 내주실 수 있을까요?

여 물론이죠. 무엇 때문에 그러시죠?

남 저는 Clean Water in Africa라는 자선 단체의 회원이에요. 저희 단체가 현재 아프리카 아이들이 음식을 먹고 깨끗한 물을 마실 수 있도록 기부를 하고 있거든요.

여 그렇군요. 아프리카에서 깨끗한 물이 부족하다는 것은 잘 알고 있어요.

남 네. 많은 아프리카 사람들이 그로 인해 죽어가고 있지요. 저희 자선 단체에 기부를 하실 의향이 있으신가요?

여 그러고 싶지만 할 수 없어요.

남 이유를 물어도 될까요?

여 제가 이미 다른 기관을 후원하고 있어서요.

해설 기부를 할 수 없는 이유를 묻는 말에 대한 가장 적절한 응답은 ② '제가 이미 다른 기관을 후원하고 있어서요.'이다.

① 아니, 그건 옳지 않아요. 다시 생각해 봐요.

③ 진짜로 무슨 일이 정말로 일어났는지 기억이 안 나요.

④ 누군가에게 도움이 된다는 건 정말 의미가 있어요.

⑤ 그 기관에 데려다 줄게요. 함께 가요.

어휘 be willing to ~할 의향이 있다   sponsor [spάnsər] 후원하다

18 적절한 응답 찾기 ⑤

M We only have a few months until we graduate.

W Time really flies.

M Exactly. We should think of what field we will specialize in and what university to enter.

W What are you going to major in?

M I'm going to major in biotechnology. I'm really

interested in this field.

W That means you've already made some plans for the future, right?

M Not really. I will figure out what I can do with my major while I am at college. What about you?

W Well, I don't know what I really want to do. I'm worried about my future.

M It's not too late to find your interest during college.

남 졸업까지 몇 개월 밖에 안 남았네.

여 시간이 정말 빨리 간다.

남 맞아. 어떤 분야를 전공할지 그리고 어떤 대학교에 갈지 생각을 해야 해.

여 너는 무엇을 전공할 거야?

남 나는 생명 공학을 전공할 거야. 이 분야에 관심이 많거든.

여 그 말은 네 미래에 대해 이미 계획이 있다는 뜻이네, 그렇지?

남 다는 아니야. 내 전공으로 무엇을 할지는 대학을 다니면서 알아내야지. 너는?

여 글쎄, 난 내가 진짜 무엇을 원하는지를 모르겠어. 내 미래가 걱정돼.

남 대학교에 가서 하고 싶은 것을 찾아도 늦지 않아.

해설 원하는 것이 무엇인지 모르겠고 미래가 걱정된다는 말에 대한 가장 적절한 응답은 ⑤ '대학교에 가서 하고 싶은 것을 찾아도 늦지 않아.'이다.

① 네가 진짜로 하고 싶은 게 뭔지 내게 말해도 돼.

② 어떻게 그 과목을 낙제할 수 있는 거지?

③ 오늘 밤에 네 과제를 끝내는 걸 도와줄 수 있어.

④ 지금 네가 하는 것은 전혀 도움이 안 돼.

어휘 specialize in ~을 전공하다 major in ~을 전공하다 biotechnology [bàiouteknáləʤi] 생명 공학

19 적절한 응답 찾기 ②

M Hi. Let me have a one-way ticket to Daegu, please.

W What time do you want to leave? There is a train that departs in thirty minutes, and the next one leaves two hours from now.

M I'd like to take the former one.

W But since all the seats are sold out, only standing-room-only tickets are available. Is that okay with you?

M There are no seats at all on the train?

W There's some space in the area connecting each train, but it'll be hard for you to sit there.

M Are there any seats available on the next train?

W Yes, there are many empty seats.

남 안녕하세요. 대구로 가는 편도 티켓 하나 주세요.

여 몇 시를 원하시나요? 30분 뒤에 출발하는 게 있고 다른 건 2시간 뒤에 여기 도착합니다.

남 전자를 원합니다.

여 하지만 모든 좌석이 매진되어서 오직 입석만 가능해요. 괜찮으신가요?

남 기차 안에 좌석이 아예 없나요?

여 출입문 옆에 공간이 좀 있기는 하지만 앉기 어려우실 거예요.

남 그렇다면 다음 열차는 가능한 좌석이 있나요?

여 네, 빈 좌석이 많이 있어요.

해설 다음 열차에 앉을 수 있는 좌석이 있냐고 묻는 말에 대한 가장 적절한 응답은 ② '네, 빈 좌석이 많이 있어요.'이다.

① 무엇이 당신에 대해서 아무에게도 말하지 마세요.

③ 내일 다시 와주세요.

④ 일어난 일에 대해서 아무에게도 말하지 마세요.

⑤ 지금 열차를 타려면 서둘러야 해요.

어휘 one-way 편도의 former [fɔ́:rmər] 전자의

20 상황에 맞는 말 찾기 ③

M Harry goes down the escalator to take the subway and sees a foreign couple on the platform. They are carrying luggage and are wearing big backpacks. They seem to be tourists. They are looking at a big map on the wall, but they look confused. Harry thinks they might need some help finding their way. In this situation, what would Harry most likely say to the couple?

Harry Excuse me. Is there anything I can help you with?

남 Harry는 지하철을 타기 위해 에스컬레이터를 타고 내려갔고 한 외국인 커플이 승강장에 있는 것을 보았습니다. 그들은 손에 수화물을 가지고 있고 큰 배낭을 메고 있었습니다. 그들은 관광객인 듯 보였습니다. 그들은 벽에 있는 큰 지도를 보고 있었지만 혼란스러워 하는 것처럼 보였습니다. Harry는 그들이 길을 찾는 데에 도움이 필요할 거라고 생각했습니다. 이 상황에서 Harry는 그 커플에게 뭐라고 말을 할까요?

Harry 실례합니다. 제가 도와드릴 게 있을까요?

해설 길을 잃어 도움이 필요해 보이는 커플을 발견한 상황에서 Harry가 할 수 있는 가장 적절한 말은 ③ '제가 도와드릴 게 있을까요?'이다.

① 옆으로 비켜주시겠습니까?

② 길을 찾는 것을 도와주시겠습니까?

④ 당신의 물건을 조심하는 게 좋겠어요.

⑤ 여기서 시청을 어떻게 가야 하나요?

어휘 platform [plǽtfɔ:rm] 승강장 luggage [lʌ́giʤ] 수화물, 짐 tourist [tú(:)rist] 관광객 step aside 옆으로 비키다

Listen and Check
p. 120

Q1	robots	Q11	False
Q2	False	Q12	for a week
Q3	read books	Q13	No
Q4	Monday	Q14	True
Q5	False	Q15	to study English
Q6	No	Q16	Yes
Q7	False	Q17	True
Q8	on the wall	Q18	their future plan
Q9	a fight with a friend	Q19	Yes
Q10	No	Q20	finding their way

해석

Q1 Jeff는 무엇에 관심이 있는가?

Q2 남자는 약속한 장소에 제시간에 도착할 것이다.

Q3 여자는 영어 능력을 향상시키기 위해 남자가 무엇을 할 것을 추천하는가?

Q4 여자는 언제 수업에 참석해야 하는가?

Q5 고객이 배달 서비스에 대한 후기를 쓰면 한 번의 무료 배달이 제공된다.

Q6 여자는 자신의 신체 검진 결과에 실망하는가?

Q7 남자는 기분이 좋은 상태이다.

Q8 여자는 그림을 어디에 걸 계획인가?

Q9 Sarah는 어떤 문제를 가지고 있는가?

Q10 여자는 벽에 페인트를 칠하려고 계획 중인가?

Q11 남자와 여자는 광고 프로젝트의 팀 멤버이다.

Q12 전시회는 얼마나 지속될 것인가?

Q13 여자는 단 맛을 선호하는가?

Q14 성인과 아이 모두 물에 뜨기 위해 이것을 사용할 수 있다.

정답 및 해설

Q15 남자는 왜 1년동안 휴학을 하고 싶어 하는가?
Q16 남자는 내일 여전히 조깅을 하러 갈 것인가?
Q17 여자는 그 자선 단체에 기부를 하지 않을 것이다.
Q18 남자와 여자는 무엇에 대해 얘기를 하고 있는가?
Q19 남자에게 대구로 가는 길에 자리에 앉는 것이 중요한가?
Q20 그 관광객들은 어떤 도움이 필요한 것처럼 보이는가?

실전 모의고사 13회
pp. 128~129

1 ②	2 ④	3 ④	4 ②	5 ④
6 ④	7 ③	8 ④	9 ③	10 ③
11 ④	12 ④	13 ⑤	14 ②	15 ④
16 ①	17 ④	18 ⑤	19 ④	20 ②

1 그림 정보 파악 ②

W Hello. What kinds of a cover are you looking for?
M I want to buy a cover for my tablet PC.
W We have two types, one that fully covers the tablet and another that has a keyboard attached to it.
M I prefer one without a keyboard. Do you have one with any small images on?
W Sorry, but we don't. But we have one with letters.
M Then I'll just take a plain white one.
W Okay.

여 안녕하세요. 어떤 종류의 커버를 찾으시나요?
남 태블릿 PC를 위한 커버를 사고 싶어요.
여 두 가지 종류가 있는데 하나는 태블릿을 전체적으로 덮어주는 것이고 다른 하나는 키보드가 부착되어있는 것이랍니다.
남 키보드가 없는 게 더 좋아요. 위에 작은 그림이 있는 것이 있나요?
여 죄송하지만 없습니다. 하지만 글자가 적힌 건 있어요.
남 그렇다면 그냥 무늬 없는 하얀색으로 살게요.
여 알겠습니다.

해설 무늬가 없는 기본형 커버를 구입한다고 하였다.
어휘 fully [fúli] 완전히 basic [béisik] 기본의

2 부탁한 일 파악 ④

W Hi. Thank you so much for coming to the autograph event.
M I'm a big fan of your group.
W We're so grateful for our fans' love.
M May I ask a favor of you?
W What is it?
M Could I get your autograph on my T-shirt?
W I'd be glad to do that for you.

여 안녕하세요. 팬 사인회에 와주신 분들께 정말 감사합니다.
남 저 당신 그룹의 열혈 팬이에요.
여 팬들의 사랑에 정말 감사해 한답니다.
남 부탁 하나만 해도 될까요?
여 무엇인데요?
남 제 티셔츠에 사인을 해주실 수 있나요?
여 기꺼이 그렇게 해드릴게요.

해설 남자가 여자가 속한 그룹의 열혈 팬이며 티셔츠에 사인해 줄 것을 부탁하였다.
어휘 autograph event 사인회 big fan 열혈 팬

3 그림 상황 파악 ④

① W Don't park your car in front of the gate.
   M What's wrong with that?
② W I can tell it's a really popular restaurant.
   M Yes. The parking lot is already full.
③ W How much should I pay for parking?
   M It's five dollars for an hour.
④ W Excuse me, sir. This parking space is only for the disabled.
   M Sorry. I read the sign wrong.
⑤ W You must stop your car when people are walking in the crosswalk.
   M I know. I was just rushed.

① 여 정문 앞에 주차하지 마.
   남 뭐가 어때서?
② 여 정말 인기가 많은 음식점인 걸 알겠네.
   남 응. 주차장이 이미 꽉 찼어.
③ 여 주차비로 얼마를 지불해야 하나요?
   남 한 시간에 5달러입니다.
④ 여 실례합니다. 이 주차 공간은 장애인들을 위한 곳입니다.
   남 죄송해요. 제가 표지를 잘못 읽었네요.
⑤ 여 사람들이 횡단보도를 건널 때에는 차를 멈춰야 해.
   남 나도 알아. 내가 조금 급했어.

해설 장애인 주차 구역에 주차하여 주차 요원에게 제지당하고 있는 상황이다.
어휘 disabled [diséibld] 장애를 가진 crosswalk [krɔ́(:)swɔ̀:k] 횡단보도 rushed [rʌʃt] 성급히 한, 서두른

4 숫자 정보 파악 ②

W How are your preparations for the speech for the seminar tomorrow going?
M They're going fine. I think I can do well since I've been practicing a lot.
W That's great. The audience will love your speech. By the way, what time does it start?
M It starts at 3:00 p.m.
W I will get there earlier than that.
M Okay. Could you call me an hour before the seminar?
W Sure. But why?
M I want to calm myself down while talking to you on the phone.

여 내일 세미나를 위한 연설 준비는 어떻게 되어가?
남 잘 되어가고 있어. 연습한 만큼 잘 할 수 있을 것 같아.
여 잘됐네. 청중들은 너의 연설을 좋아할 거야. 그런데 몇 시에 시작이지?
남 오후 3시에 시작해.
여 난 그 이전에 도착할거야.
남 알겠어. 세미나 시작 1시간 전에 나한테 전화를 해줄 수 있을까?
여 물론이지. 그런데 왜?
남 너랑 얘기하면서 긴장을 풀고 싶거든.

해설 남자는 여자에게 세미나 시작 1시간 전에 전화해 줄 것을 부탁하였고, 세미나는 오후 3시에 시작한다고 하였다.
어휘 preparation [prèpəréiʃən] 준비 calm down 긴장을 풀다, 진정

60

하다

5 언급 유무 파악 ④

W It's been a long time since we came to <u>the</u> <u>bookstore</u>.

M You're right. We were too busy to come here. Look at this! The book is about J.K. Rowling.

W She's my <u>favorite</u> <u>author</u>. I really love her books, especially the *Harry Potter* series.

M I can't agree more. Do you know how she came to write them?

W No, I don't. How could she make all those stories?

M She said the story suddenly <u>came</u> <u>to</u> <u>her</u> <u>mind</u> while she was waiting for a train at the station.

W That's awesome! I think she is one of the <u>best</u> <u>fantasy</u> <u>writers</u> in the world.

여 서점에 오랜만에 온다.

남 맞아. 우리는 여기 오기엔 너무 바빴어. 이것 봐! J. K. Rowling에 대한 책이야.

여 그녀는 내가 가장 좋아하는 작가야. 난 그녀의 책을 정말 좋아해. 특히 ≪해리포터≫ 시리즈 말이야.

남 완전 동의해. 어떻게 그녀가 그걸 쓰게 되었는지 알고 있어?

여 아니, 몰라. 어떻게 그 이야기를 만들게 되었는데?

남 그녀가 말하기를 기차역에서 열차를 기다리는 동안 갑자기 이야기가 머리에 떠올랐대.

여 엄청난걸! 나는 그녀가 세계 최고의 판타지 작가 중 한 명이라고 생각해.

[해설] 작가의 가족에 관해서는 언급되지 않았다.

[어휘] especially [ispéʃəli] 특히, 유난히 suddenly [sʌ́dnli] 갑자기
come to one's mind 머리에 떠오르다

6 장소 추론 ④

M Hi. How can I help you?

W I've <u>had</u> <u>a</u> <u>headache</u> since last night. I also have a fever.

M Well, I think you might have a cold.

W I guess it's due to <u>the</u> <u>air</u> <u>conditioner</u> at my workplace. It runs all day.

M Take these pills. You will <u>feel</u> <u>much</u> <u>better</u>.

W Thank you so much.

남 안녕하세요. 어떻게 도와드릴까요?

여 어젯밤부터 머리가 아파요. 그리고 열도 있고요.

남 음, 제 생각엔 감기 기운이 있으신 것 같네요.

여 직장에 있는 에어컨 때문인 것 같아요. 하루 종일 가동시키거든요.

남 이 알약을 복용하세요. 훨씬 나아지실 거예요.

여 감사합니다.

[해설] 여자가 증상에 대해 이야기하고 있고 남자가 약을 복용할 것을 권하는 상황이다.

[어휘] fever [fíːvər] 열 run [rʌn] 작동시키다

7 어색한 대화 찾기 ③

① M You're <u>addicted</u> to computer games.

　 W I am, and so are you.

② M I <u>feel</u> <u>so</u> <u>guilty</u> about saying something bad to my brother.

　 W You'd better apologize to him.

③ M Are you aware of the dangers of energy drinks?

W You can <u>relieve</u> <u>your</u> <u>stress</u> with them.

④ M What are some fun things to do on a rainy day?

　 W You can <u>listen</u> <u>to</u> <u>music</u> and read a book.

⑤ M It's obvious that he likes you.

　 W No way. Don't <u>make</u> <u>up</u> <u>stories</u>.

① 남 넌 컴퓨터 게임에 중독됐어.

　 여 맞아, 너도 마찬가지야.

② 남 내 동생한테 나쁜 말 한 것에 대해 죄책감을 느껴.

　 여 동생에게 사과해.

③ 남 에너지 음료수의 위험성에 대해 알고 있어?

　 여 너의 스트레스를 덜어줄 수 있어.

④ 남 비 오는 날 할 수 있는 재밌는 게 뭐가 있을까?

　 여 음악 듣고 책을 읽으면 되지.

⑤ 남 그가 너를 좋아하는 게 분명해.

　 여 말도 안 돼. 지어내지 마.

[해설] 에너지 음료의 위험성에 대해 알고 있냐고 묻는 말에 스트레스를 덜어준다고 답하는 것은 부자연스럽다.

[어휘] be addicted to ~에 중독되다 guilty [gílti] 죄책감을 느끼는
apologize [əpálədʒàiz] 사과하다 relieve [rilíːv] 덜어주다, 없애주다
obvious [ábviəs] 분명한, 확실한 make up 만들어 내다, 지어내다

8 부탁한 일 파악 ④

M Suji, <u>what's</u> <u>the</u> <u>hurry</u>?

W The free gift event is <u>about</u> <u>to</u> <u>finish</u>.

M What is the free gift?

W It's a refrigerator.

M I wish <u>you</u> <u>good</u> <u>luck</u>.

W By the way, do you <u>have</u> <u>an</u> <u>account</u> on this website?

M No. I'm not a member of it.

W Could you make one for me so that I can <u>double</u> <u>our</u> <u>chance</u> <u>of</u> <u>winning</u>?

M No problem.

남 수지야, 왜 그렇게 급해 보여?

여 무료 경품 행사가 곧 끝나거든.

남 무료 경품이 뭔데?

여 냉장고야.

남 행운을 빌어.

여 그런데 너 이 웹사이트에 계정 있어?

남 아니. 난 회원이 아니야.

여 당첨 기회가 두 배가 될 수 있게 날 위해 행사에 참여해 주면 안 될까?

남 문제될 거 없지.

[해설] 여자가 남자에게 웹사이트 계정을 만들어 경품 행사에 참여해 줄 것을 부탁하였다.

[어휘] be about to 막 ~하려고 하다

9 화제·주제 파악 ③

M Do you <u>have</u> <u>breakfast</u> before you go to school or work? Many people these days are so busy that they often <u>skip</u> <u>breakfast</u>. However, do you know that breakfast is the <u>most</u> <u>important</u> <u>meal</u> of the day? The first benefit of having breakfast is that you can <u>avoid</u> <u>extra</u> <u>calories</u> because it decreases your appetite throughout the day. Next, it <u>improves</u> <u>your</u> <u>memory</u>. Finally, it improves your mood and increases your happiness. Have breakfast and have a healthier, happier life.

정답 및 해설

남 학교를 가기 전 또는 직장을 가기 전에 아침을 드시나요? 요즘은 많은 사람들이 너무 바빠서 자주 아침 식사를 거르곤 합니다. 하지만 아침이 하루 중 가장 중요한 식사인 것을 알고 계시나요? 아침 식사의 첫 번째 이점은 하루 동안 식욕을 저하시켜서 추가적인 칼로리 섭취를 피할 수 있습니다. 다음으로 기억력을 높여줍니다. 마지막으로 기분을 좋게 하고 행복감을 높여줍니다. 아침을 먹고 더 건강하고 행복한 삶을 사세요.

해설 아침 식사의 이점에 대해 설명하고 있다.
어휘 benefit [bénəfit] 이점, 혜택   avoid [əvɔ́id] 피하다   appetite [ǽpətàit] 식욕   throughout [θru(:)áut] ~동안 쭉   increase [inkrríːs] 증가시키다, 높이다

10 숫자 정보 파악 ③

W   Good afternoon. What can I help you with?
M   I'd like to buy a sports watch.
W   For sports, one with a rubber band would be better.
M   Is that one water resistant?
W   No, it isn't. The water-resistant watch is 200 dollars, which is fifty dollars more expensive than the one without the waterproof function.
M   I'll take the one that has the waterproof function. I have a 5% off coupon here.

여   안녕하세요. 무엇을 도와드릴까요?
남   스포츠용 시계를 사려고 합니다.
여   스포츠용이라면 고무 밴드로 된 게 더 좋겠네요.
남   방수가 되나요?
여   아니요. 방수가 되는 시계는 200달러이고, 방수 기능이 없는 것보다 50달러가 더 비싸답니다.
남   방수 기능이 있는 걸로 살게요. 여기 5% 할인 쿠폰 있습니다.

해설 고무 밴드로 된 시계 중에서 방수 기능이 있는 것은 200달러이고, 5% 할인 쿠폰을 제시하였다.
어휘 resistant [rizístənt] 저항력 있는   waterproof [wɔ́ːtərprùːf] 방수의

11 할 일 파악 ④

W   I have a really cool idea for a business.
M   What is it?
W   It's building a complex building where students can study, exercise, and have a job-experience program in one place.
M   That will require a massive investment.
W   I know. There may be some big companies that are willing to make an investment here.
M   I guess you should map out some strategies to present your ideas to them.

여   정말 멋진 사업 아이디어가 있어.
남   그게 뭔데?
여   학생들이 공부를 하고 운동도 하고 직업 체험 프로그램을 한 곳에서 할 수 있는 복합 건물을 짓는 거야.
남   엄청난 투자금이 필요하겠네.
여   알아. 기꺼이 투자를 하려고 하는 큰 회사들이 있을지도 몰라.
남   그들에게 네 아이디어를 보여 줄 전략을 세워야 할 것 같아.

해설 남자가 투자처 확보를 위해 아이디어를 보여 줄 전략을 세울 것을 여자에게 조언하였다.
어휘 complex [kəmpléks] 복합 건물   require [rikwáiər] 필요로 하다   massive [mǽsiv] 엄청나게 큰   investment [invéstmənt] 투자   map out 계획하다, 준비하다   strategy [strǽtidʒi] 전략   present

[préznt] 발표하다, 보여주다

12 언급 유무 파악 ④

W   Let me introduce our animal protection group. We help owners find their lost pets by posting their photos and descriptions and find new families for abandoned pets. Right now, we are protecting twelve animals at our shelter. We provide news updates about the animals every Friday. Our group recommends that people adopt animals rather than buying them. If you're interested in volunteering at the shelter, please contact us by email.

여   저희 동물 보호 단체에 대해 소개해 드리겠습니다. 저희는 사진과 설명을 게시함으로써 주인이 그들의 잃어버린 반려동물을 찾도록 돕고 버려진 반려동물에게 새로운 가족을 찾아줍니다. 현재 저희 보호소에서는 12마리의 동물을 보호 중입니다. 매주 금요일마다 동물들에 관한 소식을 업데이트합니다. 저희 단체는 사람들에게 동물을 사지 말고 입양할 것을 제안 드립니다. 보호소에서 자원봉사를 하는 것에 관심이 있으시다면, 이메일로 연락주시기 바랍니다.

해설 자원봉사를 하고 있는 봉사자의 수에 관한 언급되지 않았다.
어휘 post [poust] 게시하다   description [diskrípʃən] 설명   abandoned [əbǽndənd] 버려진   shelter [ʃéltər] 보호소   recommend [rèkəménd] 제안하다

13 표 파악 ⑤

M   Which set should we choose for brunch?
W   How about the one with bacon and pancakes?
M   Can we have sausage instead of bacon?
W   Sure. What about soup? Do you like broccoli soup?
M   I love it. Which do you prefer to drink soda or juice?
W   I'm fine with either of them. You can choose.
M   Then let's have juice.
W   Great.

남   브런치로 어떤 세트를 골라야 할까?
여   베이컨이랑 팬케이크가 있는 건 어때?
남   베이컨 대신 소시지를 먹어도 될까?
여   물론이지. 수프는? 브로콜리 수프 좋아해?
남   좋아해. 음료는 탄산음료랑 주스 중에서 어떤 걸 선호해?
여   난 어떤 거라도 괜찮아. 네가 골라도 돼.
남   그럼 주스로 먹자.
여   좋아.

해설 소시지와 팬케이크, 브로콜리 수프와 주스를 먹는다고 하였다.
어휘 brunch [brʌntʃ] 브런치, 아침 겸 점심   either of ~중 어느 한쪽

14 화제·주제 파악 ②

W   This is what we use to keep our things in. It has different sizes and is made of different materials depending on how it will be used. Most sports brands sell it with their logos and unique designs. We usually carry it over our shoulders. This is sometimes so small that we can hold it with one hand, but we can still keep important things inside. This is an essential item, especially for students and travelers.

여   이것은 우리가 우리의 물건을 보관하기 위해 사용하는 것입니다. 용도

에 따라 크기와 재질이 다릅니다. 대부분의 스포츠 브랜드는 그들의 로고와 고유한 디자인으로 된 이것을 판매합니다. 우리는 이것을 보통 어깨에 멥니다. 가끔은 너무 작아서 한 손으로 들 수 있지만 그래도 중요한 물건을 담을 수 있습니다. 특히 학생과 여행객에게 필수인 물건입니다.

해설 물건을 보관할 수 있고 보통 어깨에 메고 다니며 특히 학생과 여행객들에게 필수인 물건이라고 하였다.

어휘 carry [kǽri] 가지고 다니다, 휴대하다   hold [hould] 잡다   essential [əsénʃəl] 필수적인   traveler [trǽvələr] 여행객

15 할 일 파악 ④

W Eunho, where should we meet tomorrow?
M The café across from school will be a good place to do our team project.
W We need to set the time, too.
M Let me do it. I'll send you a text message after I talk with the others.
W Okay. I'll wait for your text message.
M All right.

여 은호야, 내일 우리 몇 시에 볼까?
남 학교 건너편에 있는 카페가 팀 프로젝트를 하기에 좋을 거야.
여 우리 시간도 정해야 해.
남 내가 할게. 다른 팀원들과 이야기한 후에 문자 메시지 보낼게.
여 알겠어. 메시지 기다릴게.
남 알겠어.

해설 남자가 다른 멤버들에게 이야기하고 나서 여자에게 문자 메시지를 보낸다고 하였다.

어휘 across from ~의 건너편에   text message 문자 메시지

16 숫자 정보 파악 ①

W Didn't you say that you had an appointment today?
M I did. I need to go out thirty minutes before the appointed time.
W What time are you meeting your friend?
M At 1:00 p.m.
W I see. What time do you think you will be back here?
M We'll just have lunch, so I guess I'll get back by 3:00 p.m.
W I got it.

여 오늘 약속 있다고 하지 않았어?
남 그랬지. 약속 시간 30분 전에 나가면 돼.
여 몇 시에 친구를 만나는데?
남 오후 1시에.
여 그렇구나. 몇 시에 돌아올 것 같아?
남 우리 점심만 먹을 거라서 오후 3시쯤에는 도착할 것 같아.
여 알겠어.

해설 약속 시간이 오후 1시이고, 30분 일찍 나가면 된다고 하였다.

어휘 appointed [əpɔ́intid] 약속된   get back 돌아오다

17 적절한 응답 찾기 ④

W When do you feel the happiest?
M It's when I spend time with my loved ones. What about you?
W I'm happy when I focus on myself while doing what I want. It's weird, isn't it?
M No, it isn't. As everyone is different from each

other, people's ideas about happiness vary, too.
W I just feel very different than the average person.
M Being different doesn't mean being wrong.

여 넌 언제 가장 행복을 느껴?
남 사랑하는 사람들과 시간을 보낼 때야. 너는?
여 나는 내가 하고 싶은 것을 하면서 내 자신에게 집중할 때 행복해. 이상하지, 그렇지 않니?
남 아니, 이상하지 않아. 모든 사람들이 서로 다르듯이 행복에 대한 사람들의 생각도 다양해.
여 난 보통 사람들하고 많이 다른 것 같아.
남 다르다는 것이 틀리다는 것을 의미하지 않아.

해설 자신이 보통 사람들과 달라서 이상하다는 말에 대한 가장 적절한 응답은 ④ '다르다는 것이 틀리다는 것을 의미하지는 않아.'이다.
① 돈으로 행복을 살 수 없어.
② 네가 한 행동에 대해 남을 탓해서는 안 돼.
③ 무슨 일이 벌어지는 건지 알아내야 해.
⑤ 너의 스트레스 수준이 낮아서 다행이야!

어휘 loved ones 사랑하는 사람들   average [ǽvəridʒ] 평균의, 일반의, 보통의   blame [bleim] 비난하다, 탓하다   figure out 알아내다

18 적절한 응답 찾기 ⑤

W Michael, did you watch the news yesterday?
M No, I didn't. What happened?
W Two teenagers drove a stolen car and ran into another car.
M I see teen issues are getting more serious.
W Why do you think that is happening?
M I think it's due to the media and games.

여 Michael, 어제 뉴스 봤어?
남 아니, 안 봤어. 무엇에 관한 건데?
여 두 명의 십 대가 훔친 차를 운전하다가 다른 차에 충돌했대.
남 요즘 십 대 문제들이 점점 심각해지는 것 같아.
여 네 생각에는 왜 그런 일이 생기는 거 같아?
남 미디어랑 게임 때문인 것 같아.

해설 십 대 범죄 발생률이 늘어나는 이유를 물어보는 말에 대한 가장 적절한 응답은 ⑤ '미디어랑 게임 때문인 것 같아.'이다.
① 성공 말고는 어떤 것도 중요하지 않아.
② 이것에 대해 우리가 할 수 있는 건 없어.
③ 우리는 가짜 뉴스를 찾아내기 위해 노력해야 해.
④ 십 대는 어른들에 의해 보호받아야 해.

어휘 run into ~에 충돌하다   spot [spɑt] 알아내다, 발견하다

19 적절한 응답 찾기 ④

W Do you see any changes in my body?
M You seem to have lost weight. Did you start exercising?
W No, I am only eating one meal a day. It's fairly effective.
M Can you really make it through the day if you just eat once?
W Sometimes I feel hungry, but I can bear it if I can have a nice body.
M You'd better eat balanced meals to do that.

여 내 몸에 어떤 변화가 보이니?
남 너 살이 빠진 것 같아. 운동 시작한 거야?
여 아니, 하루에 한 끼만 먹고 있거든. 꽤 효과적이야.
남 한 번만 먹고 정말 하루를 버틸 수 있어?

정답 및 해설

여 가끔 배가 고프긴 하지만 좋은 몸매를 가질 수 있다면 이건 참을 수 있어.

남 그러기 위해서는 균형 잡힌 식사를 해야 해.

해설 좋은 몸매를 가지기 위해서 하루에 한 번만 식사를 한다는 말에 대한 가장 적절한 응답은 ④ '그러기 위해서는 균형 잡힌 식사를 해야 해.'이다.
① 모든 사람은 나이가 들고 살이 빠져.
② 원 푸드 다이어트가 정말 도움이 된다고 들었어.
③ 어떻게 운동을 해야 하는지 조언 좀 해줘.
⑤ 나도 지난주부터 체육관에서 운동을 하고 있어.
어휘 fairly [féərli] 꽤, 상당히 effective [iféktiv] 효과적인 make it through ~을 버티다, 헤쳐 나가다 bear [ber] 참다, 견디다

20 상황에 맞는 말 찾기 ②

M Owen and Grace are office buddies. They go to the beach on a company picnic in the afternoon. Because Owen knows that it will be hot and sunny, he brings sunscreen. However, Grace doesn't seem to expect it will be so hot. She says she's worried that she could get a sunburn. In this situation, what would Owen most likely say to Grace?

Owen Grace, you can use my sunscreen if you want.

남 Owen과 Grace는 친한 동료입니다. 그들은 회사 야유회로 오후에 해변으로 갑니다. Owen은 날씨가 덥고 햇볕이 내리쬘 것을 알고 있기 때문에 선크림을 가지고 옵니다. 하지만 Grace는 매우 더울 것이라는 것을 예상하지 못한 듯 보입니다. 그녀는 햇볕에 탈 수도 있어서 걱정이 된다고 말합니다. 이 상황에서 Owen은 Grace에게 뭐라고 말을 할까요?

Owen Grace, 원한다면 내 선크림 써도 돼.

해설 피부가 탈까 봐 걱정하는 Grace에게 Owen이 할 말로 가장 적절한 것은 ② '원한다면 내 선크림 써도 돼.'이다.
① 매년 우리는 회사 야유회를 가. ③ 나는 피부 관련 문제가 있었어.
④ 물에 휴대 전화를 빠뜨리지 않도록 조심해.
⑤ 네가 다른 사람들과 친해질 가장 좋은 시간이야.
어휘 office buddy (회사에서 특별히) 친한 동료 company picnic 회사 야유회 sunscreen [sʌnskriːn] 선크림 expect [ikspékt] 예상하다, 기대하다 get a sunburn (햇볕에) 그을리다 get close to ~와 친해지다

Listen and Check
p. 130

Q1 True	Q11 True
Q2 True	Q12 by posting photos of the pets
Q3 No	
Q4 call him before the speech	Q13 No
	Q14 True
Q5 True	Q15 at a café
Q6 No	Q16 No
Q7 True	Q17 True
Q8 make an account	Q18 teenage crime
Q9 avoiding extra calories	Q19 No
	Q20 getting a sunburn
Q10 Yes	

해석
Q1 남자는 자신의 태블릿 PC를 위해 작은 그림이 있는 커버를 사고 싶어 한다.
Q2 여자는 남자의 티셔츠 위에 사인을 해줄 것이다.

Q3 남자는 주차장에 있는 표지를 알아차렸는가?
Q4 남자는 여자에게 무엇을 요구하는가?
Q5 남자와 여자 둘 다 작가에 대한 긍정적인 인상을 가지고 있다.
Q6 여자는 남자가 에어컨을 켤 것을 제안하는가?
Q7 남자는 여자에게 에너지 음료의 위험성에 대해 말하고 싶어 한다.
Q8 남자는 행사에 참여하기 위해서 무엇을 해야 하는가?
Q9 아침을 먹는 것의 첫 번째 이점이 무엇인가?
Q10 남자는 방수 기능을 가진 시계를 필요로 하는가?
Q11 여자는 학생들을 위한 건물을 짓고 싶어 한다.
Q12 어떻게 단체는 주인이 그들의 잃어버린 반려동물을 찾아주는 것을 돕는가?
Q13 여자는 음료에 대한 특별한 선호도를 보이는가?
Q14 이것은 주로 물건을 보관하는 데 쓰인다.
Q15 남자와 여자는 내일 프로젝트를 위해 어디에서 만날 것인가?
Q16 남자는 3시간 이상 밖에 머물 것인가?
Q17 남자는 사람들 사이의 차이를 존중한다.
Q18 남자와 여자는 뉴스의 어떤 사안을 얘기하는가?
Q19 여자는 살을 빼기 위해 운동을 하는가?
Q20 Grace는 무엇을 걱정하는가?

실전 모의고사 **14회**
pp. 138~139

1 ②	2 ④	3 ③	4 ②	5 ③
6 ①	7 ⑤	8 ④	9 ②	10 ③
11 ①	12 ③	13 ⑤	14 ⑤	15 ②
16 ④	17 ③	18 ⑤	19 ③	20 ④

1 그림 정보 파악 ②

M Nicole, I heard that you designed the cover of our middle school yearbook.

W I did. Look at this cover. How is it?

M In the middle of the cover, you drew a circle, a triangle, and a square overlapping one another, right?

W You're correct. And I put the name of the school at the bottom.

M Where did you put the year?

W In the upper right corner. Can you see the year, 2020?

M I see. You really did well. It's simple and neat.

남 Nicole, 네가 우리 중학교 졸업 앨범 표지를 만들었다고 들었어.
여 내가 만들었어. 이 표지를 봐. 어때?
남 표지의 중간 부분에 동그라미, 세모, 그리고 네모를 겹치게 그렸구나. 맞지?
여 응. 그리고 학교 이름을 아래 쪽에 썼지.
남 연도는 어디에 있어?
여 오른쪽 위에 있어. 2020년이라는 연도가 보이니?
남 응. 정말 잘 만들었어. 단순하고 깔끔해.

해설 표지의 오른쪽 상단에 2020년이라는 연도를 쓰고, 중간에는 동그라미와 세모, 네모를 겹치게 그려 넣은 후, 표지 아래에 학교 이름을 썼다고 했다.
어휘 school yearbook 졸업 앨범 overlap [óuvərlæp] 겹치다, 포개다

다 neat [niːt] 깔끔한

2 부탁한 일 파악 ④

W Daniel, you look upset. Is something bothering you?
M Actually, I think you're <u>not interested in me</u> at all.
W What do you mean? We are having a date now.
M But when I talk to you, you <u>keep looking</u> at <u>your phone</u> and texting somebody.
W Sorry. It was my mom.
M Can you <u>make eye contact with me</u> during a conversation?
W Okay. I apologize to you for that.

여 Daniel, 너 화난 거 같아. 무슨 괴로운 일이라도 있니?
남 사실은 네가 나한테 관심이 없는 거 같아.
여 무슨 말이니? 우리는 지금 데이트하는 중이잖아.
남 하지만 내가 너에게 말을 할 때 너는 자꾸 휴대폰을 보고 누군가와 문자를 하잖아.
여 미안해. 우리 엄마였어.
남 대화 동안에는 나와 눈을 마주쳐 줄래?
여 알겠어. 사과할게.

해설 남자는 대화할 때 다른 행동을 하지 말고 자신의 눈을 바라봐 달라고 여자에게 부탁하고 있다.
어휘 contact [kántækt] 접촉   conversation [kànvərséiʃən] 대화

3 그림 상황 파악 ③

① W Which dish is quick and <u>easy to prepare</u>?
　 M I recommend the chicken breast salad.
② W What a mess! I should clean the kitchen floor.
　 M Then I'll clear the dinner table.
③ W I'm sorry, Dad. I <u>dropped a dish</u>.
　 M Are you all right? Be careful about the <u>broken pieces</u>.
④ W Look at these beautiful dishes.
　 M I <u>should buy one</u> for my mom.
⑤ W I'm getting wet from <u>washing the dishes</u>.
　 M Let me help you put this apron on.

① 여 어떤 요리가 준비하기에 빠르고 쉬울까요?
　 남 닭 가슴살 샐러드를 추천할게요.
② 여 엉망진창이군! 부엌 바닥을 청소해야겠어.
　 남 그러면 내가 저녁 테이블을 치울게.
③ 여 죄송해요, 아빠. 접시를 떨어뜨렸어요.
　 남 괜찮니? 깨진 조각을 조심해라.
④ 여 이 아름다운 접시를 봐.
　 남 엄마를 위해서 하나 사야겠다.
⑤ 여 설거지 하다가 젖어 버렸어.
　 남 내가 앞치마 두르는 걸 도와줄게.

해설 설거지 하다가 접시를 깨뜨린 딸을 보며 괜찮은지 묻는 상황이다.
어휘 apron [éiprən] 앞치마

4 특정 정보 파악 ②

W Wesley, do you <u>have any plans for</u> this Friday?
M Maybe I'll just stay home and read some comic books.
W <u>How about going</u> to a cat café? We can buy some snacks for the cats and <u>feed them</u>.
M You know, I love cats. Can we go today?
W Today? Sorry, but I <u>have to finish</u> my history report.
M Then what about tomorrow? I mean on Tuesday.
W That's perfect. Call me tomorrow.

여 Wesley, 이번 금요일에 계획 있니?
남 아마도 집에 있으면서 만화책 볼 거 같아.
여 고양이 카페 가는 건 어때? 고양이를 위한 간식도 사고 먹여줄 수도 있어.
남 내가 고양이 좋아하는 거 알지. 오늘 가도 돼?
여 오늘? 미안하지만 역사 보고서를 끝내야 해.
남 그러면 내일은 어때? 화요일 말이야.
여 괜찮아. 내일 전화해.

해설 월요일은 역사 보고서를 끝내야 해서 다음 날인 화요일에 고양이 카페에 가기로 하였다.
어휘 comic book 만화책   feed [fiːd] 먹이를 주다   finish [fíniʃ] 마치다, 끝내다

5 언급 유무 파악 ③

W Welcome to Twinkle Clothes Store. What are you looking for?
M I'm <u>looking for a suit</u> for an interview.
W How about this suit? It was <u>imported from</u> Italy.
M I like it, especially the indigo blue color. But it looks <u>kind of expensive</u>.
W That's the only drawback. But you can <u>buy it nowhere else</u> in Korea.
M Okay. How much is the suit?
W It's three thousand dollars.
M Wow! That's too much.

여 Twinkle 옷가게에 오신 것을 환영합니다. 무엇을 찾고 계세요?
남 인터뷰 때 입을 정장을 찾고 있어요.
여 이 정장은 어떠세요? 이탈리아에서 수입되었어요.
남 좋네요. 특히 남색이 마음에 드네요. 하지만 비싸 보여요.
여 그게 유일한 단점이죠. 하지만 한국에서는 다른 어디에서도 구입하실 수 없어요.
남 알겠어요. 얼마인가요?
여 3천 달러입니다.
남 와! 너무 비싸네요.

해설 어떤 원단으로 만들어진 정장인지는 언급되지 않았다.
어휘 import [impɔ́ːrt] 수입하다   indigo blue 남색   drawback [drɔ́ːbæk] 결점, 단점

6 장소 추론 ①

W Good afternoon. I'd like to put these coins into my bank account.
M Wow! Did you <u>gather all of those coins</u> by yourself?
W Of course. I <u>saved all my change</u> in my piggy bank for a year.
M Can you put your coins in this coin counting machine?
W Okay. [Coin-falling sounds] How much do I have?
M Just a moment. [Beep] You have 37 dollars in coins.
W That's <u>more than I expected</u>. Please put it into my account.

여 안녕하세요? 저는 이 동전을 제 은행 계좌에 저금하고 싶어요.
남 와, 이 동전을 혼자서 다 모은 건가요?

여 물론이죠. 1년 동안 모든 잔돈을 돼지 저금통에 모았어요.
남 동전을 이 동전 세는 기계에 넣어 주실래요?
여 네. 얼마 정도 나오나요?
남 잠시만요. 37달러네요.
여 예상보다 많네요. 제 계좌에 넣어주세요.

해설 1년 동안 모은 동전을 은행 계좌에 입금하고 있는 상황이다.
어휘 change [tʃeindʒ] 잔돈   piggy bank 저금통, 돼지 저금통

7 어색한 대화 찾기 ⑤

① M Snow is expected in the late afternoon today.
   W Perfect! Let's make a snowman.
② M How much is the dress in the display window?
   W It's on sale for 70 dollars.
③ M Tell me your email account password.
   W No way! That's personal information.
④ M Thank you for giving me your seat.
   W My pleasure. I'm getting off the bus soon.
⑤ M What are you doing in bed? Get ready for school.
   W I can't change the bed sheet. I'm busy working.

① 남 오늘 늦은 오후에 눈이 예상된대.
   여 좋아! 눈사람 만들러 가자.
② 남 진열창에 있는 드레스는 얼마인가요?
   여 70달러에 판매 중이에요.
③ 남 너의 이메일 비밀번호를 말해줘.
   여 안 돼! 그건 개인 정보야.
④ 남 자리를 제게 양보해 줘서 고마워요.
   여 별말씀을요. 전 곧 버스에서 내려요.
⑤ 남 침대에서 뭐하는 거니? 학교에 갈 준비를 해.
   여 침대 시트를 지금 바꿀 수 없어요. 전 일하느라 바빠요.

해설 학교에 갈 준비를 하지 않고 침대에서 무엇을 하고 있는지를 묻는 말에 일하느라 바빠서 침대 시트를 바꿀 수 없다고 답하는 것은 부자연스럽다.
어휘 display window 진열창   sheet [ʃiːt] 시트(침대에 깔거나 덮는 얇은 천)

8 부탁한 일 찾기 ④

M I can't believe that today is the last day of our trip to Boracay.
W Me neither. Our vacation went by so fast.
M We have to go back home and get back to work soon.
W I know! Now, it's time to pack our stuff. But I don't want to.
M Don't be sad. I took hundreds of nice pictures of us.
W Well done! Can you send them to me?
M Sure. I'll send them after we get a taxi to the airport.

남 오늘이 보라카이 여행의 마지막 날이라는 것이 믿기지가 않아.
여 나도 그래. 우리의 휴가는 너무 빨리 지나갔어.
남 집으로 돌아가서 곧 일해야 해.
여 나도 알아. 이제 짐을 꾸려야 해. 하지만 그러기 싫다.
남 슬퍼하지 마. 내가 우리의 멋진 사진을 수백 장 찍었어.
여 잘했어! 나에게 보내 줄래?
남 물론이지. 공항으로 가는 택시를 탄 후에 보내 줄게.

해설 보라카이에서 찍은 여행 사진을 보내 달라고 부탁하였다.
어휘 neither [níːðər] ~도 또한 아니다   pack [pæk] (짐을) 싸다

9 화제·주제 파악 ②

W Welcome to the Fancy Department Store. We have a daycare center to help you enjoy your shopping in comfort. The daycare center is located on the 1st floor near the information desk. The operating hours are from 12:00 p.m. to 6:00 p.m. All children ages 3 to 7 are allowed. You don't need to pay for it. There, three childcare specialists will look after your children safely. We promise to do our best to improve your customer experience.

여 Fancy 백화점에 오신 것을 환영합니다. 저희는 당신이 쇼핑을 편안하게 즐길 수 있도록 어린이 놀이방을 운영하고 있습니다. 어린이 놀이방은 안내 데스크 근처 1층에 위치하고 있습니다. 운영 시간은 오후 12시부터 6시까지입니다. 3살부터 7살까지의 어린이는 누구나 입장 가능합니다. 여러분은 어떠한 비용도 지불할 필요가 없습니다. 또한 3명의 전문 보모들이 당신의 아이들을 안전하게 돌볼 것입니다. 저희는 고객 여러분의 경험을 향상시키기 위해 최선을 다할 것을 약속합니다.

해설 보다 편안한 쇼핑을 위해서 어린이를 맡길 수 있는 놀이방을 운영하는 중이라고 알리는 안내 방송이다.
어휘 in comfort 편안하게   childcare [tʃaildker] 보육   specialist [spéʃəlist] 전문가

10 숫자 정보 파악 ③

W Welcome to Cutie Pet Shop. What do you need?
M I'm looking for a carrier for a small dog.
W What about this one? It's light to carry and easy to fold up.
M I like it. It's exactly what I want. How much do I have to pay for it?
W It's 35 dollars.
M Can I use this coupon? I got it from a pet magazine.
W Absolutely! You'll get 5 dollars off the total price.

여 Cutie 반려동물 용품점에 오신 걸 환영합니다. 무엇이 필요하세요?
남 소형견을 위한 캐리어를 찾고 있어요.
여 이건 어떠세요? 나르기에 가볍고 잘 접혀요.
남 좋네요. 정확히 제가 원하는 거예요. 얼마를 지불해야 할까요?
여 35달러입니다.
남 음, 이 쿠폰을 사용해도 될까요? 반려동물 잡지에서 얻었어요.
여 물론이죠! 총 가격에서 5달러 깎아 드릴게요.

해설 소형견을 위한 캐리어의 가격은 35달러이며 잡지에서 얻은 5달러 할인 쿠폰을 사용하면 총 30달러이다.
어휘 fold up 접다, 포개다, 정리하다   magazine [mæ̀gəzíːn] 잡지   absolutely [ǽbsəlùːtli] 물론, 완전히

11 할 일 파악 ①

W Let's go to the bookstore. I'll ask for a refund on this book.
M Why? Is it damaged?
W No, it's fine. I bought it yesterday, and my dad gave me the same book this morning.
M That's so funny! Then can I buy that book from you? I want to read it.
W That's a brilliant idea. I'll sell this to you.
M Okay. Here is money for it.

여 우리 서점 가자. 이 책을 환불 요청해야 해.

남 왜? 파손됐어?
여 아니, 책은 괜찮아. 내가 어제 이 책을 샀는데 오늘 아침에 똑같은 책을 아빠가 주시지 뭐야.
남 너무 재밌네! 그러면 내가 너한테 그 책을 사도 돼? 나도 읽고 싶었어.
여 멋진 생각이다. 너에게 팔게.
남 응. 여기 돈 줄게.

해설 여자가 환불하려는 책을 남자가 구입하고 싶다고 하자 여자가 수락하였다.

어휘 ask for a refund 환불을 요청하다　damaged [dǽmidʒd] 손상된, 망가진　brilliant [bríljənt] 뛰어난, 멋진

12 언급 유무 파악 ③

M Good morning, guests. We're glad to introduce the firefly-watching program to you. Participants will experience a river cruise at night to see the fireflies. We recommend that you wear long sleeves to keep your body from getting any mosquito bites. This program is conducted daily at 7:00 p.m. and lasts for about an hour and a half. It costs $25 for adults and $15 for children under 12. Children under six are not allowed due to safety reasons. If you want to take part in this program, please contact us at 012-3456-7890.

남 고객 여러분, 좋은 아침입니다. 저희는 반딧불이 관찰 프로그램을 알려 드리게 되어 기쁩니다. 참가자들은 반딧불이를 보기 위해 밤에 강 유람선 여행을 경험하실 겁니다. 모기에 물리는 것을 예방하기 위해 긴 팔을 입는 것을 추천 드립니다. 이 프로그램은 매일 오후 7시에 1시간 반 동안 진행됩니다. 어른은 25달러, 12세 미만의 아이들은 12달러입니다. 또한 6세 이하의 아이들은 안전상의 이유로 참여할 수 없습니다. 만약 프로그램에 참여하길 원하시면, 012-3456-7890으로 연락 주시길 바랍니다.

해설 반딧불이 관찰과 관련된 기념품 판매에 관해서는 언급되지 않았다.

어휘 cruise [kruːz] 유람선 여행, 순항　conduct [kándʌkt] 수행하다, 실시하다

13 그림 정보 파악 ⑤

M Look! We can select our seats online in advance.
W That's very convenient. Let's look at the seat map.
M Which one do you prefer, a window seat or an aisle seat?
W I prefer a window seat. I also need the extra legroom.
M If you want that, then we have no choice but to sit in the exit row.
W We have to pay extra for seats in the exit row, right?
M Right. You take the window seat, and I'll sit next to you.
W Okay.

남 이걸 봐! 우리는 온라인으로 미리 좌석을 선택할 수 있어.
여 정말 편리하다. 좌석 안내도를 보자.
남 창가 자리랑 통로 자리 중에서 어떤 것이 더 좋아?
여 난 창가 자리가 좋아. 또한 여분의 다리를 뻗을 수 있는 공간이 필요해.
남 그렇다면 비상구 좌석 말고는 선택의 여지가 없네.
여 비상구 좌석을 위해서 추가로 돈을 지불해야 하지?
남 맞아. 네가 창가 자리에 앉고 나는 네 옆에 앉을게.
여 그래.

해설 다리를 뻗을 수 있는 공간을 위해 비상구 좌석을 선택하였다.
어휘 legroom [ləgrúm] 다리를 뻗을 수 있는 공간　exit [égzit] 비상구, 출구

14 화제·주제 파악 ⑤

W Plastic is everywhere in our daily lives. It is a useful material for people. However, when it is thrown into the ocean carelessly, it can cause huge problems. Plastic is harmful to marine animals. Plastic takes a long time to break down. Some marine animals take plastic for food and eat it, which injures or even kills them. People should be aware of how serious plastic pollution is. If this continues, things will get even worse.

여 플라스틱은 우리 일상에서 어디서나 발견됩니다. 그것은 사람들에게 유용한 물질입니다. 하지만 플라스틱이 부주의하게 바다에 버려질 때, 그것은 큰 문제를 일으킵니다. 플라스틱은 해양 동물에게 해롭습니다. 플라스틱은 분해되는 데 시간이 오래 걸립니다. 몇몇의 해양 동물들이 플라스틱을 음식으로 오해하고 그것을 먹게 되고, 그것은 그들을 부상 입히거나 심지어 죽게 합니다. 사람들은 플라스틱 오염이 얼마나 심각한지 알아야 합니다. 만약 이것이 계속된다면, 상황은 더 악화될 것입니다.

해설 부주의하게 바다에 버려진 플라스틱이 해양 동물에게 어떻게 나쁜 영향을 미치는지를 설명하고 있다.
어휘 carelessly [kɛ́ərlisli] 부주의하게　marine [məríːn] 해양의　break down 부서지다, 분해되다　take A for B A를 B로 여기다, 잘못 알다

15 할 일 파악 ②

W Kihoon, did you hear the news that Seowoo is in the hospital?
M Yes. I got a call from her. She had a car accident. But luckily, it's not that serious.
W Why don't we go to see her?
M Sounds good. Before we do that, let's buy something for her.
W I'll buy a watermelon. That's her favorite fruit.
M I'll buy a magazine. She must be bored in the hospital.
W Okay. Let's meet in front of the hospital at 3:00 p.m.

여 기훈아, 서우가 병원에 있다는 소식 들었니?
남 응. 서우한테 전화를 받았어. 자동차 사고를 당했대. 하지만 운이 좋게도 심각하지는 않대.
여 문병 가는 건 어때?
남 좋아. 그 전에 서우를 위해 뭘 사자.
여 나는 수박을 살게. 그녀가 가장 좋아하는 과일이야.
남 나는 잡지를 살게. 병원에서 분명히 심심할 거야.
여 그래. 병원 앞에서 오후 3시에 만나자.

해설 병원에 입원한 친구를 위해 잡지를 구입한다고 하였다.
어휘 accident [ǽksidənt] 사고, 사건

16 숫자 정보 파악 ④

[Cellphone rings.]
W Hello? Who's calling, please?
M Ms. Murphy, this is the Cozy Furniture Store. Did you order a king-sized bed 3 days ago?
W Right. I visited the shop and charged it on my

credit card.

M We'd like to deliver your bed on September 7. Is that all right?

W Sorry, but I work on weekdays. Could you deliver it on September 10 or 11?

M Let me check the schedule. [Pause] September 10 is possible.

W Good. What time can I expect you?

M At around 11 a.m.

W Okay. See you then.

여 여보세요. 누구신가요?

남 Murphy씨, Cozy 가구점입니다. 킹사이즈 침대를 3일 전에 주문하셨죠?

여 맞아요. 매장을 방문해서 신용 카드로 계산했어요.

남 침대를 9월 7일에 배달하려고 합니다. 괜찮으신가요?

여 죄송하지만 평일에는 일을 해요. 9월 10일이나 11일에 배달해 주실 수 있을까요?

남 일정을 확인해 볼게요. 9월 10일이 가능합니다.

여 좋아요. 언제쯤 오시나요?

남 대략 오전 11시입니다.

여 알겠어요. 그날 뵈어요.

해설 여자가 평일에는 일을 해서 남자는 9월 10일에 침대를 배달해 주기로 하였다.

어휘 furniture [fə́ːrnitʃər] 가구   charge A on one's credit card A를 신용 카드로 지불하다

17 적절한 응답 찾기 ③

M Jaekyung, what are you doing?

W I'm writing a letter to a boy in Africa to celebrate his birthday.

M I didn't know that you have a friend in Africa.

W Actually, I've helped this boy by donating money for three years.

M You sound like an angel. I've never thought about doing that before.

W It's not very difficult at all. You can do it with your pocket money.

M Really? Just 10 dollars a month is okay?

W Of course. It's the thought that counts.

남 재경아, 뭐하는 중이야?

여 난 아프리카에 있는 소년에게 생일을 축하하려고 편지를 쓰는 중이야.

남 네가 아프리카에 친구가 있는 줄 몰랐어.

여 사실은 난 3년 동안 돈을 기부해서 이 소년을 돕고 있어.

남 너 천사 같아. 난 그것에 대해 전에 생각해 본 적이 없어.

여 전혀 어렵지 않아. 네 용돈으로 할 수 있어.

남 정말? 한 달에 10달러면 괜찮아?

여 물론이지. 중요한 건 마음이야.

해설 적은 액수의 돈을 기부해도 되는지를 묻는 말에 대한 가장 적절한 응답은 ③ '물론이지. 중요한 건 마음이야.'이다.

① 지금 돈을 모으기 시작하자. ② 언젠가 아프리카로 여행을 가고 싶어.

④ 걱정하지 마. 네 건강이 더 중요해. ⑤ 내 생일 파티에 와 줘서 고마워.

어휘 celebrate [séləbrèit] 축하하다, 기념하다   pocket money 용돈, 푼돈

18 적절한 대화 찾기 ⑤

M Natalie, how was your last weekend?

W It was terrible. I had to stay home all day.

M What happened to you?

W I suffered from food poisoning after eating some raw fish.

M I'm sorry to hear that. Are you okay now?

W Much better than yesterday. But still I don't feel very well.

M You'd better go home and get some rest.

남 Natalie, 지난 주말은 어땠어?

여 끔찍했어. 종일 집에 있어야 했어.

남 무슨 일 있었니?

여 날생선을 먹고 식중독에 걸렸어.

남 안타깝다. 지금은 괜찮아?

여 어제보다는 나아졌어. 하지만 여전히 속이 안 좋아.

남 집으로 가서 쉬는 게 낫겠다.

해설 주말 내내 식중독으로 고생했지만 지금도 여전히 속이 안 좋다는 말에 대한 가장 적절한 응답은 ⑤ '집으로 가서 쉬는 게 낫겠다.'이다.

① 그럼 함께 낚시하러 가자. ② 잊어. 네 잘못이 아니야.

③ 바다에서 수영할 때는 조심해. ④ 네가 좋은 하루를 보냈다니 기뻐.

어휘 suffer [sʌ́fər] 겪다, 고통을 받다   food poisoning 식중독   raw [rɔː] 날것의, 익히지 않은

19 적절한 응답 찾기 ③

M Doyeon, do you have time to talk?

W What's up? Do you have a problem?

M My daughter hates vegetables. She never even tries to eat them.

W Hmm... Do you remember my son Taeoh? He did the same thing. But he likes eating vegetables now.

M Are you serious? What happened?

W Taeoh and I grew our own vegetables. We planted carrots and cucumbers and watered them together.

M Wow! It must have been a great experience for him.

W It really was. You should give it a try.

남 도연아, 얘기할 시간이 있니?

여 무슨 일인데? 문제라도 있니?

남 내 딸이 채소를 싫어해. 조금이라도 절대 먹지를 않아.

여 흠… 내 아들 태오 기억하지? 걔도 그랬어. 하지만 지금은 채소 먹는 걸 좋아해.

남 정말이니? 무슨 일이 있었던 거야?

여 태오랑 나랑 우리만의 채소를 키웠어. 우리는 함께 당근이랑 오이를 심고 물을 줬지.

남 와! 그에게 정말 멋진 경험이었겠다.

여 정말 그랬어. 너도 시도해 봐.

해설 직접 채소를 가꾸는 것이 멋진 경험이었을 거라는 말에 대한 가장 적절한 응답은 ③ '정말 그랬어. 너도 시도해 봐.'이다.

① 개인적으로 그것을 추천하지 않아. ② 잘 조리된 야채가 더 맛있어.

④ 당근을 먹으면 비타민 A를 섭취할 수 있어.

⑤ 채식주의자를 위한 특식이 있어.

어휘 own [oun] 자신의   water [wɔ́ːtər] 물을 주다   experience [ikspí(ː)əriəns] 경험, 체험   give it a try 시도해 보다

20 상황에 맞는 말 찾기 ④

M Eunchan plans to move out of his parents' house. He searches for a new place, but he cannot afford one. A few days later, Eunchan happens to meet

David on the street. David says that he's looking for a roommate <u>to share the rent with</u>. David's place is nice to live, and the <u>rent seems reasonable</u> to Eunchan. So he wants to be David's roommate. In this situation, what would Eunchan most likely say to David?

Eunchan David, <u>do you want to share your room with me?</u>

남 은찬이는 부모님의 집에서 독립하기로 결정합니다. 그는 새로운 집을 찾았지만 그가 감당할 수 있는 가격이 아니었습니다. 며칠 후에 은찬이는 길에서 우연히 David를 만납니다. David는 자신이 집세를 나눠 낼 룸메이트를 찾는다고 말합니다. David의 집은 살기 좋았고 집세는 은찬이에게 합리적으로 보입니다. 그래서 그는 David의 룸메이트가 되기를 원합니다. 이런 상황에서, 은찬이가 David에게 할 말로 가장 적절한 것은 무엇일까요?

은찬 David, 나랑 방 같이 쓸래?

해설 은찬이 David의 룸메이트가 되고 싶어 하는 상황에서 은찬이 David에게 할 말로 가장 적절한 것은 ④ '나랑 방 같이 쓸래?'이다.
① 네가 혼자 산다는 얘기를 들었어. 어떠니?
② 매달 집세를 내야 한다는 것을 잊지 마.
③ 진공청소기로 방을 청소해. ⑤ 네 룸메이트랑은 잘 지내고 있니?
어휘 afford [əfɔ́ːrd] 여유가 있다 happen to 우연히 ~하다
rent [rent] 집세, 임대료

Listen and Check
p. 140

Q1	No	Q11	False
Q2	True	Q12	children under six
Q3	Yes	Q13	Yes
Q4	True	Q14	True
Q5	for an interview	Q15	No
Q6	False	Q16	by credit card
Q7	No	Q17	True
Q8	to an airport	Q18	No
Q9	three	Q19	True
Q10	a pet magazine	Q20	to share the rent

해석
Q1 남자가 중학교 졸업 앨범의 표지를 만들었나?
Q2 남자와 여자는 데이트를 하는 중이다.
Q3 남자는 여자를 걱정하고 있는가?
Q4 Wesley는 금요일에 만화책을 읽을 계획이다.
Q5 무엇을 위해 남자는 정장을 사려고 하는가?
Q6 여자는 동전을 지폐로 바꾸고 싶어 한다.
Q7 여자는 학교에 갈 준비가 되었는가?
Q8 대화가 끝난 후에 남자와 여자는 어디로 갈까?
Q9 어린이 놀이방에는 몇 명의 전문 보모가 있을까?
Q10 남자는 어디에서 쿠폰을 얻었을까?
Q11 여자의 아빠가 그녀가 구입한 책을 잃어버렸다.
Q12 안전상의 이유로 누가 프로그램에 참여할 수 없을까?
Q13 남자와 여자는 선택한 좌석에 대해 여분의 돈을 지불해야 할까?
Q14 몇몇의 해양 동물들은 플라스틱을 음식으로 오해해서 그것을 먹는다.
Q15 기훈은 자동차 사고를 당한 후에 병원에 입원했나?
Q16 여자는 킹사이즈 침대를 어떻게 계산했을까?
Q17 재경은 돈을 기부해서 아프리카에 있는 소년을 돕고 있다.
Q18 Natalie는 멋진 주말을 보냈을까?
Q19 여자의 아들은 채소를 싫어했다.
Q20 David는 왜 룸메이트가 필요한가?

실전 모의고사 **15회** — *pp. 148~149*

1	④	2	⑤	3	⑤	4	④	5	⑤
6	③	7	②	8	⑤	9	④	10	⑤
11	④	12	⑤	13	③	14	④	15	④
16	③	17	③	18	④	19	④	20	②

1 그림 정보 파악 ④

W Dad, it's so hard to wake up early in the morning. I need something to <u>help wake me up</u>.
M That's the reason why we are here. Look around and choose <u>whichever one you want</u>.
W I want something loud to wake me up. How about this one?
M The round-faced one with two bells on top? <u>Won't it be too loud</u>?
W No. I mean the square one with the red and blue light on top. I think it makes the same sound as a police car.
M Maybe it will make you wake up by thinking <u>there is an emergency</u>. Let's go with that one.

여 아빠, 아침에 일찍 일어나기 너무 힘들어요. 저를 깨우는 것을 도울 무언가가 필요해요.
남 그게 우리가 여기 온 이유지. 둘러보고 원하는 것을 고르렴.
여 저를 깨울 시끄러운 무언가가 필요해요. 이것 어때요?
남 위에 벨이 두 개 달린 둥근 시계 말이니? 너무 시끄럽지 않을까?
여 아뇨. 사각형에 빨간색과 파란색 불빛이 들어오는 등이 위에 있는 것 말이에요. 경찰차와 같은 소리를 낼 것 같아요.
남 아마도 네가 긴급한 일이 있다고 생각하면서 일어나게 만들 것 같구나. 그걸로 하자.

해설 경찰차와 같은 소리를 낼 것 같은 시계를 사고 싶다고 하였다.
어휘 loud [laud] 시끄러운 emergency [imə́ːrdʒənsi] 긴급한 상황, 비상 사태

2 목적 파악 ⑤

[*Cellphone rings.*]
M Hello, Somi.
W Hi, Chris. What's up?
M Have you found a partner for the group project? Have you <u>already completed it</u>?
W Jason and I were <u>thinking of doing</u> it together, but the teacher asked him to do it with Ted. So I am looking for a new partner now.
M Really? What about me? I have some <u>novel ideas</u> for the project. Would you like to work together with me?
W Okay, I can do that. When shall we meet?
M You have to strike when the <u>iron is hot</u>. How about this evening? Oh, don't forget to bring your laptop.
W Okay, I won't. See you later.

남 안녕, 소미야.
여 안녕, Chris. 무슨 일이야?
남 조별 과제 파트너는 구했니? 벌써 끝냈어?
여 Jason과 나는 함께 하려고 했는데, 선생님께서 Jason 보고 Ted와 과

정답 및 해설

제를 하라고 하셨어. 그래서 나는 새 파트너를 찾는 중이야.
남 정말? 나 어때? 과제에 대한 참신한 아이디어가 있거든. 함께 할래?
여 좋아, 그러자. 그럼 언제 만날까?
남 쇠뿔도 단김에 빼라고 했잖아. 오늘 저녁 어때? 참, 노트북 가져오는 것 잊지 마.
여 좋아, 그럴게. 나중에 보자.

해설 조별 과제의 파트너를 구했는지 확인하려고 전화를 하였다.
어휘 complete [kəmplíːt] 완료하다   novel [nάvəl] 참신한

3 그림 상황 파악 ⑤

① M It's a lovely night for a walk.
   W You can say that again.
② M Can I help you?
   W Sure. I need the latest tourist map for this city.
③ M Watch out! You were almost hit by that car.
   W Whew! The driver ignored the traffic signal.
④ M Let's go hiking tomorrow.
   W Cool. I can't wait.
⑤ M I guess we are lost.
   W Don't worry. We can ask somebody for directions.

① 남 산책하기 좋은 밤이야.
   여 정말 그래.
② 남 도와 드릴까요?
   여 네. 이 도시의 최신 관광 지도가 필요해요.
③ 남 조심해! 차에 거의 치일 뻔 했어.
   여 휴! 운전자가 교통 신호를 무시했어.
④ 남 내일 하이킹 가자.
   여 좋아. 기대되는 걸.
⑤ 남 우리가 길을 잃은 것 같아.
   여 걱정 마. 누군가에게 길을 물어보면 돼.

해설 지도를 보고 위치를 찾지 못해 난처해하는 상황이다.
어휘 latest [léitist] 최신의   ignore [ignɔ́ːr] 무시하다   signal [sígnəl] 신호   direction [dirékʃən] 방향

4 특정 정보 파악 ④

W You are a big fan of baseball, aren't you?
M Of course, I am. Oh, I have two tickets to the game tomorrow. Do you want to go with me?
W Really? That sounds great. In fact, I have never been to the ballpark. Will it be fun?
M Oh, I'm sure you will like it.
W What time shall we meet there?
M The game starts at 6:30. How about meeting at 6:00 at the front gate?
W I'm sorry, but I can't make it at 6:00. My piano lesson finishes at 6:00. It will probably take me 20 minutes to get to the ballpark.
M Then let's meet 10 minutes before the game starts.
W Okay. See you then.

여 너 야구 광팬이지, 그렇지?
남 물론이지. 오, 내일 시합의 표가 두 장 있어. 같이 갈래?
여 정말? 좋아. 사실, 나는 야구장에 가본 적이 없어. 재미있을까?
남 저런, 분명히 마음에 들 거야.
여 몇 시에 만날까?
남 시합이 6시 반에 시작해. 정문에서 6시에 만나는 거 어때?
여 난 6시는 안 돼. 피아노 수업이 6시에 끝나거든. 경기장까지 20분 정도

걸릴 거야.
남 그럼 경기 시작하기 10분 전에 정문에서 만나자.
여 그래. 그때 만나자.

해설 경기가 시작하기 10분 전에 만나자고 하였다.
어휘 ballpark [bɔ́ːlpὰːrk] 야구 경기장

5 언급 유무 파악 ⑤

W The famous comedian and actor Charles Spencer Chaplin was born in London, England, on April 16, 1889. His father was a vocalist and actor, and his mother was an attractive actress and singer in the light opera field. The early death of his father and the illness of his mother made it necessary for Charlie to earn a living for himself. When he was about twelve, he got his first chance to act in a stage show. Charlie started his career as a comedian when he went to the United States in 1910. In the fall of 1912, Chaplin was offered a motion picture contract.

여 유명한 코미디언이자 배우인 Charles Spencer Chaplin은 1889년 4월 16일 영국 런던에서 태어났습니다. 그의 아버지는 가수이자 배우였습니다. 그의 어머니는 경가극 분야에서 매력적인 여배우이자 가수였습니다. 아버지의 이른 죽음과 어머니의 병으로 인해 찰리는 스스로 생계를 유지해야 했습니다. 그가 약 12살이었을 때, 그는 무대에서 공연할 첫 기회를 얻었습니다. Charlie는 1910년에 미국으로 건너갈 때 코미디언으로의 경력을 시작했습니다. 1912년 가을에 Chaplin은 영화 계약을 제안 받았습니다.

해설 영화 계약은 언급되었지만 제목에 관해서는 언급되지 않았다.
어휘 vocalist [vóukəlist] 가수   light opera 경가극   for oneself 스스로   career [kəríər] 경력   motion picture 영화   contract [kάntrækt] 계약

6 관계 추론 ③

M Excuse me, but someone dropped this passport. I found it in the aisle next to my seat.
W Thank you. I'll find out whom it belongs to.
M Okay. Oh, can I have an extra blanket?
W Yes, of course. Do you feel uncomfortable?
M Not now, but when I got airsick in the past, I used to feel a little cold.
W Okay, I'll bring one for you right away.
M Thank you for your kindness.

남 실례합니다만 누군가가 여권을 떨어뜨렸어요. 제 자리 옆 통로에서 찾았어요.
여 감사합니다. 어느 분 것인지 제가 찾을게요.
남 네. 그런데, 추가 담요를 받을 수 있나요?
여 물론이죠. 불편하세요?
남 지금은 아니지만 예전에 비행기 멀미를 할 때 약간 춥더라고요.
여 알겠습니다. 바로 가져다 드릴게요.
남 감사합니다.

해설 비행기 승무원과 승객 사이의 대화이다.
어휘 passport [pǽspɔːrt] 여권   belong to ~에게 속하다   blanket [blǽŋkit] 담요   airsick [ɛ́ərsìk] 비행기 멀미

7 어색한 대화 찾기 ②

① W How often does the hotel bus come?
   M You can catch it every 30 minutes.

70

② W I bought this electric fan, but it doesn't work.
　 M You can work <u>inside</u> <u>the</u> <u>house</u>.
③ W What do you want to know about Korea?
　 M I'm very <u>interested</u> <u>in</u> <u>history</u>.
④ W What's the best way to <u>see</u> <u>the</u> <u>sights</u> in this city?
　 M Most tourists like taking the city bus tour.
⑤ W How far do you live from here?
　 M About <u>an</u> <u>hour</u> <u>away</u> by car.

① 여 호텔 버스가 얼마나 자주 오나요?
　 남 30분마다 한 번 탈 수 있어요.
② 여 제가 이 선풍기를 샀는데 작동하지 않네요.
　 남 당신은 실내에서 일할 수 있습니다.
③ 여 한국에 대해 무엇을 알고 싶으신가요?
　 남 저는 역사에 많은 관심이 있습니다.
④ 여 이 도시를 구경할 가장 좋은 방법은 뭔가요?
　 남 대부분의 관광객은 시티 버스로 관광하는 것을 좋아합니다.
⑤ 여 여기서부터 얼마나 떨어진 곳에 사시나요?
　 남 자동차로 약 한 시간 거리에 살아요.

해설 선풍기가 작동하지 않는다는 말에 실내에서 일할 수 있다고 답하는 것은 부자연스럽다.
어휘 electric fan 선풍기　sight [sait] 경치, 풍경

8　**부탁한 일 파악** ⑤

M Good afternoon, miss. What do you want to have?
W Hello. I'd like to have a *bulgogi* sandwich and an apple pie.
M Anything to drink? We have soda, juice, and lemonade.
W Two Cokes, please. Oh, I <u>want</u> <u>all</u> <u>of</u> <u>these</u> <u>things</u> <u>to</u> <u>go</u>.
M Okay. You ordered a *bulgogi* sandwich, an apple pie, and two Cokes to go. <u>It'll</u> <u>be</u> <u>ready</u> <u>within</u> 5 minutes.
W Thank you. Oh, wait. Please cancel the two Cokes. <u>I</u> <u>forgot</u> that I have some juice in my fridge.
M All right.

남 안녕하세요. 무엇을 드시겠습니까?
여 안녕하세요. 불고기 샌드위치 하나와 애플파이 부탁해요.
남 마실 것은요? 탄산음료, 주스, 레모네이드가 있습니다.
여 콜라 두 잔 주세요. 아, 전부 포장해 주세요.
남 알겠습니다. 불고기 샌드위치, 애플파이, 그리고 콜라 두 잔을 포장 주문하셨습니다. 5분 안에 준비됩니다.
여 감사합니다. 오, 잠깐만요. 콜라 두 잔을 취소해주세요. 냉장고에 주스가 있는 걸 깜빡했어요.
남 알겠습니다.

해설 주문이 끝난 후, 콜라 두 잔을 취소해 달라고 부탁하였다.
어휘 within [wiðín] ~이내에　fridge [fridʒ] 냉장고

9　**의도 파악** ④

W Dad, I think I have a fever.
M Let me see. Oh, your <u>forehead</u> <u>is</u> <u>burning</u>.
W I feel dizzy.
M Let me take your temperature. Hmm... It is almost 40 degrees. You should go to see a doctor now.
W My body is burning from the fever.

M Wait a minute. [*Pause*] Put this ice pack on your forehead <u>to</u> <u>bring</u> <u>down</u> <u>the</u> <u>fever</u>.
W Thank you, Dad. I'm aching all over.
M Don't worry. I parked the car in front of the house. Let's go to the hospital right away.
W I'm <u>lucky</u> <u>to</u> <u>have</u> <u>you</u>, Dad.

여 아빠, 저 열이 있는 것 같아요.
남 어디 보자. 오, 이마가 불덩이구나.
여 어지러워요.
남 체온을 재보자. 흠... 40도 가까이 되네. 지금 병원에 가야겠어.
여 열로 몸이 너무 뜨거워요.
남 잠깐만 기다려라. 열을 내리기 위해 이마에 얼음주머니를 올려 두렴.
여 고마워요, 아빠. 온 몸이 아프네요.
남 걱정하지 마. 집 앞에 차를 세울게. 바로 병원에 가자.
여 아빠가 있어서 다행이에요.

해설 몸이 아플 때 아빠가 있어서 다행이라고 하였다.
어휘 forehead [fɔ́(ː)rid] 이마　temperature [témpərətʃər] 온도　ache [eik] 아프다

10　**숫자 정보 파악** ⑤

W Good afternoon. What can I do for you?
M I need five 20-liter standard garbage bags. How much are they?
W They are 3 dollars each. Is that all you need?
M Do you pick up large items that <u>need</u> <u>to</u> <u>be</u> <u>recycled</u>?
W Yes, we do.
M How much will it cost to get a table <u>big</u> <u>enough</u> for four people?
W It depends on the size, but it usually costs 10 dollars. Would you like to <u>have</u> <u>your</u> <u>name</u> <u>put</u> <u>down</u> on the pickup schedule?
M No, thanks. I'm <u>just</u> <u>curious</u> <u>about</u> the cost.
W Okay. That's fine. Here are your bags.
M Thank you.

여 안녕하세요. 무엇을 도와 드릴까요?
남 20리터 종량제 쓰레기봉투 다섯 장 주세요. 얼마인가요?
여 각 3달러입니다. 필요하신 건 이것이 전부인가요?
남 재활용이 되는 큰 물건들도 수거하시나요?
여 예, 그렇습니다.
남 4인용 큰 테이블을 수거하는 데는 비용이 얼마인가요?
여 크기에 따라 다릅니다만, 보통 평균적으로 10달러입니다. 저희 수거 일정에 등록해 드릴까요?
남 아뇨, 괜찮습니다. 그냥 비용이 궁금했어요.
여 네, 알겠습니다. 쓰레기봉투 여기 있습니다.
남 감사합니다.

해설 3달러짜리 쓰레기봉투 5장만 구매하였다.
어휘 garbage [gáːrbidʒ] 쓰레기　standard [stǽndərd] 표준의

11　**할 일 파악** ④

M Jennifer, why are you <u>keeping</u> <u>all</u> <u>of</u> <u>the</u> <u>windows</u> closed?
W As you know, <u>it's</u> <u>freezing</u> outside.
M Well, keeping the windows closed makes the indoor air bad.
W To me, that's <u>far</u> <u>better</u> <u>than</u> being cold.
M But think about this... If the indoor air is not fresh,

you may get sick or <u>sneeze</u> <u>often</u>! You need to have fresh air.

W All right.

남 Jennifer, 왜 창문을 다 닫아두고 있어?

여 너도 알다시피 밖이 너무 춥잖아.

남 음, 문을 계속 닫아두는 것은 실내 공기를 나쁘게 해.

여 내겐 추운 것보다 그게 더 나아.

남 하지만 이걸 생각해 봐… 실내 공기가 신선하지 않으면, 너는 아프게 되거나 더 자주 재채기를 할 거야. 넌 신선한 공기를 가질 필요가 있어.

여 알았어.

해설 실내 공기가 나쁘면 건강에 더 좋지 않다고 하였다.

어휘 freezing [fríːziŋ] 몹시 추운　sneeze [sniːz] 재채기하다

12 　언급 유무 파악　⑤

W The Seoul Dance Festival started in 1979 and is a <u>representative</u> <u>dance</u> <u>festival</u> in Korea. It promotes Korean dance, modern dance, ballet, and other creative dance performance genres. The festival <u>lasts</u> <u>for</u> <u>a</u> <u>couple</u> <u>of</u> weeks, with performances by dance groups from all over Korea and invited arts groups <u>from</u> <u>abroad</u> as well as university students majoring in dance and performing arts. This year, the festival <u>will</u> <u>be</u> <u>held</u> in the Sejong Center from October 12 to 31. It will be a good chance for children to enjoy and understand dance performances. Don't miss this opportunity.

여 서울 댄스 페스티벌은 1979년에 시작되었고, 한국의 대표적인 댄스 축제입니다. 서울 댄스 페스티벌은 한국 무용, 현대 무용, 발레와 기타 장르의 창조적 댄스 공연을 장려합니다. 이 축제는 한국 전역의 무용단과 해외 특별 무용단뿐만 아니라 무용과 공연 예술을 전공하는 대학생들의 공연으로 2주일 정도 지속됩니다. 올해에는 10월 12일부터 31일까지 세종 문화 회관에서 열릴 것입니다. 축제는 아이들이 댄스 공연을 즐기고 이해할 좋은 기회가 될 것입니다. 이 기회를 놓치지 마세요.

해설 공연 관람 비용에 관해서는 언급되지 않았다.

어휘 representative [rèprizéntətiv] 대표적인　promote [prəmóut] 촉진하다, 장려하다, 홍보하다

13 　표 파악　③

W Happy New Year, Eric.

M Happy New Year, Subin. Time really flies.

W It sure does. Do you have <u>any</u> <u>resolutions</u> this year?

M I want to speak Chinese fluently.

W Don't you <u>speak</u> <u>pretty</u> <u>good</u> <u>Japanese</u>? You're very interested <u>in</u> <u>foreign</u> <u>languages</u>. So do you have any plans to learn Chinese?

M Every journey begins with a single step. I will memorize one Chinese character a day.

W Wow, we have <u>something</u> <u>in</u> <u>common</u>. Actually, I'm thinking of taking an online Chinese course. Will you take it with me?

M Absolutely.

여 새해 복 많이 받아, Eric.

남 새해 복 많이 받아, 수빈아. 시간 정말 잘 간다.

여 정말 그러네. 올해 어떤 계획이라도 있어?

남 중국어를 유창하게 하고 싶어.

여 너 일본어를 꽤 잘하지 않니? 넌 외국어에 정말 관심이 많구나. 그래서

앞으로 중국어를 배우기 위한 어떤 계획이 있니?

남 천리 길도 한 걸음부터잖아. 매일 한자를 하나씩 외울 거야.

여 와, 우리는 공통점이 있구나. 사실, 나는 온라인 중국어 강좌를 들을까 생각 중이야. 같이 할래?

남 물론이지.

해설 온라인 강좌를 수강할 거라는 여자의 말에 남자는 함께 하기로 하였다.

어휘 resolution [rèzəljúːʃən] 결심　journey [dʒə́ːrni] 여행

14 　화제·주제 파악　④

M This is a team sport which <u>requires</u> <u>cooperation</u> <u>and</u> <u>teamwork</u>. Six players from each team play at the same time. Players have to <u>wear</u> <u>gear</u> <u>such</u> <u>as</u> a helmet, a mouthpiece, and gloves. This game is played in three 20-minute periods and sometimes goes to overtime if <u>the</u> <u>score</u> <u>is</u> <u>tied</u>. This game is played on an ice rink, and the goalies for both teams must wear facemasks to protect themselves from the rubber puck.

남 이것은 협력과 팀워크가 필요한 팀 스포츠입니다. 각 팀의 6명의 선수들이 동시에 경기합니다. 선수들은 헬멧, 마우스피스 그리고 장갑과 같은 장비를 착용해야 합니다. 이 경기는 20분씩 3번의 피리어드 동안 진행되며 동점인 경우 연장전으로 갑니다. 이 경기는 아이스링크에서 진행되며 두 팀의 골키퍼들은 고무 퍽으로부터 자신을 보호하기 위해 안면 마스크를 착용해야 합니다.

해설 아이스링크 위에서 진행하며 6명의 선수가 장비를 착용한 채로 경기를 한다고 하였다.

어휘 overtime [óuvərtàim] 연장전　goalie [góuli] 골키퍼 (goalkeeper의 구어)　rubber puck (아이스하키의) 고무로 된 공

15 　할 일 파악　④

W Honey, you've been playing that mobile game for about 2 hours.

M I started <u>the</u> <u>last</u> <u>game</u> just 10 minutes ago. Let me <u>finish</u> <u>it</u>, please.

W No, You said that an hour ago. I'm going to turn off the Wi-Fi.

M Okay! I'm <u>logging</u> <u>out</u>. Now what should I do, Mom?

W I'm <u>vacuuming</u> <u>the</u> <u>floor</u>, and your sister is cleaning the windows. You have to take out the garbage.

M All these things? They are too heavy.

W <u>Stop</u> <u>complaining</u> and do what I say.

여 얘야, 너 지금 2시간 동안 모바일 게임을 하고 있단다.

남 10분 전에 마지막 게임을 시작했어요. 제발 이것만 할게요.

여 안 돼. 한 시간 전에도 그 말을 했잖니. 와이파이를 끌 거야.

남 알았어요. 로그아웃하고 있어요. 이제 뭘 하면 되나요, 엄마?

여 나는 바닥을 청소하고 있고, 네 여동생은 창문을 닦고 있어. 너는 쓰레기를 내놓아라.

남 이것들 전부를요? 너무 무거워요.

여 불평하지 말고 하라는 대로 하렴.

해설 엄마는 남자에게 쓰레기를 버려야 한다고 말하였다.

어휘 vacuum [vǽkjuəm] 진공청소기로 청소하다

16 　특정 정보 파악　③

M May I help you?

W Can you show me that digital camera?

M Here you are. This is the most popular model with YouTubers. It has 128GB of memory and can be connected via Wi-Fi.

W Well, it feels a little heavy.

M Would you like to see another model?

W No, thanks. It just caught my eye. Actually, I don't need it. By the way, I need a memory stick to back up my photos. How much is this one?

M This memory stick? It's 6 dollars.

W Okay, I'll take it.

남 무엇을 도와 드릴까요?

여 저 디지털 카메라 좀 보여주시겠어요?

남 여기 있습니다. 이것이 유튜버들 사이에 가장 인기 있는 모델입니다. 128기가 메모리에 와이파이로 연결됩니다.

여 음, 약간 무겁네요.

남 다른 모델을 보여드릴까요?

여 아뇨, 괜찮습니다. 그냥 눈에 띄어서요. 사실, 전 필요가 없어요. 어쨌거나 저는 사진을 백업하기 위한 메모리 스틱이 필요해요. 이건 얼마인가요?

남 이 메모리 스틱이요? 6달러에요.

여 좋아요. 이걸로 할게요.

해설 사진을 백업하기 위한 메모리 스틱을 구매하고 있다.

어휘 via [váiə] ~을 통해

17 [적절한 응답 파악] ③

[Telephone rings.]

M Hello. 112 National Police Crime Center.

W I want to report a crime.

M What happened, miss?

W I think somebody broke into my house a few hours ago.

M Was anyone hurt? Or what was taken?

W Luckily, nobody was hurt, but my TV, laptop and some jewelry are missing.

M I'll send a car there right now.

W Please hurry. I'm so scared.

M Just give me your name and address.

남 112 범죄 신고 센터입니다.

여 범죄 신고를 하고 싶어요.

남 무슨 일인가요?

여 누군가가 몇 시간 전에 저희 집에 침입한 것 같아요.

남 다친 사람이 있거나 없어진 물건이 있나요?

여 다행히도 다친 사람은 없지만 제 TV, 노트북 그리고 귀금속 몇 개가 사라졌어요.

남 경찰차를 지금 보내겠습니다.

여 서둘러 주세요. 무서워요.

남 이름과 주소를 가르쳐 주세요.

해설 범죄 신고를 하고 경찰이 빨리 와달라는 요청에 대한 가장 적절한 응답은 ③ '이름과 주소를 가르쳐 주세요.'이다.

① 무엇을 도와드릴까요? ② 문을 확실히 잠가야 했어요.

④ 다른 채널로 돌리세요.

⑤ 걱정하지 마세요. 생각하시는 것보다 흔한 일이에요.

어휘 break into ~에 침입하다 jewelry [dʒúːəlri] 보석류

18 [적절한 응답 파악] ④

W Honey, your nose is bleeding. What happened? Did you get in a fight with your friend?

M No, I'm not that kind of a boy, Mom. I just fell down on the street.

W How did that happen?

M I tripped over something when I was walking and watching a movie on my smartphone.

W Oh, I've told you not to use your smartphone while walking.

M Now I understand why you always tell me that. I'm sorry to have worried you, Mom.

W Be more careful from now on.

여 애야, 너 코에서 코피가 나. 무슨 일이니? 친구랑 싸웠니?

남 아뇨, 전 그런 아이가 아니잖아요, 엄마. 그냥 길에서 넘어졌어요.

여 어떻게 그런 일이 생겼어?

남 스마트폰으로 영화를 보면서 걷다가 무언가에 걸려 넘어졌어요.

여 오, 걸을 땐 스마트폰을 사용하지 말라고 늘 말했잖니.

남 이제 엄마가 왜 그렇게 말씀하셨는지 알겠어요. 걱정시켜드려 죄송해요, 엄마.

여 앞으로는 더 조심해라.

해설 스마트폰을 보면서 걷다 넘어져 다쳐서 엄마를 걱정시켜 죄송하다는 말에 대한 가장 적절한 응답은 ④ '앞으로는 더 조심해라.'이다.

① 넌 911을 불러야만 했어. ② 너무 심각하게 여기지 마.

③ 가서 새로운 모델을 한번 보자. ⑤ 네가 집에 돌아와서 기쁘구나.

어휘 bleeding [blíːdiŋ] 피를 흘리는 get in a fight with ~와 싸우다 trip over ~에 걸려 넘어지다

19 [적절한 응답 파악] ④

[Cellphone rings.]

M Hello.

W Hello, Steve. It's me, Jessy.

M Jessy? Wow, I was surprised that an international phone number popped up on my cellphone. Where are you?

W I'm still on vacation. I'm calling you from Ho Chi Minh City now.

M Is everything okay?

W Sure. Right now is the perfect time to travel to Vietnam.

M I'm glad you're having a good time.

남 여보세요.

여 안녕 Steve, 나야 Jessy.

남 Jessy? 와, 국제 전화번호가 표시되어서 깜짝 놀랐어. 너 어디니?

여 나 여전히 휴가 중이야. 지금 호치민에서 전화하는 거야.

남 다 괜찮지?

여 물론이지. 지금이 베트남을 여행하기에 딱 좋은 시기야.

남 즐거운 시간을 보내고 있다니 기쁘네.

해설 여행하기 좋은 시기라는 말에 대한 가장 적절한 응답은 ④ '즐거운 시간을 보내고 있다니 기쁘네.'이다.

① 우리 가족은 종종 베트남 식당에서 외식을 해.

② 멋지네! 베트남은 쌀국수로 유명하지.

③ 베트남에 가 본 적 있니? ⑤ 좋은 생각이야. 언젠가 그곳에 가자.

20 [상황에 맞는 말 찾기] ②

W When a boy stops her, Hana is on her way home. He says hello and that he is really glad to see her again. But Hana doesn't remember who he is. So she asks what his name is. He says his name is Juho. Hana tries to recall who he is, but she cannot remember him. Hana doesn't think she has heard his name before. In this situation, what would Hana say to the boy?

Hana ___Excuse me, but do I know you?___

여 한 소년이 하나를 멈춰 세웠을 때, 하나는 집에 가는 길이었습니다. 그는 인사를 하고, 그녀를 다시 만나 정말 기쁘다고 말을 합니다. 그러나 하나는 그가 누구인지 기억하지 못합니다. 그래서 그녀는 그의 이름을 묻습니다. 그는 이름이 주호라고 말합니다. 하나는 그가 누구인지 기억하려 노력하지만, 그를 기억할 수 없습니다. 하나는 그의 이름도 들어본 적이 없다고 생각합니다. 이런 상황에서, 하나가 소년에게 무엇이라고 말할까요?

하나 실례지만 저를 아세요?

해설 자신을 안다는 남자가 누구인지 기억이 나지 않는 상황에서 하나가 할 수 있는 말로 가장 적절한 것은 ② '실례지만, 저를 아세요?'이다.
① 오랜만이야 ③ 다시 만나서 반가워, 주호야.
④ 부모님께 안부 전해줘. ⑤ 미안하지만, 경찰을 부를 거예요.
어휘 recall [rikɔ́ːl] 기억을 떠올리다

Listen and Check

p. 150

Q1	False	Q12	False
Q2	No	Q13	to speak Chinese fluently
Q3	True	Q14	True
Q4	never	Q15	False
Q5	his talent	Q16	Yes
Q6	No	Q17	False
Q7	Yes	Q18	No
Q8	No	Q19	False
Q9	True	Q20	True
Q10	No		
Q11	False		

해석
Q1 여자는 둥근 모양의 알람 시계를 사기를 원했다.
Q2 선생님은 여자에게 Ted와 함께 과제를 할 것을 요청했는가?
Q3 여자와 남자는 자신들이 길을 잃었다고 생각한다.
Q4 여자는 야구장에 몇 번 가보았는가?
Q5 무엇이 Charlie Chaplin이 스스로 생계를 꾸리게 했는가?
Q6 남자는 지금 추운가?
Q7 남자에게 선풍기가 있는가?
Q8 여자는 냉장고에 콜라가 있는가?
Q9 여자의 체온은 약 40도 정도 된다.
Q10 여자는 남자에게 탁자를 수거할 것을 요청하는가?
Q11 남자는 창문을 다 닫아두고 있다.
Q12 그 축제는 한국 전통 무용의 아름다움만을 홍보한다.
Q13 남자의 결심은 무엇인가?
Q14 이 게임은 총 12명의 선수들에 의해 행해진다.
Q15 남자의 어머니는 그가 쓰레기 버리는 것을 도울 것이다.
Q16 여자는 자기 사진을 백업하기를 원하는가?
Q17 여자의 집에서 아무것도 사라지지 않았다.
Q18 남자는 그의 친구와 싸웠는가?
Q19 남자는 지금 베트남에 머물고 있다.
Q20 하나는 주호가 누구인지 모른다.

실전 모의고사 **16회**

pp. 158~159

1	⑤	2	④	3	①	4	③	5	①
6	③	7	①	8	②	9	③	10	④
11	④	12	④	13	④	14	①	15	①
16	③	17	⑤	18	⑤	19	①	20	④

1 그림 정보 파악 ⑤

W I'm so thrilled about the time capsule event!
M ___So am I___. I think it's such a great idea.
W What items do you want to put into the capsule?
M Well, I want to put some of ___my favorite toys___ in it.
W Toys? That's interesting. What else?
M My photos and some money. What about you?
W I will ___write a letter___ to the people of the future. I'll ___put in my album___, too.
M Why are you going to put it in your album?
W The people of the future will see my pictures and messages in it.

여 난 타임캡슐 행사가 매우 기대돼.
남 나도 마찬가지야. 그것은 매우 멋진 아이디어라고 생각해.
여 넌 그 캡슐 속에 무슨 물건을 넣고 싶어?
남 글쎄, 난 내가 가장 좋아하는 장난감 몇 개를 넣고 싶어.
여 장난감이라구? 그거 재미있겠다. 그 외에는?
남 내 사진과 돈을 조금 넣을 거야. 너는 어때?
여 난 미래의 사람들에게 보내는 편지를 쓸 거야. 그리고 나는 내 앨범도 넣을 거야.
남 왜 앨범을 넣는건데?
여 미래의 사람들이 앨범 안에 있는 내 사진들과 메시지들을 볼 거야.

해설 남자와 여자는 타임캡슐 안에 넣을 물건으로 신분증은 언급하지 않았다.
어휘 thrilled [θriled] 기대되는, 신나는   put in ~ ~을 넣다

2 목적 파악 ④

[*Telephone rings.*]
M Hello. Aladin Carpets. How may I help you?
W Hi. I'm calling ___to change my order___.
M May I have your name, please?
W This is Jennifer Lee. I ordered a green carpet for my living room yesterday.
M Just a second, please. I'll ___look for your order___... Oh, here it is. What do you want to change?
W Can I get the carpet on Friday instead of on Saturday?
M Okay. You want ___to change the delivery day___ from Saturday to Friday, right?
W Exactly.

남 안녕하세요, Aladdin Carpets입니다. 어떻게 도와 드릴까요?
여 안녕하세요. 주문을 변경하려고 전화했어요.
남 이름을 말씀해 주시겠습니까?
여 저는 Jennifer Lee예요. 어제 제 거실을 위해 초록색 카펫을 주문했어요.
남 잠시만 기다려 주세요. 당신의 주문을 찾아볼게요... 오, 여기 있네요. 무엇을 변경하고 싶으신가요?

여　제가 토요일 대신 금요일에 카펫을 받을 수 있나요?

남　좋아요. 당신은 배달일을 토요일에서 금요일로 바꾸고 싶으신 거죠, 맞나요?

여　정확합니다.

해설 여자는 카펫 매장에 전화해서 카펫이 배달되는 요일을 변경하기를 원하고 있다.

어휘 delivery day 배달일　exactly [igzǽktli] 정확하게, 틀림없이

3　[그림 상황 파악] ①

① M　I enjoyed staying with you and your family this summer.

　W　I hope you will visit us again sometime soon.

② M　Congratulations on winning the math contest.

　W　Thank you. I cannot express how happy I am.

③ M　The train for Gwangju has been delayed, ma'am.

　W　How long will it be delayed?

④ M　I'd like to make a reservation. Do you have any rooms available?

　W　Yes, I can give you a double room.

⑤ M　How much is this big pink bag?

　W　It's one hundred dollars. You are planning to travel abroad, right?

① 남　난 올해 여름에 너와 너의 가족들과 함께 재미있게 지냈어.

　여　네가 곧 다시 한 번 우리를 방문하기를 바랄게.

② 남　네가 수학 대회에서 우승한 것을 축하해.

　여　고마워. 얼마나 행복한지 말로 표현할 수가 없어.

③ 남　광주로 향하는 기차가 지연되었습니다, 손님.

　여　얼마나 오래 지연될까요?

④ 남　예약을 하고 싶어요. 이용 가능한 방이 있나요?

　여　네, 더블룸 이용 가능합니다.

⑤ 남　이 큰 분홍색 가방은 얼마인가요?

　여　그것은 백 달러에요. 당신은 해외 여행을 계획하시는 거죠, 맞나요?

해설 공항 출국장에서 여자가 남자를 배웅하는 상황이다.

어휘 express [iksprés] 표현하다　make a reservation 예약하다

4　[숫자 정보 파악] ③

W　Peter, what are you going to do this weekend?

M　I'm going to see an exhibition at the national museum this Sunday. Do you want to join me?

W　Sounds good. What time shall we meet?

M　Let's meet at 1:00 p.m. and have lunch together.

W　Oh, I'm sorry, but I am having lunch with my mom.

M　That's okay. Then let's meet after lunch. The museum closes at 6:00 p.m., so how about meeting there two hours before it closes?

W　All right. See you then. And we can have dinner together.

여　Peter, 이번 주말에 무엇을 할 예정이야?

남　난 이번 주 일요일에 국립 박물관에 하는 전시회에 갈 거야. 나랑 같이 갈래?

여　좋아. 몇 시에 우리 만날까?

남　오후 한 시에 만나서 함께 점심도 먹자.

여　오, 미안하지만 난 엄마와 점심을 먹어야 해.

남　괜찮아. 그럼, 점심 이후에 만나자. 박물관은 오후 6시에 문을 닫으니까, 끝나기 2시간 전에 만나는 건 어때?

여　좋아. 그때 보자. 그럼 우리는 함께 저녁을 먹을 수 있겠다.

해설 남자는 박물관이 6시에 문을 닫으므로 2시간 전에 만날 것을 제안하

였다.

어휘 shall ~ ~할 것이다

5　[언급 유무 파악] ①

W　Hi, everyone. Welcome to French cuisine class. Thank you for joining us for a 6-week course with chef Billy. You will discover the pleasures of the cooking world. The class will be two hours long without a break. If anyone can't attend this morning class, you can attend an afternoon or evening class. We cover the same material in all three classes. You can park your car in front of the center. Don't forget to bring some containers to take all the lovely French food you cook home with you.

여　안녕하세요, 여러분. 프랑스 요리 강좌에 오신 걸 환영합니다. Billy 셰프와 함께 하는 6주 수업 과정에 함께해 주셔서 감사드립니다. 여러분들은 요리 세계의 즐거움을 발견하실 겁니다. 수업은 쉬는 시간 없이 두 시간입니다. 만일 이 아침 수업에 오실 수 없으신 분은 누구나 오후나 저녁 수업 참여하실 수 있습니다. 저희는 세 강좌 모두 동일한 내용을 다룹니다. 여러분들은 센터 앞에 차를 주차할 수 있습니다. 여러분들이 멋지게 요리한 프랑스 요리들을 집으로 가져가기 위해 용기들을 갖고 올 것을 잊지 마세요.

해설 강좌에 사용되는 재료에 관해서는 언급되지 않았다

어휘 cuisine [kwizíːn] (격식 있는) 요리　chef [ʃef] 요리사　container [kəntéinər] 용기, (담는 용도의) 상자

6　[관계 추론] ③

M　Excuse me. Can I try these shorts on?

W　Well, I don't know. In fact, I'm not a sales clerk. I'm a customer, too.

M　Oh, I'm sorry. I just can't find a sales clerk.

W　Yeah, it looks really busy today. They're probably all helping other customers. I think it's okay for you to try them on.

M　I think so, too. Do you happen to know where the fitting room is?

W　Yes, it's over there near that wall.

M　Thanks. Have a nice day.

W　You, too.

남　실례합니다. 제가 이 반바지를 입어 봐도 되나요?

여　음, 저는 잘 모르겠어요. 사실 저는 판매 직원이 아니에요. 저도 역시 손님이랍니다.

남　오, 죄송합니다. 정말로 직원을 찾을 수가 없네요.

여　그래요, 오늘 이곳이 매우 바빠 보이네요. 직원 모두가 아마 다른 손님들을 돕고 있을 것 같아요. 제 생각에는 그것을 입어보셔도 괜찮을 거예요.

남　저도 그렇게 생각해요. 당신은 혹시 탈의실이 어디에 있는지 아시나요?

여　네, 저 벽 근처에 있어요.

남　감사합니다. 멋진 하루 되세요.

여　당신도요.

해설 옷가게를 찾은 여자가 역시 손님인 남자를 옷가게 직원으로 착각한 상황이다.

어휘 try on (시험 삼아) 착용하다　customer [kʌ́stəmər] 손님, 고객　probably [prɑ́bəbli] 아마도

7 어색한 대화 찾기 ①

① M What will the weather be like tomorrow?
   W I'm feeling under the weather lately.
② M Do you think we should leave a tip?
   W Oh, leave him a dollar.
③ M I'm sorry, ma'am, but can you please repeat the title of the song?
   W It's *The Secret between Us.*
④ M Did you have a good weekend?
   W Yes, it was terrific.
⑤ M I'm very sorry. All the tickets for the Saturday show are sold out.
   W No! I really wanted to see it.

① 남 내일 날씨는 어때?
   여 난 요즘 몸이 안 좋아.
② 남 너는 우리가 팁을 남겨놔야 한다고 생각해?
   여 오, 그에게 1달러를 주자.
③ 남 죄송하지만, 손님, 그 노래의 제목을 다시 말씀해 주실까요?
   여 그것은 *The Secret Between Us*입니다.
④ 남 넌 멋진 주말을 보냈니?
   여 그래, 아주 좋았어.
⑤ 남 정말 죄송합니다. 토요일 쇼의 모든 표가 매진되었습니다.
   여 안돼요! 전 정말 그것을 보고 싶었어요.

해설 내일 날씨에 대한 물음에 몸이 좋지 않다고 답하는 것은 부자연스럽다.

어휘 repeat [ripíːt] 다시 말하다, 반복하다   terrific [tərífik] 매우 좋은, 멋진   be sold out 매진되다, 다 팔리다

8 부탁한 일 파악 ②

W The news said there will be an ice show this Saturday.
M I heard that, too. Are you planning to go there?
W I would love to, but tickets are very expensive. They're almost seventy dollars each. I'm not sure I can afford to buy one.
M But it will be a good chance to see Olympic figure skating stars like Yuna Kim.
W Then would you like to see the show together?
M Okay. Let's go there and have a good time.
W Can you book a ticket for me? I don't know how to do it.
M Sure. Leave it to me.

여 뉴스에서 이번 주 토요일에 아이스 쇼가 있다고 하네.
남 나도 그 뉴스를 들었어. 그곳에 가볼 거야?
여 그러고 싶은데 표가 매우 비싸더라. 한 장당 거의 70달러야. 내가 그 정도 여유가 있을지 모르겠어.
남 하지만 김연아와 같은 올림픽 피겨 스케이팅 스타들을 보는 좋은 기회가 될 거야.
여 그럼 그 쇼 보러 같이 갈래?
남 좋아. 가서 멋진 시간을 보내자.
여 날 위해 표를 예매해 주겠니? 내가 예매할 줄을 몰라.
남 물론이야. 내게 맡겨.

해설 여자는 남자에게 토요일의 아이스 쇼 표의 예매를 부탁하고 있다.
어휘 afford to ~ ~을 감당하다

9 의도 파악 ③

W I can't believe this. The science exam was really awful.
M What are you talking about? You are so good at science. Was it really that bad?
W Yes, it was. I think I answered only half the questions correctly.
M Really? That's too bad.
W Maybe I will fail the test. What should I do?
M You don't know that yet. Besides, there's one more exam next month. If you study hard, the results will be much better.

여 믿을 수 없어. 이번 과학 시험은 정말로 끔찍했어.
남 무슨 소리야? 너는 과학을 정말로 잘하잖아. 그렇게나 안 좋았어?
여 응, 그래. 문제의 절반 정도만 정답을 맞춘 것 같아.
남 정말? 안됐구나.
여 아마도 난 이 시험에서 낙제할 거야. 나 어떡하지?
남 아직 모르는 일이야. 게다가 다음 달에 시험이 한 번 더 있잖아. 열심히 공부한다면, 결과는 훨씬 좋아질 거야.

해설 남자는 과학 시험의 결과로 낙담해 있는 여자에게 다음 시험에서 잘하도록 격려하고 있다.
어휘 half [hæf] 절반   fail [feil] 낙제하다, 실패하다   besides [bisáidz] 게다가   much [mʌʧ] ~ 훨씬

10 숫자 정보 파악 ④

M Excuse me. I'm shopping for a birthday present for my mother.
W Is there anything you have in mind?
M These earrings are great. Do you think they are good for my mother's age? She's in her late forties.
W Of course. And they're now on sale, so you can get a twenty-percent discount.
M Are you sure? I will take them.
W The original price is fifty dollars, and since you get twenty percent off, you only have to pay forty dollars.
M Good. Do you charge a wrapping fee?
W Yes, that will cost four dollars.
M Okay. Please wrap it as a gift.

남 실례합니다. 저는 엄마의 생일 선물을 위해서 물건을 고르고 있는데요.
여 마음에 두고 계신 것이 있으신가요?
남 이 귀걸이가 멋지네요. 그것들이 제 엄마의 나이 대에 어울릴 거라고 생각하세요? 그녀는 40대 후반입니다만.
여 물론이에요. 그리고 그것들을 지금 할인 중이라서 당신은 20퍼센트 할인을 받을 수 있습니다.
남 정말인가요? 전 그것들을 살래요.
여 원래 가격이 50달러인데, 20퍼센트 할인을 받는다면 40달러네요.
남 좋습니다. 포장비를 따로 내나요?
여 네, 포장비는 4달러입니다.
남 좋아요, 선물 포장해 주세요.

해설 원래 귀걸이 가격인 50달러에서 20퍼센트가 할인된 금액에 포장비 4달러가 추가되므로 총 44달러임을 추론할 수 있다.
어휘 have ~ in mind ~을 마음에 두다   in one's ~ (나이가) ~대의   discount [diskáunt] 할인(하다)   original [ərídʒənəl] 원래의, 고유한   charge [tʃɑːrdʒ] 청구하다   wrapping fee 포장비

11 할 일 파악 ④

W Excuse me. Can you help me?
M Of course. What can I do for you?
W I think I left my purse on the bus from Busan today.
M I am sorry to hear that. What time did your bus arrive here?
W About thirty minutes ago. And my seat number was 09A.
M Wait, please. Well, nothing has been turned in yet. Maybe the bus driver is around here. I'll call and ask him.
W Thank you so much.

여 실례합니다. 저를 도와주실래요?
남 물론입니다. 무엇을 도와드릴까요?
여 제가 오늘 부산에서 온 버스에서 제 지갑을 놓고 내린 것 같은데요.
남 그 말씀을 들으니 유감입니다. 몇 시에 당신의 버스가 여기에 도착했나요?
여 약 30분 전이었어요. 그리고 제 좌석 번호는 09A였습니다.
남 잠시만 기다려 주세요. 음, 아무 것도 아직 분실물로 신고된 것이 없네요. 아마도 버스 운전사가 이 근처에 있을 거예요. 제가 전화해서 그에게 물어보겠습니다.
여 매우 감사합니다.

해설 남자는 버스에 지갑을 놓고 내린 여자를 위해 해당 버스 기사와 통화를 하겠다고 하였다.
어휘 be turned in 들어오다, 입수되다

12 언급 유무 파악 ④

M Hello, everyone. I'm very happy to meet you for English class. I'm Ryan, your English teacher. Since today is the first day of class, I want to explain a few important things to keep. First, you should always carry your textbook and a notebook. The notebook is for writing practice. Second, be on time at all times. If any of you are late, we can't start the lesson together. Third, don't speak Korean in class. Helping you speak English well is my primary job. Thanks for listening, and if you follow the rules I just gave you, we'll have the best class ever.

남 안녕하세요, 여러분. 저는 여러분들을 만나서 반갑습니다. 저는 Ryan이고, 여러분들의 새로운 영어 선생님입니다. 오늘은 첫 수업이므로 지켜야 할 중요한 것들을 설명하고 싶습니다. 먼저, 여러분들은 항상 교과서와 공책을 가져오셔야 합니다. 공책은 작문 연습을 위해서입니다. 둘째로, 항상 수업 시간을 정확히 지켜주세요. 만일 여러분들 중 한 명이라도 늦는다면, 우리는 함께 수업을 시작할 수가 없습니다. 셋째로, 수업 시간에는 한국어로 말하지 마세요. 여러분들이 영어로 말할 수 있도록 돕는 것이 저의 중요한 일입니다. 들어주셔서 감사하고 여러분들이 제가 방금 말한 규칙들을 지켜 주신다면, 우리는 최고의 수업을 하게 될 것입니다.

해설 영어 수업에서 학생들이 지켜야 할 주의 사항 중 숙제 검사 방법에 관해서는 언급되지 않았다.
어휘 explain [ikspléin] 설명하다 primary [práimeri] 중요한, 주요한

13 표 파악 ④

M Hi. I'm looking for a bicycle for my 10-year-old daughter.
W Okay. For that age group, a twenty-two or twenty-four-inch wheel would be best.
M She's tall for her age, so a twenty-four-inch wheel will be better.
W Which type do you want, a foldable or regular one?
M I'd prefer a foldable one since our house doesn't have much space. How much is this foldable one?
W It is 250 dollars, including tax.
M It looks good, but it is a little costly. Do you have anything cheaper?
W In that case, you'll love this one.
M Good. I'll take it.

남 안녕하세요, 저는 10살 된 딸을 위한 자전거를 찾고 있습니다.
여 네, 그 연령대는 22인치나 24인치의 바퀴 크기가 가장 좋을 거예요.
남 그녀는 나이치고 키가 크니까 24인치가 좋겠네요.
여 어떤 종류를 원하시나요, 접이식이나 일반 종류 중에서요?
남 집에 공간이 충분하지 않아서 접이식이 더 좋아요. 이 접이식은 얼마인가요?
여 그것은 세금이 포함되어 250달러입니다.
남 좋아 보이지만 값이 좀 나가는군요. 좀 더 싼 것은 없나요?
여 그러시다면 이게 마음에 드실 거예요.
남 좋아요. 그걸로 하겠습니다.

해설 남자는 250달러보다는 싼 24인치 바퀴 크기의 접이식 자전거를 산다고 하였다.
어휘 wheel [hwiːl] 바퀴 foldable [fouldéibl] 접이식의

14 화제·주제 파악 ⑤

W They are designed to catch your eye when you watch TV or read newspapers and magazines. Sometimes they pop up on the screen of your cellphone. They tell you that a certain product is great. Their goal is to make you want to buy the product. If you believe what they are saying, you will want to buy the product. However, they don't always tell the truth about the product they're selling, so you should be careful to think wisely about it.

여 그것들은 당신이 TV를 보거나 신문과 잡지를 볼 때 당신의 시선을 끌도록 제작됩니다. 때로는 그것들이 당신의 휴대 전화의 화면에서 갑자기 나오기도 하죠. 그것들은 당신에게 어떤 제품이 좋다고 말합니다. 그것들의 최종 목표는 당신이 그것들을 사고 싶게 만드는 것입니다. 당신이 그들이 하는 말을 믿으면 그것들을 사고 싶을 겁니다. 하지만 그것들이 항상 팔고 있는 제품에 대해 진실을 말하는 것은 아니므로 당신은 그것에 대해 현명히 생각하도록 주의해야 합니다.

해설 대중 매체에서 제품을 홍보하여 사람들의 시선을 끌어 그 제품을 사도록 한다는 내용으로 보아 광고에 관한 설명임을 추론할 수 있다.
① 설명서 ② 비디오 클립 ③ 삽화 ④ 뉴스 기사
어휘 be designed to ~ ~하려고 만들어지다, 고안되다 pop up (갑자기) 튀어나오다 certain [sə́ːrtən] 어떤, 특정한

15 할 일 파악 ①

W I'm very disappointed with you, Bob.
M Why? Is there something wrong?
W Yes. I can't believe I saw you throw your milk carton on the street.
M Oh, don't worry about that. Somebody will clean the street later.
W How can you say that? That's a really bad attitude.

We should always keep our streets clean.

M I see, Kate. Don't be so angry. I'll pick it up and put it <u>in</u> the <u>trash</u> <u>can</u>.

여 너에게 정말 실망했어, Bob.
남 왜? 잘못된 것이 있어?
여 그럼. 네가 우유 용기를 길거리에 버리는 걸 봤다니 믿을 수가 없구나.
남 오, 걱정하지 마. 어쨌든 누군가가 길을 치울 거잖아.
여 넌 어떻게 그렇게 말할 수 있어? 그건 정말로 나쁜 태도야. 우리는 거리를 깨끗하게 유지해야 해.
남 알겠어, Kate. 그렇게 화내지 마. 내가 그걸 주워서 쓰레기통에 버릴게.

해설 남자는 길거리에 버린 우유 용기를 다시 주워서 쓰레기통에 넣겠다고 하였다.

어휘 milk carton (종이로 된) 우유 용기   attitude [ǽtitʃùːd] 태도

16 **숫자 정보 파악** ③

M Claire, I'm so nervous. I have an important meeting at three o'clock.

W I remember <u>you</u> <u>told</u> <u>me</u> <u>that</u> yesterday. Are you done preparing for it? You only have twenty minutes left.

M Yes, I am. It takes ten minutes to get to the office. I don't think <u>I</u> <u>should</u> <u>hurry</u> <u>up</u>.

W But you could get stuck in a traffic jam at this time. Why don't you <u>go</u> <u>a</u> <u>little</u> <u>earlier</u>?

M Yeah, you're right. I'll leave now then.

W Best of luck, Sam!

남 Claire, 나는 매우 긴장돼. 난 세 시에 중요한 회의가 있거든.
여 어제 나에게 말했던 것이 기억나. 준비는 모두 끝냈어? 이제 20분밖에 남지 않았구나.
남 그래. 사무실까지는 10분 정도 걸려. 난 서두르지 않을래.
여 하지만 너는 이 시간대에 교통 체증에 갇힐 수도 있잖아. 조금 더 일찍 가지 그래?
남 맞아. 그럼, 지금 떠나야겠다.
여 행운을 빌게, Sam!

해설 3시에 있을 회의에 남자는 여자의 충고대로 회의 시작 20분 전에 출발하겠다고 하였다.

어휘 get stuck in ~ ~에 갇히다, 움직이지 못하다

17 **적절한 응답 찾기** ⑤

W Chris, <u>what</u> <u>are</u> <u>you</u> <u>going</u> <u>to</u> <u>do</u> this Sunday? Do you have any plans?

M Yes, I'm going shopping with my sister.

W Oh, really? Where?

M Perhaps we will go to the new department store.

W <u>Can</u> <u>I</u> <u>join</u> <u>you</u>? I have to buy a present for my father. Can you help me find something nice for him?

M Of course! What time <u>shall</u> <u>we</u> <u>meet</u>? My sister and I will go to the department store together at noon.

W <u>Then I'll meet you there at the same time on Sunday.</u>

여 Chris, 이번 주 일요일에 무엇을 할 거야? 계획이 있니?
남 그래, 나는 누나와 쇼핑하러 갈 거야.
여 오, 정말? 어디로?
남 아마도 우리는 새로 문을 연 백화점에 가겠지.
여 내가 같이 가도 돼? 나는 아빠를 위해서 선물을 사야 돼. 네가 멋진 선물을 찾는 걸 도와줄 수 있어?

남 물론이야! 우리 몇 시에 만날까? 누나와 나는 정오에 백화점에 같이 갈 거야.
여 그럼 일요일 같은 시간에 거기서 만나자.

해설 몇 시에 만날 예정인지 묻는 말에 대한 가장 적절한 응답은 ⑤ '그럼 일요일 같은 시간에 거기서 만나자.'이다.
① 네가 그렇게 말하다니 매우 친절하구나.
② 난 너의 의견에 만족하지 못하겠어.
③ 좋은 생각이야. 나는 토요일이 괜찮아.
④ 실은 나는 백화점을 좋아하지 않아.

어휘 perhaps [pərhǽps] 아마도

18 **적절한 응답 찾기** ⑤

M What are you looking for?

W Oh, no! I think I left my phone <u>in</u> <u>the</u> <u>taxi</u>.

M Oh, that's terrible. Shall I call your number with my phone? Somebody may answer the phone.

W It would be of no use. It's probably off. I remember <u>the</u> <u>battery</u> <u>was</u> <u>low</u>.

M Do you remember the taxi company?

W Luckily, I remember it. Can I use your cellphone? I think I should call the taxi company and <u>find</u> <u>out</u> <u>the</u> <u>driver's</u> <u>phone</u> <u>number</u>.

M <u>Here it is. I hope you get your phone back.</u>

남 무엇을 찾고 있니?
여 오, 안 돼! 아마도 내가 택시에서 휴대 전화를 놓고 내렸나 봐.
남 오, 안됐구나. 내가 휴대 전화로 네 번호로 전화해 볼까? 누군가가 전화를 받을 수도 있잖아.
여 소용이 전혀 없을 거야. 틀림없이 꺼져 있을걸. 배터리가 별로 없었던 게 기억나.
남 택시 회사 기억해?
여 다행히도 기억이 나. 내가 너의 휴대 전화를 사용할 수 있을까? 택시 회사에 전화해서 택시 기사 아저씨의 번호를 알아내야겠어.
남 여기 있어. 난 네가 휴대 전화를 되찾기를 바랄게.

해설 휴대 전화를 빌려 달라는 요청에 대한 가장 적절한 응답은 ⑤ '여기 있어. 난 네가 휴대 전화를 되찾기를 바랄게.'이다.
① 미안해. 그곳은 7시에 문을 닫아.   ② 우리는 그 운전사의 이름을 몰라.
③ 서둘러. 우리는 시간이 부족해.   ④ 역에 도착하기까지 얼마나 걸릴까?

어휘 of no use 전혀 쓸모없는   be turned off (전원이) 꺼지다
luckily [lʌ́kəli] 다행히도, 운 좋게

19 **적절한 응답 찾기** ①

W Can you <u>live</u> <u>without</u> <u>a</u> <u>cellphone</u>?

M No way. It's very useful in my life. I can't live without one <u>for</u> <u>even</u> <u>a</u> <u>day</u>.

W Would you explain why it is so useful?

M As you know, it <u>has</u> <u>many</u> <u>helpful</u> <u>functions</u> such as sending messages, surfing the Internet, and taking photos and videos.

W I know that it's a convenient device. But <u>I</u> <u>think</u> <u>it</u> <u>also</u> <u>has</u> some bad points.

M Like what?

W <u>We don't talk face to face with others much anymore.</u>

여 너는 휴대 전화 없이 살 수 있어?
남 절대로 안 되지. 그것은 내 생활에서 매우 유용해. 나는 하루도 살 수 없을 거야.
여 왜 그것이 유용한지 설명해 줄래?
남 너도 알겠지만, 그것에는 메시지 보내기, 인터넷 검색, 그리고 사진과

비디오 촬영과 같은 많은 도움이 되는 기능들이 있어.
여 나도 그것이 편리한 장치라는 것을 알아. 하지만 나는 그것은 또한 어떤 나쁜 점도 있다고 생각해.
남 예를 들면?
여 <u>우리는 더 이상 다른 사람들하고 얼굴을 맞대고 많이 이야기하지 않아.</u>

해설 휴대 전화가 가진 단점의 예를 들어 달라는 말에 대한 가장 적절한 응답은 ① '우리는 더 이상 다른 사람들과 얼굴을 맞대고 많이 이야기하지 않아.'이다.
② 그 전화기를 사용하게 도와주셔서 감사합니다.
③ 그것은 우리에게 많은 유용한 정보를 줄 거야.
④ 그 메시지의 글꼴 크기가 좀 더 컸으면 좋을 텐데.
⑤ 나는 휴대 전화가 갖고 있는 나쁜 점에 대해 동의해.
어휘 without ~ ~ 없이 even [íːvən] 심지어, ~조차 bad point 나쁜 점, 단점

20 상황에 맞는 말 찾기 ④

W Gloria and Alice are classmates. They <u>have a history</u> <u>test</u> <u>tomorrow</u>. They decide to study together at Alice's house. They promise that they will study all night <u>without</u> <u>going</u> to <u>bed</u>. As time passes, however, both of them lie down and fall asleep. When Gloria wakes up, she sees that it's 7 a.m. and that <u>Alice</u> is <u>still</u> <u>sleeping</u> in <u>her</u> <u>bed</u>. In this situation, what would Gloria most likely say to Alice?
Gloria Alice, <u>wake up! The exam is going to start soon.</u>

여 Gloria와 Alice는 같은 반 친구입니다. 그들은 내일 역사 시험이 있습니다. 그들은 Alice의 집에서 함께 공부하기로 결심합니다. 그들은 자지 않고 공부를 하자고 약속합니다. 하지만 시간이 지나자, 그들 모두는 누워서 잠이 듭니다. Gloria가 깨어났을 때, 그녀는 아침 7시이며 Alice는 여전히 침대에서 자고 있는 걸 알게 됩니다. 이런 상황에서 Gloria는 Alice에게 무엇이라고 말할까요?
Gloria Alice, 일어나! 시험이 곧 시작될 거야.

해설 늦게까지 내일 있을 시험 준비를 하려 했으나 자신들도 모르게 잠든 후 아침에 눈을 뜬 상황이므로, 먼저 일어난 Gloria가 Alice에게 할 말로 가장 적절한 것은 ④ '일어나! 시험이 곧 시작될 거야.'이다.
① 좋은 있을 아침이야. 나에게 행운을 빌어줘.
② 내일 있을 수학 시험을 준비하자.
③ 시험을 잘 보려면 내가 무엇을 해야 하지? ⑤ TV를 끄고 가서 자.
어휘 promise [prámis] 약속(하다)

Listen and Check *p. 160*

Q1	False	Q12	No
Q2	Friday	Q13	False
Q3	Yes	Q14	True
Q4	No	Q15	No
Q5	False	Q16	because of the traffic jam
Q6	No		
Q7	No	Q17	Yes
Q8	False	Q18	call the taxi company
Q9	Yes		
Q10	No	Q19	True
Q11	False	Q20	False

해석
Q1 남자는 타임캡슐에 그의 앨범을 넣을 것이다.

Q2 여자는 카펫을 언제 받을 것인가?
Q3 남자는 여름 동안 여자의 가족과 함께 있었는가?
Q4 남자와 여자는 함께 점심을 먹을 것인가?
Q5 학생들은 수업 중에 쉴 수 있다.
Q6 남자는 탈의실이 어디 있는지 아는가?
Q7 여자는 내일 날씨가 어떨지 아는가?
Q8 여자는 표를 예매할 것이다.
Q9 여자는 그녀가 과학 시험에서 낙제할 것이라고 생각하는가?
Q10 가격에는 포장비가 포함되는가?
Q11 버스 운전사가 여자의 지갑을 버스에서 찾았다.
Q12 학생들은 공책을 숙제를 위해 들고 와야 하는가?
Q13 남자는 일반 자전거를 살 것이다.
Q14 광고의 목적은 특정 제품을 파는 것이다.
Q15 여자는 거리에 우유 용기를 버리는가?
Q16 여자는 왜 남자가 사무실에 더 일찍 갈 것을 제안하는가?
Q17 남자와 여자는 일요일에 만날 것인가?
Q18 여자는 대화 후에 무엇을 할 것인가?
Q19 남자는 휴대 전화가 편리한 기기라고 생각한다.
Q20 Gloria와 Alice는 자지 않고 밤새 공부했다.

실전 모의고사 **17회** *pp. 168~169*

1	③	2	③	3	②	4	②	5	②
6	⑤	7	⑤	8	①	9	③	10	④
11	③	12	④	13	④	14	③	15	④
16	③	17	③	18	④	19	③	20	②

1 그림 정보 파악 ③

W Good afternoon. What can I help you with?
M I'd like to <u>make a poster</u> to find my lost cat.
W The basic layout of the poster for that is that we place a picture on the left side and <u>a detailed description</u> on the right side.
M All right. Please write my phone number at <u>the bottom of</u> the poster. It's 888-1234.
W Okay. Anything else to add?
M I think it would be better to <u>indicate compensation</u>.
W I got it. You can <u>pick up your poster</u> by five o'clock.

여 안녕하세요. 무엇을 도와드릴까요?
남 제 잃어버린 고양이를 찾기 위한 포스터를 만들고 싶은데요.
여 포스터의 기본 레이아웃은 저희가 사진은 왼쪽 면에 넣고 상세한 설명은 오른쪽 면에 배치하는 것입니다.
남 알겠습니다. 포스터 하단에 제 전화번호를 적어주시기를 부탁드려요. 888-1234입니다.
여 네. 다른 거 더 추가하실 건 없으신가요?
남 보상금도 표시를 해두는 게 좋을 것 같아요.
여 알겠습니다. 다섯 시쯤 포스터 찾으러 오시면 되세요.

해설 포스터의 왼쪽에 사진을, 오른쪽에 상세한 설명을 두고 전화번호와 보상금을 표시해 달라고 하였다.
어휘 detailed [ditéild] 상세한 compensation [kàmpənséiʃən] 보상금, 보상

정답 및 해설

2 부탁한 일 파악 ③

W It's been a while since you wore that watch.
M You're right. But I have a problem.
W What is it?
M I guess my wrists have gotten a bit thicker. It's actually very tight for me to wear.
W Then you can make a hole in the watchstrap.
M Could you do that for me? I'm terrible at doing things like that.
W Sure. It's not as hard as you think.

여 오랜만에 그 시계를 찼구나.
남 맞아. 그런데 문제가 있어.
여 뭔데?
남 내 팔목이 조금 두꺼워진 것 같아. 내가 착용하기에 사실 너무 꽉 조여.
여 그렇다면 시곗줄 위에 구멍을 뚫으면 돼.
남 네가 좀 해줄 수 있을까? 나 이런 거 정말 못하거든.
여 그래. 네가 생각하는 것만큼 그렇게 어렵지 않아.

해설 남자가 여자에게 시곗줄에 구멍을 뚫어줄 것을 부탁하였다.
어휘 watchstrap [wátʃstræp] 시곗줄 terrible [térəbl] 형편없는

3 그림 상황 파악 ②

① W You look taller than the last time I saw you.
　 M That's true. I have gotten five centimeters taller.
② W Is it possible for her to ride the roller coaster?
　 M Sorry, but those who are below 130cm in height are not allowed to ride it.
③ W Oh, no. We have to wait in a long line again.
　 M We shouldn't have come here on a holiday.
④ W Do you have a membership card for the amusement park?
　 M Yes, I do. We only have to pay half price.
⑤ W I heard it is the steepest ride in the world.
　 M That makes me want to ride it more.

① 여 지난번에 봤을 때보다 너의 키가 더 커 보여.
　 남 사실이야. 5센티 더 컸어.
② 여 저 이 롤러코스터 타는 게 가능한가요?
　 남 죄송하지만, 키 130cm 미만의 사람들은 탈 수 없답니다.
③ 여 오, 이런. 긴 줄을 또 기다려야 해.
　 남 우리는 여기에 공휴일에 오면 안됐어.
④ 여 너 놀이동산 멤버십 카드 있어?
　 남 응, 있어. 우리는 절반 가격만 내면 돼.
⑤ 여 세계에서 가장 가파른 놀이 기구라고 들었어.
　 남 그 말을 들으니 더 타고 싶다.

해설 롤러코스터를 타려고 하는 아이의 엄마에게 직원이 아이의 키가 규정보다 작아서 탈 수 없다고 말하는 상황이다.
어휘 height [hait] 키, 높이 holiday [hálidèi] 공휴일, 휴일 steep [stiːp] 가파른

4 숫자 정보 파악 ②

W Did you make plans for the surprise party?
M Of course, I did. Stella said she would arrive here at 4:00.
W Everything should be ready by that time.
M You're picking her up soon, right? Please send me a message thirty minutes before you guys arrive here.

W Okay.
M Don't mention the surprise party to her.

여 깜짝 파티를 위한 계획은 세웠어?
남 물론이지. Stella가 여기에 4시에 도착할 거라고 했어.
여 그때까지 모두 준비가 되어야겠네.
남 그녀를 데리러 곧 갈 거잖아, 그렇지? 너희가 여기 도착하기 30분 전에 나한테 문자를 보내 줘.
여 알겠어.
남 그녀에게 깜짝 파티에 대해서 언급하지 마.

해설 남자는 여자에게 깜짝 파티의 주인공인 Stella가 도착하는 시간인 4시가 되기 30분 전에 문자를 줄 것을 부탁하였다.
어휘 make a plan 계획을 세우다 mention [ménʃən] 언급하다

5 언급 유무 파악 ②

W Do you know that a new ski resort opened last month?
M Really? Where is the resort?
W It's in Gangwon-do. There are a sledding slope and a water park, too.
M The resort must be huge. How's the water park?
W It's perfect for families. There are many rides for children.
M It sounds nice. Does the resort have its own website?
W Yes, it does. It's www.skyresorts.com.

여 새로운 리조트가 지난달에 오픈한 거 알아?
남 정말? 그 리조트가 어디에 있는데?
여 강원도에 있어. 눈썰매장도 있고 워터 파크도 있어.
남 그 리조트 엄청 큰가 보네. 워터 파크는 어때?
여 가족들이 가기에 최고인 것 같아. 아이들을 위한 놀이 기구가 많아.
남 좋은걸. 그 리조트 웹사이트가 있어?
여 응, 있어. 주소가 www.skyresorts.com이야.

해설 객실의 가격에 관해서는 언급되지 않았다.
어휘 sledding slope 눈썰매장 ride [raid] 탈 것 huge [hjuːdʒ] 거대한, 엄청 큰

6 장소 추론 ⑤

M Hi, Ms. Lee. Long time, no see!
W Yeah. I have been pretty busy these days. Is Jack available now?
M He's talking with one of his clients now. You can stay in the waiting room.
W Okay.
[Pause]
M How would you like to have your hair done?
W I want to dye my hair a bright color.
M I see. I recommend you dye your hair light brown. It will look good on you.
W That color could be a nice choice. Thanks.

남 안녕하세요, Lee씨. 오랜만이네요!
여 그러네요. 요즘 꽤 바빴어요. 지금 Jack이 시간이 있나요!
남 지금 고객분들 중 한 분과 대화를 나누고 계세요. 대기실에서 기다리시면 되세요.
여 알겠어요.
남 머리 어떻게 하실 건가요?
여 밝은 색으로 머리를 염색하고 싶어요.
남 그렇군요. 밝은 갈색으로 염색하실 것을 추천 드려요. 잘 어울리실 거

80

예요.

여 그 색깔 좋은 선택일 것 같아요. 고마워요.

해설 머리를 염색할 수 있는 곳임을 알 수 있다.

어휘 pretty [príti] 꽤, 어느 정도   dye [dai] 염색하다

7 어색한 대화 찾기 ⑤

① M You're talented at expressing yourself.

W That's what my father used to teach me.

② M You did a great job! Take pride in your work.

W Thank you for the compliment.

③ M Do you recognize the teacher over there?

W I'm not sure. Who is she?

④ M What's your challenge as a mother?

W It's raising my child to be independent.

⑤ M I'm having difficulty writing my essay.

W I really appreciate your help.

① 남 넌 너 자신을 표현하는 것에 재능이 있구나.

여 아빠가 가르쳐 주셨던 거야.

② 남 정말 잘했어! 네가 한 일에 자부심을 가져.

여 칭찬 감사합니다.

③ 남 저기 계신 선생님 알아보겠어?

여 잘 모르겠어. 누군데?

④ 남 엄마로서 어려운 점이 무엇인가요?

여 제 아이를 독립적으로 키우는 거예요.

⑤ 남 난 글을 쓰는 것에 어려움을 느껴.

여 도와줘서 정말 고마워.

해설 글을 쓰는 것에 어려움을 느낀다는 남자의 말에 도와줘서 고맙다고 답하는 것은 부자연스럽다.

어휘 talented [tǽləntid] 재능이 있는   take pride in ~에 자부심을 가지다   compliment [kámpləmənt] 칭찬   recognize [rékəgnàiz] 알아보다   independent [indipéndənt] 독립적인   appreciate [əprí:ʃièit] 고마워하다

8 부탁한 일 파악 ①

M Jessica, what's the matter? You look upset.

W I had an argument with one of my team members.

M What's the reason?

W She wasn't taking care of her responsibilities, so I complained to her.

M Did she change her behavior?

W Not at all.

M So how do you want to solve the problem?

W Could you give me some advice on it?

M You'd better talk with her more seriously.

남 Jessica, 무슨 일 있어? 속상해 보이는걸.

여 팀원 중 한 명이랑 말다툼이 있었거든.

남 이유가 뭔데?

여 그녀가 책임을 다하는 것 같지 않아서 내가 그녀에게 불평을 했거든.

남 그녀의 행동이 바뀌었어?

여 전혀 안 바뀌었어.

남 넌 이 문제를 어떻게 해결하고 싶은데?

여 이것에 대해 조언을 좀 줄 수 있겠어?

남 그녀랑 좀 더 진지하게 대화를 해보는 게 좋겠어.

해설 여자는 남자에게 팀원과의 갈등을 해결하기 위해 조언해 줄 것을 부탁하였다.

어휘 upset [ʌpsét] 속상한   complain [kəmpléin] 불평하다   seriously [sí(:)əriəsli] 진지하게, 심각하게

9 화제·주제 파악 ③

M How much information do you think we are exposed to every day? I'll explain how it influences our behavior. The type of information I want to focus on is advertisements. We don't recognize it, but we see hundreds of ads a day. What matters is they affect us when we make decisions on food, books, jobs, and so on. We should develop the ability to distinguish our real thoughts from ones that are formed by ads. When you have to make an important decision, question the ideas you come up with.

남 당신은 우리가 매일 얼마나 많은 정보에 노출이 된다고 생각하시나요? 이것이 우리의 행동에 어떻게 영향을 미치는지 설명 드리겠습니다. 제가 관심을 기울이고 싶은 정보의 유형은 광고입니다. 우리는 인식하지 못하지만 하루에 수백 개의 광고를 봅니다. 중요한 것은 그것이 우리가 음식, 책, 직업 등에 관한 결정을 내릴 때 우리에게 영향을 미친다는 것입니다. 우리는 우리의 진짜 생각과 광고로 인해 형성된 생각을 구별하는 능력을 키워야 합니다. 중요한 결정을 내릴 때, 당신이 떠올리는 생각을 의심하세요.

해설 사람들이 결정을 내리는 과정에서 광고가 영향을 미치기 때문에 중요한 결정을 내릴 때에는 떠오르는 생각을 의심하라고 하였다.

어휘 be exposed to ~에 노출되다   influence [ínfluəns] 영향을 미치다   affect [əfékt] 영향을 미치다   distinguish [distíŋgwiʃ] 구별하다   question [kwéstʃən] 의문을 갖다   come up with 떠오르다

10 숫자 정보 파악 ④

M I'd like to buy two tickets for the movie *Toy Story 4* starting at 4:00.

W For an adult, it's ten dollars per ticket.

M Okay. Is there a couple seat where two people can sit together?

W Yes, there is. You have to buy two tickets, and each ticket is twice as expensive as a regular one.

M I'd like two tickets for adults for a couple seat. I heard I can get fifty percent off when I pay with this credit card.

W Sorry, but we only offer twenty percent off for that card.

M I see. Here is the card.

남 4시에 시작하는 'Toy Story 4' 영화표 두 개를 사고 싶어요.

여 성인의 경우 표당 10달러입니다.

남 알겠어요. 두 사람이 같이 앉을 수 있는 커플석이 있나요?

여 네, 있습니다. 두 장을 구매하셔야 하고 한 장당 가격이 일반 표 한 장보다 두 배 더 비쌉니다.

남 커플석으로 성인 2장 사겠습니다. 이 신용 카드로 결제하면 50퍼센트 할인을 받는다고 들었어요.

여 죄송하지만, 하지만 그 카드로는 20퍼센트 할인만을 해드리고 있답니다.

남 알겠어요. 여기 카드 있습니다.

해설 커플석 성인 영화표 두 장에 대한 금액은 40달러이지만 신용 카드로 20% 할인을 받을 수 있다고 하였다.

어휘 normal [nɔ́:rməl] 일반의, 평범한   reserve [rizə́:rv] 예약하다

11 할 일 파악 ③

W I think we can follow that road sign.

M Wait a second. I wrote down how to get there in

my notebook.

W The road sign says we can turn left and walk for about ten minutes until we <u>get</u> <u>to</u> <u>our</u> <u>destination</u>.

M Well, I guess turning right is right. My notebook says so.

W Where did you get that information?

M I got it from a traveler's blog, where he shares <u>his</u> <u>travel</u> <u>experiences</u>.

W Let's not depend on what he wrote on his blog. Let's ask someone at an information center to make sure we <u>get</u> <u>accurate</u> <u>information</u>.

M That's a good idea.

여 내 생각엔 저 도로 표지판을 따라가면 될 것 같아.

남 잠시만 기다려. 어떻게 가야 하는지 내 공책에 적어 놓았어.

여 도로 표지판은 우리가 왼쪽으로 꺾어서 목적지에 도착할 때까지 10분 정도 걸어가면 된다고 하네.

남 글쎄, 오른쪽으로 꺾는 게 맞는 것 같아. 내 공책에 따르면 그래.

여 그 정보는 어디서 얻은 거야?

남 한 여행객 블로그에서 얻은 건데, 그곳에 그의 여행 경험을 공유하거든.

여 그가 블로그에 쓴 것에 의존하지 말자. 정확한 정보를 얻기 위해 정보 센터의 누군가에게 물어보도록 하자.

남 좋은 생각이야.

해설 남자가 한 여행객의 블로그에서 얻은 정보에 너무 의존을 하자 여자가 안내원에게 물어보자고 제안하였다.

어휘 road sign 도로 표지판   depend on 의존하다   information center 정보 센터   accurate [ǽkjərit] 정확한

12 언급 유무 파악 ④

W Hello. I'm <u>a</u> <u>program</u> <u>planner</u> at the company Thinking Up. Let me introduce some programs for <u>this</u> <u>summer</u> <u>season</u>. First of all, four programs, including history, arts, literature, and science, will be held. <u>The</u> <u>main</u> <u>activity</u> will be a student discussion. Each of the programs will <u>take</u> <u>place</u> from Monday to Friday at 10:00 a.m. and 2:00 p.m. for six weeks. You can <u>register</u> <u>a</u> <u>program</u> here at the company or on the website.

여 안녕하세요. 저는 Thinking Up 회사의 프로그램 설계자입니다. 이번 여름철을 위한 몇 가지 프로그램을 소개해 드리겠습니다. 우선, 역사, 예술, 문학, 그리고 과학을 포함한 네 개의 프로그램이 열릴 예정입니다. 주요 활동은 학생 토의가 될 것입니다. 각각의 프로그램은 6주 동안 매주 월요일부터 금요일까지 오전 10시와 오후 2시에 시작될 것입니다. 이곳 회사에서 프로그램을 신청하시거나 웹사이트에서 신청하실 수도 있습니다.

해설 프로그램 진행자의 명단에 관해서는 언급되지 않았다.

어휘 planner [plǽnər] 설계자, 계획자   including [inklúːdiŋ] 포함하
여 discussion [diskʌ́ʃən] 토의, 토론

13 표 파악 ④

M What are we going to do about the T-shirts for our class? Here are <u>some</u> <u>types</u> <u>we</u> <u>can</u> <u>choose</u>.

W Let me see. Considering the chilly weather, it would be better if we got <u>long</u> <u>sleeves</u>.

M I agree with you. What about the color? How about yellow?

W I heard that another class already has yellow T-shirts. So we should <u>go</u> <u>with</u> <u>blue</u>.

M That's totally fine. Blue is the color of victory.

W Do you think we should put <u>our</u> <u>names</u> on the T-shirts?

M No, I don't think so. Just <u>the</u> <u>classroom</u> <u>number</u> will do.

남 우리 반 티셔츠 어떻게 할까? 여기 우리가 고를 수 있는 몇 가지 종류가 있어.

여 어디 보자. 쌀쌀한 날씨를 고려해서 긴팔을 입는 게 좋을 것 같아.

남 네 말에 동의해. 색깔은? 노란색은 어때?

여 내가 듣기로 다른 반이 이미 노란색 티셔츠로 맞췄대. 그래서 우리는 파란색으로 가야 해.

남 완전 좋아. 파란색은 승리의 색인걸.

여 네 생각엔 티셔츠에 우리 이름을 넣어야 할 것 같아?

남 아니, 그렇지 않아. 반 번호만으로 충분해.

해설 긴팔에 색상은 파랑색이며 반 번호를 넣기로 하였다.

어휘 chilly [tʃíli] 쌀쌀한   sleeve [sliːv] 소매   victory [víktəri] 승리 do [dou] 충분하다

14 화제·주제 파악 ③

W It is a kind of book which is <u>mostly</u> <u>written</u> for children. They can <u>develop</u> <u>their</u> <u>imagination</u> and learn important life lessons through this. It sometimes tells about the <u>history</u> <u>and</u> <u>culture</u> of different countries. In addition, parents read it to their children before they <u>go</u> <u>to</u> <u>sleep</u>. We can <u>find</u> <u>a</u> <u>section</u> only for this in bookstores.

여 이것은 주로 아이들을 위해 쓰이는 책의 한 종류입니다. 그들은 이것을 통해 상상력을 키우기도 하고 중요한 삶의 교훈을 배우기도 합니다. 이 것은 때때로 여러 나라들의 역사와 문화에 대해서 말하기도 합니다. 게다가 부모님들은 이것을 그들의 자녀가 잠이 들기 전에 읽어주기도 합니다. 우리는 서점에서 이것만을 위한 코너를 찾을 수 있습니다.

해설 주로 아이들을 위해 쓰이고 아이들이 잠이 들기 전에 부모님들이 읽어 주는 것이며 서점에는 이것만을 위한 코너가 따로 있다고 하였다.

어휘 mostly [móustli] 주로, 대부분   develop [divéləp] 성장시키다, 개발하다   imagination [imæ̀ʤənéiʃən] 상상력   culture [kʌ́ltʃər] 문화

15 할 일 파악 ④

W Dad, we have <u>so</u> <u>many</u> <u>plants</u> that our house seems like a small garden.

M Is that so?

W And look at those plants in the living room. They are no longer <u>glossy</u> <u>but</u> <u>dead</u>.

M Oh, no. What is the date? I guess it's already been more than two weeks since I <u>watered</u> <u>them</u>. I need to do that now.

W Dad, let's only have as many plants as we can <u>take</u> <u>good</u> <u>care</u> <u>of</u>.

M Okay. I'll have to water them more often <u>from</u> <u>now</u> <u>on</u>.

여 아빠, 식물이 너무 많아서 집이 꼭 작은 정원 같아요.

남 그래?

여 그리고 거실에 있는 식물들 좀 보세요. 더 이상 윤기도 나지도 않고 잎이 죽었어요.

남 오, 안 돼. 오늘이 며칠이지? 물을 준지가 2주 이상은 된 것 같아. 지금 줘야겠구나.

여 아빠, 저희가 모두 잘 키울 수 있을 만큼만 식물을 키워요.

남 그래. 앞으로는 더 자주 물을 줘야겠다.

해설 여자가 거실에 있는 식물이 윤기가 없고 죽었다고 하자 남자가 물을 준 지가 오래 지나서 물을 줘야겠다고 하였다.

어휘 seem [siːm] ~처럼 보이다 glossy [glási] 윤기가 나는 dead [ded] (잎이) 마른

16 숫자 정보 파악 ③

W Is it today that you are taking the driver's license exam?

M Yes, it is. The test starts at the center at 2:00 p.m.

W It's already 1:00 p.m. Don't you have to leave now?

M Four people take the exam one by one, which means I have to wait for my turn for quite a long time.

W Then when are you going to leave?

M I'll leave twenty minutes before the exam starts.

W Make sure you don't miss it.

여 운전면허 시험 보는 거 오늘이지?
남 응, 맞아. 시험은 2시에 시험장에서 시작해.
여 벌써 1시야. 지금 나가야 하지 않아?
남 네 사람이 한 명씩 시험을 보는데, 그건 내 차례를 꽤 오래 기다려야 한다는 뜻이지.
여 그럼 언제 출발하려고 하는데?
남 시험 시작 20분 전에 출발할 거야.
여 놓치지 않도록 해.

해설 남자는 시험 시간이 2시이고, 시험 시작 20분 전에 출발한다고 하였다.

어휘 driver's license 운전면허 one by one 한 명씩

17 적절한 응답 찾기 ③

[Telephone rings.]

W Hello. This is Healing Resort. What can I help you with?

M Hi. It's Nathan Park. I'd like to cancel my reservation.

W Hello, Mr. Park. Did you check the refund policy before you made your payment?

M What is the policy?

W You can get a full refund only when you make a cancelation one month before the date of your reservation.

M How about just moving my date to another one?

W That's possible if there are rooms available.

M Okay. I'll call you back when I set the date.

여 여보세요? Healing Resort입니다. 무엇을 도와드릴까요?
남 안녕하세요, 저는 Nathan Park입니다. 예약을 취소하고 싶어요.
여 안녕하세요, Park씨. 결제를 하시기 전에 환불 정책을 확인하셨나요?
남 정책에 관한 어떤 거요?
여 예약하신 날짜로부터 한 달 전에 취소 통지를 해 주셔야만 전액 환불을 받으실 수 있거든요.
남 그럼 그냥 날짜를 다른 날짜로 옮기는 건요?
여 사용 가능한 방이 있다면 가능합니다.
남 알겠습니다. 날짜를 정하는 대로 다시 전화 드릴게요.

해설 방이 있으면 날짜를 바꾸는 것은 가능하다는 말에 대한 가장 적절한 응답은 ③ '알겠습니다. 날짜를 정하는 대로 다시 전화 드릴게요.'이다.
① 그건 내가 이곳을 마지막으로 방문했을 때에요.
② 전액 환불을 받을 수 있어서 좋네요.

④ 이 호텔이 최상의 서비스를 제공한다고 들었어요.
⑤ 저는 차라리 셔틀버스를 탈게요.

어휘 cancelation [kæ̀nsəléiʃən] 취소

18 적절한 응답 찾기 ④

M I'm concerned that my children watch too much TV.

W How long do they usually watch it?

M Around two hours a day.

W That sounds about average. What kinds of TV programs do they watch?

M They watch entertainment shows and dramas.

W How about doing other activities with them?

M What activities do you think will be fun and helpful at the same time?

W You can take a walk or read books together.

남 내 아이들이 TV를 너무 많이 봐서 걱정이야.
여 평소에 얼마나 오래 보는데?
남 하루에 두 시간 정도.
여 그 정도면 딱 평균인 것 같은데. 어떤 TV 프로그램들을 봐?
남 예능 프로그램하고 드라마를 봐.
여 다른 활동들을 그들과 함께 하는 건 어때?
남 네 생각엔 어떤 활동들이 재밌으면서 동시에 유익할 것 같은데?
여 같이 산책을 하거나 책을 읽으면 되지.

해설 재밌으면서 유익한 활동에는 어떤 것이 있는지 묻는 말에 대한 가장 적절한 응답은 ④ '같이 산책을 하거나 책을 읽으면 되지.'이다.
① TV를 보는 것에는 전혀 잘못된 게 없어.
② 네 생각이 내 생각보다 더 나은 것 같아.
③ 약속을 지키는 게 쉽지 않다는 걸 알고 있어.
⑤ 우리는 그 문제에 대한 해결책을 쉽게 찾을 수 있어.

어휘 concerned [kənsə́ːrnd] 걱정하는, 염려하는 helpful [hélpfəl] 유익한, 도움이 되는 keep one's promise 약속을 지키다 solution [səljúːʃən] 해결책

19 적절한 응답 찾기 ③

W Minhyeok, have you finished your part?

M I'm finalizing it now. What about you?

W I just started because there was something urgent I had to do first.

M You don't have enough time. You've only got two hours left.

W I know. I should have started much earlier.

M Ask me anytime you need my help.

W Then could you give me a hand after you're done with your work?

M Sure. Let me know what I can do for you.

여 민혁아, 네 분량은 다 끝냈어?
남 지금 마무리하는 중이야. 너는?
여 나는 급한 것 먼저 하느라 막 시작했어.
남 시간이 별로 없어. 2시간밖에 안 남았는걸.
여 알아. 훨씬 일찍 시작했어야 하는데 말이야.
남 언제든지 내 도움이 필요할 때면 내게 얘기해.
여 그럼 너 일을 다 끝내고나서 나 좀 도와줄 수 있을까?
남 물론이지. 내가 무엇을 해주면 될지 알려 줘.

해설 도움을 요청하는 말에 대한 가장 적절한 응답은 ③ '물론이지. 내가 무엇을 해주면 될지 알려 줘.'이다.
① 지도자가 되는 게 무슨 소용이야?

② 신경 쓰지 마. 모든 일이 순조롭게 진행될 거야.
④ 그 순간엔 난 결정을 내릴 수가 없었어.
⑤ 넌 네가 있는 곳을 늘 깨끗하게 유지해야 해.
어휘 finalize [fáinəlàiz] 마무리 짓다　urgent [ə́ːrdʒənt] 긴급한
smoothly [smúːðli] 순조롭게, 부드럽게　make a decision 결정을 내리다

20 상황에 맞는 말 찾기 ②

M Joshua and Vivian go to Vivian's house to <u>do their assignments</u> together. When they get to the house, they start to do their work. Soon, they hear <u>some loud noises</u> right outside the window. Joshua notices that there is some <u>construction going on</u> beside where they are studying. He <u>can't concentrate on</u> his studies and is sitting far from the window. He sees Vivian sitting close to <u>the open window</u>. In this situation, what would Joshua most likely say to Vivian?

Joshua Vivian, <u>do you mind closing the window?</u>

남 Joshua와 Vivian은 함께 과제를 하기 위해 Vivian의 집으로 갑니다. 그들이 집에 도착했을 때, 그들은 숙제를 하기 시작합니다. 곧 그들은 창문 바로 밖에서 나는 큰 소음을 듣습니다. Joshua는 그들이 공부하고 있던 곳 바로 옆에서 공사가 진행 중임을 알았습니다. 그는 공부에 집중을 할 수가 없고 창문에서 멀리 떨어져 앉아있습니다. 그는 Vivian이 열린 창문 옆 가까이에 앉아있는 것을 봅니다. 이 상황에서 Joshua은 Vivian에게 뭐라고 말을 할까요?

Joshua Vivian, 창문 좀 닫아줄 수 있을까?

해설 창문을 통해 공사로 인한 큰 소음이 들어오는 상황에서 Joshua가 Vivian에게 할 말로 가장 적절한 것은 ② '창문 좀 닫아줄 수 있을까?'이다.
① 여기서 공부하는 거 굉장히 편안해.　③ 난 몇 가지 문제들이 이해가 안가.
④ 불을 좀 켜자. 너무 어두워.　⑤ 지금 간식을 좀 먹는 게 어때?
어휘 construction [kənstrʌ́kʃən] 공사

Listen and Check
p. 170

Q1 on the left side
Q2 True
Q3 No
Q4 by sending a message
Q5 False
Q6 No
Q7 False
Q8 She has an irresponsible attitude.
Q9 when making decisions
Q10 No
Q11 True
Q12 student discussions
Q13 No
Q14 False
Q15 water plants
Q16 False
Q17 False
Q18 read books
Q19 True
Q20 the noise from outside

해석
Q1 반려동물의 사진은 포스터의 어느 곳에 배치가 될 것인가?
Q2 남자가 시계를 구입할 때 남자의 손목은 더 얇았다.
Q3 남자는 아이가 롤러코스터를 타는 것을 허용하는가?
Q4 여자는 남자에게 파티를 위한 신호를 어떻게 보낼 것인가?
Q5 여자는 남자에게 가족 여행으로 새로운 워터 파크를 추천한다.
Q6 여자는 그녀의 머리를 자르러 왔는가?
Q7 남자는 글 쓰는 것을 잘한다.
Q8 여자는 그녀의 팀원에 대해 왜 화가 나는가?

Q9 남자는 언제 광고가 사람들에게 영향을 미친다고 생각하는가?
Q10 남자는 그의 신용 카드로 50퍼센트 할인을 받을 수 있는가?
Q11 여자는 블로그에서 얻는 정보를 의심한다.
Q12 프로그램의 주요 활동이 무엇인가?
Q13 남자와 여자는 티셔츠에 그들의 이름을 넣을 것인가?
Q14 오직 아이들만이 이 종류의 책을 읽을 수 있다.
Q15 남자는 자주 무엇을 하는 것을 잊는가?
Q16 남자는 이미 그의 운전면허 시험을 마쳤다.
Q17 예약한 날짜로부터 일주일 전에 취소할 경우 전액 환불을 받는 것이 가능하다.
Q18 여자는 남자가 아이들과 무엇을 할 것을 제안하는가?
Q19 남자는 여자가 그녀를 도와달라고 하면 기꺼이 그녀를 도울 것이다.
Q20 무엇이 Joshua가 공부하는 데 집중하는 것을 방해하는가?

실전 모의고사 18회
pp. 178~179

1 ①	2 ③	3 ⑤	4 ②	5 ④
6 ③	7 ④	8 ①	9 ②	10 ③
11 ③	12 ④	13 ④	14 ①	15 ②
16 ④	17 ⑤	18 ③	19 ③	20 ④

1 그림 정보 파악 ①

M Did you design your business card yourself?
W That's right. At the center, I drew a coffee cup. Three tiny hearts are <u>drawn</u> on it.
M I also see one chocolate muffin to the right of the cup.
W Yes. The coffee cup and the muffin show that this business card is for a café.
M <u>Where is the name of</u> your café?
W I put the name of the café, Pause, in the upper left corner.
M I really love <u>how you designed this</u>.

남 네가 직접 명함을 디자인한 거야?
여 맞아. 중앙에는 커피잔을 그렸어. 커피잔에는 작은 하트 3개가 그려져 있어.
남 그리고 난 커피잔 오른쪽에 초코렛 머핀이 보여.
여 응. 커피잔이랑 머핀은 이 명함이 카페라는 걸 보여주는 거야.
남 카페의 이름은 어디에 있어?
여 카페 이름인 '쉼'은 왼쪽 상단에 있어.
남 네가 디자인한 이 명함이 너무 마음에 든다.
해설 명함 중앙에는 커피잔 그림, 커피잔의 오른쪽에는 머핀 그림, 카페 이름 Pause는 명함의 왼쪽 상단에 적혀 있다고 하였다.
어휘 business card 명함　tiny [táini] 작은　upper [ʌ́pər] 위쪽의
corner [kɔ́ːrnər] 구석, 모퉁이

2 부탁한 일 파악 ③

W Why are you <u>holding a bunch of flowers</u>?
M I'm thinking of making a bouquet for my sister's wedding.
W Wow. You must be a wonderful brother.
M So can you <u>teach me how to make</u> a wedding

bouquet?
W My pleasure. Do you have <u>everything you need</u>?
M Only flowers.
W Please give some scissors, wrapping paper, and ribbons to me.

여 너 왜 꽃 한 다발을 들고 있니?
남 내 여동생의 결혼식을 위해 부케를 만들까 생각 중이야.
여 와. 넌 멋진 오빠구나.
남 그래서 말인데, 결혼식 부케 만드는 방법을 알려줄 수 있어?
여 당연하지. 필요한 건 다 가지고 있어?
남 꽃만 있어.
여 가위랑 포장지, 그리고 리본을 줘.

해설 남자는 여자에게 결혼식 부케를 만드는 방법을 알려 달라고 부탁하였다.

어휘 bunch [bʌntʃ] 다발, 묶음   bouquet [boukéi] 부케, 꽃다발
scissors [sízərz] 가위   wrapping paper 포장지

3 그림 상황 파악 ⑤
① W What do you like to do for fun?
　 M <u>I enjoy skateboarding</u>.
② W I heard that you <u>had a car accident</u>.
　 M Right. Lucky for me, I was not hurt seriously.
③ W Let's <u>go skateboarding this weekend</u>.
　 M Okay. Please let me know when you want to go.
④ W How long do you need to <u>have a cast</u> on your arm?
　 M I'm not sure, but maybe for a month.
⑤ W <u>What happened</u> to your leg?
　 M I broke it while skateboarding.

① 여 넌 주로 무엇을 하면서 노니?
　 남 난 스케이트보드 타는 걸 좋아해.
② 여 자동차 사고가 났다고 들었어.
　 남 맞아. 다행히도 크게 다치지는 않았어.
③ 여 이번 주말에 스케이트보드 타러 가자.
　 남 그래. 네가 가고 싶을 때 내게 알려 줘.
④ 여 팔에 깁스를 얼마나 오랫동안 해야 해?
　 남 확실하지는 않지만 한 달 동안일 거야.
⑤ 여 다리는 어쩌다가 그랬어?
　 남 스케이트보드를 타다가 부러졌어.

해설 스케이트보드를 타다가 넘어져서 다리가 부러졌다고 말하는 상황이다.

어휘 cast [kæst] 깁스 붕대

4 특정 정보 파악 ②
W Look at this brochure. We can <u>exercise together</u> this summer.
M That's a great idea. Which class would you like to take?
W What do you think about <u>taking swimming lessons</u> together?
M Sounds good.
W There are two swimming classes <u>to choose from</u>. They are on Tuesday and Friday.
M I have to study Chinese every Friday. How about <u>taking the class on Tuesday</u>?
W Sure.

여 이 책자를 봐. 이번 여름에 같이 운동할 수 있어.
남 좋은 생각이다. 어떤 강습을 듣고 싶어?
여 수영 강습 같이 듣는 거 어떻게 생각해?
남 좋아.
여 선택할 수 있는 수영 강습이 두 개네. 화요일이랑 금요일에 있어.
남 난 매주 금요일마다 중국어를 공부해야 해. 화요일 강습을 듣는 어떠니?
여 그래.

해설 매주 화요일마다 진행하는 수영 강습을 듣기로 하였다.

어휘 take [teik] 수강하다

5 언급 유무 파악 ④
W Gold Bank is offering a <u>four-week summer</u> internship.
M Great! Gold Bank has 50,000 employees.
W If you get the job, you will make 700 dollars a month.
M That's <u>not bad for a beginner</u>.
W You can also <u>get work experience</u> in investments.
M What are the qualifications?
W <u>Anyone who graduated</u> from high school can apply.
M Well, I should apply for it.

여 Gold 은행에서 4주간의 여름 인턴십을 제공한대.
남 좋네! Gold 은행은 직원이 5만 명이잖아.
여 네가 그 일을 갖게 되면 넌 한 달에 700달러를 벌게 될 거야.
남 신입에게 나쁘지 않군.
여 또한 너는 투자 부분에서 경력을 갖게 되지.
남 자격 조건이 뭔데?
여 고등학교를 졸업한 사람은 누구나 지원할 수 있어.
남 음, 나 지원해 봐야겠다.

해설 인턴십의 총 모집 인원에 관해서는 언급되지 않았다.
어휘 employee [implɔíː] 직원, 종업원   qualification [kwàləfəkéiʃən] 자격   apply for 지원하다, 응시하다

6 장소 추론 ③
W <u>Look at the elephants</u> over there. They are so big but look so sad.
M I feel exactly the same way. Maybe they're sad because they have <u>lost their freedom</u>.
W Look at the lions. They are <u>just lying down</u> and seem to sleep all day.
M Do you think it's okay to keep wild animals here just for our pleasure?
W I don't think so. They're confined to such small spaces.
M We should <u>send them back</u> to their natural habitats.

여 저기에 있는 코끼리 봐. 엄청 큰데, 슬퍼 보여.
남 나도 같은 걸 느꼈어. 아마도 자유를 잃어버려서 슬픈가 봐.
여 저 사자 좀 봐. 누워서 종일 자는 것 같아.
남 단지 우리의 즐거움을 위해서 야생 동물을 여기에 두는 게 괜찮다고 생각해?
여 그렇게 생각하지 않아. 그들은 그렇게 작은 공간에 갇혀 있잖아.
남 우리는 그들을 자연 서식지로 돌려보내야 해.

해설 코끼리와 사자를 바라보며 동물원에서 대화를 나누는 상황이다.
어휘 freedom [fríːdəm] 자유   confine [kənfáin] 가두다, 제한하다

space [speis] 공간, 우주   habitat [hǽbitæt] 서식지

7 어색한 대화 찾기 ④

① M Do you need a hand with that?
　W Yes, please. These books are too heavy for me to carry.
② M Make sure you're not late for the meeting.
　W Don't worry. I'll make it this time.
③ M Can I borrow your bicycle? I lost mine.
　W Sure, but I need it back by this Friday.
④ M Do you want to grab a bite to eat?
　W Let's take a walk rather than get a taxi.
⑤ M How many people did you invite to your housewarming party?
　W About 15.

① 남 도움이 필요하니?
　여 응. 이 책은 내가 나르기에 너무 무거워.
② 남 반드시 회의에 늦으면 안 돼.
　여 걱정하지 마. 이번에는 꼭 지킬게.
③ 남 네 자전거를 빌려도 될까? 내 것을 잃어버렸어.
　여 물론이지. 그런데 이번 주 금요일까지는 돌려줘.
④ 남 간단히 뭐 먹을래?
　여 택시 타는 거 대신에 걸어가자.
⑤ 남 집들이에 사람들을 몇 명이나 초대했니?
　여 15명 정도야.

해설 간단히 뭘 먹을지를 묻는 말에 택시를 타지 말고 걸어가자고 답하는 것은 부자연스럽다.
어휘 borrow [bárou] 빌리다   grab a bite to eat 간단히 먹다 housewarming [háuswɔ̀ːrmiŋ] 집들이

8 부탁한 일 파악 ①

[Cellphone rings.]
M Hey, Bella. What's up?
W Where are you? Are you on your way home?
M Not yet. I'm about to play soccer on the school playground.
W Then can you drop by the stationery store on your way home?
M No problem. What do you need?
W I need some letter paper because tomorrow is Mom's birthday.
M Oh, no! I completely forgot about it.

남 Bella, 무슨 일이야?
여 어디야? 집으로 오는 중이야?
남 아직은 아니야. 학교 운동장에서 막 축구하려는 중이야.
여 그럼 집에 오는 길에 문구점에 들를 수 있어?
남 문제없지. 어떤 것이 필요해?
여 내일 엄마 생일이라서 편지지가 필요해.
남 아, 안 돼! 나 완전히 잊고 있었어.

해설 여자는 남자에게 집에 오는 길에 문구점에 들러 편지지를 사다 달라고 부탁하였다.
어휘 stationery store 문구점

9 화제·주제 파악 ②

W Good morning, passengers. As we informed you earlier, today we're going to check the escalators located in Anyang Station. It will take a week to complete. If needed, the escalators can be replaced with new ones. During the inspection, please take the stairs. There will also be extra staff members to assist passengers. We apologize for the inconvenience. Thank you for your cooperation!

여 좋은 아침입니다, 승객 여러분. 이전에 알려 드린 대로 오늘은 안양역에 위치한 에스컬레이터를 점검할 예정입니다. 완료하는 데 일주일이 걸릴 예정입니다. 필요하다면 에스컬레이터는 새로운 것으로 교체될 수 있습니다. 점검하는 동안 계단을 이용해 주시길 바랍니다. 또한 승객들을 돕기 위해 직원이 추가적으로 더 있을 예정입니다. 불편을 끼쳐 드려 죄송합니다. 승객 여러분의 협조에 감사드립니다.

해설 안양역에서 일주일 동안 에스컬레이터 점검을 실시하게 되었다고 알리는 안내 방송이다.
어휘 locate [lóukeit] 위치하다

10 숫자 정보 파악 ③

W Welcome to Sweet Bakery. What can I assist you with?
M Hi. Is this strawberry jam homemade? How much is it?
W Right. My grandmother and I made all of the products at home. The strawberry jam is 5 dollars for a small jar.
M Hmm... How much are these butter cookies?
W They cost 10 dollars per dozen.
M Then I'll take a dozen of the cookies and two jars of strawberry jam.
W Okay. I'll put them in a paper bag.

여 Sweet 빵집에 오신 걸 환영해요. 무엇을 도와드릴까요?
남 안녕하세요. 딸기잼을 직접 만드신 건가요? 얼마인가요?
여 맞아요. 할머니랑 제가 집에서 모든 제품을 만들었어요. 딸기잼은 작은 병에 5달러예요.
남 음... 이 버터 쿠키는요?
여 12개짜리 한 다스에 10달러예요.
남 그러면 쿠키 한 다스와 딸기잼 2병을 살게요.
여 네. 종이봉투에 담아 드릴게요.

해설 5달러짜리 딸기잼 두 병과 10달러짜리 버터 쿠키 한 묶음을 구입하였다.
어휘 homemade 집에서 만든   jar [dʒɑːr] 병, 단지   dozen [dʌ́zən] 12개짜리 한 묶음

11 할 일 파악 ③

M Sujin, your room is messy. Why are your clothes lying on the bed?
W Dad, I got up so late that I had to go to school in a hurry.
M It's not just today. Look at your desk. Many books are piled up on it.
W All right. Can I clean it up tomorrow? I have to finish my English essay.
M Sorry, but you have to organize your clothes on the bed first.
W Okay. After that, I'll do my homework.

남 수진아, 네 방이 지저분하구나. 왜 옷이 침대 위에 있는 거지?
여 아빠, 오늘 너무 늦게 일어나서 학교에 서둘러서 가야 했어요.
남 오늘만 그런 게 아니잖아. 네 책상을 봐. 많은 책이 쌓여 있잖아.

여 알겠어요. 내일 치워도 될까요? 영어 에세이를 끝내야 해요.
남 미안하지만 침대에 있는 옷을 먼저 정리하도록 해라.
여 네. 그리고 나서 숙제를 할게요.

해설 침대에 있는 옷을 먼저 정리하겠다고 대답하였다.
어휘 in a hurry 서둘러서 pile up 쌓다 organize [ɔ́ːrɡənàiz] 정리하다

12 언급 유무 파악 ④

M Cheonghakdong Etiquette Summer School provides various classes for students <u>to learn proper</u> etiquette. Children can <u>stay away from their cellphones</u> and the Internet and focus on themselves. Cheonghakdong Etiquette Summer School will begin on August 1 and end on August 20. It is for children ages 8 to 12. It costs one thousand dollars, <u>including meals and housing</u>. For more information, please visit www. cheonghakschool.com.

남 청학동 여름 예절 학교에서는 학생들이 참된 예절을 배울 수 있는 다양한 수업을 제공합니다. 아이들은 휴대폰과 인터넷에서 벗어나서 자신들에게 집중할 것입니다. 청학동 여름 예절 학교는 8월 1일에 시작하여 8월 20일에 끝납니다. 8살부터 12살 어린이를 대상으로 합니다. 비용은 식사와 숙소를 포함하여 천 달러입니다. 더 많은 정보가 필요하시면 www.cheonghakschool.com을 방문해 주시길 바랍니다.

해설 청학동 여름 예절 학교 담당 강사의 연락처에 관해서는 언급되지 않았다.
어휘 etiquette [étəkit] 예절, 에티켓 various [vέ(ː)əriəs] 다양한, 여러 가지의 stay away from ～에서 떨어져 있다, 벗어나다

13 그림 정보 파악 ④

M Sweetie, let's select the hotel where we'll stay on our last night in Canada.
W Our flight to Seoul is scheduled early in the morning.
M Then <u>staying at a hotel</u> near the bus station is much better.
W I can't agree with you more. And our flight doesn't include any free meals.
M Let's buy fresh bread at a bakery that morning. How about hotel A?
W I don't think so. It's <u>far from the bus station</u>. We'll take a bus to the airport.
M What about the hotel <u>across the street from the bakery</u>? It's near the bus station, too.
W That's perfect. I'll make a reservation.

남 여보, 우리가 캐나다에서 마지막 날에 머물 호텔을 선택하자.
여 서울로 가는 비행기가 아침 일찍 예정되어 있어.
남 그러면 버스 정류장 근처에 있는 호텔에서 머무는 게 좋겠다.
여 전적으로 동의해. 그리고 우리 항공편에는 무료 식사가 포함되어 있지 않아.
남 그 날 아침에 빵집에서 신선한 빵을 사자. 호텔 A는 어때?
여 아닌 거 같아. 버스 정류장에서 멀어. 우리는 버스 타고 공항 갈 거야.
남 빵집에서 길 건너편에 있는 호텔은 어때? 버스 정거장하고도 가까워.
여 완벽해. 내가 예약할게.

해설 빵집 건너편이고 버스 정류장 근처에 위치한 호텔을 예약하기로 하였다.
어휘 select [silékt] 선택하다

14 화제·주제 파악 ①

W Most wildfires are caused by people. Forest fires destroy many big, old trees and the habitats of animals. They also <u>cause damage to ecosystems</u>. So what can people do to <u>prevent forest fires</u>? Above all, people must be more careful with their actions. Make a fire in the forest only if it is absolutely necessary. Make sure you extinguish your fire before leaving. <u>Put it out with water</u> or cover it with soil. In addition, don't smoke in the forest. Don't throw burning matches on the ground either.

여 대부분의 산불은 사람에 의해서 발생됩니다. 산불은 크고 오래된 많은 나무와 동물의 서식지를 파괴합니다. 산불은 생태계에 손해를 끼칩니다. 그러면 산불을 예방하기 위해 사람들은 무엇을 해야 할까요? 무엇보다도 사람들은 자신의 행동에 주의해야 합니다. 절대적으로 필요할 때만 산에서 불을 피웁니다. 떠나기 전에 확실하게 불을 끕니다. 물을 부어 끄거나 흙으로 덮습니다. 또한 숲에서 담배를 피우지 않습니다. 타고 있는 성냥도 버리지 않습니다.

해설 산불을 예방하기 위해 사람들이 해야 할 일을 설명하고 있다.
어휘 ecosystem [íːkousìstəm] 생태계 extinguish [ikstíŋgwiʃ] (불을) 끄다 put out (불, 전기 등을) 끄다 match [mætʃ] 성냥

15 할 일 파악 ②

W Woojin, are you still <u>using paper cups</u>?
M Yes. After using them, I don't need to wash them.
W But you throw them away after a single use. Disposable products are <u>bad for the environment</u>.
M I see what you mean. The environment is <u>more important than convenience</u>.
W So why don't you <u>buy a mug</u> for the office?
M Good idea! I should buy one now. Can you go with me?
W Sure.

여 우진아, 여전히 종이컵을 쓰는 중이야?
남 응. 사용한 후에 씻을 필요가 없잖아.
여 하지만 한 번 사용하고 그걸 버리잖아. 일회용 제품은 환경에 나빠.
남 네가 무슨 말하는지 알겠어. 환경이 편리함보다 중요해.
여 그래서 말인데, 사무실용으로 쓸 머그컵을 구입하는 게 어때?
남 좋은 생각이야. 지금 하나 사야겠어. 나랑 같이 갈래?
여 물론이지.

해설 사무실에서 사용할 머그컵을 구입하기 위해 여자에게 같이 가자고 말하였다.
어휘 throw away 버리다 single [síŋgl] 한 번 disposable [dispóuzəbl] 일회용의

16 숫자 정보 파악 ④

[Cellphone rings.]
W Hello. I need to <u>change my appointment</u> for my annual physical checkup.
M Sure. Who's calling, please?
W This is Natalie White.
M Let me check the schedule. [Pause] All right. When would <u>be a good time</u> for you?
W Is April 5 possible?
M I'm afraid that day is <u>fully booked</u>. How about two days after that?

W　On April 7? Well, can you check the next day?

M　We <u>have</u> <u>time</u> <u>available</u> then. I'll change your reservation to April 8.

W　Thank you.

여　여보세요. 연 1회 건강 검진 예약을 바꾸고 싶은데요.
남　알겠습니다. 누구시죠?
여　Natalie White입니다.
남　일정을 확인해 볼게요. 알겠습니다. 언제가 좋으신가요?
여　4월 5일은 가능한가요?
남　죄송하지만 그 날은 예약이 다 찼네요. 2일 후는 어떠세요?
여　4월 7일이요? 음, 그 다음날로 확인해 주실래요?
남　가능합니다. 4월 8일로 예약을 변경해 드릴게요.
여　감사합니다.

해설 건강 검진 예약을 4월 7일 다음날인 4월 8일로 변경하기로 하였다.
어휘 physical [fízikəl] 신체의

17 적절한 응답 찾기 ⑤

M　Mom, can I <u>go to the</u> <u>aquarium</u> with my friends tomorrow?

W　Brian, you have a cello lesson tomorrow.

M　No, I don't. Ms. Hanson told me that she is <u>going</u> <u>on vacation</u> this week.

W　Really? Anyway, are you done with your vacation homework?

M　Absolutely! So can I go to the aquarium?

W　All right. Do you <u>need a ride</u> tomorrow?

M　No, thanks. I can take the bus. Can you <u>pack</u> <u>some</u> <u>snacks</u> for me?

W　<u>Okay. I'll prepare some healthy snacks.</u>

남　엄마, 내일 친구랑 수족관에 가도 될까요?
여　Brian, 내일 첼로 수업이 있잖아.
남　아녜요. Hanson 선생님이 이번 주에 휴가 가신다고 말씀하셨어요.
여　그러니? 그런데 방학 숙제는 다 했니?
남　물론이죠. 그러면 수족관에 가도 되죠?
여　알겠다. 내일 태워 줄까?
남　괜찮아요. 버스 타면 돼요. 간식을 좀 준비해 주실래요?
여　그래. 내가 건강한 간식을 준비해 줄게.

해설 수족관에서 먹을 간식을 준비해 달라는 요청에 대한 가장 적절한 응답은 ⑤ '그래. 내가 건강한 간식을 준비해 줄게.'이다.
① 너는 내 결정을 존중해 줄 필요가 있어.
② 네가 해야 할 일을 그만 미루렴.　③ 푹 쉬고 좋은 휴가 보내라.
④ 그것은 유럽에서 가장 큰 수족관이야.
어휘 aquarium [əkwέ(:)əriəm] 수족관　respect [rispékt] 존중하다

18 적절한 응답 찾기 ③

M　Why do you <u>have such a long face</u>?

W　On my way here, I <u>stepped in</u> <u>some</u> <u>gum</u>. Chewing gum is stuck to my shoe.

M　Oh, no! I know that irritating feeling.

W　The worst part is that I bought these sandals 3 days ago. They are so new.

M　Calm down. Let's <u>remove</u> <u>the</u> <u>gum</u> from your shoe.

W　But how? The shoe repair shop is closed today.

M　<u>I'll call my mom and ask her how to remove it.</u>

남　왜 그렇게 울상이야?
여　여기로 오는 길에 껌을 밟았어. 껌이 내 신발에 달라붙었어.
남　저런! 나도 그 짜증나는 기분을 알지.

여　가장 나쁜 건 내가 이 샌들을 3일 전에 샀다는 거야. 완전 새 거라고.
남　진정해. 신발에서 껌을 제거해 보자.
여　하지만 어떻게 해? 구두 수리점이 오늘 문을 닫았어.
남　<u>내가 엄마한테 어떻게 제거하는지 물어볼게.</u>

해설 구두 수리점이 문을 닫았는데 어떻게 껌을 제거하느냐는 질문에 대한 가장 적절한 응답은 ③ '내가 엄마한테 어떻게 제거하는지 물어볼게.'이다.
① 이것 좀 봐! 껌으로 풍선을 불 수 있어.　② 넌 집으로 가서 좀 쉬어야겠다.
④ 새 운동화를 사러 가자.　⑤ 단 것을 먹은 후에는 양치질을 해.
어휘 long face 우울한 얼굴, 슬픈 표정　irritating [íritèitiŋ] 짜증나는

19 적절한 응답 찾기 ③

M　I'm thirsty. Can I <u>drink</u> some <u>water</u>?

W　Of course. There's some in the fridge.

M　[*Pause*] What are these memos <u>attached</u> <u>to</u> <u>the</u> <u>fridge</u> <u>door</u>?

W　Ah, they are <u>lists</u> <u>of</u> <u>all</u> <u>the food</u> <u>items</u> in the fridge. They remind me of what I have.

M　That's a great idea!

W　It really is. With these memos, I can <u>reduce</u> <u>food</u> <u>waste</u>.

M　Brilliant! Who taught you this?

W　<u>My grandmother. She's good at organizing.</u>

남　나 목말라. 물 마셔도 되니?
여　물론이지. 냉장고에 있어.
남　냉장고 문에 붙어 있는 이 메모는 뭐야?
여　아, 냉장고에 들어 있는 음식 목록들이야. 냉장고에 무엇이 있는지 상기시켜 줘.
남　좋은 생각이다!
여　정말 그래. 이 메모 때문에 음식물 쓰레기가 줄었어.
남　기발해! 누가 가르쳐 준 거야?
여　<u>우리 할머니. 그녀는 정리를 잘하시거든.</u>

해설 냉장고에 메모하는 것을 누가 가르쳐 주었느냐는 질문에 대한 가장 적절한 응답은 ③ '우리 할머니. 그녀는 정리를 잘하시거든.'이다.
① 남은 음식은 내가 개한테 줄게.
② 내 여동생은 요리를 잘해. 마음껏 먹어.
④ 난 물이 더 필요해. 이 음식은 너무 매워.
⑤ 내일 무엇을 해야 할지 선생님께서 알려주실 거야.
어휘 remind A of B A에게 B를 상기시키다　leftover [léftòuvər] 남은 음식

20 상황에 맞는 말 찾기 ④

M　Marcus goes shopping at a department store. He <u>parks</u> <u>his car</u> in the parking lot and buys what he needs. After shopping, he returns to his car to go home. He sees that his car is <u>blocked by</u> <u>another</u> <u>car</u>. Someone has double-parked, and there's no one in the car. Marcus <u>finds</u> <u>the</u> <u>phone</u> <u>number</u> of the car owner. He wants to call and <u>ask</u> <u>the</u> <u>person</u> <u>to move</u> the car. In this situation, what would Marcus most likely say to the car owner?

Marcus　Hello. <u>Do you mind moving your car so I can</u> <u>get out?</u>

남　Marcus는 백화점에 쇼핑하러 갑니다. 그는 주차장에 차를 주차하고 필요한 것을 구입합니다. 쇼핑 후에 그는 집으로 가려고 자신의 차로 돌아옵니다. 그는 자신의 차가 다른 차에 의해 갇힌 것을 알게 됩니다. 누군가가 이중 주차를 했고, 차 안에는 아무도 없습니다. Marcus는 자동차 주인의 전화번호를 발견합니다. 그는 그 사람에게 전화를 걸어 차를 이동시켜 달라고 요청하고 싶습니다. 이런 상황에서, Marcus가 자동

차 주인에게 할 말로 가장 적절한 것은 무엇일까요?

Marcus 여보세요. 제가 나갈 수 있도록 차를 빼 주시겠어요?

해설 이중 주차한 사람에게 전화해서 차를 빼 달라고 부탁하려는 상황에서 Marcus가 자동차 주인에게 할 말로 가장 적절한 것은 ④ '제가 나갈 수 있도록 차를 빼 주시겠어요?'이다.
① 죄송하지만 당신의 차가 손상됐어요.
② 다음 기차가 언제 도착하나요?
③ 여기에서 당신이 무엇을 구입했는지 알고 싶어요.
⑤ 어디에서 차를 수리했는지 알려 주시겠어요?

어휘 parking lot 주차장　block [blɑk] 막다　double-park 이중 주차하다　owner [óunər] 주인, 소유자

Listen and Check
p. 180

Q1	Pause	Q11	True
Q2	True	Q12	Yes
Q3	No	Q13	False
Q4	Chinese	Q14	No
Q5	700 dollars	Q15	True
Q6	False	Q16	No
Q7	True	Q17	True
Q8	No	Q18	3 days ago
Q9	one week	Q19	lists of food items
Q10	two	Q20	in a parking lot

해석
Q1 여자의 카페의 이름은 무엇인가?
Q2 남자의 여동생은 결혼을 할 예정이다.
Q3 여자는 바다에서 서핑을 하다가 다리를 다쳤을까?
Q4 남자는 금요일마다 무엇을 공부할까?
Q5 만약 남자가 그 직업을 갖게 되면 한 달에 얼마를 벌 수 있을까?
Q6 사자들이 작은 동물을 사냥하는 중이었다.
Q7 남자는 뭔가 먹을 것을 원했다.
Q8 남자는 내일이 자기 어머니의 생일인 걸 알고 있었을까?
Q9 점검을 끝내는 데 얼마나 걸릴까?
Q10 남자는 딸기잼 몇 병을 구입했을까?
Q11 수진은 아직 그녀의 숙제를 끝내지 못했다.
Q12 12살짜리 어린이는 여름 학교에 참석할 수 있을까?
Q13 남자와 여자의 항공편에는 무료 식사가 포함되어 있다.
Q14 산불은 생태계에 유익한가?
Q15 일회용 제품은 환경에 나쁘다.
Q16 여자는 매년 하는 건강 검진 예약을 취소했나?
Q17 Hanson 선생님은 Brian에게 첼로를 가르친다.
Q18 Jenny는 언제 샌들을 구입했을까?
Q19 냉장고 문에 붙어 있는 메모들은 무엇인가?
Q20 Marcus는 지금 어디에 있는가?

실전 모의고사 19회
pp. 188~189

1	⑤	2	③	3	④	4	⑤	5	⑤
6	④	7	③	8	④	9	②	10	⑤
11	⑤	12	⑤	13	⑤	14	④	15	②
16	④	17	⑤	18	④	19	②	20	⑤

1 그림 정보 파악 ⑤

M Hi. May I help you?
W Hi. I'd like to adopt a pet.
M What kind of pet would you like to have? We have <u>various</u> <u>kinds</u> <u>of</u> <u>pets</u>.
W Could you recommend one for me?
M Well, how long do you stay at home? If you are a busy worker, I'd recommend a reptile.
W A reptile? Do you mean a snake or lizard?
M Yes. Compared to other pets such as dogs and cats, <u>reptiles</u> <u>are</u> <u>easy</u> <u>to</u> <u>keep</u>. And they don't make any noise.
W I see. But I don't like <u>hairless</u> <u>animals</u>.
M Then how about this cat wearing a ribbon around its neck?
W Oh, <u>it</u> <u>looks</u> <u>cute</u>. I'll take it.

남 안녕하세요, 무엇을 도와드릴까요?
여 안녕하세요, 반려동물을 입양하고 싶습니다.
남 어떤 종류의 반려동물을 기르길 원하세요? 다양한 종류의 반려동물들이 있습니다.
여 제게 추천을 해 주시겠어요?
남 음, 집에 얼마나 오래 머무시나요? 만약 바쁜 직장인이라면 파충류를 추천합니다.
여 파충류요? 뱀이나 도마뱀을 말하시는 건가요?
남 네, 개와 고양이 같은 다른 반려동물들과 비교했을 때 파충류가 기르기 쉬워요. 그리고 그들은 시끄럽게 하지도 않죠.
여 그렇군요. 하지만 저는 털이 없는 동물들을 선호하지 않아요.
남 그러면 목에 리본을 달고 있는 이 고양이는 어떻습니까?
여 오, 귀여워 보이네요. 그걸로 할게요.

해설 털이 없는 동물을 싫어한다고 하였다

어휘 adopt [ədápt] 입양하다　reptile [réptil] 파충류　lizard [lízərd] 도마뱀　hairless [héərlis] 털이 없는

2 목적 파악 ③

[Telephone rings.]
W Hello. Kim's Korean Food.
M Hello. I just bought some kimchi at your store. I think I <u>left</u> <u>my</u> <u>umbrella</u> <u>there</u>. Could you please check to see if it is there?
W Hold on, please. [Pause] Mister, someone on my staff found an umbrella <u>with</u> <u>blue</u> <u>stripes</u>. Is this yours?
M Can you see six stars when you open the umbrella?
W Let me check. [Pause] Yes, it <u>has</u> <u>six</u> <u>yellow</u> <u>stars</u>. It must be yours then.
M Thank you so much. I'll <u>drop</u> <u>by</u> soon.

여 Kim's Korean Food입니다.
남 여보세요. 제가 방금 가게에서 김치를 샀어요. 제가 거기에 우산을 두고 온 것 같아요. 우산이 있는지 확인해 주시겠어요?
여 잠시만요. 손님, 저희 직원이 파란 줄무늬가 있는 우산을 찾았어요. 손님 것인가요?
남 펼쳤을 때 여섯 개의 별이 있나요?
여 확인해 볼게요. 네, 노란색 별 여섯 개가 있네요. 그럼 그것이 손님의 것이 틀림없군요.
남 정말 감사합니다. 곧 들를게요.

해설 두고 간 우산을 찾으러 들르겠다고 하였다.

어휘 staff [stæf] 직원

3   그림 상황 파악   ④

① M   What a nice car that is!
   W   Thanks. It's the latest model.
② M   Excuse me, but you've got a flat tire.
   W   Oh, there must have been something sharp on the road.
③ M   Watch out! You almost hit another car.
   W   Don't worry about that. I'm a good driver.
④ M   You ran a red light. Can I see your license?
   W   Oh, I'm sorry. I didn't see a red light anywhere.
⑤ M   What brings you back here?
   W   I want to learn the traffic rules.

① 남   정말 멋진 차군요!
   여   감사합니다. 최신 모델이에요.
② 남   실례합니다만, 타이어에 펑크가 났어요.
   여   오, 거리에 날카로운 무언가가 있었나 봐요.
③ 남   조심해! 다른 차와 부딪힐 뻔 했어.
   여   걱정하지 마, 난 운전을 잘해.
④ 남   신호 위반을 하셨습니다. 면허증 좀 보여 주시겠습니까?
   여   오, 미안합니다. 빨간 불을 못 봤어요.
⑤ 남   무슨 일로 다시 오셨어요?
   여   교통 법규에 대해 배우고 싶어요.

해설 신호를 위반한 차량을 단속하는 장면이다.
어휘 flat [flæt] 평평한, 납작한

4   특정 정보 파악   ⑤

[Telephone rings.]
M   Hello. This is the Neo Computer Mall. What can I do for you?
W   Hello. I ordered a laptop last Sunday. It's already Thursday, but I haven't received it yet.
M   Oh, I'm sorry about that. Our delivery service is being delayed due to the road problems caused by the heavy snow.
W   Oh, I see. Then how long will I have to wait?
M   Under normal conditions, we offer the speedy delivery within 3 days, but in this case, it will take two more days. It will probably be there tomorrow.
W   Okay. I'll wait.

남   Neo Computer Mall 입니다. 무엇을 도와드릴까요?
여   제가 지난 일요일에 노트북을 주문했습니다. 벌써 목요일인데 아직까지 받지 못했어요.
남   죄송합니다. 저희 배송 서비스가 최근의 폭설로 인한 도로 통제로 인해 지연되고 있습니다.
여   아, 그렇군요. 그럼 얼마나 오래 기다려야 하나요?
남   정상적인 상황에서는 3일 이내의 빠른 배송을 제공합니다만, 이런 경우에는 이틀이 더 소요됩니다. 아마도 내일 도착할 것입니다.
여   알겠어요. 기다릴게요.

해설 내일 도착한다고 말하였다.
어휘 condition [kəndíʃən] 조건, 상황   delivery [dilívəri] 배송

5   언급 유무 파악   ⑤

W   The annual German Village Festival will run this year from October 6 to 8. The German Village was built for Koreans who worked as miners and nurses in Germany in the 1960s and returned home to settle down. The festival, launched for the first time in 2010, is now in its ninth year. Every year, visitors can look forward to enjoying a wide selection of beer and snacks. This year, visitors can enjoy traditional German performances, concerts, and parties in the evening. The German Village Festival is a unique event where visitors can experience German culture.

여   독일 마을 축제는 올해 10월 6일부터 8일까지 열릴 예정입니다. 독일 마을은 1960년대 독일의 광부와 간호사로 일한 다음, 고향으로 정착하기 위해 돌아온 한국인들을 위해 지어졌습니다. 2010년에 처음으로 시작된 이 축제는 이제 9년째입니다. 매년 방문객들은 다양한 종류의 맥주와 스낵을 즐길 수 있습니다. 올해 방문객들은 저녁에 전통적인 독일 공연, 콘서트 및 파티를 즐길 수 있습니다. 독일 마을 축제는 학생들이 독일 문화를 체험할 수 있는 독특한 행사입니다.

해설 연간 방문객의 수에 관해서는 언급되지 않았다.
어휘 miner [máinər] 광부   launch [lɔ:ntʃ] ~을 시작하다

6   관계 추론   ④

W   Excuse me.
M   Yes. What can I do for you?
W   I wonder where I can wash my hands.
M   There is a restroom on the second floor.
W   Thank you. I like the antique atmosphere here, and your coffee was good.
M   It's very kind of you to say that. Is there anything you want?
W   Can I get a free refill of my coffee?
M   Sure. I'd be glad to do that.

여   실례합니다.
남   네. 무엇을 도와 드릴까요?
여   손을 어디에서 씻는지 궁금해요.
남   2층에 화장실이 있습니다.
여   감사합니다. 여기 고풍스러운 분위기가 마음에 들어요, 커피도 맛있어요.
남   그렇게 말씀해 주셔서 감사합니다. 다른 필요한 건 없으신가요?
여   커피 무료 리필이 되나요?
남   물론이죠. 기꺼이 드리겠습니다.

해설 커피를 리필할 수 있는지 물었다.
어휘 antique [æntí:k] 고풍스러운

7   어색한 대화 찾기   ③

① W   Do you know how to make curry and rice?
   M   Of course. It's a piece of cake.
② W   Do you expect me to apologize?
   M   Yes. It was you who made a mistake.
③ W   Do you mind if I close the window?
   M   Of course, I do. You can do as you like.
④ W   I wonder if I can pass the test.
   M   Keep your chin up! I'm sure you can do it.
⑤ W   Can I get a refund on this jacket?
   M   Is there something wrong with it?

① 여   너 카레라이스 만들 줄 아니?
   남   물론이지, 식은 죽 먹기야.
② 여   내가 사과하길 원하니?

남 응. 실수를 한 건 너였으니까.
③ 여 제가 창문을 닫아도 될까요?
　남 물론, 아뇨. 원하는 대로 하세요.
④ 여 내가 시험을 합격할 수 있을까?
　남 기운 내! 난 네가 할 수 있다고 믿어.
⑤ 여 이 재킷을 환불할 수 있나요?
　남 무슨 문제가 있나요?

해설 창문을 열어도 되는지에 대한 물음에 안 된다고 하며 원하는 대로 하라고 답하는 것은 어색하다.
어휘 chin [tʃin] 턱

8 　부탁한 일 파악 ④

M Janet, are you <u>getting</u> <u>ready</u> <u>for</u> your trip to Paris?
W Yes, but I'm worried about one thing.
M What is it? Tell me.
W You know that I have two cats at home.
M Oh, do you want me to take care of them?
W Actually, one of my neighbors will <u>look</u> <u>after</u> <u>them</u>, but he said he can only do that for 2 days.
M And you need someone that <u>can</u> <u>be</u> <u>with</u> <u>them</u> for the rest of your trip, right?
W Yes. Can you do that for me?
M No problem. <u>What</u> <u>are</u> <u>friends</u> <u>for</u>?

남 Janet, 파리 여행 준비는 잘 되어가니?
여 응. 그런데 한 가지 걱정거리가 있어.
남 뭔데? 말해 봐.
여 내가 집에 키우는 고양이 두 마리 있는 거 알지.
남 오, 내가 고양이들을 돌봐주길 원하는구나?
여 사실, 이웃 중 한 사람이 그들을 돌보기로 했어. 그런데 그가 2일 동안만 그렇게 할 수 있다고 해.
남 그래서 넌 남은 여행 기간 동안 그들과 함께 있을 누군가가 필요한 거야, 그렇지?
여 맞아. 그렇게 해줄 수 있겠니?
남 걱정 마. 친구 좋다는 게 뭐겠어.

해설 남은 여행 기간 동안 고양이를 돌봐 줄 것을 부탁하였다.
어휘 neighbor [néibər] 이웃　look after ~을 돌보다

9 　의도 파악 ②

M I don't understand why Beth <u>was</u> <u>so</u> <u>harsh</u> to me.
W What happened?
M I asked her to help me with my school project, but she said no and commented that I should <u>feel</u> <u>ashamed</u> of myself. How could she say that to me?
W Well, Jake, you know that she didn't <u>mean</u> <u>to</u> <u>offend</u> <u>you</u>. I think she said that for your own sake.
M I know, but she didn't need to talk like that!
W If it were not an individual task, she <u>would</u> <u>willingly</u> <u>help</u> <u>you</u>.
M I didn't mind it at first, but she went too far.

남 Beth가 왜 나에게 지나치게 가혹한지 모르겠어.
여 무슨 일인데?
남 내가 그녀에게 나의 숙제를 도와달라고 부탁했어. 하지만 그녀는 안 된다고 말했고, 내게 부끄러워하라고 말하더라. 어떻게 나에게 그렇게 말할 수가 있지?
여 음, Jake, 그녀가 네 기분을 상하게 하려고 의도한 건 아니라는 걸 알잖아. 내 생각엔 그녀가 널 위해서 그렇게 말한 것 같아.
남 알아. 하지만 그렇게까지 말할 필요는 없잖아.

여 만약 개인 과제가 아니었다면, 그녀는 기꺼이 널 도와주었을 거야.
남 처음엔 신경 안 썼는데, 이번엔 너무 심했어.

해설 남자의 행동을 나무라는 여자에 대한 원망을 나타내고 있다.
어휘 harsh [hɑːrʃ] 가혹한　comment [kάment] 말하다　for one's own sake ~를 위해서　willingly [wíliŋli] 기꺼이

10 　숫자 정보 파악 ⑤

W Hello. This is the ABC Car Insurance Service Center. What can I do for you?
M Hello. I <u>have</u> <u>an</u> <u>emergency</u>. I left the key in my car and locked myself out.
W You want us to <u>send</u> <u>someone</u> to open your car, right?
M Yes.
W Let me check your location through the GPS on your smartphone. Hold on, please. [Pause] Thank you for waiting. We'll send our staff to you at once.
M That's great. I'll stay here. Thanks. How much is it?
W We usually charge 10 dollars for this service. Isn't this <u>your</u> <u>fifth</u> <u>time</u> <u>already</u>?
M Yes, that's right.
W In this case, you have to pay <u>an</u> <u>additional</u> <u>charge</u> of 10%.

여 ABC Car Insurance Service Center입니다. 무엇을 도와 드릴까요?
남 여보세요, 급한 일이 생겼습니다. 자동차 열쇠를 차 안에 두고 문을 닫았어요.
여 당신의 자동차 문을 열어줄 사람을 보내 주길 원하시는군요, 그렇죠?
남 네.
여 당신의 스마트폰의 GPS를 통해 위치를 확인하겠습니다. 잠시만 기다려 주세요. 기다려 주셔서 감사합니다. 저희 직원을 즉시 보내드리겠습니다.
남 좋습니다. 여기 있겠습니다. 감사합니다. 비용이 얼마인지요?
여 보통 이 서비스는 10달러를 지불하셔야 합니다. 이번이 벌써 다섯 번째시네요?
남 네, 맞습니다.
여 이 경우에는 10% 추가 금액을 내셔야 합니다.

해설 원래 요금에 10% 추가 요금을 지불해야 한다고 하였다.
어휘 additional [ədíʃənəl] 추가의

11 　할 일 파악 ⑤

W How long will it take to <u>get</u> <u>to</u> <u>our</u> <u>destination</u>?
M We're almost there. What's up? You look uncomfortable.
W I feel dizzy. Maybe I <u>have</u> <u>motion</u> <u>sickness</u>.
M Open the window and <u>get</u> <u>some</u> <u>fresh</u> <u>air</u>.
W Can't you see that I already have the window wide open?
M I mean that I'll open the windows in the back, too.
W Oh, I see. I'm <u>a</u> <u>bit</u> <u>sensitive</u> because I feel bad.
M It's okay. Do you want to get out of the car for a while?
W Yes, please. I'll be fine after I get some rest.

여 목적지까지 얼마나 걸릴까?
남 거의 다 왔어. 무슨 일이야? 불편해 보여.
여 어지러워. 아마도 멀미인가 봐.
남 창문을 열고, 신선한 공기를 마셔.

여 이미 창문을 활짝 열어놓은 거 안 보이니?
남 내 말은 뒷좌석의 창문도 열겠다는 뜻이었어.
여 오, 그렇구나. 몸이 안 좋으니까 내가 좀 예민하네.
남 괜찮아. 잠시 차에서 내리고 싶니?
여 응. 조금 쉬면 괜찮아질 거야.

해설 차에서 내려 쉬면 괜찮아질 거라고 말하였다.
어휘 motion sickness 멀미

12 언급 유무 파악 ⑤

W Korean traditional academies known as *seowon* are likely to become South Korea's 14th World Heritage site designated by UNESCO. This site, located in the central and southern parts of Korea, consists of nine *seowons*, representing the Confucian academies of the Joseon Dynasty. Situated near mountains and water sources, they favoured the appreciation of nature and the cultivation of the mind and the body. So the buildings were intended to be in harmony with the surrounding landscape. The *seowon* illustrates an historical process in which Confucianism was adapted to Korean conditions.

여 서원으로 알려진 한국의 전통 학교가 유네스코에 의해 한국의 14번째 세계 유산이 될 것 같습니다. 한국의 중부와 남부에 위치한 이곳은 조선시대의 유학 학계를 대표하는 9개의 서원으로 구성되어 있습니다. 산과 수원 근처에 위치한 서원은 자연에 대한 감사와 몸과 마음의 수련을 선호합니다. 따라서, 건물들은 주변 환경과 조화를 이루도록 의도되었습니다. 서원은 유학이 한국의 조건에 적응한 역사적 과정을 보여줍니다.

해설 지역별 서원의 특징에 관한 내용은 언급되지 않았다.
어휘 designate [dézignit] 지명하다   represent [rèprizént] 나타내다   favor [féivər] ~을 좋아하다   cultivation [kÀltəvéiʃən] 수련, 배양   illustrate [íləstrèit] 예증하다

13 표 파악 ⑤

W What do you want to do next?
M I can't do anything now. Let's get some rest for a while.
W No way. We don't have much time left. Come on. Let's go on the roller coaster.
M The roller coaster? I don't like big drops or thrill rides.
W Then how about the jungle cruise? It is much gentler and shorter than a roller coaster.
M But isn't it just for kids? I don't think that is suitable for us.
W No, not really. It is popular with everyone on this hot day.
M Okay. Let's go on it.

여 다음에 무엇을 하고 싶니?
남 지금은 아무것도 못하겠어. 잠시만 쉬자.
여 안 돼. 시간이 많이 없어. 어서. 롤러코스터 타러 가자.
남 롤러코스터? 난 갑자기 떨어지고 스릴감 넘치는 놀이 기구는 싫어.
여 그럼 정글 크루즈는 어때? 롤러코스터 보다 훨씬 부드럽고 짧아.
남 하지만 그건 아이들을 위한 것 아냐? 우리에게 맞는 것 같지 않은데.
여 아냐, 딱히 그렇진 않아. 이렇게 더운 날에 모든 사람들에게 인기가 있어.
남 좋아. 타러 가자.

해설 아이들을 위한 것이지만 더운 날에는 모두에게 인기가 있다고 하였다.
어휘 gentle [dʒéntl] 부드러운   suitable [sjú:təbl] 적합한

14 화제·주제 파악 ④

W These are some of the most mysterious and powerful forces in the universe. These are places where gravity has become so strong that nothing around them can escape, not even light. These are truly invisible. We can't actually see them because they don't reflect light. But scientists know that they exist by observing light and objects around them.

여 이것들은 우주에서 가장 신비롭고 강력한 힘 중 어떤 것입니다. 이것들은 중력이 너무 강해서 빛을 포함한 그 주변의 어떤 것도 달아날 수 없는 곳입니다. 이것들은 정말로 보이지 않습니다. 그들이 빛을 반사하지 않기 때문에 우리는 실제로 그들을 볼 수 없습니다. 그러나 과학자들은 주변의 빛과 사물을 관찰함으로써 그들이 존재한다는 것을 알고 있습니다.

해설 빛을 포함한 어떤 것도 달아날 수 없다고 하였다.
어휘 mysterious [mistí(:)əriəs] 신비한   gravity [grǽvəti] 중력   invisible [invízəbl] 눈에 보이지 않는   reflect [riflékt] 반사하다

15 할 일 파악 ②

W Do you have anything special planned for this weekend?
M I have to take care of my brothers because my parents are going to visit our relatives in Busan. How about you? Do you have something in mind?
W Um... I was thinking of going to the movies with you, but it sounds like you have other things to do.
M Wait! They are scheduled to return on Sunday morning. After that, I'll have some time to spend with you.
W Great. Then let's meet at 2:00 this Sunday afternoon.
M Okay. I can't wait.

여 이번 주말에 특별한 계획 있어?
남 부모님께서 친척을 방문하러 부산에 가셔서 동생들을 돌봐야 해. 넌 어때? 생각해 둔 게 있어?
여 음... 나는 너와 영화 보러 갈 생각을 하고 있었어. 하지만, 넌 해야 할 일이 있구나.
남 잠깐만! 부모님께서 일요일 아침에 돌아오실 예정이야. 그 후에 너와 함께 보낼 시간이 있을 거야.
여 좋아. 그럼, 일요일 오후 2시에 만나자.
남 그래. 정말 기대되는 구나.

해설 부모님께서 부산에 가셔서 동생들을 돌봐야 한다고 하였다.
어휘 relative [rélətiv] 친척

16 특정 정보 파악 ④

M May I help you?
W I'd like to get some information about these cosmetics.
M Okay. This lotion includes natural ingredients, which are especially good for dry skin. This facial mask helps you keep your skin moisturized and healthy.
W How about this one?

M Oh, this sunscreen <u>helps</u> <u>reduce</u> <u>the</u> <u>aging</u> of your skin caused by UV rays.

W So how often should I use it?

M You <u>should</u> <u>apply</u> <u>it</u> every 2 to 3 hours on a sunny day.

W Okay, give me this one.

남 무엇을 도와 드릴까요?

여 이 화장품들에 대한 정보를 얻고 싶어요.

남 네, 이 로션은 천연 재료를 포함하고 있어서 특히 건조한 피부에 좋습니다. 이 마스크 팩은 당신이 당신의 피부를 촉촉하고 건강하게 유지하는 것을 도와줍니다.

여 이것은 어떤가요?

남 오, 이 선크림은 자외선에 의해 유발되는 피부의 노화를 줄여 줍니다.

여 그럼, 얼마나 자주 사용해야 하나요?

남 화창한 날에는 두세 시간마다 한 번씩 바르셔야 합니다.

여 좋아요, 이걸로 할게요.

<u>해설</u> 마지막에 언급된 선크림을 사겠다고 하였다.

<u>어휘</u> cosmetic [kɑzmétik] 화장품   ingredient [ingrí:diənt] 원료 moisturize [mɔ́istʃəràiz] 촉촉하게 하다   aging [éidʒiŋ] 노화 apply [əplái] 바르다

17 <u>적절한 응답 찾기</u> ⑤

W Hey, Brian. How was the first day of the new semester?

M It was okay. <u>I</u> <u>already</u> <u>made</u> a new friend. He said <u>he</u> <u>was</u> <u>in</u> <u>Class</u> <u>B</u> last year.

W Really? I was in Class B last year. What is his name?

M Dave. Dave Jordan.

W The boy who lives on 17th Street?

M Maybe. There is <u>only</u> <u>one</u> <u>Dave</u> in my class.

W Oh, he's kind and fun. You are lucky to have a nice friend.

M <u>I feel the same way.</u>

여 안녕, Brian. 새 학기 첫날 어땠니?

남 괜찮았어. 벌써 새 친구도 사귀었어. 그가 작년에 B반이었다고 말했어.

여 정말? 나도 작년에 B반이었어. 그의 이름이 뭐니?

남 Dave야. Dave Jordan.

여 17번가에 사는 남자애?

남 아마 그럴걸. 우리 반에 Dave가 한 명뿐이니깐.

여 오, 그는 친절하고 재밌어. 좋은 친구를 사귀다니 운이 좋구나.

남 <u>나도 공감해.</u>

<u>해설</u> 좋은 친구를 사귀게 되어 운이 좋다는 말에 대한 가장 적절한 응답은 ⑤ '나도 공감해.'이다.
① 농담하지 마.   ② 그건 너무 불공평해.
③ 내가 할 수 있을까 걱정돼.   ④ 네 마음이 어떤지 알겠어.

<u>어휘</u> semester [siméstər] 학기

18 <u>적절한 응답 찾기</u> ④

W What are you planning to do for this coming Hangeul Day event?

M Some of my classmates and I are going to <u>make</u> <u>a</u> <u>presentation</u> on the history of Hangeul.

W Sounds great! Who came up with the idea?

M My English teacher suggested it, and <u>we</u> <u>made</u> <u>it</u> <u>together</u>.

W What? Your English teacher? Not a Korean teacher?

M Yes. She is not Korean, but <u>has</u> <u>a</u> <u>lot</u> <u>of</u> <u>interest</u> <u>in</u> Hangeul.

W <u>You have an amazing teacher.</u>

여 다가오는 한글날 행사에 무엇을 할 계획이니?

남 우리 반 친구 몇 명과 나는 한글의 역사에 대한 발표를 할 예정이야.

여 멋지네. 누가 아이디어를 생각해 냈어?

남 영어 선생님께서 아이디어를 제안하셨고, 우리가 함께 했지.

여 뭐? 영어 선생님이라고? 국어 선생님이 아니라?

남 그래, 그녀는 한국인은 아니지만 한글에 많은 관심을 가지고 계셔.

여 <u>넌 멋진 선생님을 두었구나.</u>

<u>해설</u> 영어 선생님이 한국인이 아니지만 한글에 관심이 있다는 말에 대한 가장 적절한 응답은 ④ '넌 멋진 선생님을 두었구나.'이다.
① K-pop이 한국을 유명하게 만들었어.
② 그녀도 한국어를 배울 필요가 있어.
③ 넌 항상 열심히 공부하려고 노력하는구나.
⑤ 세종대왕이 그것을 만들었어.

<u>어휘</u> suggest [səgdʒést] 제안하다

19 <u>적절한 응답 찾기</u> ②

M What are you doing?

W I'm making a UCC video.

M Wow, I didn't know <u>you're</u> <u>good</u> <u>at</u> <u>using</u> a computer.

W Not really. It is just my homework. I really don't want to do <u>this</u> <u>kind</u> <u>of</u> homework.

M When will you be finished with it?

W I'm not sure. I might work <u>the</u> <u>whole</u> <u>night</u> <u>through</u>.

M Come on. You need to refresh yourself. Let's take a walk.

W <u>I'm</u> <u>afraid</u> <u>I</u> <u>can't</u>. I have to finish this by tomorrow morning.

M <u>A short break can really help you avoid stress.</u>

남 뭐하고 있니?

여 UCC 비디오를 만들고 있는 중이야.

남 와우, 네가 컴퓨터를 잘하는 줄 몰랐어.

여 잘 못해. 그냥 숙제야. 이런 종류의 숙제는 정말 하기 싫어.

남 언제 끝나는데?

여 모르겠어. 나 밤새 일해야 할지도 몰라.

남 저런. 넌 기분 전환을 할 필요가 있어. 나랑 산책하러 가자.

여 미안하지만 안 돼. 내일 아침까지 이걸 끝내야만 해.

남 <u>짧은 휴식은 스트레스를 피하는 데 정말 도움이 돼.</u>

<u>해설</u> 산책하자는 요청을 거절하는 말에 대한 가장 적절한 응답은 ② '짧은 휴식은 스트레스를 피하는데 정말 도움이 돼.'이다.
① 얕은 지식은 위험한 거야.   ③ 나는 그곳에서 좋은 시간을 보냈어.
④ 모두 내 잘못이야.   ⑤ 네 컴퓨터 화면은 수리될 필요가 있어.

<u>어휘</u> through [θru:] 내내, 줄곧   refresh [rifréʃ] 상쾌하게 하다

20 <u>상황에 맞는 말 찾기</u> ⑤

W Mina and Julie want to eat out after a <u>hard</u> <u>day's</u> <u>work</u>. Mina and Julie go into a Korean restaurant. They decide <u>what</u> <u>they</u> <u>want</u> <u>to</u> <u>eat</u>, and Mina orders. <u>A</u> <u>few</u> <u>minutes</u> <u>later</u>, the waiter brings some *bibimbap* and *bulgogi* to them. But they are not what Mina and Julie wanted, so Mina <u>calls</u> <u>the</u> <u>waiter</u>. In this situation, what would Mina say to the waiter?

정답 및 해설

Mina　Sorry, but these are not what we ordered.

여　미나와 Julie는 힘든 하루를 보내고 외식을 하기를 원합니다. 미나와 Julie는 한국 식당에 들어갑니다. 그들은 무엇을 먹을지를 결정하고, 미나가 주문을 합니다. 몇 분 뒤에 웨이터가 비빔밥과 불고기를 그들에게 가져다줍니다. 그러나 그것들은 미나와 Julie가 원했던 것이 아니어서, 미나는 웨이터를 부릅니다. 이 상황에서 미나가 웨이터에게 무엇이라고 말할까요?

미나　최송하지만, 이것들은 우리가 주문한 것이 아니예요.

해설 주문한 음식과 다른 음식이 제공된 상황에서 Mina가 웨이터에게 할 말로 가장 적절한 것은 ⑤ '죄송하지만, 이것들은 우리가 주문한 것이 아니예요.'이다.
① 이것들이 오늘의 특별 메뉴인가요?　② 이것들은 얼마입니까?
③ 실례합니다만, 추가 주문을 할 수 있나요?
④ 접시 하나만 더 주실 수 있나요?

Listen and Check
p. 190

Q1	No	Q12	near mountains and water sources
Q2	It has blue stripes and yellow stars.	Q13	False
Q3	True	Q14	True
Q4	the heavy snow	Q15	go to the movies
Q5	No	Q16	lotions
Q6	False	Q17	False
Q7	No	Q18	the history of Hangeul
Q8	False		
Q9	Yes	Q19	No
Q10	four times	Q20	True
Q11	False		

해석
Q1　여자는 파충류를 좋아하는가?
Q2　남자의 우산은 어떻게 생겼는가?
Q3　여자는 교통 법규를 어겼다.
Q4　무엇이 남자의 노트북의 배송을 지체시키는가?
Q5　축제는 한국에 있는 독일인들을 기리기 위해 매년 개최되는가?
Q6　여자는 무료로 커피 리필을 받을 수 없다.
Q7　남자는 창문을 닫고 싶어 하지 않는가?
Q8　남자는 여자의 전체 여행 동안 여자의 고양이를 돌볼 것인가?
Q9　Beth는 남자의 학교 과제를 도와주지 않았다.
Q10　남자는 지금까지 몇 번이나 같은 서비스를 받았는가?
Q11　여자는 이미 뒷좌석의 창문을 열었다.
Q12　서원은 어디에 위치하는가?
Q13　여자는 갑자기 떨어지고 스릴감 넘치는 놀이 기구를 싫어한다.
Q14　블랙홀은 강력한 중력을 가지고 있다.
Q15　남자와 여자는 일요일에 무엇을 할 것인가?
Q16　어떤 화장품이 건조한 피부에 효과적인가?
Q17　Brian과 Dave는 작년에 같은 반이었다.
Q18　한글날 행사에서 남자의 발표 주제는 무엇일까?
Q19　여자는 컴퓨터를 사용하는 데 능숙한가?
Q20　미나와 Julie는 비빔밥과 불고기를 시키지 않았다.

실전 모의고사 20회
pp. 198~199

1 ⑤	2 ③	3 ④	4 ②	5 ③
6 ①	7 ②	8 ④	9 ③	10 ④
11 ②	12 ④	13 ⑤	14 ③	15 ⑤
16 ④	17 ⑤	18 ①	19 ③	20 ①

1　그림 정보 파악　⑤

M　Charlotte, are you still rolling the snowballs?
W　No. Look at this. The snowman is almost done.
M　You did great. I'll make him eyes with these buttons.
W　Looks nice. I'll wrap my muffler around the snowman.
M　No way! If you do, you'll catch a cold. How about making his nose and mouth with these sticks?
W　Okay. But he looks cold, too. I want to make him warm.
M　Then put my hat on his head.
W　We're done! Let's take a picture with the snowman.

남　Charlotte, 눈뭉치를 아직 굴리는 중이니?
여　아니, 이걸 봐. 눈사람은 거의 준비가 되었어.
남　잘했어. 난 이 단추로 눈을 만들어 줄래.
여　좋아 보인다. 나는 눈사람에게 내 목도리를 둘러 줄래.
남　안 돼! 만약 그랬다가는 너는 감기에 걸릴 거야. 이 막대기로 코랑 입을 만들어 주는 건 어때?
여　그래. 하지만 눈사람도 추워 보여. 난 그를 따뜻하게 해 주고 싶어.
남　그러면 내 모자를 눈사람에게 씌워 줄게.
여　다 됐다! 눈사람이랑 사진 찍자.

해설 단추로 눈사람의 눈을 만들고, 나뭇가지로 코와 입을 만들었으며 머리에 모자를 씌워 주었다고 하였다.
어휘 wrap [ræp] 두르다, 포장하다　stick [stik] 막대기, 나뭇가지

2　목적 파악　③

[Cellphone rings.]
M　Hello, Mom. What's up?
W　Ivan, where are you? Are you heading home now?
M　That's right. Do you need anything from me?
W　When I cleaned your room, I found your alarm clock had stopped.
M　Oh, is it broken?
W　I don't think so. If you change the batteries, it will work.
M　I got it. I'll stop at a nearby shop and buy some batteries.
W　Okay. See you at home.

남　여보세요. 엄마, 무슨 일이예요?
여　Ivan, 어디에 있니? 지금 집으로 오는 중이니?
남　맞아요. 필요한 게 있으세요?
여　네 방을 청소할 때, 네 자명종이 멈춘 걸 발견했어.
남　아, 고장이 났어요?
여　그런 것 같지는 않아. 건전지를 바꾸면 작동할 거 같아.
남　알겠어요. 근처의 가게에 들러서 건전지를 살게요.
여　그래. 집에서 보자.

해설 청소 중에 자명종이 멈춘 것을 발견해서 건전지를 사 오라고 전화하였다.
어휘 head [hed] 향하다   nearby [níərbái] 근처의, 인근의

3 그림 상황 파악 ④

① M Oh, is the elevator broken again?
   W I think so. We should call customer service.
② M This elevator doesn't stop at the second floor.
   W Are you sure? That's really annoying.
③ M Ouch! You stepped on my foot!
   W I'm so sorry. I didn't notice it.
④ M There are so many people in front of the elevator.
   W How about using the stairs instead of taking the elevator?
⑤ M The elevator suddenly stopped, so I got stuck in it.
   W That sounds terrible. Were you okay?

① 남 승강기가 또 고장이 났나요?
   여 그런 것 같아요. 고객 서비스 센터에 전화해야겠어요.
② 남 이 승강기는 2층에서는 서지 않아.
   여 정말이니? 정말 짜증나네.
③ 남 아야! 당신이 제 발을 밟았어요!
   여 정말 미안해요. 알아채지 못했어요.
④ 남 승강기 앞에 사람들이 너무 많아.
   여 승강기 타는 것 대신에 계단을 이용하는 건 어때?
⑤ 남 승강기가 갑자기 멈췄고 나는 그곳에 갇혀 있었어.
   여 끔찍하다. 괜찮니?

해설 붐비는 승강기에 타는 대신 계단으로 가자고 제안하는 상황이다.
어휘 annoying[ənɔ́iiŋ] 짜증나는, 성가신, 거슬리는   notice[nóutis] 알아채다

4 특정 정보 파악 ②

W Did you hear that an Indian restaurant just opened last week?
M I heard that. I really want to go to the restaurant as soon as possible.
W How about this Wednesday after school?
M Sorry. I have a piano lesson then. Let's meet on Friday.
W Let me see. Wait! I have to attend a family gathering on that day.
M Then what about this Thursday?
W That's perfect! See you then.

여 인도 식당이 저번 주에 새로 문을 열었다는 걸 들었니?
남 들었어. 가능한 한 빨리 가고 싶어.
여 이번 수요일에 학교 끝나고 어때?
남 미안해. 그때 피아노 수업이 있어. 금요일에 만나자.
여 어디 보자. 잠깐! 난 가족 모임에 참석해야 해.
남 그러면 이번 목요일은 어때?
여 완전 좋아! 그때 보자.

해설 목요일에 만나서 새로 개업한 인도 식당에 가기로 하였다.
어휘 family gathering 가족 모임   on that day 그 날

5 언급 유무 파악 ③

W Ladies and gentlemen, look at this innovative electric car, the Handy. We are so proud to introduce the Handy to you after several years of development. The Handy was produced by the Star Automobile Company in Korea in 2020. The Handy is designed for four passengers, and it can drive 500 kilometers on a single charge. In addition, the price is 25,000 dollars, which is reasonable compared to other electric cars. The Handy goes on sale next month. Don't miss this chance to protect the environment.

여 신사 숙녀 여러분, 혁신적인 전기 자동차 Handy를 봐 주세요. 수년간의 연구 끝에 Handy를 여러분께 소개해 드리게 되어 자랑스럽습니다. Handy는 2020년에 한국에 있는 Star 자동차 회사에 의해 생산되었습니다. Handy는 4인용으로 설계되었으며 한 번의 충전으로 500km를 달릴 수 있습니다. 또한 가격은 2만 5천 달러이며, 이는 다른 전기 자동차에 비해 합리적입니다. Handy는 다음 달에 판매됩니다. 환경을 보호할 수 있는 이 기회를 놓치지 마세요.

해설 정부 보조금에 관해서는 언급되지 않았다.
어휘 innovative [ínəvèitiv] 혁신적인   several [sévərəl] 여러   passenger [pǽsəndʒər] 탑승자   charge [tʃɑːrdʒ] 충전

6 관계 추론 ①

M Hello, Ms. Duncan. I'm glad to meet you. I'm Violet's father.
W Ah, nice to meet you. Please take a seat. What's on your mind?
M The other day, Violet told me that she wanted to become a mathematician.
W A mathematician? I think that's perfect for her.
M Do you think she has a chance to become a mathematician?
W Absolutely. Violet is a very talented student. If I were you, I would support her decision.
M Thank you. I'll talk to Violet more about it.

남 안녕하세요, Duncan 선생님. 만나서 반갑습니다. 저는 Violet의 아빠입니다.
여 아, 뵙게 되어 반갑습니다. 여기 앉으세요. 어떤 걱정이 있으세요?
남 요전 날 Violet이 제게 수학자가 되고 싶다고 말했어요.
여 수학자요? 그녀에게 딱 알맞네요.
남 그녀가 수학자가 될 가능성이 있다고 보세요?
여 물론이죠. Violet은 매우 재능이 있는 학생입니다. 만약 저라면, 저는 그녀의 결정을 지지해 줄 거에요.
남 감사합니다. 그것에 대해서 Violet과 더 이야기해 볼게요.

해설 Violet의 아버지가 자신의 딸이 수학자가 되고 싶다는 말을 듣고 그녀의 선생님을 만나 상담하고 있는 상황이다.
어휘 mathematician [mæ̀θəmətíʃən] 수학자   support [səpɔ́ːrt] 지지하다, 뒷받침하다   decision [disíʒən] 결정

7 어색한 대화 찾기 ②

① M Can you do me a favor?
   W Why not? Tell me what you need.
② M Why were you late for the meeting today?
   W Unfortunately, I haven't met them yet.
③ M Do you want to ride the merry-go-round?
   W Yes! I'll ride on the black horse over there.
④ M I wonder if anybody is home or not.
   W I don't think so. Look! The lights are turned off.
⑤ M This is the most crowded subway I've ever been

on.
W It's like this every day during commuting hours.

① 남 내 요청을 들어줄래?
   여 안 될 거야 없지. 뭔지 말해 봐.
② 남 오늘 회의에 왜 늦은 거니?
   여 불행하게도 난 그들을 아직 만나지 못했어.
③ 남 회전목마 타고 싶니?
   여 응! 난 저기에 있는 까만 말을 탈 거야.
④ 남 누군가 집에 있는지 아닌지가 궁금해.
   여 그런 것 같지 않아. 저길 봐! 불이 꺼져 있어.
⑤ 남 내가 탔던 것 중에 가장 붐비는 지하철이야.
   여 통근 시간에는 늘 이래.

회의에 늦은 이유를 물어보는 말에 그들을 아직 만나지 못했다고 답하는 것은 부자연스럽다.
어휘 unfortunately [ʌnfɔ́ːrtʃənitli] 불행하게도, 안타깝게도 commuting hours 통근 시간

8 부탁한 일 파악 ④

[Telephone rings.]
M Hello. Sweet Home Department Store Customer Service Center. How can I help you?
W I think I lost my cellphone somewhere in your store today.
M Where exactly were you shopping?
W I was in the Comfy shoe store.
M Okay. I'll check if the Comfy shoe store has your cellphone. Hold on a second. [Ringtone sounds] Sorry. Nobody is answering there.
W Then could you please give me the number of the shoe store? I want to call myself.
M Sure. The phone number is 012-3456-7890.

남 여보세요. Sweet Home 백화점 고객 서비스 센터입니다. 어떻게 도와드릴까요?
여 오늘 제가 백화점 어딘가에서 휴대 전화를 잃어버린 거 같아요.
남 정확히 어디에서 쇼핑하셨나요?
여 Comfy 신발 가게에 있었어요.
남 네. Comfy 신발 가게에 당신의 휴대 전화가 있는지 확인해 보겠습니다. 잠시만요. 죄송하지만 전화를 받지 않네요.
여 그러면 제게 신발 가게 전화번호를 알려주실래요? 직접 확인할게요.
남 물론이죠. 전화번호는 012-3456-7890입니다.

해설 휴대 전화를 분실해서 해당 신발 가게의 전화번호를 알려달라고 부탁하였다.
어휘 somewhere [sʌ́mhwɛ̀ər] 어딘가에

9 의도 파악 ③

W Sewon, there's something different about you today.
M I got a tan and changed my hair.
W You look great. Where are your glasses? Are you wearing contacts now?
M Nope. I lost my glasses after I got back from my vacation.
W That's too bad. You just got a new pair not too long ago, right?
M I know. I should have been more careful.

여 세원, 너 오늘 뭔가 달라 보여.
남 햇볕에 피부가 탔고 머리 스타일을 바꿨어.

여 좋아 보인다. 그리고 안경은 어디 있어? 지금 렌즈를 끼고 있는 거야?
남 아니. 휴가에서 돌아온 후에 안경을 잃어버렸어.
여 안됐다. 너 얼마 전에 새 안경을 구입했잖아. 그렇지?
남 응. 난 좀 더 주의를 기울였어야 했어.

해설 안경을 잃어버리지 않도록 좀 더 주의했어야 했다고 후회하는 중이다.
어휘 get a tan 햇볕에 태우다   contacts 콘택트렌즈   not too long ago 얼마 전에

10 숫자 정보 파악 ④

M Welcome to Betty Costume. What are you looking for?
W I'm looking for a Halloween costume for my four-year-old daughter.
M Hmm... How about this princess dress? We got this yesterday.
W Actually, my daughter wore a princess dress last year. Oh, I like that witch costume. How much is it?
M It's 50 dollars. And I think you need this broom.
W Perfect! And I like the witch hat. How much is each?
M The broom is 10 dollars, and the hat is 15 dollars.
W Okay. I'll just take the dress and the hat.

남 Betty Costume에 오신 걸 환영합니다. 무엇을 찾으세요?
여 저는 네 살짜리 제 딸을 위한 할러윈 복장을 찾고 있어요.
남 흠... 이 공주 드레스는 어떠세요? 어제 들어왔어요.
여 사실 제 딸이 작년에 공주 드레스를 입었어요. 오, 저 마녀 드레스가 마음에 드네요. 얼만인가요?
남 50달러입니다. 그리고 이 빗자루도 필요하실 거 같아요.
여 좋아요! 그리고 저 마녀 모자도 좋네요. 각각 얼마예요?
남 빗자루는 10달러이고, 모자는 15달러입니다.
여 알겠어요. 드레스랑 모자만 구입할게요.

해설 마녀 드레스와 마녀 모자를 구입하겠다고 하였다.
어휘 costume [kástjuːm] 의상, 복장   witch [witʃ] 마녀   broom [bru(ː)m] 빗자루

11 할 일 파악 ②

M Finally, by this time tomorrow, I'll be on an airplane.
W Where are you going tomorrow?
M I'm going on a trip to Vietnam. I've been waiting to go there for a long time.
W Did you double-check to see if you packed everything? Your passport, clothes, money, and other things.
M Let me see. My backpack is ready to go. And I'll go to the bank at the airport tomorrow to exchange some money.
W The exchange rate there is not very good. How about going to a bank around here today?
M Okay. I'd better go now.

남 마침내 내일 이 시간이면 난 비행기를 타고 있을 거야.
여 내일 어디로 가는데?
남 베트남으로 여행 가. 오랫동안 그 곳에 가려고 기다렸어.
여 필요한 건 다 챙겼는지 다시 한 번 확인했니? 여권이랑 옷, 그리고 돈, 기타 등등.
남 어디 보자. 배낭은 준비가 되었고, 내일 환전하러 공항에서 은행에 갈 거야.
여 공항 환율은 썩 좋지 않아. 오늘 근처 은행에 가는 게 어때?

남 알았어. 지금 가야겠다.

해설 공항에서 환전하는 것은 환율이 좋지 않아 지금 근처 은행에 간다고 하였다.

어휘 double-check 두 번 확인하다, 재확인하다   exchange [ikstʃéindʒ] 환전하다, 교환하다

12 언급 유무 파악 ④

M Hello, everyone. I'm happy to <u>tell</u> <u>you</u> <u>some</u> <u>news</u> about the museum of natural history. The museum is going to hold the Dinosaur Discovery Camp this summer. The camp will be held from July 10 to August 9. It is for elementary school students, and the <u>participation</u> <u>fee</u> is $30. The camp offers <u>fun</u> <u>hands-on</u> <u>activities</u>. For example, participants will look for dinosaur bones <u>hidden</u> <u>in</u> <u>sand</u> and then put them together.

남 안녕하세요, 여러분. 자연사 박물관에 대한 소식을 전해 드리게 되어 기쁩니다. 박물관은 이번 여름에 공룡 발견 캠프를 개최할 것입니다. 캠프는 7월 10일부터 8월 9일까지 열릴 것입니다. 이것은 초등학생을 위한 것이며 참가비는 30달러입니다. 캠프는 재미있고 직접 할 수 있는 활동을 제공합니다. 예를 들어 참가자들은 모래에 숨겨진 공룡 뼈를 찾아서 조립할 것입니다.

해설 자연사 박물관의 Dinosaur Discovery Camp가 개최되는 장소에 관해서는 언급되지 않았다.

어휘 discovery [diskʌ́vəri] 발견   elementary [èləméntəri] 초등의   participation [pɑːrtìsəpéiʃən] 참여, 참가   hands-on 직접 해 보는, 실습의   hidden [hídən] 감춰진, 숨은

13 표 파악 ⑤

M Lydia, look at <u>this</u> <u>schedule</u> <u>for</u> <u>musicals</u>. Let's go to see one.

W Sure. But not on Friday. I have to go to my English academy on Friday.

M Oh, I wanted to see *Snow White and the Seven Dwarfs*.

W Sorry. What about *The Lion King*? I hear this one is awesome. We can see an <u>amazing</u> <u>performance</u>.

M Well, I think $150 per person is <u>too</u> <u>expensive</u> <u>for</u> <u>me</u>.

W I didn't <u>notice</u> <u>the</u> <u>price</u>. Anyway, I've already seen *Little Red Riding Hood*.

M Then there's only one thing left.

W That's right. I think *The Little Prince* is a wonderful choice because we can take a picture with the actors.

M Really? That'll be a great memory.

W Let's reserve tickets now.

남 Lydia, 여기 뮤지컬 일정표를 봐. 우리 하나 보러 가자.
여 그래. 하지만 금요일은 안 돼. 난 금요일에 영어 학원을 가야 해.
남 아, 난 '백설 공주와 일곱 난쟁이'가 보고 싶었는데.
여 미안해. '라이언 킹'은 어때? 이거 멋지대. 우리는 멋진 공연을 볼 수 있어.
남 글쎄, 1인당 150달러는 내게는 너무 비싸.
여 가격을 못 봤어. 그런데 난 '빨간 모자'는 이미 봤어.
남 그러면 딱 한 개가 남네.
여 맞아. '어린 왕자'도 멋진 선택이야. 왜냐하면 우리는 배우들과 사진을 찍을 수 있거든.

남 정말? 좋은 기억이 될 거야.
여 이제 표를 예매하자.

해설 일요일에 공연하는 '어린 왕자' 뮤지컬을 보기로 하였다.

어휘 dwarf [dwɔːrf] 난쟁이   performance [pərfɔ́ːrməns] 공연, 성과   memory [méməri] 기억, 추억

14 화제·주제 파악 ③

W This is a special vehicle that can <u>operate</u> <u>underwater</u>. This is quite different from ships because it can <u>dive</u> <u>into</u> <u>the</u> <u>deep</u> <u>sea</u>. This is a sealed container which is covered with the strongest steel. People in this can breathe freely and eat food underwater. This is mainly used by the navy and is <u>typically</u> <u>armed</u> <u>with</u> <u>missiles</u>. However, this is also <u>used</u> <u>for</u> <u>tourism</u>, marine research, and undersea exploration.

여 이것은 물속에서 작동하는 특별한 운송 수단입니다. 이것은 깊은 바닷속으로 들어갈 수 있어서 배와는 꽤 다릅니다. 이것은 강철로 덮인 밀폐된 컨테이너입니다. 이 안에 있는 사람들은 수중에서 자유롭게 숨을 쉬고 음식을 먹을 수 있습니다. 이것은 주로 미사일을 장착해서 해군에서 사용됩니다. 하지만 이것은 또한 관광, 해양 연구, 그리고 해저 탐사를 위해서 사용됩니다.

해설 깊은 바닷속으로 잠수할 수 있고 해군뿐 아니라 관광이나 해저 탐사에도 이용되는 것은 잠수함이다.

어휘 sealed [siːld] 봉인된, 밀봉된   breathe [briːð] 숨쉬다, 호흡하다   navy [néivi] 해군   typically [típikəli] 주로, 보통   armed [ɑːrmd] 무장한   missile [mísəl] 미사일   exploration [èkspləréiʃən] 탐험, 탐사

15 할 일 파악 ⑤

W Honey, we <u>had</u> <u>better</u> <u>stay</u> <u>home</u> today. It's foggy outside.

M No. That's not just fog. It looks like fine dust.

W Oh, my! That's why I have a <u>sore</u> <u>throat</u> <u>these</u> <u>days</u>.

M Do you? You need to drink a lot of water. Honey, I'll go to the electronics store.

W Why?

M To buy an air purifier. We <u>need</u> <u>fresh</u>, <u>clean</u> <u>air</u>.

여 여보, 오늘 집에 있는 게 낫겠어. 바깥에 안개가 많이 꼈네.
남 아니. 저건 단순한 안개가 아니야. 미세 먼지처럼 보여.
여 저런! 그래서 요즘 내가 목이 아픈 거구나.
남 그래? 물을 자주 마셔. 여보, 난 전자 제품 가게에 다녀올게.
여 왜?
남 공기 청정기를 사려고. 우리는 상쾌하고 깨끗한 공기가 필요해.

해설 깨끗한 공기를 위해 공기 청정기를 구입하려고 전자 제품 가게에 간다고 하였다.

어휘 fine dust 미세 먼지   purifier [pjúərəfàiər] 정화 장치

16 숫자 정보 파악 ④

M Mom, I <u>got</u> <u>a</u> <u>perfect</u> <u>score</u> on my English exam.

W That's my boy! You finally did it.

M English is <u>difficult</u> <u>to</u> <u>learn</u>, but I kept trying to get a perfect score.

W Well done! It's already 2 o'clock. Now get some rest.

M Not today. I have a math test tomorrow. So can you <u>wake</u> <u>me</u> <u>up</u> 3 hours from now?

W Okay. Do you want to get up at 5?

M That's right. I need to <u>take</u> <u>a</u> <u>nap</u> for a while.

W I got it.

남 엄마, 나 영어 시험에서 만점 받았어요.

여 역시 내 아들이야! 마침내 해냈구나.

남 영어는 배우기에 어렵지만 만점을 받기 위해 계속 노력했어요.

여 잘했어. 벌써 2시네. 이제 좀 쉬어라.

남 오늘은 안 돼요. 내일 수학 시험이 있어요. 그래서 말인데요, 3시간 후에 깨워 주실 수 있어요?

여 알겠다. 5시에 일어나고 싶은 거니?

남 맞아요. 잠깐 낮잠을 자고 싶어요.

여 그래.

해설 수학 시험 공부를 하기 위해 5시에 깨워 달라고 부탁하였다.

어휘 make it 성공하다, 해내다   take a nap 낮잠을 자다

17 적절한 응답 찾기 ⑤

W What's the matter with your face? It's <u>all</u> <u>swollen</u>.

M I have a terrible toothache. My gums have been bleeding. It's painful.

W Ugh! You look really sick. <u>When</u> <u>did</u> <u>the</u> <u>pain</u> start?

M Since last month, I've had some pain because of a wisdom tooth.

W Last month? Didn't you see a dentist?

M No, I didn't. I thought it would <u>get</u> <u>better</u> <u>soon</u>.

W No way! Anyway, <u>stop</u> <u>putting</u> <u>it</u> <u>off</u> and go to the dentist today.

M All right. But I'm really scared of the dentist.

W <u>If you don't go, the pain will get worse and worse.</u>

여 얼굴에 무슨 문제라도 있어? 얼굴이 부었어.

남 심각한 치통이 있어. 잇몸에 피가 나고 있어. 너무 아파.

여 에고, 너 정말로 아파 보인다. 언제부터 그랬어?

남 지난달부터 사랑니가 아팠어.

여 지난달? 치과에 안 갔어?

남 안 갔어. 곧 괜찮아질 줄 알았어.

여 말도 안 돼! 어쨌든 그만 미루고 오늘 치과 가봐.

남 알겠어. 하지만 치과는 정말 무서워.

여 <u>오늘 가지 않으면 통증이 점점 더 심해질 거야.</u>

해설 무서워서 치과를 가기 싫어하는 말에 대한 가장 적절한 응답은 ⑤ '오늘 가지 않으면 통증이 점점 더 심해질 거야.'이다.

① 난 사랑니를 뽑았어.

② 자기 전에 방 청소를 해.

③ 지식은 지혜와 별로 관련이 없어.

④ 우리 부모님은 내가 치과 의사가 되기를 원하셔.

어휘 swollen [swóulən] 부은, 부어오른   gum [gʌm] 잇몸   wisdom tooth 사랑니   put off 미루다

18 적절한 응답 찾기 ①

M Abigail, what are you looking at on your laptop?

W I'm watching the movie *Beauty and the Beast*.

M I didn't know you're <u>interested</u> <u>in</u> romantic movies.

W To be honest, I like horror movies.

M Why are you watching it? It's <u>not</u> <u>your</u> <u>taste</u>.

W Actually, I'm <u>going</u> <u>to</u> <u>play</u> Belle from *Beauty and the Beast* in the school play.

M Wow! That's good news.

W Yes. That's why I'm watching this. I want to <u>understand</u> <u>my</u> <u>role</u> <u>better</u>.

M <u>Good idea. I'm sure it'll help you.</u>

남 Abigail, 노트북으로 무엇을 보는 중이니?

여 난 '미녀와 야수' 영화를 보고 있어.

남 네가 로맨틱 영화에 흥미가 있는 줄 몰랐어.

여 솔직히 난 공포 영화를 좋아해.

남 왜 보는 중이야? 네 취향도 아니잖아.

여 사실은 학교 연극에서 '미녀와 야수'에 나오는 Belle을 연기하게 되었어.

남 와! 좋은 소식이다.

여 응. 그래서 이걸 보는 중인 거야. 난 내 역할을 더 잘 이해하고 싶어.

남 <u>좋은 생각이야. 너에게 도움이 될 거라고 생각해.</u>

해설 자신이 맡은 역할을 이해하기 위해 영화를 보고 있다는 말에 대한 가장 적절한 응답은 ① '좋은 생각이야. 너에게 도움이 될 거라고 생각해.'이다.

② 나는 10초 안에 네 문제를 해결할 수 있어.

③ 내일 공포 영화를 보러 가자.

④ 내 생각에는 '로미오와 줄리엣'이 더 나아.

⑤ 난 축구를 하러 운동장에 가는 중이야.

어휘 laptop [læptap] 노트북, 휴대용 컴퓨터   to be honest 솔직히 말하자면   horror movie 공포 영화

19 적절한 응답 찾기 ③

M Eleanor, is there something bothering you?

W You know I'm learning Korean these days. But it's not easy to study Korean.

M Come on! It's obvious that it <u>takes</u> <u>time</u> <u>to</u> <u>learn</u> a new language.

W I know that! But after learning a new word, when I try to use it, I find that I <u>have</u> <u>totally</u> <u>forgotten</u> <u>it</u>.

M Well, you need more practice. How about <u>finding</u> <u>a</u> <u>language</u> <u>exchange</u> partner?

W Language exchange? What is that?

M It's a method where two native speakers <u>teach</u> <u>each</u> <u>other</u> their native language. You are a native English speaker.

W <u>Then I should find a native Korean speaker.</u>

남 Eleanor, 뭔가 신경 쓰이는 일이 있니?

여 너도 알다시피 내가 요즘 한국어를 배우는 중이잖아. 그런데 한국어 공부하는 건 쉽지 않아.

남 에이! 새로운 언어를 배우는데 시간이 걸리는 건 당연해.

여 나도 그건 알아. 하지만 새로운 단어를 암기하고 난 후에 그것을 사용하려고 하면 완전히 잊었다는 걸 알게 돼.

남 음, 너는 연습이 더 필요할 거 같아. 언어 교환할 사람을 찾는 건 어때?

여 언어 교환? 그게 뭐야?

남 두 명의 원어민이 서로에게 서로의 언어를 가르치는 방법이야. 너는 영어가 모국어잖아.

여 <u>그러면 나는 한국어가 모국어인 사람을 찾으면 되겠네.</u>

해설 언어 교환에 대해서 자세하게 설명하는 남자의 말에 대한 여자의 응답으로 가장 적절한 것은 ③ '그러면 나는 한국어가 모국어인 사람을 찾으면 되겠네.'이다.

① 영어로 일기를 쓰는 건 도움이 돼.

② 저는 이걸 다른 것으로 교환하고 싶어요.

④ 영어는 배우기에 너무 어려운 언어야.

⑤ 너는 매일 새로운 단어를 암기해야 해.

어휘 bother [bɑ́ðər] 괴롭히다, 신경이 쓰이다   exchange [ikstʃéindʒ] 교환   method [méθəd] 방법   native [néitiv] 원래의, 모국어인

20 상황에 맞는 말 찾기 ①

M Soyoung and her classmates are planning to make a class newspaper. Her teacher <u>divides</u> <u>the</u> <u>class</u>

into seven groups. Soyoung's group decides to meet at 6 o'clock after school. At 6:00, Soyoung arrives at the meeting spot. However, she doesn't see Eunhyuk and some other members. About 30 minutes later, <u>all</u> <u>of</u> <u>the</u> <u>members</u> <u>have</u> <u>arrived</u> except for Eunhyuk. She wants to tell him <u>to be more</u> <u>punctual</u> when Eunhyuk arrives. In this situation, what would Soyoung most likely say to Eunhyuk?

Soyoung Eunhyuk, <u>I want you to try to be on time.</u>

남 소영과 그녀의 반 친구들은 학급 신문을 만들기로 계획 중입니다. 그녀의 선생님은 학급 친구들을 7개의 조로 나누었습니다. 소영의 조는 방과 후 6시에 만나기로 결정합니다. 소영은 6시에 만날 장소에 도착합니다. 하지만 은혁과 몇몇 다른 친구들은 보이지 않습니다. 30분 후에 은혁을 제외한 모든 친구들이 도착합니다. 은혁이 도착할 때, 그녀는 그에게 좀 더 시간을 지켜 달라고 말하려고 합니다. 이런 상황에서, 소영이 은혁에게 할 말로 가장 적절한 것은 무엇일까요?

소영 은혁아, 난 네가 시간을 지키려고 노력하면 좋겠어.

해설 약속 시간에서 30분이 지나도록 은혁이 도착하지 않은 상황에서 소영이 은혁에게 할 말로 가장 적절한 것은 ① '난 네가 시간을 지키려고 노력하면 좋겠어.'이다.
② 우리는 공항으로 출발하는 게 나을 거야.
③ 너는 사진 찍기를 담당하고 있어.
④ 내가 학습 신문에 사설을 썼어.
⑤ 경제에 관해서 반 친구들에게 연설해 줘.

어휘 divide [diváid] 나누다, 분리하다 spot [spɑt] 장소 punctual [pʌ́ŋktʃuəl] 시간을 잘 지키는 editorial [èdətɔ́:riəl] 사설

Listen and Check
p. 200

Q1	True	Q11	Vietnam
Q2	his mother	Q12	30 dollars
Q3	True	Q13	Yes
Q4	take a piano lesson	Q14	False
Q5	25,000 dollars	Q15	to an electronics store
Q6	a mathematician		
Q7	Yes	Q16	Yes
Q8	False	Q17	False
Q9	False	Q18	Belle
Q10	a Halloween costume	Q19	Korean
		Q20	No

해석
Q1 눈사람을 만든 후 남자와 여자는 눈사람과 함께 사진을 찍었다.
Q2 누가 Ivan의 방을 청소했을까?
Q3 승강기 앞에 많은 사람들이 있다.
Q4 남자는 수요일에 무엇을 할 계획일까?
Q5 전기차 Handy는 얼마인가?
Q6 Violet은 무엇이 되고 싶은가?
Q7 여자는 오늘 회의에 지각했을까?
Q8 여자는 백화점에서 누군가의 휴대폰을 발견했다.
Q9 세원은 지금 콘택트렌즈를 착용하고 있다.
Q10 여자는 가게에서 무엇을 사려고 했을까?
Q11 남자는 내일 어디로 가는가?
Q12 Dinosaur Discovery Camp의 등록비는 얼마인가?
Q13 남자와 여자는 일요일에 뮤지컬을 보기로 결정했을까?
Q14 이것은 군사적 목적으로만 이용된다.
Q15 대화가 끝난 후에 남자는 어디로 갈 것인가?

Q16 남자는 내일 수학 시험이 있을까?
Q17 남자는 사랑니 때문에 치과에 갔다.
Q18 Abigail은 '미녀와 야수'에서 어떤 역할을 연기할까?
Q19 Eleanor는 요즘 어떤 언어를 배우고 있을까?
Q20 모든 구성원들은 만나는 장소에 제시간에 도착했을까?

Vocabulary Test
pp. 210~229

1회 *p. 210*

A
1 plain: 무늬가 없는, 무지의   2 convenient: 편리한
3 release: 출시하다   4 be supposed to: ~해야 되다
5 cooperation: 협조   6 iron: 다림질하다
7 atmosphere: 분위기   8 significant: 중요한
9 subscribe: 구독하다   10 diligent: 부지런한

B
1 drive you home   2 take part in practice
3 give me a hand   4 full of passion   5 stands in front of
6 helps you not to   7 The atmosphere in   8 put it on
9 takes place on   10 read an article

해석
B
1 나는 너를 집에 태워다 줄 수 있다.
2 연습에 참여해도 될까요?
3 날 도와줄 수 있습니까?
4 어떻게 하면 내가 당신처럼 열정이 가득할 수 있을까요?
5 그녀는 Kate가 앉은 자리 앞에 서 있다.
6 이것은 당신이 중요한 일을 까먹지 않도록 도와준다.
7 이 레스토랑은 분위기가 매우 로맨틱하다.
8 당신은 그것을 벽에 걸어둘 수도 있고 책상에 올려둘 수도 있다.
9 이 연간행사는 4월 15일에 열린다.
10 나는 기사를 읽고 익숙하지 않은 표현들에 하이라이트 표시를 한다.

2회 *p. 211*

A
1 knit: 뜨개질하다   2 refrigerator: 냉장고
3 seasick: 뱃멀미가 난   4 charity: 자선 단체, 자선
5 organize: 정리하다, 준비하다   6 deed: 행동, 행위
7 issue: 내리다, 발행하다   8 admission: 입장, 입학
9 infection: 염증   10 audience: 청중, 관객

B
1 donate them to charity   2 milk a cow by hand
3 take better care of myself   4 rolling from side to side
5 my ear pierced   6 need it back
7 register for the beginner course
8 feels grateful for his kindness
9 adjust your appearance   10 expected to be severe

해석
B
1 나는 옷을 자선 단체에 기부하고 싶다.
2 여러분은 말에게 먹이를 주거나 물을 먹일 수 있다.
3 나는 내 자신을 돌봐야 한다.

4 배가 심하게 흔들린다.
5 나는 3일 전에 귀를 뚫었다.
6 하지만 금요일 전까지 돌려주십시오.
7 나는 초보자 과정에 등록하고 싶다.
8 그녀는 방문하는 동안 보여준 그의 친절에 고마워한다.
9 당신이 이것을 볼 때 외모를 점검할 수 있다.
10 일기 예보에서 폭풍이 심해질 것으로 예상된다고 합니다.

3회 *p. 212*

A

1 various: 다양한　2 enroll: 등록하다　3 outfit: 옷
4 monument: 기념비　5 laundry: 세탁
6 make a point of: ~을 습관으로 삼다　7 convert: 전환하다
8 conflict: 갈등, 분쟁　9 overdue: 기한이 지난
10 reasonable: 합리적인, 합당한

B

1 Are you done with　2 Have you tried　3 the earlier one
4 is not here right now　5 looks good on you
6 laundry service is available　7 architects were hired
8 make a point of　9 offering the same discount
10 involves using nuclear reactions

해석

B

1 영어 수업은 끝났나요?
2 Korean Food World에서 먹어 봤나요?
3 더 이른 시간의 좌석 하나를 예매하겠습니다.
4 미안하지만 박사님은 지금 여기 계시지 않습니다.
5 그것은 당신에게 어울리지 않는 것 같습니다.
6 지금 세탁 서비스가 가능한지 궁금하다.
7 유명한 건축가들을 고용하여 기념비를 디자인하였다.
8 학교에 걸어가는 건 어떨까요?
9 그것은 50달러가 더 저렴하고, 똑같이 할인해 드립니다.
10 원자력은 전기를 생산하기 위해 핵반응을 사용한다.

4회 *p. 213*

A

1 cub: 새끼　2 inconvenience: 불편　3 conserve: 보존하다
4 prohibit: 금지하다　5 inspect: 검사하다　6 infection: 감염
7 discrimination: 차별　8 originate: 유래하다
9 characterize: ~을 특징짓다　10 brochure: 팸플릿

B

1 That's fine with　2 the inconvenience
3 Feel free to inspect　4 Why don't we
5 following what I'm saying　6 looking forward to seeing
7 what it looks like　8 that is what I want
9 are finally done with　10 temporarily out of stock

해석

B

1 괜찮습니다.
2 불편을 끼쳐 드려서 정말 죄송합니다.
3 편하게 살펴보세요.
4 우리 실외 활동 좀 하는 게 어떻습니까?
5 제 말을 이해하십니까?
6 그녀를 빨리 만나보고 싶다.

7 어떻게 생겼는지 말씀해 주실 수 있을까요?
8 제가 원하는 것이 아닌 것 같습니다.
9 우리는 드디어 학교 잡지를 끝냈다.
10 죄송하지만 일시적으로 재고가 없습니다.

5회 *p. 214*

A

1 transfer: 옮기다, 넘겨주다　2 representative: 대표
3 facility: 편의 시설　4 mimic: 흉내를 내다
5 motivate: 동기를 부여하다　6 systematic: 체계적인
7 automatically: 자동적으로　8 adjustment: 조절
9 satisfying: 만족스러운　10 spectacular: 화려한, 눈부신

B

1 off and on　2 raise it, eggs and
3 motivates you to work　4 Won't it be, there in
5 what type of person　6 automatically record your visit
7 Think about, interests you　8 studies and, gets up
9 friends and asking　10 keep your rental cars clean

해석

B

1 이 전등이 계속 깜박거린다.
2 농부들은 이것을 계란과 고기 생산의 목적으로 키운다.
3 무엇이 당신을 더 열심히 일하도록 동기를 부여하는가?
4 여름에 관광하기엔 거긴 너무 덥지 않을까?
5 그저 네가 어떤 유형의 사람인지 알아야 한다.
6 클릭하면 당신의 방문이 자동으로 기록될 것이다.
7 무엇이 당신을 흥미롭게 하는지를 생각하고, 하고 싶은 일을 해라.
8 Nick은 공부를 거의 하지 않고 자주 외출을 한다.
9 친구들에게 전화해서 여기에 와 달라고 부탁할 수 있는가?
10 대여한 차를 반드시 깨끗이 유지해 주십시오.

6회 *p. 215*

A

1 sweat: 땀을 흘리다　2 confirmation: 확인, 입증
3 official: 공식의, 공인된　4 disappointed: 실망한
5 commute: 통근하다　6 hand down: ~을 물려주다
7 electronics: 전자 제품　8 annual: 연간의, 매년의
9 excessive: 과도한, 지나친　10 corpse: 시체

B

1 jammed with cars　2 it was addressed
3 scheduled to be held
4 more expensive than I expected
5 hurt my knee　6 couldn't have done
7 succeeded in buying　8 attracted to the scent
9 which of those pictures　10 the elderly eat meals

해석

B

1 미안합니다. 도로가 차로 가득 차 있습니다.
2 나는 그것이 나한테 온 거라고 생각했다.
3 707번 회의실에서 회의하기로 예정되어 있다.
4 그것은 예상했던 것보다 비싸다.
5 나는 어제 실수로 넘어져서 무릎을 다쳤다.
6 당신의 도움이 없었으면 하지 못했을 것이다.
7 당신은 콘서트 표를 구입하는 것에 성공했다.
8 모기는 보통 땀 냄새에 끌린다.

9 저 그림들 중에 네 그림이 무엇인지 맞춰 보겠다.
10 당신은 어르신들이 식사하시는 것과 방 청소를 도와 드리게 될 것입니다.

7회 *p. 216*

A
1 particular: 특별한, 특정한　2 absence: 결석
3 slippery: 미끄러운　4 consist: 구성되다
5 preview: 미리 보기　6 unpack: (짐을) 풀다
7 emission: 배출 가스　8 memorize: 암기하다
9 bucket list: (죽기 전에) 해보고 싶은 일 목록　10 allowance: 용돈

B
1 give him a surprise gift　2 Both of them, pretty far
3 really terrible at　4 faithful to the basics
5 They're really popular
6 inconvenience you are experiencing
7 The preview I watched　8 babysit my cousin
9 the official writing system　10 thinking of having

해석
B
1 나는 아들에게 깜짝 선물을 해주고 싶다.
2 그들 둘 다 꽤 먼 곳에 산다.
3 나는 한자에 정말 약하다.
4 너는 언제나 기본에 충실해야만 한다.
5 그들은 운동을 좋아하는 십대들에게 아주 인기가 있다.
6 불편을 끼쳐 드려서 죄송합니다.
7 유튜브에서 보았던 예고편은 정말로 흥미진진했다.
8 월요일과 목요일엔 하루 종일 나의 사촌 Sam을 돌봐야 한다.
9 오늘날, 그것은 한국과 북한 모두의 공식적인 문자 체계이다.
10 다음 주 금요일이나 토요일에 새 학기 파티를 열까 생각 중이다.

8회 *p. 217*

A
1 paste: 붙이다, 첨부하다　2 leave: 남겨놓다, 떠나다
3 fire drill: 화재 훈련　4 animated: 만화 영화의
5 nervous: 긴장한, 초조한　6 personal: 개인의
7 frustrated: 매우 실망한, 좌절한　8 flight: 비행(편), 비행기
9 down: 낙담한, 우울한　10 gone: 사라진, 죽은

B
1 would go well with　2 have to let me
3 I could drive you　4 gestures and other movements
5 not to be late　6 helped me prepare for
7 you ever looked after　8 dangerous to walk with
9 Make sure to turn　10 so that you can learn

해석
B
1 흰색 티셔츠가 네가 가지고 있는 바지들과 잘 어울릴 것이다.
2 하지만 대신 저녁 식사 메뉴는 제가 정하겠습니다.
3 내가 버스 터미널까지 너를 데려다주면 좋을 텐데.
4 이것은 또한 의사소통을 하기 위해서 몸짓 언어를 사용하기도 한다.
5 어쨌든, 우리는 늦지 않도록 서둘러야 한다.
6 그 경험이 이번 인터뷰를 준비하는 데 많은 도움이 되었다.
7 당신은 전에 어르신들을 돌본 적이 있습니까?
8 손을 주머니에 꽂은 채로 걷는 것은 위험하다.
9 떠나기 전에 반드시 당신의 컴퓨터를 끄세요.

10 선생님들 전원은 여러분이 그 경험에서 배울 수 있도록 여러분을 잘 이끌어줄 것입니다.

9회 *p. 218*

A
1 blurry: 흐릿한, 모호한　2 maintain: 유지하다
3 promote: 홍보하다　4 strengthen: 강화시키다
5 informative: 유익한　6 productive: 생산적인
7 efficiently: 효율적으로　8 exterior: 외부의
9 assign: 배정하다　10 definition: 정의

B
1 tripped and fell　2 once a week　3 he used in
4 get it done　5 It gives us　6 kind of an effort
7 The price of, that of　8 collects information
9 get aches in　10 lets you know, spend on

해석
B
1 발을 헛디뎌서 땅에 넘어졌다.
2 나는 그것을 일주일에 최소 한번 한다.
3 나는 또한 그가 이 작품에서 사용한 색채도 좋다.
4 이번 주 안으로 끝내봅시다.
5 이것은 우리에게 알파벳 순서로 정보를 준다.
6 저 부단한 노력에 보상이 있어야 한다.
7 일찍 출발하는 표 가격이 나중에 출발하는 표 가격의 두 배이다.
8 Adam은 다양한 사이트에서 정보를 모으고 필기를 한다.
9 하지만 너무 무리해서 걸으면 다리에 통증을 느낄 수도 있다.
10 네가 하는 일들에 시간을 얼마나 쓰는지 알려준다.

10회 *p. 219*

A
1 inspection: 검사, 조사　2 business hours: 영업시간
3 portable: 휴대용의　4 hesitate: 주저하다, 망설이다
5 international: 국제의　6 stiff: 뻣뻣한
7 strain: 무리하게 사용하다　8 moisten: 촉촉하게 하다
9 except for: ～을 제외하고　10 due date: 마감일, 예정일

B
1 can't wait to go　2 have anything in mind
3 Why didn't you draw　4 to have you with us
5 drop me off on your way　6 get caught in
7 still being repaired　8 as early as possible
9 at a distant object　10 ask her to bring it

해석
B
1 나는 빨리 수영하고 싶다.
2 당신은 생각해 둔 게 있습니까?
3 산타클로스는 왜 안 그랬습니까?
4 함께할 수 있게 되어 기쁘다.
5 집으로 가는 길에 저를 내려주시겠습니까?
6 우리는 심각한 교통 체증에 갇힐 것이다.
7 배드민턴장이 여전히 수리 중인가요?
8 나는 가능한 일찍 숙제를 끝내는 걸 좋아한다.
9 30분마다 멀리 있는 물체를 보는 것도 도움이 된다.
10 엄마한테 전화해서 가져다 달라고 하는 건 어떠니?

정답 및 해설

11회 *p. 220*

A
1 invasion: 침입   2 tempting: 솔깃한, 유혹하는
3 residence: 주택, 거주지   4 report: 보고하다   5 demand: 수요
6 loyal: 충실한   7 refundable: 환불 가능한   8 literature: 문학
9 autograph: 사인, 서명   10 addicted: 중독된

B
1 difficult for me to   2 takes about 5 hours
3 been over 3 hours   4 come to the library
5 scolded by his homeroom teacher
6 should learn more about   7 toss the four sticks together
8 a couple of days ago   9 passed down up to
10 you can pay only in cash

해석
B
1 나는 단어 외우는 게 너무 힘들다.
2 진해까지는 대략 5시간 정도 걸린다.
3 내 개를 본지 세 시간이 넘어가고 있다.
4 오늘 저녁에 도서관에 올 수 있나요?
5 그는 종종 담임 선생님께 혼이 난다.
6 당신은 유명한 작가에 대해서 더 많이 배울 필요가 있다.
7 말을 옮기려면, 4개의 막대기를 함께 던지세요.
8 너는 며칠 전에 엄마에게 용돈을 받았다.
9 오늘날까지 이어진 고유한 전통이 많이 있다.
10 50% 이상 할인된 제품은 현금으로만 지불할 수 있다.

12회 *p. 221*

A
1 mass: 덩어리   2 keep one's word: 약속을 지키다
3 set: 정하다, 결정하다   4 compare: 비교하다
5 balance: 균형을 잡다   6 make up with: ~와 화해하다
7 take on: 떠맡다   8 indicate: 보여주다, 나타내다
9 float: (물에) 뜨다   10 sponsor: 후원하다

B
1 used in summer   2 plants on it   3 take on a
4 three stops away   5 start to rain   6 makes up with
7 specialize in   8 that departs in
9 sees a foreign couple   10 take a year off

해석
B
1 이것은 주로 여름에 사용된다.
2 식물 그림들이 멋지다.
3 당신의 팀이 새로운 프로젝트를 맡았습니까?
4 나는 버스 안이고 세 정거장 남았다.
5 일기 예보에서 그 시간쯤에 비가 내리기 시작한다고 한다.
6 그녀가 싸운 친구와 화해하기를 바란다.
7 우리는 어떤 분야를 전공할지 생각해야 한다.
8 30분 뒤에 출발하는 열차가 있다.
9 Harriet은 한 외국인 커플이 승강장에 있는 것을 보았다.
10 나는 이번 학기 이후에 1년 쉬면서 할 것들에 대해서 생각 중이었다.

13회 *p. 222*

A
1 disabled: 장애를 가진   2 preparation: 준비

---

3 relieve: 덜어주다, 없애주다   4 throughout: ~동안 쭉
5 strategy: 전략   6 abandoned: 버려진   7 essential: 필수적인
8 figure out: 알아내다   9 spot: 알아내다, 발견하다
10 fairly: 꽤, 상당히

B
1 love your speech   2 relieve your stress
3 keep our things in   4 get your autograph on
5 had an appointment   6 have an account
7 send you a text message   8 focus on myself
9 improves your mood   10 make an investment

해석
B
1 청중들은 당신의 연설을 좋아할 것이다.
2 너는 그것으로 스트레스를 덜 수 있어.
3 이것은 우리가 우리의 물건을 보관하기 위해 사용하는 것이다.
4 제 티셔츠에 사인을 해주실 수 있습니까?
5 당신은 제게 오늘 약속 있다고 하지 않았나요?
6 그런데 당신은 이 웹사이트에 계정이 있나요?
7 다른 팀원들과 이야기한 후에 문자 메시지를 보내겠다.
8 나는 내가 하고 싶은 것을 하면서 내 자신에게 집중할 때 행복하다.
9 마지막으로 이것은 당신의 기분을 좋게 하고 행복감을 높여준다.
10 기꺼이 투자를 하려고 하는 큰 회사들이 있을지도 모른다.

14회 *p. 223*

A
1 overlap: 겹치다, 포개다   2 finish: 마치다, 끝내다
3 drawback: 결점, 단점   4 specialist: 전문가
5 absolutely: 물론, 완전히   6 brilliant: 뛰어난, 멋진
7 break down: 부서지다, 분해되다   8 contact: 접촉
9 suffer: 겪다, 고통을 받다   10 afford: 여유가 있다

B
1 need to pay for it   2 went by so fast
3 buy it nowhere else   4 never thought about
5 not interested in me   6 charged it on my credit card
7 suffered from food poisoning
8 how serious plastic pollution is   9 to share the rent with
10 have no choice but to sit

해석
B
1 여러분은 어떠한 비용도 지불할 필요가 없습니다.
2 우리의 휴가는 너무 빨리 지나갔다.
3 하지만 한국에서는 다른 어디에서도 구입할 수 없다.
4 이전에는 난 그것에 대해 생각해 본 적이 없다.
5 사실 너는 나에게 관심이 없는 거 같다.
6 나는 매장을 방문해서 신용 카드로 계산을 했다.
7 나는 생선회를 먹고 식중독에 걸렸다.
8 사람들은 플라스틱 오염이 얼마나 심각한지 알아야 한다.
9 David는 자신이 집세를 나눠 낼 룸메이트를 찾는다고 말한다.
10 네가 그것을 원한다면, 우리는 비상구 좌석 말고는 선택의 여지가 없다.

15회 *p. 224*

A
1 emergency: 긴급한 상황, 비상 사태   2 ballpark: 야구 경기장
3 airsick: 비행기 멀미   4 fridge: 냉장고   5 temperature: 온도
6 representative: 대표적인   7 resolution: 결심

8 vacuum: 진공청소기로 청소하다   9 jewelry: 보석류
10 recall: 기억을 떠올리다

B

1 burning from the fever   2 I am looking for
3 stick to back up my   4 any plans to use them
5 perfect time to travel   6 the windows closed makes
7 to get to the ballpark   8 his first chance to act
9 good chance for children to
10 tripped over something when I

해석

B

1 나는 열로 몸이 너무 뜨겁다.
2 나는 새 파트너를 찾는 중이다.
3 나는 사진을 백업하기 위한 메모리 스틱이 필요하다.
4 당신은 어떤 계획이 있나요?
5 지금이 베트남을 여행하기에 딱 좋은 시기이다.
6 문을 계속 닫아두는 것은 실내 공기를 나쁘게 한다.
7 경기장까지 20분 정도 걸릴 것이다.
8 그가 약 12살이었을 때, 그는 무대 쇼에서 공연할 첫 기회를 얻었다.
9 축제는 아이들이 댄스 공연을 즐기고 이해할 좋은 기회가 될 것이다.
10 나는 스마트폰으로 영화를 보면서 걷다가 무언가에 걸려 넘어졌다.

16회 *p. 225*

A

1 thrilled: 기대되는, 신나는   2 try on: (시험 삼아) 착용하다
3 repeat: 다시 말하다, 반복하다   4 charge: 청구하다
5 discount: 할인(하다)   6 primary: 중요한, 주요한
7 foldable: 접이식의   8 attitude: 태도
9 luckily: 다행히도, 운 좋게   10 of no use: 전혀 쓸모없는

B

1 you help me find   2 would you like to see
3 do you want to put   4 they are good for
5 could get stuck in   6 any of you
7 both of them   8 going to see an exhibition
9 believe what they are saying
10 can't attend this morning class

해석

B

1 당신은 내가 그를 위해 좋은 것을 찾는 걸 도와줄 수 있나요?
2 그럼 그 쇼 보러 같이 갈래요?
3 넌 그 캡슐 속에 무슨 물건을 넣고 싶어?
4 그것들이 제 엄마의 나이 대에 어울릴 거라고 생각하세요?
5 당신은 이 시간대에 교통 체증에 갇힐 수도 있습니다.
6 만일 여러분들 중 각각이 늦는다면, 우리는 함께 수업을 시작할 수가 없다.
7 시간이 지나자, 그들 모두는 누워서 즐기기 시작한다.
8 난 이번 주 일요일에 국립 박물관에 하는 전시회에 갈 것이다.
9 당신이 그들이 하는 말을 믿으면, 당신은 그것들을 사고 싶을 겁니다.
10 만일 이 아침 수업에 오실 수 없으신 분은 누구나 오후나 저녁 수업에 참여하실 수 있습니다.

17회 *p. 226*

A

1 steep: 가파른   2 appreciate: 고마워하다

---

3 seriously: 진지하게, 심각하게   4 distinguish: 구별하다
5 discussion: 토의, 토론   6 accurate: 정확한
7 imagination: 상상력   8 concerned: 걱정하는, 염려하는
9 finalize: 마무리 짓다   10 cancelation: 취소

B

1 sounds about average   2 twice as expensive as
3 recommend you dye your   4 pick up your poster
5 had an argument   6 our names on
7 are rooms available   8 since I watered them
9 tells about, culture of
10 make an important, come up with

해석

B

1 단지 평균인 것 같다.
2 그것은 일반 좌석보다 가격이 2배이다.
3 밝은 갈색으로 염색하실 것을 추천합니다.
4 당신은 포스터를 다섯 시까지 찾을 수 있습니다.
5 팀 멤버 중 한 명이랑 말다툼이 있었다.
6 당신 생각에는 티셔츠에 우리 이름을 넣어야 할 것 같습니까?
7 결제를 하시기 전에 환불 정책을 확인하셨나요?
8 물을 준지가 2주 이상이 된 것 같다.
9 이것은 때때로 여러 나라들의 역사와 문화에 대해서 말하기도 한다.
10 중요한 결정을 내릴 때, 당신이 떠올리는 생각을 의심하십시오.

18회 *p. 227*

A

1 qualification: 자격   2 confine: 가두다, 제한하다
3 locate: 위치하다   4 organize: 정리하다
5 stay away from: ~에서 떨어져 있다, 벗어나다
6 select: 선택하다   7 extinguish: (불을) 끄다
8 disposable: 일회용의   9 irritating: 짜증나는
10 owner: 주인, 소유자

B

1 put them, paper bag   2 not bad for a beginner
3 piled up on it   4 stepped in some gum
5 too heavy for me to carry   6 send them back
7 more important than convenience
8 replaced with new ones   9 careful with their actions
10 drop by the stationery store

해석

B

1 종이봉투에 담아 드리겠습니다.
2 그것은 초보자에게 나쁘지 않다.
3 많은 책이 쌓여 있다.
4 여기로 오는 길에 껌을 밟았다.
5 이 책은 내가 나르기에 너무 무겁다.
6 우리는 그들을 자연 서식지로 돌려보내야 한다.
7 환경이 편리함보다 중요하다.
8 필요하다면, 에스컬레이터는 새로운 것으로 교체될 수 있다.
9 무엇보다도 사람들은 자신의 행동에 주의해야 한다.
10 집에 오는 길에 문구점에 들를 수 있습니까?

19회 *p. 228*

A

1 adopt: 입양하다   2 delivery: 배송   3 launch: ~을 시작하다

4 look after: ~을 돌보다   5 comment: 말하다
6 designate: 지명하다   7 gravity: 중력   8 ingredient: 원료
9 semester: 학기   10 refresh: 상쾌하게 하다

B

1 will you be finished   2 check to see if
3 me to take care of   4 the antique atmosphere here
5 want us to send someone   6 helps you keep your skin
7 we offer the speedy delivery   8 you planning to do for
9 that they exist by observing
10 an historical process in which

해석

B

1 언제 끝나나요?
2 그것이 거기에 있는지 확인해 주시겠어요?
3 제가 그들을 돌봐주길 원하세요?
4 나는 여기 고풍스러운 분위기가 마음에 들고 커피도 맛있다.
5 당신의 자동차 문을 열어줄 사람을 보내 주길 원하시는 군요, 그렇죠?
6 이 마스크 팩은 당신이 당신의 피부를 촉촉하게 유지하는 것을 도와준다.
7 정상적인 상황에서, 우리는 3일 이내의 빠른 배송을 제공한다.
8 다가오는 한글날 행사에 무엇을 할 계획이니?
9 과학자들은 주변의 빛과 사물을 관찰함으로써 그들이 존재한다는 것을 알고 있다.
10 서원은 유학이 한국의 상황에 적응한 역사적 과정을 보여준다.

20회   *p. 229*

A

1 annoying: 짜증나는, 성가신, 거슬리는   2 innovative: 혁신적인
3 support: 지지하다, 뒷받침하다   4 costume: 의상, 복장
5 exchange: 환전하다, 교환하다   6 discovery: 발견
7 performance: 공연, 성과   8 navy: 해군
9 swollen: 부은, 부어오른   10 punctual: 시간을 잘 지키는

B

1 only one thing left   2 should have been
3 sore throat these days   4 if anybody is home
5 support her decision   6 divides the class into
7 got stuck in it   8 stop putting it off   9 breathe freely
10 with these sticks

해석

B

1 그러면 딱 한 개가 남는다.
2 나는 좀 더 주의를 기울였어야 했다.
3 그래서 요즘 내가 목이 아프다.
4 나는 누군가 집에 있는지 아닌지가 궁금하다.
5 만약 저라면, 저는 그녀의 결정을 지지해 줄 것입니다.
6 그녀의 선생님은 학급 친구들을 일곱 그룹으로 나누었다.
7 승강기가 갑자기 멈췄고 나는 그곳에 갇혀 있었다.
8 어쨌든 그만 미루고 오늘 치과로 가십시오.
9 이 안에 있는 사람들은 수중에서 자유롭게 숨을 쉬고 음식을 먹을 수 있다.
10 이 막대기로 코랑 눈을 만들어 주는 건 어떨까요?

내공
중학영어듣기 ③
모의고사 20회

- 시·도 교육청 주관 영어듣기평가 최신 기출 경향 분석
- 확실한 내용 이해를 위한 Listen and Check
- 정확한 듣기 실력 향상을 위한 Dictation
  (발음 Tip과 표현 설명 수록)
- 매회 Vocabulary Test로 단어와 표현 복습
- 미국식 100% 와 영국식 100% MP3 파일 제공

듣기 내공이 쌓이는

다락원 홈페이지에서 본 교재의 상세 정보와 MP3 파일 및 부가학습 자료를 이용하실 수 있습니다.